FORTEAN TIMES 31–36

GATEWAYS TO MYSTERY

'The Ubiquity of the Stone', from Michael Maier's *Atalanta Fugiens* (Frankfort 1617). See FT33:12.

FORTEAN TIMES 31–36

GATEWAYS TO MYSTERY

FORTEAN TOMES
LONDON 1993

This first edition is published in
September 1993 for John Brown Publishing Ltd.

by Fortean Times, PO Box 2409, London NW5 4NP.

Fortean Times is now published every two months
by John Brown Publishing Ltd.
It is also available by subscription – inquiries to:
Fortean Times, 20 Paul Street, Frome, Somerset BA11 1DX, UK.
☎ 0373 451777.

British Library Cataloguing in Publication Data available.

ISBN 1-870870-37-9

Printed in Great Britain by
Redwood Books, Trowbridge, Wilts.

Cover illustration by Mikki Rain.

PREFACE

The six issues of *Fortean Times* in this book are reproduced facsimile, except for new running heads. Our thanks go to Steve Moore for compiling the contents lists. As before, they have been made as detailed as possible, as compensation for the lack of a full index.

They represent an exciting period of development in the history of *Fortean Times*. Great strides were made in presentation, consolidating our new format and style. Particular thanks must go to graphic designer Richard Adams, whose advice and facilities allowed us to make a quantum leap in picture quality and layout. We also owe Richard a huge debt for obtaining for us great cover artwork from such luminaries as the Polish illustrators Andrzej Dudzinski and Andrzej Klimowski, and that star of Underground comics, Gilbert Shelton.

Also in this period we began to experiment with the features that are now a familiar part of *Fortean Times*, including the first of Paul Sieveking's uproarious headline collages (FT34), and guest columns featuring Michael Hoffman, Doc Shiels, Loren Coleman and the ever-reliable Steve Moore. The quality of our articles improved too, with memorable contributions from John Michell, Michael Goss, Hilary Evans, Guy Lyon Playfair, Peter Christie, Sven Rosén, and David Fideler among others.

We want to thank all of our regular clipsters for their faith and support over the years. Among them the names of Janet and Colin Bord, Peter Christie, Valerie Martin, Paul Screeton, Anthony Smith, Paul Thomas, Nigel Watson, Roland Watson, Dwight Whalen and the prodigious Ion Will were prominent in these issues.

This period also marked an important change in my personal life. My eternal gratitude goes to my wife Sam, who worked to support us both while I concentrated on *FT* production. I had co-authored two Fortean books – *Phenomena* and *Photos of the Unknown* – the proceeds from which meant I could, at last, contribute to the family purse. In practical terms it meant we could afford a modest flat, ending the series of temporary editorial addresses, and soon our eldest boy Jonathan was born. With *Fortean Times* establishing itself, the future was looking good.

Bob Rickard
July 1993

FORTEAN TIMES 31-36 (1980-1982)

CONTENTS

FORTEAN TIMES 31 – Spring 1980

1 *EDITORIAL*

2 *WILDMAN: FACT OR FICTION. Yuan Zhenxin* and *Huang Wanpo* on the Chinese 'Wild Man', a hairy humanoid similar to the Yeti. Historical and modern accounts. Analysis of data: hair, footprints, excrement. Eyewitness accounts. Theories and speculations: that the Wild Man is an atavistic throwback, or a surviving *Gigantopithecus.*

6 *GATEWAYS TO MYSTERY (Part One). David Fideler* develops the idea of geomagnetic 'window areas' as triggers for anomalous events, with particular reference to the state of Michigan. Background. French UFOs and mythologically-relevant place-names. Forteana, fault lines and magnetic anomalies. Spook lights and the piezoelectric effect.

12 *COMIC STRIP: TELLY KINEX* by *J.H. Szostek.*

14 *THE TOUCH OF DEATH. Michael Goss* on the 'Delayed Death Touch' of martial arts lore. An alleged demonstration. The death of Bruce Lee. Hitting vital points. Iron palm and vibrating palm. *Ch'i* energy. Hypnotism. The DDT and Fortean phenomena.

21 *COMIC STRIP: FACTS YOU MIGHT FORGET...* by *Pokkettz.*

22 *ENIGMA VARIATIONS* - Ufological disputes - war with aliens paranoia - UFO 'attacks' in Spain, Scotland, USA, Canada, Australia - alien body-shapes: dogs, one-legged dwarfs, micro-organisms, skeletons - popular reactions to alien life. [*Nigel Watson*]

24 *ON THE TRAIL* - Maned mystery cats - 'African lions' sighted in California (1979), Illinois (1917,1970), Indiana (1948), Ontario (1960), Nottingham (1976), Georgia (1976), Arkansas (1977) - explanations: stray dogs. [*Loren Coleman*]

27 *TALES FROM THE YELLOW EMPORIUM* - follow-ups - First Emperor's Army (FT29:17): new museum, two further vaults discovered - Hairy Boy (FT30:45): Yu Zhenhuan up-dated, 32 hirsute persons in China. [*Steve Moore*]

28 *COMIC STRIP: PHENOMENOMIX* by *Hunt Emerson.*

30 *STRANGE ENCOUNTERS* - alien abductions, 1979 - attempted abduction, Catskill Forest Reserve - Livingston, West Lothian - Cergy-Pontoise, Paris. [*Paul Sieveking*]

32 *HEAVENS ABOVE* - total solar eclipse 16 Feb 1980: reactions from China, India, Africa - most massive galaxy - most energetic black hole - alcohol and gold in space - strange stellar object - explosions in space - the Hubble Constant - luminous object near moon. [*Paul Sieveking*]

33 *ANTIQUITIES* - early hominid footprint fossils - hominid evolution - Atlantis - miscellaneous finds. [*Valerie Thomas*]

35 *GHOSTS AND VISIONS* - council house hauntings - private house hauntings. [*Steve Moore*]

37 *SYNCHRONICITIES* - name coincidences. [*Paul Sieveking*]

39 *LIGHTS AND FIREBALLS* - ball lightning - research - accidents - sightings (1978): USSR, Australia, Ceylon - fireballs and explosions (1979):Britain, Texas, Finland. [*RJMR*]

42 *TRENDS* - encounters with little people - strange coincidences. [*RJMR*]

44 *BOOK REVIEWS* - *Poltergeists* (Gauld & Cornell) - *Mysteries of the World* (Pick) -

Witchcraft and the Gay Counterculture (Evans) - *An Account of a Meeting with Denizens of Another World, 1871* (Loosley) - *UFOs: A British Viewpoint* (Randles & Warrington) - *Gods of Aquarius* (Steiger) - *The Airmen Who Would Not Die* (Fuller) - *Researches on the I Ching* (Shchutskii) - *I Ching Numerology* (Liu) - *Maps of the Ancient Sea Kings* (Hapgood) - *Famous Americans You Never Knew Existed* (Felton & Fowler) - *The Incorruptibles* (Cruz) - *Realms of the Human Unconscious* (Grof) - *The Human Encounter with Death* (Grof & Halifax) - *Answer to Job* (Jung) - *The Naturalised Animals of the British Isles* (Lever) -*Natural and Supernatural* (Inglis) - *Ghosts over Britain* (Moss) - *Miracles* (Ashe) - *The Turin Shroud* (Wilson) - *The Wild Boy of Averon* (Lane) - *A Guide to Ancient Sites in Britain* (Bords) - *Atlas of World Mysteries* (Hitching) - *The Secrets of Easter Island* (Schwartz).

51 *CLASSIFIED EXCHANGES*

53 *LETTERS* - Leys and UFOs - a guiding light - the Oera Linda book - the Great Fishfall of 1859 - water monsters.

FORTEAN TIMES 32 – Summer 1980

1 *EDITORIAL*

2 *LETTERS* - fireballs - tulpas - mystery booms - film suicide? - Fort's name - giant kangaroo in Lancashire.

4 *THE MISSISSAUGA BLOB.* ***Dwight Whalen*** on a flaming green blob that fell from the sky in Ontario, 16 June 1979. Analysed as polypropylene. 'Explained away' as a burning frisbee. Three other blobs found nearby. Curious behaviour of the local police. Crank phonecalls. Speculations.

9 *COMIC STRIP: TELLY KINEX* by ***J.H.Szostek.***

10 *GATEWAYS TO MYSTERY (Part Two).* ***David Fideler*** continues his look at 'window areas' of strange phenomena. Michigan event compilation, 1839-1978 (UFOs, Bigfoots, phantom cats, etc.). A new approach to UFOs: geophysical phenomena and anomalies.

17 *ASK ARISTOTLE.* A selection from the 18th century *Aristotle's Book of Problems.* [***Paul Sieveking***]

18 *THE PANTHERS OF SOUTHERN AUSTRALIA.* ***Paul Cropper*** on the mystery cats of New South Wales.

21 *ON THE TRAIL* - more lion-like maned mystery cats in the USA - possible identification as survivors of the 'extinct' *Panthera leo atrox.* [***Loren Coleman***]

22 *OUT OF PLACE* - mystery cats - Scottish lions (1979-1980) - Inverness - Ayrshire - East Lothian - escapes and discoveries - other large cat reports. [***RJMR***]

26 *STRANGE TALES* - fairy-tale stories reappearing as real events. [***Steve Moore***]

28 *COMIC STRIP: PHENOMENOMIX* by ***Hunt Emerson.***

30 *OLD IVES' TALES.* ***Paul Sieveking*** presents a selection of animal and bird stories from the eccentric press-cutting collection of ***George Ives.***

32 *TALES FROM THE YELLOW EMPORIUM* - qigong - modern Chinese sorcery tales - S.E.Asian sorcery. [***Steve Moore***]

34 *AMERICA MYSTICA* - the cultic associations of the 'Son of Sam' and John Wheat Carr serial killings. [***Michael Hoffman***]

37 *COMIC STRIP: FACTS YOU MIGHT FORGET* by ***Pokkettz.***

38 *SWARMS AND MIGRATIONS* - chronology June 1979 to April 1980 - great plagues of Australia - English aphid plague 1979. [***Valerie Thomas***]

40 *TALES OF INDIA* - Kuano amphibian boy - floating stones of Riwalsar - Lucknow poltergeist - phantom guide - Vimla and the exorcist - Poona snake man - fertility sacrifices. [***Paul Sieveking***]

42 *TRENDS* - child sacrifice, 1979 - talking elephant - finger amputation coincidence - money lost and found. [*RJMR*]
45 *NEWS* -book news - monster hunts - funds - meetings.
46 *BOOK REVIEWS* - *Earth's Secret Inhabitants* (Rogo & Clark) - *This House is Haunted* (Playfair) - *Alien Animals* (Bords) - *Monsters and Mysteries* (Wilkins) - *UFO Phenomena and the Behavioural Scientist* (Haines) - *Guardians of the Universe* (Story) - *The Ancient Stones Speak* (Zink) - *Megaliths and their Mysteries* (Service & Bradbery) - *Glastonbury* (Mathias & Hector) - *Stonehenge and its Mysteries* (Balfour) - *In Search of Ancient Astronomies* (Krupp) - *The New Soviet Psychic Discoveries* (Gris & Dick) - *Dowsing* (Graves) - *The Old Stones of Land's End* (Michell) - *The Magic Zoo* (Costello) - *Islam* (Khan) - *Muslim Saints and Mystics* (Attar) - *The House of Lords UFO Debate* (Clancarty, etc) - *The Probability of the Impossible* (Moss) - *The Wolf Children* (McClean) - *Life Cloud* (Hoyle & Wickramasinghe) - *A Young Person's Guide to UFOs* (Ball) - *Ages in Chaos; Rameses II and his Time; Peoples of the Sea* (Velikovsky) - *Our Changing Planet; Future Worlds* (Gribbin) - *Dowsing: One Man's Way* (Elliot) - *The Manna Machine* (Sassoon & Dale) - *The Savage God* (Alvarez) - *Catastrophe Theory* (Woodcock & Davis) - *Instruments of Darkness* (Price) - *The First Three Minutes* (Weinberg) - *The Red Limit* (Ferris) - *The Once and Future Star* (Michanowsky).
54 *CLASSIFIED EXCHANGES*

FORTEAN TIMES 33 – Autumn 1980

1 *EDITORIAL*
2 *LETTERS* - 'whale tales' - Oashpe tulpoids - time slips - kangaroo girl - bigbird - Fortean art - manna - landscape zoo.
4 *STAY, YOU IMPERFECT SPEAKERS.* ***Guy Lyon Playfair*** summarizes his investigation of the Enfield Poltergeist.
6 *ABDUCTED BY AN ARCHETYPE.* ***Hilary Evans*** examines UFO abduction stories and places them in their psychological and mythical contexts.
10 *ASK ARISTOTLE* - a further selection from the 18th century *Aristotle's Book of Problems.* [***Paul Sieveking***]
11 *COMIC STRIP: TELLY KINEX* by ***J.H.Szostek.***
12 *GATEWAYS TO MYSTERY (Part Three).* ***David Fideler,*** joined by ***Bob Tarte,*** concludes his series on 'window areas'. Archetypal dimensions of the UFO mythos. Perception, projection and the paranormal. The evolution of the flying saucer. Myth and symbolism of the UFO experience.
18 *MAN BITES MAN. Selections from the archives of George Ives.* Chicken girls - drought and death - fossil footprints - coincidences. [***Paul Sieveking***]
22 *MYSTERY ILLNESSES* - 'mass hysteria' at Hollinwell, Notts, July 1980 - theories and explanations - similar incidents, May-August 1980. [*RJMR*]
27 *STRANGE ENCOUNTERS* - aliens in Russia ('light-bulb' UFOs; encounter with green men; abducted vet; dwarf aliens) - aliens give Mexican farmer crop-growing formula - encounter in Virginia - Jovians fail to land in Brazil. [***Paul Sieveking***]
28 *IMAGES* - simulacra - elephant rock - phantom in steel works - city-scape in microchip - religious message on eggshell - President Kennedy on lunar flag. [*RJMR*]
32 *TRENDS* - arrow impalements - graves and coffins - Mount St.Helens - religion watch: pious fraud, sacrilege, strange cults. [*RJMR*]
36 *UNIDENTIFIEDS* - Jeoff Watson's Loch Ness monster photos, 3 Sept 1978 - Morgawr. [*RJMR*]

38 *ON THE TRAIL* - giant snakes - Fawcett's Brazilian sighting - the Peninsula Python, Ohio - other American monster serpents. [***Loren Coleman***]

40 *TALES FROM THE YELLOW EMPORIUM* - two-headed people - strange birth defects - 'monkey-man' - horned woman - Taoist UFOs. [***Steve Moore***]

42 *ENIGMA VARIATIONS* - children's encounters with UFO entities. [***Nigel Watson***]

44 *BOOK REVIEWS* - *Arthur C. Clarke's Mysterious World* (Welfare & Fairley) - *Photographs of the Unknown* (Rickard & Kelly) - *The Dark Gods* (Roberts & Gilbertson) - *The UFO Handbook* (Hendry) - *The Dancing Wu Li Masters* (Zukov) - *Madoc: the Making of a Myth* (Williams) - *The Wise Wound* (Shuttle & Redgrove) - *The Life of Milarepa* (Lhalungpa) - *The Mute Strategy* (DeWitt) - *Nature Detective* (Falkus) - *Schrodinger's Cat* (Wilson) - *Beyond Death* (Grof & Grof) - *Time* (von Franz) - *Zen* (Bancroft) - *Subdue the Earth* (Walworth) - *Oedipus and Akhnaton* (Velikovsky) - *Harmonic 33* (Cathie) - *The True History of the Elephant Man* (Howell & Ford) - *The New Soviet Psychic Discoveries* (Gris & Dick) - *Voices in my Ear* (Stokes) - *Ghosts of Wales* (Underwood) - *The Necronomicon* (Hay).

52 *BOOKLET REVIEWS* - *Stars, and Rumours of Stars* (McClure & McClure) - *Rosicrucian Thoughts on the Ever-burning Lamps of the Ancients* (Westcott) - *Tales of the Hexham Heads* (Screeton) - *Pennick's Endsville Pagan Almanack* (Pennick) - *Tunnels under London* (Pennick).

53 *COMIC STRIP: FACTS YOU MIGHT FORGET* by ***Pokkettz.***

54 *CLASSIFIED EXCHANGES*

FORTEAN TIMES 34 – Winter 1981

1 *EDITORIAL*

2 *LETTERS* - *Dark Gods* review debated - golfball rain - Fortean research - Clarke's *Mysterious World.*

4 *ON SYNCHRONICITY AND THE SELF.* Jungian psychologist ***Jean Shinoda Bolen*** interviewed by ***David Fideler***. Synchronicity, ESP, Taoism and the continuity of all things.

7 *COMIC STRIP: TELLY KINNEX* by ***J.H.Szostek.***

8 *IN SEARCH OF DINOSAURS.* The official report submitted to the Congolese government by ***Dr. Roy Mackal*** and ***James Powell,*** regarding their 1980 expedition in search of the dinosaur-like monster *Mokele-mbembe.* Historical background, expedition results, conclusions and recommendations.

10 *NICKNAMING THOSE AQUATIC MONSTERS.* ***Joseph W.Zarzynski*** on an enduring obsession with giving water monsters endearing names.

13 *COMIC STRIP: FACTS YOU MIGHT FORGET* by ***Pokkettz.***

14 *ON THE ROAD AGAIN.* ***Michael Goss*** on ghostly tales of 'phantom hitch-hikers'. Recent cases, themes and folklore approaches.

17 *SYNCHRONICITIES* - coincidences plaguing show business as nature follows art. [***Paul Sieveking***]

18 *STRANGE CREATURES IN POWYS.* ***Janet and Colin Bord*** report on their personal investigation into the Welsh mystery cats of October 1980.

20 *OUT OF PLACE* - mystery cat sightings 1980 - Wales - Wolverhampton - New York - Hampshire [***RJMR***] - Puma sightings in Surrey [***Chris Hall***] - Scottish Puma. [***RJMR***]

26 *MYSTERY ATTACKS* - animal attacks on human civilisation - swarms and mass attacks - lone attacks. [***Steve Moore***]

28 *COMIC STRIP: PHENOMENOMIX (THE BORDERS OF BUFFOONERY **part one**)* by ***Hunt Emerson.***

30 *MARINE MYSTERIES* - whale beachings - listing: Jan 1979 to July 1980. [*RJMR*]
32 *FALLS* - world-wide ice-falls - listing: August 1979 to December 1980. [*RJMR*]
35 *DOOMS* - inept crimes. [*Paul Sieveking*]
37 *ON THE TRAIL* - the giant squid of Plum Island, February 1980. [*Loren Coleman*]
39 *WORDS FROM THE WIZARD* - magic, water monsters and mystery cats in Ireland. [*Doc Shiels*]
41 *NOTES FROM THE TRASHKASHIC RECORDS* - aspects of the cultural consensus - the Akashic Records - the astral plane - astral parasites. [*David Fideler*]
46 *BOOK REVIEWS* - *The Encyclopedia of UFOs* (Story) - *Observing UFOs* (Haines) - *The Janos People* (Johnson) - *The Andreasson Affair* (Fowler) - *The Spiritual Nature of Man* (Hardy) - *Shamanic Voices* (Halifax) - *Primal Myths* (Sproul) - *Incredible Coincidences* (Vaughan) - *Agricultural Records AD220-1977* (Stratton) - *Tutankhamun* (Hoving) - *The Interrupted Journey* (Fuller) - *The Book of Lists No 2* (Wallace *et al*) - *La Memoire des Ovni* (Bastide) - *Psi and the Mind* (Irwin) - *The Paranormal and the Normal* (Leeds & Murphy) - *Gaia* (Lovelock) - *The Quest for Gaia* (Pedler) - *A History of Witchcraft* (Russell) - *Godel, Escher, Bach* (Hoffstadter) - *Unknown Earth* (Corliss) - *The Dead Sea Scrolls and the Christian Myth* (Allegro).
51 *BOOKLET REVIEWS* - *The UFO Cults* (Burge) - *The Parapsychological Impact of the Accident at Three Mile Island* (Arnold) - *Quantum Jump* (Simon) - *Celestial Dynamics and Levitational Force* (Morrison).
52 *CLASSIFIED EXCHANGES*
54 *NEWS - book, pamphlet and periodical news - meetings.*
56 *CROSSWORD*
57 *HEADLINES*

FORTEAN TIMES 35 – Summer 1981

1 *EDITORIAL*
2 *THE MYTH OF DARWINISM. John Michell* inveighs against the theory that has become an orthodoxy, examining its faults, consequences and mythical qualities.
6 *THE GRACE PETT SHC: A RE-EXAMINATION. Peter Christie* re-investigates the original source material for a classic spontaneous human combustion case, from Ipswich in 1744.
10 *FIRES* - possible SHC cases, 1979-1981 - deaths and mysterious burns. [*RJMR*]
11 *ANTIQUITIES* - statue finds - ancient shipwrecks - lost cities. [*Steve Moore*]
14 *THE RUNAMO RUNES. Sven Rosén* and *Bob Rickard* outline the attempts of Finnur Magnusson to translate the 'runic inscription' found at Runamo, Sweden. His revelatory triumph (1834), showing the runes to be a poetic record of an ancient battle. Berzelius and others (1838) show the 'runes' to be no more than geological features, not writing, thus exposing Magnusson's 'translation'.
19 *AMERICA MYSTICA* - the 'Double Initial Murders', Rochester, NY, 1971-1976 - their mythical and cultic significance. [*Michael Hoffman*]
22 *ON THE TRAIL* - reflections of a travelling American Fortean - Fortean guide-books - local investigations. [*Loren Coleman*]
24 *WORDS FROM THE WIZARD* - monsters and surrealism - invoking and investigating Morgawr - sightings and personal recollections. [*Doc Shiels*]
28 *COMIC STRIP: PHENOMENOMIX (THE BORDERS OF BUFFOONERY part two)* by *Hunt Emerson.*
30 *TALES FROM MALAYSIA* - Fortean phenomena 1979 (UFOs, quakes, water monsters, manimals, phantoms) - phenomena 1981 (hysterias, undying chickens, animal attacks) - Indonesia. [*Ahmad Jamaludin*]

32 *CURIOSA* - twisted chimney photo.
33 *NOTES FROM THE TRASHKASHIC RECORDS* - TV and the cultural consensus - Carl Sagan's *Cosmos*. [*Bob Tarte*]
36 *TALES FROM THE YELLOW EMPORIUM* - Doomsday prophecy - shouting rock - Devil's triangle - angry god - ancient mummy - ant pills - trepanned mice - psi powers - hot people - tailed child and fish with legs. [*Steve Moore*]
38 *PLANTS* - crying pecan - walking mango tree - miraculous Christmas tree - smoking tree. [*Paul Sieveking*]
39 *ALCHEMY AND ELIXIRS* - miracle fuels. [*Paul Sieveking*]
41 *FALLS* - frogs - stones. [*RJMR*]
44 *SCIENTIFIC CURIOSITIES* - bacterial super-organism - magnetic and square bacteria. [*RJMR*]
45 *OUT OF PLACE* - mystery cats - Welsh puma - Dartmoor panther - Luton lion. [*RJMR*]
46 *LETTERS* - albatrosses - kangaroo correspondence - winged cats - astrology - huh? - wit and wisdom - mental weather control - teleported tank - Madonna in marble simulacrum.
49 *NEWS* - meetings - books - grants - organisations.
50 *BOOK REVIEWS* - *A Geo-bibliography of Anomalies* (Eberhart) - *Incredible Life* (Corliss) - *Excalibur Briefing* (Bearden) - *Are we Being Watched?* (Bords) - *Fenris Wolf publications* - *Broca's Brain* (Sagan) - *The Quest for Gaia* (Pedler) - *By Lust Possessed* (Lombard) - *Extraterrestrial Encounter* (Boyce) - *The Dark Side of History* (Edwardes) - *My Search for the Ghost of Flight 401* (Fuller) - *Tarotmania* (Woudhuysen) - *The Paranormal* (Gooch) - *UFOs: Interplanetary Visitors* (Fowler) - *War on the Mind* (Watson).
54 *CLASSIFIED EXCHANGES*
56 *ERRATA*

FORTEAN TIMES 36 – Winter 1982

2 *EDITORIAL*
3 *LETTERS* - fauna of dreams - the Janos case - curious hailstones - Pleistocene panthers - Welsh puma - wind blast, 1863.
4 *ANOMALISTICS: A NEW FIELD OF INTERDISCIPLINARY STUDY.* ***Roger W.Wescott attempts to draw up guidelines for an inclusive view of anomalistic phenomena and their study.***
11 *COMIC STRIP: FACTS YOU MIGHT FORGET* by ***Pokkettz.***
12 *THE RUNAMO RUNES* - bibliography to article in FT 35. [*Sven Rosén & Bob Rickard*]
13 *BEHAVIOURAL CURIOSITIES* - hermits and wildmen - hiding from wars - modern cavemen. [*Paul Sieveking*]
16 *STRANGE TALES* - heart left in cave (India) - magician revives dead (Ghana). [*Steve Moore*]
17 *EMBEDDINGS* - toads in the woodpile - frogs in concrete - frogs in pea-pods - fish in tree-trunk. [*RJMR*]
19 *MIRACLES* - bleeding BVM statue - BVM visions - sleeping coach-driver - menstruating statue of Pavarti - BVM flaps. [*RJMR*]
22 *FORTEANA CORRIGENDA* *Ion Will's* on the spot investigation of a Sri Lankan Buddhist fresco demolishes its UFO connection. [*RJMR*]
23 *MEDICAL CURIOSITIES* - do-it-yourself surgery. [*RJMR*]
26 *FALLS* - coins - sand and pollen - ice and hail. [*RJMR*]

28 ***CSAR & ASSAP. Bob Rickard*** introduces *The Center for Scientific Anomalies Research* and the *Association for the Scientific Study of Anomalous Phenomena.*

29 ***SOAPBOX*** - breeding plesiosaur colonies. [***Jasper McKee***]

30 ***COMIC STRIP: PHENOMENOMIX (THE BORDERS OF BUFFOONERY part three)*** by ***Hunt Emerson.***

32 ***PHOTOS OF THE GODS. Bob Rickard*** on alleged miraculous photos of deities and their continual recurrence in different guises. 'Christ in the Snow'. 'Christ in the Clouds'. Photos of Kwan Yin.

42 ***ON THE TRAIL*** - the summer of synchronistic species - meandering monitors - crazy crocodilians - the pattering of penguins. [***Loren Coleman***]

44 ***ENIGMA VARIATIONS*** - historical aerospatial anomalies. [***Nigel Watson***]

46 ***TALES FROM THE YELLOW EMPORIUM*** - Chinese sorcery update - lake monsters. [***Steve Moore***]

48 ***FORTEAN EXTRACTS FROM THE GENTLEMAN'S MAGAZINE*** - archaeo-Forteana from 1731 to 1736. [***Peter Christie***]

51 ***BOOK REVIEWS*** - *Vanishings* (Harrison) - *English Madness* Skultans) - *The Ancient Science of Geomancy* (Pennick) - *Signs of the Gods?* (von Daniken) - *Riddle of Hangar 18* (Beckley) - *Serpent in the Sky* (West) - *The Chemical Theatre* (Nicholl) - *Alchemy* (Coudert) - *Bigfoot* (Wylie) - *Fenris Wolf & IGR publications.*

56 ***CLASSIFIED EXCHANGES***

61 ***HEADLINES***

Fortean Times

Issue No. 31

The Journal of Strange Phenomena.

Price: 95p $2.50

Fortean Times

9-12 St Annes Court,
London W1, England.

The Journal of Strange Phenomena.

Spring 1980.
ISSN 0308.5899.

Editorial.

REPORT TO THE READERS

I've always felt that the best policy is to keep people informed of the pressures, problems and potential of FT, and to date this has worked well. The result is that FT readers are tolerant and patient, confident, perhaps, that even if there are delays or obstacles, a way would be found around them and that one way or another the journal will continue to be published. Right now we are going through an erratic patch due to the pressures of earning a living–but by the end of the year we should be firmly on course again. Now, as we emerge from a period of experimentation I'd like to take stock and to outline how we at FT see our future developing.

The experiments in format were necessary to appeal to sections of the magazine-buying market we hoped to become part of. National and international distributors wouldn't touch FT unless it conformed largely to their notions of normality. This was not restricted to format alone, but to content and regularity and frequency of publication. The only way to stabilize all these factors was to become professional, and both FT 29 and 30 conveyed this approach successfully. However as we proceded, and assured of some commercial interest, it became clear that we would need a large investment programme and access to more capital than we could raise. Apart from that it would be a full-time commitment at a time when most of FT's unpaid, part-time and entirely voluntary staff had other committments of survival priority. The idea was good, but we realized we simply did not have the personal resources in time or money to carry it out. FT30 was the product of a plan to see if we could achieve professional standards on our own. It cost well over £1000 to produce, and good though it was we simply do not have enough subscribers to justify that kind of budget per issue. But we've no regrets since we've demonstrated fairly what we could do with our subject material if we had the budget. We are not in the habit of letters of praise, but to judge from the comments of many of our readers we hit the right target. "An outstanding issue, down to and including the book reviews and letters..." *(Steve Hicks)*. "Congratulations on what I consider to be the best Fortean journal I've ever had the pleasure to study." *(Anthony Smith)*. "What the beautiful and haunting cover promises, the inside appears to deliver..." *(Mike Hoffman)*.

Cont on p13

Contents.

ARTICLES

3 **Wildman** *Yuan Zhenxin & Huang Wanpo.*
6 **Gateways to Mystery** *David Fideler*
14 **The Touch of Death** *Michael Goss.*

NOTES

30 **Strange Encounters** *UFO Muggers*
32 **Heavens Above** *New in Space*
33 **Antiquities** *Luck Dips*
35 **Ghosts** *Haunted Houses*
37 **Synchronicities** *Name Games*
39 **Lights** *Ball Lightnings.*
42 **Trends** *Recent Themes.*

COLUMNS

12 **Comix** *JH Szostek.*
21 **Comix** *Pokkettz*
22 **Enigma Variations** *Nigel Watson.*
24 **On the Trail** *Loren Coleman*
27 **Tales from the Yellow Emporium**
28 **Comix** *Hunt Emerson*

USUAL STUFF

44 **Reviews** *Hardbacks, Paperbacks.*
51 **Classified Exchange** *Journals*
53 **Letters**

Cover art by **Andrzej Dudzinski.**

Published by Fortean Times Ltd: 9-12 St Annes Court, London W1. Editor: ROBERT JM RICKARD. Editorial Assistants: STEVE MOORE, PAUL SIEVEKING, VALERIE THOMAS. Contributing Editors: DAVID FIDELER, PHIL LEDGER. Art Director: RICHARD ADAMS. Comix Editor and section heading artwork: HUNT EMERSON. Photosetting by Wordsmith Graphics, 19A West End, Street, Somerset. Reprosetting by Magic Ink, 22 Dane Rd., Margate, Kent CT9 2AA. Printed by Bija Press, Beeches Green, Stroud, Glos.

FORTEAN TIMES is a quarterly journal of news, notes, reviews and references on current and historical strange phenomena, related subjects and philosophies. A friend to all groups and magazines continuing the work of Charles Fort in investigating, studying and discussing all aspects of strange phenomena. SUBMISSION is invited of articles, artwork, cartoons, and news clippings on related subjects. The publishers can assume no responsibility for unsolicited material, but all reasonable care will be taken while in FT's possession. If material is to be returned, please enclose SAE. CORRESPONDENCE: letters-of-comment and personal experience are welcome. If replies are required please enclose SAE. The editor regrets it is not always possible to reply promptly. ADVERTISING and DISTRIBUTION ENQUIRIES: contact the editor at the above address, or ring 01 552 5466. SUBSCRIPTION INFORMATION: see p56.

Wildman: Fact or Fiction.

There have been one or two brief reports, in the Western press, concerning the 'Wild Man' of Hubei Province, in China—a creature which appears to be similar to the better known Bigfoot and Yeti. Most of these reports derive from an article published in the July '79 issue of the Peking magazine, *China Reconstructs'*, written by two researchers at the Institute of Paleoanthropology and Vertebrate Paleontology, of the Chinese Academy of Sciences, and who were members of the investigating team working in the area in 1976 and 1977.

We are grateful to the authors, Yuan Zhenxzin and Huang Wanpo, for their kind permission to reprint the original article, which we do so here, unedited, and hope will enjoy the flavour of a piece written in a somewhat unusual style...

At 1 a.m. on May 14, 1976 six cadres from the Shennongjia forestry region in Hubei province were driving along the highway near Chunshuya village between Fangxian county and Shennongjia, when they came upon a strange, tailless creature with reddish fur. The driver kept his headlights beamed on the creature while the others went forward to investigate. They got a good look at it from a distance of a few feet before it walked away. It was neither a bear nor any other animal they had ever seen before. A telegram reporting the incident was sent to the Institute of Paleoanthropology and Vertebrate Paleontology of the Chinese Academy of Sciences.

Historical References

This was not the first time such a thing had been heard of. Down through the centuries Chinese literary works and folk legends had told of big, hairy man-like creatures that walked erect on two legs, frequenting the vast forests of the Qinling-Bashan-Shennongjia mountain region in central China. Two thousand years ago during the Warring States period, Qu Yuan, (340-278 B.C.) the statesman-poet of the State of Chu, referred in his verses to 'mountain ogres.' Qu Yuan's home was just south of Shennongjia, in what is today's Zigui county in Hubei province. The Tang dynasty (A.D. 618-907) historian Li Yanshou in his *Southern History* describes a band of 'hairy men' in the region that is today Jiangling county, also in Hubei province. The Qing dynasty poet Yuan Mei (1716-1798) in his *New Rhythms* tells of the existence of a creature 'monkey-like', yet not a monkey' in southeastern Shaanxi province's Xianning county.

More recent accounts include the one by Wang Zelin, a former biology student now living in Xuzhou, Jiangsu province. He claims to have seen an unknown creature, shot by hunters, while he was travelling in southwestern Shaanxi in 1940. 'It looked like those plaster reconstructions of the Peking Man,' he recalls, 'only much more hairy, and it had an ugly protruding snout.' Peasants living in this locality also tell about encounters with strange hairy 'wild men' which 'walk upright like humans, but have faces like monkeys.'

The Challenge

The main reaction to such accounts had been one of scepticism or disbelief. But there were people intruiged enough to look into the matter. Groups of scientists, armymen and others have penetrated the vastnesses of the primeval forests in the past to see what they could find. Some, fascinated by the idea, have delved into ancient literature. Others have written to the Academy of Sciences contributing information and asking to be included in investigating teams. Still others went investigating using their own time and money.

Thus, when news of the incident on the highway near Chunshuya reached the Chinese Academy of Sciences, it was decided to organise an investigation team. Composed of science workers from Beijing, Shanghai and Hubei, Shaanxi and Sichuan provinces, a hundred people in all, and assisted by a contingent of army scouts from Wuhan, the team worked in the region during 1976 and 1977.

More Facts

On June 19, 1976, Gong Yulan, a 32-year-old member of the Qunli brigade of the Qiaoshang commune in Fangxian county and her four-year-old child were in the mountains cutting grass when they saw some such creature scratching its back against a tree trunk.

When our team questioned people in the area, the wife of the brigade leader recalled how Gong Yulan had come running to her door, all out of breath with great beads of sweat on her forehead saying, 'A wild man! A wild man!'

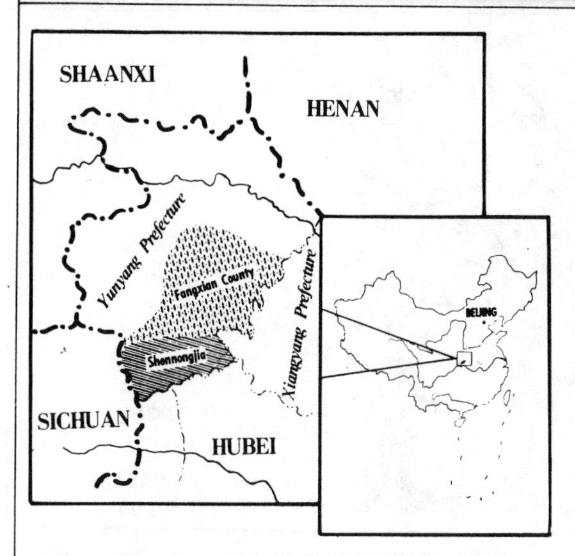

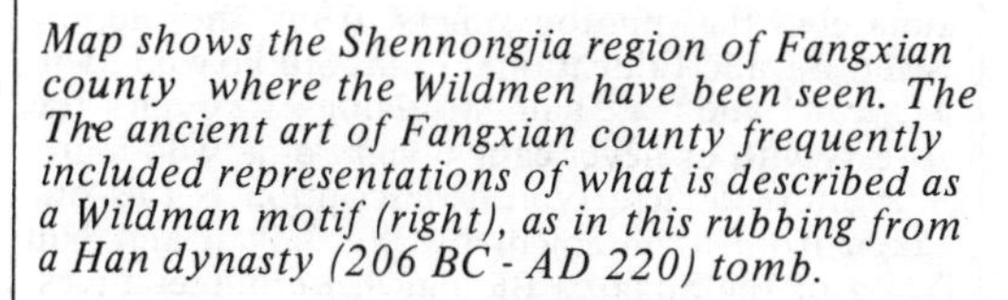

Map shows the Shennongjia region of Fangxian county where the Wildmen have been seen. The The ancient art of Fangxian county frequently included representations of what is described as a Wildman motif (right), as in this rubbing from a Han dynasty (206 BC - AD 220) tomb.

Gong Yulan led us to the spot where she had seen the creature. On the tree trunk, 1.3 metres from the ground, we found several dozen fine hairs of varying lengths. In August of the same year another group of investigators discovered two long hairs 1.8 metres from the ground on the same tree trunk.

In 1976 and 1977 our team interviewed hundreds of people — cadres, teachers, hunters, herb collectors and others, who gave vivid accounts of encounters with the 'wild men' in Fangxian county, the Shennongjia forestry district and Zhushan and Zhuxi counties.

With local militiamen and commune members the team organised several large searches. But no such creatures were found, perhaps because of the extremely rugged terrain and thick vegetation.

In two years the team investigated an area of 1,500 square kilometres, travelling a total of 6,000 kilometres. Practically every place in Shennongjia and surrounding counties where traces of 'wild men' had been reported was visited by members of the team.

We collected data on the region's geology, terrain, glaciation, meteorology, vegetation, and vertebrates including amphibians, reptilians, mammals and bird life. But on the 'wild man' we only got indirect evidence, such as hair, footprints and samples of excrement, and taped interviews with many people who claimed personally to have seen a 'wild man'.

Nevertheless we felt that the veil of mystery and legend surrounding the matter was beginning to lift a little.

Analysis of Data

Let us take a brief look at some of the data collected:

HAIR: Samples of hair brought back to Beijing and analyzed by several research departments were found to differ greatly in nature and shape from that of the brown or black bear, but resembled that of primates. This discounted the theory that it might have been a bear Gong Yulan had seen.

Could it have been some sort of primate? Investigations revealed four members of the monkey family living in the Shennongjia forests. But all of these were smaller in size and quite different in appearance from the creature described by Gong Yulan. Thus hair analysis in itself was inconclusive.

FOOTPRINTS: The question has been asked: Did you definitely see footprints of the 'wild man'? This requires more than a straight 'yes' or 'no' answer.

In those two years we came across a great many footprints of bears and other creatures large and small. Among them were a number of highly peculiar ones, similar to yet unlike those of either bears or men. A report written on the spot by investigators describes them thus:

1. The prints are of an elongated foot, wider (approximately 10 centimetres) in front and nar-

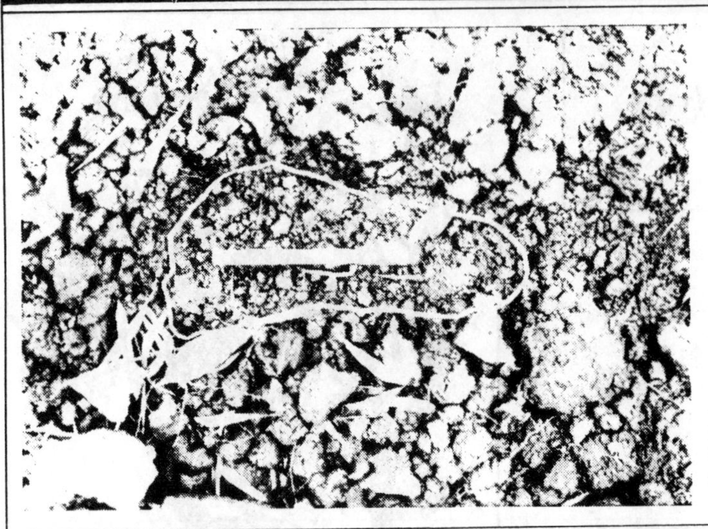

A Wildman footprint, outlined by an investigator, approximately 25cm long. (Photo: Huang Wanpo.)

rower (approximately 5cm.) at the back.
2. Toe marks are oval in shape, with one somewhat separated from the others.
3. The footprints follow each other in single file, the distance between them varying between 50cm and one metre.

EXCREMENT: In September 1976 six little piles of excreta were discovered on top of a steep rock halfway up a mountain in the Hongta commune in Fangxian county. During the period before and after this find there were four reports of signs of 'wild man' activity in this area. On three occasions — in March, May and July, 1976 — these involved a female and its child. A single adult was seen in November of the same year.

The excrement, already dry and hard, was similar in appearance to that of human beings. Analysis found bits of undigested fruit and wild chestnuts, but no animal fur or bone fragments.

Another such discovery occurred on August 30, 1977 at a place called Tielu Gully at the Panshui commune in the Shennongjia forestry region. Investigators had been told of 'wild man' footprints there and followed them. At one spot it had dug insect cocoons out of the bark of birch trees, presumably to eat them. Further along, on a hill slope and in a cave, excrement was found containing large amounts of cocoon skin.

These findings in both instances exclude the possibility of the excrement being that of humans as we know them or of a carnivorous creature. On the other hand, in each case both the quantity of the droppings and the size of remnant food particles were smaller than that of hoofed animals or bears. On the whole, the samples bore a strong resemblance to the excreta of the omnivorous primates.

Eyewitness Accounts

Some idea of the 'wild men' can be obtained from interviews with eyewitnesses. We amassed hundreds of thousands of words of these. Unfortunately, the photographers from the Beijing Scientific and Educational Films Studio who spent a year and a half trudging through the forests with us never caught sight of a 'wild man'.

A more or less typical description is this one taken from a statement by Wu Jiayan and Niu Yong of the Shaanxi Biological Resources Investigation Team in October 1977, on the reported discovery of a 'hairy man' — as the creature is known locally in the Taibai mountains in central Shaanxi province. Pang Gensheng, a 33-year-old team leader in the Cuifeng commune in Shaanxi's Zhouzhi county told them:

"In early June, 1977, I went to Dadi Gully to cut logs. Somewhere between 11 and 12 in the morning I ran into a 'hairy man' in the woods on the slope of the gully. It came closer and closer. I got scared and kept retreating until my back was against a stone cliff and I couldn't go any further. The hairy man came up to seven or eight feet, and then to about five feet from me. I raised my axe, ready to fight for my life. We stood like that, neither of us moving, for more than an hour. Then I groped for a stone and threw it at him. It hit him in the chest. He uttered several howls and rubbed the spot with his left hand. Then he turned left and leaned against a tree, then walked away slowly toward the bottom of the gully. He kept making a mumbling sound.

"He was about seven feet tall, with shoulders wider than a man's, a sloping forehead, deep-set eyes, and a bulbous nose with slightly upturned nostrils. He had sunken cheeks, ears like a man's but bigger, and round eyes also bigger than a man's. His jaw jutted out and he had protruding lips. His front teeth were as broad as a horse's. His eyes were black. His hair was dark brown and more than a foot long, and hung loosely over his shoulders. His whole face, except for the nose and ears, was covered with short hairs. His arms hung down to below his knees. He had big hands with fingers about half a foot long [a Chinese foot is 33cm] and with thumbs only slightly separated from the fingers. He didn't have any tail, and the hair on his body was short. He had thick thighs, shorter than the lower part of his leg. He walked upright with his legs apart. His feet were each about a foot long and half that broad — broader in front and narrow behind, with splayed toes. He was a male. That much I saw clearly."

Theories and Speculations

Ancient literature on the subject of the 'wild man' limited itself to accounts and descriptions, and made no attempt to look into the whys and wherefores.

Today, there are two main lines of conjecture on the origin of the purported 'wild man.' One holds that he is a 'hairy man' — an atavistic throwback of the human race; the other that he is a descendant of the great ape, *Gigantopithecus.*

Are the 'wild men' genetic throwbacks — individuals born with a lot of hair who have been discriminated against and rejected by society and forced to seek an existence in the wilds? Recent descriptions of children and adults born with exceptional amounts of facial and body hair, a feature often accompanied by longer arms than average, might seem to support this supposition.

Are the 'wild men' descendants of *Gigantopithecus,* the gigantic prehominid or manlike ape that inhabited the earth long ago, but had been considered extinct? The earliest and most recent records of these great apes in China are all in Guangxi, further to the south. But somewhere between the latter part of the Early Pleistocene Epoch (700-800,000 years ago) and Middle Pleistocene (500-600,000 years ago) they also existed in the vicinity of Hubei's Jianshi county, southwest of Shennongjia in the same mountain chain. *Gigantopithecus* bones have been found among fossilized bones used in traditional Chinese medicine and bought from local peasants by goverment trading companies in Hubei's Badong and Xingshan regions, although there is no way of ascertaining the exact period to which they belong.

On the basis of studies in comparative anatomy, the paleoanthropologist Prof. Wu Rukang says, 'Proceeding from available data, we can only say in general terms that *Gigantopithecus* had large massive bones and a huge torso, although his limbs were only slightly longer and sturdier than man's. He was probably as tall or slightly taller than modern man.'

This description is similar to eyewitness descriptions of the 'wild man' which tells of a semi-ape semi-human being that escapes classification.

What about the theory that *Gigantopithecus* has long been extinct? This may not be necessarily so. The Giant Panda, a species known to have existed side by side with the great ape for several million years, is still very much alive today. Many relic plants — all living fossils — still grow in the Qinling-Bashan-Shennongjia region. The metasequoia, the dove tree and the Chinese tulip tree, for instance, are rare species surviving from the Tertiary Period. The fact that they exist shows that this region, unlike other middle-latitude regions, did not undergo a total eradication of its ancient flora since the Tertiary Period. This is because the glaciers of the Quaternary Period (the last geological era) were, in this region, of the valley type and did not greatly affect the flora and fauna. So *Gigantopithecus*, too, might have survived.

At both low and high altitudes, the region provides an excellent ecological environment for its rich and varied mammalian species, such as serows, musk deer, river deer, several types of muntjac, masked civets, ferrets and porcupines. Such rare animals as the takin, the golden monkey and the Giant Panda live and multiply here. Also here is a white-coloured bear, which may be either an individual variation or a new species.

The centuries-old 'wild man' riddle remains unsolved. Like the Loch Ness investigators who have not yet found their monster, we still do not have enough evidence to prove — or disprove — the existence of 'wild men' in the primeval forests of China's temperate and subtropical regions. But science has been challenged, and we have taken up the challenge.

Yuan Zhenxin and Huang Wanpo.

Prof. Qian Guozhen (2nd from right) with investigation team members (Huang Wanpo.)

[FT has also received another article from the authors, in Chinese, which first appeared in the quarterly journal Hua Shi *(Fossils) (1979). This is between three and four times as long as the piece presented here, and contains further information, illustrations, and some variance of treatment, the article being aimed at a slightly less popular audience. We have had this 10,000-character manuscript translated; however, translation fees are prohibitively high, and we find ourselves forced to publish the material as a separate pamphlet. To the translation will be added an appendix containing more reports from Chinese historical literature, recent developments and whatever critical apparatus we can provide. The result should be an illustrated booklet of some 24 pages, but we regret that, with the cost of translation included, we will have to charge somewhere in the region of 75p–£1. Please do not order yet. Publication is scheduled for some time in the Summer, but the work proceeds slowly. We will make an announcement in the next issue, with full details and a firm price.* Steve Moore.*]*

Gateways to Mystery.

After many delays on the editorial side, we are very glad to begin a three-part study of a wide variety of Fortean phenomena in the state of Michigan, by **David Fideler**. Dave, an energetic and dedicated Fortean, has developed the idea of geo-magnetic 'window areas' which act as triggers or as a focus for mystery animals, UFOs and other Fortean events. Based upon historical data and primary field investigations by his Michigan Anomaly Research group, Dave builds up a phenomenological picture of his home state, and extrapolates the implications from there...

It is my belief that the researcher investigating extraordinary phenomena must be willing to pass into the traditional domains of religion, mysticism and the mysteries, art, mythology, magic and the occult. These areas, if explored without credulousness, dogmatism, and undue anxiety, may be more fruitful pathways to follow than 'science' on the road to understanding the phenomena being studied...

Robert Masters

BACKGROUND

It has been observed, on more than one occasion, that there exists peculiar haunted regions upon the face of this planet. These enigmatic 'window areas', which serve as focal points for UFO's, Mystery Animals, and all manner of unusual phenomena, are often as puzzling as the 'Things' they host.

Many serious researchers, including Michell and Rickard. have noted this:

...observed connection, dating from very early times and continuing into the present, between phantom forms, mystery lights, certain old tracks, ancient sacred centers, channels within the earth's magnetic field, geological irregularities and a seasonally recurrent force...which can be dangerous or fatal to human life. [1]

Certainly, if the records are anything to go by, in many instances we are dealing with locales that have been 'haunted' for centuries; even place names often reflect an area's connection with unusual phenomena. John Keel, who has given many samples of this in his many books and articles [2], has personally devoted considerable time investigating the Mystery Animal and UFO events that plague the area surrounding *Mount Misery* on New York's Long Island. [3;4] More recently, author Loren Coleman has dealt with the connection between 'Devil names' and phenomenal locales in his recent *Fortean Times* article. (*FT*29, p35-36).

We have an example of our own.

The area surrounding the towns of Draguignan and Les Nourrandons in southeastern France makes up one such haunted region. In 1973 a dramatic encounter with a UFO and its occupants ocurred immediately to the north of Draguignan on the slope of le Melmount - *'the evil mountain.'* [5] UFO activity, which is nothing new to the area, seems to be strangely connected with nearby *fault lines*. But perhaps even more amazing is the name of Draguignan itself, which means, literally, 'town of the dragon.' It is said the place has ancient associations with monsters.

The dragon or serpent, within the context of world mythology, has a multitude of connotations, occasionally appearing as a celestial figure, while assuming a chthonic nature in other times and places. It is the 'spirit of the waters,' often-times representative of unconscious and instinctual energies. Irregardless of the form it assumes, the serpent refers to a dynamic and volatile element, 'symbolic of energy itself — of force pure and simple.' [6] In the Hindu cosmology, for example, the *nagas* are mythical serpent kings that populate deep lakes and the underworld. When the earth quakes, it is said, the *nagas* are restless.

These projected associations, as C.G. Jung correctly observed, are common to the psychology of the archaic mind.

While it is, of course impossible to ascertain whether or not the name Draguignan resulted from the observation of weird geophysical phenomena, such a connection is suggested by the region's folklore, which seems to describe a strange form of 'telluric discharge':

...1km. from the town, along the road to Castellane, there is a dolmen: Pierre de le Fee (The Fairy's Stone). It consists of three raised stones, covered with a slab 6 metres wide, and 50 cms. thick. The dolmen is guarded by three symbolic trees: a nettle-tree, a juniper tree, and an oak, and has provided the setting for a nice legend, in which a great flame gushes out of the ground. *[7] (Our emphasis.)*

Unusual 'discharge' phenomena of this type, frequently appearing at ground level, have been observed for hundreds of years. And as surely as the serpent stirs in the 'town of the dragon,' such things are seen in the present age, although frequently within the context of UFO and Mystery Animal reports (see figure 1).

Yet, there is more, and the Draguignan phenomena are seemingly mirrored in nearby Les

Aveyron, France, 1966 *(FSR 16:5)*

Figure l - These examples of strange luminous phenomena from UFO journals may represent one category of Fortean events associated with transient electromagnetic fields. There appear to be distinct similarities between these 'UFO phenomena' and conventional 'geophysical luminosities'.

Cinncinnati, Ohio, 1973 *(Canadian UFO Report 3:9)*

Bristol, England, 1968 *(FSR 14:4)*

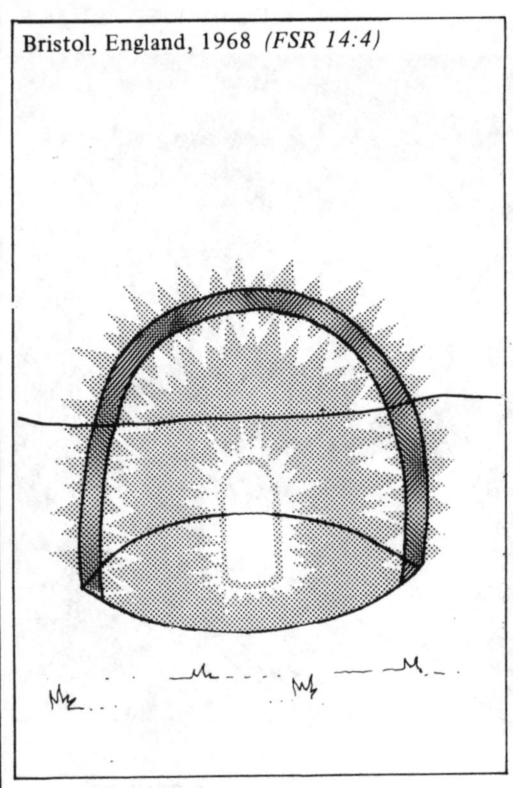

Avellino, Italy, 1977 *(FSR 25:1);*

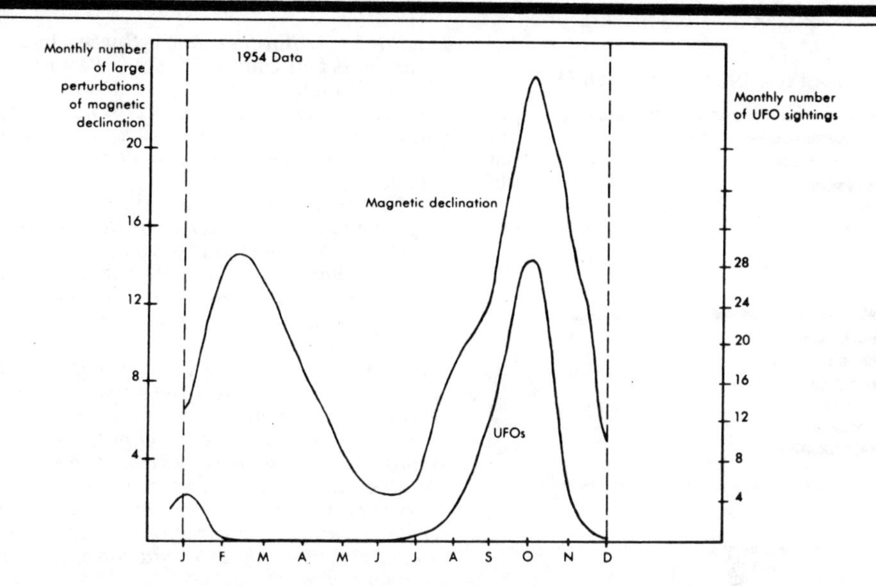

Figure 2 - Some researchers feel that the large-scale magnetic storms electrically charge magnetic variation anomalies and precipitate seismic movement in fault areas. This could give rise to 'telluric discharge phenomena' in window sectors. The figure above shows a clear correlation between magnetic storms and UFO landings in France during the 1954 'humanoid' wave. It is interesting to note that 40% of these Type 1 UFO events occurred on or within the immediate vicinity of known seismic fault lines during the disturbed period. (From C.Poher, 'Time Correlations between Geomagnetic Disturbances and Eye-witness Accounts of UFOs', FSR 20:1.

Nourrandons. For it is here that UFOs frequently land amid the fields, and old buildings have the reputation of being haunted. Perhaps they are, but we wonder: are they haunted by powerful 'mental influences,' or by some force, geophysical or otherwise, that pervades the area at times? Whatever the case, and it may prove that many factors are at play (perhaps working in symphony, we speculate), the buildings are by no means the only haunted sights. J.C. Dufor,writing in the *Flying Saucer Review* about local UFO activity, reports: 'Strangely enough, a field adjoining the scene of the flyovers and landings is called *'Close Saint-Esprit'* or *'Clos des Esprits'!' [8]* Translated, these names appear respectively as *Holy Spirit Field'* and *'Field of the Spirits'*...titles which suggest associations with otherworldly phenomena.

This entire sector seems quite active, and to the north of Les Nourrandons is the town of Valensole, site of the famous 1965 UFO landing. Indeed, something very strange is underfoot....

Forteana, Fault Lines and Magnetic Anomalies.

The 'hot spot' that we have just discussed is but one of the hundreds, if not thousands, of largely unrecognised haunted areas that cover the earth. Since these areas are remarkable for their amazing historical continuity of unusual phenomena reports, we can only surmise that *the factors responsible are relatively invariant and intimately connected with the make up of the locale.*

Evans-Wentz, in his remarkable study of Celtic fairy-lore, concluded that '....there seem to be certain favoured places on the earth where its magnetic and even more subtle forces are most powerful and more easily felt by persons susceptible to such things...' [9]

John Keel, who calls these mystery sectors 'window' areas, reports that they are often centred around seismic fault lines and magnetic anomalies in the terrestrial field. In addition, Keel observes that a person's interaction with electromagnetic fields in these 'gateways' may induce a conductive state for an encounter with non-ordinary realities.

Information which supports the connection between weird phenomena and geophysical anomalies has been gathered by researchers around the world.

For example, in 1954 the country of France experienced a massive wave of UFO reports. In all, over 200 reports of UFO *landings* from that particular 'flap' have been collected [10], many of which include accounts of the now-famous 'little men'. When certain researchers made a study of these reports in the late 1960's they discovered, undoubtedly to their amazement, that 40% of all landings occured within the immediate vicinity (1km.) of fault zones. Furthermore, a little less than 20% of all reports were situated directly over seismic fault lines, a figure much higher than statistically random distribution would offer. [11] More recently, Dr. Claude Poher, using data obtained from a French geophysical observatory,

Figure 3.

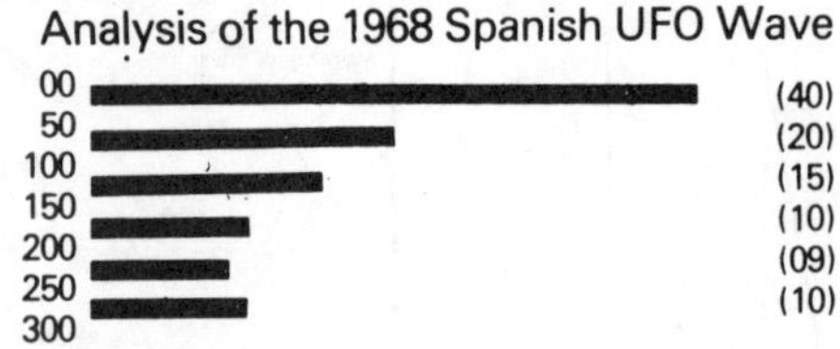

Distribution of UFO cases according to distance from seismic fault lines.

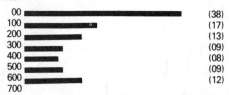

Distribution of UFO cases according to distance from magnetic anomalies.

NB: Distance is in kilometers

(SOURCE: "Conclusions of the Statistical Analysis of the UFO Wave During 1968-69," Data Net #68)

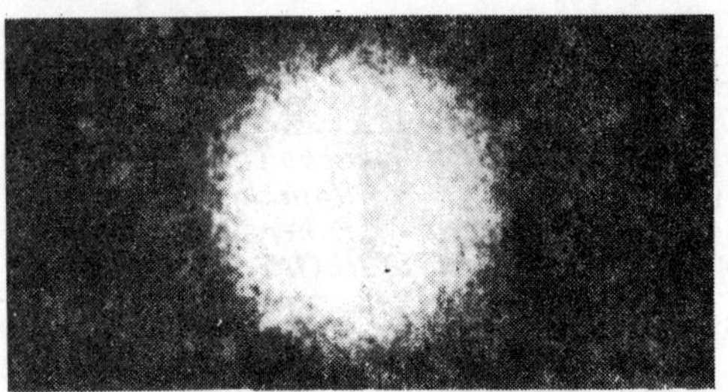

Figure 4 - The infrared photograph above is the first of seven exposures of a New Jersey 'Mystery Light' taken by a Vestigia research team. The 'SpookLight' which has made many appearances over the years appears to be related to a local seismic fault line.

Figure 5 - Within their book Space-Time Transients and Unusual Events, *Persinger and Lafreniere discuss several possible mechanisms through which large-scale electromagnetic fields may be generated in 'window areas'. One of these, the magnetic variation anomaly, is pictured above.*

A magnetic variation anomaly is a body of highly conductive material located beneath the earth's surface, which is surrounded by resistive material. During geomagnetic storms (caused by unusual solar activity), the magnetic variation anomaly, which is usually inactive, becomes charged with an electrical field in the fashion of a huge bar magnet. Smaller conductive regions, located near the surface of the earth, have the propensity to further define and focus the enormous electrical potential into smaller, localized areas. The outcome is the production of intense and transient electromagnetic fields at ground level. It is assumed that surface features such as automobiles, railroad tracks and power lines would continue to further further define the field.

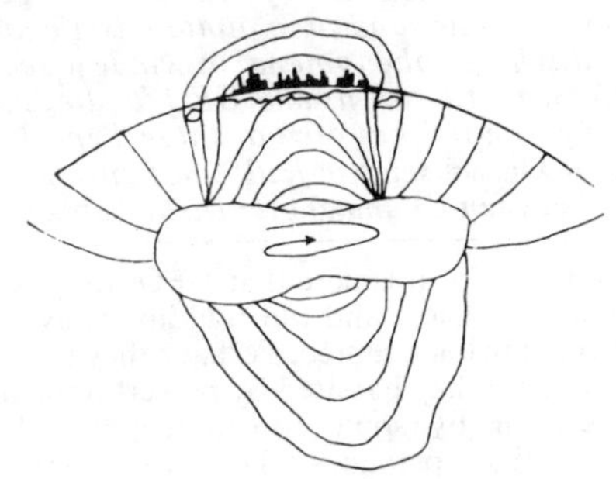

MAGNETIC VARIATION ANOMALIES

discovered that UFO activity from the period showed a distinct relationship with geomagnetic storm frequency, as seen in figure 2.

These findings are repeated elsewhere. In Spain, data collected from the 1968 wave of UFO activity shows a similar trend. [12] As the reader can see, a close relationship appears to exist between fault lines, magnetic anomalies, and UFO activity. (Figure 3).

These studies lend further support to the important work of Michael A. Persinger and Gyslaine F. Lafreniere, two Canadian research scientists who have analysed over 6,000 reports of Fortean phenomena. Their discoveries, outlined in *Space-Time Transients and Unusual Phenomena* provide the strongest support yet for the 'geophysical connection'. Beside demonstrating that Forteana cluster around fault areas in the United States, Persinger and Lafreniere discuss various mechanisms through which the phenomena may be created. Drawing upon recent discoveries in the realm of geophysics, they conclude that UFOs and other unusual phenomena are connected with large-scale electromagnetic fields that occasionally build up in certain areas of geophysical anomaly.

Unusual electrical activity has repeatedly been observed in the vicinity of fault zones, the most striking example being that of earthquake lights. That these striking, but naturally occurring, luminosities have been long observed is suggested by an old Japanese haiku:

The earth speaks softly
To the mountain
Which trembles
And lights the sky. [13]

As Dr. John S. Derr has recently observed [14], one likely candidate for electrical field production in fault areas is a little known phenomenon discivered in 1881: the piezoelectric effect. It is based on the observation that if one presses certain types of quartz crystals together immense voltages are created. Indeed, there is a quickly growing body of data which suggests that seismic pressure on quartz-bearing rocks in the vicinity of fault lines contributes directly to the production of some Fortean phenomena.

One particular noteworthy study was conducted by Vestiga, a New Jersey-based Fortean

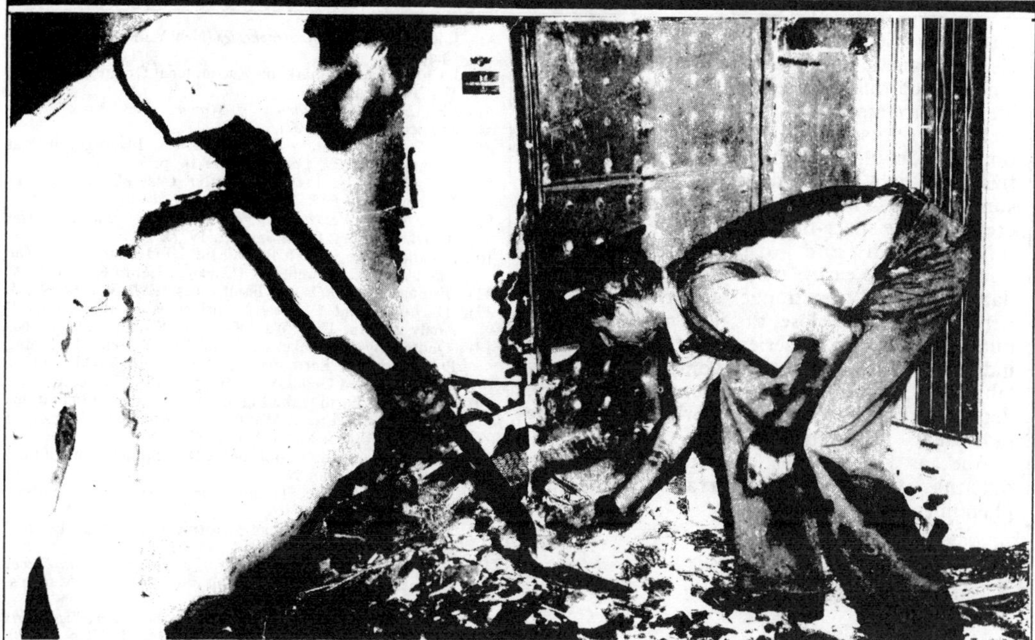

Figure 6 - When Mrs Mary Reeser, 67, of St Petersburg, Florida, 'departed this life on a pillar of fire', she spontaneously combusted just before the peak of an intense geomagnetic storm on the 1st of July 1951. The geomagnetic disturbance peaked at a value of about 1.7 on the 2nd, while the monthly average for that July was 0.82. The photo above (from St Petersburg Times & Evening Independent*) showing scant remains of Mrs Reeser and her armchair and evidence of the incredible fierce heat, inexplicably contained.*

investigations group that has actually monitored an unusual mystery light. (see figure 4). The 'spooklight', which has repeatedly appeared over a section of railroad track, appears to be associated with a local fault line and the high preponderance of quartz-bearing rock in the area. [15] In addition the group claims to have discovered a high correlation between phenomena of this type and the location of seismic fault lines.

Another mechanism possibly contributing to the generation of electrical fields in window sectors is the magnetic variation anomaly, a transient phenomenon itself. (Figure 5). Electro-magnetic fields result when underground pockets of a conductive material become 'charged' during magnetic storms. This electrical potential may then be focused to higher and higher values by smaller conductive bodies located near the surface of the earth. Therefore, we might expect to discover 'window areas within window areas', or window *clusters* resulting from the inherent nature of the magnetic anomaly itself and the smaller, more conductive 'focusing lenses'.

One might also expect to find a correlation between Fortean events and magnetic storms, as in the case of the 1954 UFO landings. Within this context, the work of Larry Arnold [16] and Livingston Gearhart [17], which links cases of spontaneous human combustion (SHC) with magnetic disturbances, is also of interest. (Figure 6). In addition, there is some interesting evidence that solar shock waves, which result in geomagnetic storms, may trigger earthquake activity. [18] Persinger and Lafreniere feel that these 'cosmic shock waves' may create small movements in fault areas, precipitating electrical field generation (a la piezo-effect), and thereby 'opening the window' for the propagation of unusual phenomena:

Solar impulses, like any impulse instituted upon a homeostatic system, would have large magnitude effects upon the phenomena discussed in the previous sections. The earth as a control system, maintains a homeostatic-like condition by a number of internal adjustment mechanisms. However, the sudden and intense 'demand' produced by a large solar flare would have the propensity to crush delicate stable-states or subsystems in the process of adjustment, and result in the instability required for the occurence of unusual events. For subsurface systems already in an unstable condition, the impulse might be sufficient to precipitate a large scale change in activity: it might be the proverbial 'last straw'. [19]

Another 'cosmic trigger' that apparently induces movement in fault areas is related to lunar position. Beside affecting ocean height, the tidal pull of the moon is large enough to lift the *crust* of the earth seven inches. Recently, several instructive papers have appeared on the connection between lunar position and earthquakes. [20; 21]

In summary, the geophysical hypothesis states that certain types of unusual phenomena appear to be inherently associated with 'window sectors' or areas of geophysical anomaly. At certain times, due to a variety of interrelated factors, powerful electromagnetic fields are produced in such areas which, according to the theory, could affect the local environment in any number of ways. These fields, representing formidable electrical potentials, could easily produce plasmas, unusual flashes of light, and strange odours. Perhaps, as some writers have suggested, 'openings' are created in the space-time continumn, allowing for teleportation and other 'bleedthrough' phenomena. Nearby witnesses might report 'landed saucers' or strange 'apparitions'. If the percipient got too close, the field might induce a quasi-hallucinatory experience in the unfortunate individual. He would then complain of being 'abducted', 'attacked', or 'taken to fairyland', depending upon the cultural world-view and the individual's private belief system.

And, as we shall see, a welter of disturbing dreams, visions, and parapsychological phenomena may follow...

David R. Fideler.

[End of part one.]

REFERENCES

1) J. Michell and R.J.M. Rickard: *Phenomena: A book of Wonders* (New York: Pantheon, 1977), p.79.
2) J. Keel: 'The Time Cycle Factor,' *FSR,* Vol. 15, No 3.
3) J. Keel: *Strange Creatures from Time and Space* (Greenwhich, Conn: Fawcett, 1970), Chapt. 10.
4) J. Keel: *The Mothman Prophesies* (New York: Dutton, 1975), Chapt. 15.
5) J. Chasseigne: 'Remarkable Encounter at Draguignan,' *FSR,* Vol.20, No. 4.
6) J.E. Cirlot: *A Dictionary of Symbols* (New York: Philosophical Library, 1962), p. 272.
7) J. Chasseigne and F. Moll: 'The Investigations at Draguignan,' *FSR Case Histories* 14, p. 5.
8) J.C. Dufor: 'A French Repeater Case: Events at Les Nourrandons,' *FSR,* Vol. 19, No. 3.
9) W.Y. Evans-Wentz: *The Fairy-Faith in Celtic Countries* (Gerrards Cross: Colin Smythe, 1977).
10) J. Vallee: 'The Pattern Behind the UFO Landings' in *The Humanoids,* C. Bowen, ed., (Chicago: Henry Regnery).
11) F. Lagarde: 'UFOs and Fault Lines,' *FSR,* Vol. 14, No. 4.
12) D. Lopez and F Ares: 'Conclusions of the Statistical Analysis of the UFO Wave During 1968-69,' *Data-Net* 68.
13) Quoted by D. Finkelstein and J.R. Powell: 'Lightning Production in Earthquakes,' General Assembly, International Union Geodesy Geophysics, 15th, Moscow, 1971.
14) J.S. Derr: 'Earthquake Lights: A Review of Observations and Present Theories,' *Bulletin of the Seismological Society of America,* Vol. 63, No. 6, 2177-2187.
15) C.L. Wiedemann: 'Results of the N.J. 'Spook Light' Study,' *Vestigia Newsletter,* No. 2.
16) L.E. Arnold: 'The Flaming Fate of Dr. Irving Bentley,' *Fate,* April 1977.
17) L. Gearhart: 'Geomagnetic Storms and Fortean Events,' *Pursuit,* Vol. 8, No. 2.
18) G. Playfair and S. Hill: *The Cycles of Heaven: Cosmic Forces and what they are Doing to You* (New York: St. Martin's, 1978), p. 109.
19) M.A. Persinger and G.F. Lafreniere: *Space-Time Transients and Unusual Events* (Chicago: Nelson-Hall, 1977), p. 219-20.
20) Playfair and Hill: *The Cycles of Heaven,* Chapt. 5.
21) R. Cooke: 'Quakes Linked to Moon's Pull,' Boston *Globe,* April 24, 1978. Cr: Loren Coleman. Also see P. Devereux and A. York: 'Portrait of a Fault Area,' pt. 2, *The News* (Fortean Times) No. 12.

TELLY KINEX

by JH Szostek.

Cont from p1

Loren Coleman made a point when he wrote: "It is superb... from suicidal pumkins to the artwork of Emerson, Woodruff and friends, the latest issue was a cosmic Fortean adventure. I think you may have outdone yourselves." That looks true, now; the economies necessary to our survival will unavoidably seem like a step backwards. Beginning this issue we are thinned to 56 pages–still more than many other journals. We will also have to be less extravagant with our covers. It is not the printing cost of a full colour cover which is prohibitive but the cost of colour separation for the plates, which can amount to £200 alone. The other economy is more invisible: we turn from the ideal of photosetting–and here we record our thanks to Tom Graves and Jan Hoult of *Wordsmith*, whose pruned-to-the-bone prices are still beyond our reach–to IBM typesetting, which we also would be unable to afford were it not for our unselfish friends at *Magic Ink*, who virtually saved us from going back to typing the issue on our old typers ourselves.

Another reader touches on another problem. Mike Grayson, even though a "recent convert to your quarterly magazine of zany, whacky humour and neo-existentialist philosophy," thought it a steal at the price. "It seems heartless to send only £3 for 4 issues of a journal of FT's quality." Other readers have enclosed donations, large and small, and their names are recorded in our Truss Fund listings. All these warming reactions spur us on to find ways to keep the quality of FT high when it would be far easier for us to lower our standards. Personally, I view our standards as both a mark of respect for our material and as a tribute to our unpaid contributors, without whom we would have a poor journal indeed. We have striven to keep the price stable, and have succeeded for nearly five of the most economically difficult years of recent times. While we have absorbed punitive price increases in our print and post bills, I urge you to realise that your £3.00 subscription is actually worth nearly 20% less due to inflation. With very great reluctance we are having to consider repricing FT just to stand still, and new prices will be announced next issue. Meanwhile we will continue to accept renewals at the old rate.

As you can see we feel confident of our future–stay with us and we'll keep FT alive.

Bob Rickard

Next Issue.

We hope to catch up on our schedule by bringing out the next issue hot on the heels of this one. Wish us luck!

We'll have a thorough look at the mystery blob that fell out of the sky over Mississauga, Ontario, by our correspondent, **Dwight Whalen**, who lives there; and an article by **Don Robbins** exposing a myth at the heart of physics, about isotopes, that has never officially been repealed.

There will be a strong accent on phantom felines with **Paul Cropper** on the mystery panthers of the Southern Highlands of Australia; part 2 of **Loren Coleman**'s review of large cat sightings in the USA; and a collection of reports and opinions on UK mystery cats by **Alan Gardiner, Chris Hall** and **David Syderserff**. Accompanying this will be our own summary of the latest mystery animal sightings in the UK, including the Scottish cats, and East Anglian ostrich!

Michael Hoffman joins our irregular columnists, under the banner *America Mystica* with an update of Son-of-Sam developments.

As we go to press we learn of fresh sightings of Morgawr, the Cornish sea serpent, and hope we can scoop a new photo of Morgawr taken this year – next issue!

William Stok.

The Touch of Death.

We are very glad to welcome to these pages **Michael Goss,** whose lively humour masks a serious interest in things Fortean, especially poltergeist phenomena. Another of his interests is the martial art of China and Japan and its attendant philosophies and folklore. Put them all together and you get this delightful assessment of occult mayhem....

This article is nothing to do with mysterious Bulgarians who lurk around London bus-stops waiting to prod dissident countrymen with poison-tipped umbrellas. It is about something equally lethal and even more peculiar.

Let us start with John F. Gilbey, a man with an unusual purpose in life. To put it simply, Mr Gilbey could be called a connoisseur of advanced methods of unarmed violence and ways to inflict grievous bodily harm upon suitably deserving cases. Highly ranked in judo and karate, he travelled the world to discover the most deadly and secret techniques of weaponless combat, and he met some pretty unusual people. He talked to one of the few surviving masters of true French savate and to Chavante Indians of Brazil who could break an attacker's arm with a short, sharp elbow lock; then there was the Liverpool man who spent at least one hour every day perfecting his 'nutting' technique, the Ganges fighter who had devoted himself to the art of kicking or hitting assailants in the groin (ouch!) and a Japanese master who could knock out a man by merely shouting at him. These and other adventures were recorded — reluctantly, as his publishers claimed — in a slim volume entitled *Secret Fighting Arts of the World* [1].

But, as Gilbey writes at the very start of his book, there was one form of combat which seemed destined to elude him: the neo-legendary 'delayed death touch', whereby slight and momentary pressure on the victim's body could cause internal damage and even terminal results. The impact and its immediate results were negligible, and it was said that the final effect might be retarded until two weeks (or longer) after the touch had been delivered. All of which seemed incredible — the sort of thing you read in comic book adverts: Fear No Man! Win Friends and Influence Your Uncle! Wipe Out Enemies with One Blow!!! — or Mr Spock's Vulcan death-grip, perhaps...

The delayed death touch would be the ultimate weapon in the potentially lethal kung fu arsenal — if it could be proved to exist. It also seems the instrument of the perfect murder. According to some martial artists, it was possible for the master to create havoc by the slightest touch of finger or palm (no punching was necessary) lightly applied to the victim's body. There were those who claimed that disruption of blood circulation, malfunction of internal organs and death could be delayed for as much as several years after the initial incident; the time factor depending entirely on the desire (and of course the skill) of the attacker.

Gilbey's problem was that while everyone interested in the Asian fighting arts had heard of the 'delayed death touch', no-one seemed to have seen it in operation. Gilbey was not interested in hearsay; he had to see the thing at first hand. The DDT remained a wild rumour, an improbable story, until 1957, when Gilbey came across a distinguished teacher of Shaolin-style boxing in Taiwan. The man's name was Oh Hsin-yang, and he told Gilbey that some of his art relied upon exact understanding of the human anatomy. For example, the blood in the body passed close to the surface at certain times of the day, so that a touch at a precise point at the crucial moment could — as Gilbey saw demonstrated — have devastating (and incapacitating) effects wholly unequal to the actual force of the blow.

Gilbey guessed that all this was in some way related to the fabled delayed death touch; Oh Hsin-yang politely confirmed that the assumption was correct. Would he demonstrate further? With due reticence the master agreed, summoning his teenage son whom, he explained, had never been given the chance to experience the technique. With little ceremony Oh placed his right index finger on a point below the boy's navel — and that was all. He then put the youth in Gilbey's care so that there could be no question of trickery, predicting that the results of the test would become apparent in three days' time at around noon.

For the next three days Gilbey and young Ah-Lin were inseparable; the boy was under close surveillance and his health seemed normal. Oh Hsin-yang did not come near him until the appointed time of noon on the third day, and he came well prepared with various medicines. Even as he busied himself about their preparation, the boy abruptly lapsed into unconsciousness. Gilbey tried his pulse and found it to be minimal, so that if Ah-Lin was only acting one would have to credit him with a superb performance. Eventually the traditional medicines and applied massage of his father restored him to a semblance of life, but Oh Hsin-yang admitted that it had been a very close thing and that his son would have to convalesce for three months. And so Gilbey left Taiwan, one of the very few Westerners ever to have seen the delayed death touch in action.

Well, this is a good story, but does it carry con-

Master Ku Yu Cheong, of Kwangsu Province (apx 1930) breaking a pile of bricks with his Iron Palm method. He could break any single brick out of the 12 at will, leaving the rest undamaged. See also the text on p18.) (From Iron Palm Illustrated *by Lee Ying Arng.)*

viction? The obvious charge — that Gilbey was a sort of Baron Munchausen without the humour — has been made with respect to several of his adventures, but it's only fair to say that within the last two decades there have been other, corroborative accounts by astute observers which suggest that Gilbey *wasn't* indulging in romantic fabrications, (ie lying). Of course, there are other possible explanations. Gilbey may have been the victim of a 'prepared experiment', set up by the wily Taiwan teacher and his son for the dubious pleasure of putting one over on an ignorant Westerner... perhaps by some secretly-administered medicine or toxic agent. There is also the hypnosis hypothesis. In addition to their familiarity with many other psychological techniques, the aforementioned masters of various schools evidently had a good working knowledge of the power of suggestion, and it is conceivable that the patent physical symptoms of the 'death touch' noted in Ah-Lin were the response to a previously-implanted hypnotic suggestion. But let's leave the hypnosis/suggestion theory for a time and turn instead to the doings of another famous martial artist, Bruce Lee.

There's nothing like the unexpected premature demise of a celebrity to start the weird tales a-flowing: the drugs/over-indulgence in sex/mysterious suicide/assassination motifs, not to mention the He's-Not-Dead-At-All-He's-Changed-His-Name-And-Is-Living-In-(X)-And-A-Pile-Of-Rocks-Was-Buried-In-His-Coffin theory. Lee, only latterly dubbed 'Black Belt Superstar' by Warner Bros.' publicity machine, was fair game. His sudden death in July 1973 was attributed by Dr R.R. Lycette of Queen Elizabeth Hospital and Prof. Ronald Teare of London University's Forensic Medicine Department to acute cerebral oedema (brain swelling) probably caused by Lee's hypersensitivity to the ingredients of an aspirin-like tranquillizer he had taken for a headache [2] ...a freakish, almost unbelievable event ill-equipped to stifle the hit-by-the-Mafia/cocaine overdose/murder-by-obscure-herbal-concoction rumours. Inevitably, the delayed death touch was implicated.

In the *News of the World* for 7 April 1974 American writer Alex Ben Block was credited as the source of a story that Lee had been murdered by some unknown master of the delayed death strike, perhaps in revenge for the film star's success in popularising the supposedly secret arts of Chinese boxing [3]. The article did concede, however, that Block was somewhat sceptical of the idea.

Consideration of the DDT leaves us gazing into a shadowy corner inhabited by venerable masters of miscellaneous mayhem who can do the most amazing things, but won't demonstrate them — due to the usual barriers of oaths of secrecy, reluctance to pander to Western wonder-seekers or because of the terrible dangers inherent in the practices themselves. Perhaps we might turn away with a sarcastic murmur of 'Oh, yeah?' were it not for the fact that said experts were occasionally reputed to display mental and physical powers which modern parapsychology suspects to be experimentally viable: psychokinesis, alternative healing systems and other illogical phenomena. In short, the phenomena of the seance and/or laboratory seem strangely similar to the sorts of things these rare individuals were seen (on *very* rare occasions) to perform.

Even so, there are problems. One can evaluate the evidence of some traditional Oriental arts such as yoga with some confidence, but the delayed death touch — by its very nature — is always going to be elusive. It might be permissible to ignore it as experimentally untestable, were it not for the respectable physical hypothesis on which it is based...

Martial artists tend to apply the phrase 'delayed death touch' in cavalier fashion to a number of (related?) techniques. Part of the confusion is semantic, or etymological, or both. I am indebted to Steve Moore — he of 'Yellow Emporium' fame — for the information that *den mur* and *dim mak,* two of the more common terms for the DDT, are in fact variant Cantonese transliterations of the same phrase, which comes out in Mandarin as *tien hsueh* [4]. Steve adds that, according to his dictionary, *tien* can mean a spot, dot or point, while *hsueh* signifies a grave, cave or (subsidiary sense) a sinus in acupuncture. He notes, too, that this same dictionary gives a curiously apposite example of the phrase's usage: in a geomantic context it can mean 'to select a good site for a grave'.

Turning to the techniques themselves, the confusion of all the possible origins of the term 'delayed death touch' is magnificent. We needn't concern ourselves too long with the 'poison hand' school, where the unpleasant practice of immersing the hand in various deleterious herbs is said to convert it into a steel-hard weapon, one scratch from which is lethal. It is less easy to set aside the 'iron palm', however. Basically, the iron palm, which is one of several styles sometimes called *dim mak*, relies upon use of herbs, medicines and perhaps heat treatments and the judicious practice of punching, or plunging the hand into, receptacles holding substances of graduating hardness — beans, rice, sand, gravel and ultimately iron filings. Strange as it may seem, the hand is said to remain soft and uncalloused even though it can deliver a lethal punch [5]. Iron palm is described as one of the 'hard' systems. Some experts like Lee Ying Arng state categorically that it is inadvisable to train in this style and the softer tai ch'i chuan at the same time, since the emphasis on strength in the former conflicts with the principles of the latter [6]. Even so, iron palmists do not appear to rely purely upon sheer force; if that's all there is to it, you'd probably save a lot of time and discomfort by getting yourself a knuckle-duster. The effects of an iron palm strike are occasionally reported to be as subtly selective in their results as those attributed to the blow from a *den mur* stylist. But this *den mur* (*den* = point of finger; *mur* = blood point) is even more esoteric in its structure, drawing upon traditional Chinese physiological lore.

Ancient anatomical principles state (says Master Alan Lee [7]) that the blood in the human body had to pass via 36 major, 72 minor and 108 subsidiary 'blood gates' in order to fill the arteries, veins and etceteras. The martial artist, knowing the location of these gates and the hours of the day when the waves of blood course through them, could by a light pressure of the finger(s), force the leading waves back on those following, causing a possibly fatal blood clot. The assassin could even make the results resemble normal malfunctions of the organism. Adepts in the art could defend against it by regulation of the pulse at times of greatest vulnerability — and in any case, the technique took years to acquire.

This, or something like it, was the principle behind what Gilbey had witnessed in the truly-rare Taiwan demonstration. But it was *not* the technique which provided the substance of the Bruce Lee assassination rumours. Block was quoted on the perils of the 'vibrating palm' attack, in which the assailant's inner energy, converted by skill and concentration into a series of resonances, vibrates at a chosen rate through the victim's body after the briefest contact, causing disruption of the major organs and death. Bet you'd like to know how they account for *this* one...

The vibrating palm utilizes a force (for the want of a better word) which the West has been encouraged to take seriously over the last few years. In Chinese it is expressed as *ch'i*, in Japanese *ki*, and one general gloss would be 'intrinsic energy'] the energy which exists, in various stages of activity, in each living being. *Ch'i* is said to originate from a point some 2 inches below the naval and to flow along 14 routes through the organism. It is alleged that the ability to control and regulate this energy enables the master of the martial arts to perform feats where strength alone would be inadequate. Its development is therefore the prime objective of both physical and mental regimens of martial arts systems.

The paths along which *ch'i* flows contain 708 separate points. Pressure on these can retard or stimulate the flow; the vibrating palm attempts to upset the rhythm of this flow by a series of resonances which, over a predetermined time, affect the operation of the internal organs, causing paralysis and/or death, but leaving virtually nothing which can be logically related to the actual assault.

Evidence for this: John Gilbey again, who watched the Ganges groin-puncher reduce the third brick in a pile of five to semi-rubble by application of 'intrinsic power' (a light touch only, please note) while bricks one, two, four and five were left intact. Reasonably enough, Gilbey summarised his reaction to the demo as 'flabbergasted'. Then in *Black Belt* for February 1972 Teoh Hood Eng recorded how he had seen the feat duplicated, the victim this time being represented by two half-inch thick roofing tiles protected by an insulating wad of bean curd, with two boards on top to add to the complications. The expert — a Malaysian kung fu man named Kah Wah Lee — claimed that he had converted his intrinsic energy by concentration into resonating waves which penetrated down through the boards and curd to the tiles beneath, shattering them.

The selective destruction of one brick in a pile seems to be a favourite trick of more than one martial artist. A skinny gentleman called Ku Yu-Cheong (d. 1962) of Kwangsu Province was famous for his ability to destroy a chosen brick from a stack of twelve (or if necessary, all twelve of them in one go). In 1928 he was alleged to have subdued an unruly horse 'in a matter of seconds' by virtue of 'a single slap on the animal's back whence the animal out of sheer agony collapsed on the floor and after a few pitiful neighs died'. I'm not sure whether it matters that Mr Ku's style was iron palm rather than *den mur*, but it is certainly odd that an Eagle Hand master who witnessed this horse-execution gave evidence that a post-mortem found no signs of external damage, but 'the internal organs of the animal were split and its backbone revealed a large bruise' [8]. The absence of such signs of surface damage suggest that, although iron palm is said to be a 'hard' or 'physical' style, it can't be divorced entirely from the *ch'i*-governed soft schools, which include *den mur*.

Do we need to invoke *ch'i* to explain the devastating effects of the vibrating palm? There are martial artists who dismiss the whole idea of the delayed death touch as an Oriental fairy-tale. They speculate that one punch from an experienced fighter *could* cause damaging shockwaves to pass via the musculature to the internal organs, as might occur if an untrained or even partially-trained person was the recipient and the punch was met by an instinctive tensing of the muscles. The point that most of these objectors miss is that we're not talking about *punches* — merely about a light, firm and momentary touch (or, as some accounts have it, a deliberate pressure of the palm). It is hard to reconcile *that* sort of attack with *this* kind of explanation.

More feasible: the damage might be said to be done, not to the physiology by conversion of intrinsic energy into resonating waves, but to the mind by suggestion; the Hypnotic Hypothesis returns, as promised a moment ago. Nearly everyone knows that suggestion (hypnotic or otherwise) can have pronounced and seemingly magical physical effects on the susceptible, and it is not unreasonable to suppose that *any* kind of touch from someone accredited with the DDT might detonate a process of self-suggested damage if the victim believed strongly in both the power of the assailant *and* the reality of the death-touch. This may be a worthy explanation, although given the existence of such a degree of belief in the victims, it is hard to see why the master should need to touch them at all; the very act of letting the target know he was singled out for doom might be enough to have him collapse in a curdled heap, bowled over by auto-suggestion.

An unexpectedly modern piece of evidence, testimony to the psychological (if not the physical) impetus of the DDT, appeared in the *Daily Mirror* of 17 February 1976. In this case there were two victims of what the paper decided to style a Kung Fu Curse, and paradoxically it was the supposed DDT master, 60-year-old Lock Ho Yin, who died. His alleged target, a 48-year-old Chinese cook named Tam Pui, resorted to methods more prosaic and less delayed when Lock hit him during a brawl on board the Royal Fleet Auxiliary 'Empire Gull', anchored at Marchwood, Hants, in September 1975. Presumably possessed of the idea that he had been DDT'd Tam delivered his own innovatory Instant-or-Pretty-Nearly-Instant Death Touch to the old man, using a long knife in place of an Iron Palm or otherwise trained hand. Not surprisingly, the cook found himself a star guest at Winchester Crown Court. A police statement attributed to Tam the words: 'I have taken my revenge. He died first and I will die later'. *Did* he die later? I'm afraid I don't know. The *Mirror* reports that he claimed to be suffering from 'a mystery illness brought on by the Kung Fu curse, which three doctors have been unable to diagnose' and ends with the note that, by his own request, he was to be deported to Hong Kong where he could seek out a doctor to remove the death curse. (In the meantime, off to Broadmoor with him). [9] If this bizarre episode shows anything, it is that belief in the DDT is still around, even in Hampshire; that it is sometimes a deeply held belief, not a superficial one — especially where Chinese cooks are concerned; and that it may encourage people to do weird things...as indeed, the brand of suggestion directed by stage hypnotistsand volunteers from the audience can be seen to make people do weird things.

On further consideration, though, the Hypnotic Hypothesis begs a few important questions. The hypnotist who raises a blister on a subject's arm by telling him that a cold spoon is in fact a red-hot spoon gets his results by manipulation of the subject's imagination — to put it at its most basic. Now, what about those broken bricks? Do bricks have imagination, and can they be hypnotised? Are tiles susceptible to auto-suggestion? [10] So long as the answer to these queries is 'Yes', we have no problems.

The concept of *ch'i*, which is integral to the DDT rationale, may not be as Orientally anomalous as it seems. I find that it has an oddly familiar ring to it. Consider: an invisible force undetectable on any type of monitoring equipment, one known only by its effects....Hmm, sounds a bit like Mesmer's 'magnetic fluid'. The much-maligned Wizard of Vienna's speculations on a universal, all-pervasive magnetic fluid, and the belief that disruptions of this fluid in the body — expressed as diseases — could be cured by 'magnetical' manipulations, won him a brief hour in the European spotlight. Naturally, when a commission from the French Academy of Science could find 'nothing to prove the existence of the animal fluid' [11] and consequently argued that, as it did not exist, it couldn't have the therapeutic benefits ascribed to it, Mesmer and his fine hypothesis were awarded the Order of the Boot and the whole concept sank into that oblivion reserved for half-explored and prematurely discredited ideas. Well, we all know

Sifu Kuang Wei-chiang demonstrates an analogue of the delayed death touch, paralysing lizards by prodding their vital points. Stroking and blowing restores normality. (Secrets of Kung Fu *1976*).

that eventually there was found a safe, less esoteric alternative to Mesmerism, and that a Manchester doctor named James Braid styled it 'hypnotism'.

In many ways it is a pity that there ever arose a situation whereby Science felt itself compelled to choose between Mesmer and Braid. Though we can applaud the (belated) acceptance of hypnotism or hypnosis, it is also true that Mesmerism posed many interesting questions which we appear to have forgotten about. For example, how did the fluid achieve so many incredible cures and stimulate so much psi phenomena, beside which our suggestion-orientated concept of hypnosis is strangely barren in its results? My personal belief, for what it is worth, is that the baby went down the plug-hole with the magnetised water: that there was a lot more in Mesmerism than the critics could see: and that something was lost when we decided to jettison animal magnetism. It may be worth finding the time to revive investigations into the existence of Mesmer's 'magnetic fluid', even if it should prove to be neither magnetic nor a fluid. And by the way, there is nothing that the French Commission could have classified as 'perceptible by any of the senses' in our modern concept of hypnosis, either — like Mesmer's fluid it is invisible, undetectable and distinguished mainly by its phenomena. [12]

But back to the mystic Orient. From Mesmerism or animal magnetism we got hypnosis; what can we hope for from *ch'i*? Maybe we've already had part of it. The mesmerists who believed that illness was a result of imbalanced universal fluid within the human system would perhaps recognise the theory behind acupuncture, where disruption or blockage of *ch'i* is identified as the source of bodily troubles, although the medium of adjustment is pins instead of passes. Manipulation of *ch'i* is fundamental to many aspects of Chinese physical arts, and it is not really surprising that there could be two completely opposed applications of the principle — the first in the beneficial practice of acupuncture and the other in the lethal technique of the vibrating palm.

Is *ch'i* really so incredible? We're living in an age when Strange Forces are abroad. Try as we will, we can't pin the damned things down, analyze or define them to everybody's satisfaction; we can suspect that they are there only because of their anomalous results. We watch them bend spoons, make objects disappear, neutralize gravity and play at poltergeists, and it is the hope of some of us that the longer they keep it up, the more chance there is that some minute but irrefutably-present reading will present itself on the screens of our infallible and sophisticated electronic monitors. But the Forces have been too capricious so far. Any attempts to explain psi in terms of an unknown (undiscovered) physical force have been disappointed by the fact that none of the mechanical detectors applied has managed to verify beyond all doubt the presence of such a force. Some of us are getting very fed up. Professor John Taylor decided some while ago that Geller-type phenomena could only be electro-magnetic in origin; having detected no evidence of electromagnetism during his recent experiments, he now declares the phenomena are *not* of electromagnetic origin and that therefore they don't exist [13] ... just as the Academy of Science Commission voted that, as animal magnetism could not be proved to exist, then its alleged therapeutic virtues were also non-existent.

Every now and then, you get the horrid suspicion that our approach is totally wrong and that the magical forces, fluids and energies are never going to show up on the kind of equipment we like to use to prove the existence of other physical forces, fluids and energies. Perhaps we ought to put more emphasis on using these forces instead of trying to verify their existence; the olden day Chinese seem to have been quite satisfied by the fact that *ch'i* provided a working hypothesis upon which acupuncture could be based, even if it couldn't be seen or measured. And if *ch'i* is the force which lies behind the enigmas of psychokinesis, levitation and some of the other curiosities which defy the scientific method, it will be interesting to note the reaction of Western parapsychologists to the challenge. The Eusapia Palladinos, Stella Cranshaws and Uri Gellers have given us more than enough trouble in terms of both what thay can do and the limitations of our understanding of what goes on when they do it. What could the average parapsychologist (if such a person exists anywhere?) make of Oh Hsin-yang or the Ganges groin-hitter? Presuming, of course that these masters could be persuaded that it is in everyone's interest that they demonstrate their powers in a suitable laboratory context. Something tells me that you wouldn't get them within a mile of a suitable laboratory context to begin with.

So there may be more to the delayed death touch than we might think. Unlikely as it may seem, the DDT is part of the broader and scarcely more comprehensible spectrum of strange phenomena, and as such it gains a little more credibility. If you want to read a relatively uncommon attempt to review the possible relationships between the world of parapsychology and the enigmatic things which martial artists claim for the advanced practitioners of their various crafts, I'd recommend Glen Barclay's *Mind Over Matter: Beyond the Bounds of Nature* as a good intro. [14] And if when you're paying for it, the sales-girl leans across the counter and gives you an innocuous-seeming lil poke on the chest...you could be in trouble, son.

Michael Goss

REFERENCES

1) Charles E. Tuttle & Co. Inc., 1963; Pan Books (paperback), London and Sydney, 1974.
2) Felix Dennis and Don Atyeo, *Bruce Lee: King of Kung Fu.* London: Wildwood House, 1974. See pp. 86-87.
3) "Star 'Killed By Kung Fu Wizards'", *News of the World* 7 April 1974, p.3. In fact, Block was mooting the DDT as only one of a *number* of peculiar 'conspiracy to murder' theories current after Lee's death. In his *The Legend of Bruce Lee* (US: Dell and London: Mayflower, 134-137, both published 1974) he quotes the words of the high-ranking American karateka Ed Parker, who stresses that the art — taught only 'to the most patient and peaceful member' took 'years to perfect'. Moreover, he concludes that 'this form...is becoming extinct. The few who know this system will take their wealth of knowledge with them to their graves.' (The full quote can be found in sensei Parker's *Secrets of Karate*, London: Barrie & Jenkins, 1964, p.33. In the USA the book was published in 1963 by Prentice Hall as *Secrets of Chinese Karate.*) Block also quotes the same Kah Wah Lee who crops up later in my article, since his claim that the DDT attacks the blood and lung structure adds pertinence to the allegation that 'Bruce Lee had strange broken blood vessels in his lungs' (Block, op. cit., p.136) Finally, both Block and Parker are mentioned in Dennis and Atyeo, op. cit., p. 89.
4) Interestingly, Ed Parker (see preceding note) writes of '*Tien Hsueh,* or in Cantonese, *Dim Muk.*'
5) A fairly detailed account of Iron Palm training is given in Alan Sutton's 'Behind Iron Palm', *Inside Kung Fu* 1: 7, June 1974, 37-39, where the art of Master Share Lew is featured.
6) Lee Ying-Arng, *Iron Palm in 100 Days.* Hong Kong: privately printed(?), no date. See p.63.
7) Iron palm, poison hand and 'blood gates' are all described by Master Alan Lee in *Official Karate*, 7:47, May 1975, pp.32-35, 49, 54.
8) These details of skillful horse-murder (equicide?) in 1928 are from Lee Ying Arng's book, op. cit., p.8.
9) "'Doomed' by Kung Fu curse', *Daily Mirror* 17 February 1976. The paper doesn't really explain just *why* Tam Pui feared the blow he received and there is no specific mention of the DDT — only of the 'Kung Fu curse'. But as he believed 'he would die a lingering death' (plus other details summarised here) it is reasonably clear that this is convenient journalese for the DDT, and we can imagine that the murderer truly believed the dead man to have been a master of this technique. Wonder what style he professed? And on the subject of cooks and kung fu, an article by Alan Sutton (*Inside Kung Fu* 2:7, June 1975, p.30) mentions that Jin Foon Mark, head chef at the New China Inn, Minneapolis, is also a master of the Southern Praying Mantis system and as such has been trained in both the arts of acupuncture and *dim mak*... showing that it is not a totally dead art, evidently.
10) The relevance of suggestion to *dim mak* is discussed in Massad F. Ayoob's 'The Delayed Death Touch: Is It Really Just A Myth?', *Black Belt* XII: 5, May 1974, 30-33, 35-36.
11) Quoted by Ralph Harry Vincent, *The Elements of Hypnotism.* London: Kegan Paul, Trench, Trubner & Co. Ltd., 1897, p.22. Vincent's book contains some fine plates showing various reptiles and amphibians flaked out in hypnotically-induced states of catalepsy; oddly enough, a photocopied article sent by Steve Moore (see illustration) reveals that kung fu students can also elicit similar paralytic responses in brute creation. They have tamed elephants and horses by means of acupuncture and (best of all) the article depicts a Bruce Lee look-alike named sifu Kuang Wei-chiang laying out a number of small 'nook snake' lizards in uncomfortably contorted postures after rendering them tractable by pressure on vital points of the body. This, it seems, is a portion of the *tien hsueh* system (see comments on alternative names for the DDT earlier in this article, and Note 4 above). Ref. Wong Dow, 'Control Of The Behaviour Of Lizard By The Kung Fu Skill Of Hitting The Vital Points' in *Secrets of Kung Fu* 1: 1, August 1976, pp.6-9.
12) 'It has always been much easier to define hypnosis by what it does, rather than what it is'. (Timothy Hall and Guy Grant, *Superpsych: The Power of Hypnosis.* London: Abacus (paperback) edn., 1978; see p.24).
This may be true, but it begs a lot of questions. You not infrequently find a circular process of reasoning, wherein hypnotists attempt to define hynosis as a state in which certain phenomena may be exhibited, and then offer the same phenomena as proof there is such a thing as hypnosis. This appears OK until you realise that you cannot convincingly explain a thing in terms of what it does and then say that what it does proves the thing exists...or (worse) that the phenomena *them*selves are synonymous with the thing *it*self. (This problem is discussed in Theodore X. Barber's *Hypnosis. A Scientific Study,* Van Nostrand Reinhold Co., 1969). As to the undetectability of hypnosis — not the phenomena, but the thing itself — we can't even argue from the evidence of EEG readings. The brain of the hypnotised subject emits waves distinct from those registered during normal consciousness, but these (I am told) are identical with others displayed when the subject is in another, non-hypnotic type of altered state of consciousness, e.g. meditation. From this it seems that we could tell from an EEG chart that a particular person was in an altered state of consciousness, but not (without external criteria or evidence) that he was in an hypnotic condition as opposed to, say, a self-induced meditational one. Hmm...
13. This summary of affairs does Prof. Taylor's point of view less than justice. For a more detailed survey and some comments on his abandonment of the EM hypothesis, see *Alpha* 1:1, January/February 1979, pp.22-24, 30-32. In addition *Alpha* states that a future issue will be summarising Prof. Taylor's latest *Nature* paper on this subject.
14. London: Arthur Barker Ltd., 1973; Pan (paperback) edn., 1975. On a much less restrained level, you may also enjoy Aaron Lee's "Sun Kung — an occult, witchcraft, conjury, magic, or just plain trickery?" (sic.) in *Real Kung Fu* 1:3, November 1975, 64-68. *Sun Kung* is a school of kung fu which appears to confer on ascetic practitioners many occult powers — the ability to swallow burning candles, geomantic skills, invulnerability to knife attacks, invisibility *and,* for good measure, the art of delivering delayed or instant death by means of the 'life and death palm' or the 'five-thunder palm'. All this in only 49 days of training! The student's studies include incantations, possession of his body by the spirit of the 'grand master' and the symbolic surrender of his soul into this same grand master's keeping. The caption to one photo explains that following one of the rituals the student "would possess a supernatural power similar to black magic".

ACKNOWLEDGEMENT
As observant readers will have spotted, I owe a big vote of thanks to Steve Moore, who sent me a large number of photocopies of articles I would otherwise have missed. Thanks again, Steve.

PROFESSOR CLASPROOT'S
FACTS YOU MIGHT FORGET...
1192: INNOCENT III IS POPE... LUIGI POZZO BLOWS HIS NOSE...
... CAUSING A NASTY NOSEBLEED!
JUS' A BIDDIT! I DOW DAT FACE!
A MORE SIGNIFICANT EVENT THAN IT MIGHT AT FIRST APPEAR... FOR POZZO'S HAY-FEVER HAD CREATED THE IMAGE OF ST. GLORIA DEL WOOLCO, PATRON SAINT OF EAR, NOSE AND THROAT...
THE HANKERCHIEF WAS DEEMED IL McCOY IN VERITAS, AND POZZO WAS INDUCTED INTO THE SEMINARY AT PAMPLONA...
WHERE HE CREATED LIGHTNING IKONS FOR THE FAITHFUL.
HA-CHOW! THAT'LL BE FIVE LIRA. BLESS YOU
GAZUNDHEID, FATHER
IN 1196, THE SEMINARY WAS VISITED BY CARDINAL ROSSO, WHO BLESSED POZZO...
... AND MIRACULOUSLY CURED HIS HAY-FEVER!
OOPS!
POKKETTZ '80
LUIGI DECIDED TO RETURN TO HIS FORMER LIFE. BUT ON THE VERY DAY OF HIS DEPARTURE, WHILST DELVING FOR A QUANTITY OF TROUBLESOME EAR-WAX...

U·F·O Commentary by Nigel Watson

WORMOLOGY

Sometimes it is harder to distinguish between the levels of absurdity inherent in the activities of UFO researchers, than it is to define the mating habits of the common worm.

Instinctively the animal urges of the British Ufologist are territorial. Each must stake his or her own geographical patch, and if anyone commits the sin of intruding into foreign territory a struggle of superhuman magnitude has to be engaged in order to settle the arguments that ensue. The glittering prospect of amassing hordes of UFO reports in competition with fellow Ufologists is the aim of these animals who have little interest in the actual content of their accumulations, blindly dividing themselves into ever smaller factions.

The inevitable result of these machinations will be covert terrorist activity between rival UFO Networks and Research Associations. The innocent members of the public who happen to be foolish enough to report seeing UFOs will be kidnapped by the first UFO commando group to get to them. UFO crusades will be fought with bitter emnity; massive fatalities and injuries will litter the annals of Ufology.

These Ufological worms burrowing into the fabric of our society are spreading their canker into the body of our basic data sources. Perhaps the stroke of a Ufological Doctor's beard will solve everything if we are not doomed!

HEAVENLY DEATH

Ufologists might fight and squabble but the flying saucer pilots laugh at this triviality. They are serious in carrying out their darkly hidden satanic mission to conquer the spirit and senses of humanity. Yes, "people are being *hurt, disturbed* and even *killed* by the UFO" according to David Sydeserff [1], who lives in the dangerous regions of Scotland. The War of the Worlds has been secretly fought between the Governments of Earth against a powerful and ambiguous enemy for hundreds of years.

US troops were drugged and sent to far off planets which they imagined to be Vietnam. Hitler was really a Venusian space pirate. Churchill was a mutant pin-stripe slug; and Stalin was a baby reptile from a tropical plant located somewhere in the direction of the Orion constellation. Real Earthmen are midgets, and are usually green coloured, but due to pollution and planetary warfare most of them have died or gone underground (you see hundreds of them every morning on the London Underground railway; they hide beneath bowler hats, and carry rolled-up umbrellas for protection).

Star Wars, Battlestar Galactica and the Black Hole are all unconscious expressions of our nightmares, which in fact offer us a glimpse of half forgotten reality. Alien ideas are erupting from our bodies and behind every cloud there is an enemy space ship waiting to invade and violate.

Gleaming meteors of death transmit unheard orders to their spies on Earth, and when the time is right the invasion will shatter the combined terrestrial Governments with one mighty blow. As an alternative of the third kind, the top strata of our society is embarking upon a Star Trek, and the traditions and hopes of humanity might yet escape the fate that lurks above us.

WAR REPORTS

As you sit in your deck-chair reading your beer-stained copy of FT you might be chuckling with glee at the silly threat of inter-galactic warfare. But there is no need for complacency; we are all in danger (even Forteans!) from marauding gangs of undisciplined bloodthirsty homicidal aliens. From every corner of the world reports are flooding in about their activities, our blind folly in ignoring them can be gauged from the following selection.

In August 1973, seven men were working on a cotton plantation in Gerena, Spain, when at between 3.30 and 4.0 am they were attacked by a UFO. A huge bright object flew low over the fields, several times, causing the workmen to duck (a tactic which might cause anyone to go quackers!). [2]

32-year-old Mr John Milroy was driving his mother from Ardersier to Croy, Scotland, on the night of 19th April 1979, when at 11:30pm they saw some lights coming towards them. The lights maintained a trajectory which was leading it towards Milroy's car, and his mother began to beg him to reverse. But instead he said that: "We decided to get out of the car and my mother took my hand and said: 'If we're going to die at least we're together.' Then I realised that although I'd revved the engine and we'd slammed the car doors, there wasn't a sound anywhere. There was no sound when I put my foot on the ground. I couldn't see any shape behind the lights in the sky. My mother and I ran towards a ditch, and when we got there everything came back to normal. The sound came back, the light went–it was fantastic."

Mr Milroy reported their sighting to the police, and the next morning he suffered from a mild case of shock, his mother was put under sedation. At RAF Kinloss, Flt. Lt., John Hunter said; "We had a Nimrod in the area between 11:15 and 11:45 last night. I think Mr Milroy saw its landing lights–they are very bright and can be seen from 20 miles away." [3] This statement of course hides the RAF's interest in keeping the hostile actions of the UFOs secret.

On the 1st August 1979, Patrolman William Shaughnessy encountered a white jelly-donut-shaped light. He was patrolling, just to the north of New York City when at 1:35am this UFO for no obvious reason buzzed his car, twice! Both times it sped to a point above his car, made a 90 degree turn, and sped away again. The light stopped the police car radio from working, but otherwise it did no other damage. [4]

Mr X notes three similar cases. [5] The first occurred on the 18th August 1979, when a private aircraft encountered a "rolling energy ball with a red radiant side and a white radiant side" 40 miles northeast of Ottawa, Canada. During the sighting the aircraft controls became jammed and the instruments went haywire.

On the 20th August 1979, a lady driver was followed by a green light (a traffic light!) when she was motoring along the Murchison Highway, Tasmania, Australia. The light caused her car to loose power, and on the completion of her journey she found that the car had used an excessive amount of petrol and that her wristwatch had stopped. [5]

Another policeman, Deputy Sheriff Val Johnson, met an aggressive UFO at 1:30am on the 28th August 1979. He was on patrol in the vicinity of Warren, Minnesota, when a brilliant light sped towards his car and hit it with such force that it shattered the windscreen, dented the hood (bonnet?), bent a couple of aerials, and broke a headlamp. The car's electric clock and the Deputy's wristwatch both lost 14 minutes, and he suffered from shock when he recovered consciousness. [5]

BODILY CONFIGURATIONS

If we are to defend ourselves we must learn to identify our enemies. This isn't easy; the space people come in all shapes and sizes. But fortunately we were able to offer a few clues for extraterrestrial body hunters everywhere.

Romeo Ernesto Suarez, tells how in 1950 he saw UFOs emerge from the sea, but his strangest story concerns a dog. He found this canine mystery in San Julian. He said: "It was dark-coloured and gave off a perfume as I never smelt again. When I stroked its back I felt kind of faint electric shock and one night, when sleeping in the stall of an 'estancia' I noticed it whimpered like a child. This called my attention but did not bother me too much in spite of my realizing it was a very strange dog." The next morning the dog had vanished, even though the doors and windows had been shut. [6] Suarez reckoned the dog was an extra-terrestrial!

On the 19th January 1977, a 9-year-old said he saw two UFOs, one of which landed in his backyard in Harrah, USA. The boy also saw two green-coloured entities in association with the UFOs, who seemed to have one eye, one "leg" and a pig-like nose. [7] Then in Mendoza, two workers during a night shift (no date is specified) met a 75cm tall dwarf who hopped on one leg. Using complicated machinery the entity suspended the two witnesses above the ground. After doing some pirouettes the dwarf flew off into the sky as if "an invisible and powerful ray" impelled it. Prof V Corradi, director of the Institute for Studies of Extrahuman Phenomena, interviewed one of the witnesses and he believed the men had seen a cyborg! But, "it must not be thought these are robots with cables and photoeletrical cells" he said, no they are sophisticated cybernetic organisms which utilize bionic laws. In 1963, Corradi says that a secret military file was opened on these creatures called "Project Cyborg" in England. [8] Funnily enough these hopping entities remind me of the Lincoln Imp who resides in Lincoln Cathedral, so these beings have quite an history.

The micro-organism which fell on Portugal on the 2nd November 1959 at Berengual [9] got its picture published in the Portuguese *Journal de Noticias*. Evidence shows it lifted weights of 350 grammes, and was a tough little chap... before it died. [10]

More extraterrestrial remains have been discovered. [11] Two members of an orchestra (on an unspecified date) found two extraterrestrial skeletons hanging from a branch, on the beach of Posorja, Guayaquil, Equador. The skeletons were two cms taller than the 15 cm skeletons found in Mexico "some years ago." [12]

UP THE POLL

Contrary to their earlier opinions American psychologists now believe (anything that fits their theories!), that humanity will not panic if the aliens landed. Dr Elliot Aronson said: "I do not believe that there will be many extreme reactions; people will not panic, they will not become aggressive, they will not leave the cities, they won't absent themselves from their wordaday world." He might have convinced himself to forget a certain radio play called "The War of the Worlds" which caused panic on the 31st October 1938 in the USA. But times change! Dr Elaine Walster thinks that aliens might give us; "things we want–universal peace, a cure for cancer, or solar energy". In return they could have, "jazz, achievement motivation... and Colonel Sanders Chicken." [13] No wonder the aliens are hostile!

In Britain the NOP Market Research Survey asked 2012 people: "If astronomers proved there was intelligent life in space, would you be alarmed or not?" 213 said they would be frightened, 13 didn't know, and 1,687 were the (brain-washed?) majority who said they wouldn't be alarmed. [14]

I tell you, humanity must watch the skies, or else the population of Earth will be wiped out by indiscriminate alien attacks! Act now before it is too late!

Nigel Watson.

Notes:
1) David Sydeserff, 'Cooperation — Now', *Northern Ufology* 68.
2) 'A Night of Fear', *UFO INFO* Dec 1979.
3) Aberdeen *Evening Express* 20 April 1979.
4) *Midnight Globe* 6 Sept 1979.
5) *Res Bureaux Bulletin* 51.
6) *La Razon* (Buenos Aires) 1 Nov 1978. Trans: Jane Thomas .†
7) *Tri-City Herald* 5 Nov 1978.
8) *La Razon* 26 Oct 1978. Trans: Jane Thomas .†
9) See my column FT29.
10) *La Razon* 9 Oct 1978. Trans. Jane Thomas .†
11) See my column last issue (FT30).
12) *Cronica* (Buenos Aires) 27 Oct 1978. Trans. Jane Thomas .†
13) *Midnight Globe* 7 Nov 1978.
14) Daily Telegraph 28 April 1979.

[Credit: Ion Will, Jake Williams, Lucius Farish's *UFO Newsclipping Service* Nos 114 & 115 (items marked†). NW.

MANED MYSTERY CATS

An "African" lion loose in California? The sightings in November, 1979, of a fully maned cat are only the most recent pages in an elusive chapter of the phantom feline mystery.

Fremont, California, the site of past reports of black panthers, is across the East Bay from San Francisco, but fringed by some of the wilder regions of northern California. At 5:27 pm, on the night of November 10, 1979, Fremont residents near the Coyote Hills Regional Park relayed to police the disturbing fact that a large male lion was roaming loose. One caller told the authorities, after swearing he was not drunk, that he heard roaring at the corner of Alvarado and Lowry Boulevards.

Soon a massive search was organised. Based on the 6:28 pm reports of several residents who saw the lion near Alvarado Boulevard and Whitehead Lane, the "safari" began in the Alameda Creek area. More than forty policemen, firefighters, animal control workers and East Bay Regional Park District personnel were involved in the unusual chase. At one point, tracking dogs and a Bay Area Rapid Transit helicopter were included.

Shortly after nine pm, Freemont Police Officer William Fontes came face to face with the big cat under the Fremont Boulevard-Nimitz Freeway overpass, as the feline meandered down the Alameda County Flood Channel. When Fontes shined his flashlight in the face of the lion, it growled but did not attack. Days later, when a local owner of a forty pound chow-chow puppy came forth claiming his dog was the lion, Fontes said: "The puppy in no way resembled the 300 to 400 pound animal observed in the flood control channel".

On the 10th of November, after Fontes' sighting, the lion was last seen near Newark Boulevard and the Turk Island Dump at about 10pm, and then the search was called off due to darkness.

Charles Johnson, maintenance supervisor at Coyote Hills Regional Park commented after the search that he thought the lion still lurked in the park. He felt the hunters did not do an adequate job in their "safari" through the park. "They didn't check that underbush while I was here," Johnson observed. "They just flew the helicopter over it and turned on sirens to scare the lion."

During the following days no one saw the lion again. Fremont Police Identification Officer Karen Burhardt, and an animal track expert from Marine World Africa USA labled tracks found in the flood channel as those of "a large cat", but the lion seemed to have disappeared from the Fremont area.

Large, maned mystery cats—seemingly male African lions—are nothing new. Reports tick back over the years, from various parts of the United States and Canada. There appears to be a direct relationship between these "African lions", and the "black panthers" we have become so accustomed to hearing about, but more on that later. Let's look at a short history of the maned mystery felines.

Soon after the turn of the century, the famous "Nellie the Lion" incidents drew headlines in central Illinois. The furor started in July 1917 when Thomas Gullet, a butler at the Robert Allerton estate southwest of Monticello, was attacked while he was in the garden picking flowers. Gullet's injuries were only a few scratches, but despite the fact the animal had been seen near Camargo a few days earlier, this event served as the stimulus for massive lion hunts.

Thomas Gullet had described "Nellie" as an "African lioness", as did the Allerton Manison's chief housekeeper. Mrs Shaw. on the 15th of July. Mrs Shaw spied "Nellie" as a 300 man posse searched for the lion on another part of the estate. But "Nellie" was not alone. Apparently, her male companion was nearby. On the 29th of July, a lion pounced the automobile in which the families of Chester Osborn and Earl Hill were riding near Decatur.

James Rutherford was driving a hay wagon past a gravel pit on the 31st of July, when he spotted a "large yellow, long-haired beast". Throughout central Illinois during the Summer of 1917, many witnesses viewed "Nellie" or her maned counterpart. Like all the other mystery cats, "Nellie" was never caught or killed, and her origin remained elusive to the authorities.

A few years later, and in a neighboring state, another fully maned lion was reported scurrying about. In the midst of a mystery cat flap in which black panthers and tawny mountain lion types were being seen, a giant animal rushed a fishing party of four adults and two children in the Elkhorn Falls, Indiana region. The incident occurred in the early evening hours of the fifth of August, 1948.

According to Ivan Toney, who lived nearby, "About 7:30 pm, a man came to the house and wanted to use the phone to call the sheriff. He said he and another man, along with their wives and two children, were fishing along the banks of the pool at the foot of the Elkhorn Falls. Their car was parked on the road near the gate leading to the falls. He said the animal came up the stream from the south. When they sighted it, they started running for the car. They reached it but the animal lunged at the car, then plowed through the fence into the sandy bar along the stream's edge."

The creature "looked like a lion with a long tail," the witnesses asserted, with bushy hair around the neck. This is a trait of the male of the African lion. Deputy Sheriff Jack Witherby examined the tracks and said they were like "nothing I have ever seen before." Witherby, after completing his investigations of the incident, issued a warning to persons in the area who fish along streams at night.

Two days after the Elkhorn Falls incident, two farm boys, Arthur and Howard Turner, saw a strange beast near a plum tree not far from the gate leading into their barnyard. On a rise of ground to their right, another animal stood 200 feet away. Arthur raised his rifle to his shoulder and blasted away. The animals wheeled around, jumped a gate and disappeared down a lane.

The Turner boys described one of the animals as "having the appearance of a lion". It was large-headed, shaggy and brown in color. The other looked like a black panther. Tracks were found, but their dog "Shep" refused to help the Turners and the authorities search for the mystery cats.

The following afternoon, farmers northwest of Abington, Indiana, watched two animals identical to those the Turner boys had seen. And the next morning, the two beasts were sighted by others in Wayne County. Although other varmint reports continued coming out of Indiana in the late forties and fifties, none specifically mentioned the maned lions again.

In June of 1960, near Kapuskasing, Ontario, Leo Paul Dallaire had yet another experience. He reported seeing an animal resembling an African lion on his farm. Dallaire said it was light tan in color, had a mane, was at least three feet tall and five feet long. The animal also had a four foot long tail with a bushy end.

Meanwhile, back in the Midwest USA, ten years later, Tom Terry and about five other people called the Winnebago County Sheriff's office to report they had seen a lion near Roscoe, Illinois.

In late May of 1970, Terry and his friends were working at the Parthenon Sod Farm on Burr Oak Road along with the owner, George Kapotas. The seven of them were loading sod onto a semi-truck one Friday morning when George saw something run by with a bag of raw meat in its mouth. The meat had recently been used to feed two stray dogs wandering around the farm. The two dogs went in pursuit of the animal. "We thought it was a dog" Tom Terry said. "It seemed kind of funny that one stray dog would steal two others' meat."

Terry and his friends climbed on the truck and saw the thief was a lion. At about the same time, Kapotas noticed the same thing. Kapotas got pretty close to the lion, but had to give up the chase. Then on the other side of the field, Terry and his friends piled into a van to join the dogs who were still running after the beast. "We found the dogs sitting by a gate across the field," Terry noted. "They didn't move. They looked shell-shocked."

Driving slowly past the dogs, the search party found the animal on the top of a hill. "He turned and looked at us," Tom Terry later told a sheriff's deputy. "He must have been eight feet long. He had a mane and a long tail. It looked... well... like a regular lion. When they got about 80 feet from it, the "regular lion" jumped a fence and disappeared. "Nobody believes me. I wouldn't believe it, if I were in someone else's shoes," Terry said.

After the local authorities were called, this all prompted a small "safari" of law enforcement officers, complete with a state police airplane, in the area of the sightings near Interstate 90. After searching for one and a half hours, they failed to find the lion. The usual teletype inquiries requesting information on escapees from circuses and animal shows elicited negative results. But a week later something caused two ponies, one horse and four calves on the Lyle Imig farm near Rockford, Illinois, to bolt through two barbed wire fences. The prowling beast left tracks described as five inches long and four and three-fourths inches wide with a span of about 40 inches between each pawprint. Larry Black of the

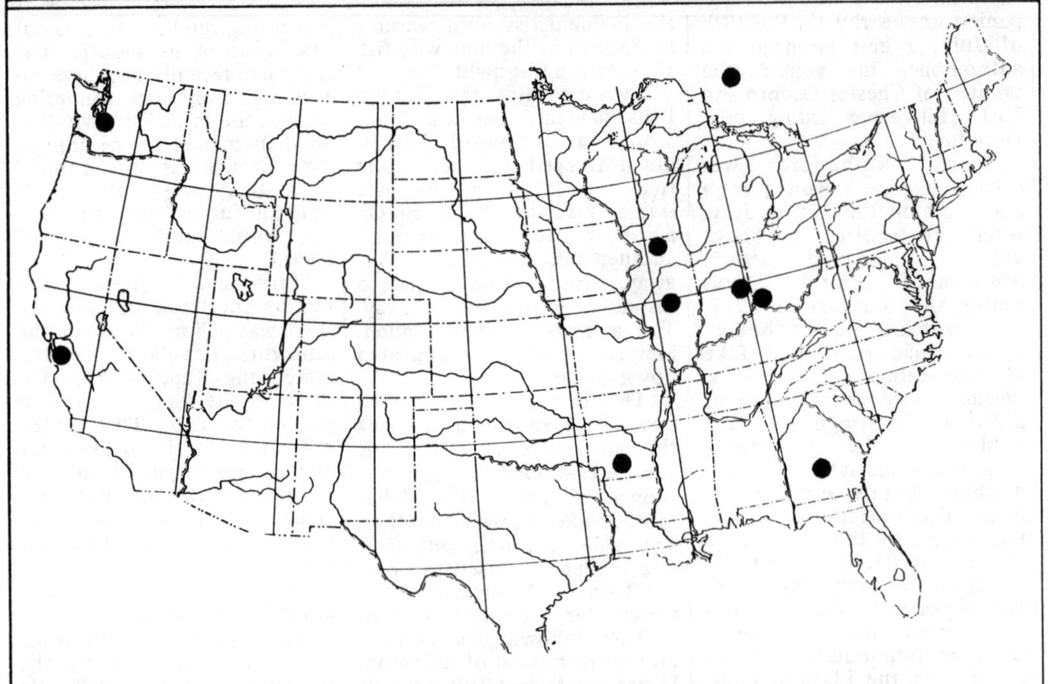

Maned mystery cats in North America - 20th century. (© Loren Coleman.)

county's Animal Welfare League said they were like those of a "huge dog" but he was baffled. He said a similar but smaller set of tracks also was found at the scene. Of the larger tracks, Black noted: "It isn't a dog's; it's something else and we're going to find out what." Lyle Imig rounded up his livestock and returned them to his farm. He said once back the "very excited animals wouldn't leave the shed".

Late in August of the same year along the east bank of the Rock River near Rockford, it seems the same "lion" was still exciting local animals. Dogs began to bark vigorously in the area after a "roar" was heard. Dorsey Hailey swears he was not kidding when he said he heard a lion roar in the vicinity of his home. "It sounded just like a lion," he said. "Like the lions they have in the Milwaukee zoo." His wife who was out hunting dewworms at the time agreed. And of course so did the neighbors' dogs who were barking. Sheriff's deputies and neighbors with flashlights searched through the late August night, but found no trace of the beast.

Robert Rickard has shown that maned lions are not strangers to England, either. (See *Fortean Times* February 1977.) During July and August, 1976, several residents of Nottingham saw what was described as a lion. One witness told the press: "It's head was down and its long tail had a bushy end." Before this English lion left, more than sixty-five people had seen it, and the police had come out with a bizarre explanation the lion was nothing more than a paper bag. Yes, a paper bag!

The same year English policemen were trying to tell the people of Nottingham they were merely seeing a paper bag with a long bushy ended tail, a farmer in Georgia, USA, watched a weird animal in his pasture. J H Holyoak was driving a pickup truck down to check on his cows in Berrien County, Georgia, that day in 1976. Suddenly, he saw this "thing" and thought it was a dog chasing his cattle. When he got within 50 to 100 feet of the animal, he noticed the "thing" resembled a half-panther, half-lion. Specifically, Holyoak said it looked like a panther all over its body except for the mane it had on its neck, just like an African lion.

H J Holyoak's son, Ken, a farmer in his own right and a University of Georgia graduate, added these details in a 1979 interview: "He told me the animal was big and was trying to catch a calf. He shot the animal with birdshot and saw blood running out of it, but it didn't do much damage. The animal crossed the fence and ran off into the woods."

Ken Holyoak noted the "lion" was seen in the forest and swampy woods between Alapaha and Enigma. (An interesting name for a town, considering the circumstances.) He felt sure his father knew what he had seen because "it was daylight, and there was no mistake about it." His father, H J Holyoak was raised in the mountains of Arizona, killed mountain lions there, and knew the difference between them and this "African lion" in Georgia.

In 1977, in Arkansas, where people at Dierks were reporting panthers as "black as the ace of spades", a maned lion attacked two dogs at Dover. Beginning with sightings at the turn-of-the-century, the authorities have been faced with trying to account for all of these maned mystery cats.

More often than not, the police in the United States try to explain away the maned lion sightings as dogs, as we saw with the Fremont 1979, case.

Such dog explanations buried the Cincinnati, Ohio's suburban Croesbeck lion report of April 1971, and the Tacoma, Washington, July, 1976, story. Indeed, the Tacoma lion was described by "all sorts of people" as having "a shaggy black mane, light brown body, and a black tuft at the end of a long tail". Police fanned out, shot off their shotguns and revolvers, endangering mainly themselves, and did not catch or kill the lion anywhere near Washington and South 56th, where it was seen. Instead, they caught a part-collie, part-shepherd dog named Jake at the city dump and labeled poor Jake, the "lion".

The answers to the maned mystery cats are beyond the sphere of dogs and escaped circus animals, however, and rest in clues found in the Pleistocene. *Loren Coleman.*

[Author's note: credit for Indiana/Ohio research, and related theoretical background, to Mark A Hall, of Minnesota.]

As this issue already carries two major articles on oriental subjects, we've decided to postpone the previously-announced changes in this column's format until next issue. Basically, I want to dispense with the current "one subject per issue" form and replace it with something looser and less structured, perhaps opening this department to other writers, if anyone would care to step forward with notes or short pieces. But for the moment, we restrict ourselves to one or two brief follow-ups...

FIRST EMPEROR'S ARMY

Since covering this in FT 29 (p17–19), there have been one or two new developments. A museum has been built on the site, in Lintong County, Shaanxi, and opened on 1st October 1979, in celebration of the People's Republic's 30th anniversary. The main exhibition hall, with a single-span roof like an aeroplane hangar, is 230 metres by 72, and covers the whole of the main pit, which itself is estimated to contain 6000 lifesize pottery figures of warriors from the 3rd century BC. Excavation is now continuing within the hall itself, and I imagine the eventual idea will be to restore the entire vault to something like its original state. A thousand figures have now been excavated (though apparently only 400 are on display in the museum so far), and they continue to show individual features without duplication; each was originally painted, though the colours are now virtually non-existent. Weapons continue to be excavated by the thousand, mostly of bronze or an alloy of copper and iron, though we learn of the finding of poisonous arrowheads made of an alloy of copper and aluminium.

Two other smaller vaults were discovered in 1976, in close proximity to the main vault, also containing warriors and horses, and these have been emptied, their contents being placed in the main museum. As to the size of these secondary pits, the number of their contents, and their geographical relation to the main vault, we have little to go on. Latest estimate is that the combined three vaults contain more than 7000 figures and horses–in view of the First Emperor's obsession with multiples of 6, one might speculate on a figure of 7200–so if you take off 6000 men and approximately 100 4-horse chariots, that leaves between 600 and 800 figures and horses in the other two pits. Maybe... *Ta Kung Pao* (HK) 27 Oct + 22 Nov 79; *Beijing Review* 14 Dec 79; *Sunday Times* 16 Dec 79; *Times* 3 Jan 80; *Chinese Literature* Feb 1980.

THE HAIRY BOY

See FT 30 (p45–47). Yu Zhenuan, now 2½ years old, continues to develop in good health and with normal intelligence, though glossy black and dark brown hair continues to grow over his entire body. Research is still going on at the biology department of Liaoning University, and a forum was held at the end of 1979, with 40 attendees and 15 scientific papers presented. Spread over 10 different provinces, 32 hirsute persons have now been found in China. *Ta Kung Pao* 10 Jan 80.

Steve Moore

PHENOMENOMIX

TALES OF MISUNDERSTANDING

HUNT EMERSON

THOK!
A SIX!

'ODZ BODKINS!
TIS A TOAD!
RIDIP!

MOST AMAZING!
I SHALL TAKE 'UN HOME WITH ME...
INDEED, MR. WEED, TIS NOT RIGHT THAT SUCH A CREATURE BE LOOSE!
SINGULAR!
I SHALL WRITE TO THE TIMES!
WHAT OF THE MATCH?
"AMPHIBIAN STOPPED PLAY"
...TEZ THEY STEAM H'ENGINES...

FOR WALLACE WEED, THIS WAS TO BE THE FIRST OF A SERIES OF REMARKABLE EVENTS!
RIDIP!

HE BEGAN TO NOTICE STRANGE LIGHTS IN THE SKY TO THE EAST....
OY-OY!

....A PAINTING HE OWNED BEGAN TO BLEED....

HE WOKE ONE NIGHT TO FIND HIS BED FULL OF FISH!

AND HE WAS VISITED BY A MYSTERIOUS STRANGER IN BLACK, WHO SAID....
BE WARNED, WEED! DO NOT SPEAK OF WHAT OCCURS!!
WALLACE HAD NO INTENTION OF TELLING ANYONE! HE HARDLY BELIEVED HIS OWN SENSES!!

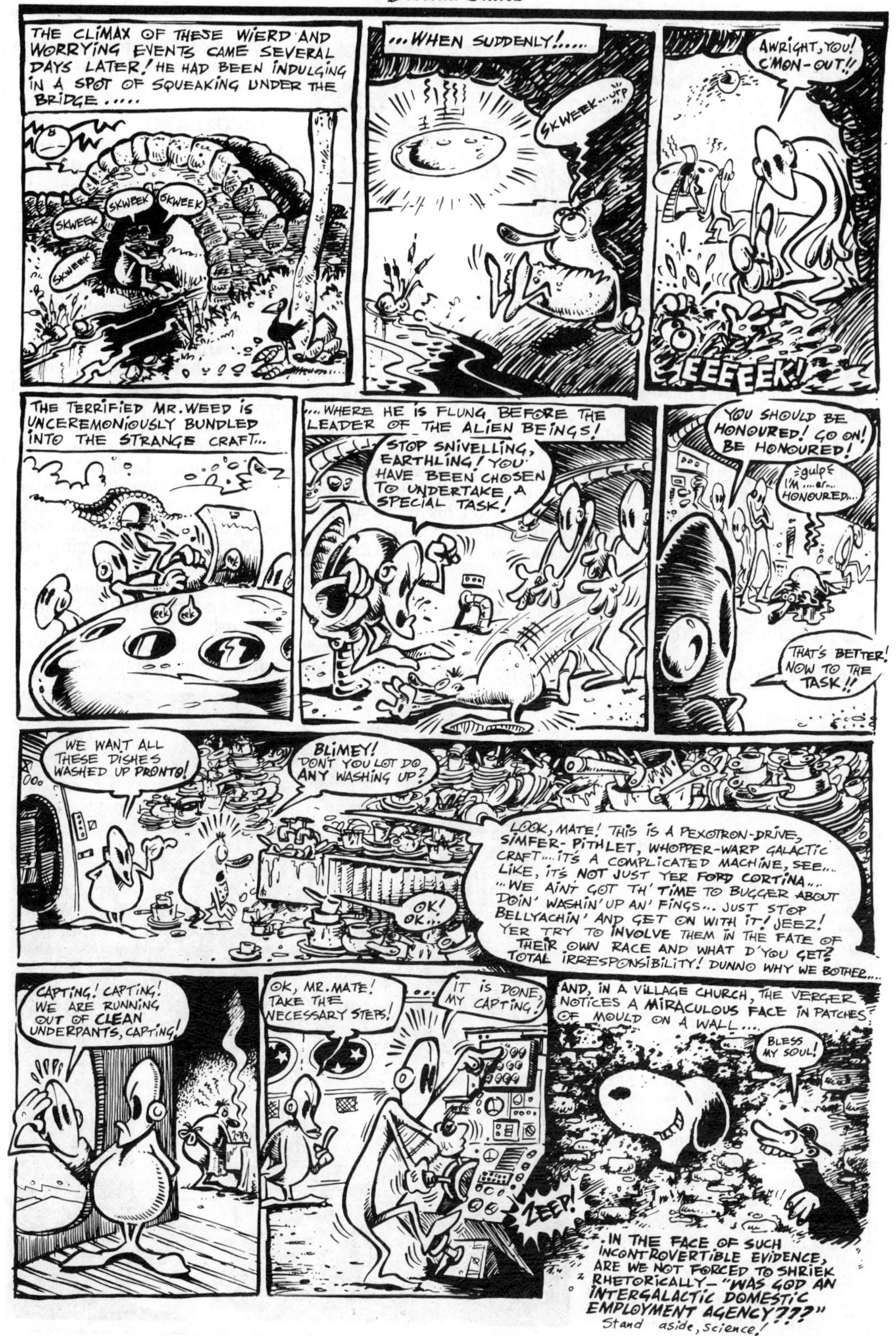
THE CLIMAX OF THESE WIERD AND WORRYING EVENTS CAME SEVERAL DAYS LATER! HE HAD BEEN INDULGING IN A SPOT OF SQUEAKING UNDER THE BRIDGE.....
SKWEEK
SKWEEK
SKWEEK
SKWEEK
...WHEN SUDDENLY!.....
SKWEEK...UP
AWRIGHT, YOU! C'MON-OUT!!
EEEEEK!
THE TERRIFIED MR. WEED IS UNCEREMONIOUSLY BUNDLED INTO THE STRANGE CRAFT...
eek
eek
...WHERE HE IS FLUNG BEFORE THE LEADER OF THE ALIEN BEINGS!
STOP SNIVELLING, EARTHLING! YOU HAVE BEEN CHOSEN TO UNDERTAKE A SPECIAL TASK!
YOU SHOULD BE HONOURED! GO ON! BE HONOURED!
gulp I'M ...er... HONOURED...
THAT'S BETTER! NOW TO THE TASK!!
WE WANT ALL THESE DISHES WASHED UP PRONTO!
BLIMEY! DON'T YOU LOT DO ANY WASHING UP?
LOOK, MATE! THIS IS A PEXOTRON-DRIVE, SIMFER-PITHLET, WHOPPER-WARP GALACTIC CRAFT...IT'S A COMPLICATED MACHINE, SEE... LIKE, IT'S NOT JUST YER FORD CORTINA... ...WE AIN'T GOT TH' TIME TO BUGGER ABOUT DOIN' WASHIN' UP AN' FINGS... JUST STOP BELLYACHIN' AND GET ON WITH IT! JEEZ! YER TRY TO INVOLVE THEM IN THE FATE OF THEIR OWN RACE AND WHAT D'YOU GET? TOTAL IRRESPONSIBILITY! DUNNO WHY WE BOTHER...
OK! OK...
CAPTING! CAPTING! WE ARE RUNNING OUT OF CLEAN UNDERPANTS, CAPTING!
OK, MR. MATE! TAKE THE NECESSARY STEPS!
...
IT IS DONE, MY CAPTING!
ZEEP!
AND, IN A VILLAGE CHURCH, THE VERGER NOTICES A MIRACULOUS FACE IN PATCHES OF MOULD ON A WALL...
BLESS MY SOUL!
...IN THE FACE OF SUCH INCONTROVERTIBLE EVIDENCE, ARE WE NOT FORCED TO SHRIEK RHETORICALLY— "WAS GOD AN INTERGALACTIC DOMESTIC EMPLOYMENT AGENCY???"
Stand aside, Science!

The age of optimism and friendly space folk of the Adamski era has faded. Here are some recent abduction — and attempted abduction — cases culled from the press....

IN NEW YORK STATE

Some time presumably in September 1979, two men (names withheld) were camping in the Catskill Forest Reserve, 100 miles northwest of New York City. They were awakened at one a.m. by noises from a strange "streamlined camper trailer", faintly luminous, with a smooth irregular shape, a mast at one end and a spinning unit mounted to it. There was also a tall luminous figure with dark "eyes" and a series of diagonal slashes on one cheek. Suddenly, three more figures appeared. They were silent and identical, except for the number of cheek slashes. Convinced that they were going to be kidnapped, the campers escaped.

A day or so later, one of the men discovered several diagonal abrasions on his back, and his friend noticed a small "burning" mark near his navel. Ufologist Budd Hopkins thought that the marks were an indication of an abduction which the campers had suppressed in their trauma. One of the men had a flashback of being "picked up"– a rare experience for a man weighing 245 pounds. (*Midnight Globe* 9 Oct 1979).

IN SCOTLAND

On Friday morning, 9 November 1979, Bob Taylor, a 60-year-old forestry foreman generally regarded as a "sensible, straightforward man", was at work on Dechmont Hill, Livingston, West Lothian, near the M8 Glasgow–Edinburgh motorway, when he encountered a silver-coloured, domed spacecraft in a clearing. Suddenly, two objects shaped like sea-mines, each with six spikes, peeled off from the craft and approached him slowly. They grabbed him by the sides of his trousers and tore them, leaving scratch marks on his thighs. He fainted, but remembers the sensation of being dragged towards the craft. Trailmarks as of dragging feet were later found. He also recalls a foul chemical smell and his red setter barking furiously.

The creatures and craft were gone when he came round, but

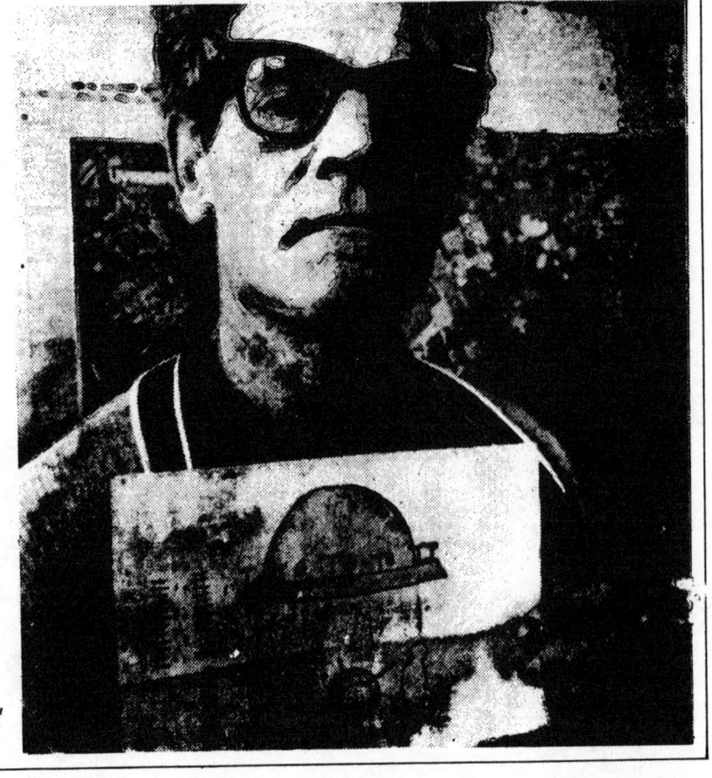

Bob Taylor, 61, with his drawing of the UFO and 'creature'. He was 'mesmerized' by the sight of the domed grey craft, which had little propellors set around its rim. 'Two figures came out, I think from underneath it. They were grey ball shapes about four ft high with 6 metal spikes on each...They were made of something like emery board. They came very quickly. I couldn't move. They came right up beside me and there was a powerful odour... choking me...I must have fainted.' Immediately after crawling home Taylor went to Bangour General Hospital, and despite suffering 'severe pain' in his head, discharged m himself before having an X-ray. 'Doctors said I would have to strip. I refused. I'd had enough.' Glasgow Herald *13 Nov 1979.*

there were a dozen or so deep triangular marks in the ground, two parallel tracks and flattened grass. Police later sealed off the area. A police spokesman said: "There are indentations on the ground as if made by the legs of some machine. But there are no marks leading to the spot, which is in quite a secluded area.

In the afternoon, two Glasgow women had watched a pale white ball in the sky for some time. "I am sure I saw it split up in half and come together again. Then suddenly it just vanished" said one. Dozens of people came forward to say they had seen swooping lights in the sky the previous evening. *S. Express* + *Scottish S. Express* 11 Nov 1979; *Sun* 12 Nov 1979; *Northern UFO* News 67; *Scotsman* 10 Nov 1979; *Glasgow Herald* 12 Nov 1979; Aberdeen *Press & Journal* 13 Nov 1979.

FRENCHMEN THROUGH THE LOOKING GLASS

At 4am on 26 November 1979, Franck Fontaine, aged 19, Salomon N'Diaye and Jean-Pierre Prevot were in Cergy-Pontoise, a Paris suburb, loading a station wagon with clothes for their stall in Gisors. "A very distinct beam of light appeared and was heading very quickly towards the ground", said Prevot. Prevot and N'Diaye went to get a camera, leaving Fontaine with the car.

When they returned, the car had been moved 200 yards and was surrounded by a "circular halo with three or four little spheres." The spheres merged, trailed upwards and vanished. They approached the car, found its door open and engine running, but no sign of Franck anywhere. A nationwide police hunt began, and Franck was the most wanted man in France, until he "refound" himself 5 days (or 7 days—the accounts vary) later in the same place. Unaware that time had passed, he headed for his friends' house to ask why they had left him. When he saw N'Diaye he said "What are you doing in your pyjamas? Five minutes ago you were ready to go to Gisors."

The last thing he remembered was seeing a light the size of a tennis ball coming down towards him and settling on the car bonnet. He felt a strong tingling in his eyes, and everything went blank. Maybe hypnotic regression will yield interesting data. When he reappeared he was wearing the same clothes, had the same amount of money on him, and appeared fit and shaved. Franck Fontaine had lost 5 (or 7) days.

The mythical structure of this event is a beautiful reversal of the abduction of Corporal Valdes of the Chilean army, at 4:15am on 25 April 1977 on the remote northern desert border with Bolivia—see FT23p6. Valdes vanished for 15 minutes in front of his men during a UFO event. He reappeared with 5 days' growth of beard, and 5 extra days on his calendar watch (which stopped soon after). He fainted, and as he came to again he said: "You do not know who we are, nor where we come from. But I tell you that we will soon return."

Last we heard, the French police were undecided whether to prosecute the three Frenchmen for "contempt of the law". Perhaps the charge could be disturbing the peace—of science. *Herald Tribune* + *Evening Mail* + *D. Telegraph* + *D. Express* 4 Dec 1979; *Toronto Sun* 5 Dec 1979; *La Razon* (Buenos Aires) 19 + 20 May 1977; *Melbourne Age* (Australia) 19 May 1977; *AP Report* 23 May 1977 + 3 Dec 1979; *D. Express* 30 Nov 1979 *Times* 28 Nov 1979.

[Credit: Anon (Edinburgh), David Britt, Paul Burd, Peter Christie, Alan Gardiner, M Howe, Mike Rickard, R Rickard pere, Sam, Paul Screeton, Dave Sutton, D Watson, Roland Watson, Dwight Whalen, Jake Williams, Ion Will.] **PRAdeGS.**

Chilean Armando Valdes (above) lost 5 days in 15 minutes; Frenchman Frank Fontaine (left) spent a timeless 7 days -- both UFOnapped!

In recent months, besides being told that the sun is shrinking by more than 8 miles a year, and that the moon is quivering by 50 yards every 3 years since a momentous meteoric bullseye on 18 June 1178, we also learned of the most massive and most energetic objects so far observed.

GLOOMY PORTENT

A total eclipse of the sun took place over SW China on the first day of the year of the Iron Monkey (16 Feb 1980) which according to tradition forebodes catastrophe. It will be the last solar eclipse visible over China until 2007. *D. Telegraph* 22 Jan 1980. The path of the total eclipse also passed over Central Africa and diagonally across India.

In India it was the first solar eclipse this century, but still an ominous event in a land where study and awe of the total eclipse by Hindus goes back 2 millenia. On the 14th day of the Royal War (apx 850 BC). celebrated in the *Mahabharata*, a darkness at noon intervened during the battle. How appropriate, then, that the eclipse this time passed over the huge bathing tank (*ghat*) at Kurukhetra, where, tradition has it, Lord Krishna delivered one of his sermons before the battle. Anticipating extraordinary attendance at this doubly propitious place and occasion, the Haryana State government claim to have spent a huge sum (given variously as £250,000 to a £million) expanding the bathing facilities at the Brahmosavar *ghat*. About two million people took a holy dip during the 75 minutes or so of the eclipse along the three-quarter-mile ceremonial bath. Doubtless the nation's forebodings were fueled by the series of tremors that swept through NW India on the 14th, just two days before the eclipse, and as the whole country prepared to take the dark day off.

In Kenya, the usual gaggle of scientists climbed Mount Kilimanjaro. In Zaire tribesmen barricaded themselves inside their huts; cooking pots broken and discarded; and pregnant women taken indoors. Across the continent cattle milled restlessly; evening choruses of birds struck up before the whole animal kingdom fell silent. In India female bees became aggressive and mentally ill patients more disorderly. Then it was over.

For some of the scientific experiments during the eclipse, see *New Scientist* 24 Jan 1980. Rest of data came from: *D. Telegraph* 13+15+16 Feb 1980; *Times* 15+18 Feb 1980; *Guardian* 16+18 Feb 1980; *Sunday Times* + *S. Express* + *Observer* 17 Feb 1980.

ASTRO–SUPERLATIVES

The most massive is a giant galaxy shaped like a catherine wheel, 600,000 light years across, six times as large as our own. Known as NGC 1961, it is 150 million light years away, and has only just been measured accurately (?), though first catalogued by Herschel in the last century. Some of its spiral arms are disfigured by blobs and lumps, suggesting a recent (250 million years ago) collision with a smaller galaxy. *D. Telegraph* 10 Mar 1979.

The most energetic is a black hole 10,000 million light years away, but only 100 million miles across. It is (?was) devouring a star a week. Much closer to home, in Sagittarius at the centre of our own Milky Way, they've spotted another one 5 million times more massive than our sun and 30,000 light years away. The centrifugal force of our galaxy spin will long prevail against the inward suck, and Prof. Martin Rees at Cambridge assures us that it will be at least 50,000 million years before we go down the plughole... *D. Telegraph* 6 Mar + 19 Mar + 5 Jun 1979; *Times of India* ? Apr 1979.

BOOZE AND BULLION

In 1974 it was announced that a huge amount of molecular ethyl alcohol had been found in the interstellar cloud Sagittarius B2 in the Milky Way. If it were condensed, it would produce "about 10,000 trillion, trillion bottles of 200 per cent proof liquor" said Dr Zuckerman at Maryland University. When we get there, however, we might find the black hole has drunk it.

Also from Maryland, this time from the Goddard Space Flight Centre in 1978, we learned that a visible blue-white star called Kappa Cancrii, in Cancer, 175 light years away, contains about 100,000 million tons of gold, in the proportion of one part per 100,000, one million times the proportion in the sun. Gold on earth is one part per 200 million. *D. Mail* 30 Oct 1974; *D. Mirror* 16 Dec 1974; *D. Telegraph* 27 Jun 1978.

COSMIC LAWN SPRINKLER

A strange object known as SS433, 10,000 light years away in the constellation of Aquila the Eagle, was found in June 1978 to have two complete sets of spectral lines with massive red and blue shifts respectively, which appeared to show that it was simultaneously coming and going at 114 million miles an hour, 17 per cent of the speed of light. The lines were later found to indicate hydrogen and helium. Experts theorised that it might be a cosmic "lawn sprinkler" squirting out jets of matter in opposite directions, or a giant disc-shaped black hole with a ring of gas spinning at enormous speed. Dr Bruce Margon at the University of California thought it was a doomed star in "some terribly weird kind of trouble." Smithsonian researchers have found that, before 1929, SS433 was essentially constant in intensity, but it then began a steady oscillation in brightness with a period of just over 160 days. So the cosmic sprinkler has been on for 50 years. *New Scientist* 18 Jan + 10 May + 31 May 1979; *Globe and Mail* 24 Apr 1979; *Christian Science Monitor* mid-Apr 1979; *Pretoria News* 25 Apr 1979; *D. Telegraph* 25 + 26 Apr 1979; *Herald Tribune* 30 Apr 1979.

STAR WARS?

In the last decade there have been around 80 unexplained explosions in deep space. A bang on 5 March 1979, 50 times more intense than any previously recorded, occurred 180,000 light years away in the large Magellanic Cloud outside our galaxy. A vast quantity of lethal gamma rays were produced in a fraction of a second and scorched across space, and were picked up by 8 widely scattered space probes. It differed from typical gamma ray bursts in that its emissions were at unusually long wavelengths.

Ray Klebesadel, a leading scientist at Los Alamos , said this event was definitely not a supernova explosion. "The odd thing is that its source was an area only about 187 miles in diameter with a whole lot of energy erupting in a fairly small sector. It resembled a high energy bomb blast," he said. Nuclear physicist Stanton T Friedman declared: "Tremendous activity of this sort could well be life out there involved in a war." Said James Oberg at Houston: "It is a legitimate theory that 'star wars' may be taking place." *Herald Tribune* 25 May 1979; *National Enquirer* 25 Sep 1979.

UNIVERSE "IS LOOKING YOUNGER"

A team at the Harvard-Smithsonian Astrophysical Observatory, led by Dr John Huchra, have doubled the value of Hubble's Constant, a number by which astronomers calculate the distance and "outward" speed of distant galaxies. This means that the hypothetical Big Bang that began our whacky reality took place only 9 billion years ago, twice the supposed age of the Earth, instead of the widely accepted 15 to 20 billion years. Since some stars are reckoned to be 15 billion years old we arrive at the whimsical situation that the universe is younger than some stars in it. *D. Mail + D. Telegraph + Eve. Standard + Herald Tribune* 15 Nov 1979; *Poona Herald* 16 Nov 1979; *New Scientist* 22 Nov 1979.

OBJECT NEAR MOON

An Indian news agency report dated 20 January 1980, describes a mystery object that shone brightly, visible to the unaided eye, close to the partially visible moon. The object was seen by many observers in New Delhi, including our man on the spot Chris Gray. An official of the Meteorological office in New Delhi scotched rumours that this was an unscheduled lunar eclipse, and at the same time apologised to assembled newsmen that they did not have appropriate equipment to hand to study it properly. Interestingly, the official said that a similar object had been seen "over the capital" [?] a few days before, but not as close to the moon as this latest one, nor was it as well illuminated. After observing the new object for an hour, the Meteorological office issues a statement to the effect that an "unusual... well-lit object situated in a westerly direction of the moon... moved in Azimuth from 249.8 degrees to 250.8 degrees in approximately ten minutes." They had no idea what it was. *Indian Express* 21 Jan 1980.

[Credit: Chris Gray, Chris Holtzhausen, Jerry Mabie, Valerie Martin, Roland Watson, Dwight Whalen, Ion Will.] PRAdeGS.

From a large pile of recent clippings we have selected two stories which caused general interest and a random collection of curious finds.

LONG LONG AGO

Early man has been capturing the headlines recently. There were two major stories last year. We begin with the less controversial; footprints in the mud of time. Fossil hominid footprints have been found on the shore of a lake in Northern Kenya. The date ascribed to them is 1.5 million years old, and this makes them the earliest example from a direct ancestor of man. (Mary Leakey discovered 3.6 million-year-old hominid footprints preserved in volcanic ash in Tanzania, but these apparently belong to a more remote ancestor of man.) The individual who made the prints walked in very shallow water. The prints left behind in the mud were preserved when flood waters deposited silt on the bed of the lake. Dr. Behrensmeyer, leader of the excavation team, stated "They recorded a behaviour pattern we had not expected to find–

wading with hippos and birds." We wonder what they did expect. *Herald Tribune* 20 Dec 1979.

The study of early man is so patchy that any new find can cause a rash of theory amending. Or in the case of Dr Donald Johanson, a whole new species. He claims that his recent finds in Ethiopia and Mary Leakey's finds in Tanzania point to an early species of man living in Africa about 3.5 million years ago. The theory is controversial on two points, firstly, because the cranium is so small he suggests that man may have split from his ape ancestors much later than is currently supposed. Secondly he claims that his new species is the common ancestor of two different hominid types; *Australopithecus Africanus* which becomes extinct and *Homo Erectus* which evolved into *Homo Sapiens*. He calls his new species.... *Australopithecus Afarensis*. Opposition is strong; other anthropologists feel that the bones belong to *Australopithecus Africanus.* We feel that *Afarensis* might not have a long life. *Time* 29 Jan; *D. Telegraph* 22 Feb; *Bangkok Post* 22 Mar; *Herald Tribune* 20 Nov; *Times* 21 Nov; *New Scientist* 6 Dec 1979.

ATLANTIS AGAIN

Early in 1979 a Russian scientist, VM Marakviev claimed to have found the remains of an ancient civilisation on the sea bed midway between Portugal and Madeira in the Atlantic. Deep water photographs were taken from the top of a submerged mountain chain. Marakviev claims that they show the remains of stone walls with fragments of a stronghold with wide staircases. These are heavily eroded and covered in marine vegetation. He says that geological evidence suggests that the submerged mountain chain may well have once been above water (of course). He also feels that this site is nearer to Plato's original description than other suggested Atlantis sites.

Opposition mustered its forces. Archaeologists rejected the claim preferring the more well-established theory that Atlantis was, in fact, the Minoan civilisation which was destroyed by the Santorini volcano. They also quoted evidence gathered from nine drillings in different sites on the Atlantic seabed that showed the land had sunk 50-60 million years ago. Marakviev promised to publish the photographs. They didn't appear. The vacuum thus caused by the absence of photographic evidence drew forth rumours. We note (*Observer* 21 Oct 1979) that Azorean officials suspect the whole set-up. They feel the Atlantis story is a cover for Russian investigations of a nearby strategic USA air-force base. Still no photos.

And so Atlantis sinks beneath the sea again leaving its tell-tale wake of confusion, unfulfilled promises of evidence and rumour. *D. Telegraph* 28+29 Mar; *Glasgow Eve. Times* 29 Mar; *Delhi New Statesman* 30 Mar; *Le Soir* 3 Apr; *Houston Chronicle Texas* 5 Apr 1979.

'It's a disgrace. It should have been let ages ago.'

MISCELLANY

Egyptian archaeologists have discovered an ancient city which they believe to be Aun, the city where the prophet Joseph lived 3700 years ago. *Saudi Gazette* 27 Aug 1979.

A blueprint for a pyramid was discovered by an East German archaeologist working on the restoration of a pyramid in the Sudanese village, Bergraviya. The plan is 2000 years old and contains a design for a platform on the summit of the pyramid. *Globe and Mail* 10 Apr 1979.

Another city find. Archaeologists digging in Jerusalem to find the remains of King David's city, have just found the remains of King David's city. Naturally! *D. Telegraph* 24 Sept 1979.

An intriguing sacrificial scene was uncovered in Northern Crete by Greek archaeologists. A skeleton with a dagger through its chest was found lying on an altar. Two other skeletons in attitudes of worship were found in the shrine room, another crushed skeleton was found at the entrance. The shrine was destroyed by an earthquake followed by a fire. This is the earliest yet example of human scrifice (3700 years old) in the Agean. *Guardian* 18 Aug 1979.

Two well-preserved female corpses interred about 3000

years ago have been unearthed in the Xinjiang region of China. They were dried by natural causes. The bodies lay on wooden planks buried in a public cemetry. *Beijing Review* 14 Jan 1980.

Finally, I had intended to round off the recent finds with a humorous little cluster of clippings dealing with grandiose plans to reconstruct some of our golden antiquities, including the Tower of Babel (!) and Stonehenge. However recent clippings with a similar theme have suggested a larger treatment than a mere punchline to an antiquities box at a later date

[Credit: Mark Ball, J and C Bord, R Maragna, Valerie Martin, Sam, Has Thomas, Roland Watson, R White, Ion Will.] VT.

Hauntings come in many forms, and in the past we have run phantom hitch-hikers, sexy spectres, fire-raising polts, and so on; perhaps neglecting the fact that the majority of ghost-phenomena are by no means so exotic. So this issue we return to basics, with a selection of recent haunted houses...

UNWELCOME TENANTS

We begin with a few council house hauntings...

Nick and Ann Read have been driven from their home in Willington, Co. Durham, by a motherly ghost. One night Ann checked on her 6-month-old son Lee, and found him sleeping peacefully in his cot, but the wrong way round in the bed, and with the covers thrown off. Ten minutes later, he had been turned round, neatly tucked up, and he was lying on a pillow taken from Ann's room. The house had been blessed, the locks have been changed (?), but nothing will persuade the Reads to return. A medium visiting the house sensed the presence of a woman whose son drowned. *Sunday People* 23 Sept 1979.

The Chawsen council estate at Droitwich, Worcs, lies half a mile from the site of a Civil War battle fought in 1642, so it's hardly surprising that any ghostly manifestations would take the form of a Cavalier: a shadowy outline, 6 feet tall, in boots, plumed hat and cape. Mrs Janet Launchbury, 26, saw him walk through a wall and disappear. Her brother Trevor, 29, saw his bedroom door opened and slammed, saw the door-handle turned, and felt a 'presence' and a drop in temperature. Curiously, Janet's daughter Sarah, 6, told of her mother sitting on the bed during the night, talking to her and holding her hand; no such event occurred. The ghost has spread its attentions to the neighbours also, and three houses have been blessed by the Rev. Andrew Pullin. Margaret Greaves had her house blessed within three weeks of moving in, after her daughter Maxine, 12, reported feeling a sudden blow on the shoulder and finding no one there. Residents are convinced that somewhere on the estate, ouija-board parties are being held, which are stirring up the ghosts. From the report we have, however, there seems no evidence of this whatsoever... but it's convenient to have something to blame it on, isn't it? *News of the World* 14 Oct 1979.

An unnamed elderly couple were transferred from their modern council flat in the West End of Glasgow after a haunting lasting three years. The flat is only seven years old, but was built on a site known as "the old haunted house". The elderly couple were aware of a family of ghosts, apparently of a doctor, his wife and three children, one of whom was handicapped; during the haunting, the old woman felt herself medically examined by the ghost-doctor, has seen the ghosts, been pushed by them, and felt the cold as they walked past. The couple's married daughter, living elsewhere, has also seen the ghosts; though the old couple's teenage granddaughter, living with them, is completely unaware of their presence, though she's puzzled when small objects are found to be moved. The flat was never blessed for fear of upsetting the ghosts and causing even more trouble. *Glasgow Herald* 14 Nov 1979.

A 90-year-old house in Lambeth, SW London, provides us with a really tangled web. Last occupant of the place as a private house was Randolph Galway, now 45: he and his wife Stasia moved in, and he became depressed and started drinking. Stasia started seeing something like a dog with horns, then after 6 weeks, left with the two children. Randolph let himself into the house one night and saw a black goat run down the stairs and into the street. He left too, stopped drinking, and reuinited with his wife.

The council bought the house, renovated and redecorated it, and two years later, in late 1979, Peter Richardson, 33, his wife Linda and their five children moved in. Linda was expecting her 6th child at the time, and the Richardsons lasted 6 weeks too. There were almost daily occurrences; dolls walked of their own accord; a doll which cried when lifted up floated through the air and duly cried; 5-year-old daughter Louise saw a woman in the kitchen; Linda saw a "cold

Two haunted families -- the McGuires, of Lowell (left); and the Frantas, of Watertown (right).

smoky sort of shadow" hovering over the bed and touching her arm. Finally, one night, a footstool moved from one side of the room to the other, a china doll hurtled toward Linda and smashed on the table; birthday cards fell over. The Richardsons fled the house and squatted an empty dwelling nearby. Someone told the Richardsons a woman had hanged herself in the house some years previously after her husband died; the police have no records of any suicide in the house.

Enter Henry (Harry) Cleverly, assitant district housing manager of Lambeth Council and psychic medium. Someone must have been stirring things up with a ouija board, says he (ho hum). Harry thinks church exorcism too prissy, so he assembled two or three other mediums and let the ghost possess him, a nasty *male* spirit was induced to leave after an hour's struggle; whereupon he was possessed by a female spirit, who thanked him...she apparently had been held prisoner by the male ghost. Just to complete the numerical symbolism, Harry is 6 feet tall, and has been a medium for 6 years. But what happened to the goat? *News of the World* 16 Dec 1979; *D. Mail* 21 Dec 1979; *Weekly News* 12 Jan 1980.

INVASION OF PRIVACY

And a few in private houses...

Mrs Patricia Franta of Watertown, Wisconsin, wrote to the *National Enquirer* (28 Aug 79) of her experiences beginning in August 1977. Five nights in a row, after putting her four children to bed and while her husband was at work, she felt a cold chill while watching TV. Then one night daughter Jackie screamed and told of somebody sitting on her bed; two nights later Jackie heard scratchings in the closet. Husband Charles would come home from work at night and see a black shadow cast across Patricia's bed. Son Jason, 2, was hurled downstairs and finger-marks were found round his waist as if someone had squeezed him. When Jason was placed on a rocking horse, it began rocking furiously by itself. Patricia's sister-in-law had heard (where from we know not) that a woman and her lover had been murdered in the house by the woman's husband. The Frantas left after 3 months.

Charles Partride of Edinburgh, his wife, two children, sister and sister-in-law set off to their holiday house in a highland glen at Strathconon. They didn't stay long: one day. Arriving in the early hours of Sunday 2nd Sept 79, Partridge and his wife set off later that day in the car to buy groceries at Dingwall. Slowly approaching a bridge, Mrs Partridge turned the wheel to the right; the car went left, and was a total write-off, though they sustained no more than bruising. Mr Partridge's sister Catherine is psychic, frequently seeing a woman who "watches over her". That night, the woman appeared in company with a small boy who warned "watch yourself tonight". Then "something evil" came into the house, following Mr Partridge, passing through him, and apparently trying to take him over. The women-spirit kept appearing and disappearing, her appearance dispelling the presence and vice-versa, as if they were battling. It was extremely cold, in spite of a blazing fire. Then a policeman turned up to ask about the accident, and they persuaded him to drive them to a hotel. As they were leaving, they saw the "presence", a man in a black cape and top hat. In the hotel, the woman appeared to Catherine again, saying the evil presence had left, but the Partridges returned to Edinburgh. *Press and Journal* (Scotland) 5 Sept 79.

The McGuire family have been living in a 125-year-old house with 12 rooms in Lowell, Boston, for ten haunted years. All the usual stuff: sound of people walking about in high-heels, crying sounds, a blanket pulled off Tom McGuire while he slept. A pet dog had to be given to friends after twice jumping through a window and once through a screen door. Main apparition mostly seen by wife Marie McGuire, is a small transparent boy in an old-fashioned sailor-suit, about 3 years old and crying his eyes out...occasionally to be heard playing a toy drum. Old trunks in the backyard barn provided a photograph of a small boy, believed to be the ghost, and a tiny gravestone was found in the shrubbery, though time had obliterated the inscription. Daughters Kathleen, 19, and Patricia, 10, have also seen the boy, and Kathleen has also seen a woman in old-fashioned clothes. Mrs McGuire has seen *another* woman at the kitchen door, wearing a hat with a flower in it, her face an "awful gray". And friends of Kathleen attending a pyjama party saw a strange woman peering in at them through a window. A priest has blessed the house. *Boston Globe* 31 Oct 79.

Tom Moore, 48, his wife and four children have been living in their terraced house in Chatham, Kent for 11 years, and they've had enough... enough of a ghost who usually stands at the top of the stairs, staring and looking furious, though on occasion he is to be heard laughing. The ghost is believed to be that of a man called Wild, who lived in the house twenty years ago, and apparently had a strong dislike of children. Things got worse since Tom pulled out an old fireplace some months ago, and found a brass bracelet, hairslide, and a few other unnamed objects. The house has been exorcised three times without avail, and now Tom, who has just about paid off his mortgage, is so desperate that he wants to give the house to the local council, if they'll only give him rented council accommodation. He really ought to know better! *News of the World* 6 Jan 80.

[Credit: Keith Beacroft, Paul Burd, Loren Coleman, B Hain, GP Lundegaard, Sam, Martin Straw, D Watson, Nigel Watson, Jake Williams.] SM.

'Who hath not owned, with rapture-smitten frame, the power of grace, the magic of a name?' mused Thomas Campbell (1777-1844). Here are some living examples of the word made flesh....

- In 1976, Alan Bird joined the Royal Society for the Protection of Birds as an assistant reserves manager. Among his colleagues at the RSPB's headquarters in Sandy, Bedfordshire, were Barbara Buzzard, John Partridge, Celia and Helen Peacock and Dorothy Rook. Peter Condor had recently retired as director. The following year, PC David Bird was investigating the theft of 10,800 eggs from a parked lorry in Bristol. And in March 1979 a police hunt for an ostrich reportedly seen near Ipswich was being led by Inspector Derek Bird. His boss was Chief Inspector Plume. We also noted Mr Woodcock, president of the Huddersfield Bird Watcher's Club and Mr Feather, president of the Colchester Pigeon Club. *Guardian* 11 March 1976; *D.Express* 19 Oct 1977; *D.Mirror* 16 Mar 1979; *S.Express* 21 &19 Oct 1975.

- Mrs A. Plumb won the stoned fruit jam section at the Witchfield Produce Show in Cambridgeshire. *D. Telegraph* 14 Sept 1979.

- Mr and Mrs Ratty of Hemel Hemstead called in a pest control officer after they found traces of mice in their loft. *Sun* 23 Oct 1979

- On 3rd August 1975, a car driven by Jean-Pierre Serre of Paris crashed into a car driven by Georges Serre of Clermond-Farrand at Riom in France. Seconds later, a car driven by Mlle. C. Serre, of Royat, crashed into the other two. The three drivers were not related and had never met. Serre is not a very common name. 120 are listed in the Paris directory among 1,200,000 entries. *D.Telegraph* 4 Aug 1975

- Robert C. H. Hershey, an employee at the Pepperidge Farm plant in Downington, Pennsylvania, was killed when he fell into a vat of chocolate. A local rescue squad had to cut through the mixing tub's steel housing to retrieve his body. *New York Times* early 1974.

- More than 1000 inhabitants of the Yugoslav island of Krk are called Zic — and 200 of them have the christian name Antun. 'It makes the sorting of letters very difficult' complained a postman....called Antun Zic *News of the World* 27 Feb 1977.

- Gough Witlam, the Prime Minister of Australia, received a report that started: 'Evidence on the need for national health protection for prostitutes was given by a probation officer, Miss Lillian Pickup.' *D. Mirror* 19 May 1975.

• Australian barman Thomas Key married Ann Lock. Twenty years later, their only child, Bill Key, married Ellen Bolt, daughter of Harry Bolt and the former Miss Evelyn Chain. In 1967 Valerie Brown of Wakefield, Yorkshire, married Alan Black. The wedding was attended by 11 Blacks, 8 Browns, 5 Whites, 5 Greens and 4 Greys. Other memorable matrimonial alliances took place between Beulah Philpott and Henry Passwater; Susan Eatwell and Douglas Burpitt; Hazel Wealthy and John Money; Miss Pepper and Mr Salt; Mr Veale and Miss Pie; Mr Adam and Miss Eve; and to cap the lot, Mr Cloak and Miss Dagger. *Titbits* 11 May 1978; *Weekend* 24-30 April 1974.

• Fire destroyed a potato chip factory in Tauranga, New Zealand, burning the stock to a cinder. The owner's name was Mr Crisp. A young girl, Giovanna d'Arco (Joan of Arc) was sitting at the fireside when a spark shot from the fire and ignited her clothes, burning her to death. The haystack of a farmer in Gippsland, Australia, burst into flames three times in 10 days. The stack would be doused by firemen but flared up again in strong winds. The farmer's name was Alan Sparks *Evening News* 20 Sept 1977; *Point de Vue-Images du Monde* 28 April 1977; Melbourne *Truth* 11 March 1978.

• Motorists fined by a Brighton court included N. Skidmore, who admitted driving with worn tyres, and I. Dunnett, who pleaded guilty to speeding. *S.People* 3 April 1977.

• The reintroduction of salmon to the Thames was planned by an official committee chaired by Hugh Fish. *D.Mirror* 23 May 1977.

• At a wedding in Sydney the bride, groom and best man were all lawyers. Their names were Lawless, Swindells and Cheetham. *Titbits* 7 Jul 1977.

• Two police officers went to arrest Mrs McDonagh in her Southampton flat on suspicion of stealing 16 packets of pork chops. Mr McDonagh pinned PC Butcher to the floor while his wife raised an axe over his head. The act of butchery was, however, prevented by the swift action of WPC Janet Dawkins. *D.Telegraph* 24 July 1979.

• On 20 August 1979 Diana Nyad waded ashore on Juno Beach, Florida, and became the first person to swim the 60 miles from the Bahamas. At the same time, Sandra Blewett was preparing yet again to swim the English Channel. She failed on three previous occasions *Int. Herald Tribune & Evening Standard* 21 Aug 1979.

• Patrick Woods, 44, was killed as he tried to break into a house in Nottingham. Police found him with his head wedged between two planks of wood in a boarded-up ground floor window. He had died through strangulation. *Guardian* 8 Sept 1979.

• An armless thalidomide boy of 17 was awarded his karate brown belt in August 1979. His name was Jerry Limb. *D.Telegraph* 11 Aug 1979.

• Christine Dedman, 17, of Squirrels Heath Avenue, Gidea Park, died after being hit by a car in Chestnut Street, Borden, Kent. *Eve. Standard* 7 Jul 1977.

• A Japanese-built container ship called the Opan Bounty was chartered to take frozen foods from Australia to Iran. Captain David Blye was in charge of the ship and William Fletcher Christian was the first officer. We have no record of a mutiny. *Reveille* 4 Nov 1977.

• On the first day of the trial of the Young Liberal Leader Peter Hain for alleged bank robbery there was some confusion and uproar. The cashier from whom money was snatched was Mrs Lucy Haines. Mr Timothy Hayne was the accountant who chased the thief. The police photographer was also a Mr Hayne, and the fingerprint officer was a Mr Haynes.

• Victoria Lard plunged 17 storeys in New York and crashed through a parked car. Her lard saved her — she weighed more than 15 stone — and she was pulled out of the wreckage alive. *News of the World* 30 July 1978.

• An Indian called Stanley Joseph Stillsmoking was indicted in Texas for attempted theft of cigarettes. *D.Mail* 22 Feb 1979.

• Jack Mount, 59, of Craven Arms, Shropshire, headmaster of the Brookside special school for maladjusted children at Ludlow, pleaded not guilty to four charges of unlawful sexual intercourse with girls between 11 and 14, two of attempted unlawful sex, and five of indecent assault, between January 1976 and May 1978. *Guardian* 9 June 1979.

Houston Chronicle (Texas) 5 Jun 1974 and 13 Mar 1975; *Minneapolis Star* 13 Jan 1977; *D. Telegraph* 7 Mar 1978; *Weekly News* 14 Oct 1979; *High Times* Jun 1979; *Titbits* 30 Jun 1979.

[Credit: Judith Gee, Mark A Hall, CM, John Michell, Valerie Martin, Peter Roberts, Margo Sagov, Valerie Thomas, Nigel Watson, Ion Will, Heathcote Williams.] **PRAdeGS.**

About 2000 years ago Lucretius and Pliny described the tricks of ball lightnings in terms just as applicable to cases today, yet their nature and even existence is still as enigmatic. The recent UFO 'abductions' in France and Scotland 'see 'Strange Encounters') had ball lightning- type phenomena in association — then we received a story from Guy Playfair which seems incredible (see 'Letters'). So a review of recent cases seemed timely....

BALL LIGHTNING

In the groves of Academe the existence of ball light ning is debated still, ignoring the garish illumination from without, where those Puckish balls whizz and flirt and pop loud enough to punctuate the learned closeted discussion. Your editor, in the course of locating possible photographs of ball lightnings for photobook of strange phenomena to be published near Christmas, inquired at the National Meteorological Library at Bracknell. Stunned with a mixture of disbelief and amusement, I heard a librarian tell me: "You won't find anything on ball lightning here. We don't believe in it!" How Fort would have chuckled!

So any would-be ball lightning hunter has to resort to other tactics. The data's there all right–it's just a question of the right approach. But if the academicians are having a hard time accepting plain old spherical lightning, they would become rabid Medievalists before the demonic shapes of spheres with twin feelers, spheres emitting rays, rods, torpedoes and dumbells, all listed, with impeccable references in William Corliss' volumes of *Strange Phenomena* (section GLB in the "G" series of *Sourcebooks*). And as if its existential conundrums were not enough, the ball lightning's behavioural characteristics have been compared to poltergeists on the one hand (see Maxwell Cade & Davis, *The Taming of the Thunderbolts* 1969), and with UFOs on the other (see Condon's *Scientific Study of UFOs* 1968/9, and numerous other "serious UFO studies, including *UFOs: A British Viewpoint* by Randles and Warrington reviewed in this issue.) At the silly end of the spectrum we find ourselves wondering if ball lights later hatch into UFOs, or are sentient. Such speculation may be necessary to account for the undoubted experiences of apparently intelligent actions by these gaily glowing globules–see the letter from Guy Playfair later this issue.

Into this provocative and delicious melange of superstitious fear and scientific curiosity I toss a pinch of the occult. *Reveille* 12 Nov 1976, and a plea for eye-witness accounts of ball lightning to be sent to a lecturer at Manchester University's Institute of Science and Technology. His name... Neil *Charman*. Someday we'll ask TOAD, our computer, if Mr Charman is still around–he might refer us to our SHC files!

BL ACCIDENTS

Our Finnish correspondent, Tuuri Heporauta, ball lightnings are not uncommon in the Finnish countryside, supported by folk traditions which warn of their danger and trickiness and advocate caution. He sent a clipping from the paper *Lapuan Sanomat* 4 September 1969, which reported a storm on that 30th August during which a truck hit a ball lightning. On the road between Tiistenjoki and Laitomaki, the driver was astonished to see the ball travelling about 3ft off the ground, then suddenly spin in front of his vehicle and explode on impact. Tuuri said that a similar incident occurred in Finland in September 1979 (an anniversary?) in which, this time, the driver deliberately rammed a large ball lightning hovering in the road before him–but Tuuri regrets he did not clip the story.

Whilst, as far as we can imperfectly recall, no one has yet been killed by a BL–the Black "Dog" of Bungay, 1577, excepted–one can believe that one of these para-electrical grenades exploding in the wrong place could cause untold damage. Precisely this concern was expressed in a letter from two men in the Amoco Oil Research Department, Naperville, Illinois, which appeared in *Nature* 263p187 (16 Sept 1976). Appealing for more information, I Ginsburgh and W L Bulkley give the brief outlines of eight cases known to them, presumably culled from accident reports, where balls of light are seen travelling up fill pipes, or across tanker decks towards compartments, just before a devastating explosion. These writers publicly express their regret that safety experts will undoubtedly continue to ignore the hazard–until, that is, a tragedy or a lab confirmation forces a recognition. We suggest, in the meantime, that workers in the oil industry be given genuine samples of thunderbolt, an old European remedy against lightning and another bone of contention among experts.

FROM USSR TO OZ

During an early morning storm, we guess in January 1978, a

"hot, bright, yellow ball" was observed in the air over the Bell Tower of Ivan the Great, part of the Archangel Cathedral of the Kremlin in Moscow. A woman worker in the cathedral saw the half-meter diameter ball enter through one of the open doors and sail across the open floor, past the iconostasis. It stopped when it reached the central door it flared up with a loud cracking noise and vanished leaving only a strong smell of ozone. *Soviet Life* Feb 1978.

Even by bizarre ball lightning standards the one that turned up at a small Australian town near Nowra, New South Wales, was unusual–one report described it as "10ft in diameter" which if true would make it one of the largest BL ever, usual sizes ranging from golfballs to several feet in diameter. Both reports agree it was multi-coloured. Bob Wright was one of several drinkers in the Fisherman's Haven, the pub of the Jervis Bay Hotel, in Huskisson, at 7pm on 19 March 1978, when the "technicolour fireball" burst through the wall of the bar. Wright said: "It had all the colours of the rainbow–the glowing lights were beautiful." This vision wasn't the product of too much Foster's; its sudden and violent appearance left too much objective evidence. Wright and his mates paused in mid-gulp when they heard a "roaring" out in the street. One got up to see what it was, when suddenly... "He was flat on his back as the thing came through the door and we ducked for cover. We could see the eastern wall of the public bar moving inward." With a screaming noise about 30 glass panels were "sucked" inward as the wall "bent". Then "the fireball tore out the opening and rolled across Owne Street." At the Avoca Guest House, the BL apparently went up the outside wall and flung sheets of galvanised iron off the roof. It went through two more houses before it vanished whence it came. When things had quietened down Wright and his pals laid into the beer "to get over the shock". One note says the Aboriginies call BLs *willy willy*. Certainly! Sydney *Mirror* + Sydney *Morning Herald* both 22 March 1978.

Our only other account for 1978 seems circumstantial. An article by V Buvanasundaran, in the Ceylon *Daily News* 10 Jan 1979, strange "balls of fire" are described accompanying the cyclone of 23 November 1978. One curious passage reads: "This tornado at Delhi descended during the day and the glow in it was mistaken to be the sheen of the metal used to fabricate the flying saucer. The damage caused by strong winds was thought to be due to the flying saucer coming close to earth." [sic] This was seen, not only by "the residents of Amparai" but "physicists in India". Still, our mirth aside, instances of both ball lightnings, and illuminations in the central tubes of tornadoes, are given by Corliss (for full citations, see GLD sections in the "G" series *Sourcebooks*). Mr Buvanasundaran goes on to mention that a similar effect accompanied the double tornado that devastated the Botale area of Sri Lanka in 1964, when eye-witnesses to the one that "crushed the Walbtali Fair spoke of a ball of fire that came down from the heavens."

FIREBALL FESTIVAL '79

As far as we know few people if any have seen the origin of ball lightning. The following letter from the *Daily Mirror* 16 Feb 1979, may describe such a rare event. Mr R George, of Exwick Road, Exeter, Devon, wrote: "During a recent thunderstorm I was sitting at a table, writing a letter, when a flash of lightning appeared to come through the window. Like a long beam, it cut across the table, then, about six inches from the table, a golden or yellow ball some five inches round appeared. It vanished as suddenly as it appeared and all was clear again."

Whether the following event involved ball lightning is not clear, but I include it here because of the Trickster elements and the tradition of shamanistic election sometimes taking the form of being hit by lightning, often resulting in a cure of some ailment. About midnight, 25th February, 30-year-old Bobby Jiminez was driving home to Porterville, California, after visiting his brother. The earlier account mentions red lights dancing in the sky which "explode" into an orange ball of fire–the later account mentions only the orange ball. Suddenly there was an orange flash and a loud roaring noise and Jiminez, who had been deaf since a bout of spinal meningitis before his third birthday, realized he could hear again. He drove to a local sheriff's office where his excitement and incoherence almost got him locked up. Jiminez speaks only a few words so the cause of his agitation took some time to figure out. Police officers said there were no reports of flashes or explosions from that area, but Jiminez firmly believes the event did happen. At the least he is delighted with his renewed faculty, and although still with a severe hearing loss, revels in the sounds of doors slamming, phones ringing etc. Dallas, Texas *Morning News* 28 Feb + 2 March 1979.

On 18 March 1979 a mystery explosion shattered the peace of Marlborough, Wiltshire. It seems to have centered on the grounds of Marlborough College, where, at 2pm, masters and pupils were just finishing lunch, when windows flew into smithereens, buildings shook and debris shot everywhere like shrapnel. A large ash tree was found with a crater at its foot, the hole penetrating a main sewer had allowed the blast to travel in the sewer 100 yards to a heavy iron manhole, and here the blast destroyed the brick lining and hurled the solid iron cover yards to embed in the lawn. The blast was heard at Pewsey, 7 miles away, knocked out telephone lines and set off alarms in Marlborough itself. But what caused the explosion? Undoubtedly something had ignited methane in the sewer, but what? A geologist on the College staff scorned the idea of a meteorite–we could make something of that, but will generously let it pass. There is a vague groping at something of greater interest to us here; the College bursar, Jack Ashbury, said: "There was a tremendous flash of lightning which zipped across the river Kennet right up to the Bath road." Later on Keith Lovatt, who lives nearby, said he was out walking his dog at the time, and might have seen something: "There was this ball of blue, just like the arc of an electric welder. It rolled over the ground and I thought it struck me. It seemed to hit all around me. I didn't realise at the time exactly where it had struck. If it was ball lightning, its effects on the ash tree are characteristic–all the bark was stripped off from top to bottom, but without scorching, while a shrub at the base of the tree was withered. Swindon, Wilts *Evening Advertiser* 19 March 1979.

Now comes a truly Fortean punchline–just over five hours later, the same day as the Marlborough blast, hundreds of people throughout Britain saw a huge meteoritic fireball flash through the sky over the West Country and Wales. Lifeboats from the Isle of Wight were launched in the belief there had been an accident in the Solent. It was about 7.45pm, lasting for many minutes, and described as a "blue-green colour, which turned to orange as it fell out of the sky" – and as bright as a blushing geologist, I'd say! Account in same paper as above.

A gigantic explosion shook houses and frightened residents in Caversham, Berks, on the night of 4th April. Several people witnessed a bright red ball crashing to the ground outside their homes on Caversham Heights. Mrs Elsie Powell, of Graveney Drive, said: "It was in the distance, behind some trees and was coming down quite slowly. It looked (bright red) like the flames a rocket gives out, but instead of going up it hit the ground." Her neighbour, pensioner Ronald Fleming, discovered the strange effects of the blast: "It was a terrific explosion, and for a while I just sat there, completely amazed, and very shaken. But then I heard the window rattling and saw the catch had broken. The explosion just pulled all the catches off. All the window catches have been sheared off at the front of the house." Investigating, he found that all the catches, made of plastic and metal, at the front of at least three other houses, had been neatly sheared in two. We note that the witnesses saw the bright ball a little while *after* the explosion, and it is not clear which of the two phenomena was responsible for the mischief. The paper gives a good quote from "a high-level weather expert at the Meteorological Office in Bracknell," "I would hesitate very strongly to relate a thunderstorm to broken window catches. It seems very unlikely that they would have been broken without the windows being smashed first. There would be no strain on the catches if the windows were closed. There is no way we could explain it." Nevertheless, this "very unlikely" damage exists. We note also that a police spokesman said Reading police had received "no reports of any strange incidents in the area." (Yawn!) *Reading Chronicle* 6 April 1979.

Tuuri Heporauta translates an incident reported in *Keskipohjanmaa*, Kokkola, Finland, 17 July 1979. On 14 July, a heavy thunderstorm raged over Tynka, in the Kalajoki region on the west coast of Finland, with much lightning damage. Between 5–6pm lightning hit an electricity pole in the yard of Mrs Aino Torvi, fusing the wires and blasting the switchgear through the air 30 meters away. The explosion left two ball lightnings (or a divided one?), one of which travelled along the ground leaving a track. The other headed straight for a pine tree, 150 meters away, and tore chips from its trunk leaving a deep cut, before it travelled to a wooden shed where it pulled off some boards and shifted the whole building from its corner-stones.

A more meek pair of ball lightnings startled a couple of Hartlepool Borough Council workmen, painting a house in Brierton Lane, Hartlepool, on 25th October. Terence Kelly said that a bright orange ball, slightly larger than a fist, and emitting fiery sparks, flew out of the sky past his arm to hit the pavement. "It just disintegrated in a shower of sparks. I looked for some kind of remains but there was nothing there." He was shocked enough to go and tell his foreman. "He just laughed and said it was nothing. Five minutes later the same thing happened to him–a fireball narrowly missed him and went into a bush. We had a look in the bush but couldn't see anything there. It was just like the first one and we have no idea what it could have been. It didn't make any noise except for a whizzing sound as it went through the air. There was no residue at all and no burn marks." Mrs Doreen Peterson, whose house was being painted, said she saw a flash of light and Terence jump back. "I thought he had fallen off his ladder." She recalls: I thought it was lightning because it was a very dark day and the weather was terrible." Hartlepool, Durham *Mail* 26 Oct 1979.

During the recent reports of the abductions–real or not–of Franck Fontaine and Scotsman Bob Taylor (see our "Strange Encounters" section) ball lightning-like effects are mentioned, lights in the former case, and the smell and burns in the latter case. One man involved in the investigation of Bob Taylor's experience is the Edinburgh-based ufologist Stuart Campbell, and following the Taylor reports, Campbell was sent an account of a ball lightning which terrified a man walking home in a quiet Glasgow street, which seems to have occurred about the time Bob Taylor was space-mugged. The unnamed man heard a hissing behind him and turned to see a football-sized object hovering above the ground a few yards away. It glowed redly and gave off a foul smell, likened to rotten eggs. In a few moments it came towards him, but he evaded it and watched, stunned, as it moved up the street, then vanished. Scottish *Sunday Post* 25 Nov 1979.

And finally—Jim Philpotts, of Guildford, Surrey, was woken from his afternoon nap by an eerie green and orange glow in his hallway. Jim, 67, said: "There was a bang, like a lightbulb exploding, and there it was, a foot across, a few inches above the ground." The ball hovered at the foot of his stairs, then faded away, leaving "a strong chemical smell." *News of the World* 16 Dec 1979.

[Credit: Tom Adams, Paul Burd, RE Cotton, Tuuri Heporauta, Nigel Pennick, Paul Screeton, Anthony Smith, Thoth, M Tuppen, Roland Watson, Ion Will. Frank Glover.] **RJMR.**

More odd aggregations of data — this time around such diverse topics as Little People and human sacrifices — proving the Pluriverse is as inscrutable as always....

LITTLE PEOPLE

Angela Elliott, Patrick Olive and Andrew Pearce, all aged 10, and Andrew's 8-year-old sister, Rosie, were walking home at dusk on 29 October, after playing in Wollaton Park, about a mile from their homes in Nottingham. Angela said: "We heard this tinkly bell. We started running and these little men in cars came out of the bushes. There were about 60 of them in 30 cars like bubble cars. They were half my size and looked old. They had greenish faces with crinkles in them and long white beards with a bit of red on the end. They were laughing in a funny way and driving over swamps near the lake. We were frightened and ran to the gate. I don't think they liked the lights outside because they didn't follow us into the street."

Andrew said he saw one of them, "with a red top and green legs," standing up in his car. "I felt something drop on me out of the trees. I think it was one of the men and I fell into the swamp." Patrick too tripped and fell into the swamp in his panic. The next day the four told their stories to their headmaster, Robin Aldridge, at Southwold Primary School, Radford. Mr Aldridge interviewed each child with a tape-recorder and got them to draw what they saw. His opinion: "I know it sounds far-fetched but they really believe in what they saw. These children are not the kind who would make up something like this." The next day (30th Oct) Patrick's 12-year-old sister, Mandy, said she saw the gnomish go-karts: "About six of them coming round the back of Wollaton Castle... just like those Patrick saw." Skeptics would say she didn't want to be left out of the fine fuss.

Although the children said they had never seen gnomes before, we note, as an interesting illumination of playground traditions and culture, that among the Nottingham children it was well rumoured that Wollaton Park was a favourite haunt of gnomes and that the place was full of them. Andrew said: "We heard that if you don't tell them where you live, they take you to their houses and keep you." Who can believe that the heart of all folklore and traditional beliefs died long ago—it's still with us today. Last word goes to Mrs Joan Olive, who doubtless was recalling washing the swamp off young Patrick and out of his clothes. She said: "I think it's a load of nonsense." *D. Mail + D. Star + D. Express* 1 Oct 1979.

We barely had time to get over our fear of being mugged in the park by gangs of goblins when a real living doll was discovered in mid-December—a 9-year-old girl who weighed about 4½ lbs and stood just over 13¼ inches tall. Her name is Stamatoula and she is perfectly formed and proportioned, but smaller than many new babies. I had to get the ruler out to check on 14 inches, and it is incredibly small for a perfect human being. The smallest person in the *Guinness Book of Records* is Pauline Musters, born in Holland in 1876, who at 9 years old was only 21.65 inches. She grew another 2 inches.

Dr Pavlos Vlachos examined Stamatoula at a children's home in Athens run by nuns

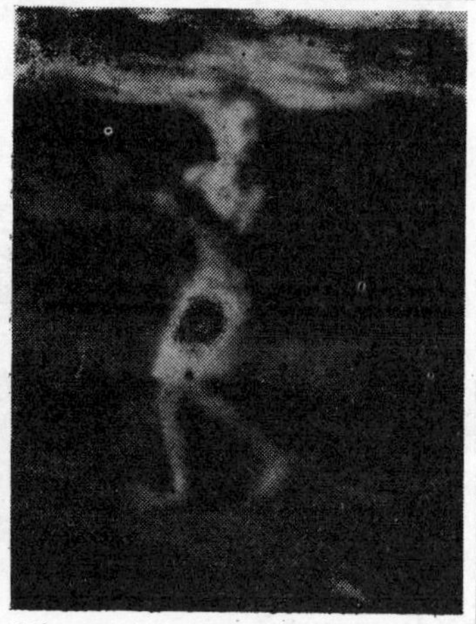

Gloria Ramsey and her brother-in-law on the beach at La Jolla, California -- but not alone. See 'Little People'. (Photo by kind permission of Bill Cox & Pyramid Guide.*)*

and identified her condition as Seckel syndrome, which often produces dwarfism with prominent nose and eyes. He said: "She has tiny, bird-like features and normal characteristics, but in miniature." She has a normal IQ for a girl her age and speaks clearly but so softly it is difficult to hear her. Her head is about the size of an orange and she has blonde hair. Her father, a poor Greek farmer, had taken her to the convent in Athens because of her condition shortly after she was born and she has stayed there ever since. The nuns have vowed to protect her from publicity. London *Eve. News + D. Star + Sun* 19 Dec 1979; *Niagara Falls Review* 24 Dec 1979.

Then we discovered the photograph accompanying this section! It was reproduced originally in Bill Cox's *Pyramid Guide* number 34 (March–April 1978), and reproduced here with their kind permission. We don't know too much about the photo, except that it was taken on the beach at La Jolla, California, and shows Gloria Ramsey, of Gardena, California, and her brother-in-law. We will be making further inquiries about the photo–stay tuned! For more details on the *Pyramid Guide* write to: Box 30305, Santa Barbara, CA 93105, USA.

[Credit: Bill Cox, Bob Forrest, B Hain, Chris Hall, Sam, Diana Senior, Dwight Whalen.] **RJMR.**

CARBON-COPY CAPERS

On 6 July, a real doctor called Roland Fakes was cleared, at a disciplinary meeting of the General Medical Council, in London, of prescribing a fatal overdose of a drug for a four-year-old girl two years previously. London *Evening Standard* 6 July 1979. Then scarcely 10 days later a genuine fake doctor turns up. Irishman and one-time meat salesman, Francis Murphy, applied successfully for a post at Redhill General Hospital, and his credentials checked out because he assumed the identity of a doctor who had gone abroad, a man with the same name as Murphy's brother. In all Murphy carried out 17 operations as an orthopaedic surgeon in 1977, but was eventually sacked for insubordination. The investigating policeman disclosed a curious and perhaps formative fact: as a child in Portlaoghise, Ireland, Murphy had lived in *No 6, Doctor Murphy Place!* London *Evening Standard* 16 July 1979; *Daily Telegraph* 17 July 1979.

At roughly the same time another scenario was not duplicated but recurred three times. A small single-engine plane carrying Ian Mackintosh, novellist and TV playwrite, Susan Insole, daughter of a former England cricketer, and their pilot Graham Barber, took off from Anchorage at 2.30pm on July 7. They had logged a flight-plan to fly to Whittier, then south to Kodiak Island. Three and a quarter hours later Barber contacted the Kodiak tower, saying that he was about 50 miles north of Kodiak and expecting engine failure. He called twice more, the last contact being only 48 miles from Kodiak and losing altitude. Then the plane vanished. Experts say that life expectancy in the frozen seas off Alaska is perhaps two minutes at the most. The plane, a Rallye 235, carried no marine life-saving equipment so it is not unexpected that although rescue planes were in the area in about 8-9 minutes no trace of survivors or plane could be found. Nor is the event itself remarkable. At least three light aircraft were posted missing without trace in the area in the last eight months. *Guardian* 13 & 14 July 1979. What makes it interesting for us is that two separate reports of similar plane crashes involving two journalists and their pilot occurred a week after the Kodiak incident, on the same day, 14 July. One accident took place on Shikoku Island, Kura Bay, Japan, while fishing the salvage of a World War 2 plane — and the other fell into the Schuylkill River, Philadelphia, while filming a charity jog. *International Herald Tribune* 16 July 1979; *TV Times* 26 Jan 1980.

[Credit: P Rogerson, N Watson, I Will.]

Hardbacks.

POLTERGEISTS
By Alan Gauld & AD Cornell.
RKP 1979; £9.95, pp406, indexes, plates.

Some writers have complained that poltergeists are performers with somewhat limited repertoires; they do the same things over and over again. The trouble is that most people who write about poltergeists have somewhat limited repertoires, too: they *say* the same things over and over again.

Since this book doesn't leave enough change from a tenner for you to buy a bag of crisps, you'll probably be looking for something different—something you haven't already had in Sitwell, Price, Thurston, Owen *et al.* An optimist may also demand, in addition to detailed analysis of the phenomena, an answer to the question posed but avoided by previous authors: "Can We Explain the Poltergeist?" On these terms, AG and ADC (as they refer to themselves throughout) *almost* manage to send us home happy and crispless.

The poltergeist aficionado will want not merely well-evidenced cases, but ones he has not encountered before—and many of them. Concentrating on those "in which we have diary accounts or other comparable contemporary records", AG comes up with some real peaches, not only evidentially "strong" but often as uncommon and peculiar as the most blase polt fan might wish. Even when introducing an old friend like the Tedworth case (rendered here under the modern name, Tidworth) he manages to avoid the usual Mompesson rehash by producing unfamiliar mss. testimonies. Others are salvaged from remote, untranslated and forgotten texts: for instance, take to your hearts the Sandfeldt case of 1722, which languished for centuries in a damnably obscure document written by an equally obscure investigator named Haenell before AG placed it in juxtaposition with the better-known Poona depredations in his chapter on "Fantastical Poltergeists". The Sandfeldt spuk showed a certain lack of finesse when, with a cordial cry of "Your health!" it threw a tankard of human excrement into the afflicted house. But even this pales when compared with the 1713 Dortmund case, tersely described by AG as "notable as perhaps the most revolting on record", while his warning that the account of a "daemon" in a Naples monastery (1696/97) is "very little known and is in addition one of the most bizarre and violent in the literature" scarcely prepares us for an attack on our credibility rare even in poltergeist cases. You'll find a similarly unusual selection of hauntings-cum-poltergeists; Canvey Island will never be the same for me now I've read about the window-smashing episodes that occurred there in 1709. Part II offers samples from the authors' personal investigations: their industrious pursuit of an East Midlands poltergeist, two prodigious water-producing specimens and a well-recorded "minor haunt" featuring a variety of imitative noises and other effects.

If nothing else, these illustrative examples dispose of the notion that polts are predictable. Other axioms, such as the distinction between hauntings *per se* and poltergeists, are challenged as well. The neo-classical division between place- and person-centred events is shown to be less convincing than functional. AG believes that in certain cases both factors need to run concurrently to produce the phenomena; a certain person may trigger phenomena in a certain place (but not in others) and having done so may leave without automatically causing them to abate. Though evidence of such place/person interaction is hard to discern, the argument at least cautions parapsychologists against assuming that poltergeist cases *always* require an agent to be on hand, or that a house will *always* be haunted regardless of who happens to be in it.

I fear the worst whenever a computer pokes its binary nose into parapsychology, but the ADC analysis of 500 cases given in Ch.12 cleverly reveals a wider range of effects than polts are generally credited with. Linked to the Appendix, this survey becomes a useful bibliography for each individual case, the relevant literature per types of phenomena and a clue to their frequency. At a glance you can see, for example, that the survey found 53 instances of poltergeist arson (11% of the total), of which 28 were pre-1874, as opposed to 77 assaults, 46 of which were post-1874... and so on. AG comments on the possible trends and patterns—also on the results of a cluster analysis of the "characteristics", which non-numerate dimbos like me will appreciate. Poltergeist behavior doesn't seem to have improved over the years, while again, the traditional hauntings/poltergeist division, "though probably valid in a general way has been in important respects misdrawn".

By the time you reach Ch.17, "The forces at work", you may find yourself in the mood for some answers–or at least for some convincing suggestions. But it soon appears that if, as the writers insist, we view both the "common" effects (rappings, minor object-movements, etc.) *and* the seemingly less credible but equally well-attested "uncommon" ones (like apportation or levitation of humans) no single theory comes up to scratch. The supposed relevance of laboratory-tested PK is trying "to explain the unknown in the terms of the unknown", ectoplasmic and electromagnetic emanations are not backed by case-evidence, Lambert's geophysical thesis is soundly trampled and even overall application of Roll's "rotating beam" theory falls short. Conclusion: "A quick answer to... 'What are the forces at work...' is that we do not have the faintest idea."

It is disappointing to find no new theories about poltergeists in this fat book. The realisation that the writers are unable to suggest any plausible source for "an agency capable of effecting its purpose in a number of ways" shouldn't come as a surprise, though I think that some of the ideas examined here would find supporters ready to stand up for them, at least with regard to certain cases. (And what about the possible sexual origins of poltergeist incidents? AG and ADC seem to have passed this nexus by.) But, while stating that in most of the 79 cases featuring some kind of intelligent communication, there is "convincing evidence" that the minds of living, human agents were the source, the authors concede that some effects (e.g., purposeful movement of larger objects, etc.) imply that we may occasionally be dealing with discarnates, though we cannot positively identify them with the spirits of particular deceased persons. Which leaves us pondering what other types of discarnates there may be, manifesting as poltergeists...

As the time hasn't arrived when we might definitely say we *can* "Explain the Poltergeist", the lack of certainty at the end of this book is not only permissible but inevitable. Perhaps the most important message in this book is that polts are capable of conforming to our cultural expectations: they're RSPK if we want them to be, or "daemons" if we are looking for daemons. What next? AG writes that "we must shortly expect the first poltergeists which function as messengers from the occupants of UFOs". If you've read Clive Harold's *The Uninvited* you may be thinking that they've already landed... *Michael Goss*

MYSTERIES OF THE WORLD

General editor: Christopher Pick.
Lyric Books 1979; £4.95, pp160, index, photos.

A lavish coffee-table book, covering a random selection of mysteries ancient and modern. The texts, by various experts, are informative and admirably open-ended. Atlantis, Stonehenge, Avalon, the Pyramids and Easter Island, the perennial favourites are all here. Tim Dinsdale gives an overview of land and sea monsters (nice to see colour reproductions of a still from the Patterson Bigfoot film, and one of Doc Shiels' Nessie pics, both from the Fortean Picture Library). John Rimmer, editor of *Magonia*, covers UFOs, with an emphasis on their psychic aspect. And Bob Rickard ponders the phenomenon of stigmata, with a wealth of case histories. I noticed that besides St Teresa of Avila, and Therese Neumann, there were at least two other notable stigmatics called Teresa... a cosmic trigger? Other chapters deal with miracles, the Turin Shroud and the Bermuda Triangle – though some of the profuse illustrations, many in colour, bear little relation to the text.

Paul Sieveking

WITCHCRAFT AND THE GAY COUNTERCULTURE

By Arthur Evans.
Fag Rag Books, Box 331, Kenmore Station, Boston, MA 02215, USA; $5.50, pp180, illos.

This book is part of a tradition rarely considered in Western "His-Story". The Tantrik double-sexed deity, the Yogini with serpentine energy manifesting from her Yoni and the rudiments of internal alchemy can be found in such works as Philip Rawson's *The Art of Tantra* and John Blofeld's *The Secret and the Sublime*. These books share with Mr Evans' *opus* a tremendous esteem and reverence for ritual sex as a sacerdotal function of the Creatrix and Her Children.

Evans depicts the marvelous weave of sexual richness and mystery that existed and thrived under pre-Christian nature-worshipping matriarchies. He relates that the oldest Anglo-Saxon deity is the goddes Wyrd (Fate), who was one of the "three sisters". Eventually they were called the "Weird Sisters" (weird originally meant fateful). It is interesting that these powerbrokers of time and destiny are portrayed by Shakespeare as double-sexed as shown by Banquo's remark in *Macbeth*: "You should be women, yet your beards forbid me to interpret that you are so."

Evans' exegesis really picks up steam when he proves that the degredation of the European fertility spirits into devils and the bringer of fecundity and vernal ecstasy, Pan, into the Christian Satan represents the same monumental loss and waste as in Euripides' great play, *Bacchae*.

Evans makes one basic point: that for most of the past 30,000 years native and natural peoples revered gays and androgynes and regarded the status assigned to them as commensurate with the health and well-being of the environment–low status for gays signified then–as now–a fragile ecosphere under attack. Evans is breaking new ground and naturally there is much to cross swords over–his contention that the Knights Templar were not gay–based on the assumption that they were executed on hysterical and paranoid charges arising out of a medieval "McCarthyite"-style period doesn't wash.

The Templars are very important in the history of gay heresies such as Catharism and Gnosticism which the author covers well. The symbol of the Templars prior to DeMolay's immolation was two men astride a horse. This was a cryptic reference to the role of horseracing in the scheme of twilight (intentional) language. After DeMolay was ordered burned the Templars fled to King Robert Bruce's Scotland where they changed their emblem to a phoenix and chose the motto, "She Burns that She May Live". To this day, the name Bruce is associated with feminist men. As for the derivation of the word "gay" as applied to male homosexuality it can be found in an intellectual current of which the Templars were, for a time, the *avant-garde*. This was alchemy, or the "gay science". "gays" owe part of their successes as well as their "new" name to a process of human alchemy still unfolding. Crowley's worship of change in the 20th century was centered on the Templar Baphomet, the bearded hermaphrodite with large breasts who resembles the weird sisters of *Macbeth*. What if the most powerfully transformative hoo-doo worked today is performed by the growing number of males who have undergone breast enlargement by silicone implantation or cannabis smoking?

Witchcraft and the Gay Counterculture is loaded with the kind of unusual anecdotes dreams, great films and better societies are made of. We learn Joan of Arc dressed in men's clothes and was primarily accused of witchcraft on account of her choice of apparrel. She was considered radiantly magnetic by the common people who sought to touch her so as to be healed or granted a vision (*sidhi*). Evans says this adulation was connected to an old tradition of gay people as shamans and healers.

Arthur Evans makes a telling point against America's alleged "First Amendment" religious freedoms. He states that open, public sex has never been allowed and hence, the central part of matriarchal nature worship is supressed and an entire European tradition denied. This book does not accept that Christianity is a particularly venerable, ancient or humble religion.

The author maintains that Christianity got its foothold among the patriarchal Roman military and then city-dwellers and the wealthy. Before this the Great Mother was worshipped as the Maker of All Things. Statues of the goddess showing her split-legged yoni in the East, and of the Sheela-na-gig motif in the West were everywhere. Witchcraft was really the one and only "old religion", a religion of women and gays, without wars or alienation, and the creed of the peasant or pagan since the root *pagani* literally denotes a country dweller. St. Augustine dedicated his *City of God* to the destruction of the *pagani*. Right down to the present the rural people have been the faithful devotees of the Goddess. As late as the 19th century, Evans informs us that the common people who did not sucker in for the alleged progress marked by coal mining and an "Industrial Revolution" were holding sex rituals at Bronze Age megaliths. The Church vigorously attempted to stamp out this remnant of what it called "obscene practices at monuments".

Witchcraft and the Gay Counterculture is a treasure-trove of startling facts which shatter "comfy" illusions and pulls no punches about the need for complete freedom from Jehova's enslavement. A distinct challenge to the chronicles of the intellectual elite, Mr. Evans' book is a welcome addition to the revisionist critique of the paid prostitutes of academia who, Evans infers, were and are a good deal less worthy than the sacred harlots of Temple *sadhana*.

Michael Anthony Hoffman

AN ACCOUNT OF A MEETING WITH DENIZENS OF ANOTHER WORLD, 1871

By William Robert Loosley; edited + commentary by David Langford.
David & Charles 1979; £4.50, pp96, photos.

The announcement by David & Charles early in 1979 that they were soon to publish an original and hitherto unknown account of a 19th-century UFO contact that occurred in Buckinghamshire, England, was received by some ufologists with great interest. A publication with such a claim merits close attention by serious researchers; they must decide if its authenticity is such that it should by general consensus be incorporated into the existing body of accepted UFO reports.

The presenter and editor is David Langford, a physicist who also writes SF. The UFO witness and author of the MS was William Robert Loosley, builder, cabinet-maker and undertaker, of High Wycombe, Bucks, who lived from 1838 to 1893 and whose strange experience occurred in 1871. Briefly, his report tells how one night he saw a bright, starlike light land in a nearby wood, and the following afternoon he walked to the area and found two apparently intelligently controlled mechanical contrivances. The smaller appeared to be specimen gathering and the larger attempted to communicate with Loosley by means of an increasingly elaborate series of visual holographic symbols which were meaningless to the simple builder and joiner. Prevented from leaving the scene of contact by the attentions of the smaller machine, he was forced to spend several hours viewing this tedious display until suddenly both machines turned their attention away from him and he was free to return to his home. Late that night he saw the bright, star-like light again land in the wood and a short while later take off again, having presumably taken the two machines aboard.

This report fills 28 pages of the 96-page book and is preceded by some 9 pages on "The Question of Proof" written by Langford who is concerned not, as one might expect, with establishing the authenticity of the Loosley manuscript, but with mulling over some of the time-worn arguments for and against the reality of the UFO phenomenon. Following the Loosley account are some 45 pages on "The Question of Interpretation". The first seven of these give background details of Loosley's life, with photographs of him with his family, shop front with name, family grave, and the desk with the hidden drawer in which the manuscript was discovered. The following pages are concerned with Langford's interpretation of Loosley's account.

At various points in the book Langford suggests that the manuscript could be a modern hoax, and he ends his introductory note with the words "...there still lurks the possibility of error or fabrication. The reader is warned." So with the editor's warning ringing in our ears, let us examine the contents of his book. First, the account itself. Does it "ring true"? My impression is that the style and expression are not authentic. The wordy phrases read more like a parody of a Pepysian diarist than a self-taught Victorian artisan. But I claim no expertise in the writings of either age. It would have been helpful and more convincing to have had the published opinion of someone whose study of Victorian writing and vocabulary could have given a clear indication on this point, but there is nothing of this in the book. Neither do I like the calm and collected way in which Loosley seems to have accepted his incredible experience, and his decision to tell no one. His behaviour during and after the experience is altogether too "reasonable".

Although no two UFO experiences are the same, they all share a certain inconsequentiality. Loosley's report is too logical and explicable to sound like a genuine UFO experience. Rather the plot reads more like a short story by H.G. Wells.

The bulk of editor Langford's "Interpretation" section consists of a detailed analysis and interpretation of the complex "communications" directed at Loosley, which he could, amazingly enough, recall in considerable detail after his incredible ordeal. Some of these analyses are of a mathmatical complexity that comes naturally to those who have an honours degree in physics, but will be largely meaningless to the general reader. The astronomical interpretations are so closely argued that one inevitably wonders which came first, Loosley's account of the pictorial symbols he saw or Langford's explanation of them.

The foregoing objections are quite subjective. But before ufologists can accept the report as genuine the following objections *must* be answered:

1. Why has no third party, expert in the study of the documents of this period, been called in by editor or publisher to authenticate the Loosley manuscript?
2. Why have the publishers not added a note to say they have seen the Loosley manuscript and consider it genuine? In view of Langford's suggestions that he may be the unwitting party to a hoax, one would expect him and the publishers to seek verification of the manuscript's authenticity, in their own interests at least.
3. Why is there no photograph of a page of Loosley's original manuscript? We are given photographs of the family, the shop front, the grave, and even a cheque from Disraeli to Loosley.* A photograph of the original text, even though the handwriting was illegible, would have indicated its authenticity. If the manuscript does exist, this omission is incomprehensible.
4. Why does Langford give no account of how he became involved in the matter, how the document came into his hands, what connection he has with Loosley's descendants, etc?

Until action is taken along the lines suggested in the four points above, the Loosley account must be considered dubious. The evidence presented for the existence of Loosley himself is reasonably convincing, but the book gives us no solid reason to believe in the existence of his manuscript and therefore we cannot believe that he ever had any experiences involving extraterrestrials or UFOs.

It may be perhaps that I am taking too solemn an attitude to what is only intended to be an academic joke at the expense of ufologists. But too often in the fields of ufology and forteana it has been shown that this year's tall story becomes the future's factual report, passed on from one hack writer to another and accepted as the truth by thousands of gullible readers. Only much later is the myth sometimes exploded, usually by the painstaking work of a researcher prepared to unravel the threads that stretch back through the years. The Hamilton calf-napping is one such story that has been exposed, though even now it is still regularly

[*Editor's note: these are indeed photos of a family, a shop front, grave, and a cheque from Disraeli to someone called Loosley, but nowhere is it shown to our satisfaction that these are the relics of the family Loosley in question.*]

appearing in so-called UFO books of the type thrown together by journalists and editors who know nothing of the subject and work simply by copying material from earlier books of dubious authenticity. Before the Loosley contact of 1871 joins the ranks of these apocryphal reports, editor Langford and his publishers should be challenged: Either satisfy the four points listed above, or admit that the book is an ingenious hoax, of interest only to readers of science-fiction. *Colin Bord*

UFOs:
A BRITISH VIEWPOINT
By Jenny Randles & Peter Warrington.
Robert Hale 1979; £5.25, pp249, index, bib, photos.

Compared to the constant flow of books on UFO topics from the USA, you'd be forgiven for thinking that Britain was devoid of UFOs, or interest in them. Apart from the unique books of Arthur Shuttlewood, there has been no British book on the subject, of any significance, since those by Eileen Buckle, and Robert Chapman, at the close of the 60s. But as any reader of FSR, or the valiant group journals, will tell you, Britain too has its share of UFO encounters, of all kinds, and in recent years over a dozen regional UFO groups in Britain have formed a loose alliance–Northern UFO Network (NUFON)–to coordinate their research and recording activities, and the authors of this book are at the center of that initiative.

This is not a history of UFOs in Britain, since about 90% of the material is drawn from NUFON investigations over the last decade–and the "viewpoint" is definitely post-Condon, post-Hynek even. Although accepting Hynek's system for classifying "close-encounters", the authors have extended it with amendments of their own to cope with graduations of "strangeness". The authors acknowledge the importance of tackling the physical evidence of sightings and encounters–photos, radar traces, ground marks, radiations, effects on animals, electro-magnetic damping of light and radio or TV waves, interference with mechanical devices, etc.–it is clear that they attracted to the "high strangeness" cases: the close proximity encounters, even abductions, by UFO beings.

These cases are so strange, one is literally at a loss to know how to account for them and deliberately or not, our authors are compelled to try various blind alleys and red herrings before settling, uneasily, on the notion that subjectivity is the key. It certainly offers a more satisfying prospect of accounting for some of the phenomena, in ways which an appeal to the occult, the Hollow Earth, the nuts-and-bolts alien civilizations, the interdimensional time-travellers and, lately, demons, does not. But I say "uneasily" because the writing (not always smooth) is ridden with the awareness that more questions are being raised than answered.

Nevertheless, this is a brave attempt, and full of valuable case material, and essential reading for all interested in ufology. The authors, in making the break from the usual UFOs-from-Outer-Space tradition, have broached, for the general reader, a whole new area and approach. If such awareness of the philosophical and psychological implications inherent in the UFO enigma are thus made more widespread, only good can come of it.
RJMR

GODS OF AQUARIUS
By Brad Steiger.
W H Allen 1977; hb £5.95, pp264, index. photos. Panther 1980; pb; £1.25.

Those who have read Brad Steiger's *The Aquarian Revelations* and *Revelation: The Divine Fire* will know what to expect from this latest offering. The greater part is a compilation of "New Age" teachings and prophecies gathered from the numerous UFO "contactees" who believe that they receive their messages from the space brothers via telepathy and trance mediumship. Interspersed with this are chapters of UFO close encounter reports, most of which are well known to ufologists. The possible relationship between these two disparate manifestations of the UFO enigma is never clearly defined nor examined. There are a number of photographs and drawings but these generally have little or no connexion with the text. A disappointing book in that such a potentially fascinating subject should be handled so ineptly that it has become exceedingly dull.
Colin Bord

One of the curiosities of this book is the chapter on "Star Maidens", an idea Steigler has promulgated sensationally in the pages of national American weeklies, and on TV. Star Maidens are identified by a rag-bag of miscellaneous symptoms by which other professions identify their witches, hysterics, misfits, mediums, shamans etc, but which, to Steiger, signify a person not-of-this-Earth. The chapter contains a long and rambling interview with a Star Maiden called Francie, which offers no convincing logic or proof of her take-it-or-leave-it pronouncements. Her awakening to her condition occurred when, as a child, beautiful, naked angels floated through the walls of her room. They have come here from a "higher dimension", "like unto Venus", for our betterment. Etc. What Steiger doesn't say is that Francie is his wife, and in the course of promoting the Star Maiden philosophy on TV, Francie's business, as a psychic, received not unhelpful publicity. For more on Star People, see Nigel Watson's column last issue.

I don't wish to imply that Steiger's approach is worthless and mercenary. I found much of the content of the "UFO prophets" very interesting as fodder for psychoanalysis, if rather banal in terms of Cosmic Revelation. Steiger also brings out in this way certain consistencies in the revelations of the Contactees, Star Children, psychics, visionaries, and those who follow the various methods of "active imagination" as Jung called it. *RJMR*

THE AIRMEN WHO WOULD NOT DIE
By John G Fuller.
Souvenir Press 1979; £5.95, pp360, index, photos.

Fuller's latest "faction", or dramatized fact, based on ill-fated R101, a huge airship, whose crash in France on the maiden flight to India, in 1929, put paid to the commercial development of the airship in Britain.

In his distinctive style, Fuller reconstructs the life of the R101; from her early days, in which the Spiritualist movement and Sir Arthur Conan Doyle became involved, relaying the ominous warnings received through seances, to the predestined disaster and its aftermath. When communications from the "spirit world" began coming through famous and reliable mediums, relating to faults in the structural design of the airship, this case for "Survival" was lifted out of the ordinary. A fascinating story which deserved to be retold, and well told in the telling. *RJMR*

RESEARCHES ON THE I CHING
By Iulian K Shchutskii.
RKP 1980; £6.95, pp320, index, bib.

I CHING NUMEROLOGY
By Da Liu.
RKP 1979; £2.95 pb, pp145, notes, charts.

Written in the 30s as a doctoral dissertation, but not published until 1960, Shchutskii's book is an important sinological work on the text and history of the *I Ching* and its associated literature; referring to, and translating sections of, a great deal of commentatory material previously unavailable in western languages. The book is specialist, technical and perhaps hard-going, but immensely rewarding; though Russian and western sinology have their differing viewpoints; and it is definitely for those concerned with history and philosophy, rather than the diviner. Professor Shchutskii had an enormous wealth of linguistic and academic knowledge; regrettably, he also had a penchant for jokes about the revolution, which eventually deprived him of his life (aged 40) and posterity of several of his manuscripts.

Da Liu's work, on the other hand, is brief, popular, and quite obviously aimed at the diviner. Based on the "Plum Blossom Numerology" of Shao Yung (1011–1077) it provides two different methods of deriving *I Ching* hexagrams by numerical means, and numerous applications, from finding lost objects and predicting the weather to long-range historical forecasting. Easy to follow and with many explanatory examples from the experience of both Shao Yung and the author, it illustrates well the many subtleties of the *I Ching* system and is full of delightful tales. One complaint, though. If Shao Yung wrote 10 poems predicting the future of China, 7 of which have come to pass, why not present the last 3? This apart, RKP are to be commended for publishing two more books well worth a place on the shelf of any student of the *I Ching*. *Steve Moore*

MAPS OF THE ANCIENT SEA KINGS
By Charles H Hapgood.
Turnstone Books 1979; £7.95, pp275, bib, notes, illos.

This revised edition of Professor Hapgood's book (first published in America in 1966) tells the story of a meticulous research project. The trail begins in 1929 when a map drawn by Piri Re'is, a turkish admiral, was rediscovered. The map caused great excitement for two reasons; firstly unlike other 16th-century maps it showed South America and Africa in correct relative longitudes, and secondly it appeared to show the coastline of Antartica, which is now concealed beneath the ice cap. Professor Hapgood undertook a seven-year investigation of this map and many others, including the medieval portolan or navigational maps. His researches led him to the conclusion that these maps were based on compilations of much earlier maps produced by an unknown ancient civilisation.

It is an excellent book and an antidote to the disgraceful distortions of Von Danikenism on this subject. The author has taken great pains, indeed, to present not only the maps, along with the red herrings, blind alleys and the frustrations encountered in such a complex task. This revised edition is very well illustrated and annotated which is a great help to the reader who is following the complicated proofs presented. Professor Hapgood knows the implications are sensational but the style of writing is restrained. He also insists that the role of the amateur has been woefully neglected by experts in all fields (three Fortean cheers!) and therefore gives credit to all people concerned in the project throughout the book. A scholarly book, beautifully produced and a model of research. Highly recommended. *Valerie Thomas*

FAMOUS AMERICANS YOU NEVER KNEW EXISTED
By Bruce Felton & Mark Fowler.
Stein & Day, NY 1979; $12.95, pp293, index, photos.

This is a gripping dictionary of absurd, hilarious and far-fetched biographies–hundreds of cranks, fanatics and blunderers–that will give you hours of pleasure. Who walked backwards across America? Which American became king of Arorai, in the Gilbert Islands? Who was the hero of the Great Boston Molasses Flood of 1919? Who invented the mint with the hole, the supermarket trolley, vaseline, or the ice-cream cone? These, and many other questions are answered here. A great gift.
Paul Sieveking

Paperbacks.

THE INCORRUPTIBLES

By Joan Carroll Cruz.
Tan Books 1977 (Box 424, Rockford, IL 61105, USA); $5.00, pp 310, bib, photos.

Of all the group of mysteries, called for convenience "the physical phenomena of mysticism", perhaps the most baffling is the incorruptibility of the remains of saints (beatified or not). Not much has been written about this obscure topic, apart from the work of Thurston, Summers and a very few others. Indeed there is little that can be said about such a startling phenomenon, except that it is very well attested, and the authorities usually confine themselves to compiling cases.

Now we have a single valuable reference work, in a book that represents a patient and considerable research effort of collating probably all the available material on the subject – ie. apart from the Vatican archive which is severely restricted. Well over 100 examples are given in the form of potted biographies, with bibliographic references, and in some cases, photographs. A good example would be the visionary of Lourdes, St Bernadette Soubirous, who died on 16 April 1879; found incorrupt on exhumations in 1909 and 1919. The sisters of the Chapel of St Joseph, in Nevers, washed and reclothed the body which was found in almost perfect condition, despite a pervading damp which had rusted one crucifix and covered another with verdigris.

Mrs Cruz examines a number of notions in her introduction. Spontaneous incorruptibility amongst ordinary corpses seems very rare, according to the testimony of sextons and grave-workmen. Natural and artificial embalming can account for only a very few cases. We are left with a mystery. According to the rules of her order, St Catherine of Bologna was consigned to the earth without a coffin, and found intact 18 days later, in 1463. After successive exposures her body can still be seen, still seated, in a huge glass urn in her chapel at Bologna, overseeing the worship more than 500 years after her death. Similarly, the most recent saint in the book; St Charbel Makhlouf (d.1898), found in perfect condition 4 months later, his grave a quagmire of mud and water. His body is not on view at his shrine in the Lebanon, but is examined each year, and so far found to be lifelike and flexible.

These examples could be compounded: saints who died from execution (like St Cecilia), or from disease, and even natural causes like old age, but whose remains defied the usual dissolution. Also significant are the number of cases (the majority) whose condition was signalled by lights around the grave, unforgettably pleasant odours, exudations of scented liquids, and whose exhumations were requested by appearing in dreams and visions to their sisters. Some mention is also made of the cures attendant upon the holy remains. The variety in details from case to case is astonishing.

But to me the most fascinating aspect are the cases where the celebrated corpse was also a stigmatic. The stigmata of St Catherine of Siena were invisible during her life, but appeared for all to see at her death in 1380. She was found still intact in 1430, after her coffin had been "much exposed to rain" in Rome. Having "survived" that, her body was promptly dismembered, with papal permission, by Blessed Raymond of Capua–Siena got her head and an arm, while Venice got three fingers. In 1487 a hand and the left foot went to chapels in Rome and Venice; the foot still distinctly marked with its stigmata during an examination in 1597. In 1501 a rib went to Florence, and in 1575 a shoulder blade was sent to a convent in Rome. This holy dismemberment is dignified by the feast-title of "Translation" – and further Translations occurred as recently as 1855, at which time her mangled remains still showed no sign of corruption despite the lapse of nearly 500 years and the grim work of the pious butchers. There are other cases where the stigmata have remained long visible in corpses which have escaped the bizarre craving for relics. There are many scholars–this reviewer among them–who have argued for the psychosomatic origin of stigmata among the living; but how then do we account for the persistence of these marks after the moment of physics death? This is only one of the many unanswered questions posed by the undeniable fact of Incorruption. As a reference book for those interested in such questions, this book is essential. It is, surprisingly, an easy read–but not, as is my wont, while eating. *RJMR*

WORTHWHILE PAPERBACK EDITIONS:

REALMS OF THE HUMAN UNCONSCIOUS *by Stanislav Grof (Souvenir Press 1979; £5.50 hb, £3.50 pb, pp257, index, bib, illus);* **THE HUMAN ENCOUNTER WITH DEATH** *by Stanislav Grof & Joan Halifax (Souvenir Press 1979; £4.95 hb, £2.95 pb, pp240, index, bib).* Grof begins his *magnus opus* based on his respected experience with the LSD research with an overview of the nature of the unconscious. *Realms* deals with the phases of birth trauma and the various levels of unconscious operation and how these affect our lives, as a background for his view of LSD as a non-specific chemical 'amplifier' of basic 'condensed' patterns of experience. The second book analyses his work with Halifax on the experience of dying patients and the use of LSD in the final phases. These important books may be ponderous but reward the reader with many insights into bizarre cases of contact with 'other' beings (demons, angels, gods, aliens etc) and other aspects of psychological experience. **ANSWER TO JOB** *by Carl G Jung (RKP 1979; £1.95, pp194, index).* Jung's immensely readable and relevant attempt to interpret beliefs and the apparent pervasiveness of implacable evil in the world at large, and manifest 'unfairness' of many aspects of everyday life. As always his writing is rich with insight, on the role of religion, archetypes and visionary experience in modern life.

THE NATURALISED ANIMALS OF THE BRITISH ISLES *by Christopher Lever (Paladin 1979; £2.95, pp600, indexes, bib, diags).* A fat, valuable guide to 'when, where, why, how and by whom the various alien vertebrate animals now living in a wild state in Britain were introduced, how they subsequently became naturalised, and what effect they have had on the environment and on the fauna and flora.' Since the book has the 'imprimatur' of many establishment naturalists, there's no sign, of course, of the baboons, wild boars, 'Surrey pumas' etc that we chronicle in Fortean Times; but they do include the wallaby colonies and many other interesting creatures, like Indian porcupines, with maps of their residence, indexes of people, species and places, extensive bibliography and a useful chronological list of these animal introductions. Belongs on every Fortean's shelf.

NATURAL AND SUPERNATURAL *by Brian Inglis (Abacus 1979; £2.95, pp579, index).* Inglis' detailed history of spiritualism takes in the overlap areas with shamanism, alchemy, witchcraft, apparitions, psi powers, animal magnetism and hypnotism, the beginnings of psychology and psychiatry, and religious movements, with much discussion of phenomena, case histories, the great mediums and investigators (and many forgotten outside the old records). Essential reading. **GHOSTS OVER BRITAIN** *by Peter Moss (Sphere 1979; 95p, pp156).* Peter Moss advertised nationally for ghost experiences and said he got 'hundreds' of replies. This book presents about 60 of the most striking and varied cases, showing that many folklore accounts may have been based on such experience in olden times. In this day of over exposed material it is refreshing to meet new material with a fresh power to stand your hair on end. **MIRACLES** *by Geoffrey Ashe (Abacus 1979; £1.50, pp206, index).* Geoffrey Ashe's idiosyncratic and meandering attempt to dissect miracles, visions, shamanism, tulpoid projections and the Turin Shroud, revisiting the themes of his earlier books on the way. Well worth reading. **THE TURIN SHROUD** *by Ian Wilson (Penguin 1979; £1.50, pp368, notes, plates).* Wilson's now classic reference on the Shroud is a concise and detailed review of all the available material. Wilson's theory is that this Shroud could be the famous Byzantine shroud known as the 'Mandylion', which vanished shortly before the Turin relic turned up in 14th century France, possibly via the Templars. Recommended.

THE WILD BOY OF AVEYRON *by Harlan Lane (Paladin 1979; £1.95, pp351, index, bib, notes).* Acclaimed as a 'model of scholarship', this book recounts the famous case of the feral boy found in a French wood in 1800, and how the study of him led to the foundation of modern techniques for teaching deaf mutes. Recommended.

A GUIDE TO ANCIENT SITES IN BRITAIN *by Janet & Colin Bord (Paladin 1979; £2.50, pp183, indexes, bib, diags, photos).* Beautifully illustrated quick reference to 136 megalithic sites around the British Isles, with background info and how to get there. **ATLAS OF WORLD MYSTERIES** *by Francis Hitching (Pan 1979; £4.50, pp257, index, bib, maps, photos).* A fair summary of some quantifiable Fortean mysteries, from selected enigmas of antiquity to monsters, relics and psi powers. **THE SECRETS OF EASTER ISLAND** *by Jean-Michel Schwartz (Sphere 1979; 95p, pp207, photos).* A reconstruction of the Easter Island culture, the statue-makers and the Birdman cult from translations of the weird script record. Interesting asides on *mana* and magic.

Classified Exchanges.

As a reader service FT welcomes mutual exchanges with any relevant publication, and copies issues received since our last issue earn a listing here. No mag — no mention: All we ask in return is a similar entry in your own journal.

FORTEAN

INFO JOURNAL — back on the track again — one of the longest established Fortean journals — current issue, number 35. Quarterly. Annual sub: $10.00 — single copies $1.75. INFO: 7317 Baltimore Ave, College Park, MD 20740, USA.

JOURNAL OF METEOROLOGY — monthly review of weather phenomena for UK, with worldwide disaster summaries etc — much of interest for serious Forteans. £9.50/yr — overseas: $22.00 surface; $28.00 airmail. J. Meteorology: Cockhill House, Trowbridge, Wiltshire BA14 9BG.

LANTERN — quarterly journal of Borderline Science Investigation Group, covering East Anglian Forteana and antiquities. £1.00/yr — overseas rates on application. BSIG: 3 Dunwich Way, Lowestoft NR32 4RZ.

NESSLETTER — monthly newsletter on sightings, personalities and events at Loch Ness, £1.75/yr — US $7.00 (other countries on application). Ness Information Service: Huntshieldford, St Johns Chapel, Bishop Aukland, Co Durham.

PURSUIT — the other long established and essential Fortean journal — published quarterly by the Society for the Investigation of the Unexplained. $10.00/yr — overseas surface $12.50, airmail $15.00. SITU: RFD 5, Gales Ferry, CT 06335, USA.

REPORT ON CURRENT RESEARCH — quarterly bulletin of David Fideler's Michigan Anomaly Research group. $5.00/yr — single copies $1.25. MAR: Box 1479, Grand Rapids, MI 49501, USA.

RES BUREAU BULLETIN — a regular, frequent digest of Canadian and other primary Forteana, from Mr. X; available on exchange or for clippings. Res Bureau; Box 1598, Kingston, Ontario K7L 5C8, Canada.

SCIENCE FRONTIERS — a brief digest of important articles in scientific literature, accompanying list of mail-order Fortean books. The Sourcebook Project: Box 107, Glen Arm, MD 21057, USA.

SIS REVIEW — specialist journal devoted to scholarly discussion of themes arising from the work of Velikovsky — the Autumn 1979 issue carries the first tributes and obituaries of the late Dr Velikovsky, who died on 17 Nov 1979. Published quarterly by the Society for Interdisciplinary Studies — write for details. SIS: 6 Jersey House, Cotton Lane, Manchester M20 9GL.

STIGMATA — quarterly report of Project Stigma, keeping a watchful eye (ugh!) on the continuing enigma of cattle mutilation. $5.00/yr. Project Stigma: Box 1094 Paris, TX 75460, USA.

VESTIGA NEWSLETTER — quarterly report of Fortean investigating group in New Jersey. Write for details. Vestigia: RD 2, Brookwood Road, Stanhope, NJ 07874, USA.

ZETETIC SCHOLAR — an independent review of claims of anomalies and the paranormal — edited by Marcello Truzzi, and already by its fifth issue becoming an indispensible sourcework; articles on attitudes to phenomena rather than on phenomena + invaluable cumulative bibliographies on Fortean, UFO and Paranormal topics. Published twice a year — $10.00 (USA & Canada) — $15.00 (foreign — single issues $6.00. Zetetic Scholar: Dept of Sociology, Eastern Michigan University, Ypsilanti, MI 48197, USA.

UFOs

APRO BULLETIN — monthly journal of US's Aerial Phenomena Research Organisation. $12.00/yr — overseas: $15.00 surface, $17.50 airmail. APRO: 3910 E Kleindale Rd., Tucson, AZ 85712, USA.
BUFORA JOURNAL — quarterly journal of British UFO Research Association. Write for details. BUFORA: 30 Vermont Rd., Upper Norwood, London SE19 3SR.
EARTHLINK — now an independant UFO magazine based in Essex, published quarterly. £2.75/yr — overseas £4.00; single copies 65p/£1.00. Earthlink: 16 Raydons Road, Dagenham RM9 5JR, Essex.
EXTRATERRESTRES — glossy journal of UFO reports and discussion in French. Write for details. Les Extraterrestres: Saint Dennis Les Rebais, 77510 Rebais, France.
IL SENZATITOLO — review journal in Italian. Write for details. Il Senzatitolo: Box 240, 42100 Reggio Emilia, Italy.
INFORESPACE — premier glossy bimonthly journal of reports, investigations and studies, from Belgian group. Write for details. SOBEPS: Avenue Paul Janson 74, 1070 Bruxelles, Belgium.
INSOLITO — journal of the main UFO and astronomical study group in Portugal, in Portuguese. Write for details. CEAFI: Rua sa da Bandeira, 331-3 Sala 32, Porto, Portugal.
IRISH UFO NEWS — quarterly reports and investigations from Ireland. £3.00/yr — overseas rates on application. IUFORA: 4 Copeland Drive, Comber, Co Down, N Ireland BT23 5JJ.
JOURNAL UFO — incorporating *Canadian UFO Report* — very good coverage of Canadian reports and investigations, published quarterly. $10.00/4 issues — single copies $2.75. UP Investigations Research Inc: Box 455, Streetsville, Mississauga, Ontario, Canada L5M 2B9.
JUST CAUSE — intermittent newsletter of Citizens Against UFO Secrecy. Write for details. CAUS: Box 4743, Arlington, VA 22204, USA.
MAGONIA — incorporating *MUFOB* — the second issue, just out, is exemplary — a quarterly journal devoted more to the UFO phenomenon in society, philosophy, psychology etc rather than UFO reports — also includes Peter Rogerson's continuing catalogue of Type 1 UFO records. £1.75/$5.00 airmail — cheques payable to editor John Rimmer please. Magonia: 64 Alric Ave, New Malden, Surrey KT3 4JW.
NORTHERN UFO NEWS — monthly summary of UK cases as gathered and investigated by the UFOIN network of groups. Write for details. NUFON: 23 Sunningdale Drive, Irlam, Salford M30 6NJ.
NYHETSBLAD — review journal of Swedish archive group, in Swedish. Write for details. AFU: Box 5046, 151 05 Sodertalje 5, Sweden.
TIJDSCHRIFT VOOR UFOLOGIE — review journal, in Dutch, of the group NOVOBO. Write for details. NOVOBO: Lijnbaan 4, 9982 HJ Uithuizermeeden, Holland.
UFO NEWSCLIPPING SERVICE — 20 page monthly collection of worldwide UFO press clippings — indispensible to serious interest. Some Forteana. For details and sample write UFONS: Route 1, Box 220, Plummerville, AR 72127, USA.
THE UFO REGISTER — primary research articles of central UFO interest, plus catalogues of 1972 and historical reports — official organ of Data Research: Contact International (UK). Write for details. Data Research: 48 Crown Rd., Wheatley, Oxford OX9 1UL.

PSI

ALPHA — regular bimonthly overview of parapsychology topics, with some UFOs, earth mysteries and Forteana thrown in — now available only by subscription. £5.00 UK; £5.75 Europe; £9.00 overseas. Alpha: 20 Regent St., Fleet, Hant GU13 9NR.
INTERNATIONAL JOURNAL OF PARAPHYSICS — quarterly journal of psychotronic research, regularly contains translations of research papers from USSR, Yugoslavia, Hungary, Romania, Poland, France, etc. Write for details. Paraphysical Laboratory, Downton, near Salisbury, Wiltshire.
METASCIENCE QUARTERLY — incorporating *The Journal of Occult Studies* — an impressive collection of wide-ranging and authoritative studies of topics, from UFOs, Tesla. $14.00/yr — foreign $16.00. MetaScience Foundation: Box 32, Kingston, RI 02881, USA.
SPECULA — quarterly journal of the American Association of Meta-science — frontline speculation on parapsychology, UFO energies and psychotronics. Write for details. AAMS: Box 1182, Huntsville, AL 35807, USA.

EARTH MYSTERIES

ANCIENT SKILLS & WISDOM REVIEW — a review journal of books and mags related to the general topic of earth mysteries. £2.00/yr — single copies 50p. Paul Screeton: 5 Egton Drive, Seaton Carew, Hartlepool, Cleveland TS25 2AT.
ARCHAEOASTRONOMY — bulletin of the Center for Archaeoastronomy. Write for details. Center for Archaeo-astronomy: Space Sciences building, University of Maryland, College Park, MD 20742, USA.
IGNEWS — bimonthly newsletter of Manchester area cryptogeologists. £2.10/yr — single copies 25p. IGNews: BM Bulletin, London WC1V 6XX.
JOURNAL OF GEOMANCY — quarterly organ of the Institute of Geomantic Research. £3.00/yr — 60p/copy. IGR: 142 Pheasant Rise, Bar Hill, Cambridge CB3 8SD.
THE LEY HUNTER — primary journal of ley and earth energy research. £3.00/yr — Europe £4.50, overseas (airmail only) $11.50/£5.45. TLH: Box 152, London N10 2EF.
NEARA JOURNAL — quarterly journal of the New England Antiquities Research Association. $5.50/yr. NEARA: 11 Elizabeth Court, North Kensington, RI 02852, USA.
TERRESTRIAL ZODIACS NEWSLETTER — free for donations, contributions or exchanges. Paul Screeton: 5 Egton Drive, Seaton Carew, Hartlepool, Cleveland TS25 2AT.

OTHERS

THE BEAST — the mag that bites back on behalf of Animal Lib. 40p/copy. The Beast: 2 Blenhein Crescent, London W11 1NN.
FANTASY MEDIA — news and reviews of fantasy in films, books, art, comix and TV. £3.00/yr — overseas $11.00. Fantasy Media: 194 Station Road, Kings Heath, Birmingham B14 7TE.
GNOME NEWS — newsletter of the Gnome Club of Great Britain. £2.50/yr — overseas £3.50. Gnome Club: West Putford, Devon EX22 7XE.
UNDERCURRENTS — bimonthly magazine of radical alternatives and community technology. £3.60/yr — overseas surface £4.50; 60p/copy. Undercurrents: 27 Clerkenwell Close, London EC1R 0AT.

LEYS AND UFOs

May I thank you for the review of *The Ley Hunter's Companion* (by Ian Thomson and myself) [FT30p56]. Janet Bord's review could hardly have been more positive and complimentary. But she does raise a mild criticism in that she feels our attempts to link UFO-incidence and ancient sites to be "weak". One or two others have hinted at this, so I would like to put on record that we have made no such attempt.

For at least a decade many authors (including Janet and Colin Bord) have made great play of the supposed links between leys and UFOs. Consequently, Ian and I could hardly write a book on leys without somewhere mentioning this hypothetical connection. We would have preferred not to as we were anxious to demonstrate the reality of straight alignments of sacred sites in the ancient world without bringing in possible fringe factors to confuse the basic issue.

In the course of producing the book we studied over 40 examples of ley-type alignments so we thought the best thing we could do was to compare these with the records of a reputable and comprehensive UFO organisation. BUFORA kindly allowed us access to their records and we did nothing other than glean accounts from these archives and relate them to the (phenomenologically speaking) random leys we had researched around England. We were entirely po-faced about this and made NO wild claims. Our correlations showed that 37.5% of our lines had had a recorded UFO-event occurring somewhere along their lengths—and some had more than one such recorded event. We felt this was significant but stated that only statistical analysis of further similar work could confirm that opinion. And so it remains.

I'm on record (literally magnetic tape) at a BUFORA lecture I gave as saying that I do not as yet accept that there is any worthwhile evidence linking UFO activity with leys. But I am more ready to accept the possibility that some ancient sites are situated in areas of above-average UFO incidence, and this probably because of the presence of certain geological characteristics.

So the UFO/ley "evidence" in the *Companion* isn't weak—it is simply presented and one makes of it what one wishes. If 37.5% on a random sample isn't significant, then it isn't.

As for the October 1977 Stonehenge UFO event: our Stonehenge—Old Sarum ley (actually Sir Norman Lockyer's line) links four sites of alleged abnormal aerial phenomena. Janet Bord quotes Jenny Randles' attitude that the Stonehenge incident involved a misperception of army flares. That may be so, but I saw the April 1978 Granada TV programme feature Jenny Randles, other experts and the witnesses and film of the alleged incident. At that time Randles seemed less inclined to disbelieve the witnesses and, moreover, it was stated in the programme that the army had been consulted as to the possibility of flares being used that night and a negative answer was obtained. If I've been misled in this particular case well, no matter—there are *at least* seven other claims of unusual aerial phenomena on this line alone remaining to be explained away!

Paul Devereux
(The Ley Hunter) London

GUIDING LIGHT

Here is my version of my Czech friend's experience, which I can assure you is as close to her account as possible, with corrections only in her English.

"My husband and I are keen mountain climbers, and we go climbing every year. One Sunday morning in November 1977 we set out to climb the highest mountain in Czechoslovakia, Mount Snezka. It was a sunny day, with no cloud in the sky, but half way to the 1,400m peak the weather suddently turned bad and it began to snow. Although I know the mountain well, after an hour or so it was clear that we were lost. We had set out at 8am, and by 3pm we were exhausted and desperate. We were now in the thick of a gale and snowstorm.

"Then suddenly I looked to the left and saw a big blue ball, which was very near me and shone with a clear and warm light. I was very surprised, and I must admit I was also very frightened. I shut my eyes, but when I opened them the ball was still there. I asked my husband if he could see it, but he could not. Then, when I stepped forward, the ball moved with me, then it turned to the right and moved slowly away from me. I followed it, as if hypnotised by it. My husband asked why I had changed direction and said it was the wrong way, but he followed me although he still couldn't see the ball.

"All the way, the ball showed us the right direction and after two hours we arrived at the town. As soon as I could see the first houses, the ball disappeared. I am convinced that it saved our lives. I cannot explain this event, but it is true."

Guy Lyon Playfair. London

THE OERA LINDA BOOK

The *Oera Linda Book* [see review of *The Other Atlantis*, FT29p50f] *is* a hoax. It was aimed at the "Frisian Academy", a provincial learned society, where Frisian particularism ran high. (Frisian is not a Dutch dialect, but a language proper. Even today, this creates problems; cf, for instance, Wales.)

The whole matter has been well researched by Dutch scholars. Still, the case against the probable author has not been conclusively proved; mindful of his academic position, he covered his traces very carefully. One day at the Royal Library in the Hague would be sufficient to get all the information, provided the researcher knew Dutch, and had some familiarity with the little world of 19th-century Dutch medievalists and their *literati* friends.

German has nothing to do with the issue, except in as far as in Germany, during the Hitler period (1938 I think it was), the text was resuscitated in a sumptuously edited translation, as an authentic document from the glorious Germanic past unjustly spurned by the Dutch people who had lost true racial feelings, etc. To us this was hilarious, because it needs only a working knowledge of Middle Dutch and Frisian to see that the language is synthetic, and the jokes, especially the etymological ones, very broad.

However–in 1954, a colleague of mine wrote: "It might well be that this masterpiece of forgery remains virulent, and that some day, for whatever reasons, the authenticity of the *Oera Linda Book* will once more be proclaimed as a fact."

Dr Mia Gerhardt. Domburg, Holland.

THE GREAT FISHFALL OF 1859

I am in receipt of your latest, and most splendid to date, issue of *Fortean Times*. You do not need me to tell you what an excellent issue this is, and that it deserves the very widest support.

My main purpose in writing is to offer some additions to Robert Schadewald's interesting article of the 1859 fish-fall [FT30p39f]. He professes not to have found Troedyrhiw on any map he has consulted. The place is mentioned in the article reproduced from the Merthyr *Telegraph*, and occurs on p.39 of FT, and again on the following page.

If Mr Schadewald cares to look on map 15 of the Bartholemew *Gazetteer of Britain* (maps section at end of this indispensible reference work), he will find Troedyrhiw plainly marked some two miles NNE of Mountain Ash. It is actually over the other side of an intervening mountain, in the neighbouring Rhymney valley. The same map also clearly marks Aberman (not Abermann) in the Cynon valley.

The above information shows that the fish fall was more extensive than a few adjacent places in the Cynon valley, that the fall occurred on both sides of a mountain (of very considerable height–over 1000 feet) dividing the Cynon and Rhymney valleys, and that, due to this now established wider distribution of the fallen fishes, newspapers that may then have existed in Pontypridd and Abergavenny (two sizeable towns known to have had their own newspapers in later decades) should also be scrutinised for accounts. The occurrence of fallen fishes in both the above mentioned valleys discloses the fact that not only was JE Gray's explanation patently ludicrous but that the "storm" discharging the fishes either covered a much larger geographical area than initially thought or it carried some fishes in the air over the mountain and down into the Rhymney valley before dumping them. Either possibility raises other factors too complex to discuss here but which Mr Schadewald (should you pass this letter or a copy of it on to him) may care to ponder and elaborate upon.

The Rev WS Symonds later moved to Pendock rectory near Tewkesbury, and I believe that many of his papers (he was a prolific author) may be either at Tewkesbury or Worcester or Malvern (all nearby). I will make some enquiries to that effect. I have consulted some of Symonds' geological memoranda at Worcester, but know that *not* all his MS went there.

Bernard Delair (Contact UK). Oxford.

[Robert Schadewald replies: My map of the Mountain Ash area does indeed show Troedyrhiw, although the name is split into two lines and buried among elevations, cairns and contour lines. Upon being told where it is, I found it immediately. As for overlooking it before, I can only plead blindness and stupidity.

The spelling of "Abermann" apparently varies. My map shows Aberaman, Aberaman

Ho and Coetgae Aberaman all within about a mile of each other.

One of these days, I'm going to get to England. Between the British Newspaper Library, the National Library of Wales, and libraries in the Mountain Ash area, I have no doubt that I'll be able to turn up additional sources. I even have hopes of resurrecting the Symonds paper from somewhere. Meanwhile, if anyone else comes up with additional sources, I'd be most grateful for photocopies.]

ABOUT FT30

A good meaty issue, as always, with a very nice cover by Una Woodruff (you see... almost Max Ernstian territory???). I love the stuff on Nessie pictures being, really, swimming elephant pictures. I didn't see the original *New Scientist* article, but recall Rip Hepple saying something about it. I don't know if you remember but, back in '76, a photographer on the "Falmouth Packet" suggested that the "Mary F" pictures of Morgawr looked very like a swimming elephant. Bloody right... they do, too! In fact, they look more like a swimming elephant than that picture of an elephant swimming off the coast of Sri Lanka! *That*... as reproduced in FT... is amazingly similar to the Heuvelmans "Long-Neck", even down to the tiny "horns". Nature imitating supernature? Another type of simulacrum?

Several witnesses have described Nessie's skin texture and colour as being similar to that of an elephant. Then there's that "Pictish Beast" (by the way, were your examples, the line drawings, taken from George Bain?)... I must have a long look at the Meigle School. Meanwhile (just for fun), remind yourself of Max Ernst's "Elephant of Celebes", a bit bovine but the word "elephant" is derived from the Hebrew *eleph*, an ox. Anyway, in the Ernst painting, a fish fall is about to happen... so watch out Schadewald!

Doc Shiels, Truro, Cornwall.

Help!

This column is free to any reader or researcher who requires help on a question or in locating source materials on Fortean topics. Just send a brief paragraph outlining your interest, on a separate sheet, including your address, to FT editorial address. An FT reader service.

Mystery Helicopters/aircraft – sighting reports, clippings etc required for in-depth research work. UK & overseas cases wanted on this enigma, first highlighted by John Keel in *OTH*. Xerox costs refunded. David Rees: 92 Hillcrest Road, Offerton, Stockport, Cheshire SK2 5SE.

Mystery smells, especially in connexion with ball lightning and weather freaks. Would appreciate photocopies of items for article. William Zeiser: 1529 N Park Ave, Indianapolis, IN 46202, USA.

Mystery airships, sightings and reports of unidentified airships etc seen over any part of the British Isles, pre-1920, but especially the years 1909 & 1913. Compiling a catalogue and chronology. Nigel Watson: 1 Angerstein Road, Scunthorpe, Lincs DN17 2LZ.

Tree Alignments – any information or sources on the Twisted beech, *Fagus tortuosa*, which occurs along a corridor from Denmark to Brittany, purportedly caused by radioactive meteorite. Mike Crowley: 7 Belmont Road, Harrow, Middx.

Devil's Footprints, Devon Feb 1855, or any similar **mystery "tracks"**, alignment of imprints in inaccessible places etc, for supplementary case material for forthcoming FT *Occasional Paper* on Devil's Footprint source material. Any illustrative material on the subject. Already have the obvious sources, Fort, Gould, ILN etc. Bob Rickard: c/o FT Editorial address.

Truss Fund.

...in which we gratefully acknowledge the valued donations sent by the following. Such heartening support helps us brave the slings and arrows of outrageous misfortune, and are applied where they will do most good.

David Appleton, Larry Arnold, MIG, Mike S Grayson, Dennis Magnus, Valerie Martin, SN Morgan, Leslie Shepard, Mike & Linda Ward, Nigel Watson, Peter Willmott, CA Worth.

FAIRY EXHIBITION

Brighton Museum are staging a major exhibition from 3 May to 13 July on the subject and influence of the fairy world and belief in the visual and performing arts.

The exhibition will include some examples of amulets for protection against fairies, "elf-shot", and even some "fairy loaves" and a bronze bell once stolen by a mermaid. Fay Godwin was commissioned to photograph six sites in Surrey associated with the Little Folk. The major attraction is supposed to be the extensive collection of paintings, engravings and drawings, many from the collections of the nation and the famous, inspired by the fairy tradition. There will be performances of fairy plays, ballets, pantomimes and operas. An illustrated catalogue will be available, and a book dealing with the whole event and displays in detail.

A lot of effort has gone into research and collection of material into an unusual subject, and we hope those of our readers within reach will make the effort to visit this imaginative venture. More info can be had from:

The Exhibitions Office,
Brighton Museum,
Brighton BN1 1UE,
England.

Isn't it time you tried *Undercurrents*?

The magazine of radical alternatives and community technology.
£3.60 for six issues from 27 Clerkenwell Close, London EC1.

Fortean Times

Issue No. 32

The Journal of Strange Phenomena.

Price: 95p $2.50

Fortean Times

9-12 St Annes Court,
London W1, England.

The Journal of Strange Phenomena.

Summer 1980
ISSN 0308.5899

Editorial.

From this issue we have a new sub rate of £4.00, or $10.00 a year ($17.50 airmail). This is the first sub increase since mid-1975. Since we believe in giving you a good deal we tried to absorb all the spiralling costs. Heroic though this was, we passed the point beyond which we were loosing revenue.

With Dwight Whalen's history of the Mississauga Blob, part two of Dave Fideler's well-received 'window phenomena' papers, some good readers' letters, some great comix, and lots more, we've put together another damned good issue, if we may be permitted to say so. We were honoured when US artist Gilbert Shelton offered to draw us a cover during his recent visit to these shores. His 'Furry Freak Brothers' have had many adventures with Fortean phenomena, so it seemed only right that he should illustrate the phantom feline friends of Fat Freddie's cat. Australian Paul Cropper reports on panther sightings in New South Wales; Loren Coleman submits an interesting theory based on recent American mystery cat sightings; and we offer a brief survey of 'lioness' sightings in Scotland this last winter.

Continued on p17

Contents.

Cover art by **Gilbert Shelton**

ARTICLES
4 **The Mississauga Blob** *Dwight Whalen*
10 **Gateways to Mystery pt 2** *David Fideler*
17 **Ask Aristotle** *Paul Sieveking*
18 **Southern Highland Panthers** *Paul Cropper*
30 **Old Ives Tales** *Paul Sieveking*

COLUMNS
21 **On the Trail** *Loren Coleman*
32 **Tales from the Yellow Emporium** *Steve Moore*
34 **America Mystica** *Michael Hoffman*

COMIX
9 **Telly Kinex** *JH Szostek*
28 **Phenomenomix** *Hunt Emerson*
37 **Facts You Might Forget** *Pokkettz*

NOTES
23 **Out of Place** *Mystery Cats*
26 **Strange Tales** *Fairytales come true*
38 **Swarms** *Squirming Hordes*
40 **Strange India** *Faraway Forteana*
42 **Trends** *Odd Aggregations*

USUAL STUFF
2 **Letters**
45 **News**
46 **Reviews**
54 **Classified Exchange**

Published by Fortean Times Ltd: 9-12 St Annes Court, London W1. Editor: ROBERT JM RICKARD. Editorial Assistants: STEVE MOORE, PAUL SIEVEKING, VALERIE THOMAS. Contributing Editors: DAVID FIDELER, PHIL LEDGER. Art Director: RICHARD ADAMS. Comix Editor and section heading artwork: HUNT EMERSON. Photosetting by Wordsmith Graphics, 19A West End, Street, Somerset. Reprosetting by Magic Ink, 22 Dane Rd., Margate, Kent CT9 2AA. Printed by Bija Press, Beeches Green, Stroud, Glos.

FORTEAN TIMES is a quarterly journal of news, notes, reviews and references on current and historical strange phenomena, related subjects and philosophies. A friend to all groups and magazines continuing the work of Charles Fort in investigating, studying and discussing all aspects of strange phenomena. SUBMISSION is invited of articles, artwork, cartoons, and news clippings on related subjects. The publishers can assume no responsibility for unsolicited material, but all reasonable care will be taken while in FT's possession. If material is to be returned, please enclose SAE. CORRESPONDENCE: letters-of-comment and personal experience are welcome. If replies are required please enclose SAE. The editor regrets it is not always possible to reply promptly. ADVERTISING and DISTRIBUTION ENQUIRIES: contact the editor at the above address, or ring 01 552 5466. SUBSCRIPTION INFORMATION: see p56.

THE FIREBALL AND THE CARPET SALESMAN

Having recently borrowed *Phenomena* from my library and enjoyed reading every page of it, I feel I can contribute a couple of strange happenings that have occurred to me and members of my family, the first being the Fireball incident.

It was during the last war, and I was staying with my grandparents here in Stokesley (near Middlesborough). They lived in a small cottage by the river, and one day we had a thunderstorm. My grandparents went to every room in the house opening every door and window, "so if the lightning comes in it can get out again." We were all sitting in the small back room when there came the biggest flash of lightning and peal of thunder that I have ever heard, and above the sound of pouring rain we heard this loud fizzing sound. I went to the back door and there on the step was this football-sized blue bubble which seemed to be spinning on its axis at a terrific rate of knots.

The draft coming caused the bubble to be drawn into the room where it floated gently into all four corners, passing under the table twice. It did not seem to emit any heat, although it fizzed and crackled and was nearly of blinding intensity. At this time we were all standing on chairs. The cutlery in the table drawer was all magnetised together.

The bubble was then caught in the through draft and left via the sitting room and front door, and as it passed the electricity meter behind the front door exploded. The bubble then gained height and speed, sped away in a great curve and smashed into the roof of a house 300 yards away. We were really alarmed at the explosion and amount of damage caused by our visitor, who seemed to us to have no more substance than a penny balloon.

In 1965 I had just bought my first car, and took my wife and two daughters out into the country for the first ride and picnic. Not far from here is a ruined castle and church, and in part of the church lies a crusader. My daughters wanted to see his tomb, and I lifted them up so that they could look inside through a grille in the door. Suddenly my wife screamed out in fright. A man had touched her on the shoulder. None of us had noticed his approach, even though the path and area we were standing on was covered in deep gravel.

The man was deeply upset and crying and I asked what was the matter. He asked us to follow him through the churchyard, which we did, and asked us to go and read the inscription on a tombstone, then return and tell him what the inscription said. The inscription read: "Here lies the body of Harold James Bell of Silloth, Cumberland. Born 21 June 1815. Died 21 June 1865, Aged 50 years."

On repeating this to the stranger, he broke down completely and after a while told us of this coincidence. He was Harold James Bell of Silloth, Cumberland. Born 21 June 1915, and that day, 21 June, was his 50th birthday. He was a sales rep. for a Cumberland company, and had been asked on that day to travel east into this area where he had never been before. Five miles from here some unknown force took over control of the car and brought him off the main roads through a narrow country lane to this place. He had been pushed and shoved by something invisible until confronted by the tombstone.

He was convinced that the event was a way of showing him that he had come to the end of his natural life, and we could not convince him otherwise. My wife was really upset over the affair, and I decided we would leave. I escorted Mr Bell back to his car (a 1964 Ford Anglia Estate), noticed various credentials, carpet samples etc, and left.

Next Monday, I told the story to my manager at work. A week later he came to me with a laugh and complimented me on telling such a good story. He and his wife, walking in the area, decided to go and see the tombstone, and couldn't find it. I was amazed at this, as it really couldn't be missed. That evening after work I returned to the graveyard, and sure enough there was no gravestone, nor sign that it ever existed. My wife and I have revisited the site many times out of curiosity. I always wonder what became of the unhappy Mr Bell. Did he and his car really exist that day? Our conversation, the atmosphere and the unreality of it all made this the strangest happening in all my life.

Ron Parker,
Middlesborough, Cleveland.

WAS IT A TULPA?

The thing that I find most unusual about collecting Fortean reports is that until you have actually experienced a Fortean event, you have that nagging sense of uncertainty that these things really do occur. I can say unequivocally that they do exist, because I experienced one in 1974. It was mid-October and I was walking home about 4 p.m. when my attention was suddenly drawn to what looked like a giant hot air balloon–white in color–about 100 feet off the ground. As I watched, it suddenly started to decay at the edge and turn black. My first thought was "My, God, someone has set the thing on fire!"

It gradually stabilized until it looked like a round black hole in the sky. I was only ½ mile from home and literally ran the rest of the way. I burst in the back door, grabbed my 8mm movie camera and managed to get about 3 ft of film exposed before it vanished in the west.

Later on, my mother informed me she had also seen the same object about the same time or *earlier* than I observed it, and it exhibited the same behaviour exactly. My only conclusion was that somehow the original object travelled backwards in time or else there were two identical objects exhibiting the same behaviour. Since that appearance in 1974, I have read about the creation of thought-forms or tulpas and wonder if somehow either myself or my mother inadvertently created one that was observed by the other. It was certainly a remarkable experience, and I can well appreciate the feelings of those who are reluctant to inform others of something weird that has happened to them. Despite myself, I was far from comfortable with whatever had happened and kept trying to mentally explain it away, even though I have collected and read about unusual phenomena for years. I have had several other unusual experiences but none were so definite and unequivocal as this one. Then too, I had the strip of movie film which although unspectacular shows a clear and definite black dot above the trees.

W. Ritchie Benedict,
Alberta, Canada.

MYSTERIOUS BOOMS IN THE WEST

Since 1977 Mr. and Mrs. Denton have heard a series of mysterious sounds in the area around Bridgewater, Somerset. Sometimes they sound like explosions, sometimes like the rumbling of thunder. On some occasions the vibrations have been felt in the house. Mrs. Denton has recorded the dates and times of these sounds in a diary. Below are extracts from their letter.

In the beginning the bangs usually occurred at 9 p.m. once or twice a week. They appeared to be coming from the West. More recently the sounds have been as many as three to four in one evening, and the direction has changed to the North West. The times range from noon to 11 p.m. One night the time was 8.1, then 8.25, another night 9.5, then 9.48. Some bangs have been loud enough to make us jump. From May 7th 1979 to June 12th we recorded only one rumble. Since the 21st December last year there have been only three or four nights when we haven't recorded any of these sounds. The last three bangs tonight (27th January) at 6.30, 8.25, and 9.20, sounded like anti-aircraft guns.

At first we thought it was due to the blastings in the quarry over Quantock hills (10 miles away by road). But we can see the hills from our window, and as it usually happened around 9 o'clock we thought it strange. Meter readings were taken, and it was put down to Concorde. This seemed to make sense at the beginning when the noise was only once or twice a week. But how can you have Concorde at 6.45 and 7.45 the same night? There has been nothing on the television about it recently, perhaps it has something to do with the army or the government. There must be people living much nearer to it than us, so why nothing has been said is a mystery.

Mr and Mrs Denton,
Bridgewater, Somerset

FILM SUICIDE?

I have a rather interesting story which can be found in the book *The Complete "Wedding March" of Erich von Stroheim* by Herman G. Weinberg (Boston: Little Brown and Co., 1974). It seems that the actor and director von S was an early Fortean because Weinberg mentions that he was interested in the paranormal and that "a favourite book of his was Charles Fort's *The Damned*" [sic]. Anyway the film "The Wedding March" when it was finished turned out to be too long and von S's backers took it out of his hands and made two films of it, *The Wedding March*, which got the director's seal of approval, and *The Honeymoon*, which did not and which he was able to prevent them (his backers) from exhibiting in the U.S. Anyway *The Honeymoon* was briefly and unsuccessfully shown in Europe and South America and dropped from sight, except that a single print was preserved at the Cinematheque Francaise, which was destroyed by fire–5 days after von S died in May 1957. In a footnote on p.95 Weinberg relates that "Langlois (the then curator of the C.F.) is convinced... that it died voluntarily... out of shame of having been disowned and not wanting to outlive its creator. A true suttee." Anyway I thought you might like the story.

Patrick Harrigan,
Rensselaer, New York

FORTUITOUS

No-one seems to have noticed that Charles Fort's name can be taken as an aglicisation of the Latin *forte*, by chance. Can this be a coincidence?

Chris Hutton Squire,
Undercurrents magazine.

Continued on p **56**

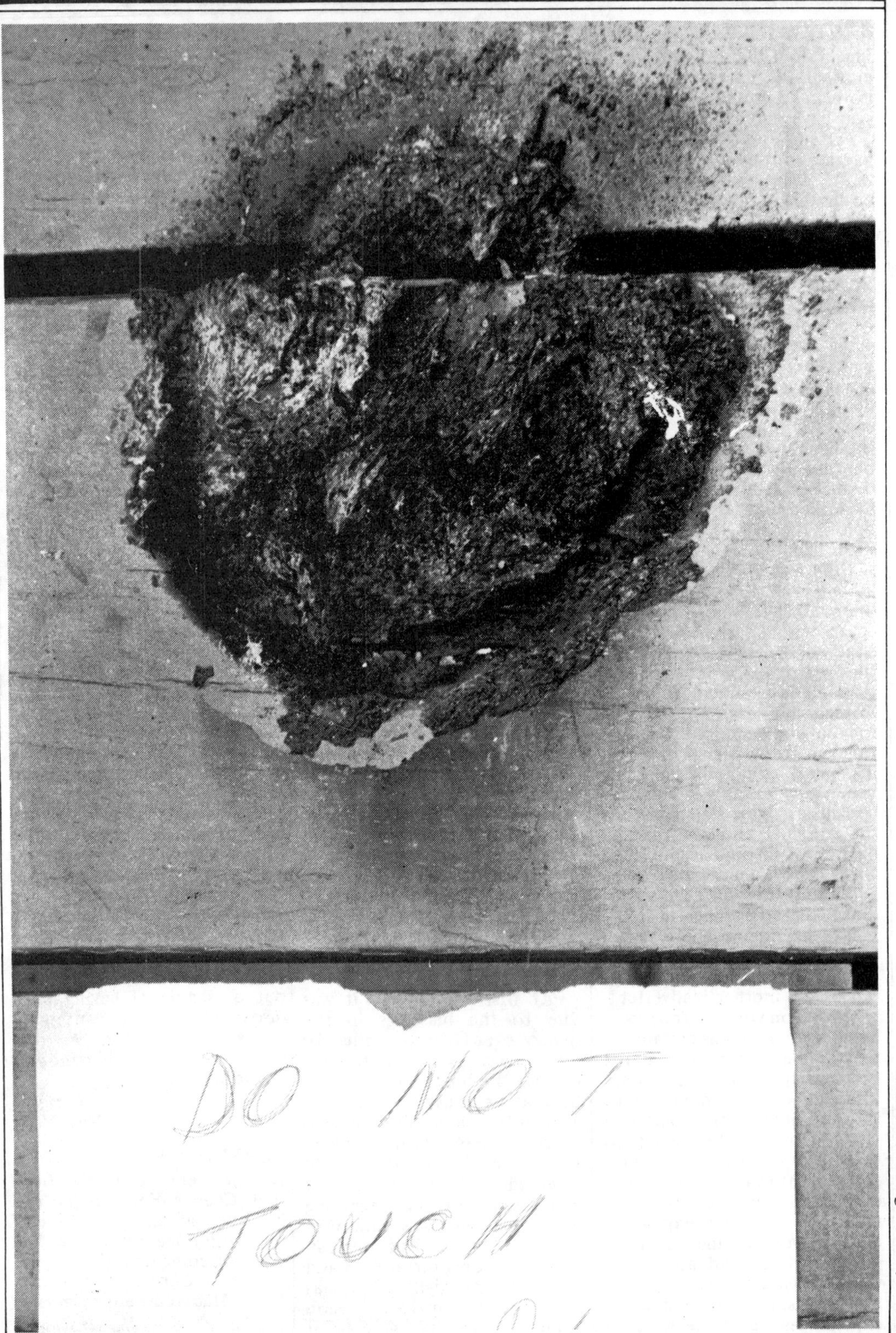

Inland Publishing Co Ltd., Canada

THE MISSISSAUGA BLOB

In June 1979, in the wake of Skylab mania, something fell out of the sky into a backyard in Mississauga, Ontario, causing great consternation. Mississauga also happens to be the home of our energetic correspondent Dwight Whalen, whose chronicle of the incident and its effects not only records the details for us, but illuminates the reactions of everyday folk and of 'experts' and media to an unexpected happening.

It was late afternoon, 16 June 1979, a hot, sunny Saturday in Mississauga, Ontario. In the backyard of his Melton Drive home, real estate broker Traven Matchett, 49, was painting lines on his ping-pong table. His nineteen-year-old daughter Donna was skimming their swimming pool 40 feet away. Behind her stood a green picnic table which something suddenly struck with a thud. Thinking the family dog had merely thumped its tail against some cedar decking, she continued undistracted. Seconds later came a crackling sound. She turned.

The next sound was Donna's scream.

A cylindrical column of flame was shooting up from a molten green mass upon the center of the table. Thinking quickly she picked up a garden hose and doused the fire as her father ran up.

"It was a picture I'll never forget as long as I live", says Matchett.

Dave Haisell and I visited the Matchetts in December to review the mystery of "The Mississauga Blob". What it is and where it came from are questions that still have not been answered to the Matchetts' satisfaction. They want to know who is responsible for the fiery mass that could have easily struck Donna, or set their house ablaze had it landed on the roof. What further disturbs them is a growing suspicion that someone else wants the same answers more eagerly than they do.

"The flame was like a blow torch, magnified, shooting up through the table," Matchett told us. He described it as a very intense light, reddish-orange with yellow streaks, perfectly cylindrical, about 18 inches high by eight inches wide. "A lot of people were puzzled when we said the top of the flame was flat," he says. "But it was. Whatever was burning was driving the flame up 18 inches–and stopped flat."

The burning substance was three or four inches high when Donna turned the hose on it.

"The fire was out as fast as I hit it with the water," she says. "There was no smoke whatsoever, just a little vapour."

The extinguished mass shrank and solidified.

"It was as hard as that immediately after," Matchett said, as he handed me his chunk of the blob. It was a small, flat, dark green mass with a fibrous, pock-marked texture, weighing about four ounces.

"Donna's first thought," says Matchett, "was that I had ignited something on the table, pulling some kind of prank. My thought was that maybe she had laid a cigarette on something and it caught fire. Then both of us realized that we had done nothing out of the ordinary to cause this thing."

Nor, he says, had his next-door neighbors. On the advice of one of them, a pilot, Matchett phoned the control tower of the Toronto International Airport to learn if the flaming mass might have fallen from an airplane. It hadn't. "They told me that if anything had fallen that hot out of plane, the plane had to be on fire," he says.

They advised him to check the nearest military air bases, and the merry-go-round began. Matchett learned that breaching the fortress of officialdom on a weekend can be impossible.

"I called the military. They couldn't give me an answer. It was Saturday; nobody was available. I called the University of Toronto. They told me to call the Ontario Science Center. I called the Science Center and they told me to call the papers, as the press might be able to send someone to at least look at it."

Matchett phoned *The Toronto Sun*, which immediately sent a reporter.

"Then I called NASA, and couldn't get through because it was Saturday."

But when the story broke in the next day's *Sunday Sun*, bedlam struck.

"This place was like Grand Central Station," says Matchett, "and it was like that for a whole week. The story just zoomed across the country. Donna was giving interviews on the phone every three minutes. There were television cameras here, newsmen, it was unbelieveable the excitement there was around here over this thing."

On Monday an inspector from the Ontario Ministry of the Environment came and took a sample of the green blob for analysis. Their conclusion: it was merely polypropylene, a widely used chemical plastic in such items as plates, ashtrays, and toys. I asked the Matchetts if something on their picnic table, a plastic dinner plate, perhaps, could have caught fire.

"We don't have plastic dinner plates," says Donna.

Her father says he remembers precisely what was on the table. "There were my reading glasses, a ceramic ashtray, a towel, a garden glove, and a book of matches. They were all there after the blob fell."

But polypropylene, the Ministry told them, is also used in frisbees. If the burning mass of plastic had fallen from the sky, possibly an incendiary set a frisbee on fire and tossed it into Matchett's backyard. The Flaming Frisbee Theory, however, starts Matchett burning, especially when he recalls the visit from the Ministry's inspector.

"This guy walked into my yard with a pencil," he says incredulously. "Not a geiger counter, not an instrument, not a thing. He lifted the blob up with his pencil and said, "It looks like a frisbee." I politely invited him to leave. He wasn't interested in listening to what it had looked like, what had happened, the heat of it, he really had no interest at all."

Matchett decided to conduct his own tests. He bought two $5 frisbees and set them on fire, the first with a blow torch. "It took about four or five minutes to ignite it and then it just burned like an old, wet rag," he says. "It melted and simmered, but didn't explode into any kind of intense fire the way the blob did." On the second frisbee he poured gasoline, stepped back, and tossed a lit match. "We watched it burn for a while and there was a lot of smoke," but when the blob burned, "there was no smoke at all."

There was, he recalls, after the blob was extinguished, "a strong acidic odor, a vinegary smell" which lingered about the yard till Monday morning. He says he was too excited, though, to pay much attention to it.

Public interest was excited, too. Quite naturally people wondered if Matchett and/or his daughter had staged the whole thing for laughs.

"The police came here and hammered questions left, right and center," says Matchett. "I told them everything I could possibly tell them. In the end I said, "Look, if you want, my daughter and I will take a lie detector test if you think there's anything we're trying to hedge or cover up. We're telling you exactly as it was."

As he told one reporter, "I'm not going to ruin my picnic table for fun."

The Matchett's weren't asked to take a lie detector test.

The Mississauga Blob, while it hasn't burgeoned or produced offspring in the classic science fiction manner, may nevertheless be evidence of an "alien invasion". When the blob story hit the news, Mrs. Dorothy Smith of Sherobee Drive–about a mile from Matchett's residence–came to him with a curious story. About a month before, she said, she found a solid, circular blob of plastic-like material in her own backyard. But unlike Matchett's green blob, hers was black. Matchett then showed her where his blob had melted between two planks of the picnic table onto his concrete patio blocks. There she saw a hardened, shiny, jet-black residue identical, she told him, to her blob.

Chuck Le Ber of nearby Brampton told much the same story. He had found a dark-colored blob of what appeared to be hardened plastic in his backyard the previous April.

Both blobs, however, met a fate hardly worthy of deadly invaders from space. They were thrown in the trash.

A third blob–a whopper–was given to Matchett by another Bramptonian, a well-to-do elderly gentleman who requested anonymity. When Donna hauled it into the room I almost expected Steve McQueen to rush in, urging all of us to flee Mississauga.

(Not again?!)

To describe it in a word: grotesque. Measuring roughly 18 inches long, 10 inches wide and 1 inch thick, it weighs about eight pounds. Its design resembles a huge pancake which someone has squeezed out of a gigantic toothpaste tube, or an enormous brain that's been flattened by a steamroller. Its surface resembles that of china, smooth and shiny. Its color is pale green, but when Matchett snapped off a couple of fragments for us, we found the blob's interior to be entirely white. Possibly it's just a mass of industrial caulking. Whatever it is, Dave plans to have a sample analyzed, with results to appear in a future issue of JUFO.

Like its Mississauga cousins, the Big Brampton Blob was allegedly discovered in someone's backyard. Why these things apparently never splatter onto frontyards may suggest a subversive, house by house, plan of conquest–today Peel County, tomorrow the World. In which case, "Follow *me*, Steve!"

Whatever these blobs are, and wherever they originate, Matchett just doesn't buy the Environment Ministry's flaming frisbee suggestion (The Ministry wouldn't speculate further, as investigation of strange falling objects is not their responsibility). Not only do frisbees not burn like he says the blob did, it's inconceivable to him how anyone could have tossed one flaming into his backyard.

"The trees at the back are about seventy feet tall. No one threw it in from that end; I was standing back there. Our hedges are about twelve feet tall;no one threw it over the hedges. In order to get it on the backyard table they'd have to stand in front of the garage, throw it over the garage and around the corner of the house to land on the table like the blob did, which is impossible. The height of that flame on the table, the intensity of it–there's no damn way anyone could have thrown something burning."

Whether anyone could have or not, Peel Regional Police were unable to turn up any clues. Matchett also gave them a sample of the blob for analysis by the Center of

Traven Matchett prods the remains of the Blob as Donna looks on. (Photo: Inland Publishing Co Ltd, Canada.)

Forensic Sciences in Toronto. In return, Matchett was refused a copy of the lab report. Instead, claiming it was a confidential document, the police nevertheless showed it to him and let him read it three times, once to himself, twice out loud to his wife. When the police left, he wrote the following from memory:

"The analysis shows the presence of two different kinds of plastic–polypropylene and polystyrene. The melted masses of plastic have no distinctive or identifying features. A microscopic analysis shows the presence of no other unusual materials. No reading above the normal background reading of radioactivity was encountered. Polypropylene and polystyrene are common plastics used for a number of manufacturing purposes in this dark green color. Plant pots and trays are found to be of this composition. However, due to the complete melting of the item no definite identification of the original source is possible. Polystyrene is readily ignitible with a match. Polypropylene is combustible; however, it is harder to ignite. When it burns, it burns with vigor."

While this largely concurs with the Environment Ministry's findings, Matchett feels the forensic lab didn't completely level with him either.

"I mean, why bring a report out here and let me read it if I couldn't have a copy of it?"

And why, he wonders, did the lab want the entire blob? Surely a sample would have been enough.

"The lab wanted everything, table and all."

Matchett chose to part with neither his table nor his blob, despite a fear that the blob might be radioactive. But the Ministry and forensic lab had no sooner assured him it wasn't than Tom Grey, Canadian Director of the Northeastern UFO Organisation, assured him it was. He took a reading about two weeks after the blob fell. He claims his geiger counter indicated a very light but harmless radioactive reading, above the normal background level, on both the blob and the spot where it struck the table. Matchett wonders how "harmless" the blob might have been on June 16, when he couldn't find any scientific personnel to check it out.

"What baffles me is that on a Saturday in June, if a spaceship loaded with little green men had landed in my backyard, nobody could have investigated it till Monday!"

When the news media blitzed the blob, Matchett grew fearful of curiosity seekers. He locked his picnic table in his garage for a few weeks and took the remainder of his blob to an undisclosed location for safe-keeping. In a short time the story lost intrigue. It became just another case of a fire-bug pitching a plate of flaming plastic into someon's backyard. And what's more inconspicuous in weekend suburbia than a person in an asbestos suit?

Public interest faded. For that, at least, the frisbee theory relieved some of the worries that had been plaguing Matchett and his family. "There were a lot of people that I never saw before roaming around here at different times of the day and night," he recalls.

The biggest nuisance was strange phone calls. "Someone called me one night and said, 'We'd like to come over and see your table.' Well, it was two o'clock in the morning! I said, 'You have to be joking,' and he said, 'No, we're not kidding. We're very, very serious.' I said, 'Well, either you're kidding or you're drunk. What's wrong with you?' The guy hung up on me. He must have been drunk or something. Or stupid. Two o'clock in the morning and he wants to come and see this table."

Dave and I wanted to see it, too, and Matchett gladly obliged. He especially wanted to show us what he described as "a circular ring of plastic-like substance, almost clear," on the underside of the planks where the flaming blob landed."

He and his daughter took us to their picnic table in the backyard. Matchett removed a bucket he had inverted over the scorch patch to protect it from the rain and snow. The blob had left a curious circular burn mark. About eight inches in diameter, only its perimeter and a silver-dollar sized area dead center showed scorched paint. The area in between was as green as the rest of the table.

"It was 20 to 30 seconds maximum from the time Donna heard the thud until the time she extinguished the fire," Matchett told us. Time enough, seemingly, for the searing blob to scorch all the paint beneath it, if not char the wood, too.

But Donna and her father describe the strange fire from the blob as cylindrical, without any flickering flames, and its top level as a sheet of glass. Also peculiar was the blob's rapid cooling and solidifying when Donna extinguished it.

"We touched it a couple of times right afterwards and it was hard," she says. "It was ice cold."

Where the blob landed it straddled two planks of the picnic table. Droplets of the flaming goo oozed through the space between them and somehow scorched the wood on the underside leaving a circular black patch a bit smaller than the burn mark on top. But that was all to be seen when Matchett turned the table over to point out the plastic ring on the scorch mark's circumference.

"Hey, it's gone," said Matchett. "It's gone. Remember the ring that was raised up there, Donna?"

"Well, it's been out in the air," said Donna. "And it has rained."

Matchett continued mystified. "There's not a thing on that. You see this mark here? he asked Dave and me, his finger tracing the rim of the scorched wood. "There was a circle of plastic-like material, a clear ring, on that."

I wondered, like Donna, if the weather was a factor.

"Could it have fallen off, and been swept away in the snow?" I asked.

"No, no, no," insisted Matchett. "It was as hard as a rock."

Donna agreed. "It looked like it was embedded right into the wood."

"We've got pictures of that and so have the police. It shows that ring perfectly," said Matchett. His voice was betraying the suspicion Dave spoke:

"It looks like somebody has taken it off for you."

"Someone has been here and taken it off," concluded Matchett. "There's no doubt about it."

The belief comes easily to him. Aside from getting crank phone calls, he thinks someone tried to break into his house, and has since had new locks installed. But in September someone did break into his real estate office. He found his file cabinets rifled and documents strewn everywhere. As far as he knows, nothing was taken, but nothing of the blob nor his papers pertaining to it were kept there.

He wishes now he'd taken more precautions with his picnic table. "Since it's starting to rot a bit anyway," he says, "I'm going to cut the burned piece out and screw on some metal strips to secure the planks." Until someone can give him a satisfactory explanation of the blob, he wants to save something of, what he fondly calls, "the most controversial table in North America."

Would space debris be the explanation Matchett's looking for? Skylab didn't fall until July 11, but a Chinese satellite, MAO 2, was predicted to re-enter the atmosphere over Michigan on Sunday, June 17. No one reported seeing it fall, however, but plastic would hardly survive the terrific heat of atmospheric re-entry.

It's not a meteorite, nor an industrial pollutant, nor did it fall from an airplane, according to the Environment Ministry.

Something from a weather balloon? Same story, says Matchett. Checking with military air bases at Camp Borden and Petawawa, he was told that none of their balloons were aloft during the middle of June.

What about amateur rocketry? There is such a hobby group in Brampton, says Matchett, but supposedly police inquiries cleared them of suspicion.

Even so, I wonder if someone could have fired a small rocket, with a polypropylene component, over Mississauga. As it spent its thrust, couldn't a chunk of it have plummeted, flaming, onto Matchett's picnic table? Though neither the Smith nor Le Ber blobs were seen to fall, or burn, who's to say a would-be Robert Goddard isn't responsible for all three of them?

(As for whatever that hideous Big Brampton Blob is, I'm fingering a rosary.)

"The Mad Missileman of Mississauga" may be a wild speculation, but surely no wilder than a pyromaniac hurling hot frisbees into people's backyards.

All Matchett wants is an explanation—a reasonable explanation—of the Mississauga Blob.

"If someone could come along and say there was a plane flying over and it was carrying such-and-such, and something caught fire and it dropped out—fine. Just show me the part, how it came about, I'll accept it. But not knowing, that's what bugs the hell out of me."

But Matchett may be stymied for a long time to come. As he recalls a neighbor telling him, "Strange things happen in this world, and you may never find out what it is. It may be as mysterious twenty years from now as it is today."

Dwight Whalen

Gateways to Mystery.

Part Two.

Based on historical data and primary field investigations by his Michigan Anomaly Research group, **David Fideler** continues his exploration of the idea of 'window phenomena', events which are triggered by or focussed upon geographic regions, exemplified by an aera of his home state, Michigan.

"We shall pick up an existence by its frogs.

"Wise men have tried other ways. They have tried to understand our state of being, by grasping at its stars, or its arts, or its economics. But, if there is an underlying oneness of all things, it does not matter where we begin, whether with stars, or laws of supply and demand, or frogs, or Napoleon Bonaparte. One measures a circle, beginning anywhere." Charles Fort

Many Forteans have read of the Sister Lakes, Michigan "Bigfoot" wave of 1964. Jim Brandon mentions the activity in his guidebook *Weird America* [22], and John Keel gives a more fullish account in his *Strange Creatures from Time and Space* [23]. Very few, however, realize that the activity took place within a mile of *Magician* Lake, a name which suggests a historical connection with the paranormal. And according to Everett Claspy, a Michigan writer, "the name goes back to the Indians." [24].

Yet, even this observation views the importance of the creature wave in relative isolation. For the entire southwest corner of Michigan's Lower Peninsula, an area which encompasses Magician Lake and environs, is a veritable hotbed of supernatural activity. In other words, this five-county area may represent a 'window' or 'gateway' through which Fortean phenomena repeatedly leak into consensus reality: a place where, because of certain physical, and perhaps even psychological factors, phenomenal reality is at its strongest point in the world of everyday affairs.

A purely mechanistic science views phenomena in isolation. Fort's viewpoint was that of Continuity, in which phenomena were perceived and studied in relation to one another. An irrational story of strange lights, or entities, or maybe both, appears in a small-town newspaper; through the eyes of isolation the offensive Absurdity is pompously dismissed. But viewed in connection with other reports of the same nature, in the spirit of phenomenology, 'singular' anomalies become an army of the Damned...

PORTRAIT OF A MICHIGAN 'FAULT AREA'

1839–Summer
MICHIGAN CITY, INDIANA
A "wild child" with chestnut colored hair is reported "running at large" in the vicinity of Fish Lake, "setting up the most frightful and hideous yells." [C-1]

1883–February 4
SOUTHERN MICHIGAN
Earthquake frightens many people; VI on the Modified Mercalli Scale; epicenter north of Kalamazoo. [G-1]

1896–
Nr. PINE LAKE
'Phantom panther' reports issue from the area. [D-1]

1897–March 31
GALESBURG, MICHIGAN
A brilliant white light appears, accompanied by "a sharp crackling sound, evidently coming from above." The phenomenon startled the witnesses, and one man reported seeing "a huge object tipped with flame at a great distance above the earth." A Mrs. Wyngate thought she heard 'voices' from above, at the time of the occurrence. The phenomenon lasted for 30 seconds. [B-1]

1897–April 10
Nr. EDWARDSBURG, MICHIGAN
An animal that resembled a panther and made a "terrible noise" was reported by men fishing on Pine Lake. The creature was blamed for a series of livestock deaths. [D-2]

1897–April 11
BENTON HARBOR, MICHIGAN
A "huge ball of fire" was seen in the sky for 15 minutes. [B-2]

GALESBURG, MICHIGAN
Two men reported seeing a quickly moving object that was "illuminated at both ends". There was a dull explosion, and the object disappeared. [B-3]

WATERVLIET, MICHIGAN
Two citizens reported seeing 'the mysterious

airship', moving rapidly toward the north-west. [B-4]

1897–April 12
SOUTH BEND, INDIANA
Several individuals reported seeing a mysterious 'airship'. [B-5]

NEW CARLISLE, INDIANA
Around 100 people saw "what they call an air-ship" going in a southwesterly direction at 8:30 p.m. It was about 500 feet up, moving rapidly, and in sight for about 10 minutes. The object gave off a bright white light, and had small red, green and blue lights of a lesser intensity. [B-6]

BENTON HARBOR, MICHIGAN
Three witenesses reported seeing a rapidly moving object with blue, red and green lights. It was headed in a northwesterly direction. [B-7]

NILES, MICHIGAN
Several individuals reported the flyover of a bright electric light, closely followed by two coloured lights, one red and the other green. [B-8]

NEW TROY, MICHIGAN
'Mystery airship' approaches witnesses; few details given. [B-9]

KALAMAZOO, MICHIGAN
About a dozen people, including the editor of the Kalamazoo *Gazette*, observed a mysterious light fly over the center of town, at a rate of speed between 45-60 miles per hour. All that could be distinguished was a reddish-green light of great intensity that was six times larger than any star in the sky. It was about half a mile high, and moving in a northerly direction. [B-10]

1897–April 14
CONSTATINE, MICHIGAN
At 10:45 p.m. several citizens saw a mysterious light, ¼ the size of the full moon, moving in a northerly direction on a zig-zag course. Its altitude varied, from 45 to 75 feet. [A-1]

1897–April 15
SCHOOLCRAFT, MICHIGAN
About five people saw a mysterious object fly over town at 10:45 p.m. One witness estimated that it was moving at 60 miles per hour. [B-11]

1897–April 17
THREE RIVERS, MICHIGAN
A number of residents saw a mysterious aerial object in the vicinity of Three Rivers. [B-12]

1897–Late April
SAILOR, INDIANA
Two farmers reported encountering a phantom form, whose body looked like that of a man, but was covered with hair. [C-12]

1897–October 31
NILES, MICHIGAN
Earthquake rattles SW Michigan. [G-2]

1899–October 10
ST. JOSEPH, MICHIGAN
Earthquake shakes area; IV on Modified Mercalli Scale. [G-3]

1901–February 6
PAW PAW, MICHIGAN
Unexplained fall of dust is reported on a perfectly calm day. [H-1]

1904–
Nr. ROLLING PRAIRIE, INDIANA
Three witnesses observed two whitish-blue objects hover within 15 feet of the ground. The objects flew toward a barn, approached each other, and then disappeared behind a hill. [A-2]

1947–July 7
SOUTH BEND, INDIANA
Two witnesses chase a "copper-colored fiery disc" in their car. The object was tree-top height, and moved at an estimated speed of 200 miles per hour. [A-3]

1947–November
STURGIS, MICHIGAN
A mysterious panther-like animal is seen by residents on several occasions. Tracks are discovered in the area which are too large to be those of a dog. [D-3]

1950–June 23
BENTON HARBOR, MICHIGAN
A DC-4, with 58 aboard, was flying near Benton Harbor on a stormy night. Witnesses on the ground saw a mysterious ball of fire in the sky, and the plane was destroyed. [B-13]

1952–April 17
CASSOPOLIS, MICHIGAN
An oval-shaped object, which traveled with a 'wobbling motion', was seen moving at a high speed. [B-14]

1952–July 23
SOUTH BEND, INDIANA
At 11:35 p.m., Captain Harold Kloth, USAF, saw two blue-white objects arc over the city. [B-15]

1954–May
LA PORTE, INDIANA
A motorist sees three round or oval-shaped UFOs moving as a unit, emitting beams of light downward. The car lights and radio failed at the time of the sighting. [A-4]

1958–July
LA PORTE, INDIANA
A glowing, oval-shaped object closely approaches the surface of Pine Lake. [A-5]

Sister Lakes, Michigan – June 1964.
Witness drawing.

SYMBOL		CATEGORY
		UFOs
A	●	Landings & Close Encounters (14)
B	○	'Flyovers' (26)
		PHANTOM FORMS
C	★	Anthropoids, Bigfoot (10)
D	▲	Mystery Cats, Phantom Panthers (5)
E	✪	Apparitions (1)
F	■	Out-of-Place Animals (1)
		GEOPHYSICAL
G	⌖	Quake Epicenters (3)
H	‡	Falls (1)
I	§	Mystery Explosions (1)

1959–
SISTER LAKES, MICHIGAN
A 21-year-old mother sees a phantom gorilla-like creature outside her home. [C-3]

1962–
SISTER LAKES, MICHIGAN
'Bigfoot' sightings are made in the vicinity of Magician Lake. The creature was nine feet tall, with "big, bright shining eyes". [C-4]

1964–June 9
SISTER LAKES, MICHIGAN
Four witnesses see an ape-like creature with brilliantly shining eyes after a thunderstorm. The percipients reported that the apparition made gurgling sounds. Later, deputies found 18-inch footprints in the area. [C-5]

1964–June 11
SISTER LAKES, MICHIGAN
Three girls encounter a mysterious, bear-like creature, that was walking upright. The authorities felt that the girls were sincere and genuinely frightened. (See illustration.) [C-6]

1964–July 13
Nr. DOWAGIAC, MICHIGAN
A married couple reported watching a large creature with reddish-brown hair from their car, in the vicinity of Dowagiac Swamp. It made to attempt to approach them, acting in a shy manner, and eventually climbed a tree. Fire department personnel who were sent to the scene discovered scratches and broken limbs on the trees. [C-7]

1964–
NILES, MICHIGAN
A Chicago motorist is attacked by "something that had red eyes, brown hair, and squeals". His automobile window was shattered in four places where the creature struck the automobile. [C-8]

1966–March 20
LA PORTE, INDIANA
A UFO that was blindingly bright chased two youths from Michigan City, Indiana to La Porte, at which location they pointed out the object to a policeman who viewed the UFO for over 15 minutes. [A-6]

FULTON, MICHIGAN
Several witnesses saw a low-level object, about the size of an automobile, which emitted five or six red lights. It was "as high up as two trees", and in view for five minutes, after which it darted off to the east. [A-7]

1966–March 28
NILES, MICHIGAN
Truck drivers told police that a brightly lit object, apparently oblong and thirty to forty feet long, approached and flew parallel to the highway for several minutes. The truck drivers

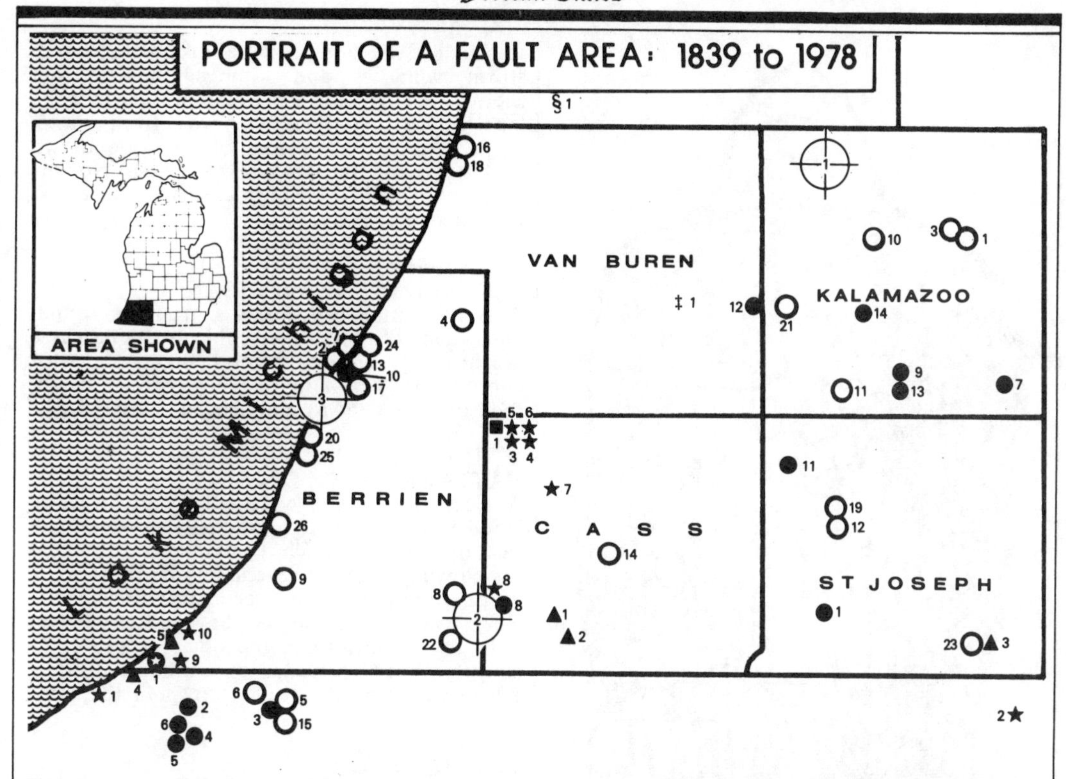

added that, when they blinked the lights of their vehicles, the lights of the UFO blinked in the same sequence. [A-8]

1966–March 31
VICKSBURG, MICHIGAN
A man driving home at 6:00 a.m. saw lights on the road ahead, and discovered a grey, lens-shaped object hovering about four feet above the surface of the road. It had one intense white light and three colored flashing lights. Driving within several feet of it, he became afraid and backed up, but the object suddenly flew over and behind him. The object left at a high speed to the east, and emitted a noise similar to "a swarm of bees". [A-9]

1966–April 13
SOUTH HAVEN, MICHIGAN
At 11:30 p.m. a man and his wife saw a cigar-shaped object with multi-colored lights, and a flame "spewing" from the rear. It was about 700 feet up, moving south to north, and then heading out over the lake. It was seen also by seven other witnesses. [B-16]

1966–April 17
BENTON HARBOR, MICHIGAN
Many witnesses, including local police, observed a UFO so bright "you couldn't look straight at it". It was 15 stories in the air, and, according to one witness, "something like a hot dog in shape". [B-17]

BENTON HARBOR, MICHIGAN
Benton Harbour Police Chief Merle McCarroll and his wife watched a silently flying object with "a large red blinking dome light" near their home. The object was not more than 100 to 150 feet above the ground, and made no noise whatsoever. [A-10]

1966–April 22
SOUTH HAVEN, MICHIGAN
Police receive several reports of a UFO with red, green, and white lights, from along the Lake Michigan shoreline. [B-18]

THREE RIVERS, MICHIGAN
Police and residents see a UFO with flashing red, green, and white lights. [B-19]

1966–December 6
HOWARDSVILLE, MICHIGAN
A woman is awakened at 6:00 p.m. by a sound "like a transformer running", causing her to look outside. There she saw a hazy red object, about 25 feet in diameter, hovering directly outside her home, and shining a white light toward the ground. According to the police report, she watched the object for about 15 minutes. During her observation, two cars passed by her house, and the light was pointed towards them as they went by. [A-11]

1967–March 7
ST. JOSEPH, MICHIGAN

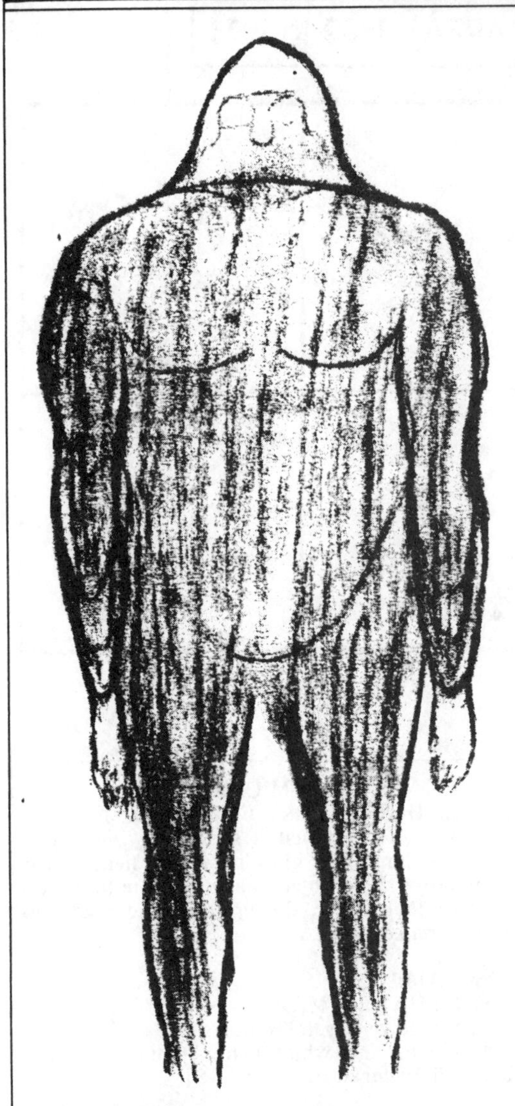

New Buffalo, Michigan – April 1976.
Witness drawing.

Two men saw an object which changed color from red to green to white, which had lights on the bottom also. It hovered over Lake Michigan, was joined by a second object, and then left. An investigation conducted by the Air Force could not account for the phenomenon. [B-20]

1968–
SISTER LAKES, MICHIGAN
Many residents spot a large, cat-like animal. An out-of-place ocelot is later shot in the area. [F-1]

1970–January 1
PULMAN, MICHIGAN
The new decade came in with a bang at 12:15 a.m. when the area around Upper Scott Lake was rocked by a gigantic explosion that broke storm windows and knocked books from shelves. A large hole was found in the ice of the lake approximately 220 yards from shore. Large, 8-inch-thick pieces of ice were blown 100 feet from the 40-foot-wide hole. No one could explain the mysterious blast, which was felt four miles away. [I-1]

1971–June 4
TEXAS CORNERS, MICHIGAN
Two boys in a canoe saw a group of round, "bell-shaped", blue-green objects flying on a northeasterly course. After being in sight for approximately a minute, they turned north, then one broke away and headed south. [B-21]

1971–October 12
MATTAWAN, MICHIGAN
At least six people watched a "bright white cloud flying in circles", gradually moving in an easterly direction. The percipients estimated the glowing mass was several hundred feet wide. At one point the object seemed to direct a thin beam of light into the sky above. After being in sight for a short time, the object appeared to land in a heavily wooded area. Three additional UFOs were reported to go down in the same area. [A-12]

1973–December 3
Nr. VICKSBURG, MICHIGAN
Three witnesses saw an object that looked like a "half-sun" at 12:30 a.m. The object moved slowly at times, and hovered at others. The witnesses followed the object by car until it disappeared in the Gourdneck State Game Area. [A-13]

1973–
NEW BUFFALO, MICHIGAN
Several 'Bigfoot' sightings and instances of parapsychological phenomena focused around the witnesses. [C-9]

1974–April 15
NILES, MICHIGAN
A UFO with bright white light and assortment of smaller, multi-colored flashing lights was chased by police cars from three different posts for 45 minutes, after which it disappeared in the southwest. The object, which was 600 feet above the ground, moved at speeds around 35-45 miles per hour, occasionally stopping to hover. It was also observed by a number of residents. [B-22]

1974–August 20
PORTAGE, MICHIGAN
Close encounter of the first kind, investigated by the Center for UFO studies. No further information available. [A-14]

1975–October 6
STURGIS, MICHIGAN

A man watched an inexplicable glowing mass, three times the size of a barn, hover mysteriously above a neighbor's home. The 'glow' suddenly disappeared. [B-23]

1975–November 19
BENTON HARBOR, MICHIGAN
Multiple witnesses watch three brilliant gold objects fly over in a V-shape, moving west to east. [B-24]

1976–April
NEW BUFFALO, MICHIGAN
Reported 'Bigfoot' and 'phantom form' activity. (See illustration.) [C-10]

1976–August
Nr. NEW BUFFALO, MICHIGAN
Several witnesses watch a "misty, glowing figure" floating outside their home, several feet above a field. One of the percipients interpreted the glowing mass as being a 'ghost', or possibly an 'angel'. (See illustration.)

1977–February
Nr. MICHIANA, MICHIGAN
Phantom panther reports. Large cat tracks are discovered in area. [D-4]

1978–August 3
ST. JOSEPH, MICHIGAN
Just before midnight, the St. Joseph Coast Guard Station received a civilian report that a long, silver, cylindrical and brightly lit object was in the sky for 30 minutes, and then headed southwest. [B-25]

1978–October 31
Nr. BRIDGMAN, MICHIGAN
Several witnesses reported seeing unusual nocturnal lights above the Cook Nuclear Power Station. Some witnesses said they saw the objects shoot beams of light toward the ground. [B-26]

Date Unknown
NEW BUFFALO, MICHIGAN
Area residents report seeing a large, panther-like animal. [D-5]

A NEW APPROACH TO UFOS

There can be little doubt that a wide variety of factors contribute to the distribution of unusual phenomena reports, such as population density, the number of available witnesses and media outlets, as well as a myriad of other sociological considerations, for any area in question. Underlying all of these 'coloring' factors are the actual mechanisms which give rise to anomalous phenomena, be they electromagnetic, physical, or psychological. In part one of this series it was suggested that at least *some* Fortean phenomena are precipitated by naturally occurring electromagnetic discharges in the vicinity of seismic fault lines and magnetic anomalies. These observations, based on findings from real-world geophysics, may account for highly localized areas, like the sector under consideration, that exhibit historical continuity in a wide variety of unusual phenomena.

Michigan Anomaly Research (MAR) was established in 1974, to empirically test the window hypothesis, using the state of Michigan as a laboratory. A data-base of several hundred reports has been assembled, and, as of this writing, statistical tests are being formulated to

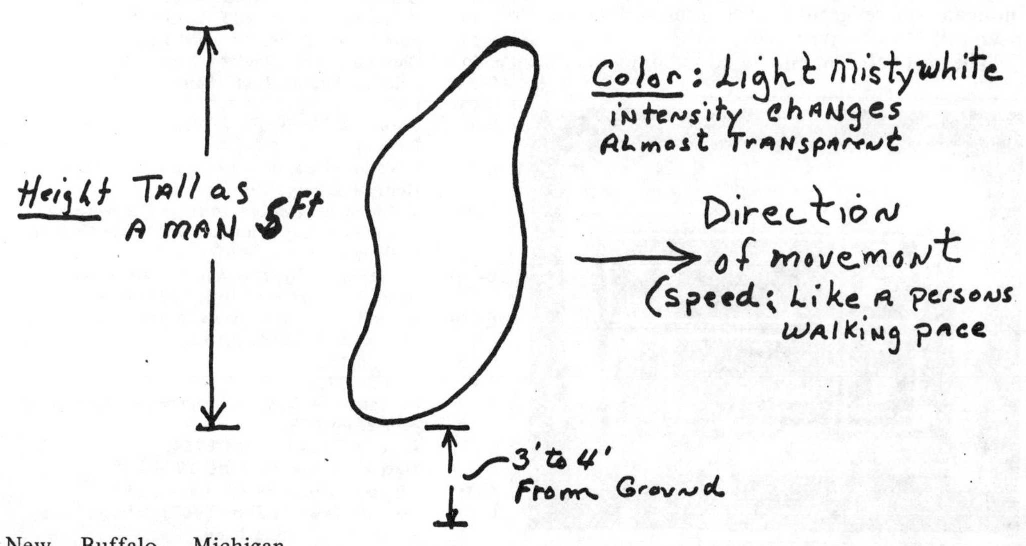

New Buffalo, Michigan – August 1976. Witness drawing.

answer the question: "Is there a quantitative relationship between geophysical phenomena and Michigan anomalies? While the above chronology is *not* an attempt to answer this question, it does appear to support the hypothesis in the qualitative, or descriptive, sphere.

For example, what is one to make of the various 'UFO' phenomena which exhibit qualities of a decidedly electromagnetic nature? The predictive model, formulated by Dr. Michael A. Persinger [25], certainly encompasses such phenomena as 'glowing clouds', entities, and plasmas, in addition to the wide variety of electromagnetic effects that appear in the above cross-section. Furthermore, if we consider the possibility that the above accounts are symptomatic of disturbances in the local geophysical continumn, the model naturally suggests the possibility that the rash of unusual phenomena experienced during the spring of 1897 represent the byproducts of accumulating seismic stress, which resulted in the earthquake of 31 October 1897.

If a relationship does exist between geophysical discharges and the type of phenomena described above, potentially valuable information may result from the deployment of specialised recording instruments to suspected window sectors. The M-1000 Magnetometer System, now employed by MAR, is designed to automatically measure and permanently record changing magnetic fields. Initial monitoring sessions, involving the simultaneous tape recordings of magnetic fluctuations and very low frequency (VLF) radio disturbances, will begin in the summer of 1980. These recording sessions will take place at the location of several precisely known 'UFO landing sites', during geomagnetic disturbances, to determine whether or not transient fields are naturally induced where ground-level luminosities have been reliably observed. [26]

The real value of the 'window' model is that it gives a true foundation to UFO research, from whence scientifically competent studies, and *tests*, may proceed. Until now, such a foundation has been missing.

Of equal importance to a purely physical model is an approach which encompasses the highly important, but sorely overlooked, psychological dimension of the UFO mythos. This brings us to the third and final part of this series, because in addition to considering the psychology of the time, place, and witnesses, we must be prepared to explore the archetypal background of the human spirit.

[End of part two.] *David Fideler*

The M-1000 Magnetometer used on MAR Fieldtrips.

REFERENCES

22) J. Brandon: *Weird America* (New York: Dutton, 1978) p.115.
23) J. Keel: *Strange Creatures from Time and Space* (Greenwich, Conn: Fawcett, 1970) p.107.
24) E. Claspy: *The Dowagiac-Sister Lakes Resort Area and More About its Potawatomi Indians* (Dowagiac: privately printed, 1970) p.7.
C-1) Philadelphia *Saturday Courier* 28 Dec 1839.
G-1) D. Bricker: *Seismic Disturbances in Michigan* (Lansing, Michigan: MI Dept. of Natural Resources, 1977) p.5.
D-1) Saginaw *Evening News* 17 April 1897.
B-1) Detroit *News* 1 April 1897.
D-2) Niles *Weekly Mirror* 14 April 1897.
B-2) Benton Harbor *Evening News* 12 April 1897.
B-3) Grand Rapids *Democrat* 14 April 1897.
B-4) Benton Harbor *Evening News* 15 April 1897.
B-5) Kalamazoo *Gazette* 14 April 1897.
B-6) Port Huron *Daily Times* 14 April 1897.
B-7) Benton Harbor *Daily Palladium* 13 April 1897.
B-8) Grand Rapids *Press* 13 April 1897.
B-9) Benton Harbor *Daily Palladium* 13 April 1897.
B-10) Kalamazoo *Gazette* 14 April 1897.
A-1) Detroit *News* 15 April 1897.
B-11) Kalamazoo *Gazette* 16 April 1897.
B-12) Port Huron *Times* 20 April 1897.
C-2) Cleveland *Plain Dealer* 1 May 1897.
G-2) Bricker: *Seismic Disturbances in Michigan* p.5.
G-3) Ibid.
H-1) *Books of Charles Fort* (New York: Dover, 1974) p.65.
A-2) J. Vallee: *Passport to Magonia* (Chicago: Henry Regnery, 1969) p.186.
A-3) T. Bloecher: *Report on the UFO Wave of 1947* (Privately printed, 1967) case No.556.
D-3) Indiana University Folklore Archives.
B-13) D. Keyhoe: *Flying Saucers from Outer Space* (New York: Henry Holt, 1953) p.18.
B-14) R. Hall, ed.: *The UFO Evidence* (Washington, DC: NICAP, 1964) p.153.
B-15) Ibid., p.161.
A-4) Ibid., p.74.
A-5) O. Hartle: *A Carbon Experiment?* (Privately printed) p.155.
C-3) Detroit *News* 12 June 1964.
C-4) Detroit *News* 11 June 1964.
C-5) Chicago *American* 13 June 1964.
C-6) Detroit *News* 11 June 1964; Chicago *American* 12 June 1964.
C-7) *Saucer News* No.58.
C-8) *Fate* Dec 1964.

C-9) MAR files.
B-22) *Police and the UFO Experience* (Evanston: Center for UFO Studies, 1975) p.3.
A-14) CUFOS news release.
B-23) Sturgis *Journal* 7 Oct 1975.
B-24) Benton Harbor *Herald-Palladium* 20 & 21 Nov 1975.
C-10) MAR files.
E-1) MAR files.
D-4) MAR files.
B-25) *International UFO Reporter* Aug 1978.
B-26) Grand Rapids *Press* 2 Nov 1978.
D-5) New Buffalo *Times* 18 Nov 1976.
25) M.A. Persinger: "Transient Geophysical Bases for Ostensible UFO-Related Phenomena and Associated Verbal Behavior", *Perceptual and Motor Skills* 1976, Vol.43, pp.215-221.
26) Individuals interested in receiving information about the M-1000 Monitor System and the MAR *Report on Current Research* may write: MAR, PO Box 1181, Grand Rapids, MI 49501, USA.
A-6) B. Steiger: *Flying Saucers are Hostile* (New York: Award Books, 1967) p.45.
A-7) J. Sherwood: *Flying Saucers are Watching You* (Clarksburg, W. Va: Saucerian Books, 1967) p.44.
A-8) F. Edwards: *Flying Saucers Here and Now* (New York: Bantam, 1967) p.28.
A-9) J. Vallee: *Passport to Magonia* p.326.
B-16) Grand Rapids *Press* 14 April 1966.
B-17) Lansing *State Journal* 18 April 1966.
A-10) *Saucer News* Vol.13, No.4, p.25.
B-18) Grand Rapids *Press* 22 April 1966.
B-19) J. Sherwood: *Flying Saucers are Watching You* p.65.
A-11) Niles *Daily Star* 7 December 1966.
B-20) Grand Rapids *Press* 23 July 1967.
F-1) E. Claspy: *The Dowagiac-Sister Lakes Resort Area* p.15.
I-1) Grand Rapids *Press* 4 Jan 1970.
B-21) NICAP *UFO Investigator* Sept 1971.
A-12) Ibid.
A-13) Kalamazoo *Gazette* 3 Dec 1973.

Ask Aristotle.

Selections, by Paul Sieveking, from *Aristotle's Book of Problems*. (1749); A kind of 18th century agony column.

Q: Why doth a Man lift up his Head towards the Heavens when he doth imagine?
A: Because the Imagination is in the fore part of the Head, or Brain; and therefore it lifteth up itself that the Creeks or Cells of the Imagination may be opened, and that the Spirits which help the Imagination, and are fit for that purpose, having their discourse thither, may help the Imagination.

•

Q: How come it Birds don't piss?
A: Because that superfluity which should be converted into Urine is turned into Feathers, for there is much moisture in the Feathers. Another reason is, they are in continual motion, therefore moisture in them is dry'd up by air or wind.

•

Q: Why hath not a Man a Tail like Beasts?
A: Because Man is a noble Creature whose property is to sit; so a Beast cannot that hath a Tail.

•

Q: Why is the Milk of brown Women better than that of white?
A: Because brown Women are hotter than others, and heat purges the Milk and so 'tis better.

•

Q: Why doth a Basilisk kill a Man with his sight?
A: The Basilisk is a very venomous and infected Beast and there pass from his Eyes venomous vapours which are multiplied upon the thing which is seen by him, and even unto the Eye of Man; the which venomous vapours of humours entring into the body do infect him, so in the end the Man Dieth. And this is also the reason why the Basilisk looking upon a Shield perfectly well made with fast clammy pitch, or any hard smooth thing, doth kill himself, because the humours are beaten back from the smooth hard thing unto the Basilisk, by which beating back he is killed. And the like is said of a Woman when she hath her monthly disease, whereof it followeth that some old Women do hurt themselves when they look upon the glasses or other firm and solid things in the time of their Terms.

Q: Why have Women longer hair than Men?
A: Because Women are moister than Men, and flegmatick, and therefore there is more matter of hair in them. And furthermore, this matter is more increased in Women than in Men from their inferior parts, and especially in the time of their Monthly Terms, because the matter doth then ascend, whereby the Humour which breedeth the hair doth increase. And *Albertus* doth say that if the hair of a Woman in the time of her Flowers be put into dung, a venomous Serpent is engendered of it.

•

Q: Why is a Man's Head round?
A: Because this is the most fit to receive anything into it, as *Aristotle* doth affirm.

EDITORIAL|*Continued*

Some of you may have noticed our Fortean column in *Alpha* magazine, the first of which appeared in their May 1980 issue. In that column we advertised that this issue of FT would carry some new photos of Nessie. They were taken on 3 September 1978 by Jeff Watson, Jeff's story deserved more space than we could allocate it in this issue, so we decided to hold it over to next issue and give it the treatment it deserves.

Bob Rickard.

THE PANTHERS OF SOUTHERN AUSTRALIA

Gilbert Shelton.

As other material in this issue demonstrates, Surrey is not the only area of the world haunted by phantom felines. We welcome **Paul Cropper,** of New South Wales, to these pages with his survey of the problem in southern Australia.

One Sunday night in 1976, Stephen Johnson was returning home from a friend's place at Cambewarra. It was about 11 p.m. at night, when he rounded a slight curve on the Illaroo Road, heading towards North Nowra. The lights of the car were on high beam, and they picked up a large pair of eyes on the left hand side of the road. As the car straightened, Stephen saw a huge cat like a panther, jet black and standing at least 2 foot high at the shoulder. He could not judge the length of the animal, as he was too stunned to obtain a decent look, and as he was travelling fairly fast was quickly past it. Further up the road he turned the car around and returned to where he had seen it, but the animal had obviously disappeared.

Stephen Johnson was not the first person from the Southern Highlands to claim to have seen an animal which closely resembled a panther. In January of the same year (1976), Hugh Ferguson of Callalo Beach had been travelling along the Forest Road to Currajong just on dusk when he caught sight of the hindquarters and tail of a large black animal disappear into the roadside bush. He described what he saw as being jet-black, with heavily set hindquarters at least 2 foot 6 inches high, and a long tapered tail.

University zoology "experts" (and I use the term loosely) will, of course, tell you that there are no "big cats" such as panthers or pumas occurring wild in Australian bush. So just what have Stephen Johnson, Hugh Ferguson and thousands of other witnesses over the last 60 years been seeing, anyway? The sheer volume of reported sightings of "panthers" (they number in their hundreds) leave us with two alternatives; either we reject all the reports, and some have been made by police officers and even members of parliament, or we accept the fact that all the evidence suggests that there are several species of large felines roaming the Australian Bush.

Let us examine a number of representative reports from one particular area long known for its "panthers"... the Southern Highlands of New South Wales, encompassing thousands of acres of virgin bushland, and roughly bordered by Mittagong in the North, Milton in the South, and the rugged Morton National Park in the West.

The first reports of a large black cat resembling a panther in this area come from 1966. Unsubstantiated rumours from several local sources say that early this year a circus truck crashed whilst travelling between Nowra and Moss Vale, and a female black panther escaped into the bush, however after checking with agricultural authorities here in Sydney I am unable to say that the talk of a crash is anything more than local rumours. Later that same year (1966) Sam Knight, who owned a property several miles north of Nowra, said that early one morning he had gone out with two cattle dogs to round up the cows for the morning's milking, when he sighted a huge black cat in one of his paddocks. Upon seeing the animal, his 2 dogs had immediately attacked it, and in the ensuing fight, both dogs were severely wounded, and both eventually fled the field, with the "panther" disappearing into the surrounding bush. Mr. Knight was quite shaken by the incident, and informed no one except his family, and immediate neighbours.

Several years after Sam Knight's encounter, a long time resident of Bomaderry was looking over the rugged Meryla Valley with high powered binoculars, when he spotted what he later described to me as "A huge black cat-like animal, bigger than a doberman" cross a bush track effortlessly in one jump, and disappear into bush towards a nearby creek. He estimated that the creature would have weighed several hundredweight.

This same man was later to have another experience that would finally convince him that the Southern Highlands panther was more than legendary. Several years after his first sighting, he was checking a small pile of burning off-cuts just on dusk on a sawmill on his property, set on the edge of thick bush.

Glancing into the scrub, he noticed several ti-trees moving just behind the isolated mill, then he heard a sound which he said resembled a cat calling to its kittens–except louder and coarser. Squinting in the dim light he saw what looked like one large shape with 2 smaller shapes following, moving deeper into the bush.

Early next morning he returned to the mill and found 3 separate sets of unusual animal tracks; 2 large sets, measuring 3½ inches by 3 inches, and 2 smaller sets. Where the tracks had approached a pile of off-cuts, the larger tracks had gone around it, and the two smaller tracks went over the top. All the separate sets of tracks exhibited 4 big forward claws. Tracks similar to those above have been discovered at many locations throughout Nowra and the Morton Bay National Park.

The recent "wave" of panther sightings, mainly centred in the mountainous area north of Nowra, began in earnest in early 1975. From then until the present day sightings by both local residents and visitors have occurred in large numbers, but only a small percentage of these have reached the press. Most "locals" are very reluctant to discuss their own experiences, mainly from fear of public ridicule, and also many fear the prospect of masses of hunters wandering around their properties armed to the teeth and prepared to shoot anything that moves!

However sincere investigators prepared to visit and talk with witnesses about their experiences will usually find many people who are prepared, after some initial reluctance, to assist them in their investigations.

In June 1979, I spent around 3 days visiting the Nowra area and talking to witnesses. One of the several people I spoke to was a Mr. Reg. Hill, who owns a property along the Tourist Road from Beaumont to Berry. Both he and his daughter have seen the animal. His own sighting occurred in early 1975, when he caught sight of a black cat-like animal disappearing into low scrub on his property. A few months later in June, his 15-year-old granddaughter was riding her horse when it suddenly baulked, and she saw a jet black animal 3 foot high at the shoulder with a long streamlined body cross an open paddock, heading north, in front of her. Later that same afternoon, Mr. Hill was speaking with another farmer who owns a property 2 miles north. Before Mr. Hill could speak of his granddaughter's sighting, the other man excitedly told a similar story.

He and his son had been out feeding their pigs around 5 o'clock when he had looked up and seen a large black animal unhurriedly ambling along a fence, past their sawmill for a couple of hundred yards. They both had watched this creature at a distance of 300 yards for at least 4 or 5 minutes. He estimated the animal weighed between 4 or 5 hundred pounds and stood 2 foot 6 inches high at the shoulder and looked exactly like a black panther. As they watched, the animal sprang 9 ft. to clear a creek, and then disappeared into the bush, leaving a perfect set of pawprints in the soft soil of the creek bank.

Upon hearing their account, Mr. Hill immediately went with several others to the bank of the creek to examine the creature's tracks. Finding the most well-defined out of several visible tracks, they covered it with a sheet of galvanised iron, and later returned to make a cement cast. The cast measures an incredible 4 inches by 5 inches, and during my investigations I was fortunate enough to secure a copy of the original cast.

From 1975 to the present day there has been dozens of reported sightings and incidents attributed to the "panther". Rather than detail all of them, an effort which would be tedious and repetitive, let us consider several interesting incidents, starting in 1976.

* In Feb. 1976, Tony Anderson of Wollongong stated he had encountered a panther-like creature several miles North of Neriga.

* Around April 1976, a Nowra man found 2 paw prints in mud near Wandandian Creek whilst prospecting. He said they were about 5 times the size of dingo prints found in the area, and both prints showed clearly the marks of claws on the foot.

* A Kangaroo Valley housewife called outside by her children watched a large black animal lope across a paddock to jump a nearby fence, run through their bull pen and eventually cross a small creek. A bull kept in the pen responded by dashing madly to the far end of the paddock. This same woman has since found several unusual scratch marks on its chicken pen, as if some animal was trying to force its way inside. A neighbour has also lost several head of cattle to some unknown predator.

* On the 15th November 1977, Ramon Sega and his son Tom, were hunting on a property in the Cambewarra Range, when they saw a large black cat-like animal staring at them with yellow eyes from the bush. Ramon said "Before it could pounce Tom shot it with his .303 rifle. He shot it through the heart, but it took the cat about a minute to die. Its tail was about 2 foot long, and it had teeth like fangs." They skinned the cat, but unfortunately for all concerned, left the carcase on the mountainside. During my stay in the area, I was able to examine the skin, and although allowing for shrinking and other changes over 2 years seemed to be nothing more than a large feral cat, however I hope to have several hairs analysed as soon as possible.

* Early in 1979, several men watched a large black animal lope quickly through a herd of cattle at Foxground, sending the herd dashing berserkly in all directions. One of the men I spoke to said it could have been a wild dog, but he did not think a dog could send a herd of cattle into complete panic as it had done, nor move as fast as this animal did.

Many of the people I have spoken to in the last few months have advanced theories as to the probable identities of the creatures involved. Some stated that they believed the animals were once panther cubs released into the bush by Americans who had them as mascots in WW II. One witness had actually spoken to American servicemen who had confirmed this to him. Several others were of the opinion that the panthers escaped from a crashed circus truck somewhere on the south coast. Those who are sceptical as to the claims of witnesses say it is nothing more than a black walleroo, such as the one captured on a property in Kangaroo Valley in May this year. While it is possible that a black walleroo could be mistaken for a panther in some instances, who could fail to identify it after watching it for 5 minutes at short range in broad daylight. Certainly not anyone who has lived in the Southern Highlands all their life, and is quite familiar with most forms of animal life found there!

While the reports I have cited above come solely from the Southern Coast of NSW, the sighting of black panthers is not a phenomenon concentrated solely in this area. Reports in my possession concerning these animals have also come from areas as far apart as the Dandenongs in Victoria, the New England area of NSW and the Central Wheat Belt of Western Australia.

Only by the further collection, study and correlation of reported sightings and other incidents by researchers and zoologists can we begin to understand the nature of our mystery felines, such as the panther-like creatures which I am convinced roam the rugged expanses of the Southern Highlands.

Paul Cropper

Note: Some names have been changed to preserve anonymity.

AN ANSWER FROM THE PLEISTOCENE

Last time in this column, accounts of mystery felines closely resembling male African lions were examined. These rare beasts are not as familiar as the "black panthers" of Fortean literature, but they are just as elusive. The folks in the International Fortean Organization have passed along yet another piece of the puzzle from, of all places, Surprise, Nebraska. The report is typical of the ones chronicled here in my recent column on the subject.

The *Omaha World Herald*, Monday, August 2, 1954, told of the latest sighting of what appeared to farmer Arnold Neujahr to be an African lion. "He reported he saw a lion as he topped a hill two miles west of Surprise," the newspaper informed. "The surprised lion, he said, dived into a ditch and disappeared into some trees. The lion had a mane, he said." (How else would one expect to find a lion seen near Surprise, Nebraska, but surprised?) One woman living in Surprise, the newspaper continued, said she saw a lion and mate running across her front yard. A similar incident took place in nearby Rising City. The Omaha paper ended by noting that these stories closely paralleled those which touched off a lengthy lion hunt near Ceresco, November 12, 1951. Ceresco is 32 miles east of Surprise.

As the other accounts mentioned in the first part of this examination demonstrated, these "African lions" have some unique traits. Indeed, the maned mystery cats seen in America have some particular characteristics which separate them from the so-called "black panthers", in whose company they are often found. Besides being social, the mysterious maned lions appear to be more forthrightly venturesome, retreating less quickly than the black panthers, but then again not attacking as frequently either. Comparing them overall, the maned lions seem more even tempered, less timid and yet not as aggressive as the hauntingly hyperactive black phantom cats. Why?

There are many levels of reality in the shadowy world of cyptozoology, and I have written elsewhere of my Jungian-like thoughts on these creatures. It is time now, however, to offer a fresh new alternative to the origins of these mystery felines. I feel there may be a concrete, flesh and blood, if you will, answer to some accounts of mystery cats in the New World. I will here explore and develop a suggestion made by Mark A. Hall of Minnesota that the "black panthers" and "maned lions" may be only two slices of the same pie, and that the answer seems to lie in the survival of relict populations of *Panthera leo atrox (Panthera atrox* or *Felis atrox*, to some), the giant American lion of the Pleistocene.

When one begins to imagine

the great felines of the American Ice Ages, thoughts usually run to the images of the sabertoothed cats. The classic Rancho La Brea painting rushes into our consciousness; *Smilodon* the lion-sized sabertooth on the back of some unfortunate grazing mammal flashes to mind. The two prehistoric animals are stuck together in the tar pits, soon to be immortalized for thousands of years in the gooey mess. But a rarer (or maybe more intelligent?) visitor lurks in the background. There, larger by a third is another cat. This cat is *Panthera leo atrox*.

Fossils of atrox have been found in forty sites, from Alaska to Peru, from California through Nebraska to northern Florida. This giant lion was killed by Paleo-Indians, and Dr. Bjorn Kurten has written of the evidence suggesting they were around until as recently as 10,370 years, plus or minus 160 years, before present. Do they persist in isolated pockets today? Why should we even consider such a notion?

Panthera leo atrox was closely related to the Eurasian cave lion, *Panthera leo spelaea*. An unbroken range of lions fringed the top of the world during the Pleistocene, with a distinctive subspecies in each hemisphere. *Pantherea leo leo*, the so-called modern lion of Asia and Africa, is the reduced remainder of *P.1. spelaea*. But the cave lion seems to have actually persisted into historic Europe. Xerxes' expedition through Macedonia in 480 B.C. had to put up with such "annoyances" as the killing of some of his draft camels by lions. Some authors of ancient Greece, Herodotus, Aristotle, Xenophon, and others, wrote of their contemporary lions. Investigators such as Dawkins and Sanford see no difference between the cave lion and the modern lion. And Dawkins, Kurten, and many others feel *spelaea* and *atrox* are identical. Because men lived for so long with the cave lion, we can learn much about these lions from the prehistoric artists of Europe, for theorists and fossils do not tell us much about what the animals looked like. One reindeer shoulder-blade from France clearly shows a cave lion with a tufted tail. F. Ed. Koby studied prehistoric drawings and sculptures of the large Ice Age cats and found two types. One was a heavily built feline with neither mane nor tufted tail; the other was a lion with mane and tufted tail. The art of palaeolithic man reinforces the idea that the prehistoric lions showed some quite clear differences between males and females. As C.A.W. Guggisberg wrote on the cave lion in art in his excellent overview: *Simba: Life of the Lion:* "Two lions in the *Grotte des Trois-Freres,* of which one is maned, turn their heads towards the viewer, and stare at him with big eyes."

The giant American lion *P. leo atrox* reflected this sexual dimorphism, as would be expected, through the different limb sizes of the fossil finds. The sexually linked differences in the cats is the key to the lock which opens the mystery of the phantom feline quest of the phantom feline question. Only lions are social. Only lions show wide physical differences between sexes.

The behaviours demonstrated by the mysterious maned cats of America are exactly what one would predict of a male *atrox*. And the more aggressive huntress *atrox* would resemble the "black panther." The latter are more frequently seen, and definitely more agressive than their maned male counterparts - following closely the pattern of the African and Asian (modern?) lions, *P. leo leo*. The black panthers, our female *atrox,* are the mystery cats consistently reported with the cubs, or young. They are downright nasty but intelligent. The strutting, careful maned male *atrox* are no dumbies, either.

And the fossil *atrox* was a bright cat. Thirty sabertoothed *Smilodons* ended up in the La Brea tar pits for every one *atrox*. Because of that amazing ratio, many an author has discussed the intellectual superiority of the lions of La Brea vs. the sabertooths. In Kurten and Anderson's *Pleistocene Mammals of North America,* for example, they also note that *atrox:* "had a larger brain, relative to body size, than any of the Pleistocene or living lions of the Old World."

Added to its intellectual abilities are various natural selective processes which would have helped *atrox* adapt as the New World changed. One of these is the tendency towards melanism on the fringes of the lions' range. One good example of this is the darkly colored (with black belly and head manes) Cape lions of South Africa. The reports of the "black panthers" may be evidence that the females have been able to effectively use this genetic adaptation. Then the stage would be set for what we find in America today . . . large maned lions doing what males do (sleeping, mating, regally walking about) . . . and aggressive black cats doing what females do (hunting, killing, raising young). Whether or not *P. leo atrox* is the answer remains to be seen but for now, it seems to fit.

Loren Coleman

"We've had it Sir! We're up against the hard-boiled variety."

Out of place animals have popped up in droves over the last 12 months. Next issue we shall hear of wallabies, racoons, ostrich, bison and bear – but for now we complete our round-up of 'lioness' sightings in Scotland, and other big cat news...

THE SCOTTISH LIONS

Sightings of "lionesses" in Scotland came thick and fast in the last half of 1979, all from regions with previous sightings [see FTs 25, 26, 28 & 30].The latest flap began in late summer with unconnected reports of livestock depradations here and there – but no one took any notice of them until the main flap was under way in November.

Except in a few cases there was no attempt to deny the existence of some species of the large cats among the wild and ancient hills and heather. Richard O'Grady, director of Calderpark Zoo, Glasgow, said he was particularly impressed by " the quality of these observations . . . some by well-known naturalists, not just people making wild statements."

Grady's own idea is that these animals – police later said they believe at least three, possibly more, were on the loose – were set free by owners who feared the consequences of the *1978 Dangerous Animals Act,* which required registration and placed heavy liabilities on owners whose pets cause trouble. An escape, for example, would cost them £400 in fines plus recovery costs. Press and police adoption of this view – that the animals were loosed recently – was soon reflected in the statements of witnesses. For example, during the Cannich incident, farmer Ted Noble's sister-in-law said: "About 2 yrs ago [ie 1977] a mysterious red animal float [like a horse-box] drove up the glen and as it passed the farm there was that very strong animal smell you associate with circusses. It could well be that some crank has turned the wild animal loose."(Scottish *Daily Record* 29 Oct 1979.) As in all mysteries rumour and conjecture play their part in this flap, and may even have coloured some of the sightings by nervous witnesses. This aspect needs proper study.

Previously we had noted two distinct areas of sightings in the northern counties; the environs of Inverness at the northern end of Loch Ness, and on the far northern coastline of Cumberland and Sutherland, where the animal became known as the 'Skerray Beast'. The lastest flap contains many sightings which suggest that the two animals (or their families) are getting closer to each other as they extend their territories. Either that or we are dealing with one or two animals who travel far and quickly, and are responsible for sightings in both areas. If it is one animal, it is covering a helluva lot of territory!

INVERNESS AREA

27 Oct 1979.
Six policemen and two gamekeepers begin a search for a lioness in a huge area 20 miles from Inverness, after Farmer Ted Noble sees a large cat-like creature stalking the ponies at Kerrow Farm, Cannich. He was "in no doubt it was a lioness." Scottish *Sunday Express, Sunday Mail* 28 Oct; Scottish *Daily Record, D. Telegraph* 29 Oct 1979. Livestock depredations in previous two months, mentioned.

According to later papers, the search, over much of the Strathglass area, failed to discover anything. *Glasgow Herald, Sun, Shropshire Star* 29 Oct; Scottish *Daily Record* 30 Oct 1979.

3 Nov 1979.
Alex Ross and Jimmy Johnstone, a train driver and his mate, spot a big cat crossing the railway line as they approached Garve, Ross-shire. The Highlands locomotives are equipped with powerful spotlights to pick out sheep, deer and rockfalls etc, so they had a clear view of the creature. Ross said: "What we saw was yellowish-brown and had a long tail." He thought it too large and the wrong colour to be a wildcat. *Nessletter* 37 (Dec 1979); Aberdeen *Press & Journal* 5 Nov; Aberdeen *Evening Express* 14 Nov 1979.

Angus Monroe, a company director of Lairg, was driving to Embo late at night on the A839 when he saw a "strange cat-like animal" on the roadside near Muie, near a built-up area. Monroe: "It was about the size of a Labrador dog, dark in colour but with a distinctive cat's face. I had just come round the bend and the lights picked up what I thought was a dog . . . I could have run it down and killed it, but you wouldn't do that deliberately. It ran in front of me – I was travelling at about 40mph – before I braked. It crossed in front of me and made off into the grass towards the River Fleet. It was definitely a cat, but the size of a big dog. I am in no doubt about that." The report goes on to add: "The animal has consistently shown up in the first week of November for the past three years, but always on the North Coast around Bettyhill and Skerray." Aberdeen *Press & Journal* 5 Nov; Scottish *Daily Record* 5 Nov 1979.

1st week in Nov 1979.
Another railway worker, Ian Macinnes, was just 70 yds from the beast as it crossed the line near Tarvie. Aberdeen *Evening Express* 14 Nov 1979.

6 Nov 1979.
Four members of a local curling club, returning at night to Stratpeffer, saw a large cat-like animal in the road in the headlights, between Muir of Ord and Marybank. It was sandy coloured and looked powerful. It stood still for a moment then jumped a fence into a field. The men got out to look but it had gone, leaving the sheep "running around in all directions." *Nessletter* 37, Aberdeen *Evening Express* 14 Nov 1979.

2nd week in Nov 1979.
Forestry Commission instruct workers not to go out alone. Forest Rangers told to carry rifles. "The rangers are armed, but they have been instructed not to shoot it. Under no circumstances would we dream of killing it. We do not believe there is a lioness, but we are taking precautions just in case."

Donnie Dingwall, greenkeeper at the Strathpeffer golf course and his assistant, Raymond Houston, found remains of a roe deer. All that was left were two legs, broken off at the knee, one stripped to the bone, and the other with some flesh left (see photo). Both, Aberdeen *Evening Express* 14 Nov 1979.

16 Nov 1979.
David Dillon, 13, was cycling to catch the school bus, when a large cat-like animal bounded across the road in front of him. "I turned and cycled like mad the half mile back home."

At Tore – not far from David's experience – a man told police that he had seen a "lioness". NB: Due to scant information, and being unable to place Tore on my map, I am uncertain about the relation of these incidents to others. The account, in Scottish *Daily Record* 17 Nov 1979, calls it the 'Rossshire lioness', but these (and the Garve sightings above) are the first sightings in Rossshire that I recall.

22 Nov 1979.
Two youths, driving towards South Clunes, in the Drumchardine area, see "strange animal" on the road 150 yds ahead of them – golden brown, long tail, standing 3ft high. It had been walking but bounded quickly across a field into some trees. *Nessletter* 37.

14 Dec 1979.
Retired forester Arthur Cadman begins setting cage-traps in forest near Cannich, where he is convinced there is a lair. He says: "I have been aware of the beast's presence for some time. I have a cast of its pawmark, and have had samples of hair and droppings analysed." Cadman said he found lamb, sheep and deer stripped to the bone. *Sunday Express* 16 Dec 1979.

17 Jan 1980.
Donald Grant, director of a meat producing firm in Dornoch, was driving between Loch Carron and Achnashellach, on the way to Dingwall from Kishorn, at 3.15 pm, when the animal ran across the road in front of him. Grant: "It was about 2ft 6in high, perhaps a little higher, very dark brown in colour and definitely a large cat. I must admit I was very surprised. I have never seen anything like it before. I got out of the car to have a look at it, but it bounded off into the rhododendrons and disappeared." Aberdeen *Press & Journal* 19 Jan 1980.

18 Jan 1980.
Farmer George Riddell follows strange pawprints in snow for more than half a mile at Beauly. Police visit scene and take photos of tracks. Riddell says he was skeptical about the reports of a 'lioness', "but these tracks are most convincing. They came right down the side-road almost to the farm buildings." Scottish *Daily Record* 19 Jan 1980.

10 Feb 1980.
Police searches end disappointingly. No signs of 'lioness'. Inspector John Graham, of the Northern Constabulary, says he has records of 19 sightings since last October, generally describing a large cat-like creature "sandy coloured, brown or black." Graham believes more than one animal may be involved because the sightings cover a large area. It is not clear whether Graham is referring to the number of reports from all over Scotland that Autumn and Winter, or 19 sightings in the Inverness region alone. He says the first sighting in the area was by an English couple in 1973, who saw a "big cat" swimming in River Naver at Strathnaver. *Observer* 10 Feb 1980. But Strathnaver is miles northwards, in Sutherland, the home of the "Skerray Beast".

AYRSHIRE AREA

Summer 1979.
The following letter, by HC Mullin, appeared in the *Glasgow Herald* 12 Nov 1979, whose sighting was some 50 miles north of Ayrshire and on the outskirts of Glasgow itself.

"I saw one on the M74 coming out from Honeywell Controls factory site at Viewpark, near Uddingston. It was early on a Saturday morning in summer, the sky was bright and visibility quite good. The animal was greyish in colour, with white tufts of hair on its side. It walked with a peculiar padding motion on big flat feet or paws. It had a very long tail, quite smooth, which swept back in a long upward curve. I thought it was an american cougar, or mountain-lion; but I'm no expert on cats. I actually stopped the lorry and ran across the road to see it going through a thick hedge. Then I realized that this was a big cat and might be partial to a bit of lorry-driver for tiffin. So I ran back to the safety of the cabin and drove off. At the end of the M74, outside Calderpark Zoo, is a telephone. I thought of phoning the police, then thought better of it."

Early Feb 1980.
Account of Mrs Anne Lockhart of Crofthead Farm, Kilmaurs, Ayrshire in undated *Glasgow*

Herald clipping, but probably sometime in mid or late Feb 1980.

"A large golden-coloured animal with a big tail . . . about twice the size of my Labrador" came into her front garden at 10am. It was well built, with a long tail, and moved beautifully at speed. It ran across the garden before jumping over two fences into fields and out of my vision. . . I didn't report the sighting to the police because I asked a number of locals if they had seen it and they had not. But I am a level-headed person. I definitely saw what I described. It was like a young lioness." Mrs Lockhart also saw pawmarks with "clearly defined claws" left in the snow.

AN EAST LOTHIAN ANIMAL

The following accounts of a mystery cat to the east of Edinburgh were investigated by David Sydeserff, and are extracted from a short MS called 'Mystery Cats of Scotland'. We decided not to publish this in full because most of the cases were already included in our listing (above). This is the first we had heard of an MA in this region, and it doesn't seem to have been seen since 1977. We note that most of the descriptions refer to a "black" animal, though the remainder of the details are often contradictory. Our thanks to David for collecting another piece of the record . . .

'I was able, during mid-1978, to personally question the witnesses of this animal seen between September '76 and Summer '77. I believe it was publicised at the time, but I cannot recall it.'

'At 07.40 one morning in September 1976, Mrs Mary Stephens (52) of North Berwick, looked out her living room window which faces the Law, a 560 ft high "hill" which lies at the south of the coastal town. She saw an animal she describes as a puma running between two dykes at the foot of the Law; it was slowing as if it had been running and did not emerge from the second dyke. The puma was the size of a dog, black in colour with the tail as long as the body. She notified the police later who found nothing. Apparently, the previous night a man was walking his dog in the area, a regular habit for this man, and his dog suddenly became frightened of something.'

'In January 1977, three Council roadmen were working at the village of Whitekirk, four miles south of North Berwick, and at noon they stopped for lunch. Walking towards their depot, they saw an animal creeping out of whins on the village common, a rough-pasture sloping ground. The mal, a puma, was 35 yards away and slightly above them. It looked like a Labrador, though with a definite cat's face; four feet in length with tail as long as the body, and stalking close to the ground, height 22 inches or so. Legs and stump of tail were quite thick and as it moved its muscles clearly rippled. Colour was Jet black. The animal stopped as it sensed the men and raised its head. The eyes seemed to have scabby rings round them, but this could have been due to reflection from the sun (weather was cold but no snow). The puma was unconcerned, as if used to humans and stalked off into the whins after "a good wee while". Police and the local farmer found nothing.

'At 03.30 one morning in February 1977, a postman was driving mail from North Berwick to Drem railway station for collection. As he was passing the village of Direlton, two miles west of North Berwick, his headlights picked up an animal bounding across the road from the low firs outside the village (on the right). The puma showed no concern to the van and cleared the road in four bounds, well ahead of the witness. It was 8 ft long, evidently well-fed with the tail as long as the body. Black in colour. The witness could not stop. Police were later informed but the witness heard no more about it.'

'The final sighting I know of was in the summer of 1977 when a married couple saw an animal on North Berwick Law from their kitchen window (over-looking the Law). Time was between 08.00 and 09.00 and the animal was like "a huge cat" with "a long bushy tail" which lay idly behind it. It seemed to be eating something amongst the whins. Then it moved and was lost to sight. A few mornings later, the couple saw the same (or similar) animal in the same place and at the same time; they are not sure if it was eating. Disappeared again behind bushes.'

ESCAPES AND DISCOVERIES

Two lionesses burst into the grounds of Southbroom Comprehensive School, Devises, Wiltshire, on 28 April 1980. They had escaped from Sally Chipperfield's Circus, on the village green nearby, and were recaptured within two hours. The children were at their lunch break when one lioness, chased by circus men, jumped through the window of a mobile classroom, sending kids screaming into the playground. Some of the kids were shocked, but the rest became quite excited as the circus men closed in. The other lioness made for the main building and dived through a double-glazed door. She was badly cut and wrecked the classroom as she paced the floor. A spokesman for Devises Police said they had not established how the animals got out. London *Evening Standard* 28 April 1980.

Such escapes make an interesting contrast to simple sightings were an escape conjectured. In our experiences escapees are usually recaptured or shot or return in a miserable condition within a very short time. Any break-out from a zoo, however small, is usually well publicized, and certainly reported to authorities who promptly issue warnings and mount their safaris. Conversely, when something is sighted and reported to the police, the first thing they do is to ring around known zoos and collectors to check they have full complements. They usually report back that none of their own animals are missing.

On the 1st Feb 1980, the area around Warminster, Wilts, not far from Devises, was searched by police marksmen and two army helicopters. Two separate reports – one of a kangaroo, and the other of a lion near the railway line just north of Warminster – caught the police by surprise. "It began to look like there had been a mass escape from a safari park," a police officer said. Ten miles away is Longleat House, with its famous collection of lions – but they had none missing, natch! The police search found nothing at all, and there the mystery lies.

Coincidentally, the item immediately below the above – in the *Sun* 2 Feb 1980 – says that a wild boar was causing havoc among the gardens of Basildon, Essex – but no mention of where it might have escaped from, or whether the police caught it.

Connoisseurs will appreciate the next item. On the night of 20 may 1980, the body of a lioness was recovered from a lake near a disused brick quarry at St Helens, Lancashire. The *Daily Telegraph* 21 May 1980 gives no other details – but we note that on the day it was reported, Mount St Helens, in Washington state, blew her top!

OTHER LARGE CAT REPORTS

Since the excellent summary of recent 'cat' sightings in the USA in Loren Coleman's column last issue [FT31pp24-27], we have heard of a "large Black cat of some kind" haunting the residents of Russellville, Arkansas. It was first sighted on 4 Jan 1980. around 10pm, by a man who said it was causing his dog and himself "problems". This was only a few minutes after locals had banded together to capture a steer found wandering behind Bo's Donut Shop [true!].

A couple of weeks later, at 1.50am on 21st Jan, a resident went to his front door to investigate the barking of dogs. In the beam of his flashlight, across the street, he saw: "a large black panther with eyes about the size of half dollars." He called police, but they didn't find anything. We almost expected to hear next of eyes the size of saucers, etc – well, almost. On the night of 23 Jan, a lady looked out of her window, alerted by dogs barking to see "an all black animal with great big eyes". At 9pm the next night the animal was seen again – but searches by police and Arkansas Game and Fish Commission officers found no sign of lairs, remains of kills, or even tracks. Russellville *Daily Courier-Democrat* 6, 22, 23 & 25 Jan 1980.

In FT30p8 I gave the impression that a black panther is a different animal from a pigmented leopard. Not so, several readers corrected. Mike Grayson wrote "The panther *is* a pigmented leopard: a melanistic mutation which occurs most frequently amongst the leopard population of SE Asia." Thanks all. Curiously, about the same time, I received a bundle of clippings from our Finnish correspondent Tuuri Heporauta, which included the news that Dutch scientists on Bali had discovered evidence of a black panther on the island, where up to now no panthers were thought to exist. The World Nature Foundation naturalists identified paw marks and clawings on trees, and even collected eye-witness accounts from the Northern part of the Indonesian island. At least eleven locals, including two Indonesian nature protection officials in the Prapat Agung area in 1974, say they have seen a black panther. This is a classic case of reemergence, or migration, or teleportation, well, of out-of-place animals anyway. I wonder why British papers didn't pick up this story? From *Keskipohjanmaa*, Kokkola, 24 Dec 1979.

[Credits: Tom Adams, Janet & Colin Bord, Richard Cotten, Chris Hall, Tuuri Heporauta, Chris Hutton Squire, J Land (we're lost your address Mr Lang; please write to our editor), Valerie Martin, David Rees, Paul Screeton, David Sydeserff, Doc Shiels, PR Thomas, D Watson, Roland Watson, Jake Williams.] **RJMR.**

Conspiracy theory of the absurd: up in heaven there's been a coup, and now Walt Disney, Hans Christian Anderson and the Brothers Grimm are running things. You don't believe it? Listen....

TWICE UPON A TIME

Barcelona: 6-foot tall, good-looking blonde Nieves (Spanish for Snow) Boira, had seven boyfriends, all below average height. People sniggered. But 30-year-old Nieves suddenly got rich... new car, new clothes... while several jewellery stores suddenly got poor: robbed, in total, of over a quarter million pounds by men below average height, with sawn-off shotguns. You guessed: Snow White and the seven bandits. Nieves masterminded (perhaps that should be "mistress-minded") the whole affair, and took most of the loot, and in return... yes, in this tale, the dwarves actually got the girl... until they all ended up in jail. *Sunday Express* 19 August 1979. And in Palma, Majorca, another young lady, Maria Bisbal, sawn-off shotgun hold-up artiste extraordinaire, pulled 14 heists; until one day she left behind a dainty high-heeled shoe, stuck in an iron grille while she fled. Enter the handsome detective: the shoe fits, 20-year-old Maria confesses all... off to court they go (judicial, that is, not royal...) *Daily Express* 3 September 79.

•

Johannesburg, S.A.: 19-year-old Oliver Grey had a lovers' tiff, tied dynamite round his waist and blew himself up; but not before scrawling on the wall "All the King's men and all the King's horses won't be able to put Oliver together again". Didn't *quite* get that right, Ollie... still... *Daily Express* 4 October 1975.

•

Legendary tales... "Helen of Papua" says the headline: 3 men killed and 80 houses burned down when hundreds of warriors armed with bows and spears fought one another over the abduction of a young woman in Papua, New Guinea. *Daily Telegraph* 28 November 1979. Narcissus: 23-month-old Leila Ahmed believed to have drowned in a pond after becoming fascinated by her own reflection. *Daily Express* 4 September 1979. And in 6th-Century China, Bodhidharma, founder of Zen Buddhism, is alleged to have escaped pusuing troops by floating across a river on a reed: in 1979, the 87-year-old "head Buddhist monk" of Laos escaped to Thailand... by floating across a river on three car tyres. *Daily Star* 7 March 79.

•

To Mary and Joseph, a carpenter, a son, born on Christmas Day. Sorry, folks, it's Mary and Joseph Austen, of Swindon, Wilts... and they're calling the kid Joseph Charles (JC?). *The Spectator* (Canada) + *Daily Mail* 26+27 December 1979. And in Longview, Texas, a clergyman walking past the Nativity scene in front of his church heard crying coming from the manger, and found a baby boy abandoned there. *Evening Standard* 4 December 1979.

•

Mrs R Shanks, 71, writes to the *Sunday People* 25 November 1979, from Mottram, Cheshire, to inform us that one night she woke to find a mouse sitting on top of her electric clock. In St Charles, Missouri, Dan Odom applied the kiss-of-life to numerous frogs, frozen in transit from Tennessee. They all survived to take part in a local frog-jumping competition and, in view of these indignities, its hardly surprising none of them turned into princes... *Schenectady Gazette* 29 February 1980.

•

Mary Sue Hubbard, wife of Scientology founder, L Ron Hubbard, jailed for 5 years for conspiring to steal thousands of Justice Dept & IRS documents. Seems old mother Hubbard planned to leave the cupboard bare... *Daily Express* 7 December 1979.

•

Or the fourth little pig... there wasn't any sign of a wolf in Perth, Ontario, but an 8-month-old pig, called Pig, burned the house down. Or so says his owner, Jack Semler. Anyway, Pig the pig, perhaps overcome with remorse, then dashed into a nearby field and promptly fainted. Or perhaps it was just excitement: Pig recovered and stood immobile for three hours, watching the house burn to the ground. *Niagara Falls Review* 1 November 1979.

•

Storks bring babies in Israel? Migrating storks caused long blackouts in Haifa, by touching electricity cables with their wings. No light, no TV. Doctors expect a significant rise in the birth rate. *News of the World* 2 December 1979. Or like the Ancient Mariner: storks nesting on the roofs are considered a sign of good fortune in the little village of Dirndorf in Austria, but over the years they got fewer and fewer, until this year there was only one... and that one only made it as far as the village outskirts. The stork decided to stop at Josef Schuttbacher's trout-farm for a final snack... quite final, because Josef shot it. Now storms and floods are expected to ruin the summer crops, women fear giving birth to deformed babies, and Josef is due for trial for killing a protected species. He also receives death-threats, has to travel ten miles to do his shopping, children throw stones at his windows, his mail is thrown in the duckpond, and no one in the village will say a word to him. *Sunday Express* 13 April 1980.

Another 'Ancient Mariner' story comes from Kumasi, in Ghana, where Mr Alhaji Alhanssan became exceedingly annoyed with a vulture that regularly stole food from his home. Finally he clubbed it to death. As he and the other occupants of the house were celebrating the demise of the scrounger, Ahanssan choked on his food and died. *Pretoria News* 7 March 1979.

•

And to end with a tall tale: James Breckon bought a packet of runner bean seed, planted them all save one, and they eventually grew to be 7 feet tall. The odd one he gave to his 8-year-old son, Calvin, and Calvin planted it in his little patch of garden, and sat back to watch it grow... and grow... and grow. Up past the sitting room window, past the bedroom window, onto the roof, to finally tangle itself round the TV aerial, 30 feet above the ground. All in two months. So far they've had ten pounds of beans from it... but no giants. *Sunday Express* 14 October 1979.

[Credit: Chris Holtzhausen, Sam, PR Thomas, Dwight Whalen, Joe Zarzynski.]
SM.

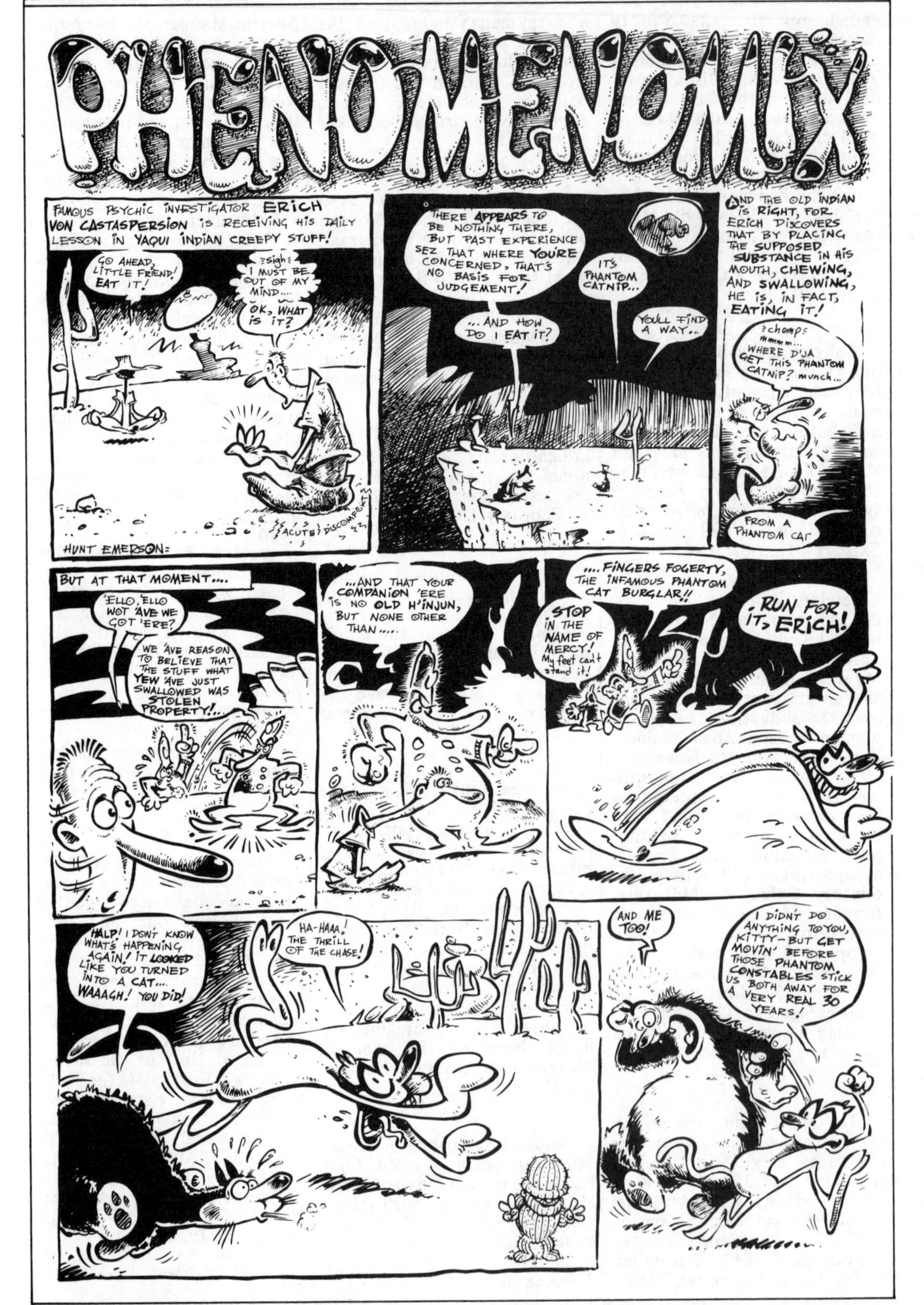
PHENOMENOMIX
FAMOUS PSYCHIC INVESTIGATOR ERICH VON CASTASPERSION IS RECEIVING HIS DAILY LESSON IN YAQUI INDIAN CREEPY STUFF!
GO AHEAD, LITTLE FRIEND! EAT IT!
sigh I MUST BE OUT OF MY MIND.... OK, WHAT IS IT?
ACUTE DISCOMFORT
HUNT EMERSON
THERE APPEARS TO BE NOTHING THERE, BUT PAST EXPERIENCE SEZ THAT WHERE YOU'RE CONCERNED, THAT'S NO BASIS FOR JUDGEMENT!
IT'S PHANTOM CATNIP...
...AND HOW DO I EAT IT?
YOU'LL FIND A WAY...
AND THE OLD INDIAN IS RIGHT, FOR ERICH DISCOVERS THAT BY PLACING THE SUPPOSED SUBSTANCE IN HIS MOUTH, CHEWING, AND SWALLOWING, HE IS, IN FACT, EATING IT!
chomp mmmm... WHERE D'JA GET THIS PHANTOM CATNIP? munch...
FROM A PHANTOM CAT
BUT AT THAT MOMENT....
'ELLO, 'ELLO WOT 'AVE WE GOT 'ERE?
WE 'AVE REASON TO BELIEVE THAT THE STUFF WHAT YEW 'AVE JUST SWALLOWED WAS STOLEN PROPERTY!..
...AND THAT YOUR COMPANION 'ERE IS NO OLD H'INJUN, BUT NONE OTHER THAN.....
....FINGERS FOGERTY, THE INFAMOUS PHANTOM CAT BURGLAR!!
STOP IN THE NAME OF MERCY! My feet can't stand it!
RUN FOR IT, ERICH!
HALP! I DON'T KNOW WHAT'S HAPPENING AGAIN! IT LOOKED LIKE YOU TURNED INTO A CAT... WAAAGH! YOU DID!
HA-HAAA! THE THRILL OF THE CHASE!
AND ME TOO!
I DIDN'T DO ANYTHING TO YOU, KITTY — BUT GET MOVIN' BEFORE THOSE PHANTOM CONSTABLES STICK US BOTH AWAY FOR A VERY REAL 30 YEARS!

gasp!
OK! HOLD IT HERE FOR A MOMENT
Gasp! HOW COME YOU GET TO BE A SLEEK STREET CAT, AND I'M A FAT OL' PUSSY?!
YOU GET THE CAT YOU DESERVE, KID. NOW LISSEN! I'LL CREATE A DIVERSION WHILE YOU GET US SOME SUPPLIES!
SUPPLIES? HMM, I AM RATHER PECKISH....
WOW! JUST THE THING! A TIN OF PUSSO-NOSH!
MEANWHILE, A DIVERSION IS CREATED....
ONE MOMENT, PARTNER IN CRIME-SMASHING! I AM ALERTED BY MY TRUSTY PHANTOM POLICE 2-WAY ETHERIC RADIO!
BEEP BEEP!
Ahem HELLO! LOUD AND CLEAR! ROGER, WILL CO, OVER, 10-4 ET CETERA!
CALLING ALL PHANTOM OFFICERS! REPORTS OF A WAVE OF UNSOLICITED APPEARANCES OF SPOOKS IN HOLIDAY SNAPS! REMAIN ABSOLUTELY MOTIONLESS UNTIL FURTHER INSTRUCTIONS! OVER AND OUT!
THAT'LL KEEP THEM OUT TH' WAY FOR A WHILE - HAVN'T YOU GOT THAT OPEN YET?
OPEN?! I CAN'T EVEN GET HOLD OF TH' DANGED THING!!!
THAT'S BECAUSE IT'S A REAL TIN, AND WE'RE PHANTOM CATS!
GRRRR!! OPEN, GODDAM YOU!!
WAAGH!
THERE'S NO USE SHOUTING AT IT - IT COULDN'T HEAR YOU ANYWAY....
I KNOW - I KNOW! COS IT'S A REAL TIN AND I'M A LOUSY PHANTOM!!
I SUPPOSE IF YA WUZ A PHANTOM TIN, WE'D BE STUCK WITH A REAL TIN OPENER!!
YUP
THE QUESTION IS... HOW AM I GONNA GET MY DINNER?!
THE REAL QUESTION IS... WHAT ARE YOU DOING TRYING TO COMMUNICATE WITH A NON-EXISTENT TIN OF CAT FOOD, ANYWAY?
Snee Hee!
FOR ONCE THE OLD INDIAN IS WRONG! IN THIS CASE THE REAL QUESTION IS "HOW AM I GOING TO GET MY DINNER?!" AND THAT'S THE END OF THIS COMIC!

OLD IVES' TALES.

Reading through the 45 hefty volumes of George Ives' press-cuttings made between 1895 and 1950, it became clear that here we had an unsung clipster hero. With his seldom-idle scissors, he bequeathed to us a stupendous collection of enigmas, fanatics, apparitions, mass hysteria, cannibals, twists of fate, transvestites and drug fiends; Ives was an old friend of Conan Doyle, and joined him on the authors' cricket team along with P.G.Wodehouse and the unfortunate J.Temple Thurston, a possible victim of spontaneous human combustion. Other friends included the radical mystic bisexual Edward Carpenter, the financier Lord Rothschild, and the pioneering sexologist and fan of Charles Fort,Havelock Ellis. **Paul Sieveking** has prepared a selection of Ives clippings, provisionally entitled ***Man Bites Man,*** to be published this year, and here selects a few stories concerning animals and birds, most of which for reasons of space, are not included in the book.

BEASTLY OMENS

In May 1905, the trawler *Etrurian* entered the port of Boston in Lincolnshire with a haul of a score or so of giant crabs, the largest of which weighed 16 pounds and measured a yard and a half across with claws extended. The claws were eighteen inches in circumference. That same month, some men were felling an oak tree at Pulham St Mary in Norfolk when a toad that had apparently been embedded in the tree for years fell out. It died after a few minutes. [1]

Later that year, an heroic pig swam four miles from Canvey Island to Southend, through rough water, thus disproving the old yarn that pigs can't swim without cutting their throats with their trotters. Around the same time, a ram in Tipperary battered Katherine Ryan to death, leaving her corpse almost unrecognisable, and a two-headed tortoise, *Terrapene Carolina*, turned up near Mount Vernon in Virginia. The heads fed seperately and alternately. [2]

FROG NEWS

It was reported in 1917 that, some years before, Colonel John J. Astor had given a large sum of money to Harvard and Yale for research on selective breeding to produce giant oxen, sheep and pigs capable of feeding on useless vegetation such as thistle and thorny cactus. He pointed out that biologists had already produced frogs two feet high. Speaking of which, there was a fall of frogs on Gibraltar's North Front sometime in 1914. Later the little fellows were covered with a shower of pink sand. Astor wasn't around by then. He had been drowned on the *Titanic*. There was another frog shower in the same place in the Spring of 1921. Reuters reported that thousands of the small hopping creatures could be seen in the hedges and aroused much curiosity. Later that year, a quarryman in Cheshire was reported to have found eight live frogs embedded in a big block of stone. [3]

SPORTING SWALLOWS

In August 1921, a swallow laid down its life for the Sussex team in a cricket match at Alton in Hampshire. The bird deflected a ball from Roberts straight down on the wicket, and fell dead on the ground. Major Bentinck was given out. The same trick was tried by another swallow in August 25 years later at a match in Bognor. This time the batsman blocked the ball. The bird achieved immortality of a sort by being stuffed and mounted with the ball. [4]

WHITE BIRDS

In 1905, a certain Mrs Holden of Hampton was resuscitated after a death certificate had been granted. Later, she described the sensations of her trance. White birds were floating about the house, and on the table a coffin was visible to her. Three years later a pair of white sparrows appeared in Willesden Infirmary grounds, and were harassed by the ordinary sparrows. In 1928, a white blackbird was seen in allotment gardens at Brancepeth Colliery, Willington, County Durham. Thirty years before, a white blackbird was shot near the same place.

The Willington whitebird report appeared in the same newspaper as the story of Mr Louis Linnett of Luton, who was savaged by an owl while motorcycling between Wollaston and Grendon in Northamptonshire. It pulled out his hair and slashed his cheek with its beak and claws. He left his machine and ran to a hedge, blinded by blood. Twice he beat off the bird which was biting his fingers. When it flew away, he was too exhausted to move, and was rescued by a passing motorist. [5]

BIRDS OF JUSTICE

In 1929 General Pattberg of Homburg on the Rhine received a carrier pigeon in the post with a letter demanding £250 to be attached to the bird and set free. If he failed to comply, he was threatened with death. An aeroplane followed the bird to a pigeon loft which was photographed and the villain arrested.

In 1930 a green parrot struck down the murderers Mesterino and Barataud in the penal colony in French Guiana—by giving them deadly parrot disease. The two men had escaped the guillotine back home, in spite of the public clamour for their execution.

About the same time in New York, another parrot trapped a murderer. The bird was renowned for its quickness in learning, and when neighbours were aroused from sleep by its shrieking "Don't papa, don't" they became alarmed and entered the apartment, which belonged to Mr and Mrs Yitkos. The wife had been killed with an axe. With the parrot's help, the police were put on the trail, and Yitkos, a New York longshoreman, confessed to the crime. [6]

WINGED CATS

In June 1933, Mrs Hughes Griffiths of Summerstown, Oxford, saw a strange black and white cat prowling round her garden. When she saw it in a room of her stables she got the Oxford zoo to come and catch it in a net. "I saw it move from the ground to a beam—a considerable distance, which I do not think it could have leaped—using its wings in a manner similar to that of a bird" she said. The fully developed fur covered wings were growing just in front of its hindquarters. Another winged cat turned up in 1939, belonging to Mrs Roebuck of Attercliffe, Sheffield. [7]

CYCLOPS NEWS

In March 1936, Dr Buck Ruxton was on trial at Manchester Assizes for the murder of his wife. The previous autumn, human remains had been found in a ravine in Moffat, Scotland. These were said to include Mrs Ruxton and a nursemaid of the Ruxton children. 43 bits remained unassigned to either body. Among these was a cyclops eye. The experts did not regard it as human. Less than a week after this evidence was presented, a lamb with a cyclops eye was born at Woodlands Farm, Apperley Dene, near Stocksfield in Northumberland. It lived for an hour and a half. In October 1938, a pig with a short trunk, resembling that of an elephant, with a cyclops eye just below the trunk, was born on a farm near Lille. The pig's 16 brothers and sisters were all quite normal. [8]

Paul Sieveking

George Ives' volumes of Newsclippings contained two photos from newspapers of winged cats.

(Above) In 1933, this specimen was found in an Oxford garden and put on display in Oxford Zoo. We tried to locate it through the Royal Zoological Society, only to learn that Oxford Zoo was closed long ago and its exhibits dispersed. Perhaps a local reader could track it down? (Sunday Dispatch 10 June 1933)

The second example comes from News of the World 30 June 1939 *(below), showing a tomcat named 'Sally', owned by Mrs. M. Roebuck, of Candow St, Attercliffe, Sheffield. Sally had fur-covered wings measuring 2ft tip-to-tip; and although he cannot fly, he is said to have cleared 5ft with his wings outstretched.*

REFERENCES

1) *Star* 16 May + 30 May—6 Jul 1905.
2) *Scientific American* 1905.
3) *Evening Standard* 21 May 1921; *Daily News* 11 Oct 1921.
4) *Evening Standard* 25 Aug 1921 + 15 Aug 1946.
5) *Daily Chronicle* 19 Jun 1908; *Daily News* 31 Oct 1928.
6) *Daily News* 11 Sep 1929; *Daily Chronicle* 1 Apr 1930; *News Chronicle* 27 Jan 1931.
7) *Daily Mirror* 9 Jun 1933; *Sunday Dispatch* 10 Jun 1933; *News of the World* 30 Jul 1939.
8) *Evening News* 10 Mar 1936; *News of the World* 16 Mar 1936; *Daily Mirror* 20 Oct 1938.
9) *Evening Standard* 7 Aug 1937; *Daily Telegraph* 7 Mar 1939.

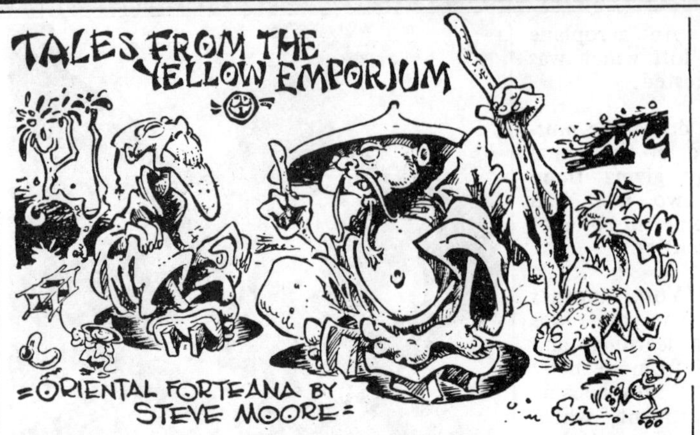

QIGONG

Firstly, my apologies to those who find the new Chinese phonetics difficult but, in common with other periodicals, I shall now be using them for the transliteration of Chinese words throughout this column. Familiar words will be placed in brackets, in their old form, after the new transliteration... for a while, at least....

We have made some mention of *Qi* (Ch'i) before, in *INFO Journal* 19,p2-5, and FT27, p19-20, as did Michael Goss in FT 31, p15, but have previously had to speak of it merely in terms of an unknown force (*Qi* is usually defined as "breath", "inner power", "intrinsic energy" etc) while expressing a pious hope that someone would provide some hard data through investigation.

Now at least we have some data on the practitioner of *Qigong* (Ch'i kung), if not the actual energy he produces (*Qigong* means simply "qi-work"). Our source is an article by Ji Wen, in *China Reconstructs* Vol. 29, No 4, April 1980, entitled "'Qigong' Exercises", and concentrates on one Hou Shuying, a 50-year old from Beijing (Peking) who has been practising qigong for 43 years. The article describes his demonstration routine: an 80cm long, 3cm square iron bar snapped with a chop of the hand, a similar bar snapped with a kick (one end of the bar was mounted in a millstone in both cases); a granite slab, 90 cm long, 40cms wide, 10cms thick, broken in two with his head; and lying on his back on the floor for three minutes with two concrete slabs weighing a total of one and half tons (that's right, *tons*! lying on his chest. . .he rocked the slabs to and fro with movements of his stomach and chest, before 26 men removed them.

Ji Wen's rationale of the process begins by quoting an "ancient theory", that *qi* is a movement of energy inside the body directed by will-power. Breathing exercises increase oxygenation of the blood and promote circulation. *Qigong* demands quick reactions, says Ji, though I confess that the only *qigong* exercises I'm familiar with seem rather passive, and these quick reactions raise the operating speed of the nervous system when controlling the muscles, thus allowing for a tremendous explosion of strength. Before discussing this explanation, let's have some data......

In directing his *qi* to his leg and breaking the iron bar, Hou's kick "was assumed to have a power of 1.5 tons". Hou, we should point out, is a wiry little 50-year old, and definitely *not* a muscle-man. Examination with sonic waves showed that when he was warming up, his muscles vibrated at a rate of 50 times greater than that of an ordinary person, and this is said to explain his sudden burst of strength.

Examination of other *qigong* masters has shown that during deep breathing exercises, they can move their diaphragm within a range 3 or 4 times greater than a normal person, some able to move it by as much as 15cms; and we are told that for every centimetre the diaphragm is depressed, 230-250 millilitres is added to the lung capacity. When Hou Shuying was warming up, his blood circulation quickened, his lung capacity enlarged, and his skin temperature rose by 2.5°C.

If *qi*-powers were restricted merely to feats of strength and breaking things, all well and good: *qi* then simply becomes a sudden burst of muscular hyper-activity. But what about the electric-like effects mentioned in FT27? A high muscular vibration rate could be brought forward as an explanation of the "electric shock" one is said to feel on being touched by a *Qigong* Master, I suppose. But what about projection of the *qi* beyond the body, or manipulating another's actions at a distance? Unless we discount these stories as untrue, we must assume some form of energy above and beyond the muscular hyper-activity promoted by Ji. Could it be that the physiological processes described above are only what goes on during the generation of a power unknown; symptoms, rather than causes? Which leaves us back where we started, still not really knowing anything about the nature of the mysterious *qi*....

And now for some news....

SORCERY

In allowing a limited return to religious freedom, the Chinese authorities have obviously found themselves with a few problems: people are taking liberties with their new liberty.

The first we hear is from the leader-column of *Ta Kung Pao* (HK) 22 March 1979, discussing an editorial in Peking's *People's Daily* about the new religious freedom: "As to feudal superstitions, they include exorcism, fortune-telling, praying for the prevention of natural disasters, geomancy and other activities. Since

Liberation such activities have been losing ground. But during the years under Lin Biao and the Gang of Four, such superstitions have staged a comeback, and they must be checked....Those who peddle such superstitions for either political subversion or personal gain must be educated and criticized, and in serious cases, strictly dealt with..."

And having been linked with the notorious Gang of Four, inevitably, the 'witches' found themselves targets of a new anti-superstition campaign, similar to the early sixties.

Not far from Shanghai lies Qilin village, Haimen County, Jiangsu Province, and there lived Jiang Xiao, the witch, and her male accomplice Ji Hailin. Jiang "posed as a divine spirit who could capture demons," and was attempting to heal a paralysed woman by ridding her of ghosts that had come back to haunt her. Unfortunately, Jiang decided that two six-year old boys, Qu Junpiang and Xu Yongping, were possessed by spirits of drowned men, and on 28 September 1979 decided to exorcise them in the village square at Qilin, in front of the assembled villagers. The exorcism began with an incantatory dance. Then the boys were beaten with branches and had boiling water poured over them. Then one was strangled, the other burnt to death. Jiang and Ji took the corpses to the office of the village leaders and put them on public display. Not surprisingly, Jiang and Ji were arrested shortly thereafter, made to attend criticism meetings, and were thought to be in line for execution, though we have heard no more on this.

This set off a flurry of press activity in China, partly reported in the west, from which we glean the following: That fortune-tellers and phrenologists had set up stalls in the streets of the city of Changsha, Hunan Province; that fake medicines were being sold at village fairs; that fortune-tellers and miracle healers in northern Guangdong Province (S. China) had made fortunes, and some of them could actually afford to build their own houses, production having fallen badly in the area because the roads to the village were packed with people seeking miracle cures; that people were travelling from place to place seeking their family records and having their fortunes told; that worshippers of "pagan gods" swarmed Jiangman municipality, bordering the Portuguese colony of Macao, arriving at the White Ribbon river to worship the gods with joss sticks, paper money and candles...*Daily Telegraph* 29 March; *Statesman* (India) 1 April; *Rising Nepal* 2 April; *Indian Express* (Delhi) 20 April; *Sunday Statesman* (India) 22 April; *Evening Standard* 14 May 1979.

At which point, enter Dr. Cyrus Lee, Professor of psychology at Edinboro State College, Pa., with a story that sounds suspiciously like hokum to me. Dr. Lee is also founder and director of the Sino-American Institute of Spiritual Psychology, but it still sounds like hokum. Says Dr. Lee, 51: there are, in China, "mystic priests" called *Gan Hsi Di* (I imagine he means *Gan Shi Di*), which means "corpse-rushers". They are especially prevelant in Hunan Province, it seems, where the mountains claim many lives, and as the Chinese believe the dead should be brought home for burial, they pay the *Gan Shi Di* a fee to bring home the body. This they do by making the dead body walk home, and Dr. Lee says he saw just such an event when he was a boy in China: dead corpses jumping, hopping and walking along the road while priests whisper incantations and gesture with symbolic paraphenalia. On the one hand, Dr. Lee says he was too terrified to go out of the house; on the other, he says that this has been going on for 2 or 3 centuries, and the locals are so used to it that it doesn't bother them. Furthermore, he tells us that the Chinese have actually filmed these zombies in mid-hop. And lastly he tells us that Chinese psychics can now send 'rays' over thousands of miles to change people's ideas, and that they did a brainwash-job on President Nixon while he was over there. This not only appeared in the *National Enquirer* 31 July 1979, but was thought worth repeating by the *Midnight Globe* 4 September 79, and it *still* sounds like hokum to me.

From an unfortunately undated clipping from the *International Herald Tribune* (February ? 1980), we learn that in December 1979, an old woman had a vision that if she went to a Buddhist shrine on the road to Chongqing in Sichuan Province (S W China) and prayed, she would be cured of an illness. She went, and a package of medicine appeared before her. This miracle brought thousands of people to the shrine to pray, including soldiers and an entire class at the local language institute, on the eve of their examinations. But, they say, only if you are a true believer will your prayers be answered..

January 1980 brought a new intensification of the anti-superstition campaign, with a new penal code providing sentences of up to 7 years for practising witchcraft or taking advantage of superstitious beliefs to carry out counter-revolutionary activities. Exorcists, however, have a sad tendency to end up on murder charges. A bed-ridden girl of Hainan Island (S.China) was diagnosed by a witch to have a demon-inspired illness. Her exorcism consisted of pouring paraffin over the girl and setting fire to her, stroking her burning hair with a broomstick and chanting spells. The girl was crippled for life; the witch awaits trial. In a commune north of Shanghai, a witch was dealing with an evil spirit known as a "water-monkey"; according to some reports, the "water-monkey" was occupying the body of a mentally ill man, who was strangled during the exorcism; according to others, it was a woman with mental trouble, declared to have a monkey-spirit in her stomach. The woman was suffocated when the witch and several other people sat on her in an attempt to squeeze the spirit out.

In Shandong Province (N. China), He Denggao's wife suffered from mental illness, and he consulted a witch. It's not clear whether she told him that his old house was the cause of the illness, and that he should move; or that his new house was the cause. Anyway, Mr. He decided to let off some firecrackers at his new place, a traditional way of exorcising demons. Alas, they were damp, and didn't go off. Bad omen, thought He, the head of the commune's construction team, so he sent for three hand-grenades that his team had for demolition work. We suspect spirit-mischief: the first two grenades went off okay; the third exploded prematurely, and blew He up. Meanwhile, in Shanxi Province, N.China, peasants were caught praying to portraits of Mao Tsetung, Chou Enlai and Zhu De, burning joss-sticks before the 3 dead leaders and telling fortunes by reading the cracks in heated oracle-bones. And in Guangxi Province, S W China, peasants stumbled on a mysterious leaflet called "The True Scripture", which appeared to have come from nowhere. You're not going to believe this, but the leaflet said that anyone who didn't make a copy of it and pass it on to someone else, would die a lingering death. A celestial chain-letter! The peasants consulted local sorcerers, and a small temple has been built. This birth of a new religion has, it seems, been affecting production in the area, so it doesn't look like it's going to be around for long... *Reuters* 22 January, *Guardian, Daily Telegraph, Glasgow Herald*, 23 January, *Shropshire Star* 26 January, *Weekly News* 2 February, *Guardian* 28 February 1980.

AND OVERSEAS

Indonesia: 40 people jailed for 8 months each for body-snatching from graveyards in South Sulawesi. The bodies were sold to traditional Chinese doctors for up to £40,000 each, who then use body-parts to make special medicines, said to bring immortality. *Gloucester Citizen* 18 January, *Daily Telegraph* 19 January 1980.

Singapore is in the grip of rumours, apparently spreading from Malaysia, that a gang of headhunters are loose on the streets and preying on children. The police deny the rumours, but there's an old superstition that a human head must be buried under a new bridge... and Singapore is building many new bridges and fly-overs at the moment. *Sunday Times* 16 March 80.

And back to Indonesia for our last tale: a 27-year old man from Sumatra married 121 times in 6 years, using 'black magic' to attract brides and get rich from their dowries. He told police he still had 4 wives left to divorce, and could only remember 28 of the women he married. Whatever this 'black magic' is, it sounds worth investigating...! *Toronto Sunday Sun* 27 January 1980.

[Credit: Janet & Colin Bord, Peter Christie, Helen Coles, Sam, Paul Screeton, Roland Watson, Dwight Whalen, Ion Will.] SM

Gannet-Westchester news reporter Maury Terry has had tremendous access to David Berkowitz (a marathon interview session at a government clinic for the insane) and to witnesses and materials in Yonkers, NY, the staging-ground for the weird SAM murders. [See FT30pp52-5].

As a result of this access, Mr. Terry has concluded that a satanic cult of which Berkowitz and John Wheat Carr were members, was responsible for the .44 killings.

The cult, consisting of 22 people, sacrificed dogs (by decapitation), drank their blood and communicated through occult codes (aka twilight language). This cryptic communication system was formulated upon an amazing sychronicity dating back to the 19th century.

The "Son of Sam" symbol [see FT30p53] contained in one of the letters he (it?) penned to journalist Jimmy Breslin, signified a pact with "descending hierarchies" and was borrowed from 19th-century occultist Eliphaz Levi. Here's what Maury Terry discovered:

> *"Two words appear across the top of the original Levi symbol. They are "BERKAIAL" and "AMASARAC". Berkowitz' nickname is "BERK". "AMASARAC" written backwards – a common Satanist ploy – is CARASAMA – "SAM CARR".*

Word inversion is not exclusively a "Satanist ploy". As this writer pointed out in a letter, in FT29, Freemasonry also uses this technique.

Sam Carr is the father of

John Wheat Carr, the alleged satanist who was probably assassinated at an "Air Force city" (Minot, ND), and Wheat Carr, a former employee of the Yonkers Police Department. Berkowitz, in a possible moment of lucidity within his programmed, hypnotic state, indicated that the dog owned by Sam Carr (who was also Berkowitz' neighbor, no less!) was "controlling him". With all respect to the holy *Vedas* ("The universe is run by dog intelligence"), could this have been Berkowitz' way of tipping observers off to the fact that members of the Carr family (two of whom were government agents – John being a US Airman at the time) were part of the control mechanism Shepherding the elephantine terror (Berkowitz) through a ceremonial murder series?

Maury Terry points out that the shooting immediately following the use of the Levi symbol happened at the "Elephas" discotheque. Mr. Terry was also able to learn that one of the Sam missives had been signed "Chubby Behemoth" and he links this, quite rightly, to "Elephas" via the Latin for "elephant". I sure wish I'd known about this monniker because what Mr. Terry has omitted is the fact that a very important ritual involving *magica sexualis* and twilight language took place at the *St. Francis* hotel in San Francisco over 50 years ago. It was here that Fatty Arbuckle, an acclaimed silent screen comedian, *raped* Virginia *Rappe* with a wine bottle, producing the "must" of the elephant. According to psychic researcher James Shelby Downard, Fatty was fulfilling the role of the "Chubby Behemoth" in this rite, intended to imprint the Dreaming Mind of the Group Mind of the millions of people who learned of it, with a subliminal message.

This twilight language usage in the SAM horror-show is not merely satanic. As I have tried to show [FT30] the SAM snuffs are obviously ceremonial and hence, when a nationally-syndicated reporter picks up this occult theme the level of disinformation present in the lone nut capture/resolution and the furnishing of "standard psychiatric motives" scenario is diminished. But to settle for a satanic label is also limiting and in a case where murder has been the object, the whole truth (or our best effort at thinking out every angle) must be the goal.

Can the satanist category fully account for the fact that cattle were mutilated in North Dakota at the time of John Wheat Carr's death there? Surely readers of Thomas R. Adams will feel an internal mental alarm go off when they learn of mutes being pawned off on satanists.

The cultic rites celebrated in Yonkers were also performed along aqueducts. In April, 1979, I wrote the "Sun of Sam" article for *FT* but it didn't appear in the States until 1980. Nevertheless, it was pointed out in those pages that SAM's letter to Breslin contained disguise-words representing the "spiritual" fecal matter or *kalas* present during magical operations. In October of 79 Maury Terry came to the same conclusion. Thanks to his familiarity with Yonkers, he also knew that the aqueduct was, at one time, the gutter of NYC. The guano-collecting Bat Tower of San Antonio, Texas, was located over a sewage center. This Tower was constructed by well-to-do Freemasons who were also members of the Anglo-Chicano Comazotz bat cult (cf. my *Masonic Assassination*).

John Wheat Carr's brother Michael was killed in an auto "accident" on October 4, 1979. Michael Carr was a member of the hierarchy of the Church of Scientology, the boss of which is LaFayette Ron Hubbard, a former associate of John Whiteside Parsons of the California Institute of Technology and the revival of the Knights Templar – the *Ordo Templi Orientis*. The OTO was into mystical toponomy (geomancy) and was synched into the absolute-zero Land's End negative sites available in California (certain areas on Mount Palomar, Griffith Park, Devil's Gate). Some of these sites would later serve as the stage for the Hillside Strangler who has been identified as Kenneth *Bianchi*, a hanger-on and "Go-fer" on the fringes of the world of police and detectives in the employ of the government.

Another onomatological symbol/sychronicity of importance is the fact that the Yonkers cult rites were conducted near a St. John place-name (St.John's hospital). The names Francis, Martin and John (sometimes preceded by "St.") are magnetic words for those practitioners of Rumpelstiltskin intentional language. Marie Laveau, the voudoo queen of legend and fact, held her hoo-doo hootenanies at Bayou St. John, New Orleans.

The method of sacrificing dogs also raised the magnitude of our interest in JOHN symbolism. Decapitation is an integral part of the 9th degree of the Scottish Rite and pertains to the ST. JOHN mania (cf. my *Masonic Assassination*).

Editor Bob Rickard reminded me a while back that German Shepherds are dogs with strong police and military associations. John Wheat Carr kept a mutilated ear from one of these police dogs on his wall. Terry says other members of the cult may have followed suit. For me such a display is most interesting in determining who was always under symbolic surveillance and by whom. It may also be a possible indicator of the level of programming experienced by the cultists. The grizzled old 19th-century American populists who fought against masonic assassinations observed how low-level initiates, when apprehended, tended to commit suicide or total self-incrimination. The old-time sleuths labeled this bizarre affliction "masonic apoplexy" and attributed it to the pioneering mind control mastery achieved by Freemason Anton Mesmer.

Let's put down our (herbal) tea-cups and do some last-minute guess-work.

I can accept that the front-group for this SAM series of sacrificial murders was a satanist outfit calculated to fulfill to the letter the worst nightmares of our orthodox Christian friends. But beyond such a Hollywood haunted-house schema is a powerful, well-oiled assassination machine, which, like the one that took off JFK, George Lincoln Rockwell (the latter through the offices of Carlos Allende), Martin Luther King, Sharon Tate, Marilyn Monroe, Don Bolles and hundreds of others, maintains the CIA, FBI and KGB in power (an enormity predicated on my reading of the signals emanating from a certain crucified snake hanging on a Tau Cross). To believe that this machine would permit the operation of another in its territory is unrealistic since the level of sophistication shown by the SAM crowd is not a commodity easily duplicated or tolerated. The notion of competing elites doesn't account for it either.

Other policemen have been implicated in the SAM tragedies including Deputy Craig Glassman. In Rochester, NY, the home-town of Kenneth Bianchi, 4 little girls were ritually sacrificed according to a twilight language every bit as terrifying and blatant as "Wicked King Wicker" in NYC (SAM). Two US Secret Service agents mysteriously appeared at the home of one of the child-victims on the day she met her demise, according to the *Rochester Times-Union*. No explanation was given for this presence. James Shelby Downard maintains that many US Secret Service agents are initiates within the cryptocracy running America.

If Maury Terry goes "for broke" in this case he can contribute to the fabled, alchemical Revelation of the Method. If he doesn't, I fear that B-Movie satanists will serve as complete explanation for the enigma that is the Son of Sam case.

If I have tended in this article toward what may appear to be a pedestrian infatuation for believing the worst about governments I can only refer readers to WH Bowart's *Operation Mind Control* (Dell paperbacks) or to the later chapters of Vallee's *Messengers*.

Also recommended is Stephen Knight's *opus* on The Ripper (which could have served as the non-fictional basis for the film *Murder by Decree* instead of the fiction which trivialised the ultimate impact of that powerfully illuminating movie, or, on the other hand, permitted its distribution).

In conclusion, I'm a kind of critically, paranoid optimist. Like that wonderful satirist Ezra Pound – who upon hearing that Harry Crosby had murdered himself and his girl-friend, described it as a "vote of confidence in the cosmos" – I believe that the Rumpelstiltskin riddle is not unbreakable. Intuition, spontaneity and a little help from the Wyrd Sisters, will prove more than a match for the Faustian tamperers and Gordian-knot slashers any day.

It's my hunch that we can throw a boomerang into the twinning mirror just by seeing that a particular door on the 33rd Street of the town of Truth or Consequences, is, at present, wide open.

"I was born to give witness
to the Truth."

Michael Anthony Hoffman

PS: To the many folks who have queried my publisher for more about FOP as both Freedom-of-Passage and FRATERNAL ORDER OF POLICE, I can only paraphrase Dr. Syntax (whom John Michell spotted on Land's End) when he was asked about the Abbey of Thelema. He said its rules were more strict than even the Catholic Church, despite the "Do Your Thing" maxim.

PPS: Will the chap who wrote me in the summer of 1978 about Bel twilight language please write again – I've lost your address.

"Thank Heaven it's Moles tomorrow!"

PROFESSOR CLASPROOT'S
FACTS YOU MIGHT FORGET
MRS. GLORIA MONEY APPEARED AT 5.35 p.m. ON APRIL 5, 1975, AT PECKHAM RYE POLICE STATION. SHE WAS SUFFERING FROM AMNESIA, AND HAD A KNITTING NEEDLE THROUGH HER HEAD.
DOCTORS EXAMINED HER, AND DEEMED THE NEEDLE INCONVENIENT BUT HARMLESS. HER HUSBAND CLAIMED HER FROM HOSPITAL TO THE DELIGHT OF THE PRESS, WHO HAILED HER AS "THE SECOND GAIL FAIRBROTHER"*...
* WHOEVER SHE WAS!
GLORIA'S BIG PRICK
HOWEVER, AN APPARENT RETURN TO RELATIVE NORMALITY WAS INTERRUPTED DURING A COMMERCIAL BREAK IN "CROSSROADS" WHEN..
CAST ON! KNIT ONE, PERL TWO...
GLORIA'S MESSAGES CONTINUED DURING DAYTIME T.V., MANY OF THEM TRANSCRIBED BY NEIGHBOR AND PATHOLOGICAL TRICHOLOGIST EDIE BONKQUE-LIGHTLY...
THEN, DURING A WELCOME BREAK IN "MR. & MRS."
CAST OFF! MESSAGE ENDS!
WHEEEP
...AND THERE THIS INCREDIBLE CASE MIGHT END WERE IT NOT FOR THE INTERVENTION OF IPSWICH TOWNSWOMEN'S GUILD, WHO USED THE EXTANT FRAGMENTS IN A CHARITY KNITTING MARATHON. SO NOW WE HAVE A GLIMPSE OF A GREATER PATTERN.
THUS ANOTHER ARCANE KEY ELUDES OUR GRASP..
...AND WE CAN ONLY SPECULATE ON ITS SIGNIFICANCE...
POKKETTZ '80

The last nine months has produced a fair-sized bundle of swarm and plague clippings. So here follows a chronology of some of the interesting clusterings of the insect and the animal world since June 1979.

JUNE 1979

Snakes plague the coastal region of Yugoslavia after an earthquake. *Athens News* 5 June.

Grasshoppers infest S. Dakota, USA. *Int. Herald Tribune* 6 June.

Packs of giant rats invade three villages in Western Java forcing people to flee. *Het Volk* 7 June.

Caterpillars (brown-tailed moth) arrive in large numbers in West Sussex, England. See FT29. *Barking and Dagenham Advertiser* 15 June.

JULY 1979

Snakes forced out of the ground by heavy rains in Madhya Pradesh State, India, kill 23 people. *Daily Mirror* 5 July.

Large insect clouds over central Texas at altitudes of 10-13,000 feet. Very unusual according to experts. *Dallas Morning News* 11 July.

Bristletails mysteriously appear in large numbers at De Von Breitenbeckers Farm, Brigham City, Utah. *Dallas Times Herald* 10 July.

Annual African Plains animal migration is the biggest for 25 years. *Daily Telegraph* 13 July.

Nine million bees in Maryland, USA, released accidentally when the container lorry transporting them crashed. *Int. Herald Tribune* 24 July.

Grasshoppers in USA spreading from S. Dakota to Oregon and Texas, threatening 1.5 million hectares of crop lands. *New Scientist* 26 July.

Aphids invade England. See below.

AUGUST 1979

Millions of cockroaches come to light in one house in Schenectady, New York. *Times-Union*, Albany, NY, 1 Aug.

A swarm of tortoises appear mysteriously on Hainault Forrest golf course. *Weekly News* 4 Aug.

Rats roam Belgrade's new suburbs as refuse piles up. *E. Standard* 9 Aug.

Cement-eating bees finally leave Mr and Mrs Joyne's house in Nottingham, England, where they had swarmed for the last 15 months. *Daily Mirror* 10 Aug.

As we go to press, the swarm of concrete eating bees which has been plagueing the home of Mr and Mrs Joynes has returned once more.

Giant snails eating the fruit trees in the Andaman and Nicobar Islands. *The Spectator* 23 Aug.

Kangaroo plague in Australia. See below.

SEPTEMBER 1979

Amphibious worms pollute the water supply at Haworth, Nottingham, England. *Daily Mail* 8 Sept.

Locusts in Australia. See below.

OCTOBER 1979

Mosquitos breeding in stagnant water at the Forum des Halles, Paris. *Int. Herald Tribune* 12 Oct.

Small black spiders infest Seaford, Sussex, England. *Daily Telegraph* 3 Nov.

DECEMBER 1979

American hard-back clams appear in large numbers in Sandwich Bay, Kent, England. None had been seen since 1960. *Daily Telegraph* 7 Dec.

Poisonous violin spiders (causing haemorrhaging) infest Johannesburg. *Omaha World Herald* 15 Dec.

JANUARY 1980

Coypu. The British Government allocates £200,000 to rid East Anglia of this pest. *Sunday Telegraph* 27 Jan.

FEBRUARY 1980

Mice plague building up in Australia. See below.

Packs of martens eating the rubber and plastic insulation on cars parked in Winterhur, Switzerland. *Sunday Express* 3 Feb.

MARCH 1980

Giant rats appear in Kensington Civil Service canteen, London. *E. News* 13 Mar.

APRIL 1980

Killer snakes in floodwaters in New Orleans. *Daily Star* 16 April.

Giant snails eat lettuce crops in Northern Spain. *Daily Mirror* 25 April.

THE GREAT PLAGUES OF AUSTRALIA

During the last year Australia has been the unhappy host to a series of swarms and plagues. Even the *Guardian* (16 April 1980) has been moved to remark about Exodus chapters 7 to 12 (describing the plagues of Egypt). Here is the sorry tale.

In April 1979 locusts descended on New South Wales, attacking not only crops but cars and houses. (*Guardian* 2 April 1979)

After the locusts came the plague of the great red kangaroo, forced out into farmland by droughts. One state issued a permit for the destruction of one million roos. The last three years of good rainfall has produced a baby kanga boom. (*Daily Telegraph* 1 Sep 1979)

In September the locusts broke out again, the eggs laid

by the previous swarm hatched out and moved in half mile wide bands across Queensland, Victoria, and N.S. Wales. The worst plague since the 1950s. (*Daily Telegraph* 1 Sep 1979) One S. Australian farmer reflecting ruefully on the kangaroo and locust plague said "First we get the bounders then we get the hoppers." (*Daily Mail* 16 Oct 1979)

But more was yet to come. Reports began in February this year of a vast army of starving mice infesting areas of S. Australia and Victoria. According to the *Australasian Express* (1 May 1980) the plague had begun twelve months previously. By mid April this year 100,000 sq. miles had been affected. The mice eat everything from putty to wedding dresses. Some desperate householders have resorted to barri cades of soap-impregnated steel wool! Even water doesn't stop them, a family reported seeing mice swimming out to their yacht. (*Scotsman* 21 Mar 1980) Mr. Barbary, a resident of Woomelang (one of the worst affected towns) said, "Poison is useless. After a while they eat it like cheese." (*Australasian Express* 1 May 1980) There has been little speculation on the origin of this plague, however bad weather in Australia has been causing drought conditions in many regions. So bad, in fact, that people are predicting the worst drought in living memory. (*Daily Telegraph* 9 April 1980, *Aust. Express* 10 April 1980)

Finally, in the midst of these large-scale movements we have a small but symbolic contribution from the termites, which have invaded the mansion belonging to the Queensland State governor, forcing him and his staff to evacuate. (*Guardian* 16 April 1980) Well, Australia, is something taking its revenge at last?

TRILLIONS OF APPHIDS

The last two weeks of July 1979 saw a plague of greenfly descending on the Eastern and Southern regions of England. The volume of the swarm (experts estimate it weighed 200,000 tons) and the speculation on its origin make this a noteworthy case in our files. (See FT29 for earlier aphid infestations.)

The first report of the green menace came from the south coast where holiday makers were forced off the beaches. An honest official at the Crop Disease and Intelligence Unit said "where they come from, goodness knows." (*Daily Telegraph* 17 Jul 1979) Farmers felt that a hard winter had killed off the ladybird, a natural predator. However, at this early stage the consensus of opinion was that winds had blown them in from North Europe (the same old explanation). The *New Scientist* (9 Aug 1979) pointed out that insect counts in North Europe were no higher than usual at this time. By 27th July the aphids were in London and Northern England, even landing at Heathrow Airport. The *Guardian* (27th Jul 1979) identified the swarm as a mixture of native and foreign aphids. However, by the end of the month, the insect had been identified as the rose grain aphid, a native species. Hot weather and other factors had caused a population explosion. They had apparently drifted out over the sea and been blown back again, although it does seem a little odd that no-one had seen this.

However, the last word belongs to the Ecological Physics Research Group at Cranfield Institute. Their research shows that the rose grain aphid is a very recent pest, which feeds on the green leaves of crops. Given the right conditions including hot weather, the population grows exponentially. Coincidentally, during the last two years, agricultural policy has recommended a 50% increase in nitrogen fertiliser, one of the effects being to turn leaves greener. (*New Scientist* 9 Aug 1979) So, in 1977 some official at the Department of Agriculture had a vision of a greener England... and in 1979 a green nightmare.

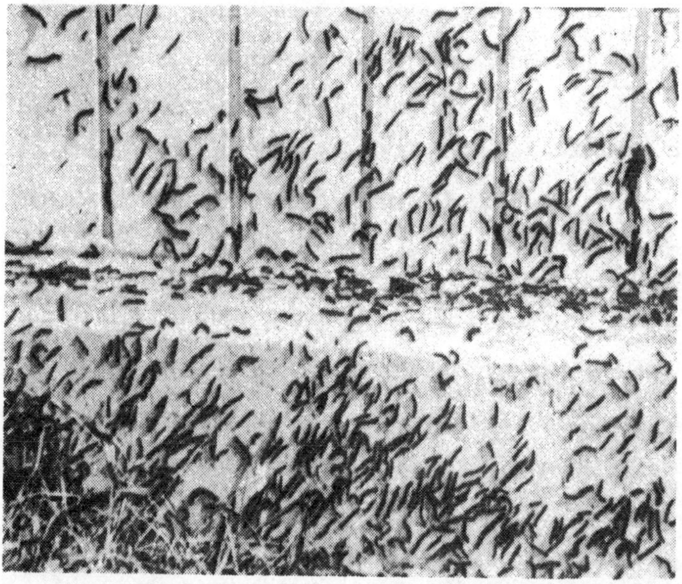

Forest tent caterpillars close East-Central School, Prince Albert, Saskatchewan on 20 May, covering the playground and building. (Niagara Falls Review *22 May 1980*).

[Credits: B. Hain, R. Watson, Paul Screeton, Valerie Martin, Alan Gardiner, C. Hall, I. Lawes, James Chambers, Tom Adams, Ronny Blomme, Stephen Simpson.] **VT**

TALES OF INDIA.

Sometimes, as we sort out the clippings received from our far-flung network of clipsters, we boggle at the quantity generated by certain countries, especially those of the Far East, which is still Virgin Territory for Fortean research. As an example we give the following collection from India, clipped during a period of less than two weeks earlier this year, by our reader Jitendra,

THE KUANO AMPHIBIAN BOY

The village of Baragdava stands on the small river Kuano in the Basti district of Uttar Pradesh. One afternoon in February 1973 the local priest caught sight of a naked boy who seemed to walk on the water. At one point he dived in, caught a large fish and ate it. Then he lay in the water and was carried downstream. The priest told the villagers of his sighting, and when he described the lad and estimated that he was about fifteen, an old woman called Somni said he was her son Ramchandra who had been carried away by the river when he was a year old.

Another villager saw him a few days later, and for a while there was considerable local interest, and people flocked to the river to see him. But he was not to be found.

Then in May 1979, Somni spotted him lying in a field. She crept up on him and recognised a birth mark on his back. He awoke and fled. A strict watch was mounted, he was caught and taken to the village. He was virtually hairless and his ebony-black skin had a greenish tinge. He managed to escape back to the river, but his experience of human society made him less reclusive, and he would come and eat bowls of spinach in water put out by the villagers.

Hundreds of villagers, police officials and hard-boiled journalists have seen him walk, run, or recline on the surface of the water, and stay below the surface for longer than ordinary humans. His insteps and toes are as hard as rock. His favourite food are raw meat, fish, frogs, marine creatures and leafy vegetables, gourds and red chillies. He reaches for food directly with his mouth.

In summer months, when the Kuano dries to a trickle, he is ill at ease; but when the river rises in floods, he is gleeful and enjoys diving in the swift current. The main puzzle is how he protects himself against the many crocodiles . . . and, of course, his alleged ability to walk on water.

Somni had a strange tale of how Ramchandra was conceived. On a stormy evening during the monsoon season, she was returning from mending a fence around the family field, as her husband was laid low with fever. She was 40 years old, a mother of three. Her way was blocked by an enormous being who seemed more like a spirit than a man. He threw her to the ground and raped her in the pouring rain. As suddenly as he appeared he vanished.

It is believed locally that a long time ago a holy man dug a well in the area. He climbed down to invoke the goddess of water, but was drowned as the well quickly filled. Some of the villagers believe that it was the spirit of this man which possessed Somni and then took the child into his watery care.

THE FLOATING STONES OF RIWALSAR

Seven huge stones defy the principle of buoyancy by floating in Riwalsar lake, in the Mandi district of Himachal Pradesh. The lake, surrounded by tall trees and high mountains, is the scene of a big fair every year on Baisakhi day, when thousands of people take a holy dip and worship the floating stones at the lakeside temple dedicated to Lomash, the local Rishi (sage). *(The Sun*, India, 23 Jan 1980.)

FEAR AND LOATHING IN LUCKNOW

In 1967 CID Inspector Guru Sharan Lal Srivastava built himself a house in Mohalla Naya Sardar Khera in Lucknow. During construction, a worker called Deena fell foul of his kinsfolk, and was hanged from a window in one of the half-constructed rooms. Whether this had anything to do with subsequent events is unknown.

The trouble began when the Inspector's wife Shanti heard stones falling in the courtyard. A whole series of disturbances followed. Fires rekindling themselves. The crashing and flying around of household goods. The tap turning on and off. Soon most of the crockery was broken. Sleeping children were moved about.

The Inspector's son Shasti seemed to become possessed. After fits and seizures his face would assume a fearsome aspect and he would issue elaborate instructions. Another child saw a whole group of snakes, raising their hoods ominously. Travelling to and from college, Shasti would often meet an aged baba who accosted him. If he were late, the baba (old man) would say "Why are you late? You must be punctual." The baba would accompany him to college or give him sweets. He seemed to vanish near a certain tree.

The Inspector's ceremonial sword started moving about, stabbing furniture and, on occasion, falling in the road outside. Clothes and bedding would catch fire.

At midday on 1st July 1975, neighbours heard the Inspector's wife screaming "Help, help I am burning!" Her son Shasti threw a quilt over her, but the fire burned on. "The evil spirit is burning me!" she cried. The fire was finally extinquished with water, but Shanti died in hospital that night.

The death inevitably brought publicity. A whole bunch of thaumaturges, exorcists and spellbinders from all religions turned up, but none could rid the house of its polt.

Finally, two reputed exorcists of Uttar Pradesh, Miyanji and Hafij from Baheri, Bareilly, heard of the case and called on Srivastiva in 1976. For several days they carried out rituals and then declared that the household could live in peace. The house, we are told, has not been plagued since then.

THE PHANTOM GUIDE

While strolling on the hill of Mahur, a pilgrim centre near Nagpur, a group of medical students were accosted by a turbaned person in a long coat who said he was a guide. He took them to some caves and gave them a tour of rock sculptures which he described in detail, but which the students were unable to see.

Later they had lunch with the guide gleefully participating. They also took about twenty photographs, but when they developed them, the guide was nowhere to be seen (according to the *Sun*, India, 23 Jan. 1980), although Rajendra Kesarwani tells us (in the *Youth Times*, 16-21 Jan. 1980) that *"the outline of his figure, highlighted by his turban"* did appear.

VIMLA AND THE EXORCIST

Mohammed Ayub Khan, an alleged exorcist from Jaipur, went to Viratnagar in February to exorcise an evil spirit from 16-year-old Vimla, who had occasional fits since her marriage six months before. The exorcist locked himself up with Vimla in a small room, lit a charcoal oven and threw some powder on it. Vimla was heard to scream and then all was quiet. When the door was broken down, Vimla was dead and Ayub Khan was unconscious. He was placed under arrest and charged with murder, along with the girl's father-in-law. *(Indian Express*, 13 Feb. 1980.)

THE POONA SNAKE MAN

Neelimkumar Khaire (28), a receptionist at the Blue Diamond Hotel in Poona, claimed a world record on 23 January this year by staying with 72 poisonous snakes for 72 hours. He undertook the ordeal to prove that snakes were not man's enemies, although three snakes had died during fierce fighting among themselves, and had been immediately replaced. About 70,000 visitors saw him moving freely among the 27 monocellate cobras, 24 Russell's vipers, 9 bindocellate cobras, 8 banded kraits and 4 kraits.

At night, when the temperature dropped dramatically, the snakes sought his body warmth, but he nevertheless managed to snatch 11 hours sleep during the three days. One observer saw snakes slide over his body 32 times on the second night. The paper *Blitz* informs us that he keeps 150 snakes in his backyard, and that he has been bitten 6000 times (!).

The world record is held by Peter Snyman (24), who spent 50 days and 7 hours with only 24 venomous snakes in Hartbeesport, South Africa, in April-May 1969. As we go to press, Mr. Austin Steven is trying to break the record - also in Hartbeesport. *Deccan Herald, Times of India* 23 Jan; *Deccan Herald, Indian Express* 24 Jan; *D.Telegraph* 25 Jan; *Blitz*, India 2 Feb 1980.)

FERTILITY SACRIFICES

On 12 September 1979, four people were hanged at Yerawada jail for the ritual murder of ten virgins.

In an obscure town in Maharastra called Manawat lived Rukmini Paradhi, a beautiful woman who was barren but wished to have children by her lover Uttamrao Barhate. She solicited the help of a quack, who declared that blood from a virgin's vagina offered to Lord Munja, the local god, would bring her fertility.

Various relatives and servants were recruited, and ten virgins were butchered between 14 November 1972 and 4 January 1974, ranging from one to thirty-five years old. One corpse was found beheaded, with the skin from the breasts and other parts removed. Rukmini remained infertile.

The town of Manawat is steeped in miracles, witchcraft and sorcery. Tree-worship is prominent. Lord Munja is supposed to be the spirit of an unmarried Brahmin boy who resides in peepal trees. He is a semi-demonaical deity, who needs appeasing at regular intervals. A peepal tree stood in the compound of Rukmini's house, and it was rumoured that a huge hidden treasure was buried under its roots. The blood offering would not only bring her fertility, but appease Lord Munja so that they could dig up the treasure.

The four that were hanged at Yerawada did not include Rukmini and her lover, who were aquitted.

Another alleged fertility sacrifice took place on 4 August 1979 in the Lawrence Road colony in Delhi, when Gunjan, the 3 year-old daughter of Pushpa Dua, was snatched from her mother and found dead in a lake. The parents had been very worried ever since the child's naming ceremony in February when a long piece of cloth containing a 10 paisa coin and some sindoor (coloured powder) dropped in the middle of the gathering from somewhere unknown. A few days later, the mother found a small package in her house containing pulses, red thread, some more sindoor and "child" written on a piece of paper. More packages were found. She became mortally afraid and went with her daughter to her parents in Jaipur, returning three days before the abduction.

Several other people had had packages thrown into their houses, always on Tuesdays, Thursdays and Saturdays. A local Tantric told them that a married couple was trying to secure the birth of a child by means of child sacrifice. Police insist that Gunjan's death was accidental, but the people in Lawrence Road disagree. *(Probe*, India, Feb. 1980.)

P.R.A. de G.S.

A selection of recent phenomenal vaguaries, clustering around unexpected themes.

SUFFER, LITTLE CHILDREN

The latter months of 1979 saw an astonishing resurgence of the ancient practice of child sacrifice. The severe drought in India in August brought out old, atavistic urges to inhumanely sacrifice. We read in the Delhi *Sunday Standard* 23 Sept 1979, that the merchants of Kota were so worried that they organised propitiation ceremonies lasting 5 days from 22 Sept. Earlier, villagers had got together to dig out the god *Gade Bhaironji*, who normally lies buried beneath their fields. Usually he grants a good rain in return for being exhumed and worshipped for a while—but this time he was obviously peeved about something. Elsewhere, another set of believers were making urgent appeals to (something called) *Neel Kanth Mahadeo*—again to no avail. By October, things were so parched in Uttar Pradesh state that nude women were sent to work in the fields at night, a tradition said to particularly interest Varuna, the somewhat unreliable god of rain. Perhaps these naked night-clad nymphs did perk up his interest, so to speak, but he obviously wasn't feeling up to the frolic. The drizzle that appeared was said, by government agronomists, to be too little too late. Even gods have their problems these days! *NY Times* 14 Oct 1979. But then a small note: In the town of Rae Bareli, 19 Oct, a woman and her husband were arrested for sacrificing a 2-year-old girl to please "a deity". The girl, who may or may not have been their daughter, was found in their house with multiple knife wounds. In fairness though, nothing is said connecting this with rain or drought—but also in fairness, we have no more news of the drought after this date. *Times of India* 20 Oct 1979.

Perhaps last year's drought began with an old man in Nairobi. A crowd of thirsty villagers beat up 75-year-old Daniel Mwavuo, accusing him of hiding the missing seasonal rain in his cooking pot. *Pretoria News* (S Africa) 21 June 1979. Compared to the witches and sorcerers of Naples the technique of those Kenyans was both crude and misconceived. It was a case of "See Naples and die!" for a goat and a crow, who were to take the Italians' complaints to the earth spirits Alias, Trilias and Silias. The drought in the area broke the next day! Melbourne, Australia *Age* 29 Aug 1979.

In February 1980 a 68yr-old tantric sadhu, Laxman Singh Giri, was charged, in Bangalore, with the murder of three children, and attacks on others, over five years. The crimes of the old, but not dear, swami came to light when police raided the burial ground at Srirampuram where the sadhu had lived for 27 years. Investigating the murders police noticed they occurred at full moons and supposed the motive was a ritual blood sacrifice to the Goddess Kali, and kept a watch on all burial gounds for unusual activities. The swami's accomplices, two men and a woman, confessed all to the police: the guru would lurk around playgrounds and later point out likely victims to them, commanding them to lure the children with sweets, cut their throats and collect the blood in a bottle. The blood was used in a rite to gain power and immortality. While he was in custody a total eclipse of the sun darkened India [16 Feb —see FT31p32] and the sadhu, who had remained silent through his interrogations, told the female accomplice that he had lost his spiritual powers. From that day he took no food or sleep, and still silent at midnight on 4/5 March died of a sudden heart attack – at least that's what it looked like to doctors. *Indian Express* 6 March; *Times of India* 7 March 1980.

That same February, in Midnapore, West Bengal, police were led to a grisly scene in a riverbank temple after following a pi-dog seen carrying the head of a 6yr-old boy. We have other accounts of children vanishing in India, in which the spectre of human sacrifice looms, but which involve a coincident – or convenient – depredation of children by wild bears and wolves etc. We'll deal with these another time.

The *Guardian* of 6 March 1980, reported the above story in the wider context of child sacrifice in India. Until the end of the last century children were slaughtered every Friday in the temple of Kali at Tanjore – and 'experts' are said to believe that human sacrifice, especially to female deities, is still widespread. Police figures showed about 100 ritual murders a year in India, of which about 80% are reckoned to have been child victims.

The summer of 1979 also saw the trial of Phuko John Kgabi on 11 charges of murder and four of attempted murder in five years. The children were mutilated in a fashion closely resembling the attacks on cattle in the USA in the last 10 years: throats cut, flesh cut from thighs and face, tongues removed and skinned in parts. Kgabi was arrested in November 1978 [see FT28p19f] with a human windpipe in his pocket. The courts at Pretoria eventually sentenced him to death on six counts, and he was hanged on 6 February this year. It was revealed that Kgabi, a former policeman had been impotent, but found himself aroused by the sight of blood during a postmortem; an experience that became an obsession. *Pretoria News* 20 March, 8 & 20 June 1979, 6 Feb 1980; *Rand Daily Mail* 19 June 1979.

Meanwhile, eyes were rollin' down in Rio. Police in Cantagalo, Brazil, had just arrested two men, Waldir de Souza and Maria de Conceicao Pontes, on suspicion of murdering a 2-year-old boy, Antonio Carlos Magalhaes, in a voodoo rite, when word got around, and the next day (22 Oct) lynch mobs howled outside the city jail. The two were accused of helping their boss, Moacir Valente, and another employee, in using the boy's blood to secure the success of a new cement business. However, during custody, they told police of five other child sacrifices and on 24 Oct, before the men could show police the victims' graves, the mob, now 2000 strong, set fire to police cars, overpowered jail guards, beat the two men and tossed them into the burning cars. Now there's two less nuts in Brazil! Vancouver, BC, *The Province* 23 + 27? Oct 1979.

But we would be wrong to single out archaic people only—the disturbing currents of puericide run deep and wild. In Halifax, Yorks, a young father—aged 23, naturally—strangled his 8-month-old son after watching *Psycho* on TV with his wife. *Times* 23 Nov 1979. In South Africa, farmer Obadia Marawa was fined for feeding his 16-year-old daughter only earth for three weeks, to teach her a lesson. *Titbits* 17 Nov 1979. Less lucky was the 2-year-old boy whose mother suffered from Munchausen syndrome—a psychopathic compulsion to fake or exaggerate or invent illnesses. Having exhausted attempts to obtain a variety of hospital treatments for created illnesses, Sheffield Crown Court was told how she stole prescription forms to obtain the drug Turinol with which she deliberately dosed her son to near death, and then reveled in the attention at the hospital. Inevitably her strategy was found out, and luckily the boy survived. She confessed: "But it's not like it seems. I love my son and I wouldn't harm him." *Sun* 11 Nov 1979. Just as tragic but this time fatal were a strict vegetarian couple whose two baby sons died of malnutrition; they were fed only organic vegetables and fruit and a seaweed preparation. The couple were convicted, in New York, of negligent homicide. *S. Telegraph* 9 March 1980. We have to wonder if the deplorable rise in baby battering, along with other assaults on the defenseless young, is part of an emerging trend, or horribly, a symptom of the general madness of our times.

Shocking as all this is, one story caught media attention. On 2nd January neighbours in an apartment block in New York heard chanting and smelled burning from inside an apartment. On investigating, a woman and her mother in the apartment said: "If you want to see the devil burn, come on in." They called the cops. Detectives from the 126th Street station found Patricia Abraham, 26, and her mother, Lucia Abraham, 56, "naked in the place performing some kind of exorcism." Firemen accompanying them found a pile of burning clothes in the bathroom, burning scraps of clothing on the kitchen cooker and pieces of burnt flesh in the oven. In one of the three bedrooms they found Patricia's 20-month-old baby, Leon Justin, with second and third degree burns over 95% of his body. He was surrounded by burning sheets and towels. The girl's mother told the cops: "God told her the baby was possessed... and she was to drive the devil out by fire." Miss Abrahams herself told police that first she threw hot water over the baby, then coated him with oil and put him in the gas oven. Doctors treating him at New York Hospital said the baby had also been starved. Leon Justin died at 8.15pm, 6 Jan 1980. *NY Post* 2 Jan 1980; *Niagara Falls Review* + *The Province* (Vancouver, BC) + *D. Star* + London *Eve. Standard* 3 Jan 1980; *Toronto Sun* 7 Jan 1980;

The toll continues... *Guardian* 17 April 1980 quotes Reuters quotes Tanzanian *Daily News,* that seven market traders have been accused of witchcraft and murder. They abducted a 7yr-old girl, skinned her and cut off her "secret parts" in the belief that they would get rich quick... In Uttar Pradesh, India, five "fanatics" who beheaded a 4yr-old girl in a magic ritual have been charged with murder. *Daily Telegraph* 23 April 1980. On the same page as this report was a note that a Pasadena man had been arrested for cutting off his 8yr-old brother's penis!

[Credits: Greg Axford, Chris Holtzhausen, Jitendra, David Macdams, Valerie Martin, Sam, Has Thomas, Roland Watson, Dwight Whalen, Ion Will, Joe Zarzynski.] **RJMR.**

ELEPHANT CALL

A 10yr-old Indian elephant, called Batyr, has astonished his keepers at Karaganda Zoo, in Soviet Kazakhstan. It began, said Boris Kosinsky, deputy director of the zoo, three years ago, when a night watchman reported the elephant talking to itself. "He just pushes his trunk into his mouth and starts talking. I though it was a joke, but I have since heard Batyr speaking many times, especially when he is in a good mood. His vocabulary is increasing fast." A recording of Batyr – saying "Batyr is good," and using verbs like "drink" and "give" – was recently played on the Kazakh state radio. *D. Telegraph* + *D. Mirror* 9 April 1980.

Three elephants were trapped when their trailer overturned on 28 April, when the Austin Brothers' Circus moved camp from , Bolton to Nelson, in Lancs. They were recovered unharmed and continued on their journey. *D. Telegraph* 29 April 1980.

A white elephant has just been born in Thailand's southern Petchaburi province, and will be presented to King Bhumibol after being "examined by experts" (whatever that means). The faded 'phant, the fourth to be found during the present reign, was instantly hailed as a good omen. *Times* 23 May 1980.

[Credits: Valerie Martin, Nigel Watson.] **RJMR.**

DOUBLE JEOPARDY

Within a few hours two famous motorcyclists faced the same decision about the same part of their battered anatomy. Nigel Boocock (left) captain of Exeter speedway team, and former England captain, severely damaged a little finger during a speedway accident on 26 May. He was given the option of a lengthy treatment to reconstruct the finger or amputation, and because he wants to get back to racing quickly, decided to lose the finger. That same day, ace biker Barry Sheen (right) was advised to lose his own little finger after he crashed during the French Grand Prix at Le Castellet. Sheen decided not to make any decision until he had flown back to England to consult his own doctors. *Daily Telegraph* 27 & 28 May 1980.

PENNIES UNSPENT

We know inflation and crisis has made much of our money worthless, but what is going on? Last summer saw some strange losses of considerable amounts of banknotes. In the first week of July workmen at a sewage works near Stanley, County Durham, found at least £300 worth of torn £5 and £10 notes. It was clear the money had gone down the drain within the previous 24 hours, and police, unable to trace it, said they were waiting to hear about a child who had torn up his father's pay packet and thrown it down the toilet. *Daily Telegraph* 6 July 1979. A few days later a man in Bath, Somerset, found £300 in £5 notes in a rubbish bin in Royal Victoria Park. They too had been torn to pieces. Police checked a list of note numbers and said they were not known to be connected with any theft or loss, and in case the two incidents were linked in some way, the Bath police forwarded information to their counterparts in County Durham. *Bath & West Chronicle* 9 July 1979.

Paul Hanny, a hotel owner in the Italian village of Soldo, was on his way to his bank to pay in 18,000 German marks collected off tourists. But he stopped off at a friend's farm for a glass of cider when the almost unbelievable happened– a cow ate most of his jacket, particularly the bit with the money in! *Guardian* 9 July 1979. Not to be outdone in this caper of crazy cash catastrophes are the Israeli police who had confiscated a big haul of counterfeit US dollars. After its use as evidence such money is usually burned, but something went horribly wrong and £20,000 worth of real banknotes ended up in smoke. *Weekly News* 21 July 1979. Nearer home, crime prevention officer, Sergeant Tony Marchant, in Shropshire, failed to stop his dogs running off with his pay cheque and chewing it to bits. Lucky for him his company replaced it, after a bank refused to accept the bits taped together. *Weekly News* 4 Aug 1979. Less fortunate was butcher Brian Ellis of Eckington, near Sheffield. He was about to set off for his stall in Sheffield's Castle Market and put a bag of about £6,000 cash on the roof of his car while he moved his son's motorbike out of the way. He remembered the bag of money much later, and in back-tracking found only some photographs which he'd placed with the money, but no sign of the cash. *Daily Mail* 14 Aug 1979.

[Credit: John Michell, Ion Will.] **RJMR.**

We would like to provide more of a noticeboard to readers, writers, publishers, conference organizers, expeditions etc, and ask anyone with a public notice to submit it for inclusion here. If we don't know about it, we can't publicize it!

BOOK NEWS

The need has long been felt for a noticeboard for news of books that are being researched, commissioned, or in the pipeline for publication. We kick off the idea with some information known to us right now, but we extend a general invitation to authors and publishers to let us know of their projects and forthcoming publications.

• Guy Lyon Playfair's recommended account of the Enfield poltergeist, *This House is Haunted*, has been bought by Stein & Day for release in the USA.

• We eagerly await the publication of George M Eberhart's massive compilation of 20,000 strange happenings on the North American continent, arranged geographically and with a comprehensive bibliography. *A Geo-Bibliography of Anomalies* will be published by Greenwood Press, Connecticut, and slated at the price of $59.95 – which seems to place it right outside the reach of mortals.

• FT editor, Bob Rickard, and book designer/Fortean Richard Kelly, have just delivered their *Photographs of the Unknown*, to be published by New English Library around October this year. The project's aim was to collect together some classical, some rare and some previously unpublished photographs which allegedly show strange phenomena, some justified, some genuinely mystifying and some known hoaxes (for the reader/viewer's edification). Throughout, the intention was to show the photos as near the original form as possible, in clarity and in colour where possible. Well over 300 photos, at least a third in full colour, deal mainly with monster, UFO, psychic phenomena, mind over matter and strange natural phenomena categories. But, the authors tell us, this has not exhausted the potential, and they would like to attempt a second volume should the publisher's and the buying public's response be encouraging.

• Janet and Colin Bord inform us they are now working on a spin-off from their successful *Alien Animals*, for the same stable Paul Elek/Granada. To be called *A Bigfoot Casebook*, it is scheduled for publication in January 1981.

• According to the *APRO Bulletin* Jan 1980, a book on UFOs by one of their field investigators is to be published in China, by Ocean Publishing Company. The author, Paul Dong, of San Francisco, was invited to explain the subject to the Chinese people by the Science editor of the *Guang Ming Daily*. The book, called *Let's Talk about Flying Saucers* will have an introduction by Coral & Jim Lorenzen.

MONSTER HUNTS

News arrives that the **Loch Ness and Morar Project** will begin their search this year, on 2nd August, by dredging the bottom of Loch Ness for possible animal remains or bones. Sediment dredging was pioneered last year at Loch Morar, and brought up many curiosities from its 1000ft bed, but no monstrous bits. They hope for better luck in the slightly shallower Ness. Project leader Adrian Shine says: "We plan to study the loch scientifically for at least three years, at different times of the year and different times of the day. But a lot depends on our getting sufficient financial support." *Sunday Express* 22 June 1980.

Jeff Watson, rapidly becoming the only contender for the Pan-British Monster Watcher Award, will be devoting his Summer to periods of shore-based watching at the following Scottish locations: Loch Ness, 12 July to 2 August, in Allsigh area; Loch Morar, 2 to 16 August along northern shore from a Morar base; Loch Shiel, 16 to 23 August from Glenfinnan base; then back to Loch Ness, 23 August to 13 September, again in Allsigh area.

FUNDS

The recently established **Fund for UFO Research Inc** – formed in 1979 "to provide a mechanism for channelling money into research projects that will increase scientific knowledge about and public understanding of UFO phenomena" – has just announced its first sponsored project: the publication of Dr Bruce Maccabee's study of the radar-visual sightings over New Zealand in December 1978. Further details, grant proposals and contributions, write to Fund for UFO Research: Box 277, Mount Ranier, MD 20822 USA.

MEETINGS

The International Fortean Organization hold their annual convention, **Fortfest 80,** this year on Saturday/Sunday 9/10 August at the Center for Adult Education, University of Maryland, at University Boulevard and Adelphi Road, College Park in the Washington DC area. Those interested in attending are invited to contact INFO: 7317 Baltimore Ave, College Park, MD 20740 – or phone; they have a number in the book under 'Charles Fort'!

Hardbacks.

EARTH'S SECRET INHABITANTS
By D Scott Rogo & Jerome Clark.
Tempo Books, NY 1979; $1.95, pp218, photos, refs, suggested reading.

You may have a difficult time locating this book. Tempo Books is one of the so-called "Juvenile presses". *Earth's Secret Inhabitants* will, therefore, be placed in some unlikely corner alongside various children's book, but do not let this become an obstacle. Jerome Clark and D. Scott Rogo have written a book worthy of adults interested in the unexplained, as well as more youthful readers.

The authors have taken on quite a chore in their attempt to survey the "earth's secret inhabitants". They include in the world's occult residents all matter of Forteana–specifically UFO's, Bigfoot, Abominable Snowmen, Nessie, Momo, phantom aircraft, alien beings, Kelly's creatures, Dover Demons, Men-In-Black, bat men, thunderbirds, Mattoon's Mad Gasser, Springheel Jack, phantom felines, mystery kangaroos, manimals, trolls, and cattle mutilators. This gallery of creatures and fellow-travellers meanders in and out of the various chapters of the book, often rubbing shoulders, for example, as in the passages about the mysterious animal killings, UFO visitations, phantom helicopter reports and monster sightings focused in Montana in 1975-1976.

This phantasmagoric approach by its very nature makes for a few shortcomings. Ivan Sanderson's work on the Himalayan yeti, and David Fideler and my examinations of the new mystery kangaroos were both reduced to only a few paragraphs. They have repeated the incorrect version of the Mike Busby story which I investigated. The black panther Bubsy wrestled did not walk on its hind feet. Such items are rare in this book, however.

A well-read Fortean will recognize the threads of old Clark, Coleman, Keel, Rickard, Fideler, Steiger and Fort data in the *Earth's Secret Inhabitants,* but Rogo and Clarks's new collection and examination of the stories is refreshing. As a secondary gain, the book can serve as a handy, ready reference guide for the casual and dedicated researcher to cases henceforth found only in out-of-print books, hard-to-obtain journals, scarce speciality magazines, and lightly attended lectures.

The Tempo editors must have had a field day with all of these Fortean cases. Because of the supposed juvenile readership of *Earth's Secret Inhabitants*, the definitions, expansions, and qualifications of specific words and phrases may appear to be cumbersome, but frankly, they are entertaining. Of course, most people know "The Pacific Northwest" does "consist of California, Oregon, Washington and parts of Canada" (p5) and sulfur "smells like rotten eggs" (p182) but by the time you are through with this book the editors and/or authors apparently wanted to make certain you knew "paraphysical" means "beyond being physical" (pages 10 and 27) or "only temporarily real" (page 29).

Discussing the origin of the name "Springheel Jack" – some felt the gasser had springs on his shoes – someone just could not resist throwing in this warning: "By the way, don't try this trick. It doesn't work, and you'll probably just break your ankles if you try it." (p105) The book's phantom parenthesizer may be trying to get a free weekend trip to Point Pleasant, West Virginia, a la Steve Martin, with this description: "That's one of those sleepy little towns where teenagers drag-race backward down Main Street on Saturday night when there isn't anything better to do." (p88) or to Dover, Massachusetts, where the Dover Demon is said to have lurked around because "it probably couldn't afford a good hotel". (page 182)

Someone has had a delightful time thinking up these gems, and readers should enjoy the ease with which this book can be read.

If the above asides are the desserts in this book, certainly the meat of *Earth's Secret Inhabitants* lies in the last chapter, "Intermediate Reality". Obviously, Rogo and Clark have changed and expanded their thinking since the mid1970's. They observe: "It is interesting to note that before collaborating on the present book, both of us had independently written books supporting a 'thought-form' sort of theory to account for UFOs and monsters• Both of us agreed at that time that an inter-relationship existed between UFOs and monsters, that somehow these phantoms are connected to our planet and to our minds, and that they might represent thought projections which had taken on a physical reality. However, it is high time that we start seriously considering the possibility that earth's secret inhabitants represent a mystery much greater than either of us had ever dreamed a few years ago". (pp196-7) that's certainly not juvenile fare.

Rejecting David-Neel's *tulpa* and Tyrrell's "idea-patterns", Clark and Rogo feel now that "UFOs, monsters and the like ....represent visitors to our world from some parallel dimension or universe." (p 196) The "window" phenomenon, they state, is a reflection of a rip in the fabric of time and space in "which all sorts of inhabitants from *that* world have entered into our own for a limited time span." (p 196)

Commenting on the notion that thought-forms would be expected to be more conventional, the authors view the creatures as "odd caricatures of the types of life-forms that populate the earth....these creatures represent the outcome of some evolutionary process paralleling life on this planet, but not exactly corresponding to it." (p 197)

Moving on, Clark and Rogo suggest another possible explanation – *The Phenomenon*, an ultimate source of intelligence which projects images outside or triggers projections inside the human mind. "Perhaps *The Phenomenon* is a medium through which these 'imaginary' entities and forces can become briefly 'real' under certain circumstances." (p 201)

"Perhaps the phantom-like monsters that freely roam our country are para-physical projections which reflect our concern about our increasing aleination from nature." Page 202)

D. Scott Rogo and Jerome Clark may be making a few mistakes in their growing insights which move them to reject "thought-forms" as a source of the creatures and their friends. First, they too narrowly restrict "forms " to those creations of our minds. The vast collective unconscious would make mince meat of a *tulpa*, and may have a life unto its own. Massive solidifying psychic projections from a grand collective unconscious may produce extremely unconventional monsterous forms whose archetypal morphs are clouded in the psyche of generations. Jung rejected the idea that telepathic images and arche-types would be clear cut. Oddly, the authors feel the glowing large eyes of ufonauts and creatures reflect a parallel universe of darkness. In overlooking the symbolic nature and meaning of this hint, they instead create an extremely "nuts and bolts", parallelistic, biological argument based on a very *earthy* bias. The arena of Forteana has room for a variety of explanations, all of which probably do play a part. The authors' ideas have much merit, and the process in the growth of their thoughts is interesting. However, the zoological *and* Jungian answers need not be forgotten or sacked to accomodate their new ideas. Some Pleistocene animals probably still prowl the Nearctic. And a few ghostly archetypes probably remain near the bedeviled places they call home. A tear in the collective unconscious may wreak havoc as surely as a window into the time-space continuum.

Clark and Rogo tell us it "doesn't really matter" whether the earth's secret residents "are inhabitants of some otherworldly dimension, thought-forms, cosmic projections, or even visitors from outer space". (p203)

Perhaps not, but certainly the authors have put a good deal of thinking behind the theories they support. If you wish to discover what they think is really important about the *Earth's Secret Inhabitants* and what we should be watching, read the book. It's a worthwhile trek into the unknown.

Loren Coleman

• See *The Haunted Universe* (New York, Signet, 1977) by D. Scott Rogo and *Creatures of the Outer Edge* (New York, Warner, 1978) by Jerome Clark and Loren Coleman.

THIS HOUSE IS HAUNTED

by Guy Lyon Playfair
Souvenir Press, 1980; £6.95, pp288, photos.

This reviewer has frequently harboured the suspicion that poltergeist cases encapsulate all the baffling enigmas that can possibly haunt the boundary between the known and the Unknown, and that once we start asking the right questions of such events the answers may well illuminate every wart and wrinkle of our existence. The more I read about poltergeists the less seems my understanding of the complexity we call 'everyday reality'. The more I have to qualify my statements about these taunting haunts, the more they seem to be special cases in which the usual protocols of our concensus reality are suspended or rearranged—but only temporarily, thank God! Poltergeists, then, provide much food for Fortean thought.

A perusal of Michael Goss' valuable bibliography of poltergeist literature (reviewed in FT 30p56) reveals that writings that actually contribute towards our understanding are very few and far between, disregarding facile media reportage and sensationalist books. The most useful books are either reports of contemporary laboratory research, or collections of summarised anecdotes, or analyses of same (e.g. *Poltergeists* by Gauld and Cornell, reviewed last issue). The subject has cried out for a book-length, up-to-date, on-the-spot, painstaking report by informed and informative investigators. I am very pleased to say that in this wholeheartedly recommended book we have one at last.

This case began in Enfield, London, on 31 August 1977,

and was featured frequently in the papers, on radio and TV. Guy Playfair, and SPR investigator Maurice Grosse, stayed with the case for months at a time during those years, and this is literally a "thud-by-crash" account drawn from miles of tape recordings (i.e. when the polt in question wasn't jinxing the recorder). Playfair has scrupulously avoided the artificial use of journalistic devices to pace and dress up the 'plot' for *Exorcist*-jaded readers after thrills. This latter practice is a cheap publishing trick, deplorably common nowadays, and has regrettably ruined several good case studies. Every conversation and incident in the Enfield account has been reconstructed from case records. The result, however true to the random unplotted plod of real-life, and whatever its literary merit, makes this book one of the most valuable documents for anyone with the slightest interest in the paranormal today, and earns my fullest endorsement.

The family involved–the Harpers (despite the use of real names in news reports, Playfair prefers to use pseudonyms to avoid further embarassment to the people involved)–consisted of a divorced mother and her two sons and daughters. The phenomenon centered on the two girls, Rose, 13, and particularly Janet, 11. A partial listing of manifestations includes: bangs on walls, fires, apparitions, moving and flying objects, overturned furniture, spoon-bending, flows of water, falls of coins, invisible assailants, apports, equipment malfunctions, doors opening and closing, strange sounds, a powerful force which would lift and hurl the children through the air, and the possible astral-projection of Janet into the house next door.

One of the weirdest aspects of the case was the abnormally loud gruff voice, coarse in tone and language, which emanated from the space near Janet. Normal ventriloquism was ruled out because the voice was heard during meals while Janet's mouth was full, and while it was taped up by Playfair or Grosse. The account is positively hair-raising at times, and one can only admire the courage and persistence of the researchers. Stage ventriloquists could not imitate the loudness of the voice, nor its complete difference from Janet's normal voice, and could not believe that a young girl could sustain such a voice (even if she could produce one) through conversations lasting up to half an hour. Yet the voice was definitely associated with Janet –sometimes 'slipping up', so that Janet said normally something the Voice meant to say, and vice versa–but never the two voices together.

Such observations added to the psychological dimensions of the case, which had all the hall-marks of a classical multiple-personality-type syndrome. The family certainly had their problems–one psychologist, Carl Sargent, was quoted in the *Daily Mirror* 31 March 1978, saying: "There's no father at home, the mother suffers from epilepsy and several of the children are disturbed." Dammit–I'd be disturbed if such things went on in my home! Here is a complex psychological situation indeed, and Playfair delineates it very well without allowing his own spiritualistic leanings to confuse the issues further. One certainly gets the impression of a *folie-à-trois* in which the two girls and younger boy unconsciously fuel each other's nervous excitement. Perhaps that nuclear group extends to the whole family because we see the ways the mother's beliefs and reactions affected the phenomena, and later on there is a suggestion that the boy was the new focus of almost identical phenomena, which fortunately for all did not persist. The communal anxiety was also influenced by the constant presence and disturbance of the investigation itself; as Playfair is the first to acknowledge, the experimenter-effect was rife in this case.

In 1978 Janet spent some time recuperating at the Maudsley Hospital. She was found normal on all counts–not even a trace of the seizures in which it took four men to hold her with great difficulty. She was allowed home, looking fitter than she had for a few years and gradually the disturbances petered out in 1979. The whole case seemed to have built up towards her first menstrual period, after which the intensity of the phenomena faded slowly.

There is no doubt, either, that the children relished being the centers of attention, and in various childish ways would attempt to prolong or revive that attention. To Grosse and Playfair, many of the ploys were quite transparent, and they coped with them as they got on with the real task of investigating the genuine events–however many visiting investigators would see no further than what they interpreted as obvious hoaxing by the children. This was presumably the verdict that they had decided upon beforehand, anyway! But as you read the book, I hope you will find, as I did, that Playfair has honestly presented the facts–sometimes from several points of view. I must agree with Playfair and Grosse that neither minor and often unjustified suspicions of childish craftiness, nor dogmatic appeals to psychological aberrations, explain away the central fact of paraphysical events seen with objective eyes and recorded by automatic equipment. Which brings me to the photographs, most of them taken by news photographer Graham Morris, one of the few people who visited the house regularly during the period of the disturbance. Morris was eager to get that definitive photo of a polt in action, and by the end of the case thought he had failed. But his persistence paid off. Grosse, in examining some of the many colour films taken on automatic cameras which could be triggered by sound, discovered that the camera had caught a mysterious double event; curtains billowing and twisting at a firmly closed window, while below it, Janet's bedclothes seem to be climbing the wall.

There are many other photos which add yet another important dimension to the book. Having just completed a period of intensive research for a forthcoming Fortean picture-book of my own, I can assure you that photos of polts in action are very rare indeed. Imagine the value then of clear photos of some of these incidents: flying toy bricks, the remains of fires, the bent spoons, moving bedclothes, pillows flying through the air, overturned furniture, the two girls wrenched from bed and flung to the floor. For me the most fascinating photo of all shows Janet in a stupor lying on top of a radio when she had just been put to bed and injected with Valium. This might be the nearest we'll get to a photo of teleportation!

Playfair writes very clearly, and with obvious compassion for the plight of this family, tortured by events beyond their comprehension. It is a thoroughly commendable effort, providing us with a unique record of a poltergeist, which, I'm sure, will stimulate analysis and debate for years to come.

Bob Rickard

ALIEN ANIMALS
By Janet & Colin Bord.
Paul Elek/Granada 1980; £7.95, pp258, photos, refs, bib, index.

Any book from the Bords is an event worthy of Fortean attention, and in this, their best book yet for Forteans, they have done us proud. It is very well illustrated – many from the Fortean Picture Library – and summarizes the Bords thoughts on mystery animal phenomena based on their accumulation over many years of stories from books, newspapers and personal correspondence with both witnesses and investigators.

The authors divide their subject matter into the primary and obvious categories of lake monsters, 'Cats that can't be caught', black dogs, giant birds and birdmen, and the Bigfoot-type creatures conveniently labelled 'Manimals'. At the same time they acknowledge the limitation of dealing with the subject generally by categories, which leave many 'unclassified' accounts, as well as those which bridge categories. The Bords are among our most thorough and eclectic writers, drawing on additional sources from the literature of paranormal phenomena, UFOs, earth mysteries and from their extensive knowledge of folklore.

What results is the most fascinating compendium of mystery animal and monster data of recent times, whose main attraction must be the wealth of modern accounts. The authors are not content to rest their case on the presentation of tired old historical accounts, except to briefly sketch the history of regional sightings or the antiquity of belief in certain kinds of animals.

And therein lies a leading question: if they've been around for a long time, why haven't they been discovered before? The answer, according to the evidence, is simple and in several parts. They *have* been seen before; the accounts being progressively shunted into the realm of folklore, or discredited as the fabrications of the ignorant, the superstitious, the gullible, and the idiotic or inebriated, or simply the products of misinterpretation and misinformation. This is as true now of sightings of the 'Surrey Puma' or Nessie, as it was of dragons or unicorns or Wildmen. It is easy to dismiss individual testimony, case by case, so that ultimately nothing is left but the establishment's view of a silly hallucinating public. But books like *Alien Animals* make a formidable and impassioned plea for viewing the subjects in as much breadth and depth as possible, so that the cumulative evidence of different peoples from different countries and different times becomes a body of data that naturalists ignore at their peril. It cries out to be accounted for, if not in their scheme of things, then in one built on the view that the sum of human knowledge does not equal the Universe.

If we accept – tentatively – the data presented, we must then ask where is the hard evidence? Where are the bones and bodies? Where are the remains of kills and lairs? Where are the live specimens to be found and how can they be trapped or studied? The Bords dwell on these questions in their last chapter, and admit the difficulty and, indeed, inadvisability of developing one all-encompassing explanation. Instead they take us on a guided tour of some possibilities – familiar to hardened Forteans, but quite probably startling to newcomers. Many witnesses have observed that the AAs were cat-like, dog-like, ape-like etc, but obviously not cats, dogs or apes etc – could they be were-animals? Several disturbing stories are related that support the idea. A strong connexion is noted between AA appearances and ancient sites, and the Bords outline the hypothesis of 'earth energy'. Many AAs both appear and behave as phantoms, an idea which in turn spawns several possibilities; that they are the spirits of dead animals from past ages; or that they materialize here from elsewhere or other realms of existence. The idea is explored that real animals are coming and going by teleportation. The ancient idea of a *genius loci* is revived in the notion that archetypal images in the human mind, perhaps even planetary mind, may physically materialize in response to forces we cannot even begin to guess at. These forms, solid one moment and ghost-like the next, are named 'tulpas', after the Tibetan tradition that tulpoid forms can be created by the power of the mind.

The authors know that

more questions are raised by their data than they can answer. Their own suspicion is that "many alien animals are non-physical, in some way linked to the witness, and needing a suitable energy source to help them materialize and to sustain them." They add in conclusion: "The only thing of which we can be completely sure, however, is that alien animals are appearing in their hundreds, even in their thousands, all over the world." The book, therefore, makes the best introduction yet to Fortean zoology. For beginners, the Bords write clearly and with unobrtusive explanatory detail; for the researcher, they include unobtrusive explanatory detail; for the researcher, they include a detailed list of references and a functional index. Highly recommended.

Bob Rickard.

MONSTERS AND MYSTERIES
by H.T. Wilkins
James Pike Ltd, Consols House, St Ives, Cornwall, 1973; £1.50 hb, pp154.

The late, prolific author Harold T. Wilkins is best known for his books on UFOs, South American mysteries, and Forteana in general. Your editor has recently discovered a 'new' collection of data compiled by Wilkins, but was unable to discover its origins beyond the fact that the UK publisher bought the copyright from the US in about 1969. The book consists of short sections a page or so long, each headed boldly, e.g., "Dinosaur Tracks Found Near Painted Desert" or "Tree Worship Blocks Road Construction in Papua". The subjects covered range far and wide, and include sea serpents, the Loch Ness Monster and others, old South American civilizations, Atlantis, unicorns and other extinct/mythical creatures, ape men, a man-eating tree and other unusual plants, the *Mary Celeste* (25 pages; some of this material repeats Wilkins' earlier *Mysteries: Solved and Unsolved*).

This book, a hardback, has an unattractive, utilitarian appearance, but it's also very cheap! It contains no index, nor any indication of sources, and many of the tales are only hearsay. But nevertheless it is an intruiguing collection of Fortean bits and pieces.

Janet Bord

UFO PHENOMENA AND THE BEHAVIOURAL SCIENTIST.
Edited by Dr Richard F. Haines.
The Scarecrow Press, Metuchen, N.J., 1979, $18.50; Bailey Bros. & Swinfen Limited, Warner House, Folkestone, Kent, 1980, £12.95, hb, pp450, references, illustrations.

After 30 years of UFO books that have been too often sensationalist in nature, a new type of book is now appearing—the serious study. This is a classic example. Its content also indicates a shift of interest away from the thing seen to the seer, and a growing realisation that many psychological factors can influence what people see or say they have seen. Edited by scientist Dr. Richard F. Haines, the book consists of 12 essays by different contributors such as Ronald Westrum, Berthold Eric Schwarz, Michael Persinger and R. Leo Sprinkle. The longest contribution is Sprinkle's investigation of the Carl Higdon case (Wyoming, Oct. 1974) with full transcripts of the interviews. But this is the only case study. The other chapters tackle such worthy subjects as "The Zeitgeist of the UFO Phenomenon", "UFO Reporting Dynamics", "Limitations of Human Verbal Behaviour in the Context of UFO-Related Stimuli" and "What Do UFO Drawings by Alleged Eye-witnesses and Non-Eyewitnesses Have in Common?" Scientists, sociologists and other researchers are not necessarily good writers, and some of the chapters are a little heavy-going. Also the value of some of the contributions to UFO research is debatable. But it cannot be denied that the UFO witness is far more important than has hitherto been generally realised, and it is good to see a book that gets down to finding out how UFO witnesses tick. The UFO researcher who feels that "the answer" is just around the corner will find this book depressing reading. It shows clearly that extreme caution is needed when handling UFO data, and that the material we do have rarely reaches a high standard.

Janet Bord

GUARDIANS OF THE UNIVERSE
by Ronald Story
270pp, illus, ref, index. New English Library £5.95

Some time ago *Fortean Times* launched the Fortean Corrigenda column in an effort to get rid of erroneous and downright fraudulent material which bogs down the serious student and generally confuses the issue for all concerned. Several authors have, albeit unknowingly perhaps, followed in *Fortean Times'* wake, among them Lawrence Kushe with *The Bermuda Triangle Mystery—Solved* and Ronald Story with his excellent examination of von Daniken's ancient astronaut hypothesis, *The Space-Gods Revealed*. Now Story has a new book in which he takes a closer look at some of the so-called 'evidence'—the Tungus ka meteorite, archaeological evidence, ancient tales like the *Epic of Gilgamesh*, and the hitherto largely unchallenged Sirius mystery. And, perhaps needless to say, the facts do not support the Danikenites' wonderful theory.

Story is objective, very objective. He bends over backwards to give Daniken's material a fair chance, but the facts speak for themselves. This is a book to buy if you have the money to spare, for even though Daniken's ideas have been blown apart, June will see his new book, *Signs of the Gods*, accompanied by an author promotion tour, and no doubt its entry into the best sellers, so seekers after truth and honesty like Ronald Story need your support. *Paul Begg*

THE ANCIENT STONES SPEAK: A Journey to the World's Most Mysterious Megalithic Sites
By David D Zink.
EP Dutton, NY 1979; $9.95, pp202.

Forteans are well aware of the lithic aberrations that stand singly or in intricately fitted arrangements as a silent witness to forgotten civilizations, that long ago engineered the planet for purposes ill understood. But they, too, are confronted with the same questions now being acknowledged by conventional archaeologists: By whom were these megalithic complexes erected? How? Why?

Those questions, too long ignored by a Bronofskian methodology that has no room for "primitive" culture capable of moving 340-ton blocks and erecting 70-foot monoliths into vast astronomical observatories, are addressed in this book. Through a lively and well-researched text, site plans, large-format photographs, and *messages from the stones themselves*, 25 of the world's most enigmatic megalithic sites reveal their stories.

While orthodox archaeologists ponder the discoveries of Thom and others about a knowledgeable and sophisticated society where none was supposed to be, Zink plunges ahead with the next giant step the rest of the archaeological community will one day have to take. Believing that "the next revolution in archaeology will involve the use of psychic data both in the field and in theorising about field results." Zink incorporates the perceptions of psychics' altered states of consciousness to suggest a new paradigm for mankind's evolution. The results are more heretical to prehistory than the premise that standing stones in the Orkneys and eastern Africa served as markstones of celestial mechanics, a fact now grudgingly admitted but unexplained by embarrassed analyzers of potsherds and flint scrapers.

The psychic impressions from the Ancient Stones are not incompatible with several recent discoveries in archaeology and geology, and furthermore touch significantly on the rediscoveries of ley lines and terrestrial-cosmic interfacings. In fact, Zink's approach suggests many new areas of inquiry based on "a worldwide engineering instinct" among ancient cultures in tune with subtle earth energies that influence a variety of physical and consciousness phenomena.

Concludes Zink: these Ancient stones "can stir up in us a healthy sense of wonder at our past, a sense of perspective on our present, and a sense of hope for our future." And so does this book. *Larry E Arnold*

MEGALITHS AND THEIR MYSTERIES. The Standing Stones of Old Europe
by Alastair Service & Jean Bradbery
Weidenfeld & Nicolson 1979; £10 hb, pp284, index, bib, maps, photos.

As the authors state in their Preface, most general books on megalithic sites concentrate on Britain and Brittany. They therefore set out to produce an illustrated guide to the megalithic sites of western Europe, and this handy sized book (8" x 5") describes and illustrates sites in France, Italy, Spain, Portugal, Malta, Sardinia, Corsica, the Balearic Islands, Belgium, the Netherlands, Germany and Denmark, as well as Britain and Ireland. Information is also given on the peoples who built the sites— their daily lives, clothing, houses, and the uses to which they put the sites. Astronomical facts and theories are presented, and mention is made of dowsing, leys, rock-carvings, and festivals. The 100+ photographs are attractive, and there are also 40 maps and plans. The text is readable and informative, and this is a book which should accompany all travellers intending to visit the countries described and with time to spare for seeking out the ancient sites. It is to be hoped that it will soon be made available to the impoverished hitch-hiking megaliths addict in a cheaper paperback edition.

Janet Bord

GLASTONBURY
By Michael Mathias & Dereck Hector.
David & Charles 1979; £3.50, pp48, photos.

STONEHENGE AND ITS MYSTERIES
By Michael Balfour.
MacDonald & Janes 1979; £6.95, pp189, bib, photos, illos.

We are seeing more and more glossy productions aimed at the general public on the theme of the mysteries of the past. *Glastonbury* and *Stonehenge and its Mysteries* are two superior versions. Neither book attempts to cover new ground, instead they both succeed in summarising their subjects and evoking the mystery and attraction that surrounds them. Dereck Hector's clear black and white photos evoke the different moods of Glastonbury very well. Michael Balfour, in *Stonehenge*, attempts a longer, more detailed description of his subject, giving equal weight to different workers in this field. It is well illustrated. It is obvious that much work has gone into the production of both these books. Long may they adorn the coffee-tables of the land. *Valerie Thomas*

IN SEARCH OF ANCIENT ASTRONOMIES
Edited by EC Krupp.
Chatto & Windus 1979; £8.95, pp279, photos, illos.

The best description of this book is provided by the editor, himself. In his introduction he states "This book is the first attempt to present systematically to the general reader the main results of archaeoastronomy to date." Dr Krupp succeeds admirably in this aim. The book includes chapters by specialists in this field; Alexander Thom and AS Thom,

John Eddy and Anthony Aveni. The chapters dealing with North American and Meso American archaeo-astronomies are very welcome to the British reader more familiar with Professor Thom's work in North Europe. A useful chapter on basic astronomy is also included. In the final chapter Dr Krupp deals with his objections to "non-scientific" theories of archaeo-astronomy. Unfortunately he lumps together Velikovsky, Von Daniken, Watkins and Michel in the same category of "astronomical fantasies". Here he takes a familiar stance based on a mixture of reasonable objections, emotion and prejudice. Surely he realises that until recently the very subject matter of his book would have been regarded as fanciful speculation. The investigation of today's vision usually provides tomorrow's orthodoxy. Apart from this quibble this is a stimulating and useful book which is strongly recommended to everyone concerned with the mysteries of the past.

Valerie Thomas

THE NEW SOVIET PSYCHIC DISCOVERIES
A First Hand Report by Henry Gris & William Dick.
Souvenir Press 1979; £5.50, pp304, index, photos.

Continuing the work begun by Ostrander and Schroeder, this book covers recent Russian research on Psi-powers and Kirlian photography, with chapters on exceptional psychic individuals, such as Boris Ermolaev, Russia's answer to Uri Geller, and master telepath Tofik Dadashev, successor to Wolf Messing. There's also good meaty sections of Russian Ufology and *Almasty*, the Bigfoot of the Caucasus–not to mention the "missing planet" Phaeton, the Tunguska event, hypnotherapy techniques and eyeless sight. A bibliography would have made it more valuable–at least for Russian readers!

Paul Sieveking

THE RELIGIONS OF TIBET
By G Tucci.
Routledge & Kegan Paul 1980; £8.95, pp340, notes, bib, chron. table, index.

For almost 80 years, anyone needing information on the religions or culture of Tibet would probably have referred to a single work. *Lamaism – the Buddhism of Tibet* by A. Waddell is a chaotic compendium of misinformation and malice written with all the authority of one who never visited a country but nonetheless was determined to demonstrate that it was inhabited by superstitious savages.

Now, praise to the Triple Gem, here is the book which Waddell should have written. Scholarly, detailed and systematic, with an exhaustive index it is a treasure-house of informed fact. Unfortunately it seems to have suffered in the translation from German and Italian and is almost impossible to read. Perhaps I am slighting the translator unduly and the fault is Tucci's but the dense academic style in which this book is written means that it is for only the most dedicated Tibetophile or those in the terminal stages of insomnia.

Mike Crowley

Paperbacks.

DOWSING. Techniques and Applications
by Tom Graves
Mayflower 1980; £1.25 pb, pp190, bib, drawings.

This informative book, which must already have proved its worth to both experienced and would-be dowsers in its earlier edition, has now been issued as a mass-market paperback. It radiates enthusiasm, and tells you all you need to know about the 'how' of dowsing. There is also information on its applications in the fields of water-divining, finding lost objects and people, agriculture, medicine, archaeology and others. Tom Graves is of course a practising dowser, and his book illustrates a fact of which more authors should be aware: that the best books are those which grow from an author's total involvement in his subject.

Janet Bord

THE OLD STONES OF LAND'S END. An Enquiry into the Mysteries of the Megalithic Science
by John Michell
Pentacle Books, 6 Perry Road, Bristol 1, 1979, pb price unknown, pp96, bib, maps, engravings, photos.

This is a very welcome reissue of a book which was first published in 1974. In it, earth mysteries pioneer John Michell presents the results of his survey of the south-western tip of England, an area rich in ancient stones. Owners of the 1974 hardback edition will wish to know what changes have been made. The author has provided a new, 4-page introduction (with an unfortunate printer's error involving the repetition of 14 lines on the last page) which explains the object of the book (to ascertain whether it is true that megalithic monuments were laid out in straight lines) and describes developments which have taken place since it was first published. The essay "Megalithic Science" has been brought forward from the end of the book so that it now, sensibly, precedes the Land's End survey. The layout of the survey (which consists of site descriptions, plans, engravings and photographs) has been tightened, which is an improvement, but the poor-quality photographs which I so disliked when I first saw the book still remain. Often unsharp and always murky, they completely fail to convey the atmosphere of the area. They are also no complement to John Michell's exciting and convincing text. The book ends with a bibliography and addenda listing extra stones. The index has been omitted, but such a book as this does not really need one.

If you are interested in leys and British mysteries and don't already have this important book, then do not miss this second chance to obtain it.
Janet Bord

THE MAGIC ZOO
By Peter Costello.
Sphere 1979; £2.25, pp222, photos, drgs, bib, index.

Subtitled 'The Natural History of Fabulous Animals', this work follows Costello's successful *In Search of Lake Monsters,* and will undoubtedly be installed in the Fortean's library, where it compares favourably with Willy Ley's *Exotic Zoology.* Costello has assembled from an impressive variety of sources the essential information about minotaurs, mermaids, centaurs, sirens, satyrs, the phoenix and the roc, giant ants, the unicorn, the manticora, Leviathan and Behemoth, dragons, basilisks, salamanders, Barnacle Geese and Vegetable Lambs, and others. His erudition – he acknowledges a large debt to Dr Heuvelmans – is rendered unobtrusive by his clear writing style. There are additional essays on the mythological roles of animals in the archaic mind, the works of the early naturalists and compilers of bestiaries, and the Fortean "Science of Unknown Animals" or cryptozoology as it has become known. The extended bibiography, by subject, is almost worth the price of the book alone.

I wholeheartedly recommend Costello's *Magic Zoo*, knowing it will give just as much pleasure to the scholars among you as it will to the non-Fortean interested in mythical animals and the curiosity they have aroused through the ages.
RJMR.

ISLAM
By Muhammad Zafrulla Khan.
Routledge & Kegan Paul 1980; £3.50, pp216, index, bib.
Here, in a book remarkably easy to read, is a clear exposition of the origins and history of Islam, and a collection of essays on the Islamic view of topics central to a modern opinion: morality, spirituality, social and economic affairs, international relations during peace and war. Other chapters deal with the conduct and duties of the Muslim. Still others expound the Islamic conception of God, Man and his place in the Universe, Revelation, and Life after Death.

The early chapters form the most succinct and erudite biography of the Prophet Muhammad I have encountered. It is rigorously straightforward emphasising only the mystical nature of Muhammad's revelation, avoiding the usual embroidery of myth, magic and miracles. Muhammad himself declared he had no supernatural powers.

The approach is dogmatic, of course, but eloquent, and there is no denying the scholarship of the author. For one who knows nothing of Islam, and would like to, like me, there can be no better place to begin.
RJMR.

MUSLIM SAINTS AND MYSTICS
By Farid al-Din Attar. Trans: AJ Arberry.
Routledge & Kegan Paul 1979, £2.50, pp287, bib notes.

This is an abridged translation of *Memorial of the Saints* written in the early 13th Century by the Persian Sufi Attar, better known for his *Bird-Parliment,* a moving allegory of the soul's quest for God. Arberry has selected 38 of Attar's 75 portraits, with material from additional sources to give a picture of each Saint in the form of a simple biography and bibliography, followed by anecdotes about the character and his teachings. These often involve miracles and are most illuminating to students of the paranormal. But as with most Sufi teachings, nothing is what it seems, and the intention of the mythologising is more symbolic than to titillate with magic. The tales bubble with alchemy, beautifully simple and simply beautiful, and can be enjoyed with delight without critically penetrating their mysticism.
RJMR.

THE HOUSE OF LORDS UFO DEBATE
Preface by Lord Clancarty; notes by John Michell.
open Head Press/Pentacle Books 1979,1980; £2.95, pp118, illos, photos.

This record of the famous UFO debate in the House of Lords in January 1979 is rapidly becoming a *genre* classic, being the authorized. record of an event, not simply of interest to those interested in the enigma of UFOs, but unique in the House's 700 year history. Lord Clancarty, perhaps known to a wider public as the UFO author Brinsley le Poer Trench, adds a preface describing the origins of his interest in the subject and his Motion for the debate. In an afterword, Lord Clancarty outlines the response to the debate, including the formation of a House of Lords All Party UFO Study Group.

John Michell, himself the author of a large number of seminal books in the UFO, Fortean and Earth Mysteries fields, has annotated the debate with explanatory notes and brief biographies of the major debaters. The publishers have added a number of photos and illustrations to make the presentation attractive.

I fully applaude the initiative of Open Head and Pentacle in putting this event on record in such an interesting and worthwhile way. Their book, already in its second printing and with a wittier cover, deserves to be in circulation for a long time to come. If you have difficulty finding the book in your shops it is available by mail order – please see the back cover of this issue.
RJMR.

WORTHWHILE PAPERBACK EDITIONS:

The Probability of the Impossible: Valuable encyclopedic review of current research into bioenergies, Astral travel and Psi, by Thelma Moss *(Paladin 1979; £2.50, pp383, index, bib, photos.)*

The Wolf Children: Charles Mcclean's study of the feral children of India *(Penguin 1979; £1.25, pp, index, notes, bib,*

Life Cloud: The now famous exposition of Fred Hoyle and NC Wickramasinghe, of the origin of life on earth in a comet crash, 4 billion years ago, which brought with it biochemicals–the seeds of all our life forms. Eminently readable with stiff patches of science. *(Sphere 1979; £1.25, pp191 index, photos.)*

A Young Person's Guide to UFOs: A competent, slim history of UFO research by Brian Ball. An unfortunate tendency to print "UFO's", is compensated, in my view, by an acknowledgement of Fort's role in prefiguring the modern UFO era *(Dragon 1979; 60p, pp96, bib, photos.)*

Reprints of three of Velikovski's 'Ages in Chaos' series by Abacus, essential reading for all interested in the catastrophic history of this planet and the revision of historical 'errors'. **AGES IN CHAOS** *(£1.75, pp 363, maps. photos, index)*. **RAMESES II AND HIS TIME** *(£1.95, pp288, maps, photos, chronology, index)*. **PEOPLES OF THE SEA** *(£1.95, pp267, photos, index)*.

Two books from the prolific John Gribbin. **OUR CHANGING PLANET** *(Sphere, 95p, pp181, diags, bib, index)* is a useful review of geophysical knowledge in the light of latest advances. Included, are chapters on the formation of the planet and its interior forces, continental drift, great fault and earthquake-prone areas, ice ages, speculation about other planets, and a potted history of geophysics and its pioneers. **FUTURE WORLDS** *(Sphere, £1.75, pp225, diags, bib, index)* a much-needed clearly-written guide to the complex theories and arguments about the future of our planet and cultures, and the social, political, economic and physical parameters of growth and decay.

DOWSING: ONE MAN'S WAY by J Scott Elliot *(Sphere, £1.50, pp159, diags, photos)*. A simple review of the history and major techniques of dowsing, by an ex-president of the British Society of Dowsers, with sections on applications and examples.

THE MANNA MACHINE by Gordon Sassoon and Rodney Dale *(Panther, £1.25, pp282, diags, refs, bib, index)*. The basis thesis – that the Hebrews' Ark of the Covenant, or 'Ancient of Days', was in fact an atomic powered pressure-cooker for algae – has been snapped up by the Von Daniken brigade as evidence of extraterrestrial intervention. Even more fascinating is the enigma of Rodney Dale, who authored the hilarious *Tumour in the Whale*, a book of tall stories, and at the other extreme, with Sassoon, wrote a learned book on decoding the Kabbalah. I can't help feeling that the first appearance of the manna machine idea as an article in *New Scientist* on April Fool's Day 1978 is some kind of clue . . . but to what, since their scholarship is genuine?

THE SAVAGE GOD by Al Alvarez *(Penguin £1.20, pp320, index, notes)* compassionate and scholarly study of suicide and the bizarre behaviour leading up to it.

CASTASTROPHE THEORY by A. Woodcock & M. Davis *(Pelican, £1.25, pp171, diags, bib, index)* a valuable layman's guide to the new science of sudden change.

INSTRUMENTS OF DARKNESS by Alfred Price *(Panther, £1.95, pp333, diags, photos, index)* an excellent history of electronic warfare, and acclaimed by the Royal Aeronautical Society as the standard reference on the subject.

THE FIRST THREE MINUTES by Steven Weinberg *(Bantam, NY, $2.50, pp177, diags, bib, index)* a layman's guide to current thinking about the origin of the universe. **THE RED LIMIT** by Timothy Ferris *(Bantam, NY, $2.25, pp204, photos, bib, index)* a layman's guide to current cosmological thinking, including the end of the universe. **THE ONCE AND FUTURE STAR** by George Michanowsky *(Sphere, £1.20, pp117, photos, index)* the cover says "Stranger than The Sirius Mystery"; this is the story of how Michanowsy identified trace signals of ancient supernova with the help of Sumerian writings.

Classified Exchanges.

As a reader service FT welcomes mutual exchanges with any relevant publication, and copies issues received since our last issue earn a listing here. No mag — no mention: All we ask in return is a similar entry in your own journal.

FORTEAN

• **Catastrophism & Ancient History** — semi-annual. Single copies $4.00. Annual sub $6.00 (USA), $8.00 (overseas). C & AH: 3431 Club Drive, Los Angeles, CA 90064, USA.

• **INFO Journal** — bimonthly. Single copies 90p/$1.75. Annual sub $10.00. INFO: 7317 Baltimore Ave, College Park, MD 20740, USA.

• **Lantern** — quarterly Forteana, folklore, antiquities and paranormalities of East Anglia. Annual sub £1.20. Lantern: 3 Dunwich Way, Oulton Broad, Lowestoft, Suffolk NR32 4RZ.

• **M-possibilities** — a Fortean newsletter for American Mensa. $3.00 for 7 issues. Michael Halm: Apt 12, 620 9th Ave N, Fargo, ND 58102, USA.

• **Nessletter** — monthly newsletter of Ness Information Service with essential data on sightings and activities. Annual sub. £2.00, N America $8.00. NIS: Huntshieldford, St Johns Chapel, Bishop Aukland, Co. Durham DL13 1RQ.

• **Pursuit** — quarterly journal of SITU. Annual sub $10.00 (USA), $12.50 (overseas. New address: SITU: Box 265 Little Silver, NJ 07739, USA.

- **Res Bureaux Bulletin** — Regular newsletter on Canadian UFOs and Forteana by the indefatigable Mr X, available for exchange or clippings. Mr X: Box 1598, Kingston, Ontario K71 5C8, Canada.
- **Science Frontiers** — brief digest of selected items from current scientific literature, with mail order catalogue. The Sourcebook Project: Box 107, Glen Arm, MD 21057, USA.
- **Second Look** — bimonthly pro-quality general overview. Single copy $3.00. Annual sub $15.00. Second Look: 10 E St SE, Washington, DC 20003, USA.
- **Strange Phenomena** — quarterly, not to be confused with a UK publication of the same name and now defunct. No info on their sub rate. Strange Phenomena: Box 19, Spit Junction, NSW 2088, Australia.

UFOs

- **APRO Bulletin** — monthly journal of Aerial Phenomena Research Organization. Annual sub $12.00 (USA), $15.00 (overseas). APRO: 3910 E Kleindale Rd, Tucson, AZ 85712, USA.
- **BUFORA Journal** — quarterly by British UFO Research Association. May 1980 issue contains a translation of the Fontaine UFOnapping case from *Extreterrestres.* Enquiries: BUFORA Membership Secretary, Miss P Kennedy: 30 Vermont Rd, Upper Norwood, London SE19 3SR.
- **Earthlink** — quarterly. Single copy 70p. Annual sub £2.75 (UK), £4.00 (overseas). Earthlink: 16 Raydons Rd, Dagenham RM9 5JR, Essex.
- **Extreterrestres** — quarterly journal of GEOS, in French. April 1980 has special investigation report of the Fontaine 'UFOnapping'; see *BUFORA.* Enquiries: Les Extraterrestres: Saint Dennis les Rebais, 77510 Rebais, France.
- **Inforespace** — quarterly journal of SOBEPS, in French. Enquiries: SOBEPS: Ave Paul Janson 74, 1070 Bruxelles, Belgium.
- **International UFO Reporter** — monthly journal of Hynek's Center for UFO Studies, ceasing publication in this form, to be issued as an insert in *Probe* magazine. Enquiries: IUFOR: 1609 Sherman Ave, Suite 207, Evanston, IL 60201, USA.
- **Journal of Transient Aerial Phenomena** — published in place of one issue of *Bufora Journal* a year. A commendable development concentrating on bringing scientific rigour to UFO investigations. Issue for March 1980 has detailed report on Bob Taylor's CE III, analysis of the Ubatuba fragment, vehicle interference reports, and Hynek on duration of UFOs. Enquire at BUFORA address above.
- **Magonia** — quarterly. The only journal at present considering the mythological, sociological and psychological dimensions of UFOlogy. Annual sub £1.75 (UK), $5.00 (overseas). John Rimmer: 64 Alric Ave, New Malden, Surrey KT3 4JW.
- **MAPIT Skywatch** — occasional personal magazine. Enquire: David Rees: 92 Hillcrest Rd, Offerton, Stockport, Cheshire SK2 5SE.
- **Northern Ufology** — quarterly report of Northern UFO Network. Enquire: NUFON: 8 Whitethroat Walk, Birchwood, Warrington, Cheshire WA3 6PQ.
- **Nyhetsblad** — newsletter of Swedish archive group. Enquire: AFU: Box 5046, S-151 05 Sodertalje 5, Sweden.
- **Tijdschrift voor Ufologie** — journal of Dutch group NOVOBO. Enquire: NOVOBO: Lijnbaan 4, 9982 HJ Uithuizermeeden, Holland.
- **Ufologia** — supplement to Italian journal *Clypeus.* Enquire: Clypeus: Casella postale 604, 10100 Torino, Italy.
- **UFO Ohio** — regional newsletter + rare book and magazine list. Annual sub: $9.00. UFO Ohio: Box 5012, Rome, OH 44085, USA.

PSI

- **Alpha** — independent bimonthly magazine of the paranormal. Annual sub £5.90 (UK), £6.00 (Europe), £10.00 (overseas airmail). Alpha: 20 Regent St, Fleet, Hants GU13 9NR.
- **EVP Newsletter** — monthly notes on electronic voice phenomena. Annual sub £1.20 (UK), £4.50 (overseas airmail). Alan Cleaver: 12 Lime Tree Ave, Old Bilton, Rugby, Warks CV22 7QT.
- **International Journal of Paraphysics** — quarterly up-to-the minute material on psychotronics and the range of paraphysical research and thinking. Enquire: Paraphysical Laboratory, Downton, Wiltshire.
- **Metascience Quarterly** — a superb review. Annual sub $14.00. Metascience Quarterly: Box 32, Kingston, RI 02881, USA.
- **Specula** — quarterly journal of the American Association of Metascience. Enquire: AAMS, Box 1182, Huntsville, AL 35807, USA.

EARTH MYSTERIES

- **Archaeoastronomy** — bulletin of the Center for Archaeoastronomy. Enquire: Center for Archaeoastronomy: Space Sciences Building, University of Maryland, College Park, MD 20742, USA.
- **Earth Energy** — an inspirational bulletin, for donations. AURA: 1548 Grace St, Lincoln, NB 68503, USA.
- **IGNews** — newsletter of the Irlam Geocryptologists. Annual sub £2.10. IGNews: BM Bulletin, London WC1V 6XX.
- **Journal of Geomancy** — quarterly organ of the Institute of Geomancy. Annual sub £3.75. IGR: 142 Pheasant Rise, Bar Hill, Cambridge CB3 8SD.
- **NEARA Journal** — quarterly of the New England Antiquities Research Association. Annual sub $5.00 (USA), $7.00 (overseas). NEARA: 4 Smith St, Milford, NH 03055, USA.
- **The Ley Hunter** — the essential quarterly magazine of earth mysteries. Annual sub £3.60 (UK), £4.50 (Europe), $11.50 (overseas airmail). TLH: Box 152, London N10 2EF.

OTHERS

- **Gnome News** — newsletter of the Gnome Club of Great Britain. Annual sub £2.50 (UK), £3.50 (overseas). Gnome Club: West Putford, Devon EX22 7XE.
- **Light Times** — "Zero gravity levity for the weighty eighties". Enquire: Light Times: 615 Ocean Front Walk 206, Venice, CA 90291, USA.
- **Occult World** — quarterly at 30p an issue. Occult World: 303 Cauldwell Hall Rd, Ipswich, Suffolk IP4 5AJ.
- **Undercurrents** — bimonthly magazine of radical alternatives. Annual sub £3.60 (UK), £4.50 (overseas). Undercurrents: 27 Clerkenwell Close, London EC1R 0AT.

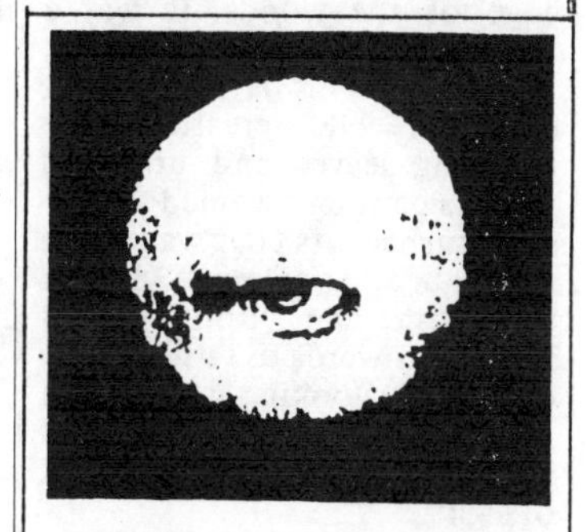

LETTERS
Continued from p3

GIANT KANGAROO IN LANCS?

The location of this sighting is a wooded area near Southport in Lancashire, called "Freshfields". It was a summer afternoon in 1967 and I had been out with my parents for a day trip. We parked in the car park and had some lunch, after which we all went onto the beach walking. On returning to the car, I myself and our dog–a cross-breed called "Smokey"–went wandering off into the woods before returning home. The area is very wooded with very tall trees of all kinds and a few small winding paths. There were not many people in the woods that day and after a while we came to a clearing (200–300 yards in length), which had a raised mound running across it.

Smokey was pulling hard but on reaching the top she calmed down. Trying to see why she had become disturbed I surveyed the area, and that is when I saw it–approximately 120 yards from me–on the edge of the woods. It was a kangaroo, its height being at least 8 ft. This is not a wild estimate. The creature was fingering leaves and branches with its paws and seemed totally undisturbed–its coat was a rich rusty brown colour. After a short time the "Roo" turned its head towards us (still on top of mound), looking at us, before it turned around and walked into the undergrowth and out of sight.

I was scared and did not wish to follow the creature, so with the dog we both ran back to my parents, who were amazed at my story. We then made contact with a policeman nearby who made enquiries, but no such creature was reported missing anywhere. After this we went to the site and indeed the area was flattened, but we never saw it again. It remains a mystery.

David Rees (MAPIT).
Stockport, Cheshire.

Small Ads.

Errata.

FT29

pp 3 & 8 – portraits of Charles Fort should have been credited "Copyright Aaron Sussman/ Fortean Picture Library".

FT30

p 11 – *Bury Free Press* should be *Suffolk & Bury Free Press*.

FT31

p 36 – photos inadvertently reversed; the Franta family, of Watertown are on the left, and the McGuires, of Lovell, are on the right.

Truss Fund.

...in which we gratefully acknowledge the valued donations sent by the following. Such heartening support helps us brave the slings and arrows of outrageous misfortune, and are applied where they will do most good.

Janet & Colin Bord; Julie Felzien; Phyllis Hall; Leo Licof; Gordon McLellan; CW Murray; Kevin Ryan; Science Fiction Theatre of Liverpool, in memory of Paul Howes; Martin Straw.

Help!

This column is free to any reader or researcher who requires help on a question or in locating source materials on Fortean topics. Just send a brief paragraph outlining your interest, on a separate sheet, including your address, to FT editorial address.

Collecting material on 'road ghosts', **phantom hitchhikers**, etc. Cases from all over the world welcomed. Mike Goss: 57 Belmont Rd., Grays, Essex.

Fortean phenomena of the **Niagara Peninsula** and **western New York State**. Compiling a sourcebook. Dwight Whalen: 2107 Harvest Drive, Mississauga, Ontario, Canada L4Y 1T7.

Moving Rocks of the Racetrack Playa. FPL would like photos of this famous phenomenon – so here's a chance to help us AND possibly earn a few bucks. But before you charge off to the Death Valley National Park, California, please check with FT editor Bob Rickard, at FT's editorial address.

Next Issue.

Well we didn't catch up on our schedule this issue but we closed the gap a little, and hopefully we'll close it a little more next time.

We announced several items last time which we were simply unable to include in this issue, and we offer our apologies to contributors and readers. The lead article will be **Hilary Evans'** thoughts on archetypes and UFO abductions, and featured on a full colour cover - if we can get that together! **Alan Gardiner** has come up with a cracking analysis of the 'Sussex Puma'. And we'll also have the regrettably delayed photos, taken by **Jeff Watson**, of a V-wake in Loch Ness in September 1978.

Among our round-ups of data will be more mystery animal sightings, monsters, falls, poltergeists, and fiery deaths.

See you then.

Fortean Times

Subscribe.

SUBSCRIPTION: Be sure of getting your issues of FT directly. A sub to FT makes a thoughtful gift that lasts the whole year, for friends, impoverished scholars and libraries, and even your enemies. Rate includes surface or second class postage, and banking exchange commission where applicable.
1 year (4 issues) £4.00/$10.00
Airmail: add £3.00/$7.50

GIFT SAMPLE: Have a sample of this issue, plus our literature sent to a friend who might subscribe — we need all the friends you can get — at these reduced rates:
Surface/UK: 75p/$1.50
Airmail: £1.50/$3.00

BACKISSUES: Limited numbers available of the following back issues: 19, 20, 25-27, 29-31. £1.00/$2.50 each.

GOOD NEWS!

At last, by popular request, reprints of early issues of *Fortean Times*. Founded in 1973 and called *The News*, these humble beginnings have become legendary - well, out of print, anyway!

Now available, high quality xerox facsimilies of the **first five** issues at **£1.00 each**, surface and second class postage inclusive. Other out of print issues in preparation.

Send order with payment to Fortean Times, c/o DTWAGE, 9-12 St Annes Court, London W1, England.

PHENOMENA

A Book of Wonders

Recommended introduction to the philosophy of Charles Fort, and the historical and thematic continuity of 57 varieties of strange phenomena, from stigmata, levitation and fairies to showers of frogs, wild children and ball lightning. By John Michell (author of *View Over Atlantis* and *Simulacra*, etc) and RJM Rickard (editor of *Fortean Times*). 216 illustrations, many collected together for the first time anywhere. Price includes post and packing.

UK: £3.10.
Surface & Europe: £3.00
Air (USA & Canada): $9.00
Air (Far East & Australia): $10.00

PAYMENT: cheques, postal orders, international money orders, made payable to *Fortean Times.* If you are in doubt, your bank will be glad to make out a cheque drawn on a British bank. These involve us in less paperwork, complications and bank charge deductions, and provide the safest method of payment for overseas subscribers. Send your order with payment to the address below. Please allow 6-8 weeks for surface mail, plus processing time.

FORTEAN TIMES, 9–12 St Annes Court, London W1, England

The House of Lords UFO Debate. Illustrated, Full Transcript with Preface by Lord Clancarty (Brinsley le Poer Trench) and Notes by John Michell.

"This record of the now-famous UFO debate in the House of Lords in January 1979 is rapidly becoming a *genre* classic, being the authorised record of an event, not simply of interest to those interested in the enigma of UFO's, but unique in the House's 700 year history."

Bob Rickard/*Fortean Times*

"Certainly it is well worth reading, and in future may well become a document of great historical interest. Reading through the views of the noble Lords, it is impossible to avoid the conclusion that Lords Tololler and Mountararat in *Iolanthe* were portrayed with the maximum of skill and minimum of exaggeration!"

Patrick Moore/*Books & Bookmen*

"The text of the debate is now available in book form, with the addition of marginal notes by John Michell which enlarge upon the UFO references made by each speaker and provide the UFO novice with the background necessary for a comprehensive understanding of the debate."

Janet Bord/*Flying Saucer Review*

"UFO's attract the bizarre and cranks, and the House of Lords has more of these per square yard than almost anywhere else."

Nigel Pennick/*Anarchist Review*

Published by *Open Head Press* and *Pentacle Books* now available at £2.95 plus 30p Post and Packing from: *Open Head Press,* 2 Blenheim Crescent, London W11 1NN. Trade enquiries apply to: *Pentacle Books,* 6 Perry Road, Bristol 1.

Fortean Times

ISSUE No. 33

The Journal of Strange Phenomena.

PRICE: 95p $2.50

UFO ABDUCTIONS

Symbols & Psychology

Enfield Polt *p10*

New Nessie Photos *p28.*

Fortean Times

9-12 St Annes Court
London W1, England.

The Journal of Strange Phenomena.

Autumn 1980
ISSN 0308.5899

Editorial.

We are probably at the most difficult period of our career. We have a chronic cash-flow problem. On paper our income should (only) just keep ahead of our expenses – but in fact we are at a time when our funds are very very low. The main reason is that subs lapse at different times and not everyone renews promptly, so our income is subject to fluctuations. Another is that the problems and expenses of running and producing a mag for a growing readership change as it gets larger. When we had 2–300 subs we had a lot of 'fat' to iron out these ups and downs. Now we are hovering around the 1000 mark – not bad for a year's growth – our non-existent resources are stretched to the limit.

Most of that 'fat' went into improving the quality prior to the increase in readers. We also spent on advertizing in the USA. New inquiries turned to subs at a rate which justified our initial expenditure – but we have not been able to restore our financial reserves. Your donations helped in the past, and now we need your help again. Or find new readers – our target is 2000 – so every one helps. (We can send free literature.)

Bob Rickard.

Contents.

Cover art by
William Rankin

ARTICLES

4 **Stay, you Imperfect Speakers** *Guy L Playfair.*
6 **Abducted by an Archetype** *Hilary Evans.*
10 **Ask Aristotle** *Paul Sieveking.*
12 **Gateways to Mystery, pt3** *David Fideler & Bob Tarte.*
18 **Man Bites Man!** *Paul Sieveking.*

COMIX

11 **Telly Kinex** *JH Szostek.*
21 **Phenomenomix** *Hunt Emerson.*
53 **Facts You Might Forget** *Pokkettz.*

COLUMNS

38 **On the Trail** *Loren Coleman.*
40 **Tales from the Yellow Emporium** *Steve Moore.*
42 **Enigma Variations** *Nigel Watson.*

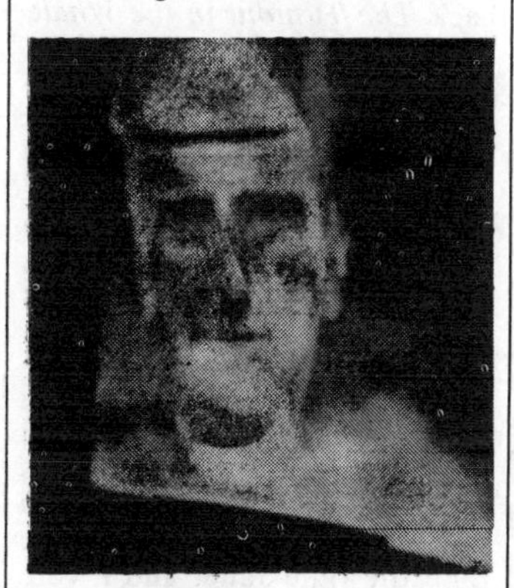

NOTES

22 **Illnesses** *Mass Hysteria.*
27 **Strange Encounters** *More C3Ks*
28 **Images** *Simulacra.*
32 **Trends** *Lumps in our Data.*
36 **Unidentified** *Nessie Hunter + Pix.*

USUAL STUFF

2 **Letters.**
20 **News.**
44 **Reviews.**
54 **Classified Exchange.**
57 **Subscription info.**

Published by Fortean Times Ltd: 9-12 St Annes Court, London W1. Editor: ROBERT JM RICKARD. Editorial Assistants: STEVE MOORE, PAUL SIEVEKING. Contributing Editor: DAVID FIDELER. Art Director: RICHARD ADAMS. Comix Editor and section heading artwork: HUNT EMERSON. Photosetting by WORDSMITH GRAPHICS, 19a West End, Street, Somerset. Reprosetting by PAULA GRAHAM. Printed by BIJA PRESS, Beeches Green, Stroud, Glos. Distributed by: *A-DISTRIBUTION*, 182 Upper Street, London N1.

FORTEAN TIMES is a quarterly journal of news, notes, reviews and references on current and historical strange phenomena, related subjects and philosophies. A friend to all groups and magazines continuing the work of Charles Fort in investigating, studying and discussing all aspects of strange phenomena. RIGHTS: all articles and artwork in FT are the copyright of the authors unless otherwise stated. Uncredited material is by the editors. The views of the contributors are not necessarily those of FT, and vice versa. SUBMISSION is invited of articles, artwork, cartoons, and news clippings on related subjects. The publishers can assume no responsibility for unsolicited material, but all reasonable care will be taken while in FT's possession. If material is to be returned, please enclose SAE. CORRESPONDENCE: letters-of-comment and personal experience are welcome. If replies are required please enclose SAE. The editor regrets it is not always possible to reply promptly. ADVERTISING and DISTRIBUTION ENQUIRIES: contact the editor at the above address, or ring 01 552 5466. SUBSCRIPTION INFORMATION: see p56.

WHALE TALES

Was that a fine Whale Tumour story of the carpet salesman in FT32 p.2? Those not familiar with WT stories should read Rodney Dale's amusing paperback *The Tumour in the Whale* in which he explains that Whale Tumour stories are unbelievable reports that the teller swears are true and happened to 'a friend of a friend' (foaf) of his, and then you keep hearing the same 'true' story from different, unconnected sources which always happened to a foaf.

It's very satisfying for the collector of WT stories to be solemnly told a favourite one by someone who *really believes* that it happened to their foaf. Like the time Janet and I were interviewing a UFO witness and the subject of psychic experiences came up. His wife told us the classic WT story that goes: 'A chap was riding along a quiet country road on his motorbike when a girl on foot signalled to him. He stopped and she asked him if he could give her a lift into the nearby town. She hopped on the pillion and off they went. Entering the town, they stopped at the traffic lights, a milk float pulled up next to them and the milkman, after looking at them for a moment, leant over and said: 'Crikey mate, you'd better get your girlfriend home quick, she looks real poorly!' (nice touch that!) At that moment the lights changed and they had to move off.

He arrived at the address the girl gave him but to his surprise found the pillion seat empty. For a few moments he was at a loss, but thinking perhaps the girl may have got off earlier and walked a short cut home, he decided to knock on the house door to check. A middle-aged woman came to the door and when he explained the situation she was by turns shocked, angry, aghast, and finally broke down. She told him that exactly a year ago to the day her daughter met her death by falling off a motorbike pillion on precisely the same stretch of road where he was stopped by the girl...'

This classic WT story was already known to us (though we did not let on), and the UFO witness's wife assured us that it had happened to a friend of her cousin, and she quite obviously believed that it had. Ron Parker's phantom toombstone report has all the marks of a Whale Tumour story, and if it isn't one already it will probably become one before long. WT stories should not be confused with reports of Fortean events, but all Fortean investigators should be familiar with the concept of Whale Tumour stories, and the best of them.

Colin Bord,
Montgomery, Powys.

OAHSPE TULPOIDS

I was particularly interested in the article 'On the Trail' by Loren Coleman, re the phantom animals. Now as there seems no other avenue to turn to get an answer to this enigma, I thought of the Ageless Wisdom Teachings and in *Oahspe: the Kosmon Bible* is a most interesting statement which could be applicable. Book of Fragapatti, Son of Jehovih. Chapter 21 verses 15 et seq. 'Nevertheless as a man may take a drop of water and put it in a vial and keep it for a long time so have I given to my exalted Angels power to take the spirit of a fish, or of an animal, suddenly dead, and reclothe it with the semblance of a body, for a season; but yet it is only a subjective existence. And even as a man letteth a stone out of his hand, and it falleth to the ground, so, when My Angels let go their hands on My spiritual animals, their spirits fall into the sea, and are seen no more. Even so also, but in a less degree, created I the trees, the grass the moss, and all vegetable things that grow on the face of the Earth. And I gave to my exalted Angels power to take the spirit out of a tree, or a bush or a plant, and to carry it away and reclothe it with corporeal substance. But to my exalted Gods I gave power to do the same things, not with one plant only, but with whole forests, and with animals and fishes and serpents. And when they do these things in Atmospherea, they are called subjective heavens.'

The above quotation could be an explanation as to why such strange animals are being seen out of their usual environment, and why some people who have had UFO contacts state that the surroundings looked so different. Oh yes, and Oahspe also gives information on falls from the skies which could explain the Fortean Falls.

Mrs Phyllis Hall,
Whangerei, New Zealand.

TIME SLIPS?

I have something interesting to report and I want you to publish this. It happens to Jack and I, both senior citizens now, sober and sane!

We go for our walk along Finchley Road, eastwards towards Swiss Cottage, circa 4–5pm, most days. We walk slowly and observantly – neither wear glasses and both have keen vision.

Several times, we see things double... a few months ago, walking past the Post Office, going east, we saw a most unusual male – tall, wearing some kind of bright red anorak, with a springy walk... no one took any notice of him... then a few yards further along the road, we saw this very same man coming out of Boots, the Chemist shop... he could not have run back in the time. We saw him twice: time-now in our time; and then time-future in our time, but time past in his.

A few weeks ago, a blind woman walked by us, (with white stick) and I drew aside slightly so as not to brush against her. Then walking on eastward, a few minutes later we saw this same woman, crossing the road at a lights crossing... again she could not have dodged past, as in both times, like the man in red, she was coming towards us. Again time-now for us seeing her first and then time-future for us, seeing her crossing the road towards us, and time-past for her!

Another time, we saw Idries Shah and girlfriend (whom we know) in this street, getting into their car, he smoking a cigar... from one side of the car and she from the near side... we walked on and then a few minutes later, saw Idries Shah and the girl walking towards us... no cigar and no car... Again coming towards us in Time now for the car incident and time future for us and time past for them!

The last occurrence was bizarre. Walking eastwards again, we saw a woman in black, wheeling an idiot woman in white in a wheel chair... woman was lolling on a side, could not sit up with a vacant face. Then walking eastwards, we saw again, coming towards us, this very same couple! This time I noticed a small cross on the woman in black... this so shocked Jack he murmured, 'I wonder how they managed that one!'

Please publish this, as I would like some talk about it, or possible explanations. We have had some other incidents like this but years ago, and these latest batch are fairly consistent within some months. It certainly adds a spice to our walks!

Is TIME stretching for us? Are we seeing into the immediate past? Which is the real sighting... first time or second time!

Judith Gee
Hampstead, London

NYMPH AWAY!

I'm afraid you can scrap the 'Kangaroo Girl' (FT25p9) from your files. But firstly, please note the correct spellings of kangaroo, and Nullarbor (= no trees). [Oops – Ed.] On excellent authority from a very close friend I am assured the 'Nullarbor Nymph' was a hoax. He was in the area for quite a while a month after the event, which was about May–June 1972. He met the people involved who informed him how the whole story had been rigged as a tourist attraction. They showed him how they caught the 'roos alive and released them for the filming. The 'nymph' did *not* live wild in the bush, nor, regrettably, did she run naked with the 'roos, though she did spend some time out there in a caravan. She, and the others involved in the hoax, left the area some months after the event.

Alf Debnam,
Bentley, Western Australia.

BIGBIRD NOTES

I believe the following to be the earliest known reference to a 'big bird' incident in the continental United States. The piece is taken from page 275 of Volume I *Annals of Albany* (NY), Joel Munsell, 58 State St., Albany, NY, 1850.

'A RARE BIRD – The citizens of Albany were entertained in November 1788 with the extraordinary sight of an 'uncommon bird'. Killed at Saratoga (NY) and sent down as a rarity. The distance from the tip of one wing to the other, when both were extended, was nine feet, two inches; the mouth was large enough to contain the head of a boy ten years old, and the throat so capacious as to admit the foot and leg of a man, boot and all. No one could decide what species the stranger belonged to, till the counsel of Dr. Mitchell of New York being called in, it was decided to be a pelican, perhaps the only one that ever extended his discoveries to this region.'

They wuz Fortean times back then too!

Joseph Trainor,
Massachussetts.

FORTEAN ART

An idea that could possibly bring in more money for FT, is to auction the original artwork used in the mag. The original of the cover by Una Woodruff [FT30] would surely be worth quite a few pounds to many people. It's an idea to think about.

Peter Horton,
Dewsbury, West Yorks.

[And a good idea too – under normal circumstances. The fact is that since we are not in a position to pay our artists their usual rates, let alone their worth, if at all, it is only right that all artwork and copyrights are returned to them. Naturally all inquiries after the works will be forwarded to the artists – it's the least we can do – Ed.]

Continued on p 56

Stay, You Imperfect Speakers.

With the investigation of the Enfield poltergeist, and the writing of his account, *This House is Haunted* (reviewed last issue), behind him, we asked Guy Lyon Playfair to summarize the case and his conclusions.

Nothing could be more Fortean than a poltergeist case. Wildly improbable events take place with outrageous regularity. Much confusion is caused. Argument rages. Scientists scratch heads, laugh nervously, and go away muttering 'childish tricks'. And the events go on taking place.

The Enfield poltergeist made itself known on the Earth plane on 31 August 1977, when furniture began to slide around, marbles and Lego bricks whizzed through the air, and knocks came from the walls of a pleasant council semi-detached house in hitherto peaceful Enfield.

Mrs Harper, a divorcee in her forties, did everything she should have done. She called the neighbours to search the house. She appealed to the local vicar and the local medium (without success). She notified the council. She did not panic.

But the phenomena went on and on, until in desperation a kindly neighbour appealed first to the police and then to the ultimate authority – the *Daily Mirror*. They, at last, did something. They spent several days covering the story, and on 10 September 'The House of Strange Happenings' made the front page. Reporter George Fallows took pity on Mrs Harper and her four frightened children and called the Society for Psychical Research, and within a week of its debut, the Enfield case had a full-time investigator on the spot. And a week later, Sherlock Holmes (Maurice Grosse) was joined by Watson (me).

There was a lot of synchronicity going on even at this stage. Grosse, a level-headed inventor and industrial designer, had repeatedly asked the SPR to find him a case to investigate in his area. On 8 September, I happened to be sitting next to him at the SPR lecture (on poltergeists, of course) at which he announced that he had found his case and would like help. A week earlier, and I would have been finishing *The Cycles of Heaven,* and a week later I would have been flat on my back on a Portuguese beach. The timing, typical of the poltergeist, was perfect.

Before long, both Grosse and I were rewarded with several close encounters of several kinds. I watched as the youngest daughter got out of a heavy armchair and took a step towards me, whereupon the chair shot along the floor after her and slammed over backwards. (Yes, I did look for hidden wires, accomplices and laser beams). A kitchen table overturned while everybody anywhere near it was in my full view, a pile of ironed clothes hopped off a table onto the floor, and my own notebook shot off a bed right under my nose, moving towards the head of the person in the bed, whose legs had not moved.

Grosse, alone in the kitchen, watched a teapot (cold and empty) rock back and forth as if doing a dance for his benefit. He saw a door open and close several times. He saw a marble shoot past him as if fired from an invisible catapult, and he saw a large sofa rise into the air and land upside down.

And there was more. Things got 'so worse', as one of the children put it, that they would happen faster than we could note them, though luckily we recorded a great many on tape. We lost count somewhere past the 400 mark, after claiming the world record previously held by William G. Roll on the Miami warehouse case of 1967, and concentrated on getting good evidence for selected events.

We began, ambitiously, with an infra-red camera kindly loaned by Pye Business Communications, whose amiable chief demonstrator came along to operate it. Result: all the lights on the tape deck went on at once, then the tape jammed solid and the whole deck had to be dismantled. Then, with everything in order, we sat and watched the girl sleeping for three hours. The Thing was camera-shy.

Photographer Graham Morris was luckier. Originally sent to the case by the *Daily Mirror,* he came back several times in his own time, with enough equipment to open a shop, and his patience and ingenuity were rewarded.• With an elaborate set-up of motor-driven Nikons, a high-speed flash charger and remote control cable, he got several photos that are not easy to

• [Many of these photos – the first, to our knowledge, to show poltergeists in action, clearly and in colour – are included in *This House is Haunted,* in B&W, and in colour in the forthcoming *Photographs of the Unknown* by Rickard and Kelly–Ed.]

explain. His best sequence of five frames shows the bedclothes being whipped off one of the girls as a curtain blows into the room and twists itself into a tight spiral. (The window was shut.) This spiral, or vortex effect, kept turning up, and may be an important clue to the mystery of poltergeist power.

Graham himself was clouted hard on the forehead by a piece of Lego just as he was taking a picture – which shows one person with arms folded, another with hands in pockets, and nobody else. A survivor of the Grunwick street theatre and several National Front marches, he had a nasty bump just over his eye for several days after this.

Then we had the knocks. They sounded as if they were made by somebody asking for attention, so we knocked back and made contact, of a sort. Using the old 'one for no and two for yes' routine, we got some interesting results. On my first attempt at communication, I spoke to the Thing from the room directly below the bedroom, where the whole family was in bed, with the light on and my recorder running.

It rapped away merrily until I asked 'Do you realise you are dead?' Then there was a brief silence, followed by total bedlam as everything upstairs was flung in all directions. The Thing must have been offended, because it never spoke to me again, at least not by knocking.

Maurice Grosse had better luck. After long and patient questioning, he learned that the rapper had lived in the house 53 years ago – it actually knocked that many times while my ear and microphone were pressed to the floor, in a curious sequence that faded in and out like a weak radio signal.

Then the knocking became disorganised, and Grosse asked 'Are you having a game with me?' Two seconds later, a cardboard box full of small cushions shot off the floor in his direct line of vision and slammed into his forehead, with impressive accuracy. A team from BBC *Nationwide* tried to repeat that one, but failed after nine or ten takes.

The most bizarre events of the whole case, which lasted about fourteen months, took place on the very day of the youngest girl's menarche, or first period. Just a coincidence no doubt. This was the day the poltergeist put on a show in public. The girl was seen floating round the bedroom, in daylight, by several passers-by, two of whom gave us very precise descriptions. One noted that the girl, plus some cushions and pillows, was being whirled around in a kind of vortex. He also noted that a large red cushion appeared on the roof of the house as he was walking along the pavement towards it. Nobody opened any windows.

On the same day, the girl alleged that she had been 'through the wall' to the house next door, and the lady from next door found one of the girl's books on her bedroom floor. We never quite sorted that one out.

Then we had the famous Voice.

For some time, there had been odd barking and whistling noises coming from the girl's direction, so one night Grosse challenged the Thing to speak. He did this on the advice of Professor J.B. Hasted, head of the physics department at Birbeck College, who is the exact opposite of the kind of scientist Fort used to get his boot into. He not only took an active interest throughout the case, but lent us his assistant, David Robertson, for two weeks, full time. David, who was in charge during the most active phase of the case, has witnessed more paranormal phenomena than any SPR member has debunked in a lifetime.

The Thing did indeed speak, in a rasping bass growl I will never forget, and then things got really confusing. Two eminent SPR members decided the girl was having us on after half an hour's research, while a well-known ventriloquist sent along by the *Daily Mirror* solved the mystery before he even got to the house. The girl was doing it with her diaphragm, he said.

She wasn't. She didn't even know what a diaphragm was. She was doing the voice, as we later proved instrumentally, with her false vocal folds, or *plica ventricularis.* This part of the larynx is not used in normal speech, and hurts like hell if you use it for more than a few seconds. Yet the girl could keep it up for hours without even clearing her throat.

The Voice never told us much of value. I had the impression of several entities crammed into an astral phone box, each grabbing the receiver from each other, and though they all sounded much the same, one or two phrases were quite impressive. Once, we were told that the speaker was 72 years old and from the local graveyard, looking for his family. He gave a name, and when I played this bit of tape on the Robbie Vincent programme on BBC Radio London, first caller on the line was a lady who said that the name given was that of her great uncle who had lived in Enfield. We are still trying to locate his grave.

The Voice would often lapse into extreme obscenity. When, just for the record, I asked if it were no more than the girl's exteriorised co-consciousness, I was told: 'Fuck off. Course I'm not.' And had we asked it if it were the devil, Beelzebub, Hitler, or whoever, I am sure it would have said yes. Then it would just have been a question of 'exorcising' it until it went away, or until the poor girl dropped dead, as on the awful Anneliese Michel case in Germany after which two priests were convicted for manslaughter.

Can we explain the poltergeist? George Owen asked the question as the title of his splendid and definitive work on the subject. The answer is no, we can't, although we know a lot more about it than we did in 1977, thanks mainly to the persistence of Maurice Grosse and

Continued on p 11

Abducted by an Archetype

From *L'Invasion Noire* (1895) by Capt Danrit. Courtesy of Mary Evans Picture Library.

The previous two decades saw a huge rise in the number of 'close encounters' reported by UFO witnesses, most of which have remained controversial because of the lack of proof or evidence that was convincing in the scientific sense. Very little account was taken of the context of the experience itself, both psychologically and mythologically. One of the most hopeful signs for the ufology of the Eightees is that this neglected trend is being reversed. We are pleased to present this thoughtful article by Hilary Evans, writer, researcher and committee-member of the Society for Psychical Research, who gives us the benefit of his wanderings among the Hills and Vallees of Magonia.

The Problem

Abducted by a UFO. That it could happen in fact would have been unthinkable until some thirty years ago (and still is for perhaps a majority of us) and if it occurred in fiction, only the most courageous story-tellers dared envisage it. Yet here we are, sober citizens of 1980, seriously sitting down and considering the possibility that dozens of alleged abduction reports could be based in reality.

We know the pattern. The abductee is walking or driving along, or even sitting at home, when there's this weird light, makes him stop what he's doing and go to investigate; he meets these weird people who take him on board this weird craft of theirs, where he's put into this weird compartment; his hosts give him some kind of physical examination, then let him go telling him he won't remember a thing. But he does, if not consciously then under hypnosis... We've read that account, or something like it, so many times, we'd hardly be surprised if it happened to us and would surely experience a sense of *deja vu* as they laid us on their inspection table.

And yet we still don't know whether stories like that have any basis in fact.

What would Charles Fort have done?

Fort believed in explanations. His four books, though they contain many attacks on scientists who conducted themselves non-scientifically, are monuments to the scientific method. Yes, you may say, and look where it got him: four fat volumes packed with anomalies still awaiting explanation, the biggest pending file of unsolved mysteries outside Scotland Yard.

If that's the scientific method, say some, we'd all be better off sitting at the feet of some Eastern guru, trying to imagine the sound of one hand clapping rather than trying to find cause-and-effect patterns in phenomena which are manifestly outside the scope of human reason. It's possible they're right, that there are some areas of experience which aren't amenable to logic-systems that we're acquainted with. But that's a desperate conclusion to come to; before that, we need to be convinced that old-fashioned cause-and-effect thinking has failed us. Personally I don't think we're anywhere near that point.

What scares people off is the seeming paradoxes inherent throughout the UFO problem, and found at their most extreme in the abduction reports. But Charles Fort delighted in paradoxes because he recognised that when you've reduced a problem to a paradox, you've got to the heart of that problem. I suggest, and I think Fort would have agreed with me, that it is precisely the outrageous character of the abduction reports which gives us our best hope of isolating their true nature.

A clue

On 26 July 1978, 37-year-old 'Gerry Armstrong' was hypnotically regressed to when, a 12-year-old schoolboy in England, he was taken aboard a UFO and examined by its occupants. His account is more or less the standard scenario outlined above, but from what he said under hypnosis I note the following: 'In a room... ain't no electric light bulb. Can't see a bulb... I can't see any bulbs. And then one go through the wall. I didn't... can't see a door.' And later, going over the material in the wakened state, he said: 'I'm being put in a room... I think it's a room. I'm trying to understand where the light is from. It's very, very interesting. We seem to walk through a wall, but there must have been a door.' [5,7]

In 1977 40-year-old Betty Andreasson was hypnotically regressed to when, ten years earlier, she was taken aboard a UFO and subjected to a number of astonishing experiences during a sequence of events which largely conformed to the standard model. From her account I note:

B: Whoosh! Another door opened. And you can't even see those doors. They just go up when they open.

Q: Can you see the source of the illumination?

B: It comes from all over the place.

Q: Can you see any welded seams on the wall or some type of seam?

B: No, it seem smooth all the way around.

Let's check the tape at that point and ask ourselves, why do the lights and the doors seem of such particular interest to both subjects and, consequently, to their questioners?

An answer is that doors and lights are things which all human homes and vehicles possess, so they're something we can relate to in an alarming situation. But so are lots of other things: why, when something so extraordinary as going on board a UFO is happening, do such trivial details loom so important? Personally, I'd be interested enough to go aboard Concorde, let alone a UFO; but I can't imagine my chief concern would be for the lighting system. Yet it's a fact that this preoccupation is almost a standard feature in abduction reports. Antonio da Silva (Brazil 1969) reported 'the lighting in the compartment was intense, of the mercury vapour type, but he was unable to detect any sources for the light, nor any openings or salient parts on the smooth surfaces. [2a] Antonio Rubia (Brazil 1977) found himself in an interior lit by an intense blue light which came from the ceiling but he couldn't distinguish the source because it seemed to come from the ceiling as a whole. [1]

And so on, and so on. All I want you to note, for the moment, is that so many witnesses pick out this particular aspect of their experience. The lights and door things are only two of many; they just happen to be the ones that set me thinking, the clues that led to the question of which is the starting-point for this inquiry: Why do the abductees' reports – not their experiences, but their *reports* – echo one another so closely?

Four kinds of report

Reports of alleged encounters between humans and non-human entities fall into four classes:

1: Stories told by real humans who describe what they allege, and apparently seemingly believe, to have really happened to them, in which they met alien and apparently non-human entities. [1, 2, 3, 4, 5, 6, 10 etc]
2: Fictional stories on the same lines, mostly dating from the pre-ufo period of the 1920s–1930s. [9]
3: Myths, usually non-specific though occasionally including purported names and locations, describing events containing remarkably similar features. [10]
4: Accounts produced experimentally in which subjects with no particular UFO background describe supposed UFO abductions under the influence of drugs or hypnosis. [8]

Study of the references indicated above reveals astonishing correspondences between these four kinds of report with such widely differing origins. For example:

• European science fiction writers in the 1920s described imaginary situations which are so close to alleged abduction reports of the 1970s as to make coincidence wellnigh unthinkable. Meheust's book is devoted to these parallels; thus he cites a French SF yarn whose hero finds himself in a small room, lit by a green diffused light emanating from no discernible source but rather from the material of the vessel itself; there are seemingly no doors or windows, but these appear when required... Compare this with Higdon [2b] who found himself in a small room, brightly lit but with no obvious source of light, or with Diaz [9] who could see no light and felt that the walls were translucent; like the SF hero he was in a small room without furniture of any kind. (To get the full impact of these parallels, the accounts should be read at length, of course.)

• Vallee [12] has devoted a book to the parallels between UFO reports and myth. Whatever we think of his thesis, his basic point is well made: it is hard not to presume some common source when Vallee bombards you with dozens of such parallels as this: Betty Hill [4] reported that during her examination a long needle was inserted into her navel... The fifteenth century Calendrier des Bergers shows demons piercing their victims' abdomens with long needles. One such parallel might be coincidence, but not this many...

• The encounters induced under hypnosis, experimentally, by Alvin Lawson and his team [8] astonished the experimenters by their close similarity to allegedly factual accounts. This is the more remarkable, since the subjects had first been screened to include only those with minimal ufological knowledge. (Clearly, as Hendry has pointed out [6] nobody these days can be expected to be completely ignorant of UFOs!) The subjects described their imaginary experiences in terms which were virtually indistinguishable from those used by the people who claimed to have actually undergone the experiences: again, you need to study the scripts at length to get the full force of the parallels, but here's a sample:

A: 'They seem to have brought me to this... it almost seems like a tube. The ceiling is about 20 feet high...'
B: 'I can see the sky up there... it's like a long tube, jagged...'
C: 'It's sort of like a tube, like I sort of feel that I'm at the bottom of a tube looking up...'

In fact, A is an experimental hypnosis subject, B is a 'real' abductee, and C is a drug-induced-hallucination subject.

In short, what we have is a situation where four kinds of report, emanating from wholly different origins, produce correspondence of coincidence-defying similarity. This argues that they are either deriving from one another, or all deriving from some common substratum, some widely, if not universally available image bank.

It is hard to see how they could be deriving from one another. To suppose a linear or sequential development, myth to SF and SF to alleged fact, leads to absurdity: how could a Brazilian farmer have access to SF stories in French of half a century before – and even if it happened by a strange chance once, how could it keep on happening?

The significance of myth

The view of Paul Misraki [10], subsequently elaborated and irresponsibly extended by Von Daniken and others, was that mythical accounts are similar to allegedly factual accounts for the simple reason that they *are* factual accounts, which have been blurred by time. However, while it may be the case that UFO abductions have been taking place throughout history, there is no good evidence to that effect, and to assume it would be highly question-begging. For one thing, the supporters of the theory need to show why we have reports from the distant past, and reports from our own day, but virtually nothing in between – why were there no abductions in the time of Shakespeare or Dr Johnson or the Victorians, periods when, though the critical apparatus of our own day wasn't available, at least we could have expected a fair standard of reporting which would help us to gauge the authenticity of the account? In the absence of any such continuing tradition, I surmise that the mythical accounts are something quite different from the factual accounts of our own time.

For our present purpose, the significance of the mythical accounts is that they were what people wanted to tell and hear. Far from being accounts of actual happenings, it is more probable that they describe precisely what does *not* happen in real life. Real life is untidy and unsatisfactory, things happen and nobody knows why, things start and don't finish, loose ends proliferate. To impose some pattern on reality is a basic human instinct, which is what keeps story-tellers and myth-makers in business.

The relation of myth to reality is that myth represents the filling of gaps in reality. Fairies and angels, and their equivalents in later cultures, are 'needed' to complete our world-picture; they, and encounters with them, are things which we feel, consciously or unconsciously, some or most or even all of us, that reality should somehow contain. If superhuman entities don't exist, mankind must invent them...

Where reality starts and ends

I think we must accept that there is a real basis for a proportion of UFO reports, and that they relate to an actual phenomenon outside anything yet classified by science. Even if we set aside all material or photographic evidence, it remains the case that we have thousands of well-presented reports, by persons apparently of sound mind and in no unusual emotional state, describing physical objects rationally and lucidly, and frequently with multiple confirmation. To dismiss such evidence is quite simply perverse.

At the same time I think we must accept that whatever reality UFOs possess, it is different from any reality we know. Their ability to change shape, to respond to individual percipients, to be seen by some and not by others, taken along with so many other logic-defying features of their behaviour and that of their occupants, means that we are up against something totally different from anything previously experienced by mankind (with the significant exception of certain categories of psychical phenomena).

If however we accept that the typical unexplained UFO report has some correspondence with reality, we really paint ourselves into a corner as regards the abduction reports: for we must choose between saying 'Ah, but they are exceptions' without any good reason for so saying, or accepting that they, too, are based on reality. Which means we have to explain how it comes about that real reports should correspond so closely with parallel accounts which we **know** to be total fabrications? We have already discounted the likelihood that they derive from one another; but what is left?

Paradox to the rescue!

At this point we have to take into account another complication which at first sight seems to make matters even worse, if possible: though, as we shall find, it actually gives us the vital clue we need, which just shows how right Fort was to be so fond of paradoxes!

The new horror we have to face is this: both Michel Monnerie in France [11] and Allan Hendry in the US [6] have established that many highly detailed sightings relate to IFOs, not UFOs. Percipients have described windows on the planet Venus and ascribed purposeful manoeuvres to the Moon! Monneries suggests that what is happening in such cases is that the sight of something unplaceable induces in some people a 'waking dream' – a state in which the subconscious overrides the conscious. This may or may not be the case: what concerns us is the fact that these percipients are clearly dredging up, from somewhere within themselves, aspects of what they expect/wish/fear to see, and plastering them into the innocent moon or whatever. The thing seen plays no part in the process: the percipient does it all.

Now you see why this apparent complication is so significant. For it shows, beyond question, that some people *do* possess inside themselves the do-it-yourself kit necessary for transforming reality into fantasy. And if IFO observers can do it, then so can UFO observers; so, perhaps, can all of us!

Conclusion

I suggest that we are justified in concluding that some, perhaps all, of us carry about, in our subconscious or wherever, all that is needed to fabricate an abduction report. What varies is the form and the circumstances. From the distant past the material survives as myth, with fairies, angels or demons as the agents. SF writers regurgitate it in the form of adventure stories: in the

1920s they tended to attribute responsibility to Mad Scientists seeking to dominate the world. We, if we are subjected to hypnosis or drugs in a lab, will regurgitate the material in the form of an imaginary encounter, now with extraterrestrial humanoids playing the leading parts.

If we experience a real-life trigger situation, whether IFO or UFO doesn't greatly matter, some of us – whether we do or don't presumably depends on our psychological make-up – may regurgitate the material in the form of an encounter decked out in the cultural clothing of the day. In Bernadette Soubirous' day it was the Virgin Mary, as was appropriate to a pious schoolgirl in a Catholic culture; earlier it would have religious-type flaming crosses in the sky, in our own day it is extra-terrestrial humanoids. Onto the public skeleton we drape our private preoccupations: Betty Andreasson [3] underwent mystical experiences personal to her personal situation, while Sandy Larson and Judy Kendall [8] suffered types of medical operations repeating real-life episodes.

I still don't know why the abductees are so preoccupied with lights and doors. But I think we can guess that if we want to know, we're more likely to learn from the psycho-analyst than anyone else. For, whether or not there is any reality underlying the abductees' stories, their characteristic features derive from some widely if not universally diffused scenario, which in its turn is made up of elements deeply embedded in all our subconsciouses.

Hilary Evans •

REFERENCES

1 Pierre Delval, *Contacts du 4me type,* 1979.
2 *Flying Saucer Review* (a) Da Silva – Vol 19 no 6 p6.
3 Raymond Fowler, *The Andreasson Affair,* 1979.
4 John Fuller, *The Interrupted Journey,* 1966.
5 David Haisell, *The Missing Seven Hours,* 1978.
6 Allan Hendry, *The UFO Handbook,* 1979.
7 *Journal UFO* (Canada) Vol 1/1.
8 *Journal of UFO Studies,* CUFOS 1979.
9 Bertrand Meheust, *Science-Fiction et Soucoupes Volantes,* 1978.
10 Paul Misraki (as Paul Thomas) *Flying Saucers,* 1962.
11 Michel Monnerie, *Et si les OVNIs n'existaient pas?,* 1977.
12 Jacques Vallee, *Passport to Magonia,* 1970.

Ask Aristotle.

More cranked-out catechism, selected by Paul Sieveking from **Aristotle's Book of Problems** (1749), for connisseurs of explanations.

•

Q: Doth Nature make any Monsters?

A: She doth, for if she did not, she would then be deprived of her End. For of all things possible she doth always purpose to bring forth that which is most perfect and best: but in the end, through the evil disposition of the matter, and influence of some special Constellation, not being able to bring forth that which she intended, she brings forth that which she can. As it happened in *Albertus's* time, when in a certain Village a Cow brought forth a Calf half a Man; then the Countrymen suspecting a Shepherd, would have burnt him with the Cow; but *Albertus* being skilful in Astronomy, said, that this did proceed from special Constellation , and so delivered the Shepherd from their Hands.

•

Q: Why doth a Man which is slain bleed when he is seen of him who killed him?

A: This proceedeth of Divine Cause, and not of a Natural, because his blood calleth for Vengeance against the Murderer; but if there be any Natural Cause of it, 'tis this: The committer of this wicked Fact calling it to mind, is very sorry for it, and repents him of it, is in anguish of Mind, and in a great heat through the strong Imagination he hath conceived, and by that means all his Spirits do stir and boil, and repair into the Instrument of the sight, and so go out by the beams of the sight of the Eyes, unto the wounds which are made, which if they be fresh, do presently fall a bleeding. Besides, this is done by the help of the Air then breathed in, which being drawn from the wound, caused it to bleed.

•

Q: How comes the Imagination of the Mother to bring forth a Black a moor, as Albertus Magnus reports of a Queen, who in the Act of carnal Copulation imagined, a Black being painted, and being in her sight?

A: Avicen says, the imagination of a Fall makes a Man fall, and the Imagination of a Leprosy makes a Man a Leper. So in this the Imagination is above the forming Power, and therefore the Child born followeth the Imagination, and not the power of forming and shaping, because 'tis weakest.

•

Q: Why is it naught to lie on the back?

A: Because as the Physicians say, It disposes a Man to Leprosie, Madness, and to an *Incubus,* where you may note, that *Mania,* or Madness, is the hurt or disturbance of the fore part of the brain, with taking away or deprivation of the Imagination: but *Incubus* (ie. the Night mare) is a Passion of the Heart, wherein a Man thinks himself to be strangled in his sleep, and something lies heavy on his Stomach, which he would put off.

Cont from p5

the co-operation of the long-suffering Harper family of Enfield.

It now seems clear that the poltergeist is a *syndrome* – a concurrence of symptoms, including a surplus of bioenergy, as (but not always) at menarche, and a climate of tension and frustration. And although neither I nor anybody else can explain how the furniture falls over, it is now possible to put forward a tentative model. Here goes:

When large amounts of energy are lost by humans, they can form a separate physical entity that takes the shape of a kind of psychic football. This is spherical and very cold. It can move around on its own, it can wrap itself around objects and travel with them – not throw them, but 'envelop' them, as Allan Kardec put it twenty years before the SPR was founded.

Imagine a gang of kids wandering around the countryside. They suddenly come across a huge empty field with a nice football in the middle. So what do they do? They kick the ball around, of course, and have a good game until they get tired. Then they go home for their tea.

Something analogous seems to happen on poltergeist cases. A gang of discarnate consciousness-packets, spirits or whatever we want to call them, wander around and come across bioenergy 'footballs' which they start to play with. If the energy-ball is strong enough, the bigger boys, good and bad, also get hold of it, for the ball is a means of interacting between our dimension and theirs.

Occasionally, these balls become visible, though usually only those controlled by good entities. (Cf. stories of glowing lights on mountains, etc.) [See Playfair's letter, 'Guiding Light', FT31p53–Ed.] Sometimes they can be dispersed, whereupon they make an awful smell as they dissolve into pools of liquid on the floor.

Naturally, we need more evidence to support this model, and the problem is that poltergeists are not cooperative. That early Scottish researcher, Macbeth, learned by the end of Act One that the unseen world reveals itself on its terms, not ours. I know just how he felt when, after the witches had done some pretty impressive forecasting, he said:

Stay, you imperfect speakers, tell me more,
...Say from whence
You owe this strange intelligence, or why
Upon this blasted heath you stop our way
With such prophetic greeting? Speak,
I charge you.

But the witches vanish. They always do.

Guy Lyon Playfair•

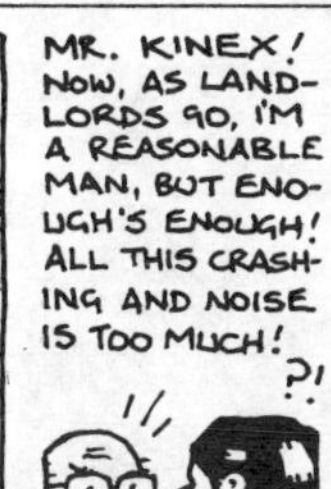

Gateways to Mystery.

In the previous two parts of this series (FT31, FT32), **David Fideler** outlined two 'gateways' into the understanding of the phenomena of a given area — by considering them in the context of the geomagnetic landscape, and temporally, by compliing chronologies of data. In this conclusion to the series David is joined by **Bob Tarte,** also of the Michigan Anomaly Research group, as they describe the third and most complex of the 'gateways' — the psychological and mystical dimension of the happenings and experiences — one which may well be more rewarding of greater study in the future.

Figure C – 'The Ubiquity of the Stone', an alchemical drawing from Michael Maier's *Atlanta Fugiens* (Frankfort, 1618).

SOME ARCHETYPAL DIMENSIONS OF THE UFO MYTHOS

If we are not dealing with space visitors at all, but with powerful imagery projected in order to alter individual belief systems, then the dream-like, hallucinatory nature of the experience begins to make more sense. We could even imagine that the object is a form of natural energy; that close exposure to it triggered the vision; and that the most important question to ask is, what effect do such visions have on the society around the witness?

Jacques Vallee.

The puzzling complexity of the so-called UFO 'phenomenon' makes it highly unlikely that any one theory or hypothesis will account for the dazzling diversity of events, rumours, and reports commonly filed under that singular and monistic misnomer. For unless we can escape the temptation of UFOlogical montheism, these phenomena will continue to be viewed through the all-or-nothing categories of extraterrestrial visitors; ultraterrestrial invaders; dark angels of Satan scaring the bejesus out of the 'born again'; or 'nothing but' astronomical misidentifications.

Following Dr Vallee's suggestion, it was conjectured in part one that *some* UFO reports result from the observation of natural telluric discharge phenomena in 'geophysical window areas'. It was further speculated that an objective 'close encounter' between electromagnetic discharge and unfortunate percipient might induce a subjective, hallucinatory flow of imagery, predetermined, and later interpreted through the predominate cultural belief systems and myths, which might account for some reports of 'UFO abductions'.

Many researchers have found it most difficult, and sometimes impossible, to draw a sharp dividing line between the psychological and objective aspects of 'the UFO phenomenon', because in the gray, twilight world of phenomenal reality, the two may be inextricably intertwined. This has also been verified in the psychological realm by the explorations of C. G. Jung, who demonstrated that apparently subjective mental phenomena are in fact moulded by archetypal factors of the objective psyche, or collective unconscious.

Perhaps the most cohesive element of the UFO 'phenomenon' is the psychological dimension, which is inseparably connected to what we may call *the flying saucer mythos.* This basic and crucial aspect is certainly the most overlooked element on the popular level, precisely because the popular treatment of flying saucers *is* the psychological dimension. In other words, the treatment of UFOs in the realm of popular culture is predetermined by a wide range of psychological factors, many of which appear to have an archetypal foundation. Secondly, the manner of treatment is *psychologically revealing.* And from this perspective, the UFO mythos is a psychic revelation of the factors which shape our view of the world, our hopes, and our fears.

PERCEPTION, PROJECTION, AND THE PARANORMAL

All reports of unusual phenomena are coloured by the psychology of the witness, the prevalent cultural world-view, and the *Zeitgeist,* or 'spirit of the times'. This is because everything that an individual perceives is, to a certain extent, a product of the observer. Likewise, the observer, within certain limits, is a product of everything he has perceived.

During the great dream known as the Middle Ages, the populace trafficked with angels, fairies, and elementals. As today, a few were taken away to the Otherworld and brought back. It was a time when the psyche was close to nature, and the soul's tendency to personify was reflected in the elusive mercurial spirits that inhabited the twilight world of an earth-centred cosmos.

There is no compelling reason to deny the objective existence of the elves, fauns, and fairies of the Otherworld (ie the unconscious), as long as we realize that these little people of the imagination are the same psychologically objective figures who populate our dreams and fantasies. Through the faculty of the imagination, our complexes and constellations of psychic energy are personified, appearing in dreams, and sometimes spilling over into the external world.

This is readily apparent in terms of the UFO phenomenon, where the questions of perception and projection are of fundamental importance, because 'everything unknown and empty is filled with psychological projection...' [89] For example, it is a well-known fact that at least 80 to 90% of all initial UFO reports result from the 'misidentification' of astronomical or man-made phenomena. What this so-called misidentification represents, in actuality, is the projection of psychic contents and qualities upon objective and external phenomena. *It is not enough to merely say that a 'misidentification' occurs when someone construes Venus as a hovering 'UFO'.* We must be prepared to take a further step, notice the blurring of mind and matter, and pursue the factors responsible, even if we are thrown up against seemingly impenetrable gateways to mystery...

THE EVOLUTION OF THE FLYING SAUCER

This quasi-physical blurring of mind and matter may be easily seen within the context of America's first major UFO wave, when many

POPULAR LIBRARY
The Book Everyone Is Talking About
BEHIND THE FLYING SAUCERS
Frank Scully

Figure A – the cover of Frank Scully's 1950 UFO book seems to reveal the psychological forces constellated by 'the coming of the saucers'.

reports were made of dirigible-shaped airships in 1897, just as man stood on the threshold of perfecting aerial flight. [90] The airship was said to be the *opus* of some Yankee inventor, who would soon release his secret to the world. A number of newspaper hoaxes fueled the epidemic of reports, and it now appears, in retrospect, that a great many individuals who saw the airship's mysterious lights in the night-time sky, were actually observing Venus and other conventional phenomena. [91]

However, any approach which dismisses UFOs – or 'airships' – as nothing more than astronomical misidentifications, fails to grasp the important, psychological significance of these phenomena, and their mythological foundations. And since neither UFOs nor airships behave like real objects, the same methods used to interpret dreams resolve many of the logical contradictions in the sightings.

•

Two significant influences on nineteenth-century thinking were the birth of modern technology and Darwin's *The Origin of Species.* Darwin contributed the idea that man is travelling an upward spiral from his primitive, animal origins. Technology, as visible proof of man's ingenuity, seemed to confirm this thought. Consequently, a hopeful future was popularly envisioned in which scientific progress might raise man to the highest state he could and should achieve. Utopia seemed not too far off.

In this context, the airships make perfect symbolic sense. They neatly embody the idea of the soaring industrial dream, where man is lifted above all wordly concerns, not by religion for once, but by the machine. The frequent breakdowns of the airships are significant, too, pointing towards the failure of technology as the ultimate problem solver.

When the airships reappeared in the middle of the twentieth century, they necessarily took on different shapes to conform to the times. The term 'flying saucer' first entered our vocabulary in 1947, after two world-shaking wars and the invention of the atomic bomb, the most destructive machine ever devised. If the airships represented our hopes for technology, the UFOs reflected the fear that it was running out of control. It was fitting, then, that the pilots of the modern 'phantom airships' were not Yankee inventors, but unimaginable aliens – as if the liberating partnership between human and machine had now been broken.

A force beyond the knowledge of our science was said to power the saucers. They moved at blinding speeds, stopping abruptly or changing direction in defiance of physical law. Orthodox science turned its back on the phenomenon, and the saucers grew more and more mystical.

'Contactees' sprang up across the country; people who claimed to have ridden the spaceships to Eden-like planets and who brought back messages with them. The Visitors, they said, had come to save humanity from itself. They warned of dire consequences for earth if we did not stop our political quarrels, and told us nuclear testing was destroying the balance of nature. [92] Some contactees called the UFOnauts 'servants of the Lord', or identified them with angels. In their mental and physical perfection, and their interest in the fate of man, the aliens were the closest thing to gods we had seen in centuries.

If the atomic bomb blew the hinges off from Pandora's Box, 'the coming of the saucers' may be equated with the return of repressed feminine values, and the archaic pagan forces (ie archetypes or 'gods') which, 30 years later, populate our entertainment media to the extent that there is no escape. This motif is most evident in figure A where the mystical saucers imposingly hover over the phallic towers of Western technology. The male/female dualism is clearly delineated here, and not only are flying saucers leaking into consensus reality, but a good deal of feminine cleavage accompanies the return of matriarchal consciousness.

In this compensatory aspect, we may envision the UFO image as a magical and anti-scientific symbol, which exerts its influence over the collective through the medium of popular culture. [93] Moreover, the rapidly escalating acceptance of flying saucers from beyond, and their god-like masters, has the propensity to undermine society's certainty in the rigidly mechanistic and arid world-view of the scientific intellect, divorced as it is from the mythopoeic foundations of imagination, art, and inspiration. Obviously some form of balance is desperately required – even in the dubious realm of 'UFOlogy' – lest one become a 'scientific UFOlogist' scouring the countryside for 'nuts-and-bolts', or an equally off-centre 'contactee cultist' riding high the astral aethers of fantasy and make believe... to nowhere.

•

There is a profoundly fascinating religious dimension to the UFO Mythos, which beckons to be noticed.

An old saying calls God a circle, 'whose circumference is nowhere, but whose centre is everywhere". As is commonly known, the circle is an archaic symbol of wholeness, and the winged disc is a traditional representation of divinity. (Figure B). In the dreams of modern individuals, circular imagery often alludes to the archetypal self, which Jung defines as both the totality of the psyche, and the psychic centre which unites the ego complex with the depths of the unconscious. We may also note that as the very pivot of psychic life, symbolic representations of the self often assume a distinctly metaphysical or 'cosmic' quality in the allegory of dream-language, owing to its central importance.

Of course, this type of symbolism reverberates throughout the history of religion and mythopoeic experience, typically appearing in the *mandala* (Sanscrit for 'magic circle'); the quaternity or cross; the divine child and saviour; the Philosopher's Stone; the square or cube; a city or temple; the sacred centre, and so on. Moreover, when these archetypal images spontaneously appear in dreams or visions, they are often surrounded by an aura of numinosity, which may evoke ambigous feelings of awe, wonder, and fear. [94]

It is the empirical observation of modern depth psychology that 'Mandalas... usually appear in situations of psychic confusion and perplexity. The archetype thereby constellated represents a pattern of order which, like a psychological 'view finder' marked with a cross or a circle divided into four, is superimposed on the psychic chaos so that each content falls into place and the weltering confusion is held together by the protective circle...' [95] Therefore, Jung found it highly significant that flying saucers (or flying mandalas, if you will), appeared spontaneously during a time of great psychic fragmentation, after the wars, and the Promethean development of nuclear technology, which still threatens to destroy the world, today more than ever.

A MYTHOPOEIC EXIT
or
FLYING SAUCER SYMBOLISM UNDER–THE–EYE

Metaphorically, and symbolically, the ubiquity of the UFO image is analogous to that of the Philosophers' Stone. (Figure C) As archetypal and poetic images of wholeness, or mandalas, both unite the celestial with the terrestrial, and other pairs of opposites. Flying saucers, as the dream machines of science fiction, are both magical and technological at once.

The visionary accounts of the 'UFO abductees' often allude to the presence of an awe-ful eye in the centre of the saucer, by which they are examined and judged. Likewise, '...Nothing can be concealed from the Stone, all is open to its view... the Stone is thus equivalent to the all-seeing eye of God." [96]

Figure B – I: Egyptian winged disc; II: Assyrian form; III: Syro-Hittite form; IV: Babylonian form.

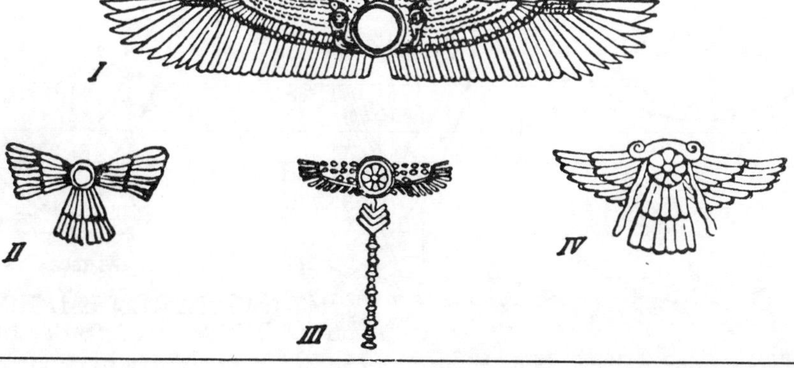

We are reminded of the four-fold mandala-vision of the prophet Ezekiel:

> '...*The wheels had the sparkling appearance of chrysolite, and all four of them looked the same: they were constructed as though one wheel were within another. They could move in any of the four dimensions that they faced, without veering as they moved.* The four of them had rims, and I saw that their rims were full of eyes all around.' [97]
> (Our emphasis.)

In his *Flying Saucers: A Modern Myth of Things Seen in the Sky,* C. G. Jung relates that: 'The centre is frequently symbolized by an eye: the ever-open eye of the fish in alchemy, or the unsleeping 'God's eye' of consciousness, or the all-seeing sun...' [98;99]

An eye-shaped symbol of a fish is the *vesica piscis*, which is formed by two interpenetrating circles, and looks like a flying saucer in profile. (Figure D) The vesica was employed by the early Christians as a symbol of the all-seeing Son, who was also known as Ikthus, which means Fish. [100] As a symbolic glyph, the vessel of the fish represents the union and reconciliation of opposites; it is the middle and intermediate realm between the two 'opposing' circles of spirit and matter.

Traditionally, this phenomenal middle realm has been equated with the human soul (ie psyche), and the world of imagination where spirit matters, or matter and spirit meet.

Christ is said to be the mediator between heaven and earth, and it is well known in art history that he appears in the mediatrix of the vesica. Further, since the temple is a gateway linking heaven and earth, and the church is known as the 'Body of Christ', a good many mediaeval cathedrals are based on the geometry of two interpenetrating circles. (Figure E)

According to the contactees, flying saucers are the gateways which lead from the terrestrial realm to the sphere of the heavenly Space Brethren. Concerning the eventual probability of interplanetary contact we will not speculate; but as connoisseurs of the poetic imagination we take delight in all systems of religious symbolism, because these are the natural phenomena of psychic expression.

It is well known, and even more widely felt, that the fire of the scientific intellect has permanently crippled the myth of Christianity. But the coming of the saucers, and each subsequent 'wave' of reports, may signal the return of the gods and daemons from the deep – washed up like the mind-boggling 'flying fish' which was recently seen by multiple witnesses, hovering 50 feet above some railroad tracks in Ventura County, California. (Figure F)

We have been developing the idea of awesome and autonomous dream symbols which leak into and influence consensus reality through the gateway of the human psyche. Within this imaginal context, the flying saucer is an eye-in-the-sky which has returned to judge humanity, while ever peering toward the future. (Figure G)

Figure D – the vessica piscis, or 'vessel of the fish'.

Figure E – Vessica geometry from Claude Bragdon's *The Beautiful Necessity* (reprinted in 1978 by the Thosophical Publishing House.)

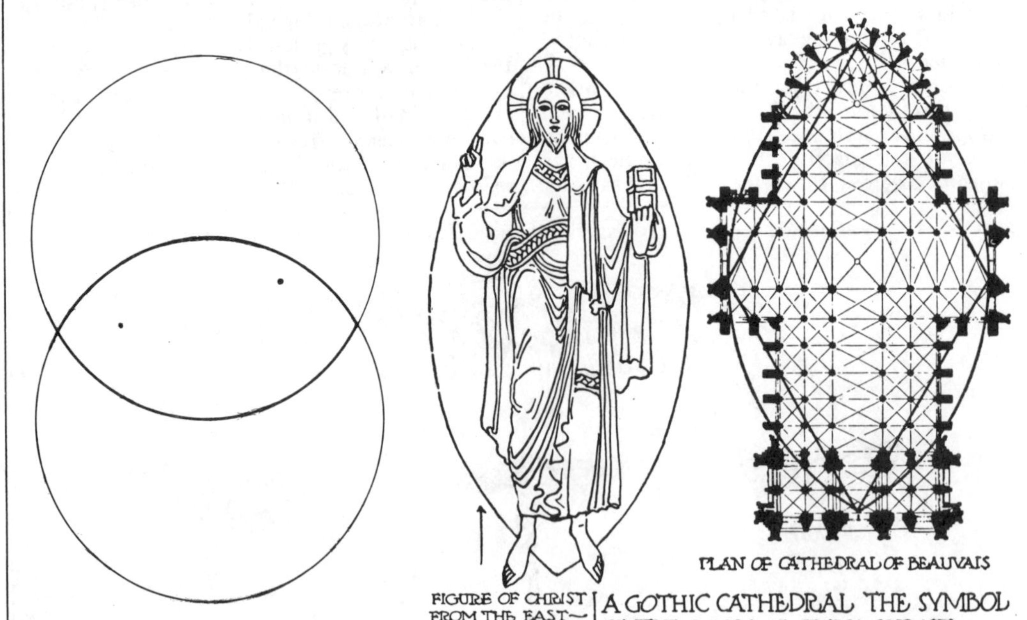

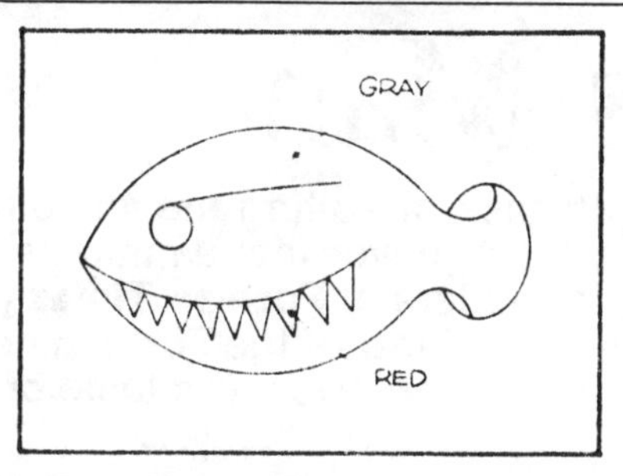

Figure F – This UFO was seen by several reliable witnesses on 31 August 1976, near Camarillo, California. (Drawing from *APRO Bulletin* Dec 1976 – APRO: 3910 E. Kleindale Rd, Tuscon, AZ 85712, USA.)

Any astrologer worth his alchemical salt will tell you that we are quickly moving from the Platonic month of the Fish into that of the Water-Bearer, who looms quite high overhead. Whether or not flying saucers are merely the psychic remnants of a dying Fish God is most difficult to say at this time, but after the Piscean flows into the Aquarian, well, then we will know for sure.

Regardless of the phenomenon's physical dimension, to a very large extent we are dealing with a mythos – a paradoxical phenomenon of the poetic faculty – which is more solid than the purely imaginary, but more ethereal than the purely physical. It would seem that the ambiguity of the Philosopher's Stone has taken to the heavens, where it forces man **on the collective level** to thoughtfully question his place in the universe, his values, and his very cosmology.

For millions of individuals, the world over, the mercurial *numinosum* of the UFO image is a doorway, or gateway, to mystery. And from this perspective, there can be no doubt that flying saucers are a phenomenon of the soul, shining out in times of social crisis and psychological transition.

David Fideler/Bob Tarte •

REFERENCES

89) C.G. Jung: *Psychology and Alchemy,* CW 12, par. 332.
90) Two good accounts of the airship reports are in D.M. Jacobs: *The UFO Controversy in America* (Indiana University Press, Bloomington, Ind: 1975), Chapt. 1; and J. Clark and L. Coleman: *The Unidentified: Notes Toward Solving the UFO Mystery* (Warner Paperback Library, New York: 1975).
91) See R.G. Neely, Jr: '1897: The Airship in Illinois', *Journal of UFO Studies,* Vol. 1, No. 1, pp 49–69.
92) Thus the UFO phenomenon, or flying saucer mythos, takes on a function analogous to the dream process itself. *'The general function of dreams is to try to restore our psychological balance by producing dream material that re-establishes, in a subtle way, the total psychic equilibrium. This is what I call the complementary (or compensatory) role of dreams in our psychic make-up...'* — C.G. Jung in *Man and his Symbols* Aldus Books, London: 1964), p. 50.
93) See J. Rimmer: 'The UFO as an Anti-Scientific Symbol', MUFOB (now *Magonia),* Vol. 2, No. 4.
94) Regarding the phenomenology of mandala symbolism, the inquiring reader may consult the following writings of C.G. Jung: *The Archetypes and the Collective Unconscious* (CW 9, part 1); *Psychology and Alchemy* (CW 12); and *Aion: The Phenomenology of the Self* (CW 9, part II). An excellent introduction is E.F. Edinger: *Ego and Archetype: Individuation and the Religious Function of the Psyche* (Pelican, New York: 1973).
95) C.G. Jung: *Civilization in Transition,* CW 10, par. 803.
96) E.F. Edinger: *Ego and Archetype,* Chapt. 10, p. 282.
97) Ezekiel 1: 16–18.
98) C.G. Jung: CW 10, par. 807.
99) Since symbolic representations of the self express the ideas of 'transpersonal' wholeness and totality, they may be qualititively identical with the image of divinity. A good example is to be found in 'The Baptism of Christ' by Aert de Gelder (1645–1727), which appears in *Fortean Times* 25. In this painting the godhead is represented as a hovering disc, with a penetrating eye poised in the center. Four beams of light descend on the figure of Christ below, thus expressing the idea of the quaternity, and the marriage of opposites.
100) Ikthus is an acronym from the Greek phrase 'Jesus Christ, Son of God, Savour', because the birth of the Fish God inaugurated the Platonic Month, or Aeon, of Pisces. Further clarifications are to be found in J. Michell's *City of Revelation* Abacus, London: 1973). Those interested in the relationships between archaic fish symbolism and flying saucers should consult Anthony Nugent's essay: 'Quicksilver in Twilight: A Close Encounter with a Hermetic Eye', in *Spring* 1978. (Spring Publications, Box 1, University of Dallas, Irving, TX 75061 USA).

CW refers to the *Collected Works of C.G. Jung,* Published by Princeton University Press, USA, and Routledge & Kegan Paul, London.

(Acknowledgements: We would like to thank Jerry Clark and Loren Coleman for *The Unidentified;* Anthony Nugent for his perceptive reflections; Allen H. Greenfield; and the entire FT staff for their splendid help.)

Figure G–'The Eye of God' (16th C woodcut).

Man Bites Man

Paul Sieveking recently finished the mamoth task of editing the 45 volume newsclipping collection of the late eccentric George Ives into a manageable book, **Man Bites Man,** now on special offer to readers of **Fortean Times** (see back cover). Last issues (FT32 p30) Paul gives us a few of the Fortean items that had to be excluded from the book — this time he gives us a taste of the goodies that made it.

CHICKEN GIRLS

A Sydney woman was fined £1 in November 1903 by an Australian police court for leaving her child to be reared in a chicken run, with the consequence that the little one could do nothing but imitate the fowls in every way, even to roosting at night.

An eminent ornithologist at the Zoological Society in London at the time commented: 'I am unaware of any previous instance of a child being raised by birds.' He did recall, however, a case in Scandinavia where a child was nursed by a pet swan after the mother had died in childbirth. *(Daily Express* 3 Nov, — 4 Nov 1903.)

More recently, a chicken child was reported in June 1980. Since birth, 10-year-old Isabel Quaresma (see photo) had lived in a chicken coop in Tabua, close to Portugal's central university city of Coimbra. Her mother is a mentally deficient rural worker who has had two other children by members of her own family. Isabel is the only child not born of an incestuous liaison. In the coop she was thrown pieces of bread and shared the chicken-feed.

Neighbours gossiped about this scandal for years, and in the end a district hospital worker took her away. She is now in a private clinic in Lisbon. She could neither talk nor was she toilet trained, and is only now learning to eat with a spoon. She gestured and made sounds like a chicken, and scratched food up with her hands. Her body is severely stunted, with a tiny head, probably due to malnutrition. One eye is clouded with a cataract, thought to be the result of a hen scratch. The psychiatrist in charge of her case is optimistic about her chances of social awakening. *Guardian* 12 Jun 1980.

DROUGHT AND DEATH

It might be supposed that propitiating the weather gods with human sacrifice was a long-lapsed activity. We noted some recent incidents last issue, but George Ives collected some even earlier twentieth century cases.

For some months in 1922–23, elders of the Mtawara tribe in Rhodesia, alarmed at the long drought and the poor crops following a season of famine, held councils led by a rain doctor. They decided on a tried and trusted remedy – a human victim burned before a suppliant people.

Isabel Quaresma, the modern 'chicken girl', emerges from the chicken coop which has been her home for eight years. (Photo: Alvares Tavares AP. Credit: Howard Wolinsky.)

The chosen one was seized, bound and publicly burned and the drought immediately broke. 63 men were subsequently charged with murder, but the apparent success of the sacrice, as the *Daily News* of 19 February 1923 points out, 'is the surest guarantee that a custom which has already sent some 70 unfortunate men to a horrid death will be continued.'

In 1927 the rain god was being over-active in Bulgaria, and the peasants thought the incessant rains had been sent as a special punishment for their sins. In one village a special committee was formed to pick out the wickedest men. Four hardened scoundrels were solemly told to prepare themselves to die. The authorities, however, got wind of this and arrested the lynching committee before they could act. *(Evening Standard* 29 Aug 1927.)

In the same area of Europe seven years later, drought struck again and rain-making rites were rife. In some villages naked girls dressed only in green leaves danced and sang in the streets and flung their garlands into neighbouring streams as a sacrifice. (Last year we noted Indian women tilling the fields naked by moonlight in order to break a drought.) At Dragovatz in Yugoslavia two youths suddenly seized a priest who had just conducted prayers for rain on the river bank and hurled him into the water to appease the pagan rain god. *(Sunday Referee* 3 June 1934.)

The inhabitants of a village in the Punjab were worried about drought in the Autumn of 1937. They kidnapped a youth from a neighbouring village and paraded him in chains down the main street to the accompaniment of beating drums. He was beheaded before the village temple and his head placed at the foot of the deity. The police subsequently arrested 25 villagers and the officiating priest. *(News of the World* 19 Sep 1937)

FOSSIL FOOTPRINTS

In August 1905 a human footprint was uncovered in an anthracite colliery at Eagle Hill, near Potisville, Pennsylvania, in which fossil snakes and ferns were plentiful. Could humankind possibly have walked the Earth in the Carboniferous period, 270 to 350 million years ago?

Another footprint was found in Eocene rocks (40 to 70 million years old) in Cyprus by two members of British Instructional Films in 1927, and was taken to Cyprus Museum. One of the men, Mr. E.W. Edwards, said: 'In a dry water course on Mount Hilarion we came upon a fragment of rock similar to the rest of the mountain, and in the fragment there was the imprint. It had filled with liquid, which had fossilized into flint.' There are many 'impossible footprints' on record. Do we rethink our geology, our history or our ideas about the nature of matter? (— 18 Aug 1905; *Daily News* 23 April 1927)

DOUBLE TAKES

In May 1907 Albert Steer left his family in Bickley with a vague word of a journey into Surrey, and the next day a drowned man's body was found near Chelsea Bridge. The description seemed to fit that of Albert Steer, and when they

saw the body at the Horseferry mortuary, his son and daughter were certain it was him.

Albert Steer had lost an eye, this drowned man was one-eyed. One of his toes had been crushed, and the body had a crushed toe. His face was marked with a dent over the eye-brow where a piece of bone had been taken away and here was the same dent in the same place.

He was duly buried with a memorial stone in the cemetary on Bromley Common. Two months later, Albert Steer turned up again, with an uneventful story of working for a gardener at Little Malden. The police still had a photograph of the corpse, and had to advertise again for friends of a one-eyed man with a broken toe and a dent above the eye-brow. *(Evening News* 3 July 1907.)

A gruesome legend was told about a pool at Chalfont in Buckinghamshire known locally as the Half Hour Pond. A girl once drowned herself there after waiting in vain for half an hour for her lover. It was said that if anyone ran round the pond three times they would see the girl's hand above the water.

23-year-old Florence Barley of New Bradwell, Bucks, had obtained work locally to be near her sweetheart, George Roberts. On being told the pond legend she laughed and said 'What a silly girl'. On 12 September 1931 she was visited by her father and gave him five shillings for her mother. The next morning she was reported missing.

After a five day search, two local workmen saw a girl's hand above the water in the middle of the pond. They cleared the weeds and recovered the body of Florence Barley. At the inquest it was declared that she had been happy and cheerful with no worries. Chalfont people were then afraid to go near the pond, and took circuitous routes home to avoid it after dark. *(News of the World* 20 Sept 1931.)

MAN BITES MAN

The above items are taken from the George Ives Archive of Press-clippings (1890–1950), from which I have selected 584 for the book *Man Bites Man.*

The topics covered include:

Armageddon Forecasts – Weird Compulsions – Animal Attacks – History of Drug Usage – Ripperism – Bizarre Pronouncements – The Welsh Revival – Witch Persecution – Quaint Trials – Fireball and Lightning Strikes – Sea Serpents – Astounding Coincidences – Hypnotism – Human Sacrifice – Visions and Predicitions – Cannibalism – Materialisations – Strange Death – Feral Humans – Human and Animal Freaks – Transvestism – Ship Mysteries – Mass Hysteria – Black Magic – Ghosts and Poltergeists – War Propaganda – Incest – Aleister Crowley – Cesare Lombroso – Edward Bulwer Lytton – Oscar Wilde –and articles by G.K. Chesterton and Aldous Huxley.

Paul Sieveking•

Our plan to devote this space to news of forthcoming books, lectures, expeditions and meetings was well received, — so authors, publishers, and organizers are invited to keep us informed. But remember there could be a publishing delay of up to 2 months — so the sooner you let us know the better.

The end of this year is proving an exciting time for British Forteans and those interested in the paranormal in all its guises. Yorkshire TV began their big budget series, 'Arthur C Clarke's Mysterious World' in 13 half-hour segments.

At our deadline the remaining programmes are: 'The Great Siberian Explosion' 14 Oct; 'The Riddle of the Stones' 21 Oct; 'Out of the Blue' 28 Oct; 'UFOs' 4 Nov; 'Dragons, Dinosaurs & Great Snakes' 11 Nov; 'Strange Skies' 18 Nov; 'Arthur C Clarke's Cabinet of Curiosities' 25 Nov. This last segment will pay specific tribute to Charles Fort.

Orbis Publishing Ltd will begin marketing their part-work *The Unexplained* nationally from mid-October, having conducted a successful trial in the Anglian region. With articles by leading Forteans and ufologists – parts 1–3 include Roy Stemman on psi, Charles Bowen on C3Ks, the Bords on manimals, Hilary Evans on the case for UFOs, Bob Rickard on SHC, Brian Inglis on hypnosis, Brian Snellgrove on Kirlian photography, etc – the series is intended to continue over the next two years. We will be following the progress of both with great interest.

BOOK NEWS

• As we go to press the following hardcover books are due for release in October. *Photographs of the Unknown* by Bob Rickard & Richard Kelly (New English Library). *The Encyclopaedia of UFOs* by Ronald Story (New English Library). *The Ark File* by Rene Noorbergen (New English Library). *Radical Occultism* by Richard Elen (Wildwood House). *Double Helix of the Mind* by Stan Gooch (Wildwood House).

• A new book is imminent from Paul Devereux, editor of *The Ley Hunter,* but no date is given for publication. It is *Earth Energies and UFOs: An Investigation of the Thor Factor,* from Turnstone Press. Readers of FT11 and FT12 will remember the articles by Paul and Andy York on the Leicestershire window areas and have some insight into what Paul will be dishing up.

• In January 1981, Granada will be publishing Charles Berlitz' *The Roswell Incident,* claimed to be a detailed encounter with a UFO, and rumoured to be about 'crashed UFOs'.

• Also in early 1981, another book from Jenny Randles, *UFO Study: A Handbook for Enthusiasts,* from Robert Hale.

NEW GROUP

We heard from John Keel that he is starting up a new Fortean Society for those interested in meeting at infrequent intervals in New York City. For more information write to – The New Fortean Society: Box 351, Murray Hill Station, New York, NY 10016, USA.

MEETINGS & LECTURES

• The new season of BUFORA lectures is as interesting and varied as usual. The venue is Kensington Central Library, Campden Hill Road, London W8 – starts at 7pm – non-members welcome if seats available. Further programme next issue.

1 Nov 80 – 'Paranormal Nuts & Bolts' by Capt Ivar Mackay.
6 Dec 80 – AGM followed by 'Odd Encounters of a Curious Kind' by Alan Watts, at 8.30.
3 Jan 81 – 'Life on Earth: A Fluke?' by Martin Heath.

• Lectures at the Society for Psychical Research, 1 Adam & Eve Mews, Kensington, London W8. (01-937 8984). No times are given so contact them for more info. Non-members £1.

11 Nov 80 – 'Psychical Research & Education' by Anita Gregory.
2 Dec 80 – 'Silent Witness', the Turin Shroud film.
8 Jan 81 – 'Minds Haunted by the Past' by Ian Wilson.

• Those interested in serious discussions of the questions highlighted by the writings of Velikovsky will be interested to learn of a lecture by Don Robbins on the 'Problems of Radiometric Dating'. It will be held at 4pm on 23 November, at the Library Association, Ridgmount St, London (nearest tube, Goodge Street), by the Society for Interdisciplinary Studies. This lecture, however, is open to non-members.

Credit: J + C Bord, David Rees. **RJMR.**

PHENOMENOMIX!

HUNT EMERSON

"...AND BAFFLING BLAZES THAT FALL FROM THE SKY OR SHOOT FROM THE GROUND!"

Moses and the Burning Soap.

Indonesian Fire Walker.

Richardson (an "entertainer") 1672

Lily White, whose clothes kept bursting into flame (Antigua, 1929)

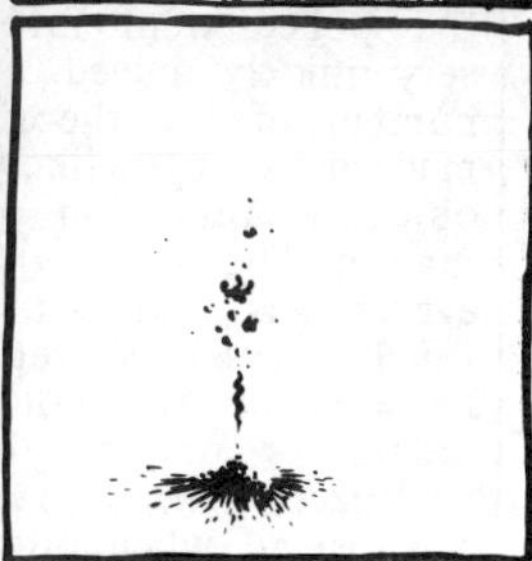

In his last book, Wild Talents (1932), Charles Fort focussed interest on the genre of 'mass hysteria' reports, and the fact that every explanation of them left more questions unanswered than answered. We were recently presented with this splendid example.

THE HOLLINWELL INCIDENT

Sunday 13 July 1980 – the day of the Hollinwell Show in fields near Kirkby in Ashfield, Nottinghamshire. It was to feature a competition between junior brass and marching bands, many of whom had travelled far in coaches to be there for the 9.30am start. They prepared for the inspection parades which began shortly after 11am. Just before midday over two hundred of the children and some adults collapsed. They were ferried by dozens of ambulances to four area hospitals, where about 259 people were examined. Nine were detained overnight–seven children and two babies. Among the symptoms reported were: fainting, running eyes, sore throats, dizziness, vomiting, trembling, weakness, numbness and a metallic taste in the mouth – but not all at once or in the same person.

In the days that followed there were many investigations and interviews. In the light of later comments, we note that the area health authorities and the police went into action very quickly indeed, so that a number of the theories were made more or less likely by the quick accumulation of information. The main sequence of events is known. Terry Bingham (variously reported to be one of the competition judges, or one of the show organizers): 'We were ready for the display when one or two children collapsed. Then a few more went, and a few more. We called off the event but others fell as they came out of the arena. Then spectators started dropping.' Another witness said: 'Some kids were catching their friends as they fell, and then they were falling down themselves... No one could understand what was happening... It was like a battlefield with bodies everywhere.' A policeman attending said: 'The kids went down like ninepins.'

One of the girls affected, Petula Merriman, 14, said: 'We were on the field in full uniform for an inspection... I've never had to stand to attention that long before. As we marched off I tried to grab hold of my drum but just fell on the floor. My friends were collapsing all around me.' Another of the afflicted, Kerry Elliott, 10, said: 'I just went all weak and got pains in my stomach and then I fainted. Everyone was falling down and some were crying. My stomach was all tight and aching. I felt better when I came round in hospital...' Her 7-year-old brother, Steven, was similarly affected.

Some of the adults fell during the height of the panic, some were taken ill accompanying their children to the hospital, and still others collapsed in wards at bedsides. Terry Bingham (whom we met above) said his own eyes began stinging and watering as he drove six kids to hospital in his car. 'I had chest pains. It was like nerve gas poisoning.' Terry Bingham is later to develop this idea. Margaret Palethorpe, 37, mother of five, three of whom were among the collapsed children, said she felt pins and needles in her tongue and lips. 'I collapsed and lost the use of one arm.' Linda Elliott, mother of Kerry and Steven (above), felt strange as she comforted her children on the way to hospital where she too collapsed. 'My arms and legs felt like sponges and it was like cramp in my stomach. That's all I remember until I came round.' Mrs Edna Wells, chairman of one band, the Ashford Imperials, said she tried to keep the children talking. '...I was helping them but I was taken ill too.'

Altogether 15 adults and 2 horses were affected, said the *Daily Star* 14 July. Horses? We'll come to that in a minute.

THE THEORIES

A good part of the fun for Forteans is to see the proliferation of theories that come in the wake of an unexpected or puzzling event, and to watch the manoeuvring of their protagonists. In this case most of the theories came in with the first reports, with a few exotic stragglers in the following few days.

Food Poisoning was the first thought of many who stood around the arena, staring in disbelief at the numbers of children keeling over. Some well-intentioned party actually broadcast urgent messages over the public address system warning people not to eat the ice cream or drink water until the source of the trouble was found. A few minutes later another warning came, this time about mineral waters. When the police moved in with health officials a short time later, they took samples of food and drink from all the stalls – but it soon became clear this theory was not tenable. Many of the children had not eaten or drunk anything which they had not brought with them in their coaches. The results of tests on the samples was a formality and proved negative in all cases. The Severn-Trent Water Authority, who supply the area, were also quick off the mark. By the end of the day they were able to say the water had 'no bacterial impurity'. The food poisoning theory was the first to be eliminated, but not in time to save the ice cream men, who for several days afterward, were subjected to taunts and jeered off estates around Kirkby in Ashfield.

By the time the police and health authorities arrived at Hollinwell a second theory was current – one which was to prove longer-lasting. It was mooted that the children had been poisoned by a **chemical insecticide** used by farmers in spraying crops. The *Daily Mirror* (14 July) was in no doubt: 'Gas Cloud KOs Children', it yelled on the front page. Some imagined a cloud of insecticide drifting across the showground – others speculated on the dust raised by the feet of several hundred marchers. Certainly, a spokesman at the Queens Medical Centre, at Nottingham, said of the children taken there, that their symptoms 'were consistent with exposure to **fumes** of some kind'. **But every lead** turned up blank. Police tracked down the farmer who owned the field: it had not been sprayed for (reported variously as 14 to 40) years. A light plane had been seen in the area three days previously (on 10 July) and it was rumoured that it was spraying the Nottinghamshire Golf Club course and woods nearby – an event contradicted by the Golf Club officials and a woodsman.

As news of the mass collapse spread across the nation via radio bulletins, the local police were telephoned by a man in Scotland who suggested that people had been affected by **high frequency radio waves.** Seek and ye shall find, is a law of phenomenology. Lo! A high frequency transmitter was found nearby at a Gas Board depot. It did not take long to eliminate this line of inquiry.

In the search for a source of fumes, the police sniffed hopefully in the direction of **a plastics fire** that caused £1 million worth of damages to a firm that made plant pots (variously reported to be 6 to 12 miles distant). Unfortunately it seems the wind was blowing in the wrong direction for this to be a likelihood.

Some reports in regional papers on the 14th suggested the cause was a **'mystery bug'**. But the term was used vaguely and soon dropped from sight. Among the culprits considered by the *Sunday Times* (20 July) was the coxsackie virus, known to be epidemic in the area. However, according to Dr Malcolm (or is it Michael?) Lewis, it causes only a mild illness with chicken-pox-like water-filled blisters, which the locals call 'blebs'. Quite a few of the children were discovered to have these 'blebs', but medically it was thought extremely unlikely that this was the cause of so widespread a reaction. One AP report that reached US papers, datelined 15 July, mentioned 'invasion from Outer Space' among other theories; *Des Moines Register* (Iowa) 16 July.

In the *Daily Telegraph* (26 July) Dr Michael (or Malcolm, in some reports) Lewis revealed that the police had investigated reports that **a UFO** had landed in an adjacent field, though the exact connexion to this mass collapse is not elaborated upon. They found no evidence for the landing, but it is interesting as an indication of the desperation or seriousness with which they were looking into every possibility.

By the end of the day police officials were drawing a blank on all avenues, and were forced to consider the possibility of **'mass hysteria'**, but they were aware that this too was a grasping at straws. At the evening press session Detective Inspector Eric Hogden said: 'The whole thing is a complete mystery. Food poisoning and mass hysteria have definitely been ruled out. A gymkhana was held in the same field later without trouble.' But Dr John Wood, director of health for the Kirkby area, said he was becoming convinced that mass hysteria was the only possibility since tests had virtually eliminated the alternatives. 'Part of it may have been one or two feeling ill and the rest getting hysteria.' Overnight the police changed their minds and were now supporting the mass hysteria hypothesis. Mr Hogden now said: 'A large number of small children had been parading and standing to attention for some time. They would also be under some pressure due to the occasion.' He suggested that hysteria spread after the first few fell ill.

AFTERMATH

Overnight (13/14 July) five of the children released from hospitals were readmitted when their symptoms recurred.

On the 16th of July three people – a married couple and a girl of 8 – none of whom were affected on the 13th, collapsed with similar symptoms and were later released from hospital after treatment. The *Daily Mail* (17 July) said that a married couple and *two* children were involved.

We also noted the collapse of two of the bands involved in the Hollinwell incident at other meetings the following weekend – see entries for 19 and 20 July in our list of possibly related incidents below.

MASS HYSTERIA

On the 16th July the *Daily Telegraph* summarized the situation: 'Tests indicate that the cause was nothing more serious than mass hysteria.' Nothing more serious... this denigration and the angry reactions of parents and organizers is typical of the general misconceptions about the nature and prevalence of hysteria and its mysterious offshoot 'mass hysteria'. Some day we will have to examine these matters in greater detail, for it is our own experience that they are tangential to many of the phenomena we investigate, and our understanding of them is critical.

As public and medical interest in outbreaks of 'epidemic hysteria' were temporarily focussed by the Hollinwell event there were several spin-off discussions. The day after the outbreak the London *Evening Standard* (14 July) contained an interview with Dr John Nicholson, of Bedford College, London University, who is also spokesman for the British Psychological Society. He referred very briefly to several cases of outbreaks among schoolchildren – including the Hazlerigg case we mentioned in our last listing of mystery epidemics back in FT8 (Feb 1975). I'm shocked I've left such an important subject alone for so long. Anyway Dr Nicholson points out that such things are fairly common to teachers, if only on a smaller scale, and mainly among girl pupils.

An article in the *Observer* (20 July) went a lot further – such happenings had hit marching band events before. All the commentators suggested that a combination of the anxiety of performing, the tension of waiting for a long period at attention may have imposed a general condition on the children, so that when one or two fell ill on parade (as is usually inevitable) the rest followed in a mounting wave of unintentional mimicry. The *Observer* writer, Denise Winn, refers to American studies of over 1000 such cases, occurring in schools and factories, in which the American National Insititute for Occupational Safety and Health has dubbed it 'assembly line hysteria'. Other outbreaks in this country have involved factories, offices, department stores, colleges and nurses' homes (the famous Royal Free Hospital incident of 1955) as well as schools; all of which are represented in our files, and all blamed on unfindable bugs, strange smells, chemicals or food poisoning but which end up quickly and conveniently forgotten as no other solution presents itself other than 'mass hysteria'. The patterns are almost identical; first one or two, which may be genuine illnesses in most cases, and then many others as the panic grips the collective imagination. One meets similar phenomena in some poltergeist cases, in historical and contemporary accounts of mass possession, and in such modern variants as 'invisible assailants'. An example of the latter is given by Scott Rogo and Jerome Clark in their recent *Earth's Secret Inhabitants* (see reviews in last issue): the phantom 'Mad Gasser' who terrorized Matoon, Canada.

In an intelligent and compassionate article on hysteria generally, Brian Inglis, writing in the *Guardian* 15 January 1980, attacked the popular misconceptions: 'that hysteria, in epidemic form, is a kind of insanity; that it affects only weak-minded or self-indulgent people, usually silly girls (girls accounting for 70–100% of victims in schools according to the *British Medical Journal);* and that consequently it is not a real disease, but something to be ashamed of.' Inglis further points out that the two main components of hysteria were known over three centuries ago: a loss of personal control (which more usually manifests in blushing, stuttering, nervous tics etc, but which in extreme cases may manifest as compulsive lying or extreme uncontrolled behaviour); and mimicry. Hysterical effects can imitate the symptoms of the whole gamut of physical, physiological and neurological disease, ranging from the sublime (hallucinations, hysterical paralysis, automatic writing, etc) to the ridiculous (hysterical pregnancies in the male (couvade). These effects can include every symptom of toxic poisoning, which happens to be a frequent delusion – or rationalization?

Both Inglis and Winn refer to American studies and treatments of mass hysteria. In the Hazlerigg, Northumbria case, in 1972, the attending doctor tried a tactic, when 168 out of 400 schoolchildren collapsed with nausea. He separated the children from each other and deprived them of vomiting bowls and the symptoms rapidly subsided – information which Dr William Thomson gave in the *Daily Telegraph* (14 July 80) the day after the Hollinwell incident. The only guidelines given to British doctors are based on giving 'firm reassurance' to the unfortunate victims.

REACTIONS

It was predicatable that parents of afflicted children and afflicted adults themselves would resist, as they saw it, being labeled hysterics. Denis Skinner, a Labour MP, whose concern seemed more for political mileage, added his weight to the lobby for a government inquiry, saying the mass hysteria verdict was 'an insult to the intelligence and another cover-up by the Establishment.' The statements of many of the people involved in the event, although intended to refute the idea of mass hysteria, only betrayed the widespread misunderstanding of its nature. The only serious questions came in consideration of the way the illness was transmitted from the children in the arena to the others. We have to account for the two babies who became ill, the spectators, the adults and several horses. We have no clear facts on the horses. A stricken horse was mentioned among the first radio news bulletins – and a line in *The Sunday Times* (20 July) says in the following gymkhana five horses became ill and one had to be destroyed. This was later denied by the organizers, and there is certainly no mention of it among the early police reports. Quite the opposite, in fact. A gymkhana was held later in the same field but without incident, Chief (or Det., in some reports) Inspector Hogden had said.

Many of the advocates of the mass hysteria idea described the conditions of the day as tension and anxiety aggravated by the long wait and hot and humid conditions. That the day was hot seems to have been an elaboration. According to one witness, Mrs Maureen Reville: 'There was no hysteria. People did not collapse all together. It was cool enough a day for most of us to have had our coats on...' *Daily Star* (17 July).

At first parents, looking for a target for their anger, hit out at the show's organizers. The chairman of one band said: 'It was disgusting the way the judges kept the children waiting so long... no wonder they passed out.' The Mansfield and North Nottinghamshire *Chronicle and Advertizer* (17 July) was very critical of the four judges and also criticized the long period of standing to attention 'while the judges inspected the children behind the ears and checked each girl's knickers.'

To confuse matters further, the *Guardian* (15 July) reported that traces of blood and protein were found in some of the children's urine samples possibly indicating kidney damage, but just which hospital this information came from is not stated. At a news conference the next day, Dr Michael/Malcolm Lewis, head of Nottingham Public Health Laboratory, said that tests on blood and urine samples for organo-phosphorus poisoning had all proved negative. Another set of contradictory facts – according to the *Daily Mirror* (23 July) Kirkby in Ashfield health officers found traces in the field of a 'cocktail of cleansing fluid and deisel fumes' which they suspect could have contributed to the mass collapse. Either the esteemed health officials are being naturally reticent or obtuse or this is another example of the bad reporting that has dogged the incident – a mixture of fumes and fluid would be a scientific curiosity in itself! However, the next day (24 July) most papers said that having run a complete battery of tests the Kirkby in Ashfield authorities had found no traces of agricultural chemicals or toxic agents, and that included the samples of grass and earth taken from all over. This seems to be a case of the old Fortean dictum of something for everyone. Just pick a theory, boys, you're sure to find something to confirm it!

The Times (24 July) said that the findings (or lack of them) by the health authorities were greeted with scorn by the anti-hysteria lobby of parents and show organizers. Terry Bingham (now described as an organizer) called the findings 'rubbish. There has been a cover-up. Some people are still feeling ill... so how can it have been hysteria?' But wait a minute! It seems to me that the organizers were on the point of being lynched, so perhaps Mr Bingham and friends have a motive for diverting attention (and responsibility) from theselves?

That should have been that – but an article in the *New Statesman* (I've not seen this, but quote a report in the *Western Mail* 8 Aug) revived and articulated the fears of the anti-hysteria lobby, hinting, not so darkly, that deliberately or not the local authorities were involved in a sinister cover-up and the children had been poisoned by organo-phosphorus compounds. (About 50 brand variants – derived from nerve gas formulas – are used as pesticides on British farms.)

Star witness in the article is – surprise, surprise – Terry

Members of the crowd attend to collapsed children. 'It looked just like a battlefield,' said one witness. (Photo: Mansfield & N. Notts *Chronicle & Advertiser.)*

Bingham. He now claims after his release from hospital – he was affected himself as he drove some kids to hospital, remember? – he steamed open a letter from the hospital to his own doctor. The diagnosis therin, he says, was 'inhalation of organic poison.' The article alleges a similar verdict was seen on the bed-chart of a girl patient, Debra Saunders. The article also said that mass hysteria could not account for the lingering or recurring symptoms, suggesting that pesticide poisoning did. This fact is not strictly true, since in reference to an outbreak of mass hysteria in an American garment factory in 1974, Denise Winn *(Observer* 20 July) says plainly symptoms were 'delayed and repeated'.

In response to the allegation of cover-up, the exasperated medics of the Ashfield District Council published their findings (or lack of them). Nor did this satisfy their critics – though the clamouring by now was coming from people with political motives. Arthur Peacock, of the Mansfield Ecology Party said; 'Everyone but Ashfield Council can see it is ludicrous to put the blame on mass hysteria.' With such a talent for sweeping generalizations he'll go far in politics. He wrote to a number of journals calling for the uncovering of 'a major public scandal'.

LAST THOUGHTS

How could it have happened? Assuming that the medical authorities are right and the conditions of the show primed the participants, they would need to be triggered. Though most reports agree that one, perhaps two, girls collapsed first, the rest following like dominoes, no report or investigation seems to have discovered or named those two. Did they fall ill of conventional causes? It is a statistical possibility.

But I note two other items of relevance. Remember the ill-considered broadcasts blaming ice-cream and minerals? Well it seems that quite early on that morning the show's organizers had to make an announcement themselves about the dangers of eating some joke jelly babies. This scare could have set the tone for the day, the other announcements only fanned the smouldering embers, so to speak. Police never found out who made the later announcements and there is a suspicion that they might have been rumours, or imagined, and not broadcast at all.

The other item is the testimony of Margaret Palethorpe, whom we met in the opening accounts. *The Sunday Times* (20 July) says she was the first person to feel ill. Two of her five children were in the Woodland Gladers band. It's pure speculation but I have mused on the possibility of her two children collapsing after seeing their mother collapse first among the spectators. Anyway, the occasion of her feeling uneasy, if not ill, was the discovery of a mass of 'blebs' on her 3-week-old baby as she changed his nappy while her children's band was waiting for inspection. The weeks after a birth can produce distinctive effects in some women. The fact that Mrs Palethorpe had remained in hospital for over two weeks after the birth might indicate that there had been some necessity for keeping her under observation. She might have been an unintentional catalyst in the drama. The mother of the other baby involved, Susan Bonsall, had panicked when she could not rouse her sleeping 2-week-old baby; a panic made worse by the chaos going on all around her. It is quite possible the babies were affected because they are more responsive than many people credit them to be.

I'll give the final word to Dr R H Lawson, who wrote a long letter to *New Scientist* (31 July) expressing his own doubts about the hysteria theory. Before he could accept it, he said, he would like to know the results of any tests of cholinesterase levels in blood, and protein in urine. He mentions the possibility of a number of the girls menstruating at the time of the incident and implies this would be a factor to consider, in the overall search for an answer, if not in the tests for toxins. Regarding the poison versus mass hysteria wrangle he says... 'they are not mutually exclusive, since one of the symptoms of organophosphorus poisoning is anxiety, and it is theoretically possible that the threshold for hysterical conversion in the crowd may have been lowered by a physical agent.'

The story was assembled from the following main sources: *D. Mail* 14+15+16+17 July; *D. Mirror* 14+17 *D. Star* 14+15+16 July; *D. Express* 14+15+16 July; *D. Telegraph* 14+16 July; *The Times* 14+15+24+26 July; *Western Mail* 14+16 July + 8 Aug; *Guardian* 14+15+17 July; London *Evening Standard* 14 July; Mansfield and North Nottinghamshire *Chronicle and Advertizer* 17+31 July + 14 Aug; *The Sunday Times* 20 July; *Observer* 20 July; *Shropshire Star* 14 July; *New Scientist* 31 July + 28 August; all 1980.

Credit: J + C Bord, Keith Chapman, J Chetwynd, Peter Christie, Mark A Hall, Nick Malloret, Valerie Martin, Sam, PR Thomas, Andy Townsend, Ion Will. **RJMR.**

OTHER RELATEABLE INCIDENTS

I thought it might be interesting to set the Hollinwell incident in the general context of similar or possibly related events of the month before and after. I note at the same time there were outbreaks of Legionnaire's Disease and others among humans, while mystery epidemics were ravaging dogs of America and gulls in Devon. More on these some other time.

• **6 May–2/3 June 1980.** Hongkong. 8 Kowloon schools

evacuated to escape 'pungent gas of unknown origin.' 10,000 students were affected during 4 separate incidents in one month. The AP report (5 June) cited on official: 'The gas for some reason appears only in schools.' *Hamilton Spectator* (Canada) 4 June 80; *Albuquerque Journal* (New Mexico) 5 June 80.

• **3 June 1980.** London. Great Ormond Street Hospital – outbreak of salmonella poisoning. 16 children in several wards affected. After rapid spread further incidents seemed to be checked by 'barrier nursing'. *D. Telegraph* 4 June 80.

• **Early June 1980.** London. Following an annual dinner on 5 June, 42 of 140 members of the Worshipful Society of Apothecaries developed hepatitis-like symptoms. 30 days after the collapse the Disease Surveillance Centre, Colindale, was called in to hunt for a hepatitis virus. 'It seems to be a virulent strain,' said the Society's grand master Sir Gordon Wolstenholme – but... 'mysteriously others were unaffected', and no sign of virus. London *Evening Standard* 23 July 80.

• **18 July 1980.** London. 6 schoolchildren on outing. One slipped backwards on an 'up' escalator, knocking others. In the panic 9 were hurt and treated for bruises and shock. *D. Express* 19 July 80.

• **19 July 1980.** South Normanton, Nottinghamshire. 6 children from the Ashfield Imperials band (involved in the Hollinwell incident) collapsed during a 5-mile charity march. Heavy traffic fumes blamed. *D. Mail + D. Star* 21 July 80.

• **20 July 80.** Manton, Nottinghamshire. 5 girls in the Kilton Concordes (another band affected at Hollinwell) fell ill during a chairty event. Quickly recovered once off the field. Only this one band affected. 'Due to cold weather and nerves', says *D. Telegraph* 21 July 80. Also, *D. Mail,* same date.

• **26 July 1980.** Mid-England. 19 children in Salvation Army band fell ill in their coach *en route* from Lincoln to Leicester for a band competition. All later released from hospital. 'The hot weather and the extremely humid day was responsible.' *D. Telegraph* 28 July 80.

• **End of July 1980.** Postol, Missouri. 100 youngsters collapse during evening services at religious camp. 'Group hysteria' and high temperatures blamed. London *Evening Standard* 1 Aug 80.

• **3 August 1980.** Cannock, Staffordshire. 27 schoolchildren collapse after eating laburnam seeds. 9-year-old Donna Shaw began eating the seeds from a tree overhanging the playground and others followed suit in a 'bizarre game of follow-my-leader'. All later released from hospital – no previous incident from this tree. *D. Telegraph* 4 Aug; *Sun, D. Star* 5 Aug 80.

• **First half of August 1980.** London. 30 members of official Australian party, here for the Centenary Test cricket series all ill or recovering from 'a nasty wave of bronchitis'. *D. Mirror* 30 Aug 80.

• **11/12 August 1980.** Folkstone, Kent. 40 army cadets on field training collapse with stomach pains. All later discharged from hospital. 'Packed lunches suspected'. *D. Telegraph* 13 Aug 80.

• **13/14 August 1980.** Colombo, Sri Lanka. 9 dead and 11 critical – suspected of drinking a poisoned 'Gal', an arrack distilled from molasses, bought from the State Distilleries. All sales suspended pending investigation. *D. Telegraph* 15 Aug 80.

• **15 August 1980.** Port Isaac, Cornwall. 12 sea cadets, aged 12–14, collapsed while walking in the town. 'stomach pains and dizziness... on the verge of unconsciousness... trouble with breathing. Detained in hospital while 22 others and 9 instructors released after hospital check-ups as unaffected. Bristol *Evening Post* + London *Evening News* 15 Aug; Bristol *Evening Post, D. Telegraph, D. Mirror* 16 Aug 80.

Credit: Valerie Martin, Sam, PR Thomas, Andy Townsend, UFO Newsclipping Service, Ion Will, Mr X's Res Bureaux Bulletin. **RJMR.**

The flow of accounts of new encounters with (something) continues unabated, as though proving it to be an endurable component of human experience. Here's the latest batch.

ALIENS IN RUSSIA
Filaments in the Firmament

A series of terrifying encounters with 'giant flying lightbulbs' in an area south of Moscow began with one on 19th August 1977 outside Serpukhov, 57 miles south of Moscow. Noted Moscow inventor S.V. Tyutin and two of his assistants were camping in a field. Suddenly they heard strange voices as if several people were talking at the same time in a foreign language – but louder than human voices.

This went on for half an hour and then, about 500 feet away, a giant 80 foot 'light bulb' started to glow with an eerie violet light. It failed to illuminate the surrounding area. The bulb slowly rose, wobbling,

Continued on p30

John Michell's article on simulacra (FT30) proved very popular — here are a few more samples of eerie spontaneous art.

(Left top): A granite rock formation, at Tadzhik, Russia, not unconvincingly like the preserved mammoths dug out of the frozen tundra in that region. From *Rand Daily Mail* (S. Africa) 16 Feb 1979. (Left bottom): In the US Steel Corporation's mill in Fairfield, Alabama, this weird face is called 'the phantom of the open hearth'. The metal-man-like face is claimed to be 'only an illusion', being part of a giant crane used to transport ladles of molten steel. *National Enquirer* 6 March 1979. (Above): A city-scape seen in an 800 times enlargement of a microchip. *Bangladesh Times* 9 May 1980.

THE CRACK OF DOOM

A simulacrum of an odd sort, that we have noted from time to time, turned up last year in the Colombian village of Tebaida, some 350 km west of Bogota. About the middle of March a peasant woman found

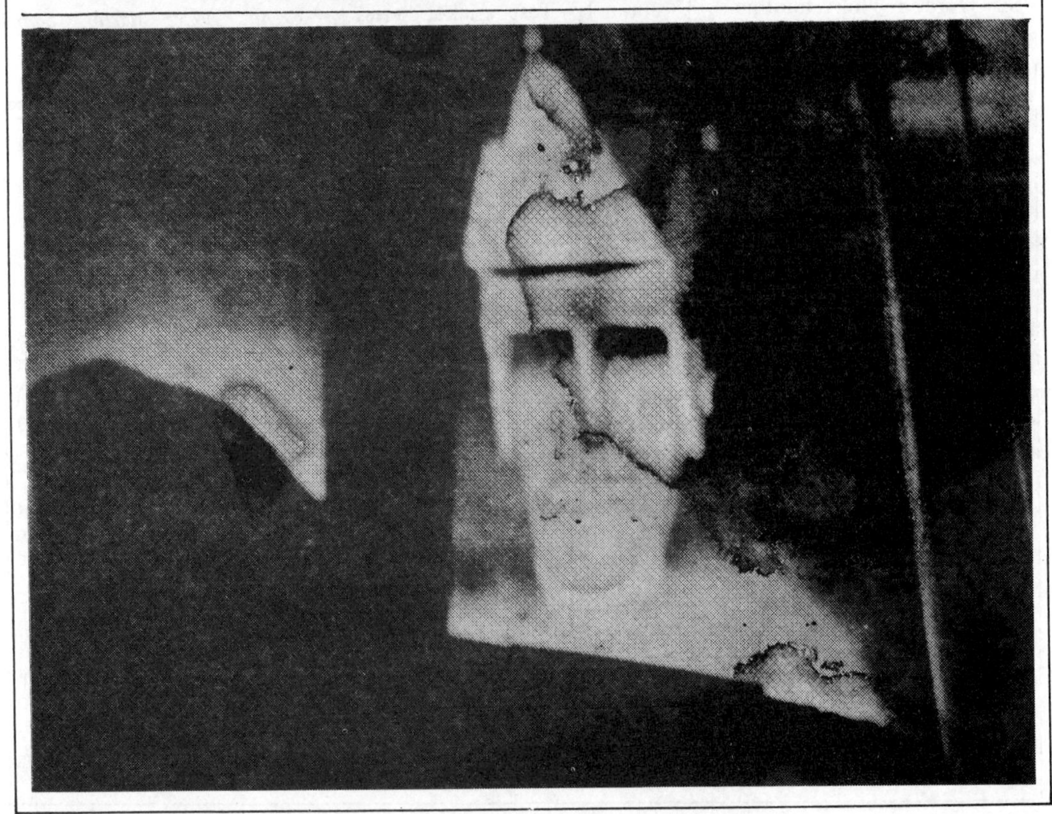

an egg in her chicken coop, with strange markings and took it to her local priest. In raised letters on the shell – presumably part of the shell – were the Spanish words: 'Juicio final. Arrepentois. Dios.' (Final judgement. Repent. God.) The priest, who was shocked, took it to his bishop – the country was reported to be agog, waiting for the bishop's judgement, never mind the Definitive one.

For other incidents of images and words in the fabric of eggs see the 'Mysterious Images' section of *Phenomena* (p58).

This story: *Pretoria News* (South Africa) 24 March 1979.

MEN ON THE MOON

As we go to press, Nigel Watson sends us a note from his local

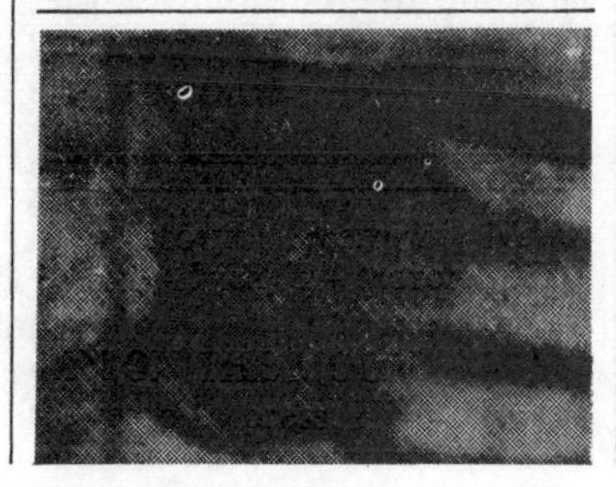

paper – *Gainsborough Journal* 26 Aug 80 – about a local collector of space memorabilia, Bob Holland, who recently noticed a profile of President Kennedy, and at least two others, in the folds of the US flag, in a photo taken on the lunar surface by Apollo 14 astronauts. He has written to NASA, asking them to explain this, and not surprisingly has not yet had an answer. We hope our enlargement here works out...

Credit: Chris J Holtzhausen, Sam, Nigel Watson. **RJMR.**

Cont from p27
and then assumed a steady, tight spiral trajectory and sailed into the sky, without sound, wind or smell. A small flourescent cloud appeared 'from nowhere', enveloped the bulb, and then both vanished.

A round area of compressed grass about 15 feet wide was found in the morning. Eight similar 'light bulbs' had been reported by the end of 1979, all under investigation by a 14-man team led by Professor Felix Yurievich Zigel.

Farmer Wolsky and the Green Men

Zigel has also studied the case of Jan Wolsky, the 71-year-old Polish farmer, which he described as 'the most thoroughly documented and authenticated report of an encounter with humanoids in the Communist bloc'. Wolsky's account has been confirmed by lie detector and twice under hypnosis.

On 10 May 1978, Wolsky was riding his horse-drawn cart through a forest near his village of Emilcin, 90 miles SE of Warsaw. 'I suddenly saw these two little men up ahead by the side of the road' he recalled. 'Their faces were a grey-green colour. They had big slanted eyes and their hands were webbed and also green. They wore little one-piece suits.'

The creatures jumped onto his cart and motioned him to continue, then to turn off the road. 'There in a clearing was a big thing like a bus, only it was hovering in mid air, moving gently up and down like a boat at sea and humming gently. My mare became nervous.' Wolsky was led to the craft. 'All of a sudden a platform whizzed down. We stepped onto it and were taken up into the thing.'

Inside, the vehicle was 'dark and empty. There were openings in the walls and I could make out rods turning like crazy. There was a heap of birds from the forest. They looked paralyzed.' Two more creatures appeared and signalled for him to take his clothes off, which he did. 'Then one of the little men came towards me with some sort of device which clicked. They moved around me with this device, making me raise my arms and stand sideways, as if they were taking pictures.'

'Then they indicated I could put my clothes back on. I did. They didn't move, so I stepped to the door and turned around, took off my cap and said, "Goodbye to you". And they bowed back and smiled.' The platform returned him to the ground and he went home.

Word of his experience soon spread, and teams of researchers arrived. They found three witnesses who saw a 'flying ship' rise up out of the forest and fly away. Local villagers said they found bird feathers all over the alleged landing site. And 'little green men' had been spotted in other parts of the region in subsequent months. Wolsky was found to be of sound mind, with eyesight and hearing above average, and a teetotaller.

The Abducted Vet and the Frayed Briefcase

Veterinarian V.G.Paltsev was hitchhiking home to Borisoglebsk, 350 miles SE of Moscow, after midnight on 16 June 1978. He spotted a softly glowing object across a field and walked towards it. When he was 50 yards away he saw that it had a transparent dome on top and inside were three short-looking men.

Paltsev said the humanoids 'had heads like eggs and very long fingers. They were working around a kind of central control console.' At 25 yards he was stopped by an invisible force field and blacked out. When he came to, the briefcase that he had been carrying was lying next to him, but it looked old and frayed.

The force field had gone, so he started walking towards the craft again. He was knocked off his feet by a blast of wind. The craft began to glow and rise off the ground. Suddenly it shot up 100 yards and then flew off. His watch had stopped, but he soon discovered, from a motorcyclist who gave him a ride, that he had somehow lost 45 minutes. During subsequent nights he kept dreaming that he had been taken for a ride in the saucer.

Under hypnosis (arranged by Professor Zigel) he gave this account: After he fell down he was gently led onto the craft by the humanoids. He became annoyed because they put his briefcase into some kind of apparatus. When it came out it looked old and frayed. After the ride, he was dragged back to the same spot where he had been lying.

All from *National Enquirer* 29 Apr + 20 May + 6 May 1980.

Dwarf Aliens visit East Prussia

Another encounter from the files of Professor Zigel took place on the morning of 4 March 1979 in Chernyakhov, 60 miles west of Kaunas in what used to be East Prussia, now part of the Soviet Union. Technical student Aleksandr Podkopaev spotted two mysterious 'domes' in fields 650 yards away. He ran towards them, and one of them lit up with a violet glow 'like a mercury lamp', rose vertically and sped away.

Under cover of the underbrush, he crept closer to the remaining dome. 'There were four little beings, like dwarfs, standing outside a flying saucer which was hovering about a yard off the ground. They had long bodies and long arms and short legs. All four were busy spreading out some shiny metallic objects on the ground – as if sorting them out before carrying them back to their ship? They wore what looked like green space suits and pointed silver-blue helmets.'

'Suddenly, as though sensing me, the four little men turned and faced me. A sort of breathing mask covered their mouths and noses. Their big red eyes were covered with gogles. I froze. The tallest of the four raised his arm, as though in salute. His arm was so long it doubled his height. He looked so funny, I even gave out a chuckle.'

Seconds later, they 'just seemed to vanish inside the dome. I could see the outlines of their bodies through the translucent sphere. The ship then seemed to cover itself with violet light and flew away.'

Research by Zigel's assistant Lyudmila Petrova discovered another eye-witness to the event – a schoolteacher who had seen the four little men from a different vantage point. And three other witnesses had observed a UFO shoot upward from the field.

David Webb, co-chairman of the Mutual UFO Network in the States, has analysed nearly 2000 cases of encounters with humanoids. 'Most numerous are those in the dwarf class' he said. 'These tend to be from two to four feet tall. Generally, they wear helmets and metallic reflecting suits.' So it looks like the Little People are still up to their tricks... *National Enquirer* 13 May 1980 + 16 Oct 1979.

THE ALIEN FORMULA FOR GIANT VEGETABLES

Farmer Jose Carmen Garcia, whose produce is the wonder of the marketplace, lives in Valle de Santiago, 260 miles NW of Mexico City, near Irapuato. Townspeople gather to see his 8 pound onions, cabbages weighing up to 60 pounds and his collard greens as big as palm fronds.

Yet Garcia, 50, ploughs his 3 acre plot behind a mule or horse, just like his neighbours, and buys the same seed at the village general store. He explains that in 1947, as a youth of 17 struggling to make ends meet on his farm inherited from his father, he met a 'very tall man. My heart stopped at his appearance. He looked like an albino, and he had gaunt, hollowed and distorted features.'

The stranger said that he had been held captive by humanoids in the interior of a nearby inactive volcano. His captors spoke unintelligible gibberish and lived on outsize vegetables.

He said he had memorised their magic formula, which he sketched on a scrap of paper. He told Garcia to concentrate on the symbols and that after a period of time, the 'message' would become clear. Then he walked away. After several sleepless nights, Garcia got the revelation – whatever it was – planted his seeds and has produced giant veggies ever since. All that he would say about his method is that he plants his seeds at night in a curving pattern, whereas other farmers plant in straight rows.

An imaginitive Agriculature Ministry official took up Garcia's challenge to prove his crop-growing prowess. He laid out two 20 acre plots near Camp de Tangasneque in Tampico state in December 1978. The competing tract was farmed by a team of Ministry experts and local farmers, using fertilizers.

At harvest time, the Ministry team averaged 30 tons per acre, compared to Garcia's 106 tons per acre.

William Robinson, information officer for the San Diego Police Department in California, was on holiday in the area when he heard about Garcia. He went to see him, and was presented with a ten-pound onion, which, as far as we know, is still in his freezer. Whatever we make of the humanoid story, there is no denying the onion or Robinson's photographs of cabbages 3 feet wide and collard greens up to 5 feet long.

After the initial UPI report in February 1980, Robinson was innundated with letters requesting more information, so he revisited Garcia on his farm. All he would add was that

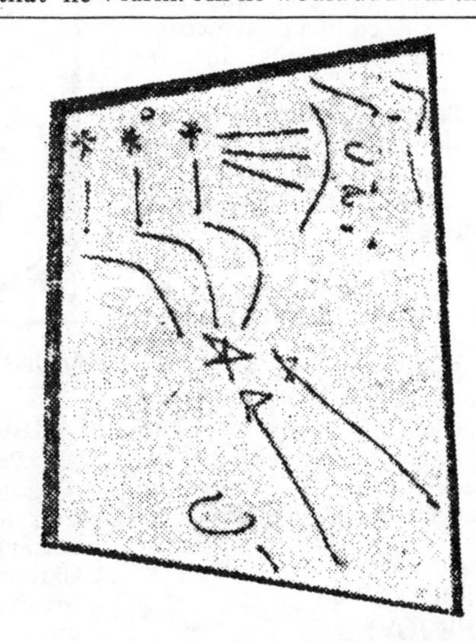

(Left) Carmen Garcia on the right, and friend, display one of his giant cabbages. (Right) The 'self-explanatory' formula given to Garcia by the 'humanoid'. (Photos: San Fransisco *Chronicle* 9 Feb 80; *Midnight Globe* 18 March 80.)

he uses a little pig manure. He said that he had given his formula, for safekeeping, to the Rosicrucian Order of San Jose, California. A spokesman there said he didn't know what to make of it. (For more on giant veg, see FT30p13). San Francisco *Chronicle* 9 Feb; Stillwater *Gazette* (Minn) 30 May; *North Shore News* (USA) 8 Jun 1980.

STRANGE TRUCK JOURNEY IN VIRGINIA

Truck driver Harry Turner left his home town of Winchester, Virginia, at 10.50pm on 28 August 1979, to make a delivery in Fredericksburg, some 80 miles away. He described what happened in the *Midnight Globe* (6 November 1979):

'The sky got real light and my radio started making a lot of noise. Suddenly, this thing grabbed me on my left side on a pressure point on my shoulder. It was like a bionic grip. I finally blacked out. But before I did, I fired eight shots from my .32 semi-automatic at it.

'I screamed: 'My God, I can't kill the thing!' Then it was like walking through a door into another world. These things wore all white with numbers on their foreheads. They talked like tape recorders running backwards, and very fast.'

Turner said he came to in Fredericksburg at 11.17 only 27 minutes from when he left Winchester. His two speedometers both read only 17 miles; yet he had used 74 more gallons of fuel than he should have (That's what it says here anyway.)

Since this event, he has been seeing a psychiatrist and has changed physically. 'My whole left side is about 80 per cent weaker. But the doctors can't find a reason for it' he concluded.

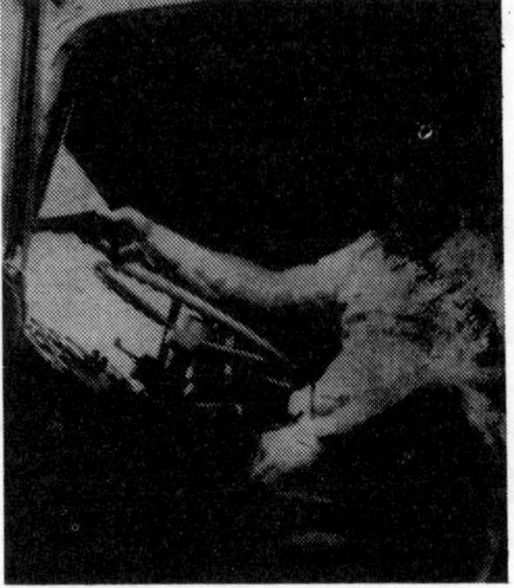

Harry Turner, in his cab, showing his gun. (Photo: *Midnight Globe* 6 Nov 1979.)

STOOD UP BY THE JOVIANS

On 8th March 1980 about 50,000 Brazilians hoping for a close encounter with a spaceship from Jupiter jammed on a ranch near Casimiro de Abreu, 120 kilometers east of Rio. Farmer Edilicio Barbosa had announced on national TV the previous weekend that he had learned by 'telepathy' that the spaceship would land on his farm at 5.20am on the 8th March, and that the Jovians would return a Brazilian helicopter pilot snatched in 1976 by the crew of an earlier probe from Jupiter. A chopper had indeed disappeared mysteriously off Brazil's Atlantic coast in that year.

The crowd waited all night, but nothing happened. Barbosa said 'the ship did not land because at the exact instant of set-down 40 people were lying right on the landing pad.' Shortly afterwards, he was nowhere to be found.

The police chief said: 'a lot of people were frustrated of course, but most are leaving calmly and we haven't had any incidents of violence. What we do have is a tremendous traffic jam.' *St Catharine's Standard* (Canada) + Vancouver *Sun* 8 Mar; *Observer* 9 Mar; *Middlesex News* (Mass) 11 Mar 1980.

Credit: Loren Coleman, Mark A Hall, David MacAdams, Sam, Ted Schultz, Dwight Whalen, Ion Will. **PRAdeGS.**

More dollops of coagulated data.

'ARROWING EXPERIENCES

At 7am on 27 Feb 1980, Alexander Hudson, 36, walked over to the ticket-clerk at the entrance to the Botanical Garden subway station, Brooklyn, NY. He had an arrow protruding from one shoulder and was bleeding badly. He told the clerk that a white van had just passed him in the street out of the back of which an archer wearing a green hood leapt, and taking aim, shot Hudson in the back. He was later said to be in a satisfactory condition after surgeons removed a solid arrow with three prongs made of razor blades. *Vancouver Sun* 27 Feb; *Guardian + D. Mail + Vancouver Sun* 28 Feb 1980.

The reappearance of an old comic-book hero (The Green Archer) as a villain raised our eyebrows a little – just enough to put us on the alert for some kind of thematic expression. Though we didn't clip it, we note that the following flight of archaic archery was a prelude to the 'bow-and-arrow' war then fermenting in the New Hebrides.

British papers for the 18th March told how Vivian Williams, 28, was shot by a 9-inch cross-bow bolt, in Liverpool, some unspecified time (a few weeks?) before this date. On trial was Gerald Wilson, 18, accused of going beserk, weilding a cross-bow 'like an axe' as he tried to kill Williams. It was said the bolt, travelling at about 125mph, would have killed Williams, were it not for his huge 'beer belly', which slowed the bolt with five inches of fat. However, the next day, Wilson was cleared by the court, who accepted his story that he never had a cross-bow, and that he accidentally wounded Williams when he poked the latter's stomach with a stick. Strange story, that! *Sun + D. Mail + D. Express + D. Telegraph* 18 March; *D. Mail + D. Express + D. Telegraph* 19 March 1980.

The *Daily Epress,* on 19 March 1980, also carried the story of the death of a motorist at the Devil's Punchbowl (!), Hindhead, Surrey, speared through the chest by a pole of wood during a collision with a stationary van.

On 23 March, a young Japanese factory worker was arrested for the murder of a young woman in Osaka, hit by an arrow fired from a passing car. She managed to pull out the arrow – made of a drill attached to a bamboo stick – and describe the incident to police, although she later died in hospital. The man claimed he was testing an invention; a cylinder-type shooting device. *D. Telegraph* 24 March; *Weekly News* 29 March 1980.

On 25th March, a police inspector and 9 constables were injured by arrows fired by tribesmen in India's Madhya Pradesh state. *D. Telegraph* 26 March 1980.

Then all quiet until 17 June, when we note that a construction worker spanned time as well as space when he used his skill in archery to solve a tricky problem at the Davis-Besse Nuclear Power Station, Port Clinton, Ohio. The problem was how to attach a power line to a fixture on a 90 metre high ceiling. Chuck Heisinger, 52, a hobbyist archer since 1939, attached the line to a hunting arrow, and fired it through a 10cm hole in the fixture while perched atop a crane 24 metres away. He was presented with the arrow, now inscribed 'The first arrow shot in a reactor building'. *Niagara Falls Review* 18 June 1980.

Credit: Michael Hoffman, Dwight Whalen, Ion Will. **RJMR.**

GRAVE HUMOUR

A run of coffin jokes began in February this year with a splendid phenomenological pun. Canon Fred Hoyle fell into a black hole – that is, a grave in Rochdale cemetary. He made ecclesiastical history by being the first vicar to claim industrial injury benefit following a funeral. *D. Telegraph* 2 Feb 1980.

A week later, police were chasing a hearse which had terrified a town. More than 20 people in Tischenreuth, Bavaria, had reported a midnight encounter with phantom undertakers. The hearse stopped in front of people out walking alone, and three men in black would take out a coffin and slowly open it. *News of the World* 10 Feb 1980.

Another coffin opened a day or two later on a fast-moving lorry between Bujumbura and Gitega, in Burundi. Five hitch-hikers leaped to their deaths in fright. It was in fact the co-driver waking up from his nap. He had closed the lid when it started to rain, and was unaware anyone had been picked up. Rochester *Post-Bulletin* (Minnesota) + *Pretoria News* (South Africa) 12 Feb; *D. Telegraph* 13 Feb 1980. A curious story came our way two months later, this time taking place in Hungary. Miklos Levay thumbed a lift into Budapest during a storm. In the back of the lorry he found an empty coffin and climbed in to keep dry. Meanwhile another hitch-hiker was picked up, and on waking Miklos lifted the lid and inquired about the weather. The frightened man broke a leg as he scrambled off the moving lorry. He tried to sue Miklos, but lost. *Weekend* 14 May 1980. Could this be another of those barroom tales, or 'whale tumour' stories, making the rounds?

On the 13th Feb, London police towed away a loaded hearse from a funeral parlour in Holloway, and the funeral was delayed for an hour and a half. An embarrassed Scotland Yard apologized to the family of the bereaved. *D. Telegraph* 14 Feb 1980.

Meanwhile in Brighton, Michigan, widow Mary Bates was suing an undertaker and coffinmaker for a million dollars because the body of her husband had fallen through the bottom of the coffin as it was being carried to the graveside. The body was 'surrounded by rags, newspapers, shredded paper and what appeared to be pantyhose.' Mrs Bates said the sight caused her emotional distress and brought on a heart attack. Cambridge *Evening News* 13 Feb; *D. Telegraph* 14 Feb 1980.

The following week, workmen digging a trench to house electricity cables for rewiring the nave of Winchester Cathedral unearthed an ancient stone coffin – believed to contain the remains of Bishop Walkelyn, who began the building of the cathedral before his death in 1098. The crumbling bones were surrounded by a shroud and well-preserved boots were still on his feet. There had been digging in the area recently, and in the fourteenth century, so the wonder was why it had not been discovered earlier.

D. Telegraph 22 Feb 1980.

Finally, the day before April First (naturally) a mix-up over the bodies of two women led to two groups of mourners attending the wrong funerals, somewhere in the new county of Avon. This was apologized for by a red-faced coroner in the Number Two district court. *D. Telegraph* 1 April 1980.

Credit: Mark A Hall, Chris J Holtzhausen, Peter Hope-Evans, Valerie Martin, Nigel Pennick, Ion Will. **PRAdeGS +RJMR.**

ST HELENS REVISITED

Last issue (FT32p26) we mentioned that the day before Washington State's pet volcano, Mount St Helens, blew her top, the body of a lioness was discovered in a disused quarry at St Helens, Lancashire. This seemed to signal a few lexilinkable events.

The *Daily Telegraph* 16 June 80 reported that hundreds of fish were found dead in a stretch of the St Helens Canal, in north west England; killed by a combination of local heat wave and parts of the canal being heated by steam outlets from factories. Apparently coarse fish cannot survive in water temperatures over 82 degrees F. We note that there were also tropical fish ('cichilds') among the survivors, whose presence in the canal seemed to be accepted by the St Helens angling association. [It is not stated, but this St Helens could be the one in Lancashire.]

'Just my luck... premature burial.'

We then clipped a story from *Midnight Globe* 5 Aug 80, telling of a phantom female hitch-hiker between Eugene, Oregon, and Tacoma, Washington, in the region of the St Helens volcano, who is threatening gallant drivers with death in the next eruption if they don't mend their ways and believe in God. This collection of stories follows the classic phantom hitch-hiker pattern – sitting in the back seat prophesying, and vanishing – and we have handed it over to Mike Goss who is researching the subject and may do an article on it for FT next year.

Finally we note four walkers were killed by passing cars in two 'unconnected' road accidents on the 30th and 31st of August. The latter occurred on Embankment Road, at St Helens, Isle of Wight. *D. Telegraph* 1 Sept 1980.

Credit: Sam, Paul Screeton. **RJMR.**

RELIGION WATCH

There seems to be activity in nearly every aspect of religious life, here and now in this 20th century AD.

- **Pious Fraud.** In San Damiano, Italy, 'Mama Rosa' Quattrini, who claimed to see the Virgin Mary in a pear tree in 1964 and have regular visions since, has had her lands, hotel, buildings and £12 million in cash, seized and frozen by the Public Prosecutor pending an inquiry. As her fame grew her family profited by and traded on the proceeds, buying land and building hotels for the pilgrims who were inevitably attracted by her ecstacies. *Reveille* 20 July 1979. Our latest notes are nearly a year later and give no extra info – looks like it'll be a long inquiry. *D. Mail* 1 Aug + *Guardian* 7 Aug 1980.

In a chapel at Craveggia, Novara, also in Italy, lies a modern sleeping beauty – Alfonsina Cottini, aged 78, who, many believe, has not woken or eaten in 12 years. Coach parties of pilgrims come from all over Europe to pray there, or to touch that part of her body where they themselves have some afflication. Nearly all, whether cured or not, leave some offerings behind. Now she is being investigated by the Bishop of Novara, as well as the chief magistrate; both are disturbed by rumours that she gets up during the night and tucks into a huge meal. We would like to know more about this case. *D. Mail* 1 Aug 80.

Should Alfonsina and Mama Rosa ever be proved frauds or not, they can thank their lucky stars (or whatever) they don't live elsewhere on this earth, for there are many places where the slightest whiff of cultism is dealt with severely. Recently we learned of the execution, in China's Guizhou Province, of Xie Xianji, aged 24, before a crowd of 10,000 people, convicted of killing 13 of his disciples. He was described as 'the leader of a bogus religious cult', and said to have 'mesmerised' his victims, convincing them 'the way to heaven is death by water'. At least four let themselves be tied up and drowned in a river – the others met their deaths in a cave. Xie was also accused of swindling them out of 1,600 yuan ($1000) in two years. London *Eve. Standard + Int. Herald Tribune* 14 Aug 80.

In Patras, northern Greece, Sister Flothee, a nun, aged 48, was jailed for smoking cannabis in her cell at the Pepolinitsis convent there. She claimed that it helped her 'participate' more in prayers, and denied that she planted the plant, maintaining that it was 'God's breezes' which wafted the seeds into the convent. *Times* 22 Aug 80.

In Bavaria, police were hunting a 50-year-old mild-mannered priest who has looted $200,000 worth of statues and other religious objects from churches in southern Germany. Police became suspicious when Rev Anton Wagner announced to his congregation he was going on a long holiday, during which items from his church in Rehling were found missing. *Globe & Mail* (Canada) 11 Aug 80.

• **Sacrilege I: Violence in the church.** A priest was killed in the presbytery of St Ethelbert's RC church, Ramsgate, Kent, on 26 May – his housekeeper later died of injuries from the same attack. London *Eve. Standard* 27 May 80. A gunman killed two and wounded 10 others when he strolled into a service in a Baptist church in Dringerfield, Texas, shouting 'This is war!' He went outside and shot himself, but not fatally. *D. Telegraph* 23 June 80. A British pastor and his wife were among five of the congregation of the Evangelical Free Church, found murdered in Bassano, near Calgary, Alberta, Canada. They were all shot by Irvin Levins, a man who resented his wife's devotion to the church – so he shot her, their two children, the pastor and his wife, and then himself. *Guardian + D. Express* 14 Aug 80.

On 12 August two rival Pakistani Moslem groups fought a pitch battle in their mosque in Rotherham, Yorks. It was a continuation of a fight begun the previous weekend when the traditionalist group locked themselves into the mosque after police were called to stop the fighting. This time the modernist group were more prepared and arrived with supporters. Soon the police were called out again and found a group of 200 still battling with iron bars, staves and bricks, and at least 14 lying injured and bloodied. *Guardian + D. Telegraph* 13 Aug 80. About a week later a similar scene occurred at the Baptist church, Mount Clemens, Michigan. Two groups disputed the election of a pastor to the church, and the two candidates turned up on the same day, armed with a loud-hailer each and tried to hold services simultaneously. 'It is a good thing to show forth thy loving kindness in the morning,' thundered Rev. Bullock. 'I was glad when they said unto me, let us go unto the house of the Lord,' bellowed Rev. Calhoun. Soon the two groups were at each other's throats, punching in the pews amid a hail of bibles. It took the town's entire police force to break it up. *D. Mirror* 26 Aug 80.

• **Sacrilege II: Blasphemy, Desecration etc.** Priests and pilgrims at the shrine of Lourdes are scandalized by the number of nudist tourists sporting in a field nearby, traditionally reserved for camping pilgrims. 'We have never seen such outrageous behaviour here before... Lourdes is not a beach,' huffed Fr Reymond Lavedan. There was another cause for concern: the shrine expected 70,000 pilgrims to turn up for a Mass and alerted the police in case some tried to take the law into their own hands. Apart from that, I suspect that pilgrims turning away because they were unable to camp would mean a loss of revenue for the shrine... *D. Mirror* 12 Aug 80.

More trouble in a Yorkshire mosque, this time at Batley. On 25 Aug two idiotic white men interrupted morning prayers when they walked in and left a pig's head on the altar. In the uproar they were lucky to get out alive. *D. Star* 26 Aug 80.

—

In the *Angelus* Aug 1980, an outraged Fr Hector Bolduc mentions several recent actions which have dismayed traditional Catholics. In Metz, France, the famous statue of the Cure of Ars (St Jean-Marie Vianney) was 'despoiled' by taking away the traditional vestments it was dressed in, replacing them with 'a gaudy modern robe' and adding 'a shaggy long wig which makes him look like a hippie.' Traditional style vestments were also the target of Modernists elsewhere. The Bishop of Turin spent many thousands of dollars replacing stained glass windows in the cathedral with new versions showing St John Bosco wearing the new and approved attire. More bizarre were attempts to replace the traditional vestments on the incorrupt bodies of St Joseph Cafasso, at Turin, and St Bernadette of Lourdes (see FT29p9) in the convent at Never. In the case of St Joseph the ecclesiastical vandals were successful, but St Bernadette proved as stubborn as she had in her life. After many attempts the sisters at Never failed to prise apart the saint's clasped hands. Their plans to call in an undertaker to break her knuckles or cut off the ends of her fingers were foiled when the plot became known and the people objected. It makes you wonder, doesn't it?

Also in August, on the feast-day of the Bodily Assumption of the BVM – the 15th? – Mrs Luis Billa, wife of a stonemason in Lomello, near Pavia, followed the custom of her native southern Italy and made a flower-bedecked shrine in her kitchen, inviting neighbours to come and pray and eat. During the gathering first one then several saw coloured tears rolling down the face of a plaster image of the BVM. It was called a miracle. As news spread, pilgrims flocked there, and Mrs Billa put up a note asking for donations to replenish the flowers and candles. Then someone – supposedly neighbours annoyed by the crowds – said they had seen Mr Billa squirting pink water onto the statue with his son's waterpistol. True or not, Mr Billa is also rumoured to have confessed the deception, saying that he didn't know why he had done it. The couple 'went on holiday' before the police could investigate – if fraud is proved to be done for gain they could face jail. The irony is that there seems to have been a genuine cure at this fraudulent shrine. Someone had gathered some 'tears' in a vial and given it to Ottorino Magnaghi, 60, a war invalid, who later threw away his crutches. Unless that too was part of a grand deception... *Guardian* 8 Sept 80.

• **Leaders and the Lost.** From A note in *The Times,* also of 2 Sept, mentions another source of religious ferment in Russia–this time something similar to the Chinese 'celestial chain-letter' mentioned by Steve Moore last issue (FT32p34). The Russian letters are rife among the Christian communities of the Volga town of Engels, the industrial city of Tula, and in Siberia. They describe a miraculous vision of a 12-year-old boy to whom 'the Lord God appeared clad in white'; and they urge the recipient to spread the message given to the boy by copying it nine times and mailing them to friends. Those who do this will gain happiness, but those who break the chains are threatened with incurable disease. The same report, in *The Times* 2 Sept 80, says that chain-letters have also started up among the Moslem communities of Soviet Central Asia, spreading a message of Moslem fundamentalism. It seems that, in view of the ferment in Iran and Afghanistan, the authorities are taking a far less tolerant view of these latter letters than the Christian ones.

Finally, police in the Philippines claimed to have crushed a cult of mountain tribesmen who believed their magical amulets would protect them from bullets. Shades of the old 'Amok' outbreaks of a few decades back! The cultists, called 'Salvatoris' after their leader, Alfredo Salvatori, who introduced the ideas of the cult to the negrito communities two years ago, killed over 300 people during this period. The police chief of Kabangkalan said Salvatori and his assistants had tricked people into buying the amulets by demonstrations with blanks in their guns. These charms were in several forms–multicoloured handerkerchiefs, oil in bottles, or old bullet shells – with inscriptions in unintelligible English, Latin and Malay. At the height of their rampage, the Salvatoris numbered about 5,000, drawn from illiterate farmers and sugar-cane workers, but many were lured away by special anti-cultist campaigns – as many as 300 surrendered in one day at Kabangkalan – and police shot about 100 others overall. (UPI) Waukegan, Illinois *News-Sun* (Illinois) 14 July 1980.

Credit: J Chetwynd, Mike Crowley, Mark A Hall, Peter James, Michael Hoffman, Peter Hope-Evans, Sam, Joe Swatek, R Watson, Dwight Whalen, Ion Will. **RJMR.**

Unlike the USA, Britain has very few Fortean investigators who regularly and persistently get out into the field, so it was with great pleasure that we have made the acquaintance of a young monster-hunter who may have pulled off the 'Shiels double' – sightings of both Nessie and Morgawr (in Falmouth Bay). Jeoff Watson, 23, a sociology student at Thames Polytechnic, spends every available penny and moment planning and carrying out sorties to regions in which in recent years there have originated reports of sea or lake monsters – the Helford estuary and Falmouth Bay in Cornwall; Lochs Shiel, Morar and Ness in Scotland; and Barmouth and Lake Bala in Wales. Once on site he establishes 'watches' interspersed by explorations, local library research and interviewing witnesses (many of whom can only be discovered and approached in person). Jeoff believes that the definitive photographic evidence of unknown water creatures the world is waiting for will most likely come from systematic shore-based observations such as his. We present some of his results and invite interested readers to contact him.

LOCH NESS 3 SEPT 1978

Jeoff's sixth trip to Loch Ness was the occasion of a series of eight photos with which many monster-hunters are greatly impressed. On the morning of 3 September 1978, Jeoff left his base in Foyers intending to cycle up to Inverness via the southern bank of the loch, stopping along the way to carry out several logged watches. He was on high ground between the power station at Foyers and Inverfarigaig, just past infamous Boleskine House, when at 2pm he noticed a curious waveform on the opposte shore, almost directly opposite Inverfarigaig, and began taking pictures. (See photos on the next page, three of which can be seen in full colour in *Photographs of the Unknown* by Rickard & Kelly, reviewed in this issue.) By the second photo a definite V-wake had formed with a motion to the right. It became more distinct and turned out into the center of the loch, almost at right-angles to the shoreline.

After the third photo, Jeoff was convinced the cause of the wake was a submerged animate object. It did not seem to be a wind effect and there was no other visible or obvious cause–some small boats in the area were moving parallel to the shoreline, but out of the picture. He moved to higher ground and resumed shooting. As it neared the center of the loch, Jeoff noticed a small dark object at the head of the wake which seemed to appear and disappear as though surfacing and submerging. By the time he took his sixth photo, the wake extended two thirds of the width of the loch and was dying out further back. As the object moved into more disturbed water Jeoff lost sight of it altogether.

During the sighting Jeoff had drawn the wake to the attention of a family parked nearby, one of whom watched through a pair of 10x50 binoculars and reported seeing 'a fin-like object' at the wake's head.

Jeoff estimates the object moved at about 10mph. The sighting lasted about two minutes. The surface conditions were fairly calm with small waves on the southern shore, and bright despite a cloud cover.

Jeoff felt sure he had captured Nessie on film, and was naturally eager to have the film developed and examined. It was promptly dispatched to Kodak. In *Nessletter* (Feb 1979) Rip Hepple compared the promising speck to the motor cruiser in Photo 5. This boat is about 25ft long and about 100yds out from the

From top to bottom, these photos are numbers 1, 4 & 5 of a sequence of 8, taken by Jeoff Watson on 3 Sept 1978, at Loch Ness, showing the mysterious v-wake he believes to be made by Nessie, first appearing as a faint white line near the far shore (top). We had planned to give these a much larger spread, but the larger we printed them the less detail could be seen in the middle tones. Colour versions can be seen in *Photographs of the Unknown.* The camera was a Chinon 35mm SLR, with 200 mm telephoto lens, using Kodacolour 400 asa film. (Copyright: Jeoff Watson.)

shore. 'Therefore the small black object is fairly substantial,' wrote Hepple. Jeoff himself got the impression of an object about 2ft long and 1ft wide.

FALMOUTH BAY

On his first expedition to the Falmouth Bay area on 20 Nov 1979, Jeoff twice saw unidentified objects in the water near Rosemullion Head, just north of Mawnan Point, taking four colour slides of the first, and two of the second. These objects occupy very small areas of the 35mm frame and almost lost in the grain enlargement and tone values – so subtle that reproduction with our limited resources would not produce any discernable or worthwhile image. Jeoff is reserved about the identity of these objects. He is inclined to think they may well be of inanimate objects, or of aquatic animals common to the area. Roger Acraman, of the Loch Morar Survey team, conducted a macro- and microphotographic analysis of the objects of the first sighting. Although he was able to identify its colour ('light purple/green') and the fact that it seemed to have two projections and two black dots on its surface, the definition or size of the image was not enough to establish any description of the object conclusively. The object of the second series, Jeoff feels, may well have been a boat.

Jeoff returned to Falmouth Bay in Feb 1980, and amongst a number of watches had another interesting sighting on 20th Feb near Polgwidden Cove, when he saw an object, with what looked like three protrusions, a neck and two humps. Later on from the same position that day he saw a floating piece of wood which looked remarkably similar, causing him to question the earlier sighting. A comparison of the slides taken of both objects suggests they were dissimilar. If the earlier object *was* a piece of wood then its profile was uncannily like that 'typical of an unknown animal' [sic]. These slides are presently undergoing analysis.

FUTURE PLANS

Although it looks like Jeoff has very little to show for many hours of field work he is far from despondent. If nothing else he considers it all good training. He keeps detailed logs of his watches and photography. He is familiarizing himself not only with the environment of the monsters, but the conditions and locations of watching and watch points. Above all he is getting to know his equipment and its results under a variety of conditions, and the relationship between the photographic record and indistinct objects seen hastily under adverse conditions. One of these days, he philosophizes, he will be in the right place at the right time and all this preparation will pay off, if not with the best shots yet of an unknown sea creature, then with photos which will yield just as valuable facts under analysis supporting this idea.

Jeoff is hoping his efforts will not only attract more people to take up shore-based watching as a hobby, but raise the standards of such observations and reporting. He welcomes serious and constructive examination of his efforts so far, and invites anyone interested to write to him at the address below. Copies of his reports and watching schedules are available to those who share his ideals.

Jeoff Watson: Flat 3, 88 Elthan Rd, Lee Green, London SE12 8UE. (Tel: 01-852 3033)

RJMR.

ON THE TRAIL OF GIANT SNAKES

In 1906, twenty years before Major Percy Fawcett vanished without a trace in the Amazon, he was sent by the Royal Geographic Society to make a thorough survey of the Rio Abuna and Acre River in Brazil. Thirty-nine at the time, Major Fawcett was known for two sometimes contradictory character traits; he was a dreamer whose dreams led him to envision lost jungle cities of fantastic wealth and splendor; he was also a scrupulously matter-of-fact military man who reported exactly what he saw in detailed and down-to-earth observations. His memoirs, striking for their contrast of visionary dreams and earthly rankness, report many strange adventures including an encounter with a giant anaconda of the Amazon. (Thanks to Dr. Bernard Heuvelmans, most of us Forteans have heard of Fawcett's various adventures, including this one.)

It was in 1907 that Fawcett ran across the giant snake. With his Indian crew, he was drifting along the Rio Negro when he spotted the snake. Fawcett reported, a great triangular head appeared at the bow of the boat, and when he shot the creature in the spine the body of the snake thrashed the water all around the boat. With great difficulty Fawcett said he convinced his crew to approach closer to the bank where the great snake lay. The Indians feared that the injured reptile would attack the boat or that its mate, as often happened, would come to destroy the hunters.

Fawcett then stepped onto the shore and cautiously approached the snake. The snake allegedly measured 45 feet out of the water and 17 in it, a total of 62 feet. The snake's diameter for such a great length was surprisingly small, only about 1 foot. The beast was not dead and emitted from its mouth an awful odor. After reporting this snake, Fawcett was told of many others including one super giant of over 80 feet that was said to have been killed by the Zrajchan boundary commission. The common length of the anaconda is usually found to not exceed 25 feet. Yet, Fawcett's tale is only one of many made by South American jungle guides and explorers who report giant snakes from 75 feet to even 150 feet in length. These creatures were said to have eyes the size of plates and a weight of several tons.

The Peninsula Python

Far from the teeming jungles of the Amazon, in the summer of 1944, a huge snake known as the Peninsula Python caused excitement along the Cuyahoga River in the wooded valley between Akron and Cleveland, Ohio. The creature first appeared on June 8, 1944, when it was seen by Clarence Mitchell sliding across his corn field and leaving a track the width of an automobile tire. Mitchell reported the creature to be about 18 feet in length.

Two days later, Paul and John Szalay reported a similar track in their fields, and two days later Mrs. Roy Vaughn called out the fire department when the giant reptile attacked her hen house. The snake climbed the fence to her chicken coop and devoured a chicken.

Now that the snake was accepted as fact, theories abounded as to where it had come from. Two years before, a carnival truck had supposedly smashed up in a cemetary in the valley, and it was speculated that the python might have escaped from this wreck. As we have discovered many times before in our investigations of 'circus train wrecks' as the source of any given mystery animal report, the story could never fully be tracked down.

The Cleveland and Columbus Zoos offered rewards for the live capture of the Peninsula Python and the news services began to carry the story which was later to arouse interest overseas from servicemen whose families lived in the valley.

On Sunday, June 25, the sirens blasted to report the creature as having been sighted up near Kelly Hill. The town emptied as numerous residents headed off to the hill in search of the Python. The hunters trampled through tangled thorn bush and burrs only to learn later that it was a false alarm.

Two days later, the snake leaped down out of a dead willow and frightened Mrs. Pauline Hopko. It also scared her milk cows, who broke their halters and ran off across the fields, and her dogs who cowered under Mrs. Hopko's skirts. Mrs. Hopko was left holding the milk pail. The snake was sighted also at this time by Bobbie Pollard and some other boys, but it disappeared before the Mayor's posse arrived on the scene.

Again, two days afterwards, Mrs. Ralph Griffin saw the snake rear up man-high in the middle of her backyard. Again, the creature avoided the posse. Then Mrs Katherine Boroutick saw it in her backyard where it came crashing down out of her butternut tree when she was out by the river throwing out some trash. The posse found broken tree limbs and another track to the river bed. Professional searchers now came into the area, and the snake was reported a few more times in the fall. However, hunters said they never got word fast enough to get a shot at the snake. By first frost, residents waited for the buzzards to find a huge carcass of a snake dead of cold, but the Peninsula Python was never sighted again, dead or alive.

Other American Monster Serpents

Throughout the United States, from the period of the Peninsula Python and before, accounts of giant snakes have circulated. Reports from the area around Bridgewater, Massachusetts, tell of CCC workers encountering huge coiled serpents along the pathways through the Hockomock Swamp. From Hastings, Michigan, come tales of the 20-foot-long Carter's

Andzrej Krauze.

'Repeat after me... Dar-win. Dar-win.'

Snake, so named because it was always seen near Carter's Lake. Near another lake, Reynold's Lake in Kentucky, local people began to take their hogs inside because of the fear their giant snake would devour their livestock after it got its fill of frogs. The era of a snake as 'large as a stovepipe' is gone merely because nobody uses stovepipes any longer, but the reports of giant snakes continue.

Recent years have had their share of monster snake accounts. The Zodiac News Service reported in January 1975 that hikers in the northern Appalachian mountains had sighted a 40-foot-long giant snake. The slithering monster had reportedly been seen by more than a dozen hiking parties since it was first viewed in 1919. Legend has it that the giant snake, which witnesses have seen on Broad Top Mountain, survives Pennsylvania's harsh winters by crawling into warm coal mine shafts. Researchers who checked out one sighting claim the monster left behind a long trough in the earth four to six inches deep.

Curtis Fuller brought the readers of *FATE* up to date on the latest giant snake report in the May 1979 issue. Fuller detailed the experience of Eileen Blackburn and her daughter (October 1978) near Cascade, Montana. The giant 20 to 30-feet-long snake reportedly had coils at least three feet across. Cascade Police Chief Earl Damon said he had other giant snake reports from area people.

Like so many other mystery animal encounters the Blackburns' had their run-in while they were traveling in their automobile. Mrs. Blackburn was not sure if she hit the giant cobra-like creature, or it struck her car.

In bygone days, the giant snakes attacked not cars, but horses. One of the classic accounts is given in John Keel's *Strange Creatures From Time and Space*. The Kenton, Ohio, individual out horseback riding was Orland Packer (not Parker, as given in Keel's book). On June 9, 1946, an eight-foot-long snake with a diamond shape on its flat head bit at Packer's horse, taking off a patch of the horse's hair. Packer was thrown, and broke his ankle. His wife reported in 1970 that her husband used crutches for two years and suffered from excessive sweating and fever long after that. As with the maladies and chronic illnesses which haunt UFO, Bigfoot, and other witnesses of strange phenomena, Packer's condition appears to be related to the giant snake he saw.

What are we to make of all this? Snakes, and serpents were very prominent in the religions of the early civilizations of the Old and New World. The snake appears to have been widely worshipped as a source of supernatural power. In the ancient cultures of the Americas, hints of the extent of the influence of giant snakes in the religions of these peoples is seen in the cult of Quetzalcoatl, the feathered serpent of the Aztecs, to the monumental earthworks of the giant Serpent Mound of Ohio. The ancients were in touch with the importance of giant serpents in their lives.

During the era of Modern Man, we have all lost contact, in varying degrees, with the meandering wonders slithering through the world. In recent years, the increase in reports and the realization of the importance of UFO's, Bigfoot, phantom panthers, and other denizens of the unknown, have merely reflected man's renewed sensitivity to the borderlands of reality.

The investigation of giant snake sightings is another step in this direction.

[Deep appreciation is given to Peter Rodman for his assistance with this giant snakes column.]

Loren Coleman•

Two Heads are Better?

Not for Zhang Zipping, 35, from a remote mountain village in Huize County, Yunnan Province. The farmer, a deaf-mute, had a second head surgically removed earlier this year. The 'parasitic' head, in some sources reported as normal-sized, but more likely about 8 inches round, was growing on the right side of Zhang's face. It had 12 teeth, hair, but the eyes, eyelids, nose and mouth were not fully developed. The cranium was normally shaped and covered an egg-sized brain, which is said not to have functioned. Plastic surgery has now restored Zhang's face, and he is said to be looking for a wife. *Sunday Sun* (Canada) + *Sunday Express* (S.Africa), 24 Feb 1980; *Ta Kung Pao* (HK) 28 Feb 1980; *Midnight Globe* 18 March 1980; *D. Mirror* 27 May 1980.

A two-headed baby was

born on 16 August 1980 in an army hospital in Tianjin, to unidentified parents. Weighing 3.3 kilos at birth, the baby has also two oesophaguses, two respiratory systems, two stomachs, but one heart, liver, anus and a normal limb-count. When the left hip is injected, the left head cries; when the left head is fed, the right head cries. *Ta Kung Pao* 28 August 1980.

Scrambled Eggs

A baby born at the Tsan Yuk hospital, Hong Kong, had four legs and four arms. It died 13 hours after birth. *South China Morning Post* (HK) 6 Oct 1979. In Manila, Phillipines, a boy with two heads, three feet and three hands born to a Filipino mother, died 5 hours later. *SCMP* 22 Jan 1980.

Small Problems

An examination operation on an 88-day-old girl, carried out at Anshan, Liaoning Province, on 4 December 1979, discovered four parasitic foetuses in a growing lump on her abdomen. In total, they weighed 325 grams. The largest was 15 cms long, and had developed hands, feet and hair. *Ta Kung Pao* 20 December 1979.

Lin Eryi, a 17-year-old male of Gutian Co, Fujian Province, complained of difficulty in breathing, and vomiting blood and human hair. Diagnosed as a tumour, the operating surgeons discovered a foetus, carried since birth, in the thoracic cavity. Weighing more than a kilogram, it had underdeveloped hair, teeth and eyes. *Ta Kung Pao* 17 July 1980.

68-year-old Wang Yinge, of Angua Co, Hebei Province, had a calcified foetus removed, which had been embedded in her abdominal cavity for 31 years. Bursting out of the womb and entering the abdominal cavity, the foetus died after 6–7 months and became calcified. It weighed 121 gms and was 11.5 cms long.

Monkeying Around

According to the Shanghai newspaper *Wenhui Bao,* local scientists have exhumed and are examining the remains of Xu Yunbao, who died in a fire in 1962, aged 23. Born in Sichuan Province, Xu's body was entirely covered in hair and bent at the waist. His skull was only 3.2 inches in diameter in birth, and he grew to be 3 feet 5 inches tall. Referred to as a 'monkey-man', Xu used all four limbs for walking, refused clothing even during the winter, and preferred raw corn to cooked food. His spinal column and limbs are said to be even more backward than that of Peking Man, though the paper denies he was either monkey or ape, while admitting he had 'a strong wild nature and liked to catch people'. His mother, 72, two brothers and two sisters are still alive, and apparently normal. *Albuquerque Journal + Arkansas Gazette* (via *UFO Newsclipping Service)* 21 April 1980.

Horny Dilemma

According to most reports *(Topeka Capital Journal* 24 May 1980; *Malay Mail* 27 May 1980; *Midnight Globe* 1 July 1980) an 88-year-old woman of Hebei Province grew two horns on the top of her head, some 6 months previusly. The larger of the horns was said to be a quarter inch long, yellowish-brown and without feeling. Dr Martin Bruber of New York declares to the *Globe* that this is a case of hyperosteosis frontalis, a bony, tumour-like growth that normally occurs on the *inside* of the skull, nearly always strikes elderly women, and that they frequently suffer from diabetes or obesity. He has, incidentally, never heard of a case where the horns grow on the *outside* of the skull, but still...

The less-restrained *New Thrill* (Malaysia) 31 May 1980, identifies the woman as 'Madam Chow' of the Chiao Ho district, Hebei, and tells us that she is in normal health (not obese or diabetic). It also tells us that the left horn first grew to two inches long, the right following suit. When both horns were that length, the tips started to turn downward, and are described as like deer-horns. The same source mentions an unidentified Japanese with 3-inch horns, and another report from China of a man with 10-inch horns, which later dropped off to leave one-inch stumps, which then started to form an 'S' shape.

THEY COME FROM *WHERE?!*

Nothing medical here, but this one's just too good to let get away...

Something's in the air over Manila, Phillipines... to wit UFOs and microwaves... and they're all coming from the Hong Giam Taoist Temple, say local residents! Seems two local evening papers have been stirring things up by reporting that 30 residents had complained to the government that harmful microwaves' had been coming from the red pagoda-like building, which is surrounded by high walls. The microwaves allegedly come from an electronic 'remote-sensing' gadget within the temple, which is also said to be responsible for releasing UFOs. Tomas Tan, 64, president of the Chinese association running the temple, says he has no idea where the reports originated from, but that he has been plagued by ugly phone calls from anonymous callers for weeks. Eventually, reporters were invited to inspect the temple, and Tan was considering libel suits. *Houston Chronicle* 15 June 1980. But there's a scenario now: 1949, and the communists are approaching... hundreds of Taoist priests climb into flying saucers, and... and...

Credit: Chris J Holtzhausen, Mark A Hall, Colin Hohnson, Sam, Dwight Whalen, Heathcote Williams. **SM.**

U·F·O Commentary by Nigel Watson

TINY FEATS

Speculation that a dead British music hall drag-artist was carrying on in an attempt to fulfil the 'show must go on' tradition, appeared when Pc Swift saw some strange clothed revellers dancing round an imaginary maypole. The location was the playing fields near Stonebridge Avenue, East Hull, and not long after the policeman saw these figures at 1.30am on 9th August 1977, they disappeared. The nearby graveyard was seen as the culprit for these ghostly happenings by the *Hull Daily Mail,* but others regarded this incident as having a relationship with fairy-lore. [1,2]

Not long after Pc Swift's sighting I telephoned him but he didn't want to say anything more about his experience. I got a similar reaction from headmaster Robin Aldridge, who had collected information about the 60 Noddy-like entities seen riding around in weird bubble cars in Wollaton Park, Nottingham, on the 29th October 1979, by some of his pupils. [3] I was equally unsuccessful when I wrote to the Nottingham UFO Investigation Society to ask if they had any information on this case. Syd Henley, on behalf of NUFOIS, replied that 'we do not investigate figments of peoples' imaginations, only UFO reports... [4] It must be great to have such psychological insight, but then I've heard that membership of NUFOIS bestows upon one all manner of abilities!

How NUFOIS would react to the following case is hard to imagine. In February 1978, I took part in a phone-in programme devoted to the subject of UFOs, which was broadcast live by Radio Humberside. Halfway through this programme a woman only identified as 'Barbara' described the details of a UFO sighting made by her 7-year-old son, whom I shall name Peter for the sake of this report.

His sighting took place on Wednesday, 18th January 1978. Fog had lingered about the fields of Anlaby school, Anlaby, near Hull, North Humberside, during the morning. However, when Peter and his three friends went to play in the schoolyard at lunch time, the weather conditions had become a lot better.

Peter started playing on one of the concrete toys in the playground when he heard a sharp whistling sound – similar to the sound produced by someone blowing into a pen top. He looked up to see a round object which had small windows in it and appeared like 'how you would imagine a flying saucer'. It was changing colours as it came down to land on the flat schoolroof.

Three people got out of this curious craft, and they walked onto the schoolroof. Peter saw that they had apparently no arms, and wore gold suits. From their backs were wires or tubes which hung from them to the craft.

Peter ran to tell his friend, who was a few yards away, about the UFO. But when they looked back at the school they saw that the three people had turned around and run back into their craft.

Then the craft took off slowly, and as it did so Peter could see through the underneath of the craft, and was able to observe the three occupants returning to their seats. Once the craft got clear of the school buildings it went away 'just like a boomerang' (though this boomerang didn't come back) and that was the last they saw of it.

On the day of the sighting Peter was rather nervous about going to bed, and he asked his sister to take him upstairs to his bedroom. Otherwise he and his three friends did not suffer any after-effects from their sighting.

The witness' mother supplied this information in a clear and precise manner without trying to sensationalize the circumstances of the observation.

Unfortunately I was unable to investigate this case due to several factors. The case is all the more interesting because exactly two months before, at 2.45pm Friday, 18th November 1977, pupils at Wawne Primary school, Wawne, near Hull, North Humberside, saw a UFO.

Fortunately headmaster, Michael Yates, was very cooperative, and within a few days of their sighting I was able to interview some of the witnesses. Mr Yates told me, 'I was talking to my wife in the staff-room when three children from her class rushed in and said they had seen something silvery in the sky.'

Altogether about twenty pupils aged between 6 and 7 years saw from the playground, a spinning object which looked like a dish upside-down with a top cupola section which had windows in it. This object was seen to move swiftly on an horizontal trajectory moving from approximately east to south. One of the children, Emma Priestly, wrote, 'On Friday I saw a flying saucer. It looked a bit like a dish upside-down and it flew to the left and then to the right. It went very fast.'

17 children in Mrs Cattle's class saw the silver-coloured

UFO from the playground, whilst three children, Robert Stevenson, Lisa Pattison and Caroline Swift, from Mrs Yates' class saw it. Because Mrs Yates' three pupils couldn't find the right words to accurately describe what they saw, she separated them and told them to make plasticine models of what they saw. The result of their work was surprisingly similar, and this seemed to indicate that they really had seen something strange in the sky.

As I wrote in my more detailed UFOIN report [5], 'It is my opinion that the children I spoke to were a good cross-section of the children who saw this phenomenon, and they kept very closely to their original descriptions of the UFO. As Mr Yates said to me, they are just normal honest schoolchildren. So it seems hardly likely that children of their age would conspire in such numbers to make up such a consistent story – and stick to it!'

So it is apparent from our brief survey that the Hull district has had its fair share of fairies (sorry, figments of the imagination) and UFO visitors. In 1978 a woman even wrote to report that in the late 1950s her son when a small boy, saw from the vicinity of their home in Hull a tin man. I have pathetically little information about this sighting, due to the witness' reluctance of being interviewed. Alright I admit it. I'm not the world's best investigative reporter, I just happen to respect the witnesses' right to remain silent and my right to remain lazy! However, it does occur to me that Hull could be the lost city of OZ, and no doubt the fairies, UFOs, and the tin man all disappeared through a process of... wait for it... osmosis.

Nigel Watson•

REFERENCES

1) *Fortean Times* No 23, p7.
2) *MUFOB* No 8, p11.
3) *Fortean Times* No 31, p42.
4) Letter from Syd Henley dated 17th February 1980.
5) UFOIN file no 7726.

Plasticine models made by UFO witnesses Robert Stevenson (top) Lisa Pattison (center): Caroline Swift (bottom). (Copyright Roger Hebb.)

Hardbacks.

ARTHUR C CLARKE'S MYSTERIOUS WORLD

By Simon Welfare & John Fairley.
Collins, London, 1980; £8.95, pp217, photos, maps, index.

This glossily impressive book is based on the TV series of the same name, as is the fashion these days. But despite the lavish production *Mysterious World* does not deliver all it seems to promise. The reader's interest has to struggle against a growing sense of *deja vu* as it is presented with familiar data in a range of familiar subjects; Bigfoot, Yeti, vitrified forts, stone circles, Tunguska incident, lake and sea monsters, UFOs, giants etc. The research is competent but not consistent – what book doesn't have its quota of errors– and the writing of Welfare and Fairley, both executives in the Yorkshire TV production company, is easy, informed and even witty. There are a few surprises for those Forteans who have read all before. The TV team spent a lot of money travelling the globe, re-interviewing witnesses to these events, and the resultant testimony and photos form islands of interest in an otherwise unremarkable text. Whereas most of the photos are incidental scenes or portraits, there are a few we are glad to see for the first time: the Midwinter sunbeam in Newgrange tumulus, some new Yeti-prints, and a splendid section of the 1973 Manchester ice-fall block seen through polarized light.

The actual role of Arthur C Clark in all this seems ambiguous and unnecessary. It is clear from book and series that Clarke did not do the research or visit the sites of these mysteries himself, and the opening statement of each series-segment – that these cases are all from Clarke's files – is highly questionable. His chief qualification seems to be his lauded science-fiction work, and the fact that he was once actively antagonistic to many of the mysteries he now seems to be endorsing. But a closer look at his contribution to the book – an introduction, a foreword, and afterwords to each chapter – shows it to be peppered with disclaimers and qualifications, and adding nothing of consequence to the main text by Welfare and Fairley.

Deliberate or not, the same hesitancy to become fully involved in the mysteries that are being presented under his name, is stronger in the TV segments, in which ACC is filmed against the background of Sri Lanka (now his permanent home) for his brief intros and cuts which serve to link the main narrative of voice-over and interviews. One senses the media-logic, which dictates, presumptuously, that a 'star' is needed to front the project if the public is to buy it, but his real accomplishments notwithstanding, Clarke seems as out of place as an entombed toad. He might as well be any British tourist, surprised on Unawatoona Beach by a film crew, and asked to make several dozen link-pieces. Inevitably the ACC interjections look superfluous, and the same goes for the book.

With the TV series behind it, there is no doubt the book will be very successful, and along the way a lot of money will be made. More's the pity, then, that the authors could not have helped their readers more. Having stoked up their interest, the book just peters out... There is no 'further reading' list, nor any indication of where the neophyte might continue his studies. There is one chapter specifically dedicated to Fort, but which has room only to look at a handful of recent cases (falls of nuts, seeds, ice and frogs), and Fort's set-pieces, the Chinese seals (stamping kind) found in Ireland and the Devil's Footprints (Devon 1855). That sources could not have been acknowledged more, nor a brief list of magazines and societies given, seems to me to be a great opportunity missed, and one which may not come on such a scale again.

RJMR.

PHOTOGRAPHS OF THE UNKNOWN

By Bob Rickard & Richard Kelly.
New English Library, London, 1980; £7.95, pp144, plates.

Anyone who believes that there is a dearth of photographs of inexplicable phenomena should take a look at this book, for Rickard and Kelly have proved that there is no shortage. However, having said that, the book does show that there is a lack of *good* photographs of many phenomena, especially those which take the observer unawares and are over all too soon. In 144 fully utlised pages the subjects range far and wide through all illustratable aspects of Forteana, and the following brief rundown can only begin to indicate the wealth of material Rickard and Kelly have managed to locate.

Water monsters have not been widely or well photographed when one takes into account the large number of sightings, and many of the pictures here show only wakes or indefinable shapes. The only 99% genuine picture of an ape-man is shown, and the rest are footprints, witnesses, etc. Falls are better represented, since once fallen the object or substance is static until it dissolves or is otherwise lost. 'Natural UFOs (e.g. lenticular clouds) and other atmospheric marvels vary in their ease of capture on film, while 'genuine' UFOs have been widely photographed but usually with an inconclusive result – a small, blurred speck against an ocean of sky. It seems that the closer a UFO is photographed, the more likely it is to be a hoax! One spread shows how Ground Saucer Watch use a computer to analyse these tantalising UFO photographs, and two spreads are devoted to a strange and colourful aerial display recorded in the Canary Islands in 1979. Psychic phenomena have been intriguingly photographed, from possession and stigmata to bleeding images, ectoplasm, thoughtograpy and kirlian photography. There are even photographs of possibly paranormal persons, including aliens, the Blessed Virgin Mary and Christ, all notoriously camera-shy, and a wider coverage of the less coy ghosts and mediumistic materialisations. 'Mind over matter' is depicted through photographs of yoga feats, psychic surgery, fire immunity, including fire-walking, spoon-bending (though one picture in the 15-picture sequence on p.124 seems to be out of place – the fourth from the end should change places with the one preceding it), levitation of objects and people, apports and poltergeists, the book closing with some of the fine photographs taken by Graham Morris during the Enfield poltergeist outbreak in 1977.

365 photographs in 144 pages is not bad value, especially when we realise that each picture shows some aspect of an inexplicable phenomenon. Each spread is crammed with pictures, many in colour, so much so that the effect is at times overwhelming, making this a book to dip into rather than to 'read' straight through. The photographs are supported by brief factual captions, and a 6-page introduction gives some background on the history and problems of photographing the unexplained.

Rickard and Kelly are to be congratulated on the extent of their research, for they have tracked down some rare material. Of course they cannot always (or even ever) guarantee the authenticity of pictures, and most of the transitory phenomena pictures could have been hoaxed by a skilled photographer. It is interesting to go through the book and try to work out how each picture could have been faked; but of course the fact that a photograph could have been faked does not prove that it was. This uncertainty does mean that the value of these pictures as evidence of anything is limited, but nevertheless their historical value is incalculable. This is a fascinating Fortean pictorial record which will appeal to a very wide range of readers, from the 'man and woman in the street' to the most knowledgeable Fortean.

Janet Bord.

THE DARK GODS
by Anthony Roberts
& Geoff Gilbertson
Rider / Hutchinson, London 1980; £7.95 hb £4.50 pb, pp266, graphs, bib, index, photos.

The Dark Gods is a continuation of the theme raised in Vallee's *Messengers of Deception.* It examines the control

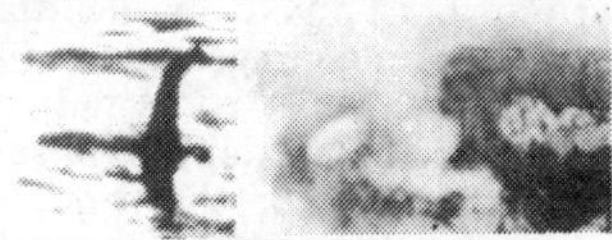

mechanism behind miraculous phenomena, 'ultraterrestrials' wielding prodigal powers, the alleged treachery of some New Age groups and gurus and the interface between politics and black magic.

The foreword is partly a hand-wringing session conducted by celebrity Colin Wilson who is worried about public reaction to a thesis predicated upon assumptions unrecognized 'by the millions'. One such axiom of Roberts and Gilbertson appears on p.28, 'In nearly every culture, past and present, the religious ethos consistently takes on a polarizing dualistic form.' Tantra, Zen and the watercourse way of the Tao contradict this sweeping generalization which is followed by the authors' assurance that their enormity does make sense.

Even though he's technically correct then, about *The Dark Gods,* the tenor of Wilson's remarks will probably contribute to the tendency among 'fringe' researchers to surround their data with sycophantic, explanatory asides. These almost apologetic constructions are intended for a public which routinely 'swallows' ludicrous media disinformation without batting an eyelash, while submitting thoughts outside the agenda to critical scrutiny worthy of a Sherlock Holmes.

Success manifests itself in a variety of ways, some of which are unconnected with media hype. The refusal to be debased by appeals to the 'sensibilities' of automatons is a sign of the ungovernable, intractable and rude visions and pattern-detection of pioneers everywhere. They are the wild ones who do not tailor their prose to Joyce Carol Oates' notion of what is literature or their epistemology to a modern public drunk alternately on petrol and alcohol. Those in a position to advance artists and writers must make intellectual space and encouragement available to the most roots/radical among them or stand exposed as accomplices of the thought police.

In the marketplace of political opinions, the authors of *The Dark Gods* take a line similar to the *nouveaux philosophes* who have challenged the Newtonian – Kantian – Enlightenment – Fuerbachian postulates in France. In the occult firmament, Roberts and Gilbertson attempt to vindicate the dire warnings and prophecies of Nesta Webster, H.P. Lovecraft, Commander William Guy Carr and their epigones.

The only consistency in this *opus* is its inconsistency and that, coupled with its view of evil, makes it a difficult book to like.

There's a High Church, Goethe – and – Mephistopheles image of Lucifer here, complete with dramatic fanfares from Gounod's orchestra and chorus. Other than at the Metropolitan Opera, I don't expect to see this guy in America, where evil is a smoke that goes with TV, chili-burgers and race wars.

In *The Dark Gods* we are suppposed to be experiencing the shattering of the misdirections, deceits and illusion which mark what the authors term 'The Trail of Klingsor' (after the villain of *Parzival*).

What actually occurs is the concealment of an important question which is reflected in the unquestioned regard Roberts and Gilbertson have for the Bible and the Jesus legend. What they don't afford us is a peek at the real identity of the god of the Old Testament. They have no curiosity about how the Jewish tribal diary managed to wangle top-billing as planet earth's holy book. Of all the stratagems the authors attribute to the 'ultraterrestrials', the Bible is not for a moment considered part of the imposture.

There is excellent hermeneutical evidence for Yahweh being a female impersonator and transsexed caricature of the Great Goddess. This racist, genocidal entity's 'sacred scripture' continues to cause untold suffering for native and natural peoples and the false-naming diabolization of megaliths and earth shrines.

In lieu of such an exigesis, we are treated to dogmatic orthodoxies such as a warning against 'organized spiritual groups' who try to bring about '...a replacement for Christ'. Why should we accept this Christian fundamentalism? Because: 'The Bible – it must be noted–tells us categorically that Christ will not be superceded...' (p.175)

While totally ignoring the neglected arcana of Antonin Artaud, Malcolm Lowry, William Burroughs and Mary Daly we are made to encounter the usual quotes from the Book of Revelation.

Bible prophets are esteemed as paradigms of illusion-shattering (p.39). The 'spiritually minded folk of the wold' are defined as those who 'rally their spirits with passages from the Bible' (p.136)

The 'Message from Myth' section discusses the sub-rosa aspects of the Grail story in a rehash of the patriarchal rip-off of women's experience. The Grail story contains mythic power stolen from women's mysteries – in this case, in the fabrication of a myth of male 'menstruation' under cover of salvational blood and immortal life. As Jean and Ruth Mountaingrove have written *(Womanspirit),* 'We [women] are the ones who bleed and are not injured; we bleed and do not die.' Roberts and Gilbertson obviously don't have an inkling of contemporary developments in radical feminist scholarship (such as Mary Daly's *Gyn/Ecology).* The authors of *The Dark Gods* even have the temerity to drag the Mother Goddess into this botched job and thus flirt with psychic backlash – She is no traitor to her daughters and no perpetrator of the draining of gynocentric transforming energy by phallocratic myth.

It is important to note that either as a result of a disconcerting ruse or an equally troubling befuddlement, the authors intersperse their sexism and Christianity with certain *pro forma* cliches connoting liberation, balance and flexibility. We read fragments about reality games, cosmic balance and paganism. But these protrude from the text like an academician's belly. They are cancelled out by the sum tenor and thrust of the book.

Many statements directly contradict others. On p.51 sex and freethinking are praised while on p.82 we are urged to avoid '...earthy, sexual license of promiscuous self-indulgence.' Throughout the book the authors display their horror of the snake and goat and automatically assign them a demonic zoomorphism. They also seem to detest Klingsor primarily because he fornicated with a married woman (p.83).

On p.139 Gilbertson says he wants to 'vindicate' mason and hypnotist Franz Anton Mesmer while on p.201 Roberts writes approvingly of the Abbe Fiard's 'tracts warning of the dangers of magicians and black occultists such as Mesmer...'

Except for a brief homily about confrontations with the control force being capable of producing 'an awareness of cosmic perspective' which can be 'liberating' (p.73), the MIB are described as 'phantom police'. Despite a selection from Brad Steiger about the 'echo-effect' of MIB phenomena (which is clouded by our Reformer-authors into a sermon on behalf of 'action'), there is little feeling for the psychology behind MIB terror and UFO contactee assassinations and suicides.

The mechanism of self-fulfilling prophesies is omitted from consideration as is the hunch that UFOs are reactive/ reflexive mind traps set for logical-positivist types who try to match wits (and egos) with the *Sidh.*

There is preaching about the need for 'a well-developed sense of humor' (p.74) but none surfaces in the pages and pages on Lovecraft, Bender and Adamski. No satire and none of the water-is-wet reality of the sacred clowning of native and natural shamanistic cultures. Hence H. P. Lovecraft is portrayed as a man haunted by undoubtedly prophetic dreams. There should be scoffers at every altar, including Lovecraft's. Why couldn't there be some relationship between the abysmally debilitating modern diet the Cthulhu-proclaimer adopted in his later years, and his nightmares?

Any disquisition on the control mechanism needs to ask such questions as:

Who faked Montezuma out of his jock strap by canonizing the 'White-god-from-the-East' prophesy which allowed a ragtag band of malarial pale-faces, under Cortez, to conquer a proud and powerful nation?

What can we learn from the relationship (if there is one) between the awe and glamour generated by the technology behind miraculous phenomena and the awe generated for modern civilization among native peoples coming into contact with gunpowder and the internal combustion engine?

The Dark Gods contains interesting tidbits for your files, on such subjects as occult politics, twilight language (shelta thari), decapitation, Albert Pike, America's 'Founding Fathers' and ley lines.

A more poetic and less dogmatic format might have rescued the authors of *The Dark Gods* from themselves. Voyants are usually easier to forgive than historians. Crusading historians are even less deserving of mercy. Roberts and Gilbertson deride what they call the 'ultraterrestrials' in a manner our shrewd peasant ancestors did not. The latter referred to the fairies as the 'people of peace' and 'the good neighbors', and in that practice lies a wisdom incapable of articulation. Let's just say that among 'stone age mentalities' there's a winking agreement undiscerned – at their peril – by moralists and modernists.

Michael Anthony Hoffman

Paperbacks.

THE UFO HANDBOOK:
A Guide to Investigating, Evaluating, and Reporting UFO Sightings
by Allan Hendry
Doubleday, NY 1979; $8.95/ Sphere, London 1980; £5.95, pp297, appendix, bib, graphs, photos, illos.

UFO skeptics will love this book. James Oberg, in the regular UFO column of *OMNI Magazine* (Sept. 1979) noted:

> Reports published by Dr. Hynek's own research center suggest that the line between UFOs and trivial IFOs may not be as clear as he would like to think. Early in 1977, for example, Hynek's managing editor, Allan Hendry, published an editorial 'to illustrate the thin veil that can exist between UFOs and IFOs.' Describing his attempt to solve some nighttime UFO reports from Las Vegas, Nevada, on January 19, 1977, Hendry recounted a series of frustrating dead ends. Then by 'sheer luck', he stumbled on the bizarre explanation: The Environmental Protection Agency had been using an illuminated balloon on a half-mile tether to collect samples of air pollution. This was the object that had set off the report, Hendry concluded confidently. But without Hendry's lucky break no amount of hard work could ever have converted that UFO into an IFO.

Hendry, in *The UFO Handbook*'s conclusion, comes to this same conclusion:

"...I am currently discouraged about the ability to take that which remains after the transient UFO event is over, the anecdotal testimony of excited witnesses and utilize it to plumb the physical, mythological, or psychological nature of any given case' (p.283) and 'It seems like a given UFO account, no matter how sensational the claims or how sincere the witnesses, always has the option of falling through as an IFO... but *never* does the evidence suddenly allow a burst of approval for even one UFO!' (p.283, Hendry's emphasis).

If this were all there were to it, there wouldn't be much reason for reading this book, other than to reassure oneself that nothing peculiar is happening in the universe. However, there is still plenty to wonder about.

Hendry uses the 1307 cases he investigated in his first year with the Center for UFO Studies; about 90% could be identified – most of them easily – as IFOs. This corresponds fairly well with the Project Bluebook which had about 95% identifiable as such. What is surprising is that most of the things people report as UFOs can be readily identified. Of the nocturnal lights that Hendry investigated 35% were stars. Apparently people don't know a star when they see it.

This book is a handbook for those who see potential UFOs. Hendry goes through the possible explanations and the way to verify facts. Using this book, almost anyone should be able to recognize most of what they see in the sky. (It is too bad that Doubleday and Sphere didn't publish it in a field notebook format instead of an unwieldy 7 x 9½" paperback. Also, the absence of an index greatly reduces its usability.)

Hendry's method, however, extends beyond a handbook. One of the innovations of Hendry's study is that, unlike most previous UFOlogists, he doesn't just consider the reports of IFOs as background noise, mere nuisances to be identified and cast aside so that the more provocative reports can be analyzed. Instead he uses the IFOs as a control group for the UFOs.

Some UFOlogists have put emphasis on the experience of witnesses to UFOs, on their reliability, professions, and so forth. However, neither character not observational training helped people report more accurately. Pilots, as a profession, reported the fewest IFOs (75%). Police did the worst (94%). The fact is that untrained observers report less IFOs than the police do.

Likewise, it is not the emotional reaction of the witness that determines validity of a report. Hendry gives the example of people who go into shock when they mistake Venus for a UFO. Their reaction is caused by their interpretation of the event and not by the object viewed. Multiple witnesses can be as wrong as a single one. In fact, more IFO reports have two or more witnesses than UFO reports.

No UFO investigation can take any report at its face value. UFO witnesses are not 'error-free' instruments. The investigator must use his ingenuity to ferret out the facts behind the experience.

Hendry gives ample tools for this determination. There are chapters on animal reactions, hypnosis, lie detectors, magnetic detectors, multiple witnesses, optics, photography, press, radar, radiation detectors, statistics, UFOlogists, UFO groups.

The chapter on statistics is the longest and most technical in the book. Hendry makes mincemeat of all the theories surrounding UFOs (including those done by researchers connected with the Center for UFO Studies). For example, he shows flaps are a function of gathering techniques rather than the number of sightings. He also discredits Jacques Vallee's statistics about UFO times and totals. This chapter alone is worth the price of the book.

The chapter on hypnosis as an investigational tool is intriguing. Hypnosis is used primarily in CE3 cases but it turns out that one doesn't have to have UFO exposure to relate an abduction scenario under hypnosis. More questions are raised than answered by this. The objective CE3 abduction may be discredited, but why is this scenario so readily available to the mind? No one has proposed an explanation to that. The only links that come to mind are found in the writing of Carl Jung.

Forteans and the obsessive newspaper clippers will want to study the chapter on the press as a tool. Hendry points out that newspapers have consistently belittled UFO reports while continuing to report sightings. UFO reports are considered human interest stories and are not subject to the same scrupulous investigation as other news reporting. This renders UFO reports in newspapers as almost worthless. That would be sad news for subscription clipping services, except probably people like me will go on collecting clippings of the unusual. Now, however, I can't take them very seriously.

In summation, this is the most unbiased and informative book on UFOs to date. Hendry attempts to look at the total picture. Any furture work on UFOs that ignores this book would be irresponsible. Hendry cautions, for instance, against blanket explanations about UFOs and explaining one unknown in terms of another (ball lightning). Finally, after several years, progress is being made in the methodology of UFO investigations.

We don't really know much more about UFOs than we did when Jung wrote *Flying Saucers*, but what has been learned as a result of the research is exciting. The central issue remains elusive, but this book illuminates things that UFO skeptics never seem to notice.

Rob Hollis Miller

THE DANCING WU LI MASTERS

by Gary Zukav
Rider / Hutchinson, London 1980; £4.50, pp352, foldout charts, polaroid filters, index, bib, notes, diags.

Not, as I first imagined, the manual of an obscure Kung Fu cult, this book presents an entertaining and readable account of modern Physics. It presupposes no previous knowledge of the subject and guides the reader gently from Galileo via Newton and Einstein to the exalted heights of Quantum Mechanics. 'Why bother?' I hear you ask, and justifiably so if you suffered as much from High School Physics as I did. The answer is that this is no mere compendium of theories, experiments and conclusions, Zukav presents his material in such a way as to convey the excitement, wonder and sheer mind-stretching weirdness which is at the heart of his subject. He claims, for example, that 'it is no longer evident whether scientists really discover new things or whether they create them'.

We are taken on a magical mystery tour of the cosmos, from quarks to black holes without the encumbrance of mathematics, for as John von Neumann said (and who should know better than he?) 'In mathematics you don't understand things, you just get used to them.'

How about a sample from the deep end of the book, the Einstein – Podolsky – Rosen effect...

Certainly sub-atomic reactions produce a 'two particle system of zero spin', that is we have two rotating electrons, protons or whatever, whose spins are always complementary, and I repeat, *always.* Imagine such a system in which particle A has a right spin and particle B must be spinning left. Now here comes the freaky bit, if we take particle A and change its spin so that now it spins left instead of right then particle B must immediately reverse its own spin. There appears to be a faster-than-light transfer of information between the two particles and this effect is assumed to be equally valid whether A and B are an inch apart or at opposite ends of the universe. How does particle B know that A has had its orientation altered? This interaction erodes commonplace notions of cause-and-effect and verges eerily on telekinesis.

Although Zukav does not attempt a thorough correlation of physics to oriental philosophy (he promises a subsequent work on that subject) there are enough passing references to Taoism, Tantrism, Zen etc. to illustrate the astounding relevance which these traditions bear to modern science. One physicist is even quoted as suggesting that in the next century, college physics courses will include classes in meditation.

A profound disservice has been done to this book by its blurb which quotes a reviewer thus: 'The most exciting intellectual adventure I've been on since *Zen and the Art of Motorcycle Maintenance".* Talk about damning with faint praise! If you are firmly convinced of the solidity of the word and would be disturbed by the suggestion that reality is rather wobbly and blurred then this book is not for you; it might drive you to think.

Mike Crowley

MADOC: THE MAKING OF A MYTH.

The legend of the Welsh discovery of America by Gwyn A. Williams.
266pp, illus, sources, index. Eyre Methuen £8.50.

Prince Madoc, who legend has it 'discovered' America in 1170, was a latecomer to those shores. The Norse were there perhaps as early as AD 700. St. Brendan 200 years before that. The Egyptians, Greeks, Romans possibly before the birth of Christ. But Madoc is important because he became the symbolic figurehead of British colonial expansion. Belief in the legend gave the British the right to challenge the Spanish monopoly in the New World.

Madoc, a scholarly book possibly hampered by the author's peculiar writing style, but one which bubbles with his enthusiasm and knowledge of the subject, is without doubt an important contribution to the literature of pre-Columban discoveries, and it is of interest to Forteans because it illustrates how once myth and legend is believed, and particularly if it is acted on, it can be as significant to history as reality.

Paul Begg

THE WISE WOUND

By P Shuttle & P Redgrove.
Penguin, Harmondsworth, Middx, 1980; £1.95, pp335, notes, bib, index.

Peter Redgrove and Penelope Shuttle have collated scientific, psychological, sociological and mythological data on this quintessentially female experience and given us valuable reference work on this important and neglected subject. They tackle it in three distinct sections: the medical and physiological realm of reproduction, fertility, gestation, maturation of the biological individual, and the cycles involved; the sociological and historical context in which menstruation is seen as 'The Curse', and how the woman relates to herself, other people, society as a whole and her psychiatrists; and finally the mythological role of menstruation, the Moon, vampirism, witchcraft and associated symbolism. There are many interesting avenues branching off from the main inquiry – eg: crime figures analysed for their menstrual component, or the strange fact that women of different menstrual cycles will tend to sychronize their periods when cloistered together (a factor that has some bearing on outbreaks of possession or 'mass hysteria' in nunneries or girls' schools.) Thoroughly recommended.

RJMR.

THE LIFE OF MILAREPA

trans. LP Lhalungpa
Paladin, St Albans, Herts 1979; £1.95, pp220, plates.

This autobiography of Tibet's most celebrated mystic and poet has occupied a central position in that country's literature since it was dictated in the early part of the 12th century.

It tells of how Milarepa, cheated of his inheritance by his grasping uncle and aunt, sought revenge on behalf of his widowed mother and sister. To this end he studied under a black-magician and returned to his home village to unleash a cataclysmic hail-storm on the house of the wicked pair. Then, over come with remorse at the sight of this wanton destruction he resolved to forsake sorcery and to seek guidance from a guru. Thus he came to meet Marpa the translator, to all the world a prosperous, married farmer but to his devoted students an indefatigable powerhouse, striving day and night to bring about their enlightenment.

In Milarepa's case, however, Marpa's guru-activity took a strange form which, if you are unacquainted with this remarkable work, I leave you to discover for yourself.

My knowledge of early South Tibetan is hardly adequate to judge the accuracy of this, the second, translation into English but anyone familiar with the earlier Evans-Wentz edition is in for a pleasant surprise. The narrative tears along at the pace of an adventure yarn and the songs with which Milarepa has ornamented his tale take on fresh clarity and meaning. For example compare the following:

'Within a certain unseen region of the Heavens,
The Perfect Buddha, expert in subtle argument,
Hath propounded many subtle and profound Apparent Truths;
And there one findeth ne'er the time to know the Real Truths:
Avoid, O Rechung, subtle argument.
(Evans-Wentz version)

In the invisible realm of the heavens,
There is a Buddha who skillfully uses falsehoods,
Guiding sentient beings toward relative truth.
Little time have they to realize ultimate truth.
O Retchung, abandon concepts.
(New Lhalungpa translation)

This book is essential reading, not merely to Forteans. If you have any pretensions to culture this belongs on your bookshelf alongside Dante's Divine Comedy, Shakespeare's Complete Works and your *Perishers* annuals.

Mike Crowley

THE MUTE STRATEGY

by Dave DeWitt
Sunbelt Press, Box 1331, Belen, NM 87002, USA, 1979; $3.00, pp239.

This is definitely a mandatory book for paranoids, Forteans and afficianados of the horror-story. The plot is hokey bacon-and-eggs Americana: Rancher Bob and Sherriff Lou protecting the cringing womenfolk against phantom helicopters, headless corpses, MIBs, government cover-ups and the high-tech horrors who carve prostitutes and livestock.

But it is also a non-dogmatic examination of the phenomenon which has bedeviled humanity from earliest times—though some would argue that the cattle mutilation waves which struck amid the fabled shadows and mythic proportions of the American West in the 1970s, have a particularly ominous message.

What exactly is the American spirit-of-place? DeWitt hints at the answer through a Van Helsing-type academic 'monster-hunter's' classroom reading, D.H. Lawrence's *The Plumed Serpent.*

In that brilliant novel, Lawrence suggested that America is the 'great No' to the European, Asian and 'even African' yes. Fans of this viewpoint see the American West as a kind of alchemical crucible of death: the scene of the first atomic bomb blast, the snuffing of John Kennedy and the comings and goings of numberless thanatos cults whose hell-hole of dark inspiration is the death lore of Mayan-Aztec myth.

DeWitt opts for this perspective rather than the tedious Billy Graham/Hal Lindsay-style warnings about B movie Satanism, which always struck this writer as Barnumesque and for the 'cowans'.

As for the 'message', Mr. DeWitt is brave enough to point a finger at the possible connection between UFOs and the US government (the latter either covering up the mutes or actually assisting in these evisceration orgies). He doesn't mention the hunch that a group of egomaniacs who combine Black Magic with modern technology may be firmly entrenched in the highest echelons of Washington. Neither does he touch on the old legend that evanescent entities can materialise on this plane of existence with the help of human and animal blood and entrails.

If there's a message it might be for women: cows are an ancient symbol of the human female and perhaps, in some bizarre way, the rape-mutilation of Earth Mother is somehow related to the attack on cows. Maybe the prophesy is telluric, 'to proceed further on this course of planetary rape will result in unthinkable consequences for women'.

All Hallows Eve or just destiny in the lower case? *The Mute Strategy* is stimulating reading and a refreshing break from the received opinion routinely encountered in this American media ghetto.

Michael Anthony Hoffman

NATURE DETECTIVE
By Hugh Falkus.
Penguin Books, Harmondsworth, Middx, 1980; £2.95, pp256, photos.

An essential book for any British naturalist, or Fortean who has to take into account the huge variety of wildlife in his investigations. This large format book is crammed with photos of the tracks of insects, animals, snakes and birds; ground marks and other evidence of hiding, feeding, living, breeding, eating, killing and hibernating. Fascinating and informative and a delight to both active and armchair 'detectives' of all ages.

RJMR.

SCHRODINGER'S CAT
by Robert Anton Wilson
Pocket Books, NY 1979; $2.50, pp256, glossary.
Robert Anton Wilson does to the novel what Roeg does to the movies. Using the theories in quantum physics Wilson's characters are connected by information not space-time, a theory already used to evaluate UFOs by Jacques Vallee in *Messengers of Deception.* Wilson's characters are paranoids and his informational 'bits', his set-pieces are often hilarious. So is it *Illuminatus:*? Yes and no. Some of the people are from that pasture, subtly and suitably changed. Hopping off with the stupidity of Terrans as though viewed from the future, *Schrodinger's Cat* leads us to the brink of nuclear splat, but in *The Universe Next Door*, which is the second-take of *S's Cat*, the story becomes infinitely more complicated. Or simple, depending on how one views the Universe. H. P. Lovecraft's still there and so are the fnords. CIA, the FBI, conspiracies, cover-ups, bizarre sexual gymnastics? Yep. Magick, space beings, robots, drugs, a taxidermed phallus... you name it.

Wilson's last novel is novel, though his early style reminds me of the delightful technique of Vonnegut: Is Wilson really a character in the book or did he really write it? Tarot, psychology, the I Ching: '...Rhoda was originally renowned back in the '60s for her own curious mutation of old-fashioned Dixieland 'scat-singing'; what few realised was that her riffs were not mere Jabberwocky but actually fragments of the Enochian Keys used by Dr. John Dee, Mr. Aleister Crowley and other magicians. People who came out of Civic Monster concerts seeing auras, hearing strange voices, catching odd fugitive galimpses into fairlyland and Oz, or seeing the djinns gathered about the throne of Allah, attributed this to the heavy marijuana fumes always circulating in the air at rock concerts'. Or, 'Justin Case suspected that the FBI was tapping his phone. However, 9,000,000 out of the 20,000,000 primates in New York also suspected the FBI of tapping their phones. Case just happened to be one of the 8,000,000 who were correct in this suspicion'. Is this a good or a bad book? I really couldn't say because having been exposed to Bell's Theorum, which moots that any two particles which come into contact will continue to influence each other, no matter how far apart they subsequently move, I cannot possibly hold any objective viewpoint. But then who can? Possession, ESP, racism, Purity of Essense, Richard Nixon, 23 skidoo...

David Sutton

BEYOND DEATH
By Stanislav and Christina Grof.
TIME
By Marie-Louise von Franz.
ZEN
By Anne Bancroft.
All: Thames & Hudson, 1980; £3.95, pp96, plates, illos, bib.

Three worthy additions to the acclaimed 'Art and Imagination' series. Each carries a short essay by the author/s, followed by heavily illustrated sections following various related themes. First class visual stimulation of the imagination—solid enough to be tantalizing, and light enough to be digestible.

RJMR.

WORTHWHILE PAPERBACK EDITIONS:

SUBDUE THE EARTH *(Granada, London, 1980; £1.25, pp221, index).* Ralph Franklin Walworth's challenge thrown at the feet of geologists, Darwinists and paleontologists. Disputes the Creation, the fossil record, and the evolution of this planet as scientists would have us know it. Deserves to be read by all for its bold and different points of view.
OEDIPUS AND AKHNATON *(Abacus, London, 1980; £1.95, pp206, plates, refs).* Velikovsky's journey into Greek and Egyptian mythology, the enigmas of which he deciphers with his impressive and scholarly insight. Fascinating.

HARMONIC 33 *(Sphere, London, 1980; 95p, pp204, tables).* Bruce Cathie's over-the-top exposition of a world-wide grid of power used by UFOs, and of the geophysical upheaval that results from damage to this grid by atom-bomb tests.

THE TRUE HISTORY OF THE ELEPHANT MAN *(Penguin, Harmondsworth, Middx, 1980; £1.25, pp223, plates, appendices, bib, index).* As timely preparation for the forthcoming film on the life of Joseph Carey Merrick, Michael Howell and Peter Ford prepared this excellent biography of one of the most pathetic freaks of modern times. Merrick was horribly distorted yet his inner nature commanded love, respect and admiration from all who knew him in the Victorian society that had rejected him earlier in life.

THE NEW SOVIET PSYCHIC DISCOVERIES *(Sphere, London, 1980; £1.50, pp448, plates, index).* Impressive compendium of official and unofficial Soviet paranormality by Henry Gris and William Dick who travelled extensively in Russia meeting the gifted psychic and their researchers. **VOICES IN MY EAR** *(Futura, London, 1980; £1.00, pp224, plates).* The autobiography of Doris Stokes, well-known London medium, and some of her adventures.

GHOSTS OF WALES *(Corgi, London, 1980; £1.25, pp218, photos, bib, index).* As a companion to his other gazetteers of Scottish and London ghosts, this new book by Peter Underwood belongs on every ghosthunter's shelves.

THE NECRONOMICON *(Corgi, London, 1980; £1.25, pp184, appendices, illos, bib).* The most aesthetically satisfying and intelligent attempt yet to recreate Lovecraft's famous reference work — this time decoded with a computer from fragments of aged parchment and discussed by Colin Wilson, Robert Turner and David Langford, edited by George Hay.

RJMR.

Booklets.

STARS, AND RUMOURS OF STARS by Kevin & Sue McClure *(available from the authors at £1 or $3, inc postage; 8 Scotland Road, Little Bowden, Market Harborough, Leicestershire, UK.)*

The McClures have done us all a great service by re-examining the Great Welsh Revival of 1904–5. The authors are active members of the Society for Pyschical Research, which devoted nearly a whole volume of their *Proceedings* to discussion of the strange 'spiritualistic' phenomena that attended the preaching of Mary Jones and a few others. Although the SPR interest was prompted by accounts of apparitions and strange lights, it was the work of Charles Fort which urged that the Revival and its signs be seen in a general context of all the other curious events going on simultaneously, such as the UFO and mystery airship sightings of the day, strange animals on the loose, some spontaeous combustions, and so on. As the authors point out in their introduction, the story of the 'Egryn Lights' is relevant to the researchers of UFOs, Bigfoot, psychical research, spiritualism, and Fortean phenomena, and has been cited by a number of them 'in the same breath as Fatima, as UFO of the religious kind.' We all know the way less scrupulous authors distort poorly researched data into new and erroneous myths, and it is the avowed intention of the McClures to prevent this happening in this case – or at least to remove the excuse for it. Accordingly, they lead us into the witness testimony via a chapter on the historical and sociological context of the Revival (one of many it seems). The eye-witness testimony is gathered from contemporary sources, who had it direct from the witness... and in most Fortean research that's as close as you'll get. Most of the quotes are referenced and there is a small bibliography. Thoroughly recommended.

RJMR.

ROSICRUCIAN THOUGHTS ON THE EVER–BURNING LAMPS OF THE ANCIENTS by W Wynn Westcott. A reprint from *The Freemason* (1885). *(Price 35p. Available from David Medina: 6 Grant Court, 18 Spencer Hill, London SW19 4NY.)* A brief tour of classical sources and their Rosicrucian interpretation. Fascinating.

RJMR.

TALES OF THE HEXHAM HEADS by Paul Screeton *(60p, from the author at: 5 Egton Drive, Seaton Carew, Hartlepool, Cleveland TS25 2AT.)* The stone heads, found at Hexham in 1972, are said to be ancient Celtic in origin (disputed) and the catalyst in a series of frightening visions of a wolf-headed man seen by, among others, Dr Anne Ross, the Celtic scholar. Paul Screeton summarizes their history, the debate on their origin, and the psychic phenomena that they undoubtetly triggered. Fascinating and recommended.

RJMR.

PENNICK'S ENDSVILLE PAGAN ALMANACK *(50p).* **TUNNELS UNDER LONDON** *(65p).* Two more studies from the prolific duplicator of Nigel Pennick. *(Published by Fenris-Wolf: 142 Pheasant Rise, Bar Hill, Cambridge CB3 8SD.* The *Almanack* collates the Odinist, Pagan, French Revolution and other calendars, as well as the Civil Calendar of the Common Era, equinoxes, solstices and feast days etc. etc. Very handy. *Tunnels* is a tour-de-force of research, especially since officialdom is tight-lipped about the existence, number and use of many of these tunnels.

RJMR.

FACTS YOU MIGHT FORGET

ALIEN MENTORS (Part 1)

Classified Exchanges.

As a reader service FT welcomes mutual exchanges with any relevant publication, and copies issues received since our last issue earn a listing here. No mag — no mention: All we ask in return is a similar entry in your own journal.

FORTEAN

- **Creature Chronicles** – quarterly Ohio-based coverage of manimals and mystery animal sightings. Available for exchange. Ron Schaffner: Box 12049A, Cincinnati, OH 45212, USA.
- **Forteana** – quarterly journal of the Scandinavian Fortean Organization, in Danish. Changed from a newspaper format to one more like the old FT. New address; SCANFO: Skindergade 19, 1159 DK-1157 Kobenhavn K, Denmark.
- **Full Moon** – a new journal covering Fortean, folklore, UFOs etc subjects from the Hawaiian Islands. Juicy Fortean chunks of food for thought. USA $7.00/yr; foreign subs please inquire for rates. Jacob A Davidson: 1981-B St Louis Drive, Honolulu, Hawaii 96816, USA.
- **Journal of Meteorology** – a monthly source of sound weather data and records, with many articles on Fortean related meteorology. Annual sub: £11.50; overseas £13.00. Inquiries to J. Meteorology: Cockhill House, Trowbridge, Wiltshire BA14 9BG.
- **Lantern** – quarterly Fortean and folklore journal of East Anglian mysteries. Consistently of interest. UK & Europe £1.20/yr; USA $5.00. BSIG: 3 Dunwich Way, Oulton Broad, Lowestoft, Suffolk NR32 4RZ.
- **New Atlantean Journal** – quarterly of the New Atlantean Research Society, covering parapsychology, UFOs, pyramids, ancient enigmas and Forteana. USA $7.00; Overseas surface $10.00, airmail $15.00. NAJ: 5963 32nd Ave North, St Petersburg, FL 33710, USA.
- **Nessletter** – monthly newsletter of the Ness Information Service. Sightings and gossip from the Scottish and other monster-haunted lakes. £2.00; USA $8.00/yr. NIS: Huntshieldford, St Johns Chapel, Bishop Aukland, Co Durham DL12 1RQ.
- **Res Bureaux Bulletin** – regular coverage of Canadian UFOs and Forteana generally by one of Forteanisms' most devoted men. Now discontinued per se, and incorporated into INFO Journal. But Mr X would still like to exchange clippings or data. Mr X: Box 1598, Kingston, Canada K7L 5C8.
- **Science Frontiers** – brief digest of current scientific articles of relevance, with mail-order catalogue. Sourcebook Project: Box 107, Glen Arm, MD 21057, USA.
- **Second Look** .– a pro bimontly of consistent interest and quality covering the whole range of Fortean interest. Single copies $3.00 inc p+p. Second Look: 10 E St SE, Washington DC 20003, USA.
- **Zetetic Scholar** – a half yearly review of criticism and bibliography covering the whole range of Fortean interest. ZS is thick, relevant, scholarly, interesting and generally a damn fine monument to the energies of its editor, Marcello Truzzi. Makes FT editor want to give up (but he won't of course!). Well worth the sub price of $12.00/yr (N America only), overseas subs apply for rates. Zetetic Scholar: Dept of Sociology, Eastern Michigan University, Ypsilanti, MI 48197, USA.

UFOs

- **APRO Bulletin** – monthly journal of the Aerial Phenomena Research Organization. News, investigations, articles. Annual sub: USA $12.00: overseas $15.00. APRO: 3910 E Kleindale Rd, Tuscon, AZ 85712, USA.
- **BUFORA Journal**–quarterly of the British UFO Research Association. Inquiries to BUFORA Membership Secretary 30 Vermont Rd, Upper Norwood, London SE19 3SR.
- **Hypotheses Extraterrestres**–quarterly journal of GEOS, in French. Inquiries to Les Extraterrestres: Saint Denis les Rebais, 77510 Rebais, France.
- **Inforespace** – quarterly journal of SOBEPS, in French. Inquiries to SOBEPS: Ave Paul Janson 74, 1070 Bruxelles, Belgium.
- **Investiation** – a new journal, of the UFO Investigation network formed to increase the standards of investigation in the UK, edited by Martin Keatman. The first issue contains a fascinating bedroom invasion of 'little dolls'. Subs: £1.50 for 3 issues. UFOIN: 31 Stuart Close North, Walton, Stone, Staffs ST15 OJU.
- **Journal of Transient Aerial Phenomena** – another step towards more scientific and systemized ufology, published by BUFORA's research dept. Inquire at BUFORA's address above.
- **Magonia** – quarterly. The pioneering British UFO journal that has consistenly explored the sociological, psychological and mythological dimensions of UFOs. Currently featuring the work of Nigel Watson, and na engrossing discussion of the ethics of UFO Investigation. Annual sub £1.75; overseas $5.00. John Rimmer, 64 Alric Ave, New Malden, Surrey KT3 4JW.
- **MAPIT Skywatch** – informal journal of UFO discussion. Much of interest. Inquiries to David Rees: 92 Hillcress Rd, Offerton, Stockport, Cheshire SK2 5SE.
- **MUFON UFO Journal** – monthly journal of the Mutual UFO Network. News, articles, investigations. Annual sub: N. America $8.00; overseas $9.00. MUFON: 103 Oldtowne Rd, Seguin, TX 78155, USA.
- **Northern UFO News** – monthly summary of UK cases reported to NUFON. Solid data. Inquiries to Jenny

Randles: 8 Whitethroat Walk, Birchwood, Warrington, Cheshire WA3 6PQ.

• **Tijdschrift voor Ufologie** – journal of NOVOBO, in Dutch. Inquiries to NOVOBO: Lijnbaan 4, 9982 HJ Uithuizermeeden, Holland.

• **Notiziario UFO** – journal of the Centro Ufologico Nazional, in Italian. Inquiries to CUN: via Vignola 3, 20136 Milano, Italy.

• **UFO Newsclipping Service** – a montly collection of facsimilie clippings on UFO, manimal and Fortean reports from worldwide papers. Well worth it if you can afford it. For more details see the ad on this page.

PSI

• **EVP Newsletter** – monthly notes, interviews, data etc on the 'electronic voice phenomenon'. Recent issues report on experiment at Rollright Stones. Annual sub £1.20; overseas airmail £4.50. Alan Cleaver: 12 Lime Tree Ave, Old Bilton, Rugby, Warks CV22 7QT.

• **International Journal of Paraphysics** – quarterly on latest psychotronic and paraphysical research. Inquiries to Paraphysical Laboratory, Downton, nr Salisbury, Wilts.

• **Specula** – quarterly journal of the American Association of Metascience. Much of Fortean interest. Inquiries to AAMS: Box1182, Huntsville, AL35807, USA.

EARTH MYSTERIES

• **Ancient Mysteries** – Editor Nigel Pennick reminded me recently that I had ignored the title change (formerly the *Journal of Geomancy)* in our last issue. A truly eclectic and splendidly eccentric journal, published by the Insitute of Geomantic Research. Annual sub £3.75; overseas $9.00, airmail $12.50. IGR: 142 Pheasant Rise, Bar Hill, Cambridge CB3 8SD.

• **Ancient Skills and Wisdom Review** – a review journal for all related topics. Annual sub £2.00; overseas $5.00. Paul Screeton: 5 Egton Drive, Seaton Carew, Hartlepool, Cleveland TS25 2AT.

• **Earth Energy** – informal journal dedicated to the restoration of 'the ancient Golden Age'. Inquiries to AURA: 1548 Grace St, Lincoln, NE 68503, USA.

• **IG News** – a bimonthly folklore, occult and earth mysteries magazine. Annual sub £2.50; overseas $5.00. IG News: BM Bulletin, London WC1V 6XX.

• **NEARA Journal** – quarterly of the New England Antiquities Research Association. Annual sub $5.00 (USA); overseas $7.00. NEARA: 4 Smith St, Milford, NH 03055, USA.

• **Quicksilver Messenger** – a new magazine of the earth mysteries of SE England. Inquiries to Chris Ashton: 26a Wilbury Ave, Hove, Sussex.

• **Stonehenge Viewpoint** – a regular newsprint journal of archaeology, astronomy etc related to earth mysteries. Inquiries to SV: 2821 De La Vina St, Box 30887, Santa Barbara, CA 93105, USA.

• **The Ley Hunter** – an essential journal of earth mysteries. Annual sub: £3.60, Europe £4.50, overseas airmail $11.50. TLH: Box 152, London N10 2EF.

OTHERS

• **Kingdom Voice** – Prophecy and related phenomena. Inquiries to Kingdom Revival Crusade: Riverside Cottage, Bridgend, Harpford, Sidmouth, Devon EX10 ONG.

• **Undercurrents** – monthly magazine of radical alternatives. Annual sub £3.60; overseas £4.50. Undercurrents: 27 Clerkenwell Close, London EC1R OAT.

• **Walrus** – the 'official organ of the nonmaterial world'. Indescribable melange of anarchistic and radical delight, once again from the demented typer of Nigel Pennick. Inquiries via Fenris-Wolf: 142 Pheasant Rise, Bar Hill, Cambridge CB3 8SD.

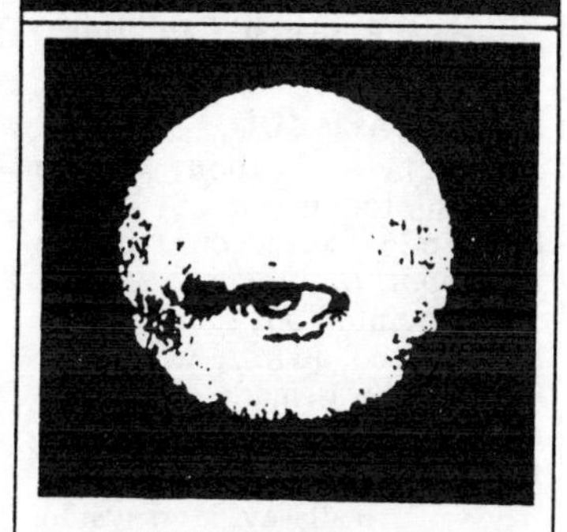

LETTERS
Continued from p3

MORE ON MANNA

[You asked for] info on Rodney Dale and *The Manna Machine* (FT32p54). Dale used to live in Bar Hill and I knew his son, who borrowed Charles Ponce's Garnstone book *Kabbalah* from me for his father's research into Macroprosopus and his heavy friends. Dale also visited the director of the place I work at – the Culture Centre of Algae and Protozoa – in order to get gen on how to grow Chlorella with nuclear light, and was promptly shown the door! Of course, algae would snuff it instantaneously if subjected to a light of such intensity, not to mention the radiation – and anyway, there is a maximum growth rate which, for physical reasons of protein and cellulose 'manufacture', cannot be accelerated, certainly not enough to feed the Hebrew masses of Sinai in such a small culture vessel. I knows it – I grows it!

Nigel Pennick,
Institute of Geomantic Research, Cambridge.

LANDSCAPE ZOO

Relevant to the body of the lioness found at St Helens (FT32p26), an account in the *Liverpool Daily Post* 22 May 1980, pointed out that the lake and disused quarry, where the discovery was made, are adjacen to, of all places, Elephant Lane!

Graham McEwan,
Wallasey, Merseyside.

Truss Fund.

...in which we gratefully acknowledge the heartening support of the following whose donations will be applied where they will do most good.

Larry Arnold, Mike Grayson, Robyn Gurney, Nick Malloret, SN Morgan, Don Robins, Leslie Shepard (omitted from FT31).

Next Issue.

Despite our attempts to catch up this issue is late, and the next will be too. You have our apologies, and assurance that we will continue, if erratically (because of current workloads.)

Next issue: ice falls, beached whales, inept crimes + more unofficial wildlife + monsters.

Among other articles we'll be feature Joe Zarzynski on the names of water monsters. We also begin an occasional series of interviews with people who have helped found our field of Fortean studies, or whose work we feel will be an influence on its development. David Fideler kicks off the series for us with a scoop that gives us great pleasure – an interview with Dr Jean Shinoda Bolen, author of *The Tao of Psychology,* and wife of the editor of *New Reality* magazine.

Plus many other goodies.

Help!

This column is free to any reader or researcher who requires help in locating source materials, or questions answered, on Fortean topics. Just send us the details or query on a separate sheet of paper with your name and address, keeping it brief. An FT reader service.

- I would like to hear from anyone who has information on **animal mutilation** reports in the British Isles. Tommy Blann: 1002 Edmonds Lane, Apt 152, Lewisville, TX 75067, USA.

- I'm researching evidence of **small human beings** (eg. in the archeological record) especially, but not exclusively, in the Americas. Any information would be appreciated. I'll be happy to pay postage and copying costs. Ted Schultz: Box 910, Berkely, CA 94701, USA.

- Peter Costello is researching a book on the **Piltdown Man hoax**, and would appreciate any references to confessions or promised exposures of the deed or leads to unresearched material. Peter Costello: 15 Wellington Place, Dublin 4, Ireland.

- Dennis Rush would like to contact FT readers or other in the Middlesborough area interested in **meeting**, discussions, investigations etc. Dennis Rush: 21 Marton Moor Rd, Nunthorpe, Cleveland.

- Richard Kelly is researching for a book of photographs which capture dramatic, bizarre, memorable and interesting **'moments in time'**, and would welcome any ideas, suggestions or leads FT readers might care to offer. Richard Kelly: 36 Litchfield Gardens, London NW10.

- Loren Coleman is collecting accounts of **people killed by meteorites** and would appreciate any references to known material. Loren Coleman: 115 Chilton St, Cambridge, MA 02138, USA.

Fortean Times

Subscribe.

SUBSCRIPTION: Be sure of getting your issues of FT directly. A sub to FT makes a thoughtful gift that lasts the whole year, for friends, impoverished scholars and libraries, and even your enemies. Rate includes surface or second class postage, and banking exchange commission where applicable.
1 year (4 issues) £4.00/$10.00
Airmail: add £3.00/$7.50

GIFT SAMPLE: Have a sample of this issue, plus our literature sent to a friend who might subscribe — we need all the friends you can get — at these reduced rates:
Surface/UK: 75p/$1.50
Airmail: £1.50/$3.00

BACKISSUES: Limited numbers available of the following back issues: 19, 20, 25-27, 29-31. £1.00/$2.50 each.

GOOD NEWS!

At last, by popular request, reprints of early issues of *Fortean Times*. Founded in 1973 and called *The News*, these humble beginnings have become legendary - well, out of print, anyway!

Now available, high quality xerox facsimilies of the **first five** issues at **£1.00 each**, surface and second class postage inclusive. Other out of print issues in preparation.

Send order with payment to Fortean Times, c/o DTWAGE, 9-12 St Annes Court, London W1, England.

PHENOMENA
A Book of Wonders

Recommended introduction to the philosophy of Charles Fort, and the historical and thematic continuity of 57 varieties of strange phenomena, from stigmata, levitation and fairies to showers of frogs, w‥d children and ball lightning. By John Michell (author of *View Over Atlantis* and *Simulacra*, etc) and RJM Rickard (editor of *Fortean Times*). 216 illustrations, many collected together for the first time anywhere. Price includes post and packing.

UK: £3.10.
Surface & Europe: £3.00
Air (USA & Canada): $9.00
Air (Far East & Australia): $10.00

PAYMENT: cheques, postal orders, international money orders, made payable to *Fortean Times*. If you are in doubt, your bank will be glad to make out a cheque drawn on a British bank. These involve us in less paperwork, complications and bank charge deductions, and provide the safest method of payment for overseas subscribers. Send your order with payment to the address below. Please allow 6-8 weeks for surface mail, plus processing time.

FORTEAN TIMES, 9–12 St Annes Court, London W1, England

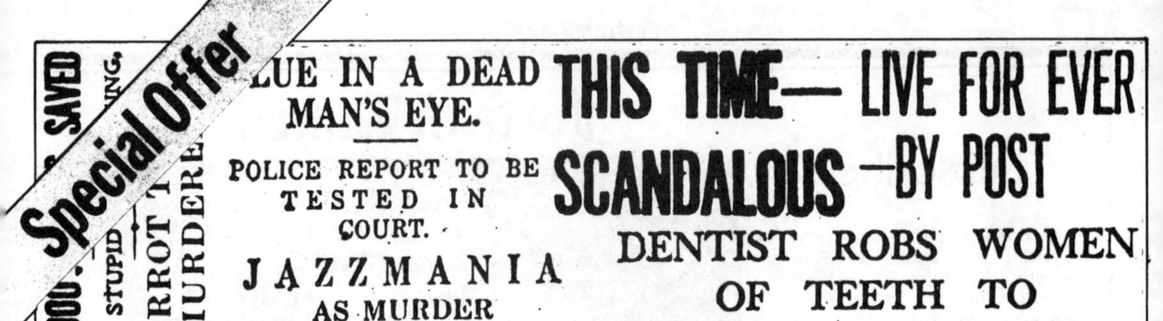

CLUE IN A DEAD MAN'S EYE.

POLICE REPORT TO BE TESTED IN COURT.

THIS TIME— LIVE FOR EVER

SCANDALOUS —BY POST

JAZZMANIA AS MURDER COMPLEX.

DENTIST ROBS WOMEN OF TEETH TO SATISFY A 'CRAVING'

STIGGINS OF THE ARCTIC.

ESKIMOS DRIVEN TO RELIGIOUS MANIA.

CAT WITH WINGS!

SCIENCE PROVES WOMAN INFERIOR.

BESTIAL ORGIES IN SICILY.

CAKES OF GOATS' BLOOD AND HONEY.

Bride was 'man' for 50 years

Cow 'Mothers' Deadly Snake

MAN BITES MAN

INNKEEPER'S DEATH AFTER QUARREL WITH CUSTOMER

MAN BITES MAN

The Scrapbook of an Edwardian Eccentric

George Ives

MONUMENT TO SATAN.

HANGMAN FOUND STARVING

THREE DELUDED DAUGHTERS.

MOTHER'S SKELETON IN KITCHEN.

TABLE SPREAD WITH FOOD FOR HER.

SHOWER OF FROGS.

DRUG THAT LEADS TO INSANITY

Schoolchildren Victims of a Deadly Weed.

Ripperism

SNOW SNUFF' DANGER

ANGELIC SOULS TO ORDER

PRISON FOR SUNDAY TENNIS PLAYING.

WEIRD MIDNIGHT WATCH.

DAY OF DOOM.

AMERICAN FANATICS AND THE

HANGMAN FOUND STARVING

75 YEARS IN THE DARK.

"SEA-SERPENT" CAPTURED

SURPRISE AT A SEANCE

MATERIALISATION OF A LIVING MAN.

Ghost Bus of Kensington

Negro Shot to Give Week-End Party "a Little Excitement"

ELECTRIC BOY.

MAN SHARES LIONS' FAMILY LIFE

NATIVE OUTCAST BEFRIENDED IN THE WILDS

AMATEURS WHO SIN FOR PLEASURE.

WHAT KNOWLEDGE HAS DONE.

FREAKS IN A LONE KENTISH FARM.

WIRELESS CLUE.

MAN BITES MAN The Scrapbook of an Edwardian Eccentric
Edited by Paul Sieveking and Published by Jay Landesman Limited.
Offered to *Fortean Times* readers at the special price of £6.00 including postage (UK, Europe & Surface) and £10.00 (Overseas airmail) or dollar equivalents. Cheques made payable to: *Fortean Times*, DTWAGE, 9-12 St. Annes Court, London W1.

Fortean Times

ISSUE NO. 34 | The Journal of Strange Phenomena. | PRICE: 95p. $2·50

+ Phantom Hitch-hikers; Mystery Cats; Beached Whales; Ice Falls; Synchronicity.

At last available. *Fortean Times Occasional Paper No 1:* WILDMAN. A compendium of information on the Chinese equivalent to the Yeti and Bigfoot. Three articles newly (and expensively) translated from the Chinese for the first time, with explanatory material and critical apparatus. Includes new photographs, 12 illustrations and monster-pictures from old Chinese books. 24 pages. FT format.

Main Contents:

- A CHALLENGE TO SCIENCE: the Mystery of the Wildman, by Yuan Zhenxin and Huang Wanpo. A much-expanded version of the article by the same authors that appeared in FT31, including considerably more technical information and further case material.
- I WITNESSED A 'WILDMAN' MOTHER AND CHILD IN THE CHESTNUT FOREST by Fan Jingquan. A lengthy eye-witness account from the early 50s.
- DOES THE 'FLYING SAUCER' EXIST by Zhou Xinyan. A curiosity item demonstrating the Chinese attitude to UFOs and containing some material relevant to the 1976–77 Wildman investigation.
- Also an introduction and Appendix: A BRIEF BESTIARY OF CHINESE HILL–MONSTERS; the latter a dictionary compilation of ancient cases and theories from traditional Chinese literature, by Steve Moore.

£1.00 (US $2.50) each UK and world surface mail; or US $4.50 airmail. Cheques, etc, payable to: **Fortean Times, DWTAGE, 9-12 St Annes Court, London W1.**

MAN BITES MAN.

MAN BITES MAN – The Scrapbook of an Edwardian Eccentric. Edited by Paul Sieveking and published by Jay Landesman Ltd. Large format. Hard-cover. 160 pages. Profusely illustrated with 584 facsimile items from the press-clipping albums of George Ives, from 1890 to 1950. The weird, the dubious, the heroic, the horrific, and the hilarious.

We are fortunate indeed that (Ives's) treasured volumes . . . have been plundered for our delight by Paul Sieveking with his keen eye for the bizarre . . . Plunge one's hand where one may in this treasure-packed bran pie, one's fingers clutch something of value, each item carefully dated.
Arthur Marshall/New Statesman

It's a really strange collection, and a treat for a particularly odd relative.
Steve Grant/Time Out

(Ives's) obituary in The Times *said that though the Ives cuttings were trivial on the surface, they did 'record important changes in public opinion'. That is a respectable enough excuse for wallowing in* Man Bites Man.
E.S. Turner/
Times Literary Supplement

It all makes a wonderful, cockle-warming tome. Edwardian eccentrics are much more fun that Edwardian country ladies.
John Ezard/Guardian

Offered to *Fortean Times* readers at the special price of £6.00 (US $15.00) including p+p UK and world surface mail; or £10.50 (US $26.00) overseas airmail. Cheques, etc, made payable to: **Fortean Times, DTWAGE, 9-12 St Annes Court, London W1.**

Fortean Times

9-12 St Annes Court
London W1, England.

The Journal of Strange Phenomena.

Winter 1981
ISSN 0308.5899

Editorial.

SCHEDULE

Despite our attempts to get back on schedule, only three issues were published in 1980, as in the year before. We call ourselves a quarterly and that is what we want to be – however matters are not always as we wish them. Since FT is run by unpaid voluntary and spare-time labour the first call on the energies and time of FT staff is the earning of their daily break, a chore which can take a lot out of you. Add to that the complexities of writing, editing, administering and publishing FT, each aspect of which has expanded dramatically in the last few years to become fulltime jobs in themselves. The nett result is that we are regrettably unable to *guarantee* four issues a year. Instead we will make the simple promise that a sub will last for four issues, and do our best to make that coincide with a year.

SURVIVAL METER

Many magazines do not like to divulge their circulation data, but we have always believed in being open with you, the reader. It has been suggested that if we did so readers would feel more involved in our fate– so here we go. The mailing list for this issue contains 907 paid subs, and about 100 necessary

Continued on p56

Contents.

Cover art by **John Stalin**

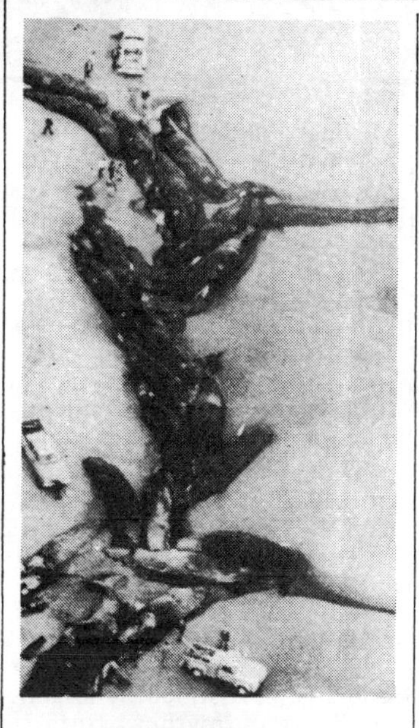

ARTICLES
4 **On Synchronicity and the Self** *Dr Jean Bolen/ Dave Fideler.*
8 **In Search of Dinosaurs** *Dr Roy Mackal/ James Powell.*
10 **Nicknaming those Aquatic Monsters** *Joseph Zarzynski.*
14 **On the Road Again** *Michael Goss.*
18 **Strange Creatures in Powys** *Janet & Colin Bord.*

NOTES
17 **Synchronicity** *Nature follows Art.*
20 **Out of Place** *1980 Cat Flaps.*
26 **Attacks/** *Animal Saboteurs.*
30 **Marine Mysteries** *Beached Whales.*
32 **Falls/***Ice Bombs.*
35 **Dooms/***Inept Crimes.*

COLUMNS
37 **On the Trail** *Loren Coleman.*
39 **Words from the Wizard** *Doc Shiels.*
41 **Notes from the Trashkashic Record** *David Fideler.*

COMIX
7 **Telly Kinex** *JH Szostek.*
13 **Facts You Might Forget** *Pokkettz.*
28 **Phenomenomix** *Hunt Emerson.*

USUAL STUFF
2 **Letters.**
46 **Reviews.**
52 **Classified Exchange.**
54 **News.**
58 **Subscription info.**

Published by Fortean Times Ltd: 9-12 St Annes Court, London W1. Editor: ROBERT JM RICKARD. Editorial Assistants: STEVE MOORE, PAUL SIEVEKING. Contributing Editor: DAVID FIDELER. Art Director: RICHARD ADAMS. Comix Editor and section heading artwork: HUNT EMERSON. Photosetting by WORDSMITH GRAPHICS, 19a West End, Street, Somerset. Reprosetting mostly by PAULA GRAHAM, c/o BCM IT, London WC1N 3XX; and MAGIC INK, 22 Dane Road, Margate, Kent CT9 2AA. Printed by BIJA PRESS, Beeches Green, Stroud, Glos.

FORTEAN TIMES is a quarterly journal of news, notes, reviews and references on current and historical strange phenomena, related subjects and philosophies. A friend to all groups and magazines continuing the work of Charles Fort in investigating, studying and discussing all aspects of strange phenomena. SUBMISSION is invited of articles, artwork, cartoons, and news clippings on related subjects. The publishers can assume no responsibility for unsolicited material, but all reasonable care will be taken while in FT's possession. If material is to be returned, please enclose SAE. CORRESPONDENCE: letters-of-comment and personal experience are welcome. If replies are required please enclose SAE. The editor regrets it is not always possible to reply promptly. ADVERTISING and DISTRIBUTION ENQUIRIES: contact the editor at the above address, or ring 01 552 5466. SUBSCRIPTION INFORMATION: see p56.

THE DARK GODS REVIEW (FT33p45f)

Anthony Roberts writes:
Michael Hoffman's visciously innacurate review of my co-authored book *The Dark Gods* is such an insensitive, biased travesty that it sadly calls for a detailed refutation. This is a distasteful matter for any busy author but in this instance, for the sake of the book's overall 'message', (and this author's integrity) it's a necessary requirement. There is a disturbing current tendency for certain reviewers to expend most of their prose jerking off on their own pet theories in the disguise of an 'objective' critique. I get the distinct impression that Hoffman has lurched into this morally dishonest ego-trip. From his published material in previous issues of *Fortean Times* it would appear that this elitist obscurantist is fanatically dedicated to the boringly fashionable matriarchal/pagan/gay witchcraft syndrome, with voyeuristic overtones covering the workings of black occultism. These crowded and frenzied indulgences can hardly give one confidence in his ability to be objectively assessive of a book devoted to UFO's in a philosophically ecumenical Christian context, leavened by an attempt to discuss the rationale of evil.

There are of course many criticisms that can be levelled against *The Dark Gods* for its bizarre subject matter is such as to have confused and coerced the human spirit for millenia. Alas, Hoffman misses all the valid faults and instead settles like a hungry (and desperate) vulture upon some very thin pickings indeed. As *every* comment he makes about the book is at least inaccurate, it is obvious that a fully detailed reply is impossible owing to lack of space. However, to comment on his major 'sins' as they swirl up through the verbal sewerage might be found productive. For instance, in the quote about dualism it must be noted that I say *nearly* every religion has dualist overtones, not all. But even the Tantric, Zen, Taoist philosophies proferred by Hoffman as non-dualistic have as main spring-points polarizing 'opposites', sometimes described as yin and yang! And again, the Bible contains a distilled synergetic synthesis of myth as truth in the Poetically codified form of Tolkienian 'sub-creation'. It's a beautiful, esoterically structured guide towards an all embracing understanding of God's love and purpose. Its *interpretation* by liars, cheats and general all-round charlatans has only debased its true mystical coinage for shallow minds like Hoffman's.

At this point it is opportune to move on to the hysterical feminism of the Grail section of the review.

The Grail Mysteries in final form are a careful synthesis of *all* aspects of religious experience and expression. To describe the cosmically transcendent, yet earthly harmonizing mysteries of the 'True Grail of God' as a mere rip-off of woman's 'monthlies' reveals a paucity of imagination (and scholarship) that beggars description! I am familiar with most current trends in 'radical feminist scholarship' and I reject many of them as being biasedly authoritarian misconceptions as bad (and as prejudiced) as the ruined patriarchal system they denigrate. Before the matriarchal 'Age of the Goddess' there was the libertarian Golden Age of harmonious reconciliation of the male/femal principle (yin and yang), and this is well proved by the legends of Atlantis and the dual (balancing) geomantic iconography found in the antediluvian Terrestrial Zodiacs. So much for Mr. Hoffman's drearily parochial feminist apologetics! I don't know about 'academicians' bellies' but Hoffman seems to have been well hit by the flaccid tits of the Great Hag!

Now to the so-called 'contradictory statements'. I do praise responsibly supportive sex and free thinking (admirable pastimes) but I only condemn licence and promiscuous self-indulgence because I have seen their cruelly selfish effects on relationships (mainly among occultists, witches and gays). Sex and free thinking that develops spirit and harmonizes human interaction, yes. Where it corrupts, damages, blights and destroys, no. We detest the Klingsorian puppet, not because he fornicates, but because he is a conscious tool of discarnate evil and a blasphemous mocker of true Creation. Gilbertson is out to 'vindicate' the existence of the etheric force that Mesmer played around with, not the morals (or magic) of the practitioner. The MIB patently do more harm than good; look at the grisly record, etc., etc.

We are accused of having no sense of humour. Has Hoffman

never heard of irony! The whole book is designedly ironic and is meant to make one wince not guffaw. As for satire, Bender, Adamski, etc. were supreme self-satirists (albeit sinister) and an endless stream of simple jokes and puns must be left for the James Joyce's of this world (or the Zen Buddhists). As to HP Lovecraft, here Hoffman really excells himself in ignorance. HPL's dream nightmares are proved accurate through a deep Quabbalistic interpretation, as Kenneth Grant has shown in his books. But more important, the key dream/visions (and the nighmares) all occurred *before* his early teens when he was being well looked after (and fed) by his over-solicitous mother and two adoring aunts! This is stated categorically in his collected letters. Lovecraft mined his own archetypal instincts ever after but the 'Dark God' influences flooded into his subconscious while his bodily functions were reasonable (or as reasonable as that strange human 'erratics' physiology could ever be).

To briefly answer Hoffman's plaintive questions at the end of his review:

The conquistadores had an easy massacre because of the persistent legends of a 'White God from the east' who would one day return and inaugerate a new Golden Age. These legends descend directly from Atlantean traditions and are best elucidated in Lewis Spence's neglected classic *Atlantis in America* (Ernest Benn, 1925) which contains the fruits of over 30 years painstaking research. There is no overt Dark Gods control mechanism invention here!

The 'awe and glamour' generated by the technology of miraculous phenomena, and the awe of so-called primitive peoples for gunpowder and all the other sickeningly technological gee-gaws, is an awe mainly based upon fear. Fear, as Lovecraft stated, is one of the strongest (and most manipulable) of all human emotions. Fear is the mind killer that blunts perception, poisons spirituality and distorts intuitive logic, therefore making 'soul control' so much easier. Of course control is the name of the Dark Gods' game!

Finally, I apologise to Hoffman for not writing poetry but do not recant on my attempt to make a crusade out of aspects of religious history. Most orthodox history is lying bunk but the archetypal academic shits, are the pure base notes of the pristine Hymn of Creation. They are constantly being rendered 'off key' by the Dark Gods and their human 'species traitor' allies. Gilbertson and I *do* deride the negative aspect of the 'ultraterrestrials' and remember, the ancients called some fairies 'people of peace' and 'good neighbours' only because they were terrified of them and their marked penchant for damaging homo sapiens in both physical and metaphysical ways. My own study of 'fairies' in their positive aspect is *Atlantean Traditions in Ancient Britain* (Rider, 1977). Some readers consider that a poetic and knowledgeable work, not devoid of some fragments of wisdom. Perhaps Hoffman would like to peruse it as an antidote to the confusion and mental indigestion the 'Dark Gods' seems to have ignited in his muddy synapses. 'The lady doth protest too much methinks'.

ANTHONY ROBERTS
Fulham, London.

Michael Anthony Hoffman rejoins:

Mr. Roberts begins his refutation with remarks about dishonesty. When negotiations regarding my review occurred and the possibility of revising my critique was one of my options, a friend of Mr. Roberts' wrote me, that, '. . . he (Mr. Roberts) said he liked your other writings in *Fortean Times . . .*'

To suggest that Taoism, Tantra and Zen have dualistic overtones because they recognise the existence of yin and yang, is like saying Charles Fort was a fan of Cagliostro because he considered him a symbol of the inherent trickiness of the phenomenal universe. If there is a phenomenal universe, the centrifugality and centripetality or yin and yang arise. Dualism portrays these principles as fixed, mutually antagonistic representations of good and evil. Non-dualism understands that opposites are constantly changing into one another and rides these polarities into vital harmony.

Mr. Roberts doesn't deal with the accusation that the Biblical Male Mother is one of the transsexual gender-benders he takes satisfaction in sneering at (cf. for example, the etymology of one of Yahweh's many names, El Shodai).

Mr. Roberts doesn't come to terms with the oceans of blood and acres of raped and butchered children Yahweh ordered his Chosen to annihilate. Instead, he prefers to wax eloquent over the 'distilled synergetic synthesis' and 'Poetically codified form'. As Dottie Shank has stated, 'It's not what gets said or written in the seminaries – its the actual reign of terror that comes down on the peasants that really counts.'

Of course, this slaughter of the Earth Mother's nature worshippers by Yahweh's tribe is a misinterpretation by 'liars' and 'cheats' of a 'beautiful, esoterically structured guide' and only 'shallow minds' would find anything troubling about *Ezekiel* chapter 9, verses 4–7, for example.

Whenever I hear or read someone talking or writing about 'liberation' and 'love', I quickly tap my money-holder to make sure it's still in my pocket. I intuited a similar current in *The Dark Gods* and noted it in the review: lip-service to balance, flexibility, the Goddess, paganism, quotations from Wm. Blake on 'images of truth' – all as a

Continued on p43

On Synchronicity and the Self.

David Fideler

Charles Fort's philosophy, which reminds one of Taoism and Neoplatonism, revolved around the conceptual pivot of 'Continuity', for he envisioned the cosmos as a continuous organism, greater than the sum of its parts. Unlike a purely mechanistic science, which views the universe as a glorified pinball machine awaiting dissection and study, Fort was more interested in the 'underlying oneness' of all phenomena and the relationship between the parts, more so than the actual parts themselves.

Through this perspective of 'Continuity', Fort was able to account for unity in diversity, in the same way that all islands merge into a common ground of being, the deeper one descends.

In a similar fashion, C.G. Jung's model of the psyche accounts for both the individual and universal aspects of human experience, in a manner strongly reminiscent of Fort's perception of the phenomenal world. Within the Jungian framework the light of self-reflecting consciousness is seen as the apex of psychological evolution, or to continue the analogy, the highest point on an island. But because all phenomena are continuous, and merge into one another, it is not enough to accept the highest point without examining the bedrock below. So descending to the 'shoreline', we encounter the personal unconscious, or the active, changing repository of an individual's psychological experiences. And if we are to conceptually descend deeper still, where all islands merge into one another, we enter the domain of the collective unconscious, or the basic and primordial psychological matrix which all individuals share in common. This is the 'objective psyche', and may be seen as the repository for all the archaic and universal patterns of psychological experience.

Of interest to many Forteans is Jung's controversial idea of synchronicity, or 'meaningful coincidences' which suggest an 'acausal connecting principle' at work behind the inner worlds of the mind, and external reality as we know it. Call it Tao, Continuity, or synchronicity, the pattern which connects the inner with the outer is the topic of **Dr Jean Shinoda Bolen's** new book, *The Tao of Psychology*. Here Dr Bolen (pictured above) explores the implications in an inner-view with FT Contributing Editor **David Fideler**.

There is something formless yet complete
That existed before heaven and earth.
How still! how empty!
Dependent on nothing, unchanging,
All pervading, unfailing.
One may think of it as the mother of all things under heaven.
I do not know its name,
But I call it 'Meaning'.
If I had to give it a name, I should call it 'The Great'.

Lao-tzu,
Tao Teh Ching, XXV

FT: *To begin with, could you describe the general types of synchronistic events?*

Dr. Bolen: The common, most everyday variety is when you have a thought in your mind and an outer event verifies, or connects with, that thought. So it's that single moment when you think about someone, and the phone rings, and it's that other person calling you. That is the garden-variety example of synchronicity, or telepathy, where there is a connection between an inner thought and an outer event. It could be an inner thought, or vision, or a dream, but there is essentially an inner event and an outer event going on simultaneously.

Another kind is the connection between an inner event and an event that occurs later on. And that's the common situation where you have a dream one evening and the person that you haven't thought about in a long time, who is in your dream, shows up in your office the next day... a 'coincidental meeting'.

FT: *What type of mental reactions are commonly evoked by this type of phenomenon? And what situations are conducive to synchronistic phenomena?*

Dr. Bolen: Synchronicity seems to occur most in people who are emotionally charged by something going on in themselves. In actual life the chances are that you have more 'hits' — or synchronistic experiences — when you are in turmoil, or when you are caught up in a kind of creative inspirational period, or you are just more alive either out of conflict, or anxiousness, or because you're in love, or because you're caught up in a project or something that really turns you on. It's when you step out of the more superficial levels of consciousness and go deeply into yourself that there seems to be more outer and inner types of connections. So that all of those highly charged times provoke, or inspire, or resonate with synchronistic events, as do psychological states in which there is a tremendous amount of turmoil. Sometimes a person who is really afraid of losing touch with reality will experience more synchronicity, and that will increase the fear. That in itself can be pretty spooky.

FT: *Do you feel that there is a relationship between synchronicity and the feeling of* deja vu?

Dr. Bolen: The subjective feeling of eeriness, the kind of tingle up the spine feeling that happens with *deja vu* often accompanies a synchronistic event. There often is an eerie feeling when you are aware of synchronicity. The difference is mainly semantics. In a synchronistic event the person is required. There has to be a meaningful coincidence in which the person knows that events are eerily connected together, and must be conscious of a connection between a thought and an event, or a dream followed by an event. And *deja vu* could be a synchronicity, but by definition *deja vu* is that feeling of familiarity in a new situation that one couldn't have known about before. It may be a forgotten synchronicity, but they are two different kinds of events. Probably a good number of *deja vu* experiences are due to preceeding dreams that are forgotten.

FT: *Jung conjectured that telepathy was a synchronistic phenomenon. Do you think that phenomena like ESP are primarily qualitative, and that parapsychologists might be mistaken in their search for an 'electromagnetic medium' of 'thought transference'?*

Dr. Bolen: The difference between Jungian synchronicity and parapsychological ESP is really the significance of the event, or the emphasis the person has on the event. Usually synchronicity goes along with 'meaningful', as in meaningful coincidences. So the person involved in a synchronistic event is not interested in proving it happened. He or she is interested in what the meaning of the connection is. A parapsychologist is interested in proving that it happened, that a telepathic thought was in fact conveyed, and then to figure out how it was conveyed is the problem of the parapsychologist.

The person who is interested in meaningful coincidences doesn't dispute ESP. That person really isn't interested in the scientific side of it, but in the personal meaning of it. Both the Jungian-oriented synchronistic event and the ESP event are the same event often. But the viewpoint that is taken depends on whether you are interested in proving a phenomenon or interested in figuring out what the meaning of it is.

I see ESP as falling under synchronicity, and from the psychological viewpoint I'm not interested in proving the electromagnetic hypothesis. My scientific side is interested in how the parapsychologists figure it out. I personally feel from the research side that it isn't going to be an electromagnetic vehicle, because scientifically distance doesn't seem to make a difference, time doesn't make a difference, and putting people in lead-lined boxes doesn't seem to make a difference. Maybe at some level we truly are all one, so that if something is happening in one person at a distance it is immediately registered because we are, in some way actually all one.

FT: *It has been said that in the same way our dreams utilize images from waking reality, so too is waking reality partly made from the stuff of dreams. In* The Tao of Psychology *you devote a chapter to the 'waking dream' aspect of synchronicities. What does this tell us about the phenomenon in general, and its relationship with the archetypal self?*

Dr. Bolen: To me the dreaming psyche and the connection between the person and the synchronistic event are all one and the same. We dream in symbols about charged emotional events or situations that concern us. And often dreams seem to be a re-stated way of metamorphizing the difficulty that we are in, and often dreams proceed beyond that to offer some insight into what might be going on in the situation. In the same way a synchronistic event will often reflect the inner conflict. Both may be pictures, really, of what is of concern inwardly, or is being repressed, or is not being paid attention to.

More specifically, if we are engaged in a relationship with someone and we're trying just to look at the rosy parts of it, but keep a lid on the fact that there's a lot going on that worries us, and it's not really as good a situation.

Take a woman, for example, who keeps denying to herself that this man will never marry her, and that he's hanging on and all that, and prefers to repress that awareness for quite a while as she gets into her hopes that he is going to marry her. Well, the dream life that she has will often point out to her that she's in this kind of situation where it's not going to work out. The man is doing something hostile to her in the dream world. In a synchronistic mode she may keep running into women who are like her, and become aware of this. So she goes to a beauty parlor and sits next to a woman who is three years down the road with a similar situation, and is all distraught about it. And she may go home and get a phone call from an old friend who is describing the same thing, and it's like she can't get away from the fact presented to her outside of herself that she should pay attention to something. Inner and outer worlds seem to keep presenting to her what is happening.

Also, she may consult the *I Ching* and get, like one woman I know, a repeated 'The Marrying Maiden' [Kuei Mei, Hexagram 54], which reminded her that her position was no better than that of a concubine.

FT: *Could you describe the relationship between Jung's concept of the self, and the reconciliation of opposites characteristic of Taoism?*

Dr. Bolen: When I think about the self, I think of it in relationship to what people have experienced when they are aware of being in touch with the self. And that subjective feeling is always conveyed as a sense of wholeness and okayness, as if the various parts of one's inner self are healed, and the person feels together. When you are sort of humming along and feeling in harmony there is a reconciliation of the many parts inwardly.

The usual use of psychological terms assumes that everything we are talking about occurs between your ears somehow, and is a totally inward psychological experience. Jung's idea of archetypes goes beyond that, though, and assumes that it isn't just an inner psychological state, but is a relationship to something that other people experience. And in terms of the archetype of the self, or the archetypal level in general, Jung is talking about our connection with everything else as well. It's very much like the subatomic particles that physicists use. Everything in the universe is connected to what he is calling the archetypal level.

Well, the Tao is just talking about the same thing. And if everything in the universe is connected, in a way there are no opposites. There are just different forms.

FT: *If meaningful coincidences imply a connection between our inner states of consciousness and what we encounter externally, what is the message of synchronicity and the experience of the Tao?*

Dr. Bolen: The message is almost always intuitively felt. You can think about it afterwards and see the big picture, but what is marvelous about the synchronistic event is the feeling of connectedness that occurs in the actual moment. So the message that comes through, even in the most everyday event, is one of not being isolated and alone, or separate from other people, or other events. But what strikes you in that moment is the momentary insight — or in some ways, enlightenment–that I am connected with other people, I am connected to the universe, and I am not alone. The message of synchronicity at its deepest level is one of being connected with the Tao, and in that sense we are all connected.

•

THE TAO OF PSYCHOLOGY: Synchronicity and the Self by Jean Shinoda Bolen, MD., was published in Britain by Wildwood House, London, 1980; £3.25 pb, pp111, refs, index.

Telly Kinex
HELL! I USTA BE DUMB!
..I REMEMBER PRAYIN' FOR THIS SORT OF WEATHER WHEN I WAS A KID! LORD!!
GOSHALMIGHTY!! WHAT AM I DOING GRUMBLING WHEN I SHOULD BE EXPERIMENTING?!
WHAT A TERRIFIC OPPORTUNITY FOR TESTING MY GIFT!
HUP!
BEGONE!
THUMP! THUMP! THUMP!
WOW! IF ONLY THIS STUFF STAYED ALL YEAR..
END

In Search of Dinosaurs.

In October 1980 many news agencies reported on an expedition into the remote jungles of the Congo to search for dinosaurs. The expedition began in February that year and was led by **Dr Roy Mackal,** of the University of Chicago and author of *The Monsters of Loch Ness* (1976), and Texas zoologist **James Powell.** Although they have described their adventure in various US popular science mags, we thought it would be a good idea to put their original report to the Congolese government on the Fortean record, and with their permission to do so. Dr Mackal's latest book, *Searching for Hidden Animals* was published by Doubleday in September 1980. Mackal & Powell hope to return to the Congo in Aug 1981 to renew their search.

Mackal-Powell Likouala Expedition Report (Original Text)
26 February 1980
Impfondo, Africa.

PURPOSE:

To establish in so far as is possible whether the reports of the *Mokele-mbembe* refer to a myth or real animals. If the latter to determine whether the animals are extinct or still in existence and to obtain as much information as to their nature and habitat as possible.

BACKGROUND:

In 1776 the Abbe Lievan Bonaventure Proyart published a book entitled *Histoire de Loango, Kakongo, et autres royaumes d'Afrique, redigee d'apres les memoirs des prefects apostoliques de la Mission francaise* which contained reports received from several prelates, attempting to establish their missions in the area bounded by the west coast of Africa, the Congo River in the south, Camerouns in the north, and the Oubangui River in the east. This area includes roughly what is now the Peoples Republic of the Congo, Gabon, and Cameroun.

Abbe Proyart reported that the missionaries, while passing through a forest, observed the track of an animal which they did not see, but which must have been monstrous: The marks of the claws were noted on the ground, and these formed a print about 90 centimeters in circumference. The arrangement of the footprints indicated that the animal was walking, not running, and that the distance between its footprints was 2.1 to 2.4 meters. The Belgian zoologist, Bernard Heuvelmans, estimates that this establishes the size of the animal as intermediate between that of a hippopotamus or rhinoceros and an elephant. He points out that only the largest elephants carry their feet at a distance of 2.1 to 2.4 meters apart. None of these animals, of course, has claws.

Later, Alfred Aloysious Smith ('Trader Horn') wrote of reports of a similar animal which he heard about while trading up and down the Ogooue River in Gabon in the late 1800s. He was told that the *Jago-nini* was still in the swamps and rivers. He states that he believes this animal to be the same as the *Amali,* whose footprints he had observed, about the size of a frying pan with three claws. He also states that there are drawings of the animal in Bushman caves.

More information comes from Captain Freiherr von Stein zu Lausnitz, leader of the Likouala-Congo Expedition of 1913–1914. This is the region now known as the Republique Populaire du Congo. The information consists of reports by experienced guides and trustworthy Africans. The reports refer to the Lower Oubangui, the Sangha, the Ikelemba, and Congo.

'Its preferred habitat would seem to be the frequent deep pools excavated by whirlpools at sharp, narrow bends in the rivers.

'By choice, the creature is said to retire into the depths of the numerous caves hollowed out below the water level in the clay banks. Even in broad daylight it climbs the shore in search of its strictly vegetable food. The favourite plant of the beast is a sort of riverside liana, with large white flowers, which secretes a rubbery latex, and bears nut-like fruits resembling applies. At the SSombo River he was shown, beside a heavy growth of these plants, a great breach which the animal had opened up in the dense vegetation lining the bank, in order to get at its food. However, since there were also numerous tracks of other animals it was impossible to recognize any particular spoor with certainty.'

'The animal is said to have a smooth skin, brownish-gray in color. Its size approximately that of an elephant, or at least that of a hippopotamus. It seems to have a long, flexible neck, and a single tooth, but a very long one, which was sometimes described as a horn. A few also spoke of a very long tail, as powerful as a crocodile's. Canoes approaching the beast are immediately attacked and capsized, and the occupants killed, but not eaten.'

In 1938, a German scientist, Dr. Leo von Boxberger, obtained similar reports.

In 1976 and 1979 James Powell, while studying crocodiles in Gabon and Cameroun, heard additional reports in these areas.

RESULTS:

From discussions with over 30 Congolese (including pygmies) in the Impfondo and Epena areas we were able to confirm practically all of the details described earlier, including the alleged food plant of the animals, the *molombo.* of which we obtained a specimen and which has tentatively been identified as a species of *Landolphia.*

Eyewitness descriptions establish the largest of these animals as up to 15 meters in length, long snakelike head and neck 2–3 meters long, long tail, reddish brown to gray in color. Thickness of long neck ranging from the size of a man's arm to the thickness of a man's thigh. In some cases a rooster-like comb was described as being present on the head.

A number of miraculous aspects were attached to the more factual descriptions, including the widespread belief that if a *mokele-mbembe* is observed nothing must be said about the event or death will follow. This belief of course contributes to the difficulty of obtaining information.

A number of other reports of strange animals were obtained. It is not clear whether these refer to different animals or are different versions of the *mokele-mbembe.*

Most importantly we were able to confirm and establish more details concerning a vague report at Impfondo that two or three animals had entered Lake Tele near Epena some 20–25 years ago and that one of the animals had been killed there.

We obtained reports at Epena that two animals had entered Lake Tele in 1959 and returned to the Bai River (also known as the Tibeke). The animals apparently moved back and forth between the river and the lake disturbing the fishing activities of the pygmies. They proceeded to construct a stake barrier across the molibo (one of the 4 or 5 riverways connecting the lake to the river, through which the animals were traveling in and out of the lake). As one of the animals was at the barrier attempting to enter the lake the pygmies speared the animal killing it. It was then cut up, the task being described as endless because of the long head-neck and tail of the animal. It was alleged that all those participating in the killing (and eating?) of the animal died. Apparently the pygmies in the area are very reluctant to discuss the episode.

CONCLUSIONS

From the reports received we conclude that *mokele-mbembe* refers to a real animal, not a myth, although a variety of magical or miraculous aspects are attached to the tradition. Our survey of the Impfondo and Epena areas suggests that the original more widespread range of these creatures has been greatly reduced during the last two hundred years and now is centred in the Epena district along the Likouala aux Herbes, Lake Tele, and the Bai River and tributaries. The animals appear to have been rare even in the recent past and may now be extinct, although we obtained eye witness reports as recent as 1979.

From the descriptions of the animal, we conclude that they are a species unknown to science as a living form.

RECOMMENDATIONS

On the basis of the information obtained, and the possibility that a few animals may still exist, further investigations should be made in the Epena district in order to make observations and obtain photographs of these creatures, if possible. This will require an extensive, time-consuming, well-funded expedition, involving the Congolese government and scientists in various fields.

A high priority should be the construction of a concrete highway between Impfondo and Epena, of some 90 kilometers, suitable for regular vehicular traffic. This would not only aid further research, but would benefit the Congo immensely by facilitating the development of the interior of the Likouala Region.

ACKNOWLEDGEMENTS

We wish to express our gratitude to the Congolese government and its officials for their help, encouragement and splendid cooperation in this study. We wish to thank all the Congolese people who so kindly provided information and services to us, especially the hospitality of the people of Epena and Impfondo.

Specifically, we wish to thank the officials of Impfondo, the Commissar Politique, M.A. Mouele, the Secretary-General, M.G. Nzombo, and the President of the District of Epena, M.S. Kolonga.

Also the Permanent Congolese Commission at the United Nations and the invaluable aid of Pastor Eugene Thomas and his wife, Sandy, for permitting us to use their home as a base of operations, and to Pastor Thomas, as a guide, interpreter and for liaison with Congolese government officials.

Lastly, we wish to thank the U.S. Ambassador, William L. Swing, and John Archibald, Cultural Attache at the U.S. Embassy at Brazzaville, for their help and interest in our study.

•

Dr Roy P. Mackal, James H. Powell Jr.

Nicknaming those Aquatic Monsters.

We welcome to these pages someone who has a wide knowledge of today's monster-hunting fraternity and their quarries around the world. **Joseph W Zarzynski** is a teacher, of Saratoga Springs, New York, and has spent the last six years in pursuit of 'Champ', the monster on his doorstep, in Lake Champlain. He has coordinated Lake Champlain investigations, lectured, and is working on a history of Champ, besides being a *Fortean Times* Special Correspondent.

The use of nicknames has existed in English-speaking countries for many centuries. Even during Anglo-Saxon days, surnames were rarely employed and nicknames were affixed to help identify a person's name. The Greeks had a word 'hypokorisma' which meant 'calling by endearing names'. Adopted into the English as 'hypocorisms', it means nicknames [1].

In the Spring, 1979, issue of *Pursuit* magazine, Joseph S. Haas, Jr. lists well over two hundred reported habitats of aquatic monsters [2]. It would be utterly foolish to state that all these bodies of water are the homes of monstrrous creatures. This article is intended to briefly review some of the more famous reported water monsters and to examine their appellations and how they were derived.

Nessie, Morag, Champ, Ogopogo, Manipogo, Igopogo, Ponik, Caddy, Chessie, Slimy Slim (Slimey Slim), Wee Oichy, and Whitey are just a few aliases for those phenomena called aquatic monsters. These are the specific nicknames of lake monsters, sea serpents, and even a river monster to name but a few. Or if you care not for these sometimes humorous pseudonyms, you might call them-kelpie (Scottish), 'waves without wind' (Scottish), an niseag (Scottish), pooka (Irish), piast (Irish), Bunyip (Tasmanian, Australian), skrimsl (Scandinavian), soe-orm (Scandinavian), or just plain monster.

The most famous lake monster, the Loch Ness Monster, is universally known as Nessie. The use of the common epithet, monster, for the creatures of Loch Ness began in 1933. Dr. Evan Barron, editor of the Inverness *Courier* newspaper, Scotland, changed one of the key words in a May 2, 1933, story on a sighting of a large creature in Loch Ness. When Dr. Barron reviewed Alex Campbell's article on the sighting, the editor remarked, 'Well, if it is as big as Campbell says it is we can't just call it a creature, it must be a real monster.' [3]

1975 witnessed another title bestowed upon Nessie. As a result of underwater photographs being taken of one of the creatures in Loch Ness in 1972 and 1975, Sir Peter Scott 'knighted' Nessie – *Nessiteras rhombopteryx*. Nessiteras comes from 'Ness', the name of the loch, and 'teras', the Greek word meaning wonder. 'Rhombopteryx' is from the Greek 'rhombos', which denotes a diamond shape, and the Greek 'pteryx', meaning a fin. Thus, Nessiteras Rhombopteryx means the Ness monster or wonder with the diamond-shaped fin. Sir Peter Scott hoped that conferring this scientific nomenclature upon the Loch Ness Monster would make it eligible for environmental protection [4].

Scotland's Loch Morar is deeper than Loch Ness and is the reputed home of Mhorag (Morag in the Anglicised form). The Scots believed that to see Morag meant an omen of death for a member of the Gillies, MacDonnells, and MacDonalds clan [5]. Elizabeth Montgomery Campbell and Dr. David Soloman record in their book, *The Search for Morag,* an old Scottish ballad about the fabled beasties:

Morag, Harbinger of Death,
Giant swimmer in deep-green Morar,
The loch that has no bottom...
There it is that Morag the monster lives [6].

North America's Lake Champlain in New York, Vermont, and Quebec is the home of the Champ creatures. It appears that the tide of feminism has even penetrated the depths of Lake Champlain. Champ is one of the nicknames for the Lake Champlain Monsters, a 20–30 foot serpentine creature. The term, Champ, has been criticized by one Champlain Valley feminist as being too male chauvinist and not too innovative a nickname.

Lake Okanagan is possibly the residence of Canada's most famous lake monster. The Indians around Lake Okanagan in British Columbia called the creature, 'Naitaka' or 'N'ha-a-aitk', which meant 'The Lake Monster' or 'Lake Demon' [7], however, the white residents of Lake Okanagan Valley soon adopted their own nickname for their sinuous lake friend.

At a luncheon on August 23, 1926, a parody was sung that immediately captured the public's attention. The special verse went:

I'm looking for Ogopogo
The bunny-hugging Ogopogo
His mother was a mutton, his father was
a whale.
I'm going to put a little bit of salt on his tail.
I'm looking for the Ogopogo [8].

The Vancouver *Daily Province* published the headlines: 'Ogopogo Now Official Name of the Famous Okanagan Sea Serpent' on August 24, 1926. And so, was born the nickname, Ogopogo. It was immediately accepted as a more popular name than the Indian names because Ogopogo was easier to pronounce than Naitaka [9].

The Winnipeg *Tribune* newspaper of Nov. 6, 1976 outlined the story behind the naming of Canada's Lake Manitoba monster, the Manipogo. Tom Locke, a provincial land inspector, is credited with nicknaming Manitoba's lake monster (it has also been seen in Lake Winnipegosis). Locke and several other people saw the monster at Manipogo Beach, about 30 miles north of Ste. Rose on Lake Manitoba, on August 12, 1960 [10]. Thus, was born the flashy nickname Manipogo, Manitoba's elusive lake monster.

Another Canadian 'pogo' lake monster is Igopogo, which takes up residence in Lake Simcoe, a large lake, not too far from Toronto in Ontario, Canada [11].

Quebec province in Canada has its famed Ponik, the Lake Phenegamook Monster. This lake near the Maine border is about 6½ miles long and was the scene of a scientific expedition in 1957. Dr. Vadim Vladykov, who was working for the Canadian government, launched a scientific search for Ponik [12]. The expedition met with limited success, but 'ponik beer' brewed by a local brewery, did triumph at a recent anniversity parade at Lake Pohenegamook [13].

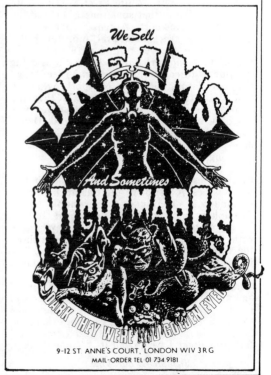

Sea serpents, too, have their affectionate nicknames. Caddy is the Vancouver Island sea serpent named after Cadboro Bay, where it has often been seen to surface. Caddy is the shortened form of Cadborosauras. This was the name given to the sea serpent by Archie Willis, the news director of the Victoria *Daily Times* in the 1930s [14].

During the summer of 1978 and the spring of 1980 Washington DC in the USA was humming over its new-found topic for cocktail parties: Chessie, the Chesapeake Bay Monster. Mr. Donald Kyker, a retired CIA official, claimed his 1978 sighting of Chessie was that of a 15 to 20-foot-long object moving against the tide [15]. Chessie's nickname is derived in part from Chesapeake and from the Loch Ness Monster's nickname Nessie. Many other reports of Chessie were reported by people living at the mouths of the Potomac, Rappahanock, and Pautuxent rivers. All those rivers empty into the Chesapeake Bay [16].

The Crystal mountain water of Payette Lake in Idaho allegedly has its monstrous creature, too. However, local citizens around Payette

Lake have had a problem in finding a suitable name for their monster. It has been called by several cognomens: Slimy Slim (Slimey Slim), the McCall Monster, the Payette Lake Monster, and most recently, Sharlie. The nickname McCall Monster is taken from the town of McCall, which lies on the shore of Payette Lake. Since 1953, most residents along the lake have referred to their monster as Sharlie. In that year the Payette *Star News* organized a campaign to christen their monster. $75 was awarded to a Lee Isle Hennefer Tury of Springfield, Virginia, formerly of Twin Falls, Idaho, for her name suggestion [17]. Thus, the controversy over which name to call the beastie should finally have been settled.

Another Scottish loch may be the home of a monster. Loch Oich is part of the Great Glen of the Scottish Highlands. It has a long tradition of monster reports. Peter Costello in his book, *The Search for Lake Monsters,* relates an account in 1961 where a hoax contrived by a journalist was printed in the Scottish *Daily Express* newspaper. The paper alluded to the Loch Oich Monster as 'Wee Oichy' [18]. Whether or not this Scottish loch has a monster can endlessly be debated, but it certainly has a nickname for itself.

I would certainly be remiss if I did not mention a river monster. The White River in Arkansas is purportedly the domain of Whitey, the White River Monster. Elwood D. Baumann in his book, *Monsters of North America,* states that sightings of the White River Monster date back to 1850 and that sometime after that the residents of Newport, Arkansas, penned the title, Whitey, for their river monster [19].

Reports of the description of Whitey vary. A 1937 newspaper account described it as being 'as wide as three automobiles and 35 feet long.' [20] Mr. Earnest Denks of Newport, Arkansas, told the Arkansas *Gazette* in 1971 that the creature he sighted in the White River was probably over 1,000 pounds in weight. 'Denks named the creature 'the eater' because according to Denks, it looked as if it 'could eat anything, anywhere, anytime.' [21]

If all these nicknames and aliases seem to have confused the reader, place yourself in this man's shoes. A visitor to the Champlain Valley sat quietly at a bar lounge that overlooked Lake Champlain and pondered its famed aquatic beast. In attempting to strike up a conversation with the bartender, the visitor naturally chose the topic of that 'something' in the lake. The inquisitive tourist inquired of the bartender, 'Sir, what do you citizens around here call that thing in the lake?' The jovial barkeep turned and with a stoic look replied, 'Well, you can call it the Lake Champlain Monster, the Lake Champlain Sea Serpent, Champ, Champy, Sammy, or... you can call it just... Monster! But you don't have to call it... "something"'.

Joseph W. Zarzynski

Author Joseph Zarzynski aboard the schooner Richard Robbins *in August 1978, searching for the Lake Champlain Monster. [Photo: JW Zarzynski.]*

REFERENCES

1 William & Mary Morris; *Morris Dictionary of Word and Phrase Origins* (New York, 1977) p399.
2 Joseph S Hass Jr; 'Lake Monsters', *Pursuit* 12:2 (whole no 46) pp56-57.
3 Nicholas Witchell; *The Loch Ness Story* (Baltimore, Maryland, 1974) p29.
4 Robert H Rines, Charles W Wyckoff, Harold E Edgerton & Martin Klein; 'Search for the Loch Ness Monster', *Technology Review* (Cambridge, Mass, March/April 1976) pp39-40.
5 Elizabeth Montgomery Campbell & David Solomon PhD; *The Search for Morag* (London, 1972) p81.
6 ibid; introduction.
7 Mary Moon; *Ogopogo* (N. Vancouver, Canada, 1977) p11.
8 ibid; p13.
9 ibid.
10 'Whatever Happened to ... Manipogo?', *Winnipeg Tribune* 6 Nov 1976.
11 Betty Sanders Garner; *Canada's Monsters* (Hamilton, Ontario, 1976) p51.
12 Dean Rhodes; *Daily News* (Bangor, Maine) 29 April, 2+5 May 1977.
13 *Wall Street Journal* 12 Nov 1977.
14 Garner; pp68-82.
15 *New York Times* 19 Nov 1978, P69.
16 *The Courant* (Hartford, NY) 23 Nov 1978.
17 *Idaho Statesman* (Boise, Idaho) 16 Oct 1977, pC1.
18 Peter Costello; *In Search of Lake Monsters* (Bungay, Suffolk, 1974) p157.
19 Elwood D Baumann; *Monsters of North America* (New York/London, 1978) pp30-33.
20 *Commercial Appeal* 9 July 1937.
21 *Arkansas Gazette* 25 June 1971.

Author's note: I would like to thank the following people for their contributions towards this article: George W Earley, Tony Healy, Gary Mangiacopra, John Ray, Dwight Whalen and Marian Zarzynski. Also a thanks to the folks at Fortean Times for kindly publishing this article. **JWZ.**

PROFESSOR CLASPROOT'S
FACTS·YOU·MIGHT·FORGET.
ALIEN MENTORS — PART TWO (2)
GOOD EVENING...
CONSIDER, IF YOU WILL, THE APALLING BEHAVIOUR OF ALIENS PASSING THROUGH IN THE PAST FEW DECADES...
...YEAH, WE GO LOOKING FOR ORDINARY, MIDDLE CLASS FAMILIES ON CAMPING TRIPS AND SCREW UP THEIR CAR ENGINES
ANOSMIUM FUELETHROX -Frog Nebula-
...WE CARRY A FULL WARDROBE OF FUNNY COSTUMES. WE JUST PUT 'EM ON AND GO STAND OUTSIDE THEIR WINDOWS
TREVOR NZETXYLTO -Dunroamin, Sirius-
WE'D HAD THIS AMAZING CHICKEN VINDALOO WITH CHILLI AT THE 'BISTRO BETELGEUSE', AND... WELL, Y'KNOW... I HAD TO STOP OFF PRONTO AT TUNGUSKA...
NAME AND ADDRESS WITHELD
SO WHERE ARE THE "SUPERIOR CIVILISATIONS" OF OLD? ARE WE SIMPLY LESS RECEPTIVE?
I SUPPOSE YOU CALL THIS RACKET ART!
MOST AUTHORITIES AGREE THAT THE BULK OF ALIENS' VISITS COME FROM THE DIRECTION OF THE CRAB NEBULA. HERE IS A COMPUTER MAP OF THE EARTH FROM THAT POINT, AS IT WAS 2700 YEARS AGO (THE TIME OF EZEKIEL). EARTH IS MARKED WITH A CROSS (X), AND NOTE THE POSITION OF THE THREE COMETS. THESE WOULD APPEAR TO FLASH IN A CRAB-PLANET'S SKY...
QUAD GREEN STAMPS
• THUS OUR VISITORS ARE THOSE EITHER SO MEAN OR SO STUPID THAT THEY ARE USING STAR MAPS AT LEAST 2700 YEARS OUT OF DATE! NO WONDER THEY SEEM SO MOODY.
RESEARCH©

On the Road Again.

Following his article on the bizarre 'Touch of Death' of Oriental martial arts – in *FT31*– **Michael Goss** returns with an examination of those travelling apparitions known as 'phantom hitch-hikers'. The subject is regarded by more orthodox psychic researchers as belonging to the realm of Folklore, and by folklorists themselves as a curiosity of native belief. As Mike Goss shows, the theme is still active today.

If ever a ghostly series is in need of a new script, it must be the Phantom Hitch-Hiker. Since Steve Moore recorded the latest peregrinations of this famous phantasm of the highways and byeways in *FT*24 (Winter 1978), he/she/it has been in constant motion: hitching lifts from unsuspecting motorists... chatting amiably with them, offering names and addresses, plus all the info they need to subsequently confirm their passenger was dead and buried at the time, *or* giving vent to dire prophesies... and of course vanishing inexplicably from the speeding vehicles. The localities change, the act doesn't.

In 1942/43 a pair of folklorists named Beardsley and Hankey contributed two important papers on the PH-H to the *California Folklore Quarterly*. Analysing 79 stories of the type, they established a set of motifs to which the ghost conformed and instead of a logical chronological listing for the sex cases reported in the press since late 1979, I thought it might be fun to adapt their technique for this round-up of itinerant wraiths. With one major proviso– B&H didn't think that any of the 'true accounts' they handled in their study were anything more than relocated folk-stories, pieces of fiction kicked round from one place to another, refurbished with new names (etc) and then put out on the long, hard road again. I've no doubt some of the following *may* come under this ruling, but – curious as it might seem – I also believe at least one (and possibly more) do not. Inasmuch as any ghost story is 'genuine' or 'really happened', a few PH-H tales can be instances of apparitional fact imitating ghostly fiction.

So to the six cases, presented *a la* Beardsley and Hankey...

HITCH–HIKER CELEBRATES ANNIVERSARY OF HER DEATH

A dirt-common motif amongst ghosts in general, the habit of celebrating the anniversary of death with a 'manifestation' is firmly supported in practice when it comes to any PH-H sample. The oft-seen young lady of Blue Bell Hill is a pretty good instance of an apparition repeating her last, fatal motor journey on the very day at the same hour it occurred; what little fresh data I have on her is reserved to the end of this column, but in the meantime how about the Strange Ride of Andre Coetzee, whose tale (courtesy of UPI) was headed 'Motorcycle Ghost Makes Presence Felt' in the *Middlesex News* (Framingham, Mass) of 11 April 1980, page one (Cr: Loren Coleman).

20-year-old Andre was breezing along on his motorbike near the Barandas turn-off outside Uniondale, South Africa, on Good Friday 1980. The article doesn't state whether the rider had prior knowledge of the accident at this spot which ended the life of a woman on Good Friday over a decade before, but the first sign of alarm he had was his hair standing on end – inside his crash-helmet. Then 'something or someone' grabbed Andre round the waist, thus inspiring him to accelerate to 80 mph to get rid of whatever it was. The presumed ghost signified its displeasure by belting him viciously on said crash-helmet three times, but when the bike reached 100 mph it gave up and removed its hateful presence.

The writer nowhere states that our hero actually *saw* anything, but the incident is put in perspective by the mention of 'several reports in recent years' of other motorcyclists who've had a blonde female hitch-hiker vanish from the rear seats of their machines. The story is briefly summarised in Jerome Clark's 'Update' column in the August 1980 issue of *Fate Magazine* (see page 78)... not surprising, as the same publication had already printed Cynthia Hind's well-researched and rather convincing article on the Uniondale PH-H on pp54–49 of their July 1978 edition.

HITCH–HIKER IDENTIFIED FROM PORTRAIT OF DEAD GIRL

B&H speak of stories where the ghost either leaves a 'proof-item' – an article of clothing, books, bags or (for drowned specimens only) pools of water and bits of seaweed – behind in the car, via which the driver can be led to someone who confirms the PH-H was (x) who died so many months/years ago. Not so far removed is the motif where the witness arrives at the door of a likely candidate and identifies his former passenger from a portrait of the householder's deceased daughter.

So it was for our second motorcycling hero, policeman Mahmood Ali, who stars in Prakash Chandra's report of the Peshawar, Pakistan case that wandered into the *Sunday Express* of 2 December 1979 (p13) 'Was that a ghost sitting on the speed cop's pillion seat?'; also summarised in *Psychic News* 8 December 1979). The pretty girl in white had melted from Ali's pillion by the time he reached the village where she said she lived and after back-tracking without seeing her, he repaired to the police station—to learn he was the fourth man to undergo this experience but the first one still alive to boast about it. The other three young men had all smashed into a truck (the *same* truck?) while searching for the absconding lady. Suspicions on the part of local villagers drew Ali to the former home of 20-year-old Nassera Begum, killed by a truck when walking on the road to find her lover and supposed now to be exacting spiritual revenge on the strangers she met there. A convenient photograph of the dead girl, matching the PH-H 'eyelash for eyelash', confirmed that the villagers knew what they were rumour-mongering about.

A happy ending: Nassera hasn't been seen again. All very well for the obligatory police spokesman to claim there must be a rational, non-ghostly explanation, but you may prefer the wisdom of the soothsayer. *He* believes the girl's spirit was pleased with (or fooled by) the handsome young officer Ali who – wonder of wonders! – is 'not unlike Nassera's lover... She is at peace at last.' Yeah, well...

PROPHETIC HITCH–HIKERS

These come in all shapes, sizes, ages and sexes; their prophesies ranging from thoughts on the Apocalypse to gleeful remarks on localized plague and earthquake, *et al* (which as far as I can see never come true). One common conversational theme is religion and one popular mode of dress that of a nun. This extreme form of PH-H behaviour has been rife in *two* USA locations over the past year, which the following show:

(a) The '"Vanishing Rider" a Christ Angel?' case given in the *Binghampton Press* 26 July 1980 (cr: J. Zarzynski) takes us to Little Rock, where we meet State Trooper Robert Roten. He has been trying to locate actual witnesses of the hitch-hiker given to lecturing motorists about the Second Coming of Christ and then disappearing under the usual unusual circumstances. As you'd expect, the clean-cut, well-dressed young male — a veritable 'highway apostle' (sic) — has been encountered by many friends of friends... but where are the first-hand accounts? Luckily, Trooper Roten has found two reports filed with the police, one for 29 June 1980 from a woman on US 65 (between Pine Bluff and Little Rock) and the second for 6 July on Interstate 30 (between Benton and Little Rock). The officer points out he has two problems: 'It's not a violation of the law and no hazard is involved...' and even though (contradictorily?) it *is* illegal to hitch lifts, how is he supposed to arrest a hiker who can vanish at will?

This story was also picked up by the *Sunday People*'s man in New York, Jeffrey Blyth, whose 'Riddle of the Car-hitch Traveller' in that paper for 5 August 1980 (page 5; cr: Steve Moore) adds that the PH-H also discussed such current affairs as the holding of the American hostages in Iran before proclaiming, before vanishing, that Christ was about to return again. Mr Blyth combines this PH-H episode with yet another, current on the other side of the continent, namely:—

(b) 'Hitch Hiking Angel Haunts Motorists' (as Bob Borino declares in the *Midnight Globe* 5 August 1980), but this time the scene is Interstate 5 (between Tacona, Washington and Eugene, Oregon). Here's the prophetic PH-H at her most deceptive: a sweet old lady aged about 50–60, in expensive clothes *or* a nun's habit. Note, too, her refinement of the vanishing act: she makes it look harder by first occupying the rear seat of the car and then removing herself during speeds of 55 mph and upwards. The sources mention that God and religion, warnings to the driver to Repent or he'll die in an accident, and a prophesy are her choice of subject matter; the last of these is at least topical, for she promises another eruption of Mount St Helens, which I understand misbehaved itself in this way before the PH-H encounters, back in May 1980.

This prophetic element is clarified by the experience of a 24-year-old University of Oregon graduate, Pat Bragan – the only one from 'dozens' of motorists actually named and quoted by Mr Borino. The PH-H informed the witness that the eruption had been God's way of warning the people of the North-West to repent and return to Him – or die in the next bit of volcanic action (for which no date is given). Pat Bragan politely waited for her to continue and when she didn't looked behind to

John Western

see... nothing and nobody. Exit one very shaken driver. American readers of *FT* might like to keep a watchful eye on the temperament of Mount St Helens.

THE HITCH–HIKER JUST VANISHES

B&H would regard stories where the PH-H says nothing (gives not so much as an address) and does little more than cadge a lift and vanish to be truncated, spoiled versions from which the critical 'corroboration' element of the hitcher's identity and deceased status have been lost, resulting in a less conclusive and less effective variant. Personally, I regard these atypical accounts as being closer to the authenticated apparitional encounters on file at the Society for Psychical Research and similar organizations and if not any more explicable, then more credible. So much so, that when I read Sally Staples's 'Was it a ghost that hitched a lift and...?' in the *Sunday Express* of 21 October 1979, I made arrangements to go to Dunstable to interview the witness, a carpet fitter named Roy Fulton.

The story I heard from him (which matched the *S.Express* write-up very closely indeed) was that a few weeks before he had been driving back from Leighton Buzzard after a darts match when, close to the village of Stanbridge, Bedfordshire, he stopped his Mini van to give a lift to a hitch-hiker: a pale-faced young man with short, dark curly hair, dark trousers and a white shirt which had an old-fashioned round collar. No conversation took place. When asked where he wanted to go, the man pointed in a direction that could have meant Totternhoe or Dunstable, and Mr Fulton (assuming the guy was a deaf mute or something) simply drove on, keeping the van at about 45 mph. Two miles down the road he tried to break the ice by offering his passenger a cigarette and there are no prizes for guessing what he didn't see when he turned to do so. Roy drove direct to his local, The Glider, where he told his story over a large Scotch – which, by the way, he doesn't normally drink.

I spoke to the other people mentioned in the article – to the Dunstable Police Inspector, to the landlord of the pub – and both confirmed they believed the story was *bona fide*. Equally valuable was the assistance of Ms Anne Court, whose original article, 'Night Ride Riddle of Hitch-Hike Ghost!' in the *Dunstable Gazette* of 18 October 1979 (page 7) first attracted the attention of Fleet Street; in fact, it seems the Staples account was based entirely on notes and other materials provided by Ms Court. Now, Ms Court also accepts the word of the witness and I'm inclined to say that, as far as one can be positive about the authenticity of *any* ghostly incident resting solely on the testimony of one single person, I find the Stanbridge case convincing – not as a piece of relocated folklore but as a paranormal fact.

Plug: those who read both *FT* and the *Dunstable Gazette* may have spotted a reference to 'psychic investigator Michael Goss' and his 'forthcoming book' on phantom hitch-hiker cases in an issue of that paper for 1 May 1980. Don't get over-excited, fans... the book is more or less finished, but is still to forthcome, due to problems relating to the parlous state of the present British literary scene (ie, can't find any-one to publish it). However, perhaps things will look better after the next eruption of Mount St Helens.

Finally, I'm a little disappointed to have what accountants style a 'nil-return' on the latest doings of the Blue Bell Hill PH-H. This lady, uncrowned queen of British road-ghosts, hasn't been up to her tricks lately – or if she has, journalists have not been cognisant of the fact. Indeed, the only recent clipping of interest (*Kent Messenger* 26 September 1980, p6, and thanks to Dick Allen!) includes her in a short-list of unlikely tales regularly offered to the press as facts which rest upon the unworthiest of evidence – 'whale tumour stories', Rodney Dale terms them. After a promising career, the Blue Bell Hill girl is fading back into folklore once again and I fear her admirers will have to be content to sit pensively in the gloom, mulling over the deeds reported by Steve Moore in *FT*24. And yet, at time of writing, the alleged anniversary of her death approaches apace — and who knows, she may be out to prove us all wrong?

•

Michael Goss

Post script – Following my appeal in the 'Help' column in FT – it really does work; I'd like to thank all the people who wrote to me or sent cuttings on recent PH-H escapades, as follows:

- Martin S. Kottmeyer of Carlyle, Illinois, who drew my attention to a wealth of material in *Indiana Folklore*, not least of which are Lydia M. Fish's "Jesus on the Thruway" (1976) and Wm. A. Wilson's "The Vanishing Hitchhiker' Among The Mormons" (1975).
- Donald K. Johnson of Downey, Calif., who sent a clipping from the *Eugene Register-Guard* of 1 August 1980.. a story dating from way back in 1951, yet featuring a PH-H which sounds oddly like the specimen now bothering Eugene and Tacoma (as above).. who spent 11 hours with truck driver Hugh Cavalli until his increasingly religiose and personal prophecies caused the driver to utter the nearly-classic line: 'Who the hell do you think you are, fella, Jesus Christ?'. (The PH-H denied it, but vanished after claiming to be "A man of vision". Whose vision?
- Bill Zeiser of Indianapolis, who contributed a comprehensive cutting on the Little Rock PH-H from the *Indianapolis Star* of 26 July 1980.
- and from down in Sussex (Lewes, to be precise) Alan Gardiner, who came up with some material on the Pyecombe White Lady, who is part and parcel of a promisingly-frequent British PH-H series.
- Also, my thanks to Paul Screeton of Hartlepool for additional material, Miss G. M. Gardner, of Everett, Washington State, and Chris Holtzhausen, of Pretoria, South Africa.

Art follows nature – or so we were told in school. But in the course of collecting and collating hundreds of clippings we often get a *deja vu* type of feeling that sometimes this whacky world of ours is getting lazy, or running out of ideas, peering over mankind's shoulder to half-inch a few plots . . .

The London version of *Dracula* had to move out of its rehearsal hall because it had been pre-booked by the National Blood Transfusion Service. (Undated clipping.)

•

Fire broke out during the witch-burning scene in Arthur Miller's *The Crucible* and gutted an arts centre in Istanbul. The Astral 2 Cinema in Soho caught fire after showing *Erotic Inferno* and *Hot Acts of Love.* Hours after the premiere of Cheech and Chong movie *Up In Smoke* at the Plaza 2 Cinema in Lower Regent Street, the adjoining Plaza 3 caught fire. *Sunday Times* 29 Nov 1970; *D.Mail* 29 Jul 1976; London *Eve.Standard* 19 Oct 1979.

•

An open-air reading of Shakespeare's *The Tempest* in Manchester was stopped by a cloudburst, as was an open-air rehearsal of Handel's *Water Music* at Redland in California. The conductor brough back the sun with *Hymn to the Sun.* The St Matthew's Parish Players had to cancel their open-air performance of the mystery play *Noah's Flood* in a Tolworth pub car park when they were washed out by torrential rain. *Reveille* 3 Sep 1976 & 10 Jun 1977; *D.Star* 16 Jun 1980.

•

The baby son of a couple staying in Julie Christie's farmhouse in Wales was drowned in a shallow pond. Six years before, in the film *Don't Look Now,* Julie Christie played the mother of a child drowned in a pond. Constable Frank Podmore who gave evidence at the inquest bore the same name as one of the pioneers of The Society for Psychical Research, who was found drowned in a pond. *Shropshire Star* & *D.Mail* 2 Apr; *Eastern Daily Press* 3 Apr 1979.

•

An actress who auditioned for the lead role in a play called *Hammer* was bludgeoned to death in New York by the playwright with a sledge-hammer. *Guardian* 12 Apr 1978.

•

A thousand pound antique throne was smashed to bits by heavy waves after it had been set up on a beach for a King Canute cigar advertisement. *D.Mirror* 25 Apr 1978.

•

The star of the film *Les Chiens* about the growing use of Alsatians in France was bitten and terrorised by an Alsatian outside a restaurant. *Guardian* 15 Mar 1979.

•

In the film *The China Syndrome* made before the Three Mile Island nuclear accident, a character remarks that a cloud of waste would wreak death and destruction over 'an area the size of Pennsylvania'. Earlier in the year, a local magazine had a fictional story called *Meltdown at Three Mile Island,* and even got the date right – 28th March. *D.Mail* 30 Mar & 2 Apr 1979.

•

Arch-criminal Jean-Charles Willoqet was arrested in a Paris flat by the Anti-Gang Squad while watching *The Anti-Gang Squad* on TV. And a drive-in cinema in Fort Wayne, Indiana, was robbed during a screening of *Drive-In,* a film about a hold-up at a drive-in cinema. *Sunday Times* 7 Dec 1975; *Houston Post* 24 Apr 1979.

•

During filming of a robbery for *Straight Time* outside a jewellers in Hollywood, thieves held up the staff and got away with £250,000 worth of gems. Everyone – staff, film crew, actors and spectators – thought the thieves and the manager shouting for help were part of the film. *Weekend* 5–11 Apr 1978.

•

Producer Irwin Allen seems to be in tune with the cosmos. When his *Poseidon Adventure* opened, the Queen Elizabeth capsized. When his *Towering Inferno* premiered, three skyscrapers caught fire in Brazil. And his film about a volcanic eruption – *When Time Ran Out* – coincided with the Mount St Helens eruption. *D. Mail* 28 May 1980.

•

Novelist Bill Granger's first thriller concerns an IRA plot to blow up the yacht of a British lord and cousin of the Queen while he is sailing in the Irish Sea. *The November Man* was published as a paperback less than three weeks before IRA bombers assassinated Lord Mountbatten on his yacht off the northwest coast of Ireland. In the thriller, the American hero foils the plot at the last moment. *Toronto Star* 29 Aug; *Int.Herald Tribune* 30 Aug; London *Eve. News* 24 Aug 1979.

•

Credits: *Janet & Colin Bord, Brian Hain, Chris Holtzhausen, Kurt Lothmann, John Michell, Peter Rogerson, Sam, Paul Screeton, Doc Shiels, Dwight Whalen, Nigel Watson, Ion Will* • **PRAdeGS.**

A view of Pant-y-Drain Farm, Llangurig, Powys, showing the sort of landscape which might provide food and cover for a mystery animal living wild. [Photo: Fortean Picture Library.]

Strange Creatures in Powys.

Late October 1980, newspapers picked up a story of police surrounding a barn, in Wales, cornering a 'lion' or 'puma'. This incident was followed by others, and although inconclusive in itself, establishes contemporary mystery animal activity in the Welsh hills. **Janet and Colin Bord** report on their investigation.

On the morning of Thursday 23 October 1980, farmer Michael Nash of Pant-y-Drain farm, 2½ miles south of Llangurig in Powys, Wales, was working near his barn when he heard a distinct snoring sound coming from among the straw bales. He had noticed the same noise a number of times recently, and his son later remembered that he had also heard the noise as long before as the previous Friday. A large and unusual footprint, plus traces of others, were found on the muddy ground in front of the barn. Mr Nash, who has 3,000 sheep on his 1,500 acre farm, had had at different times during the past ten days four sheep killed in a manner which was not typical of dogs. He decided there was a strange animal among the straw, so he informed the police. They arrived a little before 2pm and, having sized up the situation, they called up armed reinforcements to keep a watch for the creature. As dusk fell they set up calor gas lamps. Mr Nash suggested that they fence in the open side of the barn with gates to contain the creature in the event that it should break out, but the police thought this unnecessary. At 5.45pm the police, evidently hoping to avoid an all-night vigil, decided to drive the animal out and in the words of the farmer 'they hammered hell out of the asbestos [side of the barn] when they heard it snoring'. They failed to flush the beast and Mr Nash thinks that it was probably scared and disturbed, and crept out unnoticed. At 12 noon on Friday the 24th, the police went in among the bales of straw and found the empty lair, with wet straw where the creature

Farmer Michael Nash talking to Janet Bord at Pant-y-Drain Farm. The footprint he preserved from the rain is under the box; and the mystery animal's 'lair' begins with the burrow near the foot of the rightmost pillar. [Photo: Fortean Picture Library.]

had been urinating, and some 3-4 inch long droppings as well as the owl pellets which were reported in the press. These large droppings were not saved and were apparently lost among the straw in the barn.

On Friday night when the police and media had gone, Mr Nash went to the barn and could hear the animal snoring again. He shone his torch around the bay where it had been, and the noise stopped. He later revisited the barn two or three times, going there quietly and without showing a light, but he did not hear the noise again. He thinks the animal had returned on the Friday evening, but was disturbed by his torch and finding its lair disturbed it had decided to sleep elsewhere. Late on Thursday night after the police activity of banging the side of the barn, some friends of Mr Nash phoned him to say they had seen a peculiar animal beside the main road which lies across the fields about half a mile to the east. This was at 11.30pm, and Mr Nash thinks it may have been the creature.

Two weeks earlier a neighbouring farmer had had two of his sheep killed, but when we contacted him for the details he said that he thought the wounds looked very much like the work of a fox, or possibly a dog, having in past years seen similar depredations from foxes which were subsequently shot. Those sheep of Mr Nash's which were attacked had had pieces of flesh bitten out of them while they were still alive, and one animal badly injured in this way had had to be shot. The others had died of their injuries. This type of attack is apparently not typical of a dog. Some 25 miles away, farmers on the outskirts of Newtown, the largest urban area in mid-Wales, have been suffering losses from their flocks caused by dogs which their owners allow to run free. Dogs have been seen attacking sheep and killing them, and at least one dog has been shot while doing this.

On the evening of Saturday 25 October we telephoned Mr Nash who gave us details of what had been happening. He also informed us that he had the best footprint preserved under a box, and that we should call soon if we wanted to see it because it was likely to be washed away by all the rain. We therefore drove to Llangurig on the morning of Sunday 26 October and Mr Nash showed us the footprint and the place where the animal had burrowed into the straw. We photographed all the visible evidence. The footprint, which we measured, was 5 inches long by 3½ inches wide.

It is interesting that Mr Nash told us he had heard of a man living in Newtown who was known to keep a wild animal in his back yard, but who had recently been detained in one of HM's prisons and the animal was no longer there. Also Mr Nash reported that a circus had passed by on the main road a quarter of a mile away about a week earlier.

When we spoke to the police a few days later, they obviously wanted to minimise the whole incident. They had checked with all nearby police forces for reports of escaped animals, but with negative results, and they thought it might be a large dog that had left the footprint in the mud. They said that nothing other than owl pellets were found among the straw in the barn, and that a local RSPB official had suggested that the snoring noise was made by owls. They also said that the person who had kept an unlicensed wild animal in his shed lived in the Cardigan area, and as far as they knew the local council had had the creature put down. Anything on the loose and killing sheep was, as far as they were concerned, most likely to be a dog. Mr Nash had told us that he had heard of a woman who had seen a cat-like creature between Churchstoke and Sarn some 10 miles east of Newtown. The police remembered this incident but had no available record of it, or of the woman's name. They had visited the spot, but had seen nothing. They thought she may have seen a fox crossing the road. Later a report revealed that the sighting had occurred in good daylight, not at night as the police seemed to think.

To sum up: There have been several sightings of strange animals in this general area.

1. The curator of Dudley Zoo saw a big cat in the West Midlands in July 1980 – see letter from M.J. Williams cited below under 'Wolverhampton Sightings'.
2. A district nurse saw a 'lynx' near Churchstoke, Powys, on the England/Wales border on 29 September 1980. Churchstoke is 40 miles west of Wolverhampton.
3. The presence of an unknown animal was reported by Mr Nash at Llangurig on 23 October 1980. Llangurig is 30 miles south-west of Churchstoke.

The mystery footprint at Pant-y-Drain Farm (printed upside down to facilitate interpretation of the relief). After the submission of this report by the Bords, FT sent copies of these and other photos to the world's leading cryptozoological expert, Dr Bernard Heuvelmans. His verdict was that it was certainly made by a member of the dog tribe, and not by a large cat. This judgement was also offered by Dudley Zoo. [Photo: Fortean Picture Library.]

Whether the same creature accounts for all three reports is uncertain. The distances between the locations do not make this impossible, and the terrain is largely rural, often wild country. At Llangurig the only 'concrete' evidence is the footprint.

•

Janet & Colin Bord

The last half of 1980 saw a remarkable increase in the reports and varieties of cryptozoological comings and goings. The greatest attention, however, was drawn by mystery big-cats; the Llangurig incident reported above by the Bords, and only days later the capture of a puma not far from Loch Ness. We attempt a summary of the developments in Wales, the Midlands, the South, and in Scotland – a time when it seemed the British landscape was alive with pumas, lynxes, cheetahs and lionesses.

AFTER THE BARN STORM

As a consequence of the abortive seige of Farmer Nash's barn, the Newtown police called off their search for the creature, at the same time admitting that something had savaged sheep and left prints. Whatever-it-was was still out there!

About a month later – on 25 Nov – the Powys Beast was spotted by Ernie Lloyd, of Coedcae . Farm, Cwmbelan, about 6 miles from the Nash farm. Mr Lloyd described a strange cat-like creature moving in leaps and bounds' across his fields, just 300 yards from where he stood. He and a neighbour, Kenneth Vaughan, discovered a dozen paw marks on the hillside. They sound very similar to the footprint at the Nash farm, being: 'about the size of a small palm.' Police joined the search for a while, taking photographs and paw-casts.

One of these casts was sent to Dudley Zoo, where it was 'positively identified as that of a large dog', according to a letter to Janet & Colin Bord from the Zoo's superintendent, MJ Williams, and 'very similar', except a little larger, to that photographed at the Nash farm. The implication here is that the Llangurig Beast is also a 'large dog'. We can be sure that Mr Williams weighed the evidence carefully, for he himself encountered a large puma-like creature back in July near Wolverhampton – we shall hear his story later (below).

Meanwhile, the national papers for the 27th Nov, made such fun of the 'Puma that woofs' (etc), jumping to the conclusion that the animal that made the prints, was the same one that savaged the sheep, or that was seen by the various witnesses. There was no conclusive proof linking these details to one animal – indeed, according to police Inspector Ralph Ford, the farmers 'are not 100% sure of what it is, but they are convinced [what they saw was] not a dog.' Farmer Lloyd went further; with a lifetime's experience of dogs, he said, 'I insist it was more like a big cat.'

It is still out there.

Shropshire Star, Bristol *Evening Post, D.Telegraph, D. Express* 26 + 27 Nov; *South Wales Argus, Guardian* 27 Nov; *Western Mail* 27 + 29 Nov; *County Times & Express* 29 Nov 1980.

By mid-December other circumstantial evidence was suggesting to all the skeptics that the Welsh beast or beasts was/were just dog/s. About 30 miles to the southwest, over craggy Welsh mountains, three animals attacked flocks of sheep near Llanpumpsaint, Dyfed, leaving 10 dead and others dying or injured. This was on 26th November. The animals seen attacking the sheep were identified – we don't know how positively – as dogs. *Western Mail* 28 Nov 1980.

About 13 December, a beast is seen – or a were-beast is seen again – at a farm not far from Llanidloes, this time by Mrs Gwenda Bound and her 11-year-old daughter. It was described as a not-too-ferocious reddish brown dog-like animal. At their farm gates at Coed Cochion Mawr, Cwmbelan, the Boundes' dog went up to it and sniffed it. It ran off when people appraoched, leaving prints said to be like the Nash farm print, but smaller, with 'at least one large pointed claw. Naturally the papers claimed this also solved the Nash farm incident, as well as Farmer Lloyd's beast, in spite of the fact that Lloyd saw something quite different: 'a gray puma-like creature.' This was enough to kill the mystery in the eyes of the media – and lo! in self-fulfilment we have heard no more of mystery beasts in Wales since. *D.Telegraph* 26 Nov; *Shropshire Star* 15 Dec; *County Times & Express* 20 Dec 1980.

WOLVERHAMPTON WONDERS

The Wolverhampton *Express & Star* for 23 July 80 reported, with vague details, that there had been a number of sightings of a 'puma' or 'cheetah' in the wooded region of a canal tow-path and disused railway line between Compton and Aldersley, not too distant. The animal was said to be about 30 inches high and 'orange and yellow'. A large search was mounted, involving Mike Williams, a superintendent at Dudley Zoo, armed with a tranquilising gun. *D.Star, D.Mirror* 26 July; *Sunday Mercury* 28 July 1980.

The unsuccessful search was called off on the 26th July – but a few days later Mr Williams was called out again, and this time saw it for himself. In a letter to Janet & Colin Bord, dated 4th Dec, he gives his own account:

'In July this year at Wolverhampton, a school teacher on holiday was walking near a disused railway line and saw an animal come out onto the grass field alongside. He had a good view of it for nearly 5 minutes. A lady exercising her dog also saw it, she ran off exclaiming that it was a wild animal and the gentleman concerned agreed and phoned the local police. He was *adamant* that what he had seen was a Puma, I was called in and the description which he gave me certainly fitted that of a Puma, round cat-like head, pricked ears, short thick legs, heavy tail held low, brown in colour and the size of a large dog. His attention was drawn by the sound of crows mobbing it, the animal bounded down the field for 30 yards then came back and lay in the long grass at the side of the railway track watching him, then disappeared, he was about 50 yards away at the time. The teacher claimed to be an amateur naturalist and had seen foxes etc many times, so there was no doubt in his mind that what he had seen was not a fox or dog. As you can imagine over the next few days various sightings were reported along about 3 miles of this disused railway line.'

'After a reported incident whereby a large brown animal had attacked a dog whilst being walked by a child, I was called out again, with me was our Senior cat keeper with over 10 years experience of Lions, Tigers etc. We were on our own, searching along the same disused railway line, but about 2 miles from the original sighting by the teacher, when we noticed something looking at us about 200 yards further on. It disappeared and then we heard birds mobbing something in the thick cover and an animal emerged onto the track about 300 yards in front, it was a large animal which had a round head, was level across the back, heavy tail held low, and when it turned to look at us it was very narrow, everything about it was cat-like, but we couldn't get nearer than about 300 yards.'

'I left Alan our cat keeper watching it whilst I ran back to alert the police of a possible sighting. The police organised a search and within 10 minutes they had observers on raods and bridges in the area. Alan had followed the animal for about 15 minutes and then lost it. The subsequent search by police of this section of the railway track was blank. Both Alan and myself were of the opnion that the animal we saw was too large to be a fox, and had a lot of typical cat characteristics about it, but as we could not get close enough we could not give the police a positive identification. If it had been a large brown dog it would surely have been found during the big police search.'

'If we could find proof that a Puma had escaped or been released within a reasonable area of Wolverhampton then I would have said that we had seen it. As we have no evidence of an illegally kept animal on the run then we must be a bit skeptical at this stage. This is what I have told the police.'

These were not the only sightings of phantom felines in the Midlands. It seems we now have a genuine Cheshire Cat! Quoted in *Northern Earth Mysteries* No9 (Oct 1980) is a clipping from the *Stockport Advertiser* for 4 Sept 1980, which mentions sightings of a mystery cat-like animal in the Handforth area. It is described variously as 'a black cat-like animal, bigger than a cat, with a more pointed face', 'a large white cat', and 'the size of an Alsatian with pointed ears, a cat-like body and tail'. Handforth farmer, Christopher Shenton, thought it was a 4-year-old stag until he had a clearer view!

Our latest information involves a police hunt for a 'panther-like creature' in South Warwickshire. According to Chief Inspector John Price, of Evesham police, a Mr Cotton, of Pebworth, was walking along the road to Long Marston, on 23rd November, when he saw the animal – 'jet black, as big as a fox, and with a long bushy tail' – catch one of the moorhens by a pond and run off. Since then it has been seen by a Long Marston resident, Michael Marshall, on 3rd December. He was at Birds Commercial Scrapyard, when 200 yards away, he saw 'a jet black animal, about 3ft long, with a long tail', which ran off at speed. Marshall adds: 'It was definitely not a dog, but more cat-like in appearance. As far as we know the search was fruitless. *Gloucestershire Echo* 4 Dec; Sun, Bristol *Evening Post* 10 Dec 1980.

AND IN NEW YORK!

As the Welsh episode entered its closing stages something stalked the streets of New York in sympathy. On 12 Nov, a 200-pound young male lion was netted in a driveway in a quiet part of Queens. Police were unable to trace an owner or record of an escape. A spokeswoman for the ASPCA said they received four calls, each claiming to have lost a lion. She added: 'That means we have three lions out there on the loose.' P'raps they came to Wales, or Scotland, or Surrey, for a while?

You know how we like names lexilinked to appropriate cases – well the ASPCA woman was named Alayne Lyons! *New Standard* (London) 12 Nov; *Middlesex News* (Framingham, Mass) 14 Nov 1980.

New York Times 9 Dec 1980 – two lion cubs had been found wandering free in the city and turned over to the ASPCA. They had discoverable origins: the pet shop from which they had been bought by inconsiderate owners was traced by police. But wait a minute – if these cubs relate to the three loose lions (above) then one is still unaccounted for.

SOUTHERN SIGHTINGS

To supplement the report by Chris Hall (below) on Surrey sightings, we prefix this motley of mixed mystery moggies seen elsewhere in the southern counties.

On 15th June, about 3am, Patrick Doughty approached the Queens Hotel [Queens, again!], Farnborough, Hampshire, to begin his cleaning job. About a mile from the hotel, on the A325, he swerved his car to avoid 'a large brown spotted animal, travelling at high speed . . . I put the lights on full beam and watched as it cut across my path and nip between some railings before disappearing into some bushes. My first reaction was that it was a large dog.' He looked again. 'It was far too big. Its body was about 4ft long and it had a pair of huge, very powerful-looking front legs. In the beam . . . I was able to pick out spots on its body, which was a browny colour.' No puma this time – 'I'm fairly certain it was a cheetah.'

Later that same morning – 4.15am — the cheetah — or something in the shape of a cheetah – was seen by John Bedwell, the hotel's night porter. He described a lightly-coloured big cat 'with pointed ears' bounding alongside a wall. Police were called, and nothing found. Our own first impressions are that unless we are dealing with a were-cheetah, cheetahs don't normally have pointed ears or huge front legs– quite the reverse in fact, smaller front legs and rounded ears. Oh well . . . London *Evening Standard* 15 July; *D.Mirror* 16 July; *Aldershot News* 18 July 1980.

Chris Hall writes: 'For what It's worth the Queens Hotel (SU 868534) is haunted by the ghosts of a small boy and a woman. It's also next to Cockadobby Hill [dobby = goblin], a tumulus, and yes a ley line through the tumulus goes slap through the hotel, but does not follow the part of the A325 in question . . . Just for the hell of it, the Great UFO hoax of 1967, by Farnborough students, was put together in the hostel opposite.' Chris also noted that, appropriate to this sighting, the sun too had spots at this time!

If it was the same were-animal that appeared at Bodiam, on the Kent/Sussex border, it had trans-moggy-fied [sorry!] into a 'black panther'. At 10.20pm, on 3rd December, Lawrence Sharpen was turning his car at the Curlew Inn cross-roads, Bodiam, when his head-lights picked out a 'massive . . . pair of yellowy-orange eyes . . . I switched to full beam and had the perfect vision of a black cat-like animal running on the grass verge . . . past the car.' *Sussex Courier* 13 Dec 1980.

Credits: *Janet & Colin Bord, Peter Christie, Loren Coleman, Joan Elsmore, Peter Hope-Evans, Alan Gardiner, Chris Hall, J Lang, Paul Screeton, David Sutton, PR Thomas, Andy Townsend, Ion Will, Steve Wrathall* • **RJMR.**

PUMA SIGHTINGS IN SURREY

[The following summary was compiled by Chris Hall . . .]

At about 5pm on June 27 Mrs Vivien Wilkinson looked from the window of her home in East Horsley and saw a tawny-coloured feline creature at the end of her garden. It was about 30 yards away, and loped across the lawn and through a gap in the fence. She added that it was higher than a red setter, with a thick tail reaching to the ground. 'I am familiar with country animals but have never seen anything like it. I am entirely satisfied that it was a big cat', she said. She did not report the incident to the police, but did contact the *Advertiser* some weeks later after a reader reported a very similar animal. Her husband had seen something very similar in almost the same place five years ago. Last November a deer was savaged in a nearby field. The newspaper, in a large article, reviewed the legend.

The letter which led to this article was from Mrs Auriol Earle, an associate lecturer at Surrey University, who wrote from 1 Western Down, Guildford Road, Guildford. She and her husband were walking near Pockford on July 20. They had taken a footpath from Vann's Lane across fields when they heard a dog barking persistently nearby.

They were 'amazed' to see a creature 'lope up the hill' about 50 to 100 yards away, and disappear into the wood. Mrs Earle said she is 'country born and bred and can recognise a fox, deer and most breeds of dog and cat by their shape, colour and movement, but I could not identify this animal. It was dark honey-coloured, paling to a creamy-white belly, of size and length of leg similar to a red setter. Its movement and tail were feline. Was this the Surrey Puma?'

Their Jack Russell terrier ignored it, which is strange for the dog usually chases anything. The gap and track where the animal passed was obviously well used, too big for a fox, too small for a deer. She offers to point it out to anyone interested.

London Zoo were approached by the *Advertiser,* where a spokesman said this was 'highly unlikely' to be the same animal as was in the area in the 1960s, for pumas do not live that long. At the time there seemed to be only one animal so breeding is ruled out.

There had been no reports of escapes to Surrey police, and no licenses have been issued by either Surrey County Council or Waverley Borough Council for exotic animals. 'If someone kept one illegally, we would probably hear about it on the grapevine', remarked a police spokesman.

In mid-August the paper reported that five cats had gone missing recently from Purford Place near Send. (NB may be a misprint for Pyrford.)

Mrs Mary Alexander of Castle Street, Guildford, thinks she can explain the puma. On August 31 she was travelling to Guildford on the A281 at Birtley Green. The headlights illuminated a large yellow animal. This was enough to intrigue all four people in the car to turn back for another look (If only more witnesses would do this). Thus they saw it three times in all.

Mrs Alexander writes: 'Its tail and manner of moving were very like those of a big cat; its head, build and length of leg made it clear that it was a dog . . . and one could easily imagine it to be a puma. It appeared to be a cross-breed of some type, with similarities to a Great Dane but the tail was longer and thicker than any I have seen on a dog. Its eyes glowed green in the lights as it trotted along unconcerned by the traffic. It was on our near-side for two of the views, and all the occupants of the car are convinced it was a dog, although not a type with which they were familiar. Could *this* be the Surrey Puma?

For anyone looking for correlations, a 'mammoth-sized' UFO was seen over Wiseley from the A3 on the weekend of 20/21 September. And 'glowing orange bars' were seen over Knaphill in July. Both UFOs are being taken seriously by the Surrey Investigation Group for Aerial Phenomena.

On September 30 the puma was back, this time at Bramley. A 14-year-old shcoolboy saw it a few feet away when cycling to a yough club at about 8.30 pm. Car headlights showed the animal standing on the road-side verge. It was beige and looked like a puma. It made off towards Cranleigh. Bramley has also been plagued by a mystery hum for most of the summer.

Mr GS Elliot of Palmers Cross, Bramley, wasted no time in saying something about this. He write: 'I am sorry to have to disillusion your readers, but [the puma] is undoubtedly a very large lurcher dog, part Irish wolfhound I suspect, which unfortunately is not kept under proper control by its owner and is allowed to roam the neighbourhood at will. It is of such size that I initially mistook it at a distance to be a deer. The risk to sheep flocks must be significant and I am sending a copy of this letter to the superintendent of police.'

At least Surrey people come up with explanations which are possible. No one has suggested a paper bag yet!

Sources: *all from* **Surrey Advertiser.** *East Horsley, 8 Aug 1980 p3. Pockford, 25 July 1980 (letter) p13, 8 Aug 1980 p3. Missing cats, 15 Aug p2. Birtley Green dog, 12 Sept 1980 (letter) p12. UFOs, 26 Sept 1980 p8. Bramley puma, 3 Oct 1980 p1. Mr Elliot, 10 Oct 1980 (letter) p13. Bramley Hum, 31 Oct 1980, 7 Nov 1980.*

•

Chris Hall

SCOTTISH PUMA – SAGA OR FARCE?

Since our extensive round-up of Scottish sightings (up to Spring 1980) in FT32p23f, the subject occupied the media stage again with the shock news of a puma-capture at Cannich in late October. Here is our chronology . . .

• The first intimations of the coming ruckus came on 24/25 July, when Marcus Pacitti, of Aberdeen, and a friend, were walking in Achnashellach Forest, Ross-shire, and were confronted with what they first took to be a stag – again?! See last of the Midland sightings above – but which 'must have been a puma'. Scottish *D. Record* 26 July 1980. On 30 July 1980, the *Daily Express* said there had been two sightings in the 'past few days' – but no details.

• Since his first sighting in October 1979 [see FT30p23] farmer Ted Noble, of Kerrow Farm, Cannich, in Strathglass, Inverness-shire, continues to see a puma, and to find sheep with their throats ripped and bones crunched. Near the beginning of August 1980 he saw it again. The police, having searched the area before and found nothing, do not respond. Noble and a neighbour decide to set their own traps. Scottish *Sunday Mail* 17 Aug 1980.

• 6 Sept 1980 – An Australian tourist and his wife, returning to Invernesss after visiting the Highland Gathering at Braemar, saw what appeared to be 'a heavily built black lioness . . . with a long tail'. This was at 6.45pm, near Corgarff, Inverness-shire, on the Ballater to Tomintoul road, not far from the infamous 'Devil's Elbow'. Aberdeen *Press & Journal* 9 Sept 1980.

• 25 Oct 1980–Back in Ross-shire. Shock! . . . the 'puma' is shot! Double shock! . . . it's a dog! Two workers on the Crannich Estate, Ardross, near Alness, tracked for two miles a black beast they believed to be a panther, responsible for attacking sheep, lambs and even deer. When shot, they discovered it was a feral cross-bred Alsatian/Collie. The 'Great Highland Puma Mystery' is pronounced 'solved'–p'raps. *The Scotsman* 27 Oct 1980; which includes a photo (too dark to reproduce) of the unfortunate dog looking suitably villainous.

• 29 Oct 1980 – Several days later, at Rancho Noble, another mystery cat is in the bag. Using a sheep's head as bait, Ted Noble finally captures his puma. It was a triumph of vindication: 'People were beginning to think I was nuts the way I was obsessed with capturing this animal.' The media pounced on this one and gnawed its bones on the front pages. The authorities could never take seriously the idea of a puma on the loose, nor the claims of many witnesses – now here, in a cage, was a real live puma (see photo), a genuine *felis concolor.* Ted, and his son Julian, were carrying out their daily check of the trap when they heard growling and knew they were successful. The trap was near the cottage of pensioner, Mrs Janet Chisholm, who had seen the beastie a number of times, and encouraged Ted.

Naturally many papers claimed the end of another 'Mystery of the Glens', while a few others – notably *The Scotsman* – reported that Ted 'and others who have seen the tracks . . . think the puma may be one of two. Farmer Arthur Cadman, Ted's neighbour, said the second puma was lighter in colouring. Mrs Chisholm even claimed she had seen *three puma cubs* in the area.

As darkness closed in, Eddie Orbell arrived – he is director of the Highland Wildlife Park, near Aviemore. He was one of those dismissive 'experts' who pooh-poohed the idea of a puma on the loose, preferring to believe that witnesses were misinterpreting carelessly or inadequately observed more common animals. Anyway, Orbell had been asked by police to give this one a home. 'I will obviously have to eat my words,' he said sheepishly to reporters. He turned up with a stun-gun, but stories of the beast 'snarling and spitting' to the contrary, he didn't need it. The puma went quietly. No one smelled a rat, just yet . . .

Biggest coverage was in the Scottish *Daily Record;* other sources include *The Times, Guardian, D.Telegraph, D.Mail, D.Star, D.Express, The Scotsman, Shropshire Star,* all of 30 Oct 1980.

• 30 Oct 1980 – As we could have predicted more questions were raised than answered by the capture of the puma at Noble's farm. Whether people normally expect life to be simple I don't know, but certainly the media strains itself fit-to-bust to present matters simply, in the belief that people wish it that way. Nothing is simple in real life; things are rarely black and white, or what they seem, and usually involve a million loose ends. In this case over simplification and sloppy journalism distorted the picture, and in turn distorted the reactions to that first distorting. For the whole comedy of errors read the actual Press reportage, and weep! Here is the straight poop . . .

Eddie Orbell pulls the plug on the spectacle. Far from eating his words, he huffs: 'I've never believed there was such a thing as this legendary "Highland Puma". I can't believe this animal has been roaming wild since 1973 . . .'

What alerted him? The puma, it seems, far from being a terror-of-the-glens for seven (other reports say four) years, was elderly, rheumatoid in one leg, lame, well-groomed, overweight, so tame it purred for visitors to the Wildlife Park the next day, and generally too domesticated to have survived in a wild environment. 'I fear somebody may have played a hoax on Mr Noble', said Orbell, suggesting that some rash owner had released his unwanted pet only days, or even hours, before the capture. Pure speculation, but police, worried by the growing muttering of 'Hoax!', called off their search for the remaining one of more pumas that only hours before they had been so ready to believe existed in the area. *D.Mail, D.Record, D.Star, D. Express, D.Telegraph, Guardian,* Aberdeen *Evening Express,* all 31 Oct 1980.

• 31 Oct 1980 – The easy way out would be to believe that someone planted the puma in Ted Noble's trap. Any suggestions of feral pumas gives the authorities a headache. But Ted won't keep quiet, bristling with indignation at suggestions that he might even have been party to the 'hoax'. He receives timely support from Bob High, secretary of the local Farmers' Union, who saw the developing media circus as diverting attention from the *real* issue – the continuing depredation of livestock. He says many farmers, particularly in the Eastern Highlands, have seen the puma and will not speak out for fear of being made a laughing stock. Who can blame them, looking at the example being made of Ted Noble. *D.Record* 1+3 Nov 1980.

• 3 Nov 1980 – A curious development – David Carter, serving a 2-year sentence in Winchester prison, claims he released two pumas – a male and a female – in October 1979, in the same area and about the same time as Noble had his first sighting. Noble passed Carter's letter to the police. Carter said his feline Adam and Eve came to him from a friend who went abroad, and he himself kept them for a while, setting them free when he knew he would be imprisoned. Evidence in his letter suggests his pumas would now be about three years old, whereas various 'experts' gave Ted Noble's puma an age of between 6–10 years. Could Carter have taken his corroborating details (ie time and place, etc) from the news reports a few days previously? *D.Record* 4+5 Nov 1980.

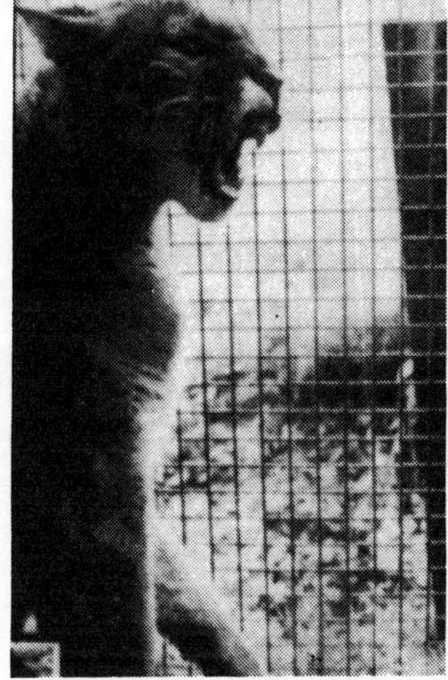

This so-called 'Highland Hellcat', caught in a trap on Ted Noble's farm, at Cannich, on 29 Oct 1980, turned out to be quite a pussy-cat. [Photo: Daily Record *30 Oct 1980.]*

• Police confirm that a David Carter did indeed send a letter from Winchester prison. That's it! There was no confirmation of Carter's story in any subsequent news report, but we have no idea whether this was because the story did not check out, or because police did not want to take the matter further. *The Scotsman* 5 Nov 1980.

• *D.Record* 6 Nov 1980: 'Expert's hoax claim shattered'. A line guaranteed to grab a Fortean's attention. The Institute of Terrestrial Ecology, at Banchory, Aberdeen, analysed droppings from Noble's puma, made within hours of capture, proved the puma had indeed been living wild, contrary to the opinion of Eddie Orbell. Dr Hans Kruuk, of the ITE said: 'It has been living wild for some time . . . living off what one would expect in the wild.' One of the two droppings 'One was 95% deer hair . . . with 4% rabbit remains and 1% sheep . . . The second was 99% sheep with 1% rabbit.' However, Dr Kruuk agreed that since the beast was very tame, it must have lived in captivity for some time. Also, *The Scotsman* 6 Nov 1980.

• Police began to take matters seriously again, saying they have obtained a list of depredations from farmers, and of witnesses in the Cannich area.

Also, George Rafferty, a vet from Grantown-on-Spey, examines the captive puma and largely agrees with Orbell's opinion, although he says its lameness is from a 'muscular complaint' not any detectable injury. 'It has certainly spent most of its life in captivity. If it has been living rough I do not think it can have been doing so for very long because of its bodily condition.' This is the last we have heard on the subject to date, since media interest in the complex wrangle evaporated very suddenly. *D. Record* 10 Nov; *The Scotsman* 11 Nov 1980.

• 16 Nov 1980– However, the mystery marches on . . . Two sheep found savaged near Garve, in Ross-shire. According to Dr Kruuk, they were killed in a way 'very typical' of puma. Garve is about 20 miles (as the crow flies) north of Cannich and well within a puma hunting range. Farmer Eddie Smith, who lost one of the sheep, says: 'I feel that a second puma is on the loose'. But who listens to country farmers? Thus, circumstantially, Ted Noble is vindicated yet again. *D.Record* 17 Nov; *The Scotsman* 18+20 Nov 1980.

• 3 Dec 1980 – Our story takes its most interesting turn yet. 19-year-old Wendy Mann, a hotel chef at Drumnadrochit on Loch Ness sees a 'cat-like beast' running across the Lewiston road, not far from Castle Urquhart. 'It was a lioness or a puma. It couldn't have been anything else', she said. *D.Record* 5 Dec; Aberdeen

Continued on p 34

The war between man and nature continues; and if the battles are not always red in tooth and claw, they can at least be downright inconvenient. Here are a few animal saboteurs . . . for added humour, see also our selection of 'headlines' on this subject on the inside back cover.

MASS ATTACKS

• **Mice**: The San Ofre nuclear power station, California, closed down by mice which shorted the electrical system. *Daily Mirror* 12 November 1979.

In Arlingsaas, Sweden, a van carrying hundreds of mice to a hospital for experiments never made it. The cunning little devils would keep *breathing* . . . until the windscreen steamed up, and the van went off the road! *D.Telegraph* 27 Nov 79.

• **Rats**: Hordes of rats, apparently breeding for nine years in an excavated lot at Park Row and Ann Street, Manhattan, suddenly swarmed out without apparent cause, to bite women and jump on cars, gnawing windscreen wipers and vinyl roofs. Health officials fenced off the site with wire mesh and put down poison. *Niagara Falls Review* 12 May 79.

Between 300 & 600 telephones were disconnected in Cheltenham, Glos, when rats gnawed through an underground cable. *Glos. Citizen + D. Mirror + D. Star + D. Telegraph* 7 Jan 80.

A lobster farm on the island of Houat, off the Brittany coast, France, attacked by what must have been an almighty horde of rats: 5,000 lobsters eaten in one night! *Sunday Express* 13 Jan 80, *Surrey & Hants News* 29 July 80.

• **Rabbits**: Ellsworth Air Force Base, South Dakota: rabbits and squirrels causing chaos in the secured weapons area by setting off security alarms. The rabbits were also breeding like crazy and burrowing into missile mounds, cause cave-ins. The Air Force were intending to go hunting . . . with bows and arrows! *Toronto Sun* 11 May 80.

The ancient monument of Stonehenge, Wilts, in danger of falling down due to the burrowing of a vast army of rabbits. Officials digging wire fence into the ground to keep the invaders out. *D.Express* 4 July 80.

• **Squirrels**: Air-raid sirens set off at Toronto, apparently due to squirrels gnawing through circuit wires (one of these days, a rodent's going to start World War III!) *Toronto Sun* 30 May 80.

New York State: hundreds of paranoids convinced their phones are bugged . . . the cause of the mystery crackling turns out to be squirrels sharpening their teeth on the wires. Five miles of cable need replacing. *D.Mail* 8 Aug 79.

• **Pigs**: New South Wales, Australia: thousands of pounds worth of damage caused by rampaging wild pigs, killing lambs and trampling crops. *S. Express* 11 May 80.

• **Rooks**: A spate of power cuts on the Isle of Man blamed on flocks of sexy rooks homing in on power-lines to whoop it up in the mating season. *D.Star* 25 July 80.

• **Insects**: A swarm of bees invaded the control tower at an airfield at Tabora, West Tanzania, driving out the air traffic team. A pilot found the controllers cowering under a tree after he landed. *The Star* (Sheffield) 19 Oct 79.

Gaevle, Sweden: swarms of wasps systematically eating the yellow paint off outhouses in a district of semi-detached homes. *D.Telegraph* 25 July 80.

• **Worms**: Half a mile of British Rail track threatened, where it runs across the Mawddach Estuary, near Barmough, Wales, as worms eat the track's wooden supports. Damage costs £2½ million to repair. *Guardian* 18 June 80.

• **Mackerel**: A Norwegian supertanker, the *Moscliff* held up for 22 hours in the English Channel, some time in December 1979, when it ran into a huge shoal of mackerel. The ship's engine stopped automatically when thousands of mackerel were squeezed through the strainers of the cooling system intake. About a ton of minced mackerel had to be removed before the ship could get underway again. London *Eve. Standard* 10 Jan 80.

LONE RANGERS

• **Spiders**: Cambridge (Canada?): Firemen responded to an alarm call from the fire-detector at the home of Mervyn Orr, but there were no flames. Instead, they opened the detector and found a spider which had spun its web between the ionization chambers and set off the alarm. *Toronto Star* 27 Nov 79.

• **Fish**: Brierley Hill, West Midlands: All Herbert the Trigger-fish wanted to do was burrow into the sand at the bottom of his 400-gallon tank, in Chris Parson's shop. Amazing what an 8-inch fish can do: the coral reefing in his tank collapsed; heating elements fell against the half-inch thick glass; the six-foot tank shattered; the gushing seawater blew up a compressor; ruined carpets, destroyed stocks, killed 8 valuable fish. £5,000 of damage (Herbert survived). *D.Mirror* 30 Oct 79.

• **Mice**: Manea, Cambs: a mouse chewed through electric wires and caused a £1,500 fire in a grain store. *D.Telegraph* 20 Sept 80.

• **Birds**: Thousands of commuters from Liverpool Street Station, London, delayed 20 minutes after a pigeon flew into overhead power lines between Gidea Park and Shenfield, causing a break in electricity. London *E.Standard* 19 Oct 79.

A crow flew into powerlines in Japan, halting 20 high-speed trains. *D.Mirror* 9 April 80.

Trains halted for 2 hours at Stoke on Trent when a crow's nest on an electricity cable cut power. *Weekly News* 8 May 80.

An owl pecked through the cooling cable and blew a 132,000 volt cable near Black Carr Woods, Bradford, causing £13,000 damage. *D.Star* 5 Aug 80.

A kestrel perched on an overhead railway power cable as a train passed underneath caused a short-circuit, blowing masonry from an overhead footbridge and halting main-line services at Crewe for more than an hour. *D.Telegraph* 27 Dec 79.

Gifhorn, W Germany: Armin Grothe's new £60,000 house was built on the hunting ground of a stork, and the latter got rather annoyed, swooping in at night to attack. Three windows smashed at last count. *D.Mirror* 26 June 80.

• **Lizards**: Dar Es Salaam, Tanzania: two lizards caused water shortages when they crawled into an electricity junction box and short-circuited water pumps. A snake had pulled the same trick the previous year. *Reuter Report* 22 Jan 80.

• **Cats**: Cindy the cat managed to climb up an electricity pylon, causing workmen to black out the village of Streatley, Luton, for 20 minutes while they rescued her. *Weekly News* 5 April 80.

• **Dogs**: The Piccadilly Line of the London underground was brought to a halt during the morning rush hour when an alsatian dog went for a walk . . . for six miles along the tunnels between Wood Green and Holborn stations. *D.Telegraph* 29 Dec 79.

• **Sheep**: At North Wooton, near Shepton Mallet, Somerset, a 200 lb pregnant ewe ran away from the flock, apparently saw its own reflection in the window, and promptly leaped through the glass pane. Finding itself in the lounge of Mr Leslie Tincknell, a homely place with a fire just lit in the grate, it promptly proceeded to run amok, covered in blood and broken glass, causing £1,000 damage to curtains, carpets and a three-piece suite. Mr Tincknell and his wife, in the kitchen didn't hear a thing. *D.Express + D.Mail + D.Telegraph* 26 Nov 79.

More trouble with a ewe at Beeches Farm, Hesket Newmarket, Cumbria. Miss Ella Todhunter was up a step-ladder painting the kitchen walls when she heard her brother Joe and his son Arthur having trouble with a sheep outside. Leaving the paint-pot at the top of the ladder, she went out to help. The sheep promptly made a break for it, ran into the kitchen, tangled itself with the step-ladder and covered itself with white paint. Ella, Joe and Arthur proceeded to chase the sheep round the kitchen, leaving a trail of footprints and a pool of paint in the middle of the carpet; and naturally, the furniture got painted every time the sheep touched it. They finally got it outside and started to load it on a truck when its painted fleece slipped through their fingers. Off went the ewe again, this time entering the kitchen through the (closed) window . . . and landed right in the pool of paint. Round and round go the pursuers; round the kitchen, out into the hall, back into the kitchen . . . white paint everywhere. Yes, they did finally get it onto the truck. *S.Express* 4 May 80.

• **Deer**: Cockeysville, Maryland: obviously outraged by the hunting licences on display at Fred Forsyth's sports shop, a deer hurled itself through the front window, smashed a glass cabinet and several fishing rods, and was finally cornered and shut up in a storage room. When two policemen arrived, the deer leaped through another window and escaped back to the woods. *Herald Tribune* 23 Oct 80.

• **Moose**: Saulte Sainte Marie, Ontario: a moose leaped through the window of a launderette, scattering customers and laundry as it rampaged around, before jumping back out the window and departing for the woods, leaving a trail of laundry. *D.Telegraph* 19 May 80.

• **Horses**: Stray horses made a meal of Alex Curtis' Piper turbo plane when he left it at Doncaster racecourse, causing £2,000 damage as they chewed both wings, the rudder, and anti-static devices. *D.Star* 20 Aug 80.

• **Bulls**: A bullock escaped from Cambridge cattle market and rampaged for 36 hours before recapture; during which time it dented two police cars, demolished a brick wall, trampled down 6 gardens and knocked down a cyclist who broke an ankle. *D.Telegraph* 29 Nov 79.

'Bull Wrecks China Shop' reads the headline (honest!). The 18-month-old bull escaped from a cattle market in Otley, Yorkshire, and headed for Peter Jordan's shop, coming in through the door like a normal customer but then knocking over cabinets of china, crushing coffee tables and destroying lamps and ornaments. It was finally lured away with a young heifer. *D.Telegraph + D. Star* 25 Sept 80.

• **Elephants**: And finally, biggest of all . . . voting had to be suspended at a polling station in central Tanzania when an elephant strolled in, scattering voters and officials. Maybe it mistook the place for a phone booth . . . wanted to make a trunk call, y'see (Sorry).

Credits: *Paul Burd, Helen Coles, Chris Hall, GPL, Valerie Martin, Sam, Paul Screeton, Dwight Whalen* •SM.

PHENOMENOMIX
"IT IS WITH TREPIDATION THAT I COMMENCE THIS NARRATIVE.... FEAR OF AWESOME CONSEQUENCES TO THE STATE OF MY IMMORTAL SOUL THAT THE REVELATIONS I AM ABOUT TO MAKE WILL BRING UPON ME.... NEVERTHELESS, I CAN NO LONGER REMAIN SILENT! THE WORLD MUST KNOW OF THE TERRIBLE DANGER THAT AWAITS THE INNOCENT WHO VENTURES TO CROSS.....
...THE BORDERS OF BUFFOONERY!
"MY TALE BEGINS IN THE SUMMER OF 1955. I WAS A FREELANCE APPRENTICE ON HOLIDAY BY THE SEA..."
...where the brass bands play tiddly om-pom-pom... HMM! WOTS THIS?
KWAK
"IT WAS A BROOCH OF CURIOUS DESIGN..."
"I WAS INTRIGUED BY THE TRINKET, AND MADE A FEW ENQUIRIES OF THE LOCALS AS TO ITS ORIGIN."
'ERE, SUNSHINE, EVER SEEN ONE OF THESE BEFORE? 'OW MUCH D'YOU FINK IT'S WORTH?
...TELL YOU WHAT, CHUM - I'LL LET YOU 'AVE IT FOR THIRTY BOB!
"WHEN I AWOKE, I WAS IN SOME SORT OF COMPARTMENT! THERE WAS NO APPARENT LIGHT SOURCE, AND DOORS KEPT APPEARING AND DISAPPEARING!"
AHA! GOT ONE IN THE RIGHT PLACE AT LAST! NOW, YOU! WHERE DID YOU GET THIS BADGE?
I... I FOUND IT! gulp! WOT IS IT? I DON'T KNOW WHAT IT IS...
IT'S THE SECRET SYMBOL OF THE ANCIENT ORDER OF BUFFOONS!
WE RULE DA WORLD, MAN...
YES, WE RULE THE WORLD... AT LEAST, NOT US, EXACTLY... NOT WE TWO.... I MEAN, WE OWE OUR ALLEGIANCE TO TH' GRAND BUFFOON!
WE'S KINDA BUFFOONETTES YA MIGHT SAY..
Hey, Lon! Whip me up a window, will ya?..
HOW'S THAT! YUP! WE'VE RUN THINGS FER AGES! WORKING SECRETLY FROM POSITIONS NEAR THRONES, WITH TECHNOLOGY ALWAYS IN ADVANCE OF THE REST OF THE WORLD, WE'VE BEEN RESPONSIBLE FOR EVERY MAJOR SPANNER IN THE WORKS IN HISTORY!
AN' WE MANIPULATE HISTORY LIKE DIS!

NOW LET ME GET THIS STRAIGHT! I'M ABOARD A FLYING SAUCER RUN BY AN ANCIENT SECRET SOCIETY THAT RUNS TH' WORLD!
'AT'S RIGHT!
OK, SO HOW MANY OF YOU LOONIES ARE THERE AROUND?
A FEW! WE CAN ALWAYS TELL A BUFFONIC BROTHER BY OUR SECRET SIGNAL....
THE BUFFONIC NUDGE! ...geddit?...
...BUT ALREADY YOU KNOW TOO MUCH!....
"WHEN I AWOKE, I WAS IN A CAVERN, THE VAST SIZE OF WHICH WAS DOMINATED BY A BIZARRE AND NAUSEATING ALTAR...."
'ERE! WHAT'S THE DIFFERENCE BETWEEN A HORSE AND A HAIRBRUSH?
EEEP!! ...er... I dunno...
WELL, THERE YOU ARE! NOW, YOU WANT TO KNOW OUR HISTORY!
NO, I WANT TO GO HOME....
...YOU'LL FIND THAT OUT LATER! FIRST, I'LL TELL YOU SOMETHING OF OUR METHODS!
WE OPERATE SUBVERSIVELY ON TWO LEVELS....
...PSYCHOLOGICALLY, BY DESTROYING THE BRAINS OF ENTIRE POPULATIONS WITH WEAPONS SUCH AS THE KNOCK-KNOCK JOKE,...
YOU FIENDS!
...AND TECHNOLOGICALLY, WITH OUR SUPERIOR POWER SOURCE – NUCLEAR RIDICULE! -an explanation of which follows...
"IN NUCLEAR FISSION, SUB-ATOMIC PARTICLES ARE ACCELERATED, AND SMASHED WITH GREAT FORCE INTO OTHER HAPLESS PARTICLES..."
Say a prayer, atom!
"...NUCLEAR RIDICULE INVOLVES SUBSTITUTING SUB-MICROSCOPIC CUSTARD PIES FOR PARTICLES. THE DEBUNKING AND EMBARRASSMENT RECEIVED BY THESE EGO-INFLATED PARTICLES PROVIDES THE POWER TO OPERATE MACHINES WHICH YOU MERE MORTALS CAN ONLY APPRECIATE AS MAGIC!"
...BUT ALREADY YOU KNOW TOO MUCH!...
HAVEN'T YOU GUYS EVER HEARD OF CHLOROFORM??!
BLONG!
continued next issue!..............

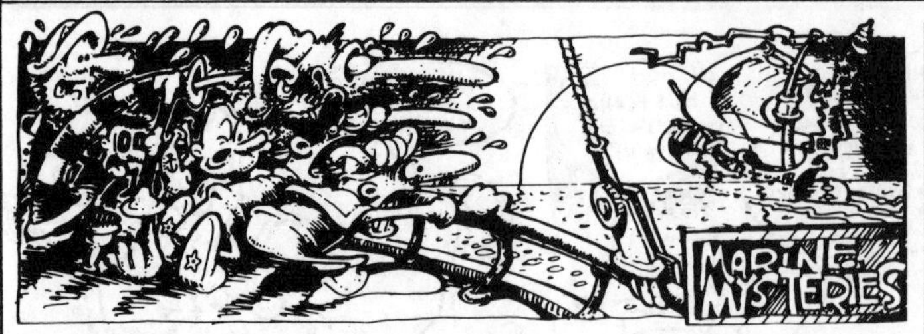

We have not presented any material on whale beachings for some time. Despite constant research and concern the cause of the beachings remains a mystery.

ON THE BEACH

The sight of a stranded school of whales must be numbered among the most pathetic scenes on this earth, made worse when individuals who are valiantly towed back out to sea turn and beach themselves again. They can take several days to die; their lungs and internal organs crushed by their body bulk, no longer supported by their natural buoyancy, or lying in pools of their own blood leaking through the cuts and blisters sustained by their beaching or by exposure to the air and sun. As a consequence of the flock of scientists descending on the beaching at Florence, Oregon (see listing below), to take their samples, marine scientists now have a better picture of what happens to a beached whale. The main cause of death is not asphyxiation, as previously thought, but slow cooking! Deborah Duffield, assistant professor of biology at Portland State University, said, on the anniversary of the Florence beaching, that whales produce a high degree of metabolic heat, normally dispersed through their flukes and flippers – but once out of water their internal organs are cooked in their own heat because air was a much poorer conductor of heat than water. *Oregonian* (Portland, Oregon) 21 June 1980.

But these esteemed vulture-scientists could offer no insight into *why* whales should beach themselves in the first place – a question that has puzzled many marine biologists and generated many theories. Some suggest suicide; or that they are following a squid (a favoured food) into warmer waters; or that they were following a leader who was ill and disoriented; or searching for a leader who had died and drifted away; or they were suffering from parasite infestations of their 'sonar' organs; or that an undersea quake had disoriented them. Martin Sheldrick, curator of marine mammals at the British Museum (Natural History), was interviewed in the *Daily Express* 19 June 1979, about his opinion of the various theories. He said there was no evidence to support the idea of mass suicide. Nor does he rate parasites of the ear. 'I have examined many strandings and have always cut open the sinuses of the dead whales to look for parasites. So far I've found no stranding that could have been caused by them.' He has known sick whales to come inshore to warmer waters to recuperate, but thinks the idea of a mass illness unlikely. He believes that beachings are probably caused by the whales being fooled by their sensitive sonar, and notes that most strandings involve deep-water ocean-going species who may be inexperienced and confused by the different sonar effects when they come into shallow waters, and follow their leader to their death.

In the Baja California case (see listing), Millie Payne, of the American Cetacean Society, suggested that perhaps one whale got itself stranded and sent out a distress call. Whales are known to be extremely loyal, and in coming to the rescue, landed themselves in the same predicament. *Sunday Express* 14 Jan 1979. The only other theory, mentioned during the Florence beaching by one *AP* report of 18 July 1979, was that the animals had come too far inshore during a high tide and had been caught by the change of tide. I find it hard to believe that intelligent marine beings would not know about changing tides, or be that slow to react when they realized their danger. The persistence with which whales, towed back to sea, return to certain death, suggests some kind of volition... or else possession! One could also ask if they were trying to get away from something in blind terror – or if they could be depressed by the pollution of their environment by the (supposedly) more intelligent creature on earth? Some time soon we will dip into our 'Marine Mysteries' file and attempt a correlation with mystery sounds and other underwater disturbances, many of which must be manmade – perhaps secret military experiments – which are producing dramatic effects in surprising places.

BEACHINGS – A LISTING

We are told that there are about 50 strandings a year on coasts around Britain; most of them single whales, and about half of those dead or dying before they reach our shores. Beachings of single whales therefore seems a natural and understood phenomenon. Much more rare and interesting are the mass beachings, the reason for which continues to mystify.

As a preface to the following listing of the mass beachings known to us over the last two years, we would like to mention a little synchronicity. Early in 1980, on successive days, 6 dead whales were washed up in different parts of England's southern coast – 11 Feb at Bembridge and 12 Feb at Brook, both on the Isle of Wight; 13 Feb, Barton-on-Sea, Hants; 14 Feb, Southsea, Hants;

15 Feb, Hastings, Sussex; and 18 Feb at Marine Parade, Hythe, Dorset. The species are not positively known or mentioned by the press – but there are hints that the first was a sperm whale and the last a baby blue whale, the rest being pilot whales. They had all been dead a long time and drifted in like stragglers from disaster far out in the ocean's depths. Cause of death was unknown; the favourite theory – arsenic poisoning, allegedly from the wreck of the *Aeolian Sky* (4 Nov 1979, off Portland, Dorset), was discounted after forensic tests (see papers for 20 Feb 1979). The coincidences we noted were, first, the conjunction between Portland, Dorset, and Portland, Oregon, in connexion with whale deaths; and second, that only the day before the first of the British beachings the *Sunday Telegraph* (10 Feb 1980) mentioned the launch of a nationwide campaign to save stranded whales, porpoises and dolphins.

An aerial view of the Florence, Oregon, beaching.

- **2nd week Jan 1979** – Mulege, Baja California, Mexico – 56 sperm whales. *S. Express* 14 Jan 79.
- **16 June 1979** – Florence, Oregon – 41 sperm whales. Reports said sperm whales rarely seen off Oregon coast, and claimed this was the largest stranding in the US (or is it *on* the US?). Greenpeace said that due to the depleted numbers of sperm whales this was 'a major loss to the whales.' They consisted of males and females between 2–35 years old; there were no infants in the group. *AP* 17 June; London *Eve. Standard* 18 June; *Int. Herald Tribune + D. Express* 19 June 1979.
- **15 July 1979** – Point au Gaul, Newfoundland – 170+ pothead whales. They were in two groups on the shore. Fishermen in boats managed to discourage another group of 60+, heading them off into deep water. *Int. Herald Tribune* 17 & 19 July; Manchester *Eve. News* 18 July 1979.
- **24 August 1979** – Trigalow Beach, Western Australia – 13 killer whales. Discovered early morning by camping fisherman woken by their 'squeals and grunts'. Bently said a school of about 400 had been in the area all week. 'They did not appear to be hurt or sick, they were just washing around in the shallows.' Two years previously 19 sperm whales beached on the same spot. Melbourne *Age* 29 Aug 1979.
- **1 July 1980** – Treachery Head, New South Wales – 60+ pilot whales. This beach north of Sydney is said (by report) to be 'a favourite beaching place for whales'. Sometime, when TOAD becomes operational, we'll run a check on repeated beachings at specific locations. *Int. Herald Tribune* 2 July; *Times* 3 July 1980.

Credit: Greg Axford, Lionel Beer, Donald Boates, James Chambers, Loren Coleman, Dave Fideler, Bob Forrest, Alan Gardiner, Paul Pinn, Sam, Paul Screeton, Ion Will.
RJMR.

Our last aggregate of ice-bombs fell within *FT27*. We have accumulated another impressive wad of data-on-the-rocks . . . Next time in 'Falls' we'll have frogs and veg.

30 August 1979, Virginia – a large hole was punched through the roof of Lewis Simms' home, near Fredericksburg, 75 miles south of Washington DC, by an object from the sky which was described as '30 inches wide' and 'as big as a five gallon bucket.' Simms' neighbour, David Brooks, witnessed the fall: 'I was standing outside washing my car when I heard a noise... like something travelling at high speed. When I looked up, it was coming in at an angle over my neighbour's house. It made a whistling noise then it crashed through their roof.' The Simmses were out when Brooks went to investigate. He found another hole in the dining room ceiling, insulation scattered everywhere, and lumps of ice on the carpet. He gathered some fragments and put them in his freezer. Federal Aviation Authority (FAA) spokesman Fred Farrar said nonchalantly that the ice-bomb was probably the result of 'a defective airplane toilet system', and, he said, it happens so often he would have 'accepted the incident without even viewing the evidence.' Just which of the many interpretations of this statement he meant we don't know! Farrar added helpfully: 'It could have been more serious... a chunk [that] size could certainly have killed someone.' *Washington Post* 30 Aug 1979.

22 September 1979, Sweden – A man working in a potato field at Kinna, some 20km east of Lanuetter airport, was narrowly missed by a large chunk of blue ice which embedded itself into the ground near him, splitting into three pieces. The original was estimated to weigh about 6kg and be about 25cm in diameter, being roundish in shape. These details were sent to us by local UFO investigator Bengt-Olof Liden, from the *Boras Tidning* 23 + 25 Sept 1979. Liden learned of the case too late – police had taken away fragments and let them melt away in the station's bathroom!

15 March 1978, France – A block of ice said to weigh 25 kilos, fell into a field near Abbeville, Somme. Farmhands in the hamlet of Becquerel heard a 'violent detonation' about 10.30am and rushed to the field, where they found the huge block, intact, in a crater. It melted in a short time under the hot sun. Fragments were sent for analysis but no more has been heard. *Le Soir* 16 March 1978.

14 April 1980, Hampshire – While ground level temperature soured to an unseasonal 72°F, the home of the Fox family, at Lyndhurst was ice-bombed, at about 3pm. The Foxes were out at the time the bucket-sized lump of ice smashed through roof and ceiling, splitting a rafter and strewing large ice pieces over their bedroom floor. Other fragments were found in the garden. A neighbour claimed he heard a whistling noise and looked up to see 'a vapour trail' leading to a 'loud explosion over Fox's roof.' Edward Fox kept a piece in his freezer, but no one called to take it for analysis. Civil Aviation Authority (CAA) men were said to be trying to trace a plane that might have dropped the ice. Kenneth Treasurer, of the New Forest District Council responsible for the property, alluded to 'similar incidents of falling ice in Ringwood last year [1979], and in Cadnam in the previous year [1978],' but said he had no further details. We interpret: these cases too were from planes which proved untraceable! *D.Star, D.Express, D.Telegraph, Sun, South Wales Argus* 15 April; *New Milton Advertiser & Lymington Times* (Hants) 19 April 1980.

1 May 1980, Yorkshire – in a letter to us a young UFO investigator, David Clarke, of Handsworth, Sheffield, says that on this day a block of ice measuring roughly 1 ft by 2 ft fell next to him on his lawn on an otherwise cloudless summer's day. It shattered and melted away in half an hour. He did not notice any planes in the sky – nor, sad to say, did he photograph the celestial remains.

9 May 1980, California – Another witness washing his car; this time Matthew Grossman, of Lido Beach, who was shocked when a six-inch chunk of ice shattered his shatterproof car roof. He says he saw a 4-engined plane above at the time, but could not identify it. An FAA investigator examined one of the pieces of ice Grossman preserved in his freezer, and said he 'believed' it came from a plane. It could be that *this time* we have a genuine case of ice-from-a-plane... p'raps. *Newsday* (NY) 10 May 1980.

End of May or first days of June 1980, Denmark – 'Frozen object' hits lawn 'at 150 mph', at Aarhus, just missing mother and daughter. 'Scientists' say it comes from plane loo. No other details. *Sunday Mirror* 8 June 1980.

28 July 1980, Warwickshire — In the early hours, a huge ice chunk punched a hole in the roof of Mrs Edith Sweet's home, in Leamington Spa, emerging through her bedroom ceiling and shattering the floor. Despite widespread coverage, appallingly few details reported. *D.Mirror, D.Star, D.Express, D. Telegraph, Shropshire Star, Bristol Evening Post* all 29 July 1980.

17 August 1980, Pennsylvania– A large block of ice falls from sky into country club swimming pool at Glen Mills. No more known. London *Evening News* 18 Aug 1980.

26 August 1980, Massachusetts –12-year-old John McClennan, playing in front of his home in Holliston, at about 11.45, heard a 'whoosh' and saw three white blurrs hit the ground about 20ft away. Terrified, he ran indoors, then he and his family investigated. There were three balls of ice – 'one as big as a softball, the other two as large as baseballs' – with a yellowish surface and pink center. They were removed to the family freezer, and from thence, by state police, for analysis. The analysis was given later as: '99% water and 1% vegetable matter'. John remembers no plane in the vicinity, and an FAA spokesman, Stan McDonnough, confirmed that Holliston is five miles from the nearest flight corridor. McDonnough, deputy public affairs officer of the FAA, alluded to the usual theory of ice forming on planes, but — unusual for official spokespersons – acknowledged that this did not really account for this incident; plane-ice is mainly in sheet form, not spherical, and does not carry vegetable matter, he said. *Middlesex News* (Framingham, Mass) 11 Sept 1980.

11 October 1980, Essex – At 5.15pm, Ray Wood and friends, on the second fairway of the golf course at Romford, were shocked when a 'huge' block of ice landed a few yards away. 'We had just played our second

(Above) 14 April 1980 – Mrs Jennifer Fox gazes at her ruined ceiling holding one of the culprit's remains. [Photo: Copyright Simon Rowley.] (Below) 28 Sept 1980 – Keith Fox inspects the 2ft hole in his bedroom ceiling. [Photo: Copyright Western Morning News.]

shot and there was a hissing noise, then an almighty thud. We turned around and there were lots of ice chunks, each about the size of a cricket ball. We stood in amazement for a few seconds. The ice block left an enormous hole in the ground.' One of the friends estimated the original size was at least 'two foot square'. London Weather Center said: 'It could only be hail, or ice falling from aircraft.' A hail event consisting of one large hailstone would be an interesting and unusual datum in itself, but beyond their automatic reflex/response the weather men showed no interest at all. Ray said: 'There wasn't an explanation. The sky was blue, without a cloud in sight, and there were no planes about.' *Evening Echo* (Essex) 19 Sept 1980 – also investigated by Essex ufologists, see report in *Earthlink* winter 79/80.

28 September 1980, Devon – At 8.50am, Mrs Sandra Fox was in bed, in her Plymouth home, her two children playing on the bedroom floor, when the ceiling exploded showering ice and debris over the whole room. They could see the sky through the hole in the roof. The main chunk 'embedded itself' in the floor just two foot from the children. 'It could have been very nasty,' she said. At the same time, a second ice-bomb plunged into the bungalow of elderly Miss Winifred Pidgeon, at nearby Rosborough, while she was having breakfast in her kitchen. A neighbour, who witnessed the fall while pegging out her washing, said she heard five distinct noises 'like the screaming of shells' before she saw one block of ice hit Miss Pidgeon's roof. No aircraft were noticed at the time. We could have here a comparatively rare event of a multiple icefall–if the five noises represent five hurtling chunks, then only two are accounted for; the others probably fell, unobserved, into fields. We also note some incidental wordplay: this is the second recent case involving a family by the name of Fox (see back to 14 April 1980, above); and the curious conjunction of Fox and Pidgeon in this story!

Apart from the sources mentioned below, these details were confirmed to us by local UFO investigators Terry Cox and his wife, in a report dated 7 Oct 1980. Terry learned that council repairmen, who arrived to put a tarpaulin over the roof damage, also removed the ice. We know of no photograph of, or attempt to analyse, the fragments – a regrettable omission in view of the uncorroborated intelligence that one of the pieces was so large it took two men to carry it out of the Foxes' house. Once again the plane-theory was trotted out, and once again was seen the pseudo-miracle of something so insubstantial apparently satisfying all concerned – everyone except Forteans, of course! *Western Morning News* 2 Oct; *Shropshire Star* 3 Oct 1980.

Terry Cox also supplied the following information. 'In the same area of Rosborough, at about midnight on the 2nd October, following the icefall, Mrs Dawn Swinburne, of Marchants Way, saw four UFO-type objects in the clear night sky flashing white and blue. After remaining stationary for a few minutes the lights moved off in a westerly direction towards Cornwall. At the same time she was aware of a high-pitched whine. Her sister, who lives nearby and who was outside tending her pony shortly before the time of this sighting, 'felt a presence' which, for no apparent reason, made her neck-hairs rise.

9 Dec 1980 – Kenneth Anderton holds the 1½lb 'ice ball' which dented his garden. [From Birmingham Evening Mail

9/10 December 1980, Birmingham – The Anderton family, of Kings Norton, find a 12-inch circumference lump of ice in a dent on their back lawn. It had arrived during the night, narrowly missing their greenhouse. It weighed 1lb 6oz. The paper calls it a 'hailstone' – a spokesman for Birmingham University meteorology department said it fell off an aircraft. Take your pick... or neither. *Birmingham Evening Mail* 10 Dec 1980.

16 December 1980, Merseyside– a 90-year-old widow, Mrs Mary Nickson, escaped certain death when a 'football-sized' boulder of ice crashed into her West Kirby house, bursting through her bedroom ceiling showering her with plaster and ice. A spokesperson for Liverpool's Speke Airport said: 'The last time this happened the ice was found to be the contents of an aeroplane lavatory.' We suspect that if this spokesperson was pressed he would not be able to name the case, which, if it existed, would be the first time such a positive identification had been proved. This is typical of the way 'experts' bamboozle an unknowing public, suggesting mysteries have been solved when they are only referring to *theories* and not fact. So it goes. Motto: Be vigilant. *Western Mail, Shropshire Star, D.Mirror* 17 Dec 1980.

Credits: *Janet & Colin Bord, Keith Chapham, David Clarke, Loren Coleman, Terry Cox, Michael Diamond, Dan Goring, Peter Hope-Evans, Bengt-Olof Liden, Henri Premont, Al Rosenzweig & Phyllis Benjamin, Simon Rowley, Sam, Jeff Saward, Paul Screeton, Paula Simons, David Sutton, PR Thomas, Andy Townsend* • **RJMR.**

Although not really Fortean in the strict sense, the following stories of hopelessly muddled Fate appeal to our Fortean humour. This is a selection from our 'Inept Crime' file . . .

AMERICAN DISASTERS

• Back in 1978, Willard Dillon had a bad day in Chicago. He dropped his gun twice during the hold-up of a local store, shot and missed a customer who gave chase, ran out of petrol and had to push his getaway car into a gas station where the attendant refused to serve him because it was closing time. Then he was arrested.

• In July last year, a gunman grabbed 180 dollars from a Los Angeles shop. As he fled, the bag containing the money burst scattering the cash, his shotgun fell apart leaving the butt behind and his mask fell off. 90 minutes later he returned with his driver to pick up the pieces, and walked into the arms of the police. *Rand Daily Mail* 23 Mar 78; *Eve.News* 9 Jul, *Guardian* & *Glasgow Herald* 10 Jul 1980.

BRITISH BUNGLERS

• Two men raided a jeweller's shop in Dorchester and drove off in a getaway car. After a while they got lost in the one-way system, gave up in despair and started to hitch. They were in court in June.

• In October another man was being chased by police in Southend. He took a wrong turning into the central police station car park and was trapped there when the gates were shut.

• The previous month, three bandits laid wait for a wages van in North London. They had remembered the pickaxe handle and the crowbar . . . but where were their balaclava disguises?! Two of them rushed down to the shops to buy new ones, but when they returned the wages van had been and gone. All three got four years, nonetheless. *D.Telegraph* 13 June; *Eve.News* 20 Oct; *D. Mirror* 13 Sep 1980.

TARTAN TERROR

• In October, seven men calling themselves the 'Scottish Republican Socialist League' were jailed for their inept antics. During the robbery of £100,000 from a security van, two of them got locked in, and they had to get the driver to let them out. A mask slipped from the face of a raider and he was subsequently recognised by a witness. An electronic bug was wrongly connected to a wire leading to an explosives depot and cut the firm's telephone.

Attempting to blow up the Scottish Assembly Building in Edinburgh, they forgot where the building was, failed to load their guns, and were frightened off by an inquisitive bus party and a drunk who kept poking his head into their car.

Seeking advice from the IRA, they were scornfully rejected. The 40-pound home-made bomb they took with them so scared the IRA experts that they all ran from the building after one look at it. Ten minutes later it exploded, but only blew out the windows of the room. They telephoned the fire brigade to put out the flames and were arrested. *D. Telegraph* 23 Sep, 15, 16, 19 Oct; *Guardian* 15 Oct 1980.

TOY GUN ANTICS

• Clive Bunyan burst into a store in Main St, Cayton, near Scarborough and brandished a toy revolver. He got the shop assistant to hand over £157 from the till, and fled. He had his motorbike parked for a fast getaway and wore his full-face crash helmet as a mask. He had forgotten, however, that around his helmet in inch-high letters were the words 'Clive Bunyan – Driver'. He was easy to find. In November he was ordered to do 200 hours community service.

• Edward McAlea of Liverpool went into a jewellers in that city with a stocking mask on; pointed a revolver at three men and warned them 'This is a stick-up. Get down.' They didn't bother, because all of them saw a red plastic stopper in the muzzle and realised it was a toy. After a scuffle, McAlea escaped, pulling the mask from his face. The jeweller recognised him as a customer of the previous day. *D.Star* 15 Nov; *D.Telegraph* 9 Feb 1980.

• The gun in the following episode might have been real, but it was all the same to David Sell. Mr Sell, an assistant bank manager in Watton, Norfolk, was leaving work when a masked man drove up and told him to open the bank door. Mr Sell ignored him. Another man pointed what appeared to be a Sten gun and warned him he would fire. Mr Sell ignored him too, and kept walking. The masked men drove off. *D. Telegraph* 8 Aug 1980.

SAFE WORK

• David Barber from Bath worked all night on a steel and concrete reinforced safe at the Cheltenham Co-op, and finally broke through to find that it had been unlocked all the time, and was empty anyway. By this time it was daylight, and to make himself inconspicuous he joined a group of joggers on a run around some waste ground, but he was still carrying his bag of burglar's tools. He hid it, schoolboys found it and police bugged it. They nabbed him after a chase. He was already on bail for trying to smuggle morphine from

India.

• The night raid on the safe of a leisure centre office in Chichester, Sussex, began cunningly enough. The gang stole a £3,000 speedboat, used water skis to paddle it across a lake, picked up their gear and paddled back to the office. But they had mistaken welding gear for cutting equipment and sealed the safe shut. The staff had to attack the safe with a hammer and cold chisel for an hour to get it open again. *D.Telegraph & Sun* 7 Mar; *D.Mirror* & *D.Star* 26 Aug 1980.

FINGERED

• During a smash-and-grab raid on a Zurich jeweller, the thief had his finger cut off by broken glass as he scooped up a tray of rings. The police identified the finger from their files and arrested the thief within two hours. Another man had left his finger behind in the mouth of his strangled victim in Ogden, Utah, in July, but I don't know if they have caught up with him. *Sun.People* 19 Oct; *Malden News* (Mass) 11 Jul 1980.

CAUGHT NAPPING

• Thomas Schimmel came home in Texas City, Michigan, to find his pocket watch and rifle missing. He called the police who came to investigate, then headed for bed, where he found the 19-year-old theif fast asleep.

• Three youths in Amherst, Nova Scotia, stripped down several cars in a used-car lot overnight and stuffed several hundred dollars worth of parts into the boot of their own car. They fell asleep in the car, only to be awoken by police.

• Lazaros Alberis, 25, was discovered in an Athens cinema sleeping over the cash register which he had tried to open with a pair of scissors. *Midnight Globe* 23 Jan 1979; *The Globe & Mail* (Canada) 5 Feb; London *Eve.News* 7 Aug 1980.

THE FLORIDA BUM

• A man kept his motor running and the parcel well in view as he passed a note to the Florida drive-in bank's cashier. She frowned, squinted and went away to get help. 'I got a bum,' the note read. 'I can blow you sky height. This is a held up.'

As bank staff puzzled over the scrawled ultimatum, the man's nerve broke and he fled. Some hours later he was back at another drive-in bank. This time the note was typewritten for clarity, but the words were still wrong. The cashiers still couldn't make them out and the man fled again, leaving behind his 'bum' – a broken transistor radio. *D.Mail* 15 Oct 1980.

MUGGER RUINS SUICIDE

• A 35-year-old Johannesburg woman had been sitting in her car writing farewell letters while carbon monoxide poured into the vehicle through a hose attached to the exhaust, when a man dragged her out, threatened her with a knife and stole about £20. She managed to drive away, but crashed into a fence and was being treated in hospital for minor injuries and depression. *D.Telegraph* 22 Jan 1980.

CARRY ON SPYING

• *Izvestia* on 27 March last year accused two CIA agents, Weatherby and Corbin, of concealing electronic sensing and broadcasting devices inside an artificial tree stump to spy on a Soviet defence installation. The agents gave the game away by their ignorance of Russian flora: their fake pine stump was put in an aspen grove, something very rare in Russia. *Times* 28 Mar 1980.

Credits: *James Chambers, J Chetwynd, Judy Cordell, Chris Hall, Chris Holtzhausen, Sam, Andy Townsend, Roland Watson, Dwight Whalen* • **PRAdeGS.**

Continued from p 25

Evening Express 8 Dec 1980.

Curiously, that same day, a Drumnadrochit grocer, Jimmy Cameron, stopped his van at a layby on the A82 (to Inverness), after making one of the few sightings of Nessie in 1980. 'It was like a submarine with its periscope up and only 60ft from the shore'. In the few seconds before he stopped, he saw 'its head and neck were about 3ft out of the water and behind was a long body. Its skin was black and appeared smooth . . . By the time I had parked the beast had disappeared without a trace'. This was his first sighting of Nessie in the 32 years he has used this road. But what was going on – a meeting of monsters? Aberdeen *Evening Express* 8 Dec 1980.

• 7 Dec 1980 – Sighting of a 'puma-like' animal' in Glen Urquhart, between Cannich and Loch Ness. Retired shipping company director, Ralph Duggan, and his wife, encountered the beast on the banks of the River Enrick, near Balnain – just a few miles from the previous sighting. Duggan found prints, took photographs and made casts. One of these was said to 'match' (read 'be similar to') those of Noble's puma. Since Noble's puma had a good alibi, is this further confirmation of at least one other puma in the area? Aberdeen *Evening Express* 8 Dec; Aberdeen *Press & Journal, D. Record* 9 Dec 1980.

That is all we know to date. If all this has left you confused, bear with it – the next instalment may be unfolding right now!

Credits: *Norman Adams, Janet & Colin Bord, James Chambers, Peter Christie, Brian Hain, Chris Hall, Peter Hope-Evans, David Houston, Alan Gardiner, Mike Rickard, Paul Screeton, Doc Shiels, Martin Straw, David Sutton, PR Thomas, Andy Townsend, Roland Watson, Ion Will. Special thanks to J Lang for a valuable extensive coverage; and to David Smith who sent in a full-page comic based on the Corgarf incident, which unfortunately arrived too late for inclusion* • **RJMR.**

A BIRTHDAY GIFT FOR JULES VERNE

Almost forgetting for the moment all thoughts of Moby Dick, we now gazed at the most wondrous phenomenon which the secret seas have hitherto revealed to mankind. A vast pulpy mass, furlongs in length and breadth, of a glancing cream-colour, lay floating on the water, innumerable long arms radiating from its centre, and curling and twisting like a nest of anacondas, as if blindly to clutch at any hapless object within reach. No perceptible face or front did it have; no conceivable token of either sensation or instinct; but undulated there on the billows an unearthly, formless, chance-like apparition of life.

Herman Melville, in *Moby Dick*

With the above passage, Herman Melville's fictional pursuit of the great white whale paid homage to a far greater mystery, the many-armed sea monster, the *Kraken,* an animal stranger than fiction. Melville in *Moby Dick,* and Jules Verne in *20,000 Leagues Under the Sea,* were writing — in admittedly sensational terms —of antiquity's *Kraken,* a beast marvelled by the ancients, as we do the Loch Ness Monster today. We now know the tales of Homer's *Scylla,* Norway's *Kraken,* and Patagonia's *Cornet* were most probably the giant squid, *Architeuthis.*

There is some reason, however, for the continued reverence of the giant squid in modern times. *Architeuthis* is an extremely rare denizen of the deep seas, and certainly remains a mysterious one. That a giant squid should wash up on the shores of Plum Island early in February 1980, having not been seen near Massachusetts for some sixty-one years, has raised more questions than it has answered.

The discovery was one of those lucky scientific breaks naturalists wait a lifetime to make. Good fortune, indeed, for the inquiring staffs of the New England Aquarium and the Smithsonian Institution that this modern eighth wonder of the zoological world should beach itself on the well protected sands of the Parker River National Wildlife Refuge. Normally the Plum Island sanctuary is only a tranquil haunt for beachcomer and bird-watcher. Wildlife Ranger Al Zelly was therefore surprised when making his rounds that first Saturday morning in February to come upon the carcass of a giant squid. The ranger contacted the New England Aquarium, according to Liz Kay, Publicity Director, and as soon as they rounded up ten men, the 450 pound cream-coloured, tentacled pile of mush was taken by stretcher to Boston.

The squid was, so to speak, only a shadow of its former self. The massive mollusc was not as large as it once had been. Although its body measured some eight feet, plus eight more feet of pieces of tentacles, the two whip-like tentacles, as well as the ends of all of the other tentacles were missing. Dr. Kenneth Boss, a Harvard University biology professor with a special interest in mollusc zoology, told me he thought the tentacles may have been eaten off at the ends before the giant squid finally settled on the sands. Dr. Clyde Roper of the Smithsonian said the squid may have measured more than thirty feet in length before its unexplained death.

Giant squids are closely related to the little common squids so well-known from Japanese and Italian cookery, and have just larger versions of typical squid equipment — saucer-sized lidless eyes, a huge bird-like beak, large suction cups on its two long whip-like arms, eight tentacles, plus a jet-like apparatus used mainly for locomotion but also capable of squirting out the classic cloud of ink. Beyond its appearance, not much is known about the giant squid despite the efforts, for example, of Jacques Yves Cousteau, since the days of Jules Verne. The giant squid's digestive system (including the one from Plum Island) are usually found empty because they seem to work so fast. There are one or two reports of giant squids eating baby whales according to the research of another Frenchman, zoologist Dr. Bernard Heuvelmans, but more often than not, the squid serves as the entree for the whale.

In the bad ole days of whalers and factory whaling vessels, the killing of sperm whales often produced some amazing finds in the whales' stomachs. In 1895, Albert I of Monaco described the events which occurred after the killing of one such whale:

The ship now afloat in a hectare of reddish water, through which ran rivulets of a deeper hue as blood poured from the animal. The more intense color was dissipated, then blended into various tints, as clouds coming down from the mountains are confounded with fog on the plains.

The whale's gigantic head was alongside our stern, and its lower jaw, hanging loose

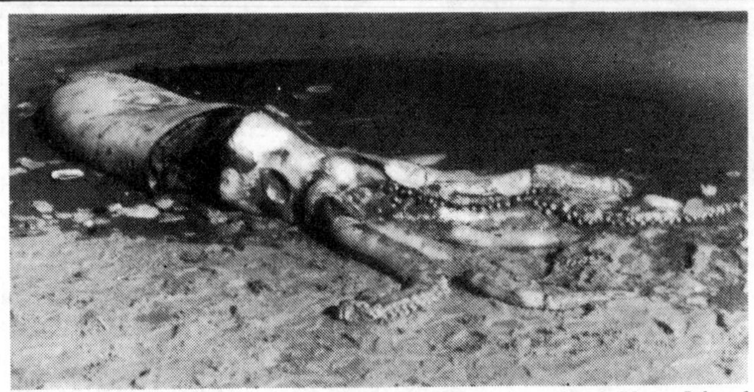

The remains of the squid, washed up on a beach at Plum Island, February 1980. [Photo: Carla Skindler, New England Aquarium.]

now that the muscles had relaxed, was moved by the action of the waves. I could see the mouth, likeayawning cavern. And I saw it vomit out, one after another, the bodies of several cephalopods – octopuses or squids – of colossal size. These, apparently, were the fruits of the whale's final plunge to the depths, following which it had been harpooned on the surface; a recent meal which had as yet hardly been affected by digestion.

Prince Albert had his naturalists gather the contents of this and many other whales' stomachs. Remarking on the investigations of the 'unpleasant mass' from the stomach of the abovementioned whale, Price Albert noted:

Toward the end, the naturalists' stomachs revolted in a faint echo of the event which, the day before, had given these treasures to science during the final spasms of the dying whale.

Prince Albert's scholars described many unknown species of giant squid as the result of their thorough though distasteful examinations. Others have made similar finds. In fact, one of the largest giant squids on record, a 65-footer, was discovered in the stomach of a sperm whale. Squid appears to be the sperm whale's favourite meal.

But Plum Island's giant squid apparently met its death in some other fashion. Beachings of giant squids in the Northeast are nothing new, but the reasons behind them are a puzzle. In Bernard Heuvelmans' indepth study on the subject, *Dans le Sillage des Monstres marins: Le Kraken et le Poule colossal,* he chronicles, among other items, the grand series of strandings and sightings of giant squid, on and near Newfoundland and Labrador, from 1871 to 1879. By comparison, the Plum Island squid is small fry. Dr. Heuvelmans notes one giant squid was recorded to have had an arm, alone, measuring 42 feet in length. Some fifty or sixty of the Newfoundland giant squids were cut up for cod bait before they could be examined and measured. Others were eaten by fish and gulls. The few which were properly inspected included the biggest stranded squid ever accepted by science — the Thimble Tickle specimen — with a body twenty feet long, arms 35 feet long, eyes 18 inches across, and a beak nine inches in diameter. Professor Addison Verrill of Yale took a special interest in these Newfoundland beachings, and his published works on the dead giant squids declared there were two distinct species involved.

But why the apparently senseless mass suicides Heuvelmans writes of in Newfoundland, or the recent one at Plum Island? Theories abound. Some feel a possible explanation may lie in the 'cold wall' where the Labrador Current meets the Gulf Stream. One researcher, C.G. Robson, found the giant squid tends to seek a water temperature of 10°C. Therefore, if a giant squid crosses the cold wall, it will naturally try to rise near the surface to reach warmer water but will only find the water is colder, and begin to die of cold. This may have been the cause of the Plum Island squid's death. The jet stream's continental weather changed radically around the first of February 1980 to a more normal winter pattern for the Northeast USA. The six previous weeks of moderate, dry temperatures may have seduced the giant squid into going farther north than it regularly would have. After the jet stream change, the squid may have been caught in colder waters and died.

Another interesting theory for the giant squid beachings comes from Frederick Aldrich, professor of zoology at Memorial University in St. John's, Newfoundland. His opinion is that every third decade the giant squid shows up in increased numbers, and then a rash of strandings and sightings occur. Professor Aldrich believes the next big wave will be in the 1990s. Perhaps Plum Island was their first beachhead. The squids may be choosing Massachusetts, not Newfoundland, as their next stomping grounds. Perhaps.

Whatever happens in the future, right now on exhibit indefinitely at the Harvard Museum of Comparative Zoology, you can view a true sea monster. Under the strange yellow lighting of the display, gaze for a moment at the beast, and look at a wonder few people have seen. Even Jules Verne who wrote of the giant 'poulps' with such emotion in *20,000 Leagues Under the Sea,* never viewed one, only read of the legend of the *Kraken.* It seems more than mere chance, then, that the ocean would choose a time so close to February 8th, Jules Verne's birthday to cast ashore such a treasure.

•

Loren Coleman

Killorglin's *Aonach an Phuic* is said to be the oldest fair in Ireland, where a great he-goat is crowned as the only king of Kerry and of all Ireland, a truly pagan Celtic king, the horned one. On Gathering Day, five members of the Shiels tribe, having travelled from Cornwall, France and Germany, came together in Sheehan's Bar where we fell in with the gypsy dukkerers, became beautifully drunk, and began to feel the magic coming back to us.

Three wild days and nights were spent at Puck Fair, playing music, clowning and conjuring, in the pubs and streets. During that time, we met Seamus Craagh ('Famous Seamus' the West Cork fiddler), and Eileen and Mary O'Donaghue (the Kerry gypsy-witches).

A couple of days after leaving Killorglin, I was walking down Killarney's High Street, when I heard a girl's voice, speaking Irish, behind me. *'Sin e an draidoir a chonaice-amair ar an aonach'* ('That's the magician we saw at the fair.') I turned and was greeted by Eileen and Mary. *'Conas taoi?* How's the Doc?' 'All the better for seeing you two,' says I, full of charm. Well... we met up with my wife, Chris, and my daughter, Meg, and had a couple of jars in Courtney's. It was then that Mary surprised us by asking: 'Will you be trying to conjure up a dragon from Lough Leane?' 'Why would I do such a thing?' I asked, innocently. The gypsy girls laughed and Eileen said, 'We know all about you and your family, Doc Shiels. We can even tell you your mother's maiden name, and we know you've raised dragons in Cornwall and Scotland.' 'That's amazing!' said I. 'Not really,' Mary replied, 'we had a long chat with your son, Ewan, at Killorglin, and he told us enough to make you a perfect punter for the palm reading.' 'Bloody tricksters!' I yelled. 'We're in the same game as yourself,' said Eileen, with a completely beguiling smile, 'and we are going to help you raise that *payshtha...* just for the crack.'

So that evening we pitched our tents in a secret place on the wooded shores of the lough, built a fire, cooked a huge pot of stew and tickled our brains with a drop of the pure stuff. Just before midnight, the O'Donaghue sisters began to sing a weird song. I didn't understand a single word of it, a strange, lonely air, ending very suddenly. A strong wind blew up, howling through the trees and lifting spray from the lough waves. I piled more logs on the fire which roared bright as a furnace. Then I spoke my own special words and the four women, sky-clad, walked into the water, calling up the *piast bestia.*

No water dragon showed itself... or, at least, we didn't see one. The storm grew more violent, the wind screaming through the woods like a banshee, tree-branches creaking and snapping, and strange animal sounds, barking and crying. Those four brave witches ran, shivering, ashore and quickly dressed, huddling round the fire, grabbing the poteen. 'Sod this for a game of bloody soldiers!' growled Chris, most unmagically. Then it began to rain. We buried the fire and took to our fiercely flapping tents.

The next day dawned, bright and calm. Mary and Eileen sang a morning song and we breakfasted on good Limerick rashers washed down with strong tea. Only Meg volunteered to take

Doc Shiels in the tall hat, and fellow busker at the Puck Fair, Killorglin, Co Kerry. [Photo: Courtesy of the Bord Failte (Irish Tourist Board.]

a dip that day. Still, no water monster raised its head in our sight, but, as Meg was swimming, a large black and white bird flew up from the lake and soared overhead for a minute before vanishing behind the trees. It was the size and shape of an albatross... that is to say, it *seemed* to be. It was, most definitely, *not* a swan, goose or heron. Its sudden appearance surprised us. I mean, we expected to raise a dragon but none of us thought we would see an albatross. Mary and Eileen insisted that it was an *ean sidh*... a fairy bird. I don't know, it looked like a flesh and feather albatross to me, however unlikely a visitor to the Killarney lakes such a bird might be.

Later in the day, we tramped into town to make some money. The gypsy girls danced as Meg and I... accompanied by Ashley Drees, mandolin-picker... played Kerry slides and polkas. We collected enough for that night's drink and the next day's food. Eileen and Mary set off for the Jug o' Punch to see Pecker Dunne, the legendary tinker fiddler and banjo player (Pecker, by the way, looks like a Sasquatch); Meg and Master Drees went to busk the Laurels pub; Chris and I went into Mrs Courtney's bar where we found Seamus Creagh and his girl friend, Pauline Dodds.

Seamus and Pauline had a strange tale to tell. Around twelve, the previous night, they had been driving into Ballyvourney when a large animal stepped into the road, in the full glare of the car's headlamps. 'Grey in colour. Shaggy coat. Tufted ears. Big... it looked just like a lynx... but you don't get lynxes in County Cork!' They were both extremely puzzled by the Ballyvourney Beast. As soon as they got home, Seamus and Pauline searched through an encyclopaedia until they found a picture of an animal which looked like the one they had seen... a lynx. I asked them to write out a statement and sign it (with FT in mind). Now, at that time, neither Seamus nor Pauline had any idea that I was a monster hunter; but the fact that they encountered their Hibernian Lynx at the very same time that we were trying raise a beastie in Lough Leane is, I'm sure, significant. We had first met Seamus in Killorglin, while we were re-building our shamanic confidence at the court of King Puck. A psychic connection had been established between us. Ballyvourney (Baile Bhuirne... the town of the stone place) is an ancient and magical village, having strong connections with the 'old religion'. Over one of the windows of the medieval church is a *sheela-na-gig*, a sure sign of paganism. It's just the sort of place for a mysterious creature to appear.

We talked of ancient sites, fairy raths and standing stones. I said to Chris that it would be good if we could spend some time on the Iveragh penninsula... the Ring of Kerry... which is full of such things. 'We need a rich American tourist to turn up and offer to take us round the Ring,' I joked. Seamus and I started to play, fiddle and tin whistle, jigs and reels. Within fifteen minutes, a big man came into the pub saying, 'I've travelled thousands of miles to hear some true Irish music. That's great!' This was our rich American (Irish-American to be exact), John, from North

The Dingle peninsula is riddled with ancient sites and standing stones, etc. During the heavy rainstorms of that weekend, one of these stones – at 'Buailtin na Deirce', Baile Bhointin, near Baile an Fheirtearaigh – ceased to stand. This photo of the fallen stone is from The Kerryman *15 Aug 1980.*

Dakota, who put a fiver in the hat, bought a vast amount of Guinness and, sure enough, offered to take us round the Ring of Kerry in his hired mini-bus.

Next day I hugged the stones of Iochtar Cuach.

The day after, I met a Sligo fiddler who said he'd seen my two mad sons in Dublin, astounding the crowds on Stephens Green with fire-spitting, bizarre songs and dances. Mary and Eileen were with them.

And the day after that, Chris, Meg, Ashley and I returned to our secret campsite by Lough Leane. Late at night, we were visited by a salmon-poacher, an old man, who, quite casually, told us that he'd seen the lough *payshtha* earlier that evening. 'What kind of animal is it?' I asked. 'It is no kind of animal at all,' he replied, 'it is a spirit, a ghost... *puca*... it has no solid form.' I asked him how many lakes, in Ireland, were haunted by such spirits. 'Every last one,' said he, 'and that's the truth, so it is.'

So it is.

•

Doc Shiels

Post script: Ireland certainly seems to be jumping with phenomenal zoological happenings. I just received the following note from a Miss Kathleen O'Shea, of Cork City, who heard about my interest in weird beasties from musician Tom Casey.

"Dear Mr Shiels. . . I have been told that you would like to know about something that I saw last month near Smerwick, on the Dingle peninsula (Corcaguiney), Co Kerry. It was Saturday the 9th August, around 4 p.m. I was walking towards Ballyferriter. The sky was dark with rain clouds. All at once it began to rain very heavily. I began to run to find shelter - then from behind a ditch [Cork usage, for a hedge] just a few yards before me, a giant black animal like a bat flew up. I screamed and fell forward. When I dared to open my eyes and stand up on my feet it had gone. I ran all the way to Ballyferriter . . ." In addition to the 'Beast of Ballyvourney' we now have the 'Big Black Bat of Ballyferriter.' This happened, of course, on the very day that Chris and I rolled into Co Kerry from Cork. Doc

. . . There are dragons beneath our cities, primordial energies greater than the power of our bombs. Two thousand years of Judeo-Christian soul-shaping and three centuries of crusading scientific intellect have gone into their interment. We had assumed them dead forgotten their presence, constructed our social order atop their graves. But now they wake and stir . . .

Thodore Roszak
Where the Wasteland Ends

This column is devoted to exploring the archaic subterranean forces which uneasily writhe behind the plastic facade of our throw-away civilization, and leak into consensus reality through the shallow holes of popular culture more often than we would like to admit. The Age of Electricity has liberated the double-faced power of the mercurial serpent, and it is all too easy these days for entire armies of media-ocrats to disco-dance their lives away to the collective beat of the Video Kundalini. 'Science does not remove the fear of the Gods' because the pagan dragons of instinct, or the transpersonal patterns of psychological experience, are much larger than the purely individual.

So with spear in hand, we seek to expose these spirits of the underworld who pull the strings of men; perhaps by barbing them repeatedly they will become less of a sinuous danger and more of a Cosmic Joke. To succeed we must cultivate a mind-revealing humour of the Lower Astral, or an occult comedy of cultural artifacts, psychic parasites, and video pathologies.

Only by acknowledging the Mind Parasites will we *ever* be safe!

THE AKASHIC TRASHED

To the contemporary occultist the world is composed of different 'planes' or levels of reality which range from the purely physical to the windy realms of the higher astral. Somewhere in between these qualitative poles is the etheric world of the Lower Astral, or the universal flux of cosmic libido, unstable Thought Forms, and other psychic refuse.

The occult description is not without value if it is (1) understood as metaphor (2) recognised as a perversion of traditional cosmology and (3) the 'astral plane' is seen to correspond to what we nowadays call the unconscious.

Occultism went from bad to worse when a German Theosophist with the name of Rudolf Steiner clairvoyantly tuned-into what he called 'the Akashic Records', where everything that has ever happened is permanently recorded in an Astral Data Bank, merely awaiting those who have the eyes-to-see! Some Forteans, such as Ion Alexis Will, call this etheric cesspool the Trashkashic Records, for the simple reason that *every singular mundane event* is said to be recorded. Obviously, there is no quality control in heaven!

TOWARD A PSYCHOPATHOLOGY OF THE LOWER ASTRAL

The universal foundation for the Astral Parasite motif in popular culture lies in the psychological realm, or to be more precise, in the existence of feeling-toned psychological complexes which may escape self-recognition. According to archetypal psychology, complexes are normal mental phenomena and the very origin of self-consciousness itself. But some complexes may have a negative, possessive influence. A flimsy ego and lack of self reflection – often apparent in mediums and contactee types – produces a type of personality that is easily overcome and modulated by the subterranean dragons.

Regarding the autonomy of mental complexes, Carl Jung observes the following in *The Structure and Dynamics of the Psyche:*

'. . . In a word, complexes behave like independent beings, a fact especially evident in abnormal states of mind. In the voices heard by the insane they even take on a personal ego-character like that of the spirits who manifest themselves through automatic writing and similar techniques.'

Jung's experiments with his mediumistic cousin formed the basis of his PhD dissertation *On the Psychology and Pathology of So-Called Occult Phenomena,* and were instrumental in the development of his later theories. The essay is essential reading for anyone pondering the nature of 'mediumistic' phenomena, the UFO contactee-syndrome, or any other form of Suburban Shamanism.

Psychic tapeworms and soul-sucking etheric larvae oftentimes assume and flaunt extravagantly fanciful garb. Lower Astral complexes may assume complete personalities, organically unfolding over a period of time, only to pass themselves off as Spirit Guides from beyond the Veil who spill the straight poop of eternal salvation to little-old-ladies-in-tennis-shoes. Among a hipper crowd they appear as inter-galactic Intelligences in league with the almighty Space Brothers, and pass off useless tidbits of saccharin advice which merely reflects the spirit of the time and the personal beliefs of any passive dupe who indiscriminately opens himself up to the Trashkashic Realm.

Such communications tend to be psychologically-revealing 'confessions' of the recipient's mental state, and often reflect compensatory phenomena at work beneath the surface. Modern day archetypal psychologists such as James Hillman are quick to point out that our complexes crystalize around archetypal cores; thus analytical therapy is often devoted to exploring the 'god' or daimon underlying a particular constellation of related psychological manifestations.

THE HISTORICAL DIMENSION

By no means should any reader of Colin Wilson automatically assume that the idea of 'The Mind Parasites' is a recent development. To the Christian gnostics, etheric lamprey and possessive complexes (ie passions) were imagined as daimonic animal spirits which latched onto the soul as 'Appendages', often influencing human behaviour for the worst. The gnostic mythos of astral appendages is preserved for us by Clement of Alexandria, an early Church Father, who reported the following nearly 2,000 years ago:

'The Basilidians are accustomed to give the name of appendages to the passions. These essences, they say, have a certain substantial existence, and are attached to the rational soul, owing to a certain turmoil and primitive confusion.

'On to this nucleus other bastard and alien natures of the essence grow, such as those of the wolf, ape, lion, goat, etc. And when the peculiar qualities of such natures appear round the soul, they cause the desires of the soul to become like to the special natures of these animals, for they imitate the actions of those whose characteristics they bear.'

If the psyche is a house divided, the existence of possessive complexes demands a moral responsibility, and so we find Isidorous, a son of Basilides, writing in his book, *On an Appended Soul:*

'Were I to persuade anyone that the real soul is not a unit, but that the passions of the wicked are occasioned by the compulsion of appended natures, no common excuse then would the worthless have for saying, 'I was compelled, I was carried away, I did it without wishing to do so, I acted unwillingly'; whereas it was the man himself who led his desire towards evil, and refused to battle with the constraints of the appendages. Our duty is to show ourselves rulers over the inferior creation within us, gaining the mastery by means of our rational principle.'

Nor was the subject of Astral Parasites overlooked by the ever-controversial magician, qabalist, and complex-ridden religionist Aleister Crowley. Some of his best writing concerns itself with the etheric scuz likely to be detected in the vicinity of spiritualists, who attract archetypal complexes and blundering unconscious 'intelligences' like ectoplasmic magnets. In *Magick in Theory and Practice* Crowley warns that spiritualists:

'. . . deliberately invite all and sundry spirits, demons, shells of the dead, all the excrement and filth of the earth and hell, to squirt their slime over them. This invitation is readily accepted unless a clean man be present with an aura good enough to frighten the foul denizens of the pit.

No spiritist, once he is

wholly enmeshed in sentimentality and Freudian fear-phantasms, is capable of concentrated thought, of persistent will, or of moral character.

They are contagious as Syphilis, and more deadly and disgusting. Unless your aura is strong enough to inhibit any manifestation of the loathly larvae that have taken up their habitation in them, shun them as you need not mere lepers! *[Crowley's emphasis.]*

Fooling with spiritualism, automatic writing, or ritual magick is a good way to open the individual up to forces larger than man. So is daytime TV. And playing around with Ouija Boards is a shit-sure way to pick up Astral Parasites.

•

David Fideler.

Author's Credits: *to Ion A Will for 'Trashkashic Records' and 'Suburban Shamanism'; Colin Wilson for justifiable paranoia; JR 'Bob' Dobbs for "Science does not remove the fear of the Gods." NEXT TIME: 'The Video Freak Show' by Bob Tarte.*

LETTERS

Cont from p3.

cover for misogyny, dualism and ersatz illumination. This intuition is confirmed by Mr Roberts' alleged 'refutation', when he writes so insultingly about the Great Hag, Kali/Hecate, after posing as Her admirer in *The Dark Gods.*

He says matriarchal paganism is fashionable. He should know. He himself jumps on the bandwagon in his Grail writing with its references to Robert Graves and the 'great prehistoric religion of the Goddess'. No talk of 'flaccid tits' there!

I agree with Mr. Roberts. Among a certain crew of clever aspirants to the title of Deep Thinker are quite a few glad-handing pseudo-Goddess worshippers. The last representatives of a dying White Man's world are playing at a masquerade which they advertise as guaranteed to produce the unmasking of the counterfeits among us. Since, as Mary Daly writes, self-deception is the essence of doublethink, the whole process culminates in an even greater counterfeit.

My review of *The Dark Gods* was austere because I spotted an illusion-compounding process presented as illusion shattering. The truth or some half-way credible version of it is too desperately needed in this nuclear age to be wishy-washy with those who muddy the waters further, under the pretext of revelation. While the court intellectuals, and ruling class educated, mouth cliches stolen from feminist discourse in order to more effectively propagandize their hatred of women (just as Trilateral Commission brochures spout ecological buzz words in order to continue their pollution and plunder), only the most mind-bombed would conclude that women and this planet are doing nicely, thank you.

We live in a profoundly misogynist 'culture' where the rapist and invader mentalities rule. Mr. Roberts is correct when he writes that some radical feminists' fidelity to the Goddess lacks balance. It's the same thing with the Petro rites of Haitian vaudon or with the inmates of the Gulag. One should not demand dispassion and objectivity from the viciously oppressed targets of starvation, rape, mutilation and murder. If you say 'nigger' to a black man, you'll get a black power punch in the mouth in return, not an invitation to intellectual dialogue. If one supports the psychic damage done to women and their allies by the male god imagery of the Bible, the response from radical feminists will probably not be too harmonious by Mr. Roberts' standards.

I urge anyone the least interested in discovering the game Mr. Roberts and other supposed code-breakers and myth-explainers are up to, to please study Mary Daly's incredibly insightful, pioneer-

Continued on p 44

LETTERS
Continued

ing *Gyn/Ecology* (Boston: Beacon Press), and especially the section, 'Deadly Deception: Mystification Through Myth'.

Even though Mr. Roberts' 'UFO-book' is too high for a mere gumshoe like this writer, I notice he doesn't bother with my remarks about UFOs as reflexive mind-traps or MIBs as part of the mechanism of self-fulfilling prophecies. These are probably too pedestrian to elicit a comment from so lofty a UFO authority as Anthony Roberts.

As for contradictions: if all of Lovecraft's 'key dreams' occurred before his teens, when he was 'well-fed', how is it that Mr. Roberts states on p.51 of *The Dark Gods* that 'the fruitition' of Lovecraft's psychic imaginings happened at the end of his life? It is the impact of the atrociously enervating modern diet Lovecraft consumed in this period, upon his creative vision that was precisely my point in the book review. Like others who follow a formula while engaged in a field (strange phenomena) that is supposed to be generally lacking in them, Mr. Roberts derides the mystery of women's menstruation as the basis for the Grail. In the same vein, because a connection between diet and behaviour is in vogue, Roberts has another laugh at the ancient wisdom that 'we are what we eat'. I predict that one day the analysis of the food eaten by Lovecraft, Fort, you or me will have great utility as a tool for understanding as yet unexplained biographical mysteries (cf. 'The mystery of Nikola Tesla' in the Oct 1980 *East West Journal;* $2.50; *EWJ*, 17 Station St., Brookline, MA 02146).

Patriarchal occult chroniclers reverse myth and reality. They call not-looking 'seeing'. They say Medusa is a horrid female who, if looked upon, will turn people to stone. But the change-of-era time has arrived and we have the strength now to reverse the reversers. It is time to see that what they have tatooed in our minds as myth is actually an internalized cop screeching again and again, 'The Man's version is THE version'.

They thought they had buried Her forever. Well, surprise, Jack. What you've tried so hysterically to repress is everywhere on the rise. In Karen Lindsay's words, 'It is those who do not look/who are turned to stone'.

Michael Anthony Hoffman
Geneva, New York

GOLFBALL RAIN?

Lacking any tenable explanation for the following experiences, I pushed them to the back of my mind until, recently I read in *Phenomena* about the fall of golf balls in Florida in 1969 (p18).

In April 1976 when tracing a disused footpath I was crossing rough and unfrequented ground about one mile west of Saundersfoot, South Wales, at an altitude of about 150 feet, map reference SN230052, when I noticed a golf ball in the grass and looking around I picked up about a dozen within a small area. I thought at first that the balls might have been lost by a careless and affluent golfer practicing but later I decided that no golfer in his senses would practice on such rough ground when there was a smooth field a few yards away so returning to the place a few days later and searching more carefully I discovered more balls making about 30 in all. Many of the balls had been trampled into the ground by cows which use the place and were barely visible so probably more could have been found by digging. The balls varied from apparently new, clean ones to badly battered; I gave them away to local golfers. The place where I found them is on the side of a valley which slopes at about 30 degrees. It is rectangular, about 50 by 30 yards and is in the corner of a large field but separated by a hedge with gaps in it. The surrounding hedges are wide belts of brambles with shrubs and trees. I found no balls outside this area.

I considered the possibility that these balls could have been transported from Tenby golf links, a distance of about 3¼ miles, by magpies which flock in this area during the spring. Though I have never seen seagulls there I thought they might have done it. The seagulls around here dig cockles out of the sand; carry them up to a height of about 30 feet and then drop them. Apparently this causes them to open. I wrote to the Royal Society for the Protection of Birds about this but their reply was that it was unlikely that birds were responsible.

I continued to visit the place during 1975 but found no more balls. Much rain prevented me struggling through mud to reach the site during January and February but when I got there in early April there was a new supply of balls just as in the previous April and again I collected about 30. I then looked forward to a regular supply of balls each April but since 1976 I have not found any.

I realise that this is a weak case. No one saw the balls arriving and no one saw me collect them and I could have planted them there myself, so I doubt that you can make use of it even though the fact that it occurred twice makes it extra mysterious. **A. T. Ryland,**
Saundersfoot, Dyfed.

A LETTER TO FT READERS

When I first saw a copy of FT in 1976, naturally one of the things to catch my eye was the attention given to what I considered a rather amusing piece of local lore: that there be pumas in Surrey. Soon the amusement turned to intrigue and a part-time study, which went on until autumn 1980. The events since then have been nothing but embarrassing.

It was easy to assume that the impressive list of sightings compiled by FT was the complete story. I simply watched the local papers for current reports. But that impressive list wouldn't be the same if it weren't for the likes of you and me. Press cuttings from readers and having people on the spot with local knowledge is the life blood of the magazine.

It happened on a visit to Farnham library for something else. I noticed they held back files of the *Farnham Herald,* a newspaper absent from the FT references. This was strange, for many of the early sightings of the puma were around Farnham.

It was surely worth a look. And the result was embarrassing, for so much data was there that it spurred me on to check the files of other local papers. There are now over 50 more accounts on file with Forteans, just from a small area of the Surrey Hampshire border.

It is embarrassing because the information has been sitting in local libraries for 15 years, just waiting for someone to look. Yet I had simply assumed there was nothing to look for. Finding this data is, to me, as much an admission of failure as an achievement.

How much more undiscovered data is lying around the country in libraries just waiting for an enquiring Fortean to look? Volumes! My message to every reader of FT is that there is more to our subject than reading the magazine. Finding historical data is fascinating!

True, it takes time, and can be tedious if nothing turns up for half an hour. But the excitement of finding accounts, the challenge of locating an obscure reference, makes up for all of that. Staff at libraries and local newspapers are unbelievably helpful usually. All sorts of unexpected people show an interest. (But be careful of what you say in local newspaper offices if you don't want to make news yourself!)

Near to everyone of us is masses of unrecorded Forteana. Why are you still reading this when you could be halfway to the library?

Chris Hall
Fleet, Hampshire.

[I couldn't have put it better —Ed.]

PUNDIT PANNED

Keep up the good work, with a mag that may not be as glossy or colourful as Mr Clarke's book or TV series, but which certainly does not 'gloss' over the strange wonders of this earth.

Stephen Wrathall
Knaresborough, North Yorks.

Having just viewed 'Arthur C Clarke's Mysterious World' on the box, and recently read of your lack of credit in the programme in the *New Musical Express,* I was inspired to produce the enclosed cartoon [below]. Well, *someone* had to!

Nick Malloret
Portsmouth, Hampshire.

[Thanks to you and others who wrote in in sympathy after the article in NME *aired our beef with the Yorkshire TV production team, that we received no credits for the crucial help we gave to the researchers especially in the early stages. Simon Welfare, the programme's producer, said in fairness that others had been left out too. On reflection that's not much of a defence. Our complaint was on behalf of a small number of people known to me who helped the programme readily and eagerly, at short notice sometimes, and with material that would otherwise have taken them much time and money to obtain for themselves. We did this, also, to help publicise our various magazines or projects, grateful for the opportunity since we have no resources of our own which could match broadcasting on such a scale. Although no promises of credits were given, we were not discouraged from our naive belief that the usual protocols of acknowledgement would be honoured – if not in the programme itself, then in the book, which had more space for such things. Indeed there is an acknowledgement section in the book but a great many names have been omitted. I know from personal experience that omissions are inevitable, but considering their resources and manpower the YTV team cannot claim the usual excuses of the overworked, hardpressed author. But let it pass. . . the sadness is that I and others will not be so quick or trusting (or cheap) in future when those smiling media men come calling, asking for your urgent help with disarming and deceptive geniality—Ed.]*

THE ENCYCLOPEDIA OF UFOS
Edited by Ronald Story.
Doubleday, NY / New English Library, london, 1980; £12.95, hb, p440, photos, appendices, bib.

OBSERVING UFOs
By Richard F Haines.
Nelson-Hall, Chicago, Il, 1980; $21.95 hb, $10.95 pb, pp300, plates, illos, glossary, bib, index.

Following Allan Hendry's *UFO Handbook* (reviewed last issue) this has been a bumper time for serious UFO books. Over the last decade or so such books were so few and far between that critics would regularly bewail the lack when faced with yet another 'subjective' account of the contactee kind. If this is a trend then it seems to imply that there has been much stocktaking of late among ufologists. A new breed of investigator is emerging: one who is less gullible, less impatient to get into print, more rigorous in his methods and with less allegiance to the standard theories of the day. The 'new approach' is not overtly scientific—the direction in which the salvation of ufology was once thought to lie — but owes more to the painstaking methods of current anthropology and social psychology, and regards scientific and medical theory and equipment as a means rather than an end.

Whereas Hendry's book provided the clearest exposition of current thinking among such ufologists, Story's *Encyclopedia* is a much needed guide to who these people are, their personal views, the cases they think important, and the host of 'special interests' that goes to make up the complex family of people and ideas called ufology. Although it is a pretty heavy tome – 440 pages of large format – Story obviously had to draw the line somewhere, and everyone will find their own list of omissions. The coverage of British ufologists is erratic omitting such key figures as the MUFOB (now *Magonia)* group (John Rimmer, Peter Rogerson and Roger Sandall), John Michell, Arthur Shuttlewood, FW Holliday and the Bords. Among Americans who have contributed to the emergence of 'new ufology' there is no mention of David Fideler and Allen Greenfield; or of Trevor J Constable and Isobel Davis. Among groups and subjects that might have rated a mention how about 'British Ufology', Warminster UFOcal, the T Lobsang Rampa story, crashed saucers and alleged alien bodies, UK's own UFOIN/NUFON, underwater USOs, SITU, Vestigia and even ourselves, FT?

Nevertheless, the *Encyclopedia* is worth it if you can afford it, well illustrated with diagrams, photos of personalities and a colour UFO photo section. The appendices contain a chronology of events in the history of ufology (up to 1978); a list of periodicals; a dictionary of events in the history of ufology (up to 1978); a list of periodicals; a dictionary of acronyms and abbreviations; and a practical bibliography.

Observing UFOs on the other hand is highly specific, being a handbook for the serious investigator, covering such essential topics as the relationship with the witness, interviewing techiniques, evaluating testimony and other kinds of information, some notes on basic physical and psychological optics, identifying IFOs and effects in photos. It has been written for an American market—eg: recourse to hypnosis and polygraph testing are more common in the States – but European readers should learn much from the methodology advocated by Haines.

RJMR.

THE JANOS PEOPLE
By Frank Johnson.
Neville Spearman, Suffolk, 1980 £5.25, hb, pp198, photo, illos, index.

THE ANDREASSON AFFAIR
By Raymond E Fowler.
Bantam, NY, 1980; 95p/pb pp242,.photos, illos, index.

'Look how the world's poor people are amazed
At apparitions, signs, and prodigies,
Whereon with fearful eyes they long have gazed,
Infusing them with dreadful prophesies.'

Shakespeare
Venus and Adonis

I hate to disagree with Frank Johnson, but I doubt that his account of *The Janos People* would earn him a fortune as a science fiction author if he had the imagination to invent such a story, as he asserts. As a work of fact is is even more unsatisfactory. I can believe in the existence of Margaret Thatcher or Santa Claus but even my gullibility is stretched to breaking point when I'm expected to believe that there are approximately 10 million Janos people waiting to make Earth their home.

The Janos people are descended from Nordic European ancestors who ventured into space a long time ago, and eventually they settled on an Earth-type planet which they called Janos. Their highly developed civilization was a virtual utopia until a naughty nearby moon, Saton, broke-up and rained-down on Janos. Millions were killed immediately, the rest of the planet's inhabitants died from the results of radioactive fallout because their nuclear power stations exploded when showered with the remains of Saton. Fortunately the Janos space fleet was unaffected by this planetary disaster, and so several thousand years ago these interstellar refuges went in search of a new home. Eventually their fleet came into contact with Earth, and now they want to be repatriated.

The prime evidence for these facts is supplied by an alleged experience which took place on the 19th June 1978 in the county of Oxfordshire, England. John, his wife Gloria, his sister Frances, and daughters Natasha (aged 5) and Tanya (aged 3), were riding in a car when they saw a UFO following them. Suddenly their journey seemed unreal and strange, and they discovered that they had taken fifty-five minutes longer than usual to arrive home. A week later John became ill and dreamt of a UFO encounter. Days later Frances had a similar kind of dream. Their daughter, Natasha, also began having 'UFO' dreams. This lead the intrepid Johnson to believe 'that a genuine CE4 had taken place'. Like any ufologist worthy of such a title, he wheeled-in his nearest friendly hypnotist. From long and gruelling hypnotic sessions, with both John and Frances, the story of this family's ride inside a flying saucer and meeting with representatives of the Janos people emerged.

In contrast to Johnson's treatment of *The Janos People* Fowler presents *The Andreasson Affair* in a much more perceptive and critical light.

The bulk of the Andreasson affair occurred in the home of the Andreasson family, which was located in South Ashburnham, Massachusetts, USA. Mr James Andreasson was seriously injured in a car crash on the 23rd December 1966, and because of his hospitalisation his wife's parents Waino and Eva Aho, aided the running of the large household. Hence, on the night of the 25th January 1967, Mrs Betty Andreasson, her children Becky, James Jr., Mark, Scott, Todd, Bonnie and Cindy, along with her parents, were present when the electricity failed and strange lights began to shine through the kitchen window. Everybody in the house, except Betty, went into a state of suspended animation. Four aliens entered the house, who were led by a being called Quazgaa. After some conversation about the bible they escorted Betty to her backyard where a mist shrouded flying saucer was waiting for them.

Inside the saucer Betty was subjected to a frightening examination, during which a long silver needle was pushed into her left nostril and another into her navel. In another part of the saucer she was placed into a strange 'cold' chair, then she was placed in a similar type of chair, though this time a cover was placed over her body and tubes were supplied to her mouth and nostrils, then a liquid was pumped into her 'immersion' chair which completely shrouded her body. This womb-like experience was further emphasised when Betty explained how afterwards she and two aliens travelled down a long dark tunnel. Emerging from the tunnel she found herself in a totally red coloured environment. After travelling through the wonders of this place, she was guided into a beautiful green environment.

In the green environment Betty encountered a bright crystal realm, before it stood a huge bird. This vision filled her with terror, and she became very hot. The bird was replaced by a fire which diminished into a pile of ashes, these took on the form of a big fat grey worm. This ancient motif of immortality and resurrection, was followed by an enigmatic conversation between Betty and a booming disembodied voice. This voice told her that she had been chosen but the time wasn't right to tell her why, though she was told that her faith in Jesus Christ would bring about an explanation when the time is right. Betty was very fearful, but the voice said: 'I can release you, but you must release yourself of that fear through my son'.

As Betty relived this experience under hypnosis, Fowler noted that 'The words "through my son" suddenly became the catalyst for the most moving religious experience that I have ever witnessed'. After this encounter she was returned to the saucer, and to her home.

The experience of Fowler and Johnson in dealing with such complex and confusing 'UFO' experiences is revealed by their approach to their respective investigations. Both of them resort to hypnotic regression techniques rather too readily, especially since it is clear neither of them have any great knowledge of how this might affect their subjects (victims!). For instance, Fowler asserts that people can be 'turned off and on like biological tape recorders!' when subjected to hypnosis. However, unlike a tape recorder the human mind manipulates in complex and subtle ways its perception of the physical environment and translates it into a manner amenable to the individual's mental environment. Perhaps as a mark of respect for UFO percipients and fellow ufologists, UFO investigators should at least attempt to discover some of the fundamental principles of hypnotic regression before they inflict these techniques upon unsuspecting and trusting members of humanity who allege to have 'lost' a few minutes of their life or to have dreamed of UFOs.

Their traditional approach to UFO investigation also reveals itself in their concentration on the witness descriptions of the 'physical' aspects of the encounters. In particular Fowler and his associates produce an excellent account of the sequence of events, as described by Betty Andreasson under hypnosis, and the details of the physical properties of the Ufonauts and their craft. But the value of such material when taken to such extremes is rather debatable, especially when other areas of the encounter are totally neglected.

It is interesting to consider both encounters as the manifestation of crisis apparitions which haunted these people at a time of great emotinal upheaval and helped them to metaphorically confront and transcend their personal problems.

Fowler devotes a lot of space to describing the beliefs and values of Betty Andreasson, and it is noteworthy that when she met Quazgaa (and God?) that she was under a lot of emotional strain. We can list these factors as being; (a) her husband was in hospital, (b) her parents moved in with her (an obvious source of conflict!), (c) the normal problems of running a large household, (d) long-standing marital problems. These factors could have created enough tension to inaugurate her encounter which revealed to her a vision of death and rebirth within the context of her Christian convictions, yet delivered in the psychologically and socially acceptable format of the UFO enigma.

Johnson doesn't disclose much about how he went about his investigation, or much about the background details of the family. However, their encounter did take place after they attended a family funeral which could have created some emotional distress within the percipients. This distress could have been amplified by the UFO sighting and their subsequent meeting with Mr Johnson. This sequence of events followed by an illness which initiated the 'UFO' dreams, could indicate that emotional distress, the influence of Johnson (many elements of their story reflect his own prejudices and preconceptions), and an illness, strongly favoured the emergence and evolution of their elaborate encounter story.

In both cases the UFO encounters serve a value-expressive function, which offer the individuals concerned an identity and role in a society where anonymity predominates. Also the UFO myth supplies a frame of reference and orientation for their personal values which cannot be easily satisfied by traditional religious institutions.

It is a sad reflection on British ufology (and the validity of UFOIN) that Johnson should become a convert to the disconnected and rambling Janos saga. Indeed, he asserts that subjectivity doesn't play a role in this case because; 'All experiences have a subjective element' hence 'it would be arrant nonsense to deduce from this that the world before my eyes exists only in my subjective mind'. Equally it would be arrant nonsense to believe that the girl with green nipples I dreamed of a few nights ago actually exists! I doubt that any rational argument is likely to change his peculiar perception of the origin of the UFOs.

Fowler can only be congratulated for his detached and impartial approach to a case that puzzled and worried him. Although his preconceptions and those of his colleagues intrude, they never eclipse the elucidation of a fascinating case history.

The Janos People and *The Andreasson Affair* illuminate some of the most puzzling aspects of the UFO phenomenon, but it is obvious that more radical and rigorous attempts have to be made to discover the dynamics of such encounters before any real progress can be made in coming to terms with this data.

Nigel Watson

THE SPIRITUAL NATURE OF MAN

By Alister Hardy.

Oxford University Press, Oxford, 1979; £6.95 hb, pp162, appendices, bib, index.

Sir Alister Hardy has been consistently interested in the natural scheme of things, and since he founded the Religious Experience Research Unit in Oxford in 1969, has supervised several widespread surveys to discover the extent and role of religious experience in the lives of people of every profession, age and intelligence. Although he is a Darwinian, in that he believes such experiences have some evolutionary advantage, this book is more simply an analysis of the first 3000 first-hand accounts of an uplifting or illuminating experience accumulated by the Unit, followed by a discussion of various analyses.

Extracts of many cases are given as examples of the various types and themes of the experience in all its varieties, from a non-specific euphoria to a vision of Christ, from out-of-the-body adventures to apparitions and telepathy or clairvoyance, from healing to exorcism, and from a realisation of inner wholeness to a sense of the experience having come from 'outside' one's self. A whole chapter discusses the 'Antecedents or triggers of experience', which may contain far-reaching implications for study of UFO close-encounters.

In essence it seems that what is called a 'religious' experience may also be experienced in non-religious terms (ie a feeling of timelessness, strength, calm, peace, hope, indifference (detachment), harmony, release, etc etc) so that freed from a rather stereotyped view of a Saul-on-the-Damascus-road type of vision many more people have such experiences in their lives than previously estimated. Indeed, based on one of Hardy's questions, David Hay, of the Religious Experience Research Project at Nottingham University, found that about 62% of a random sample of people confessed to such experiences–about 41% expressing them in religious terms. Both Hardy and Hay would say the actual percentage of people who have had such experiences, whether they led to any personal development or not, is probably very much higher. If, as Hardy suspects, we are all born with the potential to mystical experiences, then some work must be done on identifying the factors which brutalise or repress that faculty. Similarly we must be more aware of the 'triggering' factors, and that some experiences take forms which are (underneath the different symbols) not unlike contactee experiences, if we are to understand the contactee experience in terms of the human being who experiences it.

RJMR.

SHAMANIC VOICES

By Joan Halifax.
Pelican / Penguin Books, Harmondsworth, Middx, 1980; £2.95 pb, pp268, plates, bib, refs.

PRIMAL MYTHS

By Barbara C Sproul.
Rider / Hutchinson, London, 1980; £5.50 pb, pp373, refs, index.

Joan Halifax has made a fascinating book out of a selection of accounts of visions and initiations in the words of the shamans themselves. Despite the variant symbolism and language conventions the structure of experiences is remarkably consistent from Siberia and North America, to Africa and Australia, from Greenland and Borneo to Mexico and South America. Much of it was gained first-hand.

In their initiations many shamanic traditions recreate symbolically the creation of the world. In Barbara Sproul's book we have in one volume the primary myths about the origin of the gods and their creation of the world and man collected together from the traditions of Japan and China, Africa, the Near East, Europe, India, North America, Central and South America, Australia and the Pacific, and Siberian and Eskimo myths.

RJMR.

INCREDIBLE COINCIDENCES

By Alan Vaughan.
JB Lippincott, NY, 1979; $10.00 hb, pp256, notes, index of cases.

This book is about those 'periods of life when everything is up for grabs', as Vaughan puts it. We've all experienced the power and variety of coincidence or chance in our lives, both at high-points and in everyday doings. We know that recourse to the 'magic' words 'only chance', or 'pure coincidence' is a superstitious and intellectually dishonest action, and does not diminish the true mystery of such events.

Vaughan writes in an engagingly relaxed style, using 152 cases (referenced) as springboards for his own thoughts and theorising–and some of the stories are truly incredible. Vaughan even operates his own classification system: Chance Encounters of the First Kind (CE-1s) are essentially trivial involving knowledge or observation of an event which is odd yet meaningful. CE-2s are less easy to identify, but have the dimension of a *personal* meaning. CE-3s seem wholly out of the realm of accident, involving a degree of intentionality, such as being unable to find a rare book you need, and then on an unfamiliar route home finding it lying on the pavement in your path (Case 92, as happened to Lawrence LeShan, author of *Alternate Realities).*

There is little that should be said about this delightful book, except that it is a shame it is not yet in print in the UK–but if you find it, read and enjoy!

RJMR.

AGRICULTURAL RECORDS AD 220–1977

By JM Stratton.
John Baker, London 1978 (2nd edition); £5.50 hb, pp259, appendices.

This book is both fascinating and infuriating. It is an invaluable souce of Forteana – particularly to those meteorologically minded, but does tend to become merely a list of statistics and dry, humourless reportage in the modern years section at the end of the book. The earlier years are most informative, less 'involved' in their transcription. Where the reports are brief they are enjoyable, but where they become lengthy are tedious – presumably agricultural historians will go a bundle on this book though (eg. Wool was 9s 8d per tod in 1288 and only 4s 4d in 1437–courtesy of the useless information department).

Anyone wishing to relate their phenomenological studies to the prevailing meteorological conditions of the time will find this book worthwhile.

Once or twice matters Fortean creep into the columns and this is what is so good about it. Detrimental though, is the complete lack of indexes. One can pick this book up and open it at random and find some interesting data and a methodical poring over it will reward the reader in relating phenomena to meteorology.

Examples are called for: 971 'Another very cloudy year, the sun being hidden most of the time for 6 months.' 1119 'A severe earthquake recorded in Gloucestershire and Worcestershire on September 29th.' 1644 'An exceptionally heavy thunderstorm occurred in the Midlands on May 15th during which enormous hailstones, bigger than walnuts, fell.' 1658

'On September 3rd another very violent gale occurred, this was the day of Oliver Cromwell's death and the coincidence attracted considerable attention and comment'. 1748 'In one (violent thunderstorm) at Crawfurd, Scotland, on June 27th, a flash of lightning killed 320 Ewes. A swarm of locusts reached England on August 4th settling on vegetable crops.' 1821 'On September 1st a fall of snails occurred at Thornbury, Gloucestershire, covering 6 acres of land ankle deep!' etc, etc.

Alan Gardiner.

TUTANKHAMUN: The Untold Story
By Thomas Hoving.
Penguin Books, Harmondsworth, Middx, 1980; £2.50 pb, pp384, plates, notes, index.

Hoving, a former head of the prestigious Metropolitan Museum in New York, became so obsessed with the story of the discovery of Tut's tomb and treasures that he devoted years to investigating every aspect and record. The result is a piecing-together of the remarkable events before and after the tomb's celebrated opening, and perhaps the truest picture of the excavation team's bickerings and other tragedies.

RJMR.

THE INTERRUPTED JOURNEY
By John G Fuller.
Souvenir Press, London, 1980; £6.95 hb, pp340.

It is now 14 years since the first publication of Fuller's detailed account of perhaps the most famous UFO-abduction case of all, involving Betty and Barney Hill on the night of 19th September 1961, as they drove through a remote part of New Hampshire. Since that time Barney has died, Betty's psychic powers have flowered, and the world's press has reported many other cases (of varying authenticity). Fuller, while working for *Look* magazine, was given the assignment which led to the fullest cooperation of the Hills, including access to the tapes and records of their lengthy sessions with Boston psychiatrist Dr Benjamin Simon – vital documents which form the main part of this account.

It is astonishing to realise that a book so important to ufology has never seen print in the UK, until now. This edition carries a new foreword by Fuller, and comments here and there where subsequent events have clarified matters or added new information. We learned from a recent edition of *Skywatch* that Dr Simon died not too long ago – although he never expressed any opinion on the 'objective reality' of the Hills' experience, he will be remembered for his professionalism, for taking them seriously, for treating their confusion with kindness, and for providing ufology with one of the most dramatic and full records of the hypnotic regression of two contactees.

RJMR.

THE BOOK OF LISTS No 2
By Irving Wallace, David Wallechinsky, Amy Wallace, Sylvia Wallace.
Wm Morrow, NY, 1980; $12.95 hb, pp529, index.

Apart from saying it is a treasure trove of trivia and odd facts, it defies description. Belongs alongside its predecessor (which it does not duplicate) and the People's Almanacs, on every Fortean reference shelf.

RJMR.

LA MEMOIRE DES OVNI by French UFO researcher and FT reader, Jean Bastide. (Mercure de France, 26 Rue de Conde, 75006 Paris, France.) Bastide examines UFOs in history, folklore and legend, from Argonauts to Humanoids. Unfortunately in French only. Inquiries to the above address.

RJMR.

PSI AND THE MIND
By HJ Irwin.
Scarecrow Press, Metuchen, NJ/ Bailey Bros & Swinfen, Folkestone, Kent, 1980; £6.30 hb, pp173, bib, index.

THE PARANORMAL AND THE NORMAL
By M Leeds & G Murphy.
Scarecrow Press/Bailey Bros & Swinfen, 1980; £9.45, pp239, diags, glossary, bib, index.

The subtitle of Irwin's book is 'An Information Processing Approach'. Amazing how well-meaning academics can transform a fascinating subject into something as dull as ditchwater! It will be of most use to those doing a thesis on the size of symbols and image-retention in psi tests on high verbals, or some such . . .

The Leeds and Murphy book is no less academic in content, but written for humans to read. Murphy, a one-time president of the SPR, and Leeds have seen many developments of the subject – not all of them to the good – in the many years they have been interested and involved in research; and this is their attempt to put their own knowledge into a perspective of the history of the study of psi. A good state-of-the-art book.

RJMR.

GAIA
By JE Lovelock.
Oxford University Press, Oxford, 1979; £4.95 hb, pp157, bib.

THE QUEST FOR GAIA
By Kit Pedler.
Souvenir Press, London 1979; £5.50 hb, pp231.

The concept of a Mother Earth was old, even before the Greeks named her Gaia. In the mid-1970s it was reformulated by scientist James Lovelock, who brought together his interest in every science — from astronomy to zoology' – to give a scientific expression to the idea that the whole Planet Earth is a single living entity; its contingents, oceans, plant and animal life, geological, electrical and chemical processes all intereacting on a vast scale in this huge organism.

This book is about how he came to this conclusion and what he thinks it implies for the sciences and for the future of mankind as well as of Gaia herself.

Kit Pedler's *Quest* is less personal and is more politically in the ecologists' camp in aiming to make us aware that as a species we had better make our peace with Gaia before either we destroy the planet or ourselves, or *She* destroys us. Most of the book is an examination of the ways in which we could save energy, materials, lives and wellbeing by learning to live more efficiently and economically and harmoniously.

RJMR.

A HISTORY OF WITCHCRAFT
By Jeffrey B Russell.
Thames & Hudson, London, 1980; £7.95 hb, pp192, illos, notes, bib, index.

You'd think the last thing the world needed was *another* book on witchcraft, so what makes this one different. For one thing it is written by Russell, a very erudite professor of history, whose *Witchcraft in the Middle Ages* (1972) is one of the standard references on the subject. His declared intention is to provide the general reader with an authoritative and accurate history of witchcraft up to the present day, which puts all its variants into a common perspective, as an alternative to those 'popular books that clog the occult sections of bookshops'. The result is very worthwhile.

RJMR.

GODEL, ESCHER, BACH
By Douglas R Hoffstadter.
Penguin Books, Harmondsworth, Middx, 1980; £5.95 pb, pp777, photos, illos, bib, index.

Another book that defies description. Hofstadter takes the mathematical theorems of Godel, the graphical paradoxes of Escher, and the complex musical structures of Bach to weave one of the most original explorations ever of the mystery of human thinking. Along the way he employs all manner of jokes, poems, Lewis Carroll, zen, neurophysiology, Zeno's paradoxes, linguistics, high-energy physics, number and information theory, 'reasoning about reasoning about reasoning', the Greek 'dialogue' technique of philosophical exposition, non-Euclidian geometry, artificial intelligence, DNA—a veritable never-ending and rotating 'golden braid' of delightful argument. GEB won him the Pulitzer Prize. I'm not surprised. It will be valued by all who discover it.

RJMR.

UNKNOWN EARTH: A Handbook of Geological Enigmas
By William Corliss.
Sourcebook Project, Glen Arm, MD 21057, USA, 1980; $19.95 hb, pp833, illos, index.

The latest fat addition to the famous series of Handbooks essential to any serious Fortean. As before this is a collection of out-of-date, rare and obscure source material, the product of a huge search among backfiles and library shelves. The subjects covered by this weighty tome are: anomalies of strata and geology; mounds, craters and other weird topographical oddities, including 'Continental Drift'; unusual rocks, including ringing rocks and those that move; biological anomalies in geology and the fossil record, including odd survivals and 'Arctic Muck' and the mammoth's graveyard; terrestrial magnetism and its enigmas; geochemistry and nuclear geology, including bizarre chemical and nuclear processes and their results; and a whole section on myths and legends about or involving all these subjects.

We repeat our endorsement of this series of volumes — they belong on the shelves of every school or university, or at least every Fortean who can afford it.

RJMR.

THE DEAD SEA SCROLLS AND THE CHRISTIAN MYTH
By John Allegro.
Abacus/Sphere, London, 1981, £2.50 pb, pp248, plates, appendix, index.

A more comprehensive assessment of the discovery of the scrolls, their restoration and translation, and their implications for the history of the Middle East and Christianity. Allegro describes the emergence of 'orthodox' Christianity from a period in which the Essene order was ruthlessly repressed and many of its beliefs and rituals were institutionalised into the new Christianity. The price was the loss of the Essene faith, with its 'genius for individualism', according to Allegro, and the foundation of the early Church upon false assumptions about the 'heresies' over which it triumphed.

RJMR.

Booklets.

THE UFO CULTS
By Weldon Burge.
Pamphlet Publications, Box 41372A, Cincinnati, OH45241, USA, 1979; price unknown, pp37, bib.

One man's view of UFO cultism and their dangers to lives and society in the wake of the Jim Jones tragedy. Brief, well-informed, sensible.

RJMR.

THE PARAPSYCHOLOGICAL IMPACT OF THE ACCIDENT AT THREE MILE ISLAND
By Larry E Arnold.
ParaScience International, 1025 Miller Lane, Harrisburg, PA 17110, USA, 1980; $5.30 (overseas airmail), $1.00 (US & Canada) pb, pp106, illos, appendices.

On 28 March 1979, the name of Three Mile Island was added to the growing list of disasters making our very existence more precarious. Larry Arnold, one of America's leading Forteans, has prodigiously gathered together all the omens of the drama – dreams, visions, apparitions, precognitions, alleged miracles and some curious synchronicities (like the detail of the film of a similar nuclear accident *The China Syndrome),* which occurred days, even years, before the fateful moment.

RJMR.

QUANTUM JUMP: Answer to the UFO Mystery
By Peter Simon.
Peters Press, Box 752, Houlton, ME 04730, USA, 1979; $2.00, pp28, bib.

Any publication sent to us with a covering letter saying it is the 'answer to all your problems', and self-described as 'The 28 Page Bible', has a lot to live up to. It turns out to be the predictable ramblings of a youth who in his enthusiastic discovery of ufology, mysticism, some enigmas of physics, and psychic phenomena sets out to cure the world of its ills. I'm not knocking it–most thinking, concerned and compassionate individuals go through this stage during adolescence. Earnest and pretentious.

RJMR.

CELESTIAL DYNAMICS AND LEVITATIONAL FORCE
By Robert Morison.
Ascent Publications, 34 Elm Grove, London N8 9AH; 50p, pp12.

The text of a lecture to BUFORA (3 June 1978) on the implications for science and levitational forces of UFO phenomena, which, in Morrison's view employ such forces.

RJMR.

Classified Exchanges.

As a reader service FT welcomes mutual exchanges with any relevant publication, and copies issues received since our last issue earn a listing here. No mag — no mention: All we ask in return is a similar entry in your own journal.

FORTEAN

• **Bigfoot Co-op** - a bimonthly newsletter of manimal sightings, footprints, etc. Write to Bigfoot Co-op: 14602 Montevideo Drive, Whittier, CA 90605, USA.

• **Bigfoot Times** - an exchange newsletter of the Southwestern Gigfoot Research Team, including items of general Bigfooteana and news. Contact Danny Perez: 10926 Milano Ave, Norwalk, CA 90650, USA.

• **Frontiers of Science** - formerly called Second Look – a pro bimonthly of consistent interest and quality covering the whole range of sceince, pseudo-science, fringe-science interest, including some Forteana. The current issue – 2:6 (Sept/oct 1980) – contains a long-waited and much-need article on the series of experiments which proved the need for caution in hypnotic regression of UFO contactees, by Dr Alvin Lawson himself. Lawson hypnotised non-contactees, gave them a scenario for a UFO sighting and found that ordinarily the unconscious mind is quite capable of creating experiences remarkable like the tales told by contactees [See also the article by Hilary Evans last issue of FT]. Single copies $3.00 inc p+p. Annual sub $15.00 Second Look: 10 E St SE, Washington DC 20003, USA.

• **Full Moon** - Hawaiian journal covering Forteana, folklore, UFO's etc. Juicy Fortean chunks of food for thought. USA $7 /yr; foreign subs please inquire for rates. Jacob A. Davidson: 1981-B St Louis Drive, Honolulu, Hawaii 96816, USA.

• **Journal of Meteorology** - monthly review of weather data and records, with many articles on Fortean related meteorology. Annual sub: £13.50; overseas £15.00; airmail £20. Inquiries to J. Meteorology: Cockhill House, Trowbridge, Wiltshire BA14 8BG.

• **Kronos** - serious and scholarly journal of discussion of the issues arising from Velikovsky's work. Quarterly. $15 /yr; overseas $20. Kronos: Glassboro State College, Glassboro, NJ 08028, USA.

• **Lantern** - quarterly Fortean and folklore journal of East Anglian mysteries. Consistently of interest. Annual sub: UK & Europe £1.20; USA $5. BSIG: 3 Dunwich Way, Oulton Broad, Lowestoft, Suffolk NR32 4 RZ.

• **M-Possibilities** - a Fortean newsletter for American mensa. Write to Michael Halm: 620 9th Ave N, Apt 12, Fargo ND 58102, USA.

• **New Atlantean Journal** - quarterly newsprint journal of the New Atlantean Research Society covering parapsychology, UFO's, ancient enigmas, Forteana. Annual sub: USA $5; overseas surface $12, airmail $15. NAJ: 5963 32nd Ave N, St Petersburg, FL 33710, USA.

• **Nessletter** - monthly newsletter of the Ness Information Service. Sightings and gossip from the Scottish and other monster-haunted lakes. Annual sub: £2; USA $8, NIS: Huntshieldford, St John's Chapel, Bishop Auckland, Co. Durham DL12 1RQ.

• **Pursuit** - quarterly journal of SITU. Annual sub $10; overseas $12.50. SITU: Box 265, Little Silver, NJ 07739, USA.

• **Science Frontiers** - brief digest of current scientific articles of relevance, with mail-order catalogue. Sourcebook Project: Box 107, Glen Arm, MD 21057, USA.

• **SIS Review** - specialist journal devoted to scholarly discussion of themes arising from the work of Velikovsky. Published quarterly by the Society for Interdisciplinary Studies - write for details. SIS: 6 Jersey House, Cotton Lane, Manchester M20 9GL.

• **Stigmata** - occasional report of Project Stigma, investigating the continuing mystery of (mainly) US livestock mutilations. Single issue: $1.50; annual sub $5. Project Stigma:, Box 1094, Paris, TX 75460, USA.

• **Der Ukendte** - Danish glossy quarterly on mysteries of all sorts. Write to Der Ukente: Nordvestvej 8, DK 4470, Svebolle, Denmark.

UFO's

• **AESV Bulletin** - quarterly in French by l'Association d'e tude sur les soucoupes volantes. Inquiries to AESV: 40 rue Mignet, F-13100 Aixen-Provence, France.

• **AFU Newsletter** - in Swedish and English. Write to Archives for UFO Research: PO Box 11027, S-600 11 Norrkoping 11, Sweden.

• **APRO Bulletin** - monthly journal of the Aerial Phenomena Research Association. News, investigations, articles. Annual sub: USA $12; overseas $15. APRO: 3910 E.Kleindale Rd, Tucson, AZ 87512, USA.

• **BUFORA Journal** - quartly of the British UFO Research Association. BUFORA's research department also publish the Journal of Transient Aerial Phenomena, concentrated on bringing scientific rigour to UFO investigations. Inquiries to BUFORA Membership Secretary, 30 Vermont Rd, Upper Norwood, London SE19 3SR.

- **Earthlink** - quarterly. Single copy 70p. Annual sub: UK £2.75; overseas £4. Earthlink: 16 Raydons Rd, Dagenham, Essex RM9 5JR.
- **Il Senzatitolo** - review journal in Italian. Write for details: IS, c/o Alberto Lazzaro, Box 42100, Reggio Emilia, Italy.
- **Inforespace** - bi-monthly journal of SOBEPS in French. Inquiries to SOBEPS: Ave Paul Janson 74, 1070 Bruxelles, Belgium.
- **Magonia** - quarterly. The poineering British UFO journal that has consistently explored the sociological, psychological and mythological dimensions to UFO's. Currently featuring articles by Roger Sandell on conspiracy theories and contactees. Annual sub: UK £1.75; overseas $5. John Rimmer, 64 Alric Ave, New Malden, Surrey KT3 4JW.
- **MAPIT Skywatch** - informal journal of UFO discussion. Much of interest. Inquiries to David Rees: 92 Hillcrest Rd, Offerton, Stockport, Cheshire Sk2 5SE.
- **MUFON UFO Journal** - monthly journal of the Mutual UFO Network. Annual sub: N. America $15; overseas $16. MUFON: 103 Oldtown Rd, Sequin, TX 78155, USA.
- **Northern UFO News** - monthly summary of UK cases reported to NUFON. Annual sub: UK £3.60. Inquiries to Jenny Randles: 8 Whitethroat Walk, Birchwood, Warrington, Cheshire WA3 6PQ.
- **Notiziaro UFO** - official journal of the Centro Ufologico Nazionale in Italian. Inquiries to CUN: via Vignola 3, 20136 Milano, Italy.
- **Tijdschrift voor Ufologie** - journal of NOVOBO in Dutch. Inquiries to NOVOBo: Lijnbaan 4, 9982 HJ Uithuizermeeden, Holland.
- **UFO Newsclipping Service** - a monthly collection of facsimile clippings on UFO manimal and Fortean reports from papers worldwide. Well worth it if you can afford it. For more details see the ad on this page.

PSI

- **EVP Newsletter** - bimonthly notes, interviews, data etc. on the "electronic voice phenomenon". Inquiries to Alan Cleaver: 12 Lime Tree Ave, Old Bilton, Rugby, Warks CV22 7QT.
- **International Journal of Paraphysics** - quarterly on latest psychotronic and paraphysical research. Inquiries to Paraphysical Laboratory, Downton, Nr Salisbury, Wilts.
- **Specula** - quarterly journal of the American Association of Metascience. Much of Fortean interest. Inquiries to AAMS: Box 1182, Huntsville, AL 35807, USA.

EARTH MYSTERIES

- **Ancient Mysteries** - the journal of geomancy, lost knowledge and Ancient Enigmas. Published by the Institute of Geomantic Research. Annual sub: £3.75; overseas $9; airmail $12.50. IGR: 142 Pheasant Rise, Bar Hill, Cambridge CB3 8SD.
- **Ancinet Skills and Wisdom Review** - a review journal for all related topics. Annual sub: £2; overseas $5; airmail $12. Cheques payable to Paul Screeton: 5 Egton Drive, Seaton Carew, Hartlepool, Cleveland TS25 2AT. He also publishes an occasional Terrestrial Zodiacs Newsletter.
- **Archaeoastronomy** - quarterly. Annual sub: US $10; overseas $13. Write to the Center for Archaeoastronomy, Space Sciences Building, Univ. of Maryland, College Park, MD 20742 USA.
- **Caerdroia Project Newsletter** - about turf and other mazes. Inquiries to Caerdroia Project: 53 Thundersley Grove, Thundersley, Benfleet, Essex.
- **Catastrophist Geology** - occasional journal about discontinuities in Earth history, in English. Inquiries to Johan B. Kloosterman, Caixa Postal 41.003, Santa Teresa, Rio de Janeiro, Brazil.
- **IG News** - a bimonthly folklore. occult and earth mysteries magazine. Annual sub: £2.50; overseas $5. IGNews: BM Bulletin, London WC1V 6XX.
- **The Ley Hunter** - an essential journal of earth mysteries. Annual sub: £3.60; Europe £4.50; overseas airmail $11.50. TLH: Box 13, Welshpool, Powys, Wales. (Note new address.)
- **NEARA Journal** - quarterly of the New England Antiquities Association. Annual sub: USA $5; overseas $7. NEARA: 4 Smith St, Milford, NH 03055. USA.
- **Pyramid Guide** - bimonthly newsletter. Pyramidology in all its aspects. Annual sub: USA $9; overseas airmail $13. Write to Life Understanding Foundation, 741 Rasarita Lane, Santa Barbara, CA 93105, USA.
- **Quicksilver Messenger** - about earth mysteries in S.E. England. 45p per issue. Write to Chris Ashton: 26a Wilbury Ave, Hove, Sussex.
- **Stonehenge Viewpoint** - a bimonthly newsprint journal of archaeology, astronomy and geology related to earth mysteries. 2 year sub: N. America $7; overseas £3 (12 issues). Inquiries to SV: 2821 De La Vina St, PO Box 30887, Santa Barbara, CA 93105 USA, or via the Ley Hunter.

OTHERS

- **Gnome News** - newsletter of the Gnome Club of Great Britain. Annual sub: UK £2.50; overseas £3.50. Gnome Club: West Putford, Devon, EX22 7XE.
- **The Cauldron** - a pagan newsletter. now in its fifth continuous year. Single issues 25p; annual sub £1. Cash or POs only. The Cauldron. BCM Box 1633, London WC1V 6XX.
- **The Stark Fist of Removal** - newsletter of the SubGenius Foundation, a stunningly hilarious cult which sends up all the others. Pull the wool over your own eyes. The world ends tomorrow and you *may die*! Get the SubG Pamphlet No. 1, Stark Fist and assorted bits for $5. The SubGenius Foundation: PO Box 140306, Dallas, TX 75214, USA.
- **Undercurrents** - monthly on radical alternatives. Annual sub £4.20, overseas £5.20. Undercurrents: 27 Clerkenwell Close, London. EC1R 0AT.

BOOK NEWS

• Kit Pedlar's analysis of a range of 'supernatural' events, past and present, in the light of today's frontier science, *Mind Over Matter,* will be the basis for a TV series of the same name. The book, by Thames/ Methuen – no news of date of series.

• Janet & Colin Bord's UFO book written for children, *Are we being watched?,* will be released in February by Angus & Robertson.

• John Michell and Bob Rickard are hard at work on *Phenomena II* (working title); a 'sequel' to their successful introduction to Fortean phenomena and philosophy, *Phenomena,* for the same company, Thames & Hudson. The second book will concentrate mainly on phenomenal zoology and other curiosities of natural history.

• Colin Wilson & John Grant team up to produce *The Directory of Possibilities* – a guide to the fringe of human knowledge – from Webb & Bower in June.

• W Raymond Drake tells us he has completed another volume in his stupendous 'ancient spaceman' series – *Titans in Antiquity,* mainly centred on Africa this time, with a bibliography of 331 references. Despite being quickly accepted for publication by ATE, in Barcelona, and Armenia, in Milan, British publishers have not yet responded.

• Morris Leon Berg is completing *Strange Fire,* which he describes as a historical study of the ability of some individuals to create fire, and which begins where Harrison and Gaddis leave off. He is looking for a publisher.

• Nigel Watson is also looking for a publisher for his close study of several British contactees, based on personal investigations. The MS's working title is *Portrait of Alien Encounters.*

• Nigel Pennick, prodigious pamphleteer and editor of *Ancient Mysteries,* has finished his eagerly awaited book on underground tunnels, deneholes and subterranea of all kinds, their lore, legends and history. Entitled *The Subterranean Kingdom* it is scheduled from Turnstone in June.

• The definitive account of the recent New Zealand UFOs, *The Kaikoura UFOs,* by Capt Bill Startup (the main witness) and Neil Illingworth, is expected soon from Hodder & Stoughton.

• *Photographs of the Unexplained,* by **Bob Rickard** and **Richard Kelly** – a valuable photo reference for UFO, paranormal and Fortean material – will be released in paperback form by New English Library this April. It is hoped that we will have a small stock to sell through FT. Some copies of the hardcover edition are still available. Please apply for rates.

PAMPHLET NEWS

• Apart from his compendious *Geobibliography,* of which we are expecting a review copy, George Eberhart has turned his librarian skills toward a complete index for *Pursuit,* the journal of the Society for the Investigation of the Unexplained. The index covers every issue up to and including volume 11 – ie 1967 – 1978 – and is subdivided into the following indexes: Subject, Geographic, Species, Author, Review, Obituary, and an index of Fortean Irony. This 'freak of human endeavour' is available to SITU members and non-members for $1.50 in US funds. Payment with order to, SITU/Pursuit: Box 265, Little Silver, NJ 07739, USA.

• Sid Birchby informs us that while his extensive and long-awaited report into mystery noise phenomena is being pummelled into report-shape, he has produced an interim summary of the scope of his investigations. Titled *The Hummadruz* (hum + drone + buzz) it is available to anyone who sends 30p (or equivalent) to cover the cost of copying and postage. Sid Birchby: 40 Parrs Wood Ave, Didsbury, Manchester M20 0ND.

PERIODICALS

• *Alpha* have published their last issue for now (No9, Oct 1980), possibly finally. Editors Roy Stemman and David Harvey will be well remembered for their brave efforts in trying to launch a general Fortean + UFO + psychic research magazine on the newsstands, but alas those newsstands turned out to be the rocks upon which the project foundered. Although they ceased newsstand distribution with issue 5, to become solely subscriber based, the debts incurred by the high print-runs of those early issues made the project more and more financially precarious with each new issue. We, at FT, know these problems only too well – there but for the Grace of God ourselves! Still . . . David and Roy have promised the world has not heard the last of them, and we wish them well in their new adventures.

• Depressing news also came from Canada, where the normally indefatigable Mr X has been forced by circumstances to wind up his Res Bureaux as a legal entity, and to cease publication of the *Res Bureaux Bulletin,* for years the purest Fortean newsletter on this earth. One tenth of the subs he needed to meet costs and the withholding of the usual postal rates and tax exemptions accorded by the Canadian Government to Canadian publications, are blamed. Mr X says he will continue to put out the occasional *Chaos,* a journal devoted to Fort's sources. His researches will continue – including his development of a computer database, we hope – and we can expect articles from him in various periodicals. The material normally generated for the defunct *RBB,* will now appear in *INFO Journal* . . . but that too seems to be having difficulties. Oh dear . . .

MEETINGS Etc

• This year's *Festival for Mind-Body Spirit* will be held at Olympia, London, over 20–28 June. Enquiries about programmes, ads or stands to, Mind & Body: 159 George Street, London W1H 5LB.

• BUFORA lectures at Kensington Central Library, Campden Hill Road, London W8, start at 7pm – non-members welcome if seating available.

4 April – 'UFOs without Prejudice', by Ian Watson, author of *Miracle Visitors.*

9 May – 'The Janos People', by Frank Johnson.

6 June – 'What does it all mean?', by Sir John Whitmore.

• The second London International UFO Congress will be held on 24/25 May 1981, again at the Mount Royal Hotel, Marble Arch, London. For details and lecture programme send a stamped self-addressed envelope to, The Hon Secretary, BUFORA, 6 Cairn Ave, London W5 5HX.

• US Forteans, or those visiting Chicago, might like to take advantage of the 'Chicago supernatural tour' organized by Richard T Crowe. Visit old cemetaries and Indian burial grounds, the route of a hitch-hiking ghost, and other haunts and landmarks, including the tomb of 'The Italian Bride', whose body was found incorrupt 6 years after death. Contact Rich Crowe: Box 29054, Chicago, IL 60629, USA.

Help!

This column is free to any reader or researcher who requires help in locating source materials, or questions answered, on Fortean topics. Just send us the details or query on a separate sheet of paper with your name and address, keeping it brief. An FT reader service.

• I am looking for records, clippings etc of Fortean phenomena **in Lancashire, Greater Manchester and Merseyside.** Any help appreciated. Paul Thompson: 47 Leybourne Ave, Southport, Merseyside PR8 3EL.

• Am collecting articles supporting **Ancient Astronaut** theories. Also: footprints, enigmas in coal, etc. Willing to exchange material or help someone else write. Mike Marki: 9 Chautaugua Ct, Oil City, PA 16301, USA.

• I need help with my weekly column, 'Texas Strange', and welcome any information or clippings subject to two impositions: they must deal with Texas or have happened to a Texan. Send details to Dennis Stacy: Box 12434, San Antonio, TX 78212, USA.

• I am researching for a book on **earthquakes** all over the world, and would like to hear of sources, or receive clippings, or correspond with interested parties. Senora Zitha Rodrigues de Chavez: Av.1. Zaragoza 1046-D-402, Col. Pantitlan, Mexico 9DF.

• Anders Liljegren is searching for any reports of unidentified or **mysteriously behaving aeroplanes**, new and old, for an on-going study of **'ghost-fliers'**, particularly in the 1930s. The project includes previously unpublished in-depth investigations and documents now released by the Swedish Secretary of War. Write to Anders Liljegren, Archives for UFO Research: Box 11027, S-11027, Norrkoping, Sweden.

• FT's editor would like to complete FT's collection of *Doubt*. Already have Nos 36-31. If willing to sell please write in

• Am looking for a copy of the biography of Fort by Damon Knight. Will accept (temporarily) any hints on Herbert Spencer/Charles Fort rules of **'super-checkers'**. Also wish information on **Fort's influence on Sci-Fi, Fortean societies and magazines,** and **19th C journalistic hoaxes.** Jean-Louis Brodu: 186 Lea Rd, Wolverhampton, West Midlands.

• Am looking for information on fairy tales – especially **fairies in Wales.** Would appreciate any direction or advice anyone could give. Bob Taylor: 731 Hagley Road West, Quinton, Birmingham B32 1AJ.

• I am compiling a survey of **Fortean phenomena in Scotland** for the decade 1970–1980. I will be going through backfiles of several newspapers for this period, but need help and advice on other sources, data and materials. Eg: where can I get these geomagnetic maps I hear about? Roland Watson: 96 Eskbank St, Glasgow G32 6XS.

Continued from p 1

freebies. Since the last issue, 202 people have lapsed and not yet renewed, while in the same period we have gained 113 new readers. The above figure puts us about 300 short of the 1200 paid subs we need to break even. The shortfall is thankfully helped by the sale of back issues and books, and of course valuable donations.

Bob Rickard.

Truss Fund.

...in which we gratefully acknowledge the heartening support of the following whose donations will be applied where they will do most good.

David Appleton, Sid Birchby, Miss M Carruthers, Nick Cohn, Tim Dinsdale, Hilary Evans, Michael Ferrier, Alan Gardiner, Dr Mia Gerhardt, Roger Gibbons, Mike Grayson, John Harvey, John Hitchens, Phyllis Hall, JP Kain, Kevin McClure, Graham McEwan, Olivier Pecquet, Steve Roberts, Tom H Sakai, Udo Schlegel, Raymond Sinclair, Stephen Spriggs, Paul Thompson, WK Vannan, Roger Waddington, Mike Ward, Douglas Watson . . . and Judith Gee, who suggested the idea of a Library Fund from which we can augment our intended library development. A good idea that, but more on it in the next issue.

Next Issue.

Next issue will contain, among other things, a reflection on Darwinism by **John Michell**; a special feature on the enigma of the runes at Runamo, Sweden, which turned out to be merely cracks in the stone after they were 'deciphered' by a renowned rune scholar, by **Sven Rosen**; and an illustrated feature on photos of Christ, by **Bob Rickard**. We also hope to have more data sections than we have recently, plus all the usual departments and columns.

Crossword.

This crossword was created for us by **Mrs Myra Sagov.** The first correct solution received will win a mystery prize – answers next issue. If you would like to see this a regular feature, let us know.

ACROSS

1. In the throat they are gruff (5
6. Greeting on beer's start place for kettle (3)
8. Island loses note in moron (6)
9. Leased awry a closed letter (6)
11. 'Bird thou never wert' (Keats) (6)
12. I am before agreement in shock (6)
14. Without trumpethead night is near (4)
15. Inner way leads to unbalanced person (10)
19. Always attached to neither (3)
20. Mystic creatures used to be animals (10)
21. Love for Narcissus again (4)
25. Ring out of hood goes to earth (3)
26. Change more suitable for a candle (5)
27. Blocked though led by officer commanding (8)
28. Rash pie for unusual females (7)
30. Judge in a redeeming feature (4)
31. Charm i.e. twisted gives vision (7)
32. Soon the article before no French (4)

DOWN

1. Truth is stranger (7)
2. To be avoided by Ben using Pogo on moor (4,3)
3. See 11 across (6)
4. Drop backwards gives air (3)
5. Perfect circle reached by man (4,4)
6. Hardy has more than one head (5)
7. Live with sound of query to cast a spell (7)
10. Thy logs are haunting (7)
13. Human cry used by owl? (7)
16. The poet is one letter short (3)
17. Marched on to the Devil (9)
18. Lilliputian ends with angle (8)
20. Church following humour produces broom-stick lady (5)
22. Male contains love for garden tool (3)
23. Uneven manifestation gives strange warning (3,4)
24. A line not at all familiar (5)
29. Known as son (3)

Solution next issue.

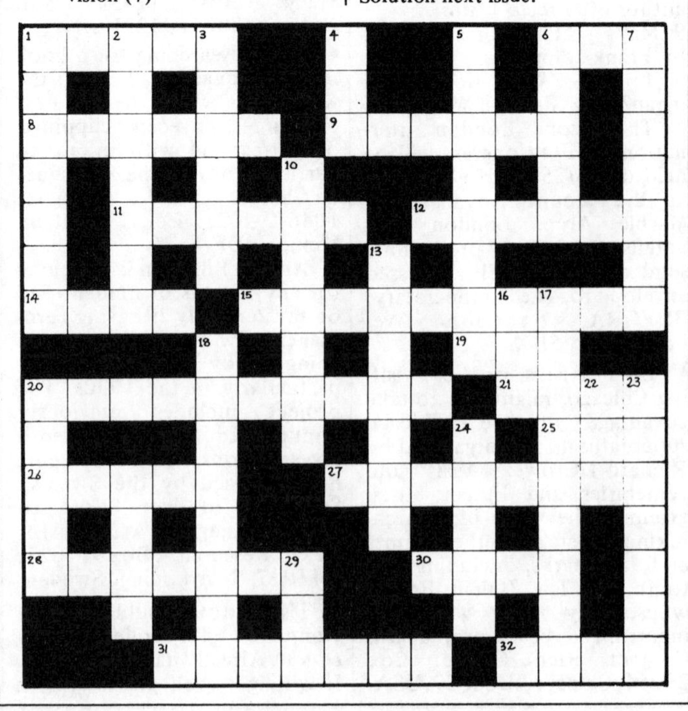

Headlines. An occasional feature. No 1: Animal Attacks.

CHICKEN HOLDS WIFE PRISONER

Amy Carter flees elephant

MOUSE STARTS FIRE

GULLS FORCE DOWN AIRLINER

Government experts are examining the carcases of more than 60 gulls involved in a bird strike which forced a holiday charter jet with 120 people on board to land after take-off from Mancrester Airport yesterday.

Baboons Attack Armored Truck

Cape Town, South Africa (AP) – A gang of baboons halted an armored payroll truck by pelting it with rocks, but eventually let the battered van proceed.

Nuke alert set by squirrels?

SPIDER EVICTS A FAMILY

RABID JACKALS ATTACK FARMERS

Mice close atom plant

Squirrel terrorises a village

A FIGHTING-MAD squirrel is terrorising villagers in East Bridgford, Notts.

After six attacks in four weeks which have left victims clawed and bitten, resi... have called in ... past c...

Bull kills a serenader

Mice have nibbled their way through a year's supply of Communion wafers stored in a church at the R.A.F. base in Wattisham, Suffolk.

WOMAN SHOT BY COW

CROW CAUSED HOLD-UP

DINGO SEIZES BABY GIRL

By Our Melbourne Corresp...

A dingo, a wild ... week-old girl ... ne... ...es Rock ... trlaia ... day ... night tha... ... child's life.

Man is shot —by a pig

Pc SAVAGED BY SQUIRREL

Rat population found thriving on radioactive contamination

Reptile Kills Australian

HEN SHOOTS THE HUNTERS

BULL WRECKS CHINA SHOP

Thugs Bunny the fighting rabbit is causing chaos at Emory and Maggie Aspinall's Florida home. He's chased off their two pet poodles and now the postman is refusing to call until Thugs is muzzled.

Woman dies in monkey horror

'MATTED MASS OF HAIR' ON FLOOR WAS DOG

MOOSE PUTS LAUNDRETTE IN A SPIN

ELECTRIC OWL...

An impudent otter

KILLER DONKEY ON THE LOOSE

Dog bites car

Reign of terror —by hedgehog

Snake strangles showman

Zebra goes berserk at Delhi zoo

Dead widow eaten by 10 pet cats

Spiders turn savage

By Our Science Correspondent

Spiders belonging to two of the 540 species in Britain have started to bite people. Scientists are investigating the new phenomenon.

Scientist eaten by monsters

Jakarta, Oct 2. A French scientist believed to have been eaten by prehistoric monsters on the

Terrified residents flee the Torridge Road kamikaze owl

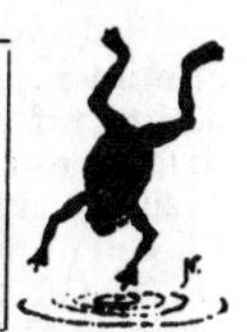

Fortean Times

ISSUE No. 35 The Journal of Strange Phenomena. PRICE: £1·00. $2·50.

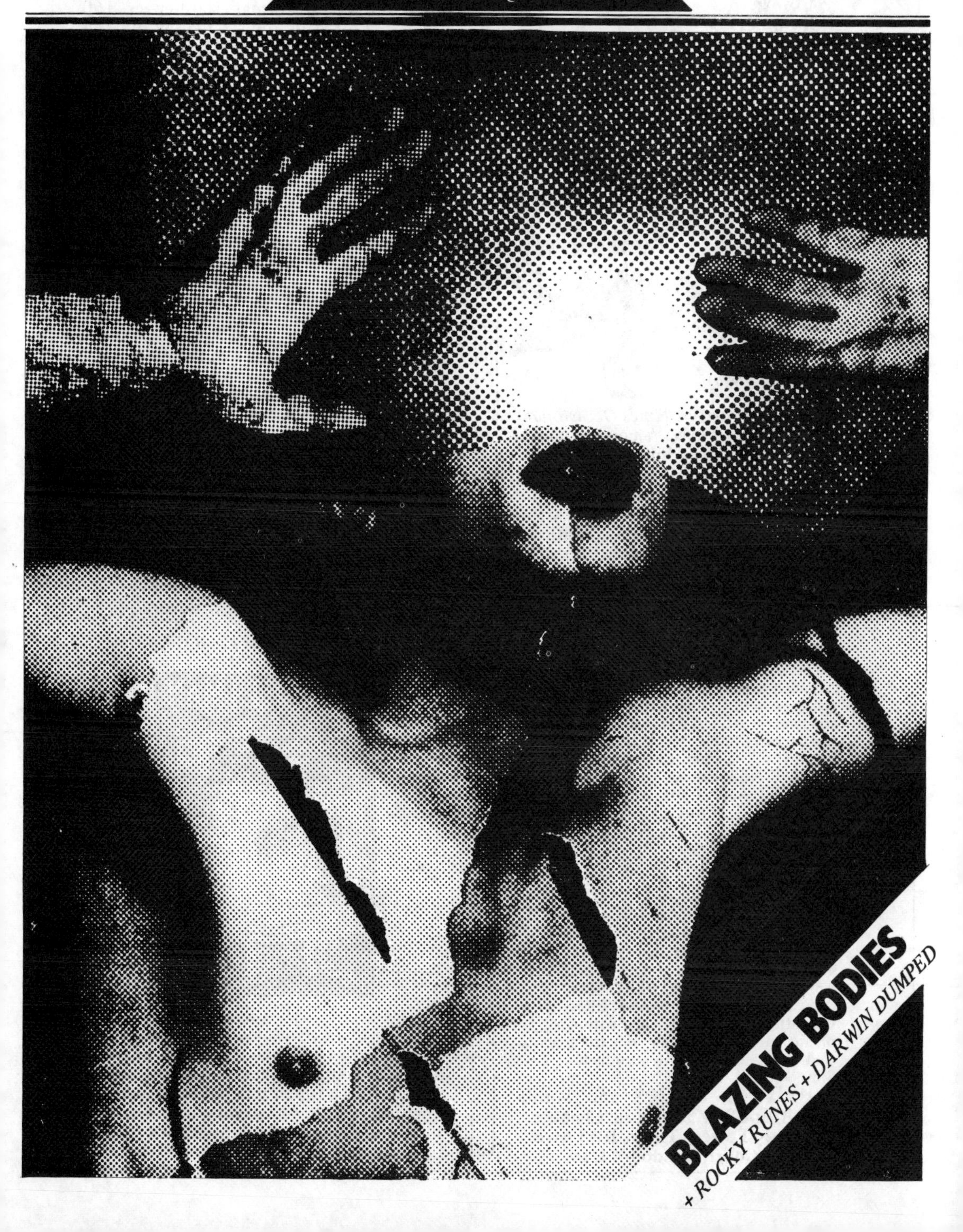

Fortean Times

BM-Fortean Times
London WC1N 3XX.

The Journal of Strange Phenomena.

Summer 1981
ISSN 0308.5899

Editorial.

APOLOGIA
We apologize for the long delay to this issue caused mainly by demands upon your editor's time both in trying to finish a book and in complications of his domestic life. We simply do not have the financial resources to send out over 1000 letters of explanation as we would like, and have to rely on your trust and goodwill Rest assured that work continues in the silent gaps, however slowly, and that we'll get back on schedule eventually. There is no shortage of interesting material and we are eager to get it to you.

CROSSWORD
The word without a clue (oops!) was *pyre*. Disregarding this, there were five correct solutions received – the first opened being from **John Gillam,** who receives the mystery prize. Several people objected to the crossword taking up precious space that could have carried more Weird Stuff, so we are dropping it. Oh well... we'll try anything once.

ADVANCE RENEWAL
Will anyone renewing their subscription by letter before the lapse of their extant sub please indicate that they are

Cont on p 35

Contents.

Cover art by
Andrzej Klimowski

ARTICLES
2 The Myth of Darwinism *John Michell.*
6 The Grace Pett SHC: A Re-examination *Peter Christie.*
14 The Runamo Runes *Sven Rosen + Bob Rickard.*
30 Tales from Malaysia *Ahmad Jamaludin.*

NOTES
10 Fires *SHC.*
13 Antiquities *Dug-up Data.*
38 Plants *Strange Trees.*
39 Alchemy *Magic Fuels.*
40 Heavens Above *Stars and Stuff.*
41 Falls *Frogs + Stones.*
44 Out of Place *Mystery Big Cats.*
44 Science Curiosities *Bizarre Bacteria.*

COLUMNS
19 America Mystica *Michael A Hoffman.*
22 On The Trail *Loren Coleman.*
24 Words From The Wizard *Doc Shiels.*
32 Notes From The Trashkashic Record *Bob Tarte.*
34 Tales From the Yellow Emporium *Steve Moore.*

COMIX
28 Phenomenomix *Hunt Emerson.*

USUAL STUFF
47 Letters.
50 Reviews.
53 Classified Exchange.
58 Subscription Info.

Our new address:

Our old one was care of the *Dark They Were* bookshop in Soho, which recently closed down. This is a good opportunity to express the gratitude of all of us at FT to Derek Stokes, Overlord of DTWAGE, and his staff, for all their friendly help during our long association. Effective immediately, FT has the following memorably brief postal address:

BM — FORTEAN TIMES
London WC1N 3XX, England

Sir Arthur Woodward (centre) and Charles Dawson (right) at Piltdown, Sussex, scene of the discovery of the bogus relics of the 'missing link'.

The Myth of Darwinism.

The last few years have seen growing numbers of writers, philosophers and even biologists expressing doubts about the prevailing dogma of Darwinism, and even the so-called neo-Darwinism. **John Michell,** co-author of *Phenomena,* and author of *Simulacra* and the forthcoming *Megalithomania,* believes Darwin's theory of Evolution to be a pernicious myth used to shape and justify low-mindedness in all aspects of modern life. Is there a remedy?

Of all the subjects I have ever written about, the one that always brings the most lively response from readers is that of evolution and Darwinism. Some people seem quite upset that one should doubt Darwin's theory, and the tone of their letters is often that of people who feel their deepest religious convictions are being challenged. Many writers have identified the Darwinian faith as a form of secular religion. More exactly, it is a cosmogony or creation myth, and it has the same magical, fairy-tale appeal as have all traditional cosmogonies. In Darwin's myth, cells of their own accord group themselves to form more complicated organisms, these separate themselves into species, and finally one of these, an ape-like creature, develops a higher consciousness and becomes a human being. As a fairy tale it seems harmless enough, but higher claims have been made for Darwin's account of the evolution of life: that it is literally true as biological fact and that it illustrates the ruling principle in the universe of spontaneous organisation and growth. This principle is represented in human nature by our agressive, inventive characteristics which have made us the 'fittest' of all races and thus the legitimate rulers of creation.

The way things have happened over the last

hundred years has been so closely related to the progress of the Myth of Darwinism that it is impossible to make sense of it without considering the nature of this myth, its origin and the ideas and actions it has tended to prove.

Every culture has its conventional cosmogony or creation myth which serves to explain how everything from the beginning of the world to the appearance of life and human consciousness first came about. These various myths both reflect and influence the cultures they belong to, and determine the ways in which people think and relate to their surroundings. The myth sanctifies the action. Most educated people at the time when Darwin's *Origin of Species* was published in 1850 believed that civilization was advancing towards a kind of rationalistic millenium. Intoxicated by the discoveries in science, psychology and economics which followed, many of them came to believe that their class and race held all keys to the future, and they looked forward to the approaching triumph of order, empire and moralistic religion throughout the world. They saw history as a pyramid of accumulated knowledge with themselves at its tip, and they regarded nature similarly, as a hierarchy which ascended from slugs and snails and puppy dogs' tails to apes, savage men, tame men, English men and, on top of the whole pile, the English professor type, Charles Darwin, using the priestly language of science, who created the desired myth to justify the established prejudices of his generation. Darwinism quickly prevailed, not because it passed any scientific tests, but because the idea behind it so exactly coincided with the ideas of the ruling classes, races and interests of the time. From a speculative biological theory it soon became elevated to dogma ('The evolution of life is no longer a theory. It is a fact. It is the basis of all our thinking.' – Sir Julian Huxley, 1959), and disbelievers were stigmatised as heretics or worse.

The new myth of human nature as an accidental development from animal nature rapidly defeated the only rival in the field, the outworn myth of God's Creation in 4004 BC. All educated people acknowledged that it was now scientifically established that man was a beast at heart. His instincts were those of a savage beast, and it was only the power of modern, rational civilization that kept those instincts in check. This type of civilization had been developed by the white races alone. They had evolved further than all others. They represented the peak of humanity. They had achieved their pre-eminence by the operation of natural selection, the 'survival of the fittest', and it was therefore necessary in future to ensure that natural selection kept on operating in their favour and against the dark soul of the African and the primitivism of the shaman and mystic. Kindly people sent off trousers, missionaries and Presbyterian morals to help raise the benighted natives. Others, more 'realistic', understood that the primitives were beyond help. They had lost out in the race to be the 'fittest', and nature had alread passed sentence on them. Primitive people, wrote Leonard Woolf as recently as 1937, are 'the flotsam and jetsom of human history. They are the middle term between the life of animals and the life of civilization.' On this understanding, colonials in all continents believed that killing off the aboriginals was not really murder since these people were only on the way to becoming fully human.

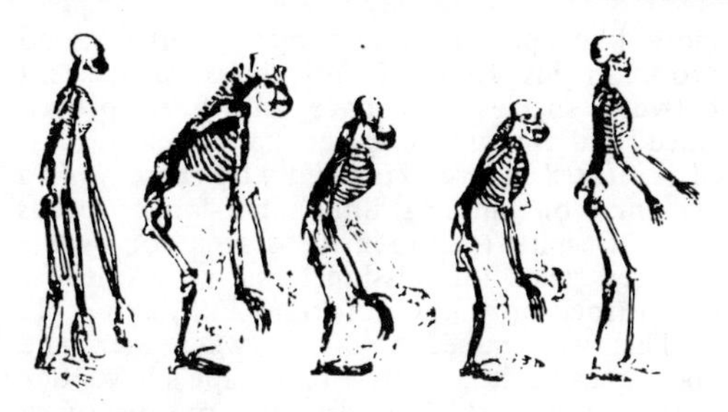

Thomas Huxley's chain of human descent. The long-armed creature on the left is a type unknown either to biologists or fossil-hunters, and was drawn from Huxley's imagination. Between the ape types and the man (on the right) there are no known links. Later, such chains always featured the Piltdown ape-man. Scientists have now abandoned this convention, but similar chains continue to illustrate evolutionist propaganda books for children.

The rise of Darwinism led to genocide as directly as did the rise of Nazi ideas in Germany. Hitler was a staunch Darwinian, and his obsession with making his own race the 'fittest' was no personal aberration, but derived from the scientific orthodoxy of his time. And we can trace his ideas on racial breeding back to one of its prime sources. 'What an extraordinary effect might be produced on our race if its object was to unite in marriage those who possessed the finest and most suitable natures, mental, moral and physical!' wrote Francis Galton, Darwin's cousin and close colleague, in 1865.

To help bring this about, he proposed keeping a register of 'superior' families who should be encouraged to interbreed, and thus 'further the ends of evolution more rapidly and with less distress than if events were left to their own course.' Darwin himself agreed that Galton's proposal was the 'sole feasible' way of proceeding. 'The object seems a grand one' he wrote, yet he feared that Galton was too idealistic and that people would never co-operate intelligently with a rational breeding policy.

Darwin's theory began as biological speculation. He himself looked rather like an ape, and it occurred to him that people were no more like apes than, say, pigs. There was no proof in his time of any lines of descent between species, nor have any been proved since; and Darwin's excuse, that the scantiness of the fossil record explained why there was no evidence of 'missing links', no longer holds good. Despite the intensive search for over a hundred years for missing links, only one has ever turned up – the notorious Piltdown skull.

This was indeed a link between men and apes, because it consisted of an ape's jaw stuck onto a human skull by one or more dishonest evolutionists who were desperate to prove their case. The leading suspect as the hoaxer is Teilhard de Chardin who tried to make a religion out of evolutionism. Piltdown was the sacred relic of this faith. All the other ape-man candidates – Java man, Peking man and those from Africa were constructed by evolutionists out of bone fragments, sometimes from pieces of different individuals scattered round a site. The illustrations here below show how the trick is done: some ancient bone fragments, much plaster and a great deal of imagination. From these objects, which have much in common with the fake mermaids once exhibited in museums, are 'reconstructed' the hairy monsters featured in the text books of evolutionist propaganda for children.

People say 'Oh, of course evolution happens; you can see it in action', and they point to local variations within species, and those made by breeders and gardeners and such effects as melanism in moths which have developed dark wings in response to industrial pollution in their habitats. But such changes are micro-effects within species. They do not affect the essential type. Some species, dogs and pigeons (which Darwin bred) for example, are more variable than others, but even they have limits. You can breed a strawberry as big as a small tomato but never as big as an orange, and there is a certain point beyond which you can not breed horses to run any faster or cows to produce more milk. Every individual deviates from its type, but when this deviation becomes exaggerated either the individual is sterile or its offspring revert back to the norm. As to melanism in moths, the blackening of their wings turned out to be a temporary, local adaptation, and as polluted areas were cleaned up the moths' wings began to lighten and to display again their previous patterns.

Micro-changes do not, as is often assumed, mount up so as to produce a change in the species with a new strain arising which cannot breed with the original stock. Scientists have tried to prove otherwise by experiments with fast-breeding fruit flies. A hundred or more generations of these insects were exposed to radiation to induce mutations. Flies were produced with legs on their heads and of different shapes and sizes, but if these were capable of breeding at all, their offspring tended to look as normal fruit flies should look. Evolutionists emphasise micro-changes involving one species developing into another. It has never been known to happen, and no one has discovered a way in which it possibly could happen.

Not only Piltdown but Darwinism itself is an almighty fraud. The first inkling I had of that came from reading Gertrude Himmelfarb's *Darwin and the Darwinian Revolution* (1959) in which she exposed the extraordinarily dishonest, bullying tactics which Darwin and his followers used to promote his theory. Professor Himmelfarb's very sharp, scholarly book was as good as suppressed by being ignored by the academic critics. Almost all the anti-evolutionist literature at the time was produced by fundamentalist religious writers. From reading these, it appeared that most of them were successful in discrediting Darwinian evolution theory, but they had difficulty in establishing their own belief in a quite recent Creation. Easily the best critique of Darwinism, purely as a biological theory, is Norman Macbeth's *Darwin Retried*. This author is not concerned with proposing an alternative creation myth; but he demonstrates, clearly and with good humour, how completely Darwinism has failed to stand up to any of the tests applied to it, and he quotes the best Darwinian authorities to show how modern science has quietly abandoned the classical evolution theory – just as the pre-Darwin geologists had quietly abandoned the creation theory – while continuing to profess allegiance to the Myth of Darwinism. Macbeth comments that his book was noticed only by the religious people, not by the scientists to whom it was addressed. A teacher or scientist, particularly in Britain, who openly questions Darwin's theory still does so at the risk of his or her own career. Yet the tide is rapidly turning as the weakness at the foundations and the misleading or evil effects of the Darwin Myth become more apparent. In this year's lecture to the British Association, John Durant delivered a withering attack on Darwinism, particularly in its social effects, tracing back to its influence the idea of the 'beast in man', that assumption which has been adopted by popular myth-makers such as Ardrey and Lorenz, and which is used to justify repression of human nature on the grounds that it is essentially bestial and aggressive. On the question of ape-men Durant observes that 'all the fossil evidence concerning human origins which has been obtained to date could easily be assembled for inspection in a single small room.' And all this evidence is equivocal. As Charles Fort said, we could just as easily 'prove' from it that apes are descended from men. For a good anti-Darwin view of the controversy see M. Bowden's recent *Ape-Men; Fact or Fallacy*.

So to the important question. If Darwinism

is an inadequate biological theory and destructive in its effects as myth or paradigm, with what should it be replaced? Perhaps we do not need a formal creation myth at all. The attitude to nature commonly recommended by the wise is to observe it as it is without worrying about what it has been or how it might become, to discern its essential fitness, the beauty of its parts and of the whole and the subtlety of its interactions. There is no enduring monstrosity in nature, nothing in the process of becoming, but everything as it apparently should and must be. It is *as if* nature was created as a perfect and living organism, harmonious and self-regulating, and since it appears that children and good and simple people like, and are therefore entitled to, a picturesque creation myth, it may be that that aspect of things should provide its basis. Why see nature, as did the sickly Darwin, as a perpetual, painful struggle of survival and supremacy; why emphasise *that* aspect and make it into a paradigm for life and society as a whole, when the other principle, that of symbiosis, the mutual dependence, co-operation and delight that neighbouring species manifest to each other, is at least as evident in nature as well as being a far more profitable subject for human study.

Perhaps the Fall of Man is a better myth than Man's Rise to Civilization. Are we fallen angels, with aspirations to regain paradise, or upstart apes, creatures with aggressive instincts which made us supreme and which we need to cultivate to fulfil our destinies as invaders of the planets? Both are myths, and we are free to adopt whichever we choose. The question of scientific evidence is neither here nor there, because such evidence always tends to arrange itself in accordance with the dominant myth of the time. The creation myth influences not only science but the entire mode of thinking among the people who adopt it. The social effects of Darwinism are not the unpredictable side-effects of the evolution theory; they are central to it as the inevitable products of Darwin's way of looking at things – so different, for example, from William Blake's. Nor was Blake a 'mere' poet and mystic. His perceptions were conditioned by and expressed in terms of an ancient cosmogeny and philosophy from the tradition that historically appeals to the highest poetic instincts in people and derives from the most long-lasting stable civilizations in antiquity. In other words, there are some ancient examples of creation myth which seem to have worked, and modern truth-seekers or myth-makers might do well to consider these rather than continue over-awed by the exclusive claims of the evolutionists.

•

John Michell

This article has been reprinted from Resurgence, *via* Quicksilver Messenger *(Autumn 1980, with kind permission.*

Sunday Times, 12 November 1972

Observer, 12 November 1972

By an amusing coincidence, both the Sunday Times *and the* Observer *commissioned artists to draw the ape-man as he appeared in life. The artists were both advised by equally eminent but rival scientists, and the two results (above) were both published on the same day. If only one version had been published, I might have believed it.*

(Below) Another example of different reconstructions from the same data. The original in this case was some skull fragments labelled Zinjanthropus.

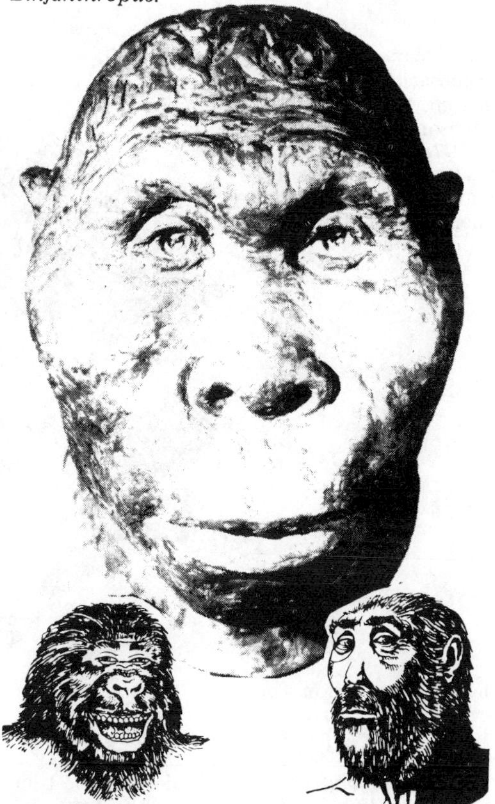

Drawn for a scientific journal.

Drawn for National Geographic, Sept 1960.

Reconstructions of Zinjanthropus head. Two newspaper drawings compared to a clay model made by Harry L. Shapiro, head of the anthropology department of the American Museum of Natural History (photo from Shapiro's Peking Man, *1974.)*

The Grace Pett SHC: A Re-examination.

Setting a research example to us all **Peter Christie** has looked into one of the best-known and most-quoted case of SHC, involving Grace Pett who became the, uh, toast of Ipswich in 1744. To judge from the refreshing amount of new information Peter has uncovered we encourage a re-examination of old stories generally.

Colin Frajbis

Some years ago I purchased a paperback entitled *Fire from Heaven*, written by Michael Harrison and first published in 1976. [1] This, as most readers will probably know, deals with the phenomenon of spontaneous human combustion (or SHC). One of the cases quoted concerned a Grace Pett of Ipswich who apparently suffered this weird form of death on April 9th 1744.

Since reading the book I had for some time been considering following up this story. My interest lay in two aspects of the case – the Fortean side and the archival side. As a keen student of Fortean phenomena any case of SHC, especially one so famous as this, was clearly worthy of investigation. Likewise as a keen family and local historian I was interested in tracking down the records concerning the story and discovering if other material about the case and its history could be located.

The initial source I had to work on was Harrison's book where there are three references to the case. The first of these reads, 'When they found Grace Pett, of Ipswich, 'like a half burned wooden log, a heap of cinders covered with white ash', a paper screen standing within a few inches of the fierce fire which had consumed Mrs Pett was unscorched.' The second reference refers to Grace as 'dedicated to drunkenness', whilst the third, somewhat prophetically, refers to the fact that 'few dedicated researchers toil on without any original discovery as the reward for their dedication' and then goes on to cite a forensic medicine book that refers to the case. Also in this third reference was the valuable statement, 'Outside of a newspaper report the first mention of this case is to be found in Sir David Brewster's *Letters on Natural Magic* (1832).' [2]

This book by Harrison thus gave me three leads – the volume on forensic medicine, the newspaper report and Brewster's *Letters*. As chance would have it an old archaeologist of my acquaintance had given me a copy of this latter book. My copy was the fifth edition dated 1842. The full title is *Letters on Natural Magic addressed to Sir Walter Scott, Bart.* It covers a whole variety of strange occurrences and phenomena, eg:

'Remarkable effects produced by intense light.'

'Spectre of a deceased friend sitting in an easy chair.'

'Images of cows seen in the air.' etc etc.

A whole chapter is given over to the phenomena related to fire and this includes the case of Grace Pett. As this gives a good coverage of the case I will quote it at length here,

'So recently as 1744, a similar example of spontaneous combustion occurred in our own country, at Ipswich. A fisherman's wife, of the name of Grace Pett, of the parish of St. Clement's, had been in the habit for several years of going downstairs every night, after she was half undressed, to smoke a pipe. She did this on the evening of the 9th of April, 1744. Her daughter, who lay in the same bed with her, had fallen asleep, and did not miss her mother till she awaked early in the morning. Upon dressing herself, and going downstairs, she found her mother's body lying on the right side, with her head against the grate, and extended over the hearth with her legs on the deal floor, and appearing like a block of wood burning with a glowing fire without flames. Upon quenching the fire with two bowls of water, the neighbours, whom the cries of the daughter had brought in, were almost stifled with the smell. The trunk of the unfortunate woman was almost burned to ashes, and appeared like a heap of charcoal covered with white ashes. The head, arms, legs, and thighs, were also much burned. There was no fire whatever in the grate, and the candle was burned out in the socket of the candlestick, which stood by her. The clothes of the child on one side of her, and a paper screen on the other were untouched: and the deal floor was neither singed nor discoloured. It was said that the woman had drunk plentifully of gin overnight in welcoming a daughter who had recently returned from Gibraltar.'

This sums up the main points well but I wondered where this report had come from? I was unable to locate a copy of the book of forensic medicine and so fell back on the 'newspaper report'. This was not difficult to locate – during the 1740s Ipswich only boasted one newspaper, the weekly *Ipswich Journal*. A run of these is kept at the Ipswich branch of the Suffolk Record Office where I consulted them. Turning to the relevant date I was excited to discover the following;

'On Tuesday Morning (April 10) a Woman in St Clement's Parish was found burnt to Death in her own House. This unhappy Affair was attended with several extraordinary circumstances, but they are so variously related, that we cannot at present give our Readers any particular Account of them.' [3]

However, a determined search through succeeding issues for the next six months revealed no further references to the 'unhappy Affair'. One wonders why such a 'newsworthy' story was not followed up?

Whilst in the Record Office I took the opportunity to search the earliest surviving rate-books for St.Clement's parish (1750) and these revealed five Pett households all labelled as 'Poor' – clearly Grace came from a humble background.

Checking through Clarke's *Ipswich* [4] I found that the author had referred to the case and gave as his source a journal known as the *Ipswich Magazine*. Research soon revealed that this was a short-lived magazine only published for the one year of 1799. Luckily, copies of this still exist and in the Bury St.Edmunds branch of the Suffolk Record Office I turned to pages 100-103 and pages 140-144 which concerned the case. The first of these references is a letter addressed 'To the Editors' which throws a new light on the case altogether. It is worth quoting at length;

'GENTLEMEN— The following narrative will probably amuse some of your readers: though many may think it a falsehood, it is an absolute fact, and there are still living, in this town, witnesses to the truth of it. [The story as told by Brewster is then given]... The poor old woman had the reputation of being a witch among some of her ignorant neighbours; and at that time a neighbouring farmer, one Garnham, had some of his sheep taken in an odd way: they were supposed to be bewitched, and he was advised to burn one of them. The farmer was much too wise to entertain such an idea; but his wife, more credulous in such matters, resolved to try the experiment. Accordingly, on the very night that this woman was burnt, Mrs. Garnham, after her husband had gone to bed, made their head man bring in a diseased sheep, and make a great fire and burn it to death.

This circumstance gave encouragement to the report of the poor old woman's being a witch; and they thought sufficient reason was found why her feet and ankles were not burnt, as it was reported, that the feet of the sheep were not, and that they were fixed in the ground when the animal was burnt. This was not true; for the poor creature was burned in the backhouse. Its four legs being tied together, it was laid on the hearth, and a miserable death it had; for soon after the fire began to burn fiercely about it, the bandage on its legs was burnt off, and the distressed sheep jumped up, and ran from the fire: the man then ran a pitch-

fork into its body, forced it into the fire again, and held it there till it was destroyed.

J.S. Ipswich'

Who J.S. was I am unsure but further research would probably elicit an answer and might possibly explain how he or she came to know these further, and very circumstantial, details of the case.

'A comment from someone signing themselves 'B' appended to the above letter decries the gullibility and unchristian attitudes of the people involved, adding that the sheep was burned on the directions of a Mr. Winter, a well-known conjuror or white magician of the area at that time. The writer adds that:

'We have made many inquiries into this affair, of persons who lived near Mrs. Pett, and who saw her ashes lying on the hearth and floor. Their relations agree in most parts with the foregoing; but state, that some ship-carpenters going to work about five o'clock in the morning, saw a great light in the room, broke into it, and found her in a blaze: they then procured some bowls of water from a pump which was near the door, in the street; on throwing it on the body it made the same hssing as if thrown on red-hot iron. Thus was the fire extinguished, but not till the body was reduced, as related above, to ashes.

These persons agree too in adding that Mrs. Pett was seen to pass hastily over Bishop's Hill, on her way to Mr Carnham's at Purdis Farm, about two miles from Ipswich, where she made a violent noise, and that, not being answered, she was seen to return over the same hill. But this part appears not well substantiated, and perhaps is merely a tradition, which might have originated in a superstitious reverence for the conjuror, who it seems had predicted that the witch would come to the place where the animal was burning; and had given his injunctions that every one there should be silent. Most accounts agree that there could be no fire or light, at the commencement of this phenomenon, though some say Mrs. Pett rose for the purpose of smoaking tobacco; but this is improbable, or the circumstance of the situation of the pipe would certainly have been mentioned.

The entry of Grace Pett's burial, in the register-book of St. Clement's parish, Ipswich, is April 12, 1744.

B.'

Of great interest was the next paragraph after the above which read.

'A drawing which was taken in the room, with the woman lying in the situation in which she was first discovered, may be seen at Mr. Bucke's Surgery, Cornhill, Ipswich. On the back of the frame reference is made to Medical Extracts, *page 93.'*

I have been unable to find out any more about this drawing which would rank as the earliest illustration of a case of SHC. The second reference in the *Ipswich Magazine* is a general review of various cases with a note that the Pett case had been printed in *Philosophical Transactions.*

After these exciting discoveries I was left facing an apparent brick wall. I knew of references in the *Philosophical Transactions*, a forensic medicine book, and also something called *Medical Extracts* none of which I could lay my hands on, and in the case of the latter I could not even identify.

Wondering where to turn next I remembered that the premier collection of books covering the history of medicine was to be found at the Wellcome Institute for the History of Medicine in London. I wrote to them explaining my problem and was delighted to receive back a very full answer from Robin Price, the Deputy Librarian.

He had identified *Medical Extracts* as being *Medical Extracts: on the nature of health, with practical observations:and the laws of the nervous and fibrous systems, by a friend to improvements* by R.J. Thornton which was published in London in 1796. The Pett reference was on page 93 of Volume 1 and, after relating the basic facts, went on to say,

'These remarkable instances of the quick combustion *carried on in the body, if I may be allowed to continue the expression, is adduced only as exceptions to Dr. Thornton's general rule, that within the body there is always carried on a* gentle combustion, *productive of the vital flame.'*

In addition to this reference the librarian had been good enough to locate a copy of the forensic medicine book, this was *Elements of Medical Jurisprudence* by T.T. Beck (London 1825), and had sent me a photocopy of the relevant pages 313-314. This has some strange variations to the usual story e.g. Mr. Pett is said to be a fishmonger instead of a fisherman, it is the daughter who quenches the flames not the passing ship-carpenters etc.

The most interesting document the library sent me, however, was a photocopy of the article in the *Philosophical Transactions of the Royal Society of Gt. Britain* (1744-45 p.463). This said that the first account of the case came in a letter from Mr. R. Love of Ipswich to his brother George Love an apothecary in Westminster. This letter was dated 28 June 1744 and was read to the Royal Society on November 8th of that year. The article quotes part of the letter and adds that on November 15th a Dr. Lobb read two more letters on the same case to the Society – one from the Rev. Notcutt of Ipswich to a Mr. Gibbons and the other from Mr. Gibbons. These letters are dated a month later than Mr. Love's. Mr. Gibbons had interviewed Mrs. Pett's daughter and two other people who had been in the house at the time of the fire, one of whom was named as Boyden.

The article says that the 'grease' from the body, 'had so penetrated into the Hearth, as not to be scour'd out, yet they observed that the Deal-Floor was neither singed nor discolour'd.'

Intrigued at these new details I wrote to the Royal Society and received a very courteous reply plus, to my astonishment, a photocopy of Mr. Love's original letter – the earliest report on the case that exists! I have reproduced this below as it is of such interest. (The spelling is that of the original.)

'Brother— I attended ye Coroner's Inquest yt sat on ye old woman that was burnt, I had no Curiosity to see ye body, not then looking on it any way extraordinary. the evidence (as I remember) was, the Daughter Deposed that her mother (the deceased) went up Stairs when she ye Daughter went to bed abt 10 o'Clock and ye deced after loosing her Stais took a Candle and went down Stairs, to Smoke a pipe in private as ye Daughter then Supposed, and next morning abt 6 was found burned on ye Brick hearth in ye Kittching or comon Keeping room, where no fire or fewell had been ther than ye Candle and ye Pipe an her mean wearing apparell and yt she was not in liquor nor addicted to drink Ginn, and yt ye Candle Stick was Standing by her, so far for ye Evidence before ye Coroner, the Jury viewed ye body and found it accidental death, But I have since heard it said by those who were curious in examining ye matter, whereof Mr Cornelius now at London was one, that ye feet and lower part of ye Leggs were not burnt with [?] ye Stockings on ye parts remaining, not Singed; very little of ye parts of ye Leggs yt were burnt lay on ye wood floor the rest of ye body on a Brick hearth in ye Chimney; part of the Head not burnt a Body of ffire in her breast in ye morning found, which was Quenched with water, her bone chiefly calcined and ye whole so farr reduced to ashes as to be put in ye Coffin wth a Shovel and yt she & her Daughter were much addicted to Ginn.

The matter extraordinary seems to be ye burning in such a manner without any other fewell but ye Clothes on her back, tho' there was a long time to do it in. It seems ye Leggs were burnt so farr only as were covered by her petty Coats, as she lay on ye floor.

Yrs R: Love. 28: June 1744'

This is a much fuller account than is given in the printed *Transactions* and adds new evidence especially with regard to the area burnt.

At the same time as I had been hunting down this information I had also been writing to Mr. Steward, the editor of the newly-published *Suffolk Bibliography* [5] which listed as entry number 3224 *Grace Pett. A tale of witchcraft* by Elizabeth Cotton (c.1875). No location for this book was given but Mr. Steward directed me to the Suffolk Record Office which holds all his original material and they supplied me with the source of his information. This was a private book collector who owned a copy and this gentleman, Mr. Tony Copsey, very generously sent me a complete photocopy of the book. It adds little to the story being based on the account given in Clarke's *Ipswich* but it is lavishly illustrated with many etchings of local scenes and events in the case which accompany a long series of verses recounting Grace Pett's demise. Typical of these is,

'The Sheep are Dying at Purdies Farm,
We carry out Dead both by Night and Day;
Witchcraft alone could work us such harm,
And GRACE PETT has been seen near the Fold to stray.'

and

'Next Day in Her Cottage at Ipswich found,
All charred to Ashes but Feet and Hands
Grace Pett lies dead on the Unscorched ground,
And the Plague is stayed upon Purdies Lands.'

To summarise then – the many articles and features on the case of Grace Pett can be traced back to two sources – one the letters from Messrs. Love, Notcutt and Gibbons written contemporaneously with the case, and second the article in the *Ipswich Magazine* written apparently from eye-witness accounts some 50 years later. The basic outline of the story is the same in both sets of sources and the very unusual nature of the death appears to be borne out. The strong presumption of witchcraft and its defeat by white magic has been ignored by all previous modern writers on the subject.

My original intention of seeking out as much information as I could can, I think, be said to have been successful to a great extent. I hope the story of how I did this will provide other readers with ideas and possibly even encourage them to research other famous Fortean cases of the past.

•

Peter Christie, BA. M.Phil.

REFERENCES

1) Michael Harrison, *Fire from Heaven* (London 1976).
2) Sir David Brewster, *Letters on Natural Magic* (London 1823).
3) *The Ipswich Journal* 14 April 1744, p3 col 2.
4) GR Clarke, *History and Description of the Town and Borough of Ipswich (Ipswich 1830).*
5) AV Steward, *A Suffolk Bibliography* (Ipswich 1979).

Author's Note: Other references to the Pett case have been found during this research: eg *The Gentleman's Magazine* (1746), an article in *East Anglia Daily Times* in 1975, and other obviously derivative items in various histories of Suffolk. I have searched for the original coroner's report on this case but this is now lost, as are any personal diaries or records of the main writers specified in the *Philosophical Transactions* report. I am now searching for personal details of Grace Pett (birth, marriage, children, etc) and hope to report my findings when they are more complete than at present - PC.

The fires of spontaneous combustion smoulder on today, flaring into a reported case now and then. We make a plea for professional help in beginning a study of this very real mystery.

We have not dealt with the subject of possible spontaneous human combustion (SHC) for some time, and have accumulated quite a pile of interesting and non-so-interesting material. At various times your editor has tried to obtain more details of a case, or a copy of the Coroner's report, only to be told by police and/or Coroner's Office that it was none of my business.

The best case in point is the fiery death of Mr Henry Thomas, a 73-year-old widower, of Ebbw Vale, in Welsh Gwent. It seems he failed to turn up for a Sunday lunch with his daughters' families, on 6 Jan 1980, and so his two sons-in-law went to his home, and failing to get an answer, broke in. In the smoke-filled living-room they saw a pile of what looked like clothes and charred bones. Somehow these remains were identified as their father-in-law. Det-Constable Terance Russell said to the inquest that he saw the skull was partially burnt and the rest of the body almost totally consumed. He was surprised to see so little damage to the rest of the room, considering the intensity of such a fire. A TV set was still on, its plastic knobs distorted by the heat, and a settee not three feet from the armchair in which Mr Thomas had been sitting was 'completely untouched' by the flames. A Home Office pathologist, Dr J S Andrews, said that death was caused by almost total burning. The fire which had consumed the body, he said, had done little damage, even in the vicinity of the body. A fire-side rug on which the body was lying was 'two-thirds untouched by the flames'. A neighbour said he had seen Mr Thomas sitting near the fire the night before (5th Jan). The Gwent County Coroner, Colonel Kenneth Treasure, was reported in the *South Wales Argus* 8 Feb 1980, from which we have this account, to have concluded: that Mr Thomas was sitting in his chair by the fire when his clothing was set alight 'by ashes'. There were ashes still in the grate, but no other evidence of burning except in the area close to the body, which was almost totally reduced to cinders. Col Treasure thought that Mr Thomas could have fallen forward striking his head on the grate.

Those who have read of SHC before will recognise here the classic scenario and effects. I wished to know more about the evidence of Dr Andrews and the fire officers, so I traced the address of the Gwent Coroner and wrote. I hoped that a copy of his report would shed light on the apparently unnoticed (or at least uncommented-upon) detail of intact clothing seen by the constable amid the charred bones. And could not Mr Thomas have begun flaming while in his chair, and got up on reflex, but was consumed, uh, in a flash by the time he hit the carpet? The unadulterated clues and evidence was not forthcoming. Col Treasure's very brief reply said: 'I regret I do not feel able to give you the information you ask for as you do not appear to be an 'interested party' within the meaning of the appropriate regulations.' Well, what *is* the definition of an interested party, I'd like to know? And why so *post-facto* cagey when the Press were obviously allowed into the inquest, where (one fervently hopes) all the evidence was heard?

Naively, I have assumed that a coroner's report is in the public domain – perhaps we have a solicitor among our readers who can confirm or correct this, and suggest avenues by which honest inquiries can be made of the authorities. Inquiries at police HQs equally end up negatively – usually with the impression that you are some kind of ghoul. It's no good saying one is investigating SHC, because this is not recognized and any explanations sound quite improbable – despite classical descriptions in forensic textbooks. Claiming that one is editor of a journal unknown to them is also unproductive, although disguising one's inquiry (which I did in the above case) as an investigation of the 1–2% of annual fire-deaths statistically listed as 'cause unknown' sounds a lot more acceptable. Fortean investigators in the USA –– like Larry Arnold –– have had wonderful cooperation from the authorities concerned in fire-deaths, including the acquisition of valuable evidential photos, but so far nothing like that has been achieved in Britain. Not that I know of anyone here – apart from Peter Christie, on the literary side (see his Grace Pett article) – who has investigated a British SHC. If we have any doctors among our readers interested in research or investigation of this subject, please contact the editor. It is about time we had a thorough scientific study of the subject and FT would be glad to make its files available.

In the meantime here is a summary of the known facts in some other recent cases. Please bear in mind that we do not claim these are SHC cases – conclusive proof is absent and depends on the needed investigation – but their circumstances merit consideration as *possible* SHCs.

•

At the inquest on Mrs Lily Smith, a 76-year-old widow, of Greenfield Cottage, Hutton-le-Hole, Yorkshire, the Ryedale Coroner, Mr Henry Blakeston, said that her body was so consumed by fire that it was impossible to identify or say how she died. However, since she had been in the habit of bolting herself in her cottage, refusing entry to all except her son, the Coroner was satisfied that the remains were of Mrs Smith, found after a fire at the home on 25 Jan 1979. The postman raised the alarm that morning, and calling two neighbours and a farmer, they broke in. There was thick smoke but no sign of flames, and they could not find Mrs Smith. A constable was called, and, as he later testified, he found a pair of legs (presumably burned off between thigh and hip) under a wooden dining chair near the fireplace, and on the chair itself, where a body would be sitting, was a heap of charred bones.

By way of explanation a Kirkbymoorside fire officer said Mrs Smith had been in the habit of sitting in front of the fire with her feet on the hearth, and that in his opinion 'something fell either out of the fireplace or down the chimney.' He produced photos of the scene saying that the fire had eventually gone out 'for lack of oxygen' because of its fierce burning.

Although an open verdict was returned on Mrs Smith's death, the Coroner seemed satisfied with the fire officer's explanation, but I'm afraid it only makes me more curious. The lady's legs were nearest the fire and thus most accessible to any spark or brand leaping from that direction, yet these alone survived the conflagration. It was suggested the fire was so intense that it used up the oxygen and put itself out, yet there is little evidence of other damage in the room. Indeed the fire had been intense enough to reduce Mrs Smith to cinders and yet left the wooden chair on which she sat substantially intact.

Yorkshire Evening Press 15 Feb 1979.

•

Our next report comes from Singapore. On 4 August 1980, a Chinese delivery man, Leong Weng Chai, saw smoke coming from a 7th-floor window. Rushing up, he heard voices behind the door and managed to open it. Madam Saemah Sapari was on fire, struggling and shouting, so he took off his shirt and tried to beat out the flames as he took her to safety. Returning, he heard a child crying, and rescued the woman's son, Mohammed, aged 6. His clothes were on fire too. Both were badly burned and died later. Before she died, Madam Saemah made a statement to the effect that at 5.20 pm that day she had been watching TV when her son shouted from the bedroom. Going in she saw the bed on fire. She said she pulled her son off the bed and put out the fire, then carried him to the staircase herself. No explanation is given for the conflicting accounts. The State Coroner, Mr Seng Kwang Boon, returned an open verdict, saying that he could not discover how the fire started, or how both were burnt.

Straits Times (Malaysia) 27 Jan 1981.

•

Vicky Gilmour, 19 was in the girls' room of a disco in Darlington, Co. Durham, when she burst into flames. The burns almost killed her, as friends tried to beat out the flames, and she will need extensive skin grafts to her face and body. In the belief that a cigarette ignited her light Indian cotton dress, a consumer organization tried setting alight pieces of Vicky's dress and other similar dresses with cigarettes – they just smouldered. A spokesman for the

Colin Frajbis

Department of Trade said: 'We've known for a long time that cotton can catch fire. But for a dress to go up in flames like this is a mystery.'

In some respects this is similar to the story of Phyllis Newcombe, who burst into flames while leaving a ballroom floor in Chelmsford, in 1938, only Phyllis died in hospital later. (She was *not* reduced to cinders in seconds as many writers allege.) In this case too, the dress was tested by flicking cigarette butts at it, to no effect.

News of the World 16 Nov 1980.

•

A week later – 22 Nov 1980 the badly-burned body of a man was found at the wheel of a car in a lay-by at High Ercall, on the north edge of Telford, Shropshire. It was suggested he might have committed suicide, but a police spokesman admitted there was little damage to the car itself.

Birmingham *Evening Mail* 22 Nov 1980.

•

Mrs Frances Kenworthy's nephew broke into her Lockwood, near Huddersfield, Yorkshire, home when he got no reply, on 4th Dec 1980. He found her on the kitchen floor, dead with burns, and called the police. Sgt Bert Booth, a Coroner's Officer, said Mrs Kenworthy had extensive burns 'but the clothing she was wearing was not marked.' A few items in the room were said to have been scorched and there was a burnt hole in the hearth-rug, 'but nothing to suggest a serious outbreak.' The report mentions that the lady's husband had died a month previously – this may have some relevance due to the high number of depressed or recently widowed old ladies among possible SHCs.

Huddersfield Examiner 5 Dec 1980.

•

On 3 May 1981, Mrs Sandra Braddock, mother of four, staggered to the door of her home at Warth-on-Dearne, near Rotherham, Yorkshire, in flames. After treatment for burns she said she had been lighting a cigarette when she, or her clothes, burst into flames. She was quite unable to account for it. Once again we read of a flaming Yorkshire widow!

Daily Star 4 May 1981.

•

In looking through our file of unpublished accounts, we found two worthy of mention. The first involved students in a rag-stunt pedal-car race, at Whitchurch, near Bristol. On the day of the race, 27 Feb 1972, some 200 students were treated for 'mystery face and eye burns'. The report adds: 'More than 300 people were burned in the same event four years previously [1968]. The cause was never discovered.' It is not clear whether this involved a sudden flash of flame, as in the case of John Scourfield (above), or there was some kind of mass collapse. Stinging sensations, choking as if stifled, and rashes are frequently reported in 'Mass hysteria' type cases. Another possibility might be a shower of acid, but this would be doubly remarkable if it twice coincided with a charity event. Story from the *Sun* 28 Feb 1972.

The second story concerns Sally Flack, 18, of Saltdean, Sussex. While on a local bus journey her trousers turned into hot pants – literally. Alarmed passengers called to her that her pants were on fire. Unaccountably, they were smouldering. She frantically slapped her thighs and legs, put out the fire, and continued her journey. Brighton Council refused to recognise her claim for compensation. *Daily Mirror* 3 Aug 1977.

•

Our file held another curio from the 'Pig-ignorant' column by Peter Laurie in *New Scientist* 23 March 1978. Having just read and approved of *Phenomena*, wherein John Michell and your editor briefly delve into the historical perspective of SHC, Laurie recalls that he had 'actually seen such a thing' while staying with Glasgow firemen researching an article on firefighting. One morning a fire was reported from an old people's home. 'In a ground floor room, where there were three beds, an old man had been sitting by the windown on a hardwood chair... The nurse had seen him happily smoking in the sun; when she came back ten minutes later he was gone. There was a pile of ashes on the floor; the ceiling of the room was black with greasy smoke; there was a strong smell of roasting... The immediate explanation was that he had dozed off, or had a heart attack, and his cigarette had set his dressing-gown on fire.'

Admirably, Laurie did not swallow this uncritically, and questioned the nature of a process which could accomplish such rapid and complete destruction. 'You have a hundredweight of meat, a hardwood chair, and a cigarette. With no other aids you have to burn the meat and the chair so that not one scrap remains unconsumed. You may not chop up the chair and build a fire – you may light this uncompromising arrangement in only one place. Few of us would get our Brownie badge under such conditions.' He ends with the expectation that the coroner could only draw the obvious conclusion – 'After all, who wants to clutter up a coroner's court with such bizarre and unscientific stuff? If there is no crime there is no reason to make much inquiry.'

Our trouble is that, not content with the 'obvious' we want to know more. As said earlier, any doctor or lawyer who would like to join us would be more than welcome.

Credits: Anon, GW Butcher, D Colley, AR Cook, Jenny Dawson of Orbis Publications who passed clippings to us following your editor's articles in *The Unexplained,* Chris Hall, Shanla Lawford, Kenneth Mays, S Maxted, Andy Townsend, Mike Tuppen **•RJMR.**

Even in our archaeology file we find things turning up in runs and clumps. Here are a few lively lumps from history's lost-and-found dept.

THAT YOU, STATUE?
A 700-year-old bauxite figurine found at the Cahokia Mounds State Park, Illinois, 6 inches wide, 8 inches tall, showing a woman carrying a hoe, kneeling on a jaguar-headed snake whose tail splits into two vines carrying gourds. *Tulsa World* 7 June 80.

The head of a 7-foot limestone statue of Mercury found at Uley, Gloucestershire, dated 150 AD. *S Times* 21 Sept 80.

A Roman sculpture of 3 flaxen-haired women found at Lincoln. *D Telegraph* 11 Dec 80.

A 2nd-century BC marble statue of the goddess Cybele found by Turkish archaeologists near the Syrian frontier. *D Telegraph* 9 Jan 81.

Three 19-foot statues found on the sea-bed between Baia and Lucrino, near Naples, near the submerged ruins of Cicero's villa. Said to portray mythic monsters 'like the one-eyed Cyclops', but we have no better identification than this. *D Telegraph + Guardian* 15 Jan 81.

A gilt-bronze figurine of a Druid, 13 cms high and probably made in Gaul in the 2nd century, found at Erith, Cambridge. The figure wears a double cassock-like garment and an outer robe, has a snake coiled round one hand and an egg-shaped object in the other, believed to be the 'serpent-stone' of Druidic tradition. *D Telegraph* 17 Jan 81.

A small bronze statue of Mercury found by treasure-hunters at an undisclosed site in N Wales, along with figurines of 3 dogs, a bracelet, and 550 coins of the 3rd and 4th centuries AD. Speculation is they might come from the lost town of Varae. *S Times* 18 Jan 81.

A rock-cut tomb, dated between 250 and 190 BC, found at Canea, Crete, containing gold jewellery and 21 female figurines worked in clay. *D Telegraph* 12 Feb 81.

SUNK JUNK
Some ships that accidentally became submarines:

Numerous Roman ships found by divers at the entrance to Ambrakikos Bay, NW Greece, believed to be the remains of the fleet belonging to Mark Antony and Cleopatra, sunk in the battle of Actium, 2 Sept, 31 BC, by ships of Octavius (afterwards Emperor Augustus). The ships are said to be in good condition, stuck in mud in shallow water. *D Telegraph* 9 Oct 80; *Western Mail* 10 Oct 80. And while on the subject, a submerged palace belonging to Antony and Cleopatra found 40 yards offshire at Alexandria by Canadian psychic George MacMullen. *Weekend* 7-13 May 80.

The wreck of one of Christopher Colombus' ships, the *Pinta*, believed found off the Turks and Caicos Islands in the Bahamas. She's alleged to have sunk 7 or 8 years after Columbus' expedition, on a return voyage. *Burlington Free Press* 13 Oct; *D Mail + Herald Tribune* 14 Oct 80.

72 wooden hulks found by sonar, 2 metres under mud in 25-metre deep water off Nagasaki, Japan, believed to be Kublai Khan's fleet, sunk by typhoon during his second attempted invasion in 1284. A Mongolian sword, bronze Buddha and stone pots also found. Melbourne *Sun* 11 Dec 80; *S Express* 21 Dec 80.

LOST CITIES
An unknown city found by Soviet frogmen at the bottom of the Baltic Sea. Timber street-paving, remnants of houses and ceramics found. Mention of another submerged city found earlier near the east coast of the Caspian Sea. *Hameen Sanomat* (Finland) 10 April 80.

A 5th-century BC Etruscan city, possibly Kelousion, found near Magliano in Tuscany, Italy. Streets, houses, fragmentary pottery found, and evidence of burning, probably by the Romans. *D Telegraph* 16 Oct 80.

A second diving expedition planned to the submerged town of Dunwich, off the Suffolk coast, for 1981. Three churches have been found so far, and they're hoping to find another 17. *D Telegraph* 18, 27 Dec 80.

Ruins of a submerged city found in Lake Titicaca, on the Peru/Bolivia border, believed to be prior to 900 AD. Roofless walls and a possible temple found, with architectural resemblances to the city of Tihuanaco, which stands on the lake shores. Roads also found. *The Sault Star* (Canada) 3 Jan 81.

A Sabine town, thought to be Crustumerium, found between two hills on the Salarian Way, 10 miles from Rome. It was last heard of in 447 BC, and now shards of pottery or roof-tiles, streets, and a long subterranean tunnel, thought to be a sewer, have been found. *Guardian* 4 March 81.

Credits: Chris Hall, Mark A Hall, Tuuri Heporauta, Valerie Martin, Paul Screeton, PR Thomas, Howard Wolinsky, Joe Zarzynski • **SM.**

The Runamo Runes.

When an 'expert' makes a monumental blunder in his own field of expertise the reaction of the scientific or academic establishment often exemplifies Hynek's dictum, that 'Science isn't always what scientists do'. Our Swedish correspondent **Sven Rosen** outlines one such tragi-comic episode, involving an Icelandic professor who let his imagination get the better of him.

FPL/Sven Rosen

This engraving, from Erik Dahlberg's Suecia Antiqua *quite realistically shows the runes in the forest clearing at Runamo. In the centrer is depicted the attempt by the scholars of King Valdemar I to unravel the riddle, and above them the arms of the Counts of Blekinge. In the foreground a man in 17th-century dress points to the only runic word which can be read easily: 'Lund'. The remaining runes are the product of a code invented by Dahlberg or his engraver: starting left, you have to substitute the preceeding letter of the runic alphabet, except those runes upside-down which need the succeeding letter. The result refers cryptically to the battle of Bravalla, which Dahlberg thought was fought in 395 AD. 'Lund' refers to the very old belief that King Harald Hildebrand did not die at Bravalla, but later at Lund.*

One of the earliest descriptions of the mysterious rock-runes at Runamo, Sweden, is by Saxo Grammaticus, and sets the scene usefully:

'In the [province of] Blekinge, there is a ridge with a path extending [along it], and the path is dotted over with peculiar written characters. All the way from the sea into the wilderness of Varend this path can be seen, along which two lines extend for a long distance, one line on each side of the path. The interspace between the lines is narrow, and its surface is furrowed by runic inscriptions. Although the path sometimes leads across the mountains and sometimes leads through the valleys, traces [remnants] of runic writing can be seen along the entire path.'

Although Saxo's picture is considerably exaggerated, these markings exist, and can be seen today, not over hill and dale, but in a few clearings in wooded areas at Runamo, about 3km outside Brakne-Hoby, in Blekinge. The 'path' is formed by a vein of trap-rock running through masses of granite forming the floors of these clearings. We are concerned with one part of this granite-sandwich where the markings are particularly prominent, as though in ages past some demented chicken had staggered along the still-plastic streak. There may be other inscribed areas but these are lost, long eroded or buried beneath the changing floor of the forest.

For centuries these strange runes were held in awe. About the middle of the 12th century, when Saxo was a youngster, the Danish King Valdemar the Great (d.1182) ordered their investigation. He was 'so confused' by them, recorded Saxo, 'that he wanted them to be translated, and for that purpose he commissioned learned men to go across the mountain [ridge] and to track out, in a scrupulous way, all the runes that were to be found, and to reproduce them by carving their likenesses into wooden tablets. But they could make no sense out of it.' Exactly when no one really knows, but local folktales appeared associating the runes with the legendary Battle of Bravalla, at which an invasion force led by Harald Hildetand, King of Denmark, was defeated by the Swedish King Ring.

The Runamo inscription, then, presented an exciting enigma for historians. It was long the opinion of academics that at Runamo Nature had fashioned a 'meander' – a snake-body. wriggling over the landscape – and some ancient rune-masters had taken advantage of this spontaneous form and filled it with indecipherable Viking poetry. Although many scholars, both learned and foolish, attempted translations – some resulting in a few fragments almost equally as incomprehensible – they usually had as much success as did Valdemar's brains-trust. Until 1833.

In the summer of 1833, the Danish Royal Society appointed a committee to demystify the runes once and for all. What we might call the 'Second Royal Expedition' was headed by Finnur Magnusson, a reputable professor at the University of Copenhagen. He hailed from Iceland, and called himself Finn Magnusen when in Denmark. The summer spent in measuring and copying the lengthy inscription – the main part was about 22 metres long – was a resounding success.

Then came the hard part, as Magnusson struggled to decipher the runes. Night and day for the next ten months he tried every conceivable trick at his disposal but the more obsessed he became the more elusive the solution seemed. By May 1834 he was utterly frustrated and almost on the edge of total despair. As he records in his own book, and again in the anthology of local historical papers known as *Brakne-Hoby*, Magnusson noticed a rune which

THE BATTLE OF BRAVALLA

Based on his interpretation of the 'runes', Magnusson believed that King Harald Hildetand, King of Denmark, raised an army of heroes from Denmark, Friesland (Holland), Ireland, England and Sachsland (Germany), and invaded Sweden by sea, marching inland from Runamo (see map), where they paused only to carve the runes. Harald's army was defeated at Bravalla by the combined Swedish-Norwegian force of King Sigurd Ring of Sweden.

The exact date of the battle is a historical mystery – one modern scholar, Ake Ohlmarks, believes it was fought in 750 AD, whereas Magnusson, among others, put the date some time in the 5th century. It is known that Bravalla, in Varend, is a prehistoric burial ground, about which battle traditions survived among countryfolk into the 19th century. Modern historians tend to site the Bravalla of the sagas in Ostergotland, in central Sweden, far away from Runamo.

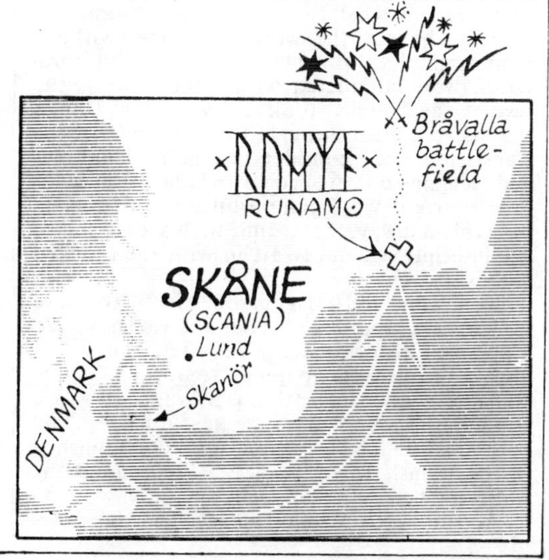

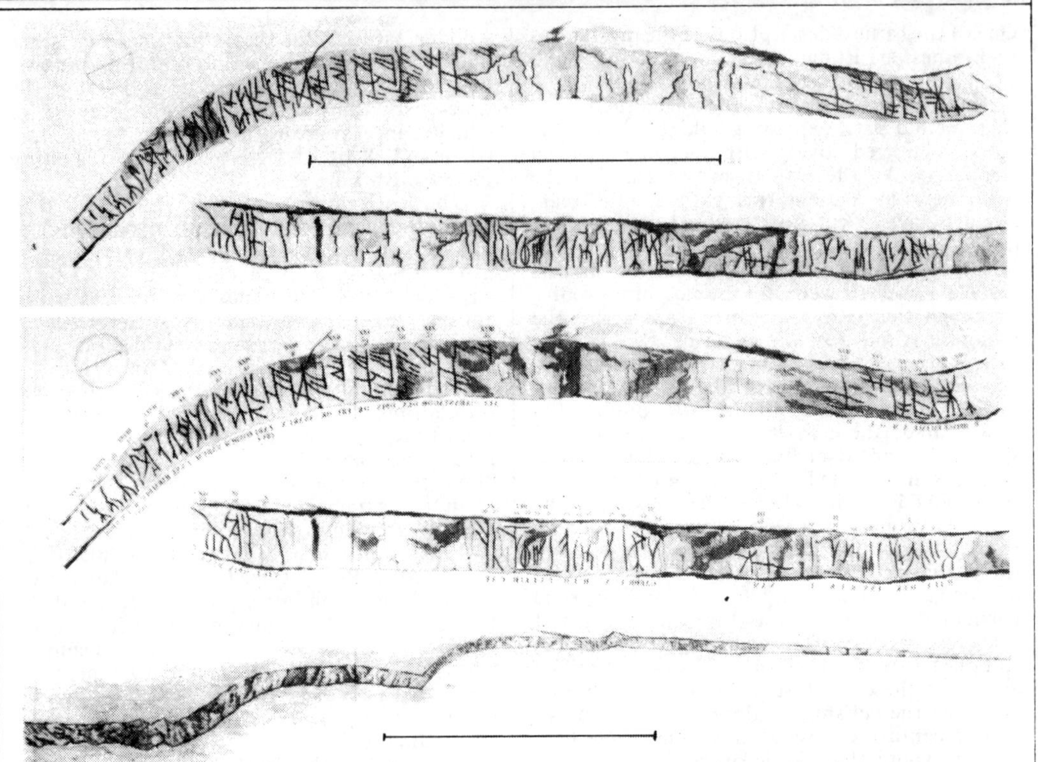

FPL/Sven Rosen

Two versions of the most interesting portion of the 'runic meander'. The top scale (emphasized) measures 3 Alen, or ells (approx 1.8 metres). **A**: *Magnusson's engraving of the original markings and cracks.* **B**: *His interpretation. Compare with 'A' for alterations, suppressions and emphasis of lines to bring out the 'runes'.* **C**: *A view of the major part of the meander, measuring, on the ground, about 64 feet by about one foot wide. The scale (emphasized) shows 10 Alen (approx 6 metres).*

looked as though it had been inscribed as a mirror-image. Suddenly the complete solution flashed into his mind 'with no particular hardship', and in what is described as a 'trance' or 'ecstasy' he put the words on paper without hesitation. The principle parts of the interpretation were completed within the hour – the rest of the 'details' took a few weeks! Unlike the inspired breakthrough, the latter part of the translation was considerably more laboured, and Magnusson evoked a whole variety of interpretive devices quite arbitrarily, to explain or explain away, according to his theories of the inscription s and to fit in with the revealed details.

Not only did Magnusson claim to have broken the cryptic code, but the text revealed a poem of historical value and literary merit. It also confirmed the popular traditions linking Runamo with the battle at Bravalla. It was a triumph of modern antiquarian scholarship, and with great hullabaloo the results were published in the Danish Royal Society's *Proceedings* the following year.

According to Magnusson's belief, the runes had been carved by Harald Hildetand's men on their march north to Bravalla (see 'Bravalla' box). His visionary breakthrough had pierced the markings' disguise and showed clearly that the inscription was in a very difficult runic system mainly based on the so-called *bindrunes*, in which complex heiroglyphs or 'monograms' are formed by superimposing the individual runic letters of a name or word (see 'Bindruna' box). The coded inscription, then, was almost entirely in mirror form, right to left, and when read by Magnusson seemed to present four regular stanzas composed of half-lines in the alliterative metre known as *fornyrdislag*. The only coherent portion contains a magical spell for victory for Harald, rendered thus in Old Norse:

Hildekinn riki nam...
Garðr in hio
Uli eið gaf

vigi Oþin runar
Hringr fai
fall a mold

Alf(ar) astagoð
Ola (...)
Oþin ok Fri
ok Asakun
fari //iraf
fiandum varum
unni Haraldi
urin sigr.

Hildekind captured the kingdom
Gardar carved the runes
Ola took the oath
[space for oath?]
May Odin hallow the sorcery
May King Ring
fall in (the) dust
[inscription indistinct]
Elfs, gods of love
[must leave?] Ola
Odin and Frey
and the race of AEsir
must lay waste, lay waste
our enemies
give Harald
great victory.

[square brackets = supposition by Sven Rosen.]

To Magnusson, whose speciality was Old Norse literature, the style of the poem was obviously the primary form of *fornyrdislag* metre, also called *Starkadarlag;* and since the legendary creator of this style, a poet called Starkoddr, had lived at the court of Harald according to some sagas, Magnusson was convinced he had also identified the author of the victory-prayer. The poem even provided a hitherto unknown diminutive ('Hildekind') used by Harald when young. Ola (or Ole) was Harald's son, who, according to Olaus Magnus, became king after the regency of Harald's bravest commander-in-chief, a female warrior called Hertha.

There followed a period of euphoria as the scholastic world warmed to the professor's achievement. By finding historical evidence for what was previously only considered legend he had extended the glorious histories of Denmark and Sweden by hundreds of years. There was great nationalistic pride in the discovery, for both Danes and Swedes. But this was the lull before the storm. Magnusson had been wholly wrong, and the embarrassment of the Danish and Swedish establishments helped to shake their science into the 20th century.

Beginning in 1838, several notable scientists showed conclusively that the marks, believed for centuries to be runes and so admirably translated by Magnusson, were merely freaks of nature. The 'inscription' was formed by natural cracks and scratches in the rock. There is some dispute between the two nations over who should be credited with the demolition job. The great Swedish chemist and geologist Berzelius was the first to air his criticism in 1838, but the Danes give most of the honour to their great archaeologist and geologist JJA Worsae, who did not publish until 1844. From the beginning Magnusson had the support of his Runamo-expedition colleague, JG Forchhammer, a Danish geologist, but against them Berzelius was joined by his fellow Swede Sven Nillson, a reputable archaeologist, geologist and zoologist.

BINDRUNA AND LONNRUNOR CODES

Magnusson can be forgiven for thinking the marks he surveyed were coded runes. They do look remarkably like two code systems in particular, and it was these that formed the main tool for deciphering the Runamo runes. One method is called lonnrunor *which demands a thorough knowledge of the alphabetical order of runes, and of the runic families. There are three such families, named after their first letters Frey ᚠ , Hagal ✱ , and Tyr ↑ , (not to be confused with Thor). To baffle illiterates the third family was often treated as the first and vice-versa. In these codes a rune was denoted by a rune-like number combination. Assuming we wanted to code the third letter , this letter would become 2:3 (ie. third letter in the second family), which in turn could be represented in a variety of ways:*

The other and main method employed by Magnusson is far more arbitrary, and involved the dismantling of bindrunes, *or monograms, made up of superimposed runes. One of the best examples is a mark he calls 'King Ring's monogram':*

According to Magnusson the dots and lines to the left indicate a name of six letters (3+3). Unlike in Chinese calligraphy there is no fixed order to the component strokes, so you can please yourself about the order of dismantling. And bearing in mind that some of the runes would be reversed, Magnusson derives, from right to left, the Norse spelling of Hringr:

The arbitrary quality of Magnusson's interpretations using the bindruna *method can be illustrated with a nice little irony, writes Sven Rosen. Assuming for a moment , perhaps in a parallel universe, that a Professor Ring was eager to prove the historical existence of a King Magnusson, using the same monogram. Prof Ring would assume, from the dots and lines, a name with nine letters (3x3), and derive them thus:*

M A G N U S S O N

Lo! The ancient King Magnusson is rediscovered!

Forchhammer attempted to defend Magnusson sometime in 1838 or 1839, according to the Danish encyclopedia *Salmonsens* (we were unable to locate this refutation). A rather stilted entry in the Swedish encyclopedia *Nordisk Familjebok*, under 'Runamo', claims that only Berzelius 'had the courage to doubt Magnusson's interpretation', and adds begrudgingly that Worsae only came to the same conclusions years later.

Berzelius had gone to Runamo in 1836 to see for himself. He describes the landscape there as 'wild' and not very populated. Visitors had to hire guides, as he did, to take them to the hard-to-find clearings where the mysterious meander could be seen. Despite Saxo's picture of a rune-spangled path leading from Blekinge by the sea into the wilderness of Varend, the vein has never been a prominent, or even clearly visible, feature of the landscape. Berzelius mentions only two places in the forest where the *lindorm* – (runic meanders were often called this after the *lindorm*, a sinuous venom-spitting crested dragon) – could be seen bearing rune-like markings.

Berzelius was well aware during this visit that the marks were not made by human hands, and out of devilish curiosity he queries the guide on their meaning. In all innocence the guide replied that there had only ever been one man in the whole district wise enough to read the runes, and he could only do so while standing on his head! The wise-man was evidently not Magnusson, but some local sage or psychic who participated in the magical mystique of the 'inscription' to the full satisfaction and need of the countryfolk thereabouts, probably using the marks to inspire his visions and prophesies. A curious posture needed to dispell a magical illusion is an ancient and universal folktale motif, and interestingly appears to apply to Magnusson's 'breakthrough' of reading the runes back-to-front. No doubt this occurred to, and amused, Berzelius. August Strindberg found malicious pleasure in citing this story from Berzelius as an illustration of country simplicity.

Throughout this affair no one ever criticised the literary quality of the 'revealed' stanzas (which Sven Rosen assures us are impressive in the original Old Norse), which brings us to an interesting point or two. Before he left Iceland for Denmark, Magnusson helped found a literary society dedicated to 'the purification of the Icelandic language'. He started out as a poet using traditional forms, but his efforts as a lyricist have been almost forgotten, there being little trace of them in modern literary histories. Ironically then a poetic vein linked Magnusson with Runamo, and his creation of the *Starkadarlag* stanzas was at once his triumph and his ruin. Since there has been no criticism of them poetically, it is impossible to tell, at this distance, whether their literary merit was more impressive as long as the legendary Starkoddr was believed to be their author.

Magnusson's critics and supporters were divided in a curious fashion: all his critics were from the natural sciences (as such subjects as varied as zoology, chemistry, and geology were in the same faculty in those days), and all his supporters were from the historical and literature fields. Such was Magnusson's professional standing amongst his academic colleagues that, despite the extreme embarrassment of endorsing an empty discovery based on a huge error of judgement, no one ever questioned his honesty or accused him of fraud. Many of his apologists bent over backwards to excuse or explain his apparent success in deciphering nonsensical random marks, and pointed out that the eminent geologist Forchhammer again and again reassured Magnusson that the marks were indeed runes.

There is no doubt Magnusson quickly became obsessed by the idea that the 'inscription' was a secret rune code, and that is exactly what he found. Runamo had an atmosphere of enchantment and Magnusson fell under its spell. Its glamour was such that, even in places where there were no 'runes', one could easily imagine the last lingering traces of an erased writing. In his book on Swedish antiquities, Erik Dahlberg summarized the attraction of the 'inscription': it was on a huge scale and looked very ancient. Though the *lindorm* is scarcely more than a foot wide, Saxo believed it to be a path, and thought the writing had been eroded by the footsteps of generations. Magnusson is not the first, nor, we predict, the last scientist or scholar to have run aground on nature's simulacra, or to have read into such spontaneous forms their 'heart's desire'. In the last decade or so we have seen Barry Fell stick his neck out over his interpretation of pre-Colombian rock inscriptions in North America, not to mention the bizarre readings of sectioned rocks by Richard Shaver, who saw there, in picture-form, scenes confirming his belief in Atlantis and the subterranean kingdom of the 'Dero'. (For these and many other examples see the works of John Michell, in the bibliography.)

However, Magnusson was defiant. In his own massive – (it needed both arms to carry it when Sven consulted it) – and detailed book, *Runamo og Runerne* (1841), he hit back at his critics. He maintained to the last that he was perfectly able to read the runes and the learned geologists were fools. Magnusson joins the select band of academics hounded to death at the center of a scandal, but unlike the pitiable Johannes Beringer in the 1720s, he could hardly be said to have died of shame.

•

Sven Rosen — Bob Rickard

NOTE *– Somehow the bibliography for this article got lost in the post. Just as well really, because we've run out of room. We'll include it next issue --* ***Ed.***

'The Double Initial murders' took the lives of four little girls via rape and strangulation, between 1971 and 1976, in Rochester, NY, which was once known as the 'Mysterious City' [1] and is today the corporate headquarters of Kodak and Xerox. The children's deaths fit a pattern which one psychiatrist called 'laying a trail of esoteric clues to match wits with the police.' [2] One of these 'clues' was the occurrence of double initials in each of the children's names. Another might be the fact that the killings took place in the months of November and April only.

The first victim's name is a common one among Spanish people (she was Puerto Rican) and is also a kind of *cant* language treasure-trove. Her name was Carmen Colon. Carmen can mean enchanted. Colon signifies the anus, among other things. In *FT30* we looked at the importance in sorcery of the word 'wicker' and of its appearance in the 'Son of Sam' case as one of the names used by the murderer(s). In *FT32* we noted, *en passant*, that many of the murders committed by the Hillside Strangler -- who is a native of Rochester — took place on sites 'sacred' to the *Ordo Templi Orientis* (OTO), the successor-group to the medieval Knights Templar.

Let's run this OTO angle along with the details of the 'Double Initial' murders through our symbol computer and see what we can come up with.

In Latin, colon has the aforementioned meaning as the small intenstine and, alternatively, as the 'dove of love'. The dove is the central symbol of the OTO. [3] Of course, like so many other potent images, the dove is also important to a whole spectrum of groups including 'Churchianity'. But it is the OTO's obsession with sex, sacrifice and ritual which causes us to pursue the dove glyph down blood-sprinkled corridors.

In the famous 'North African working', OTO chief Aleister Crowley was sodomized as part of a rite meant to invoke Choronzon, an entity Elizabethan soceror Dr. John Dee described as 'that mighty devil'. Another part of the ritual entailed the sacrifice of three doves and it was from the blood of these *feathered colons* that Choronzon supposedly materialized. [4]

According to the *Cabalah*, 'everything lies veiled in numbers'. Choronzon's is given as 333, a multiple of magic 33.

Carmen Colon was abducted on Route 33. Her body was discovered near Churchville (the first letter of that town corresponds to her initials). The second victim, Wanda Walkowicz, was found in the village of Webster. Little Wanda had flaming red hair. In a popular comic book for children, the lead character's name is Wanda the Witch. [5]

The third victim, Michelle Maenza, lived on Webster *Crescent* St. and attended Rochester School *33*. Maenza's corpse was located in the town of Macedon, in Wayne County. [6]

The fourth and last child killed was Michelle McMurray. She varies from the pattern in a couple of ways. First, the site where her body was discovered did not correlate with her initials -- Child St. -- though certainly it fits the 'motley drama' as a whole. Second, her place as fourth victim disrupts a numerological set which had been advanced with precision in all the other deaths. 'C' is the third letter of the alphabet, 'M' is the 13th and 'W' the 23rd. To continue the progression by going through the alphabet again, 'G' is the 33rd letter. There was no 'G' victim. [7]

The police in Rochester attempted to discredit the ceremonial aspects of 'Double Initial'. One headline in a local newspaper typified the mindset. It read, 'Police Discount Slaying Coincidences'. [8] When Michelle McMurray's body was recovered there was a public outcry demanding the release of the blood type found in the rapists semen, to ascertain whether or not it corresponded to the semen found on the first three children. The Rochester cops refused. [9] In a particularly revealing piece of stupidity, the head of the 'Double Initial' investigation, Michael Iaculli, stated, 'We decided a long time ago the initials had nothing to do with it.' For the past six years Rochester Police have insisted that the killer responsible for the first three deaths committed suicide in 1974, although they refused to name this mystery man.

When Rochester native Kenneth Bianchi was arrested as the monster responsible for the Hillside Strangler murders in California and Washington (state), this writer considered him immediately as a suspect in 'Double Initial'... which was not exactly a Holmes-ian caliber deduction to be sure, but one, unbelievably enough, the Rochester authorities refused to consider. Their Chief of Detectives, Anthony

Fantigrossi, maintained, for the entire first year of Bianchi's capture and subsequent incarceration, that Bianchi had iron-clad alibis for his whereabouts during the 'Double Initial' murders. [10] The Police Chief in the state of Washington where Bianchi was apprehended never interrogated Bianchi about 'Double Initial' because Rochester Police told the Washington cops firmly that Bianchi was not a suspect. [10]

In this writer's first article for *FT30* I mentioned the possibility that the Hillside Strangler and the killings in Rochester had possible links to US officialdom. I am still troubled by the fact that 'Son of Sam' hit-man David Berkowitz referred to one of his fellow pseudo-satanist cultists (John Wheat Carr) as a 'child molestor'. [11] One of the 'Son of Sam' cryptic notes was signed, 'John Wheaties, Rapist and Suffocator of Young Girls', even though none of the 'Sam' victims were raped or suffocated. Intuition made me wonder if maybe there wasn't some kind of occult network responsible for ritual killings which was somehow mixed-up with the government... not really a heck of a lot of hard evidence, however.

Then, in late 1979, a gutsy, former policewoman named *Rosemary* Leary traced Kenneth Bianchi's High School graduation photograph and compared it with a police composite drawing of the 'Double Initial' murderer. She and many others have noticed the striking resemblance. At nearly the same time, Forensic Serologist Donald D. Gordon blew away the Rochester cops' suicide mystery man explanation. Gordon demonstrated that the suicided individual was a 'secreter' (a person whose blood type shows up in their semen). The sexual fluid found on the Rochester children was that of a non-secreter (blood type does not show in semen). Kenneth Bianchi is a non-secreter.

There is evidence that Rochester Police had their own report about the secreter revelations in January 1979 but as late as October 1979 were still insisting Bianchi didn't do it and that the suicide mystery man was the culprit. [10] Early in 1980 Chief Fantigossi was confronted with this discrepancy and reportedly 'became angry' at the question. It has also been learned that when Bianchi lived in Rochester, he kept '20 to 30' pornographic pictures of little girls 'cut out like paper dolls' under his bed mattress. [12]

At the time of his arrest, Bianchi was employed as a Captain in the Whatcom Security Agency, a private rent-a-cop company. According to researcher Mae Brussell, 'Son of Sam' trigger-man Berkowitz obtained the infamous 'Bulldog .44' handgun which reigned terror on New York City, from a private security guard in Houston, Texas. In his book *The Private Sector*, investigative reporter George O'Toole points out that the private security industry has the strongest possible ties to official police agencies.

Mark Chapman, accused assassin of John Lennon, was a security guard. It should be recalled that Berkowitz was a New York City auxiliary policeman who has sued the US Army for disabilities he incurred while in military service (his homicidal capacity).

John Wheat Carr was a member of the US Air Force. His sister worked for the Yonkers Police Department. His father owned the dog Berkowitz said 'controlled' him. John Wayne Gacy murdered *33* boys in the Chicago area. He was a powerful politician (like former San Francisco Housing Authority Commissioner Jim Jones). He was photographed with the wife of US President Jimmy Carter, and was wearing a US Secret Service badge at the time. Gacy dressed alternately in clown suits and cop uniforms and drove an automobile he had specially outfitted to resemble a police cruiser. [13]

On the day she died, two US Secret Service agents were spotted at the home of Wanda Walkowicz. [14] The fiery Wanda was considered a 'tough' little child who was very leery of strangers. Would she have gotten into a car if a policeman had asked her to? We know Bianchi posed as a policeman in Los Angeles to gain his victim's confidence.

Psychic detective James Shelby Downard believes that we are in the 'Must Be' stage in what he calls 'The Long Journey of the Alchemist'. In this human alchemy, 'all that is hidden must be made manifest'.

On one level we can say that this police-criminal interface is merely coincidence or the quite natural masquerade a criminal would adopt in order

John Wayne Gacy pictured in May 1978 with Rosalynn Carter at a Democrat meeting. The larger of Gacy's two lapel badges is the insignia of the Secret Service.

to more easily obtain his terrible goals. Maybe so. But I'm interested in the cermonial trappings attending these 'immolations' – trappings the criminals had to go to great lengths to devise, and expose themselves to great risks in order to execute.

I'm interested in the effects of the blurring of distinction between cops 'n' cons when mixed with ancient words of power, archetypes, numerology and geomancy and given wide publicity, on the Dreaming Mind of our Group Mind. I am reminded of Joyce Maynard's comment that 'No villain is more frightening than the one you supposed to be your friend.' Probably the only villain to prove the exception to Maynard's rule is the one who intentionally drops clues as to his real identity in order to achieve a most subtle *haute* mind control.

In the original script for the film *The Cabinet of Dr. Caligari* the hypnotist who controlled the murderer was also the head psychiatrist at the insane asylum. Like Oswald, *Ruby*, Sirhan, James Earl *Ray* and Arthur Bremer before him, Kenneth Bianchi was a student of hypnotism. In his apartment, police discovered a hypnotism textbook and a pamphlet from the Bellingham Hypnosis Center. [15] Bianchi even posed as a hypnotist in a newspaper advertisement in the *LA Times* in which he offered 'five answers' for $25. [15]

Returning through a circle 'to the self-same spot' – we began this little piece with a Black Magical Order headquartered in California. On Halloween, 1977 a victim of the Hillside Strangler was carefully 'placed' (just as the 'Double Initials' had been) near Devil's Gate Reservoir. [16] It was here that the OTO performed its rituals. [17] The same OTO worshipped a Lovecraftian Choronzon-like *llogior* believed to reside in the Griffith Park / Arroyo Seco / Rosebowl node. Other victims of the Hillside Strangler were left in the Griffith Park and Suicide Bridge areas – places heavily imbued with sex and death 'vibes' (Griffith Park is one of the main 'gay' make-out assignation-spots).

And there's yet another 'coincidence': the OTO also established a chapter in 1915 on Mount Palomar. Palomar means dove-cote in Spanish and flocks of doves used to congregate on the mountain back then.

Was there some kind of geomantic and ritual significance in the placing of some of the bodies of the victims of the Hillside strangler in places revered by black arts groups? Is it possible that ceremonial murders and the tremendous magical powers they are supposed to conjure are still going on in our modern world of rocket trips, plastic bags and instant coffee?

Well, maybe not, maybe the whole thing is just a bad movie from which we will one day awake. It certainly resembles one. Horror-movie star Peter Lorre's daughter was almost a victim of Bianchi, who flashed a police badge at her and ordered her into his car. She had an appointment with some other destiny, though. [18]

Answers? Perhaps they can be found in the questions buried in movies such as *Chinatown*. I, for one, have my answers in the lines of that patron, secular-saint of sleuths everywhere:

> 'And the angels, all pallid
> and wan,
> Uprising, unveiling, affirm
> That the play is the tragedy
> 'Man',
> And its hero the conquering
> Worm.'

•

Michael Anthony Hoffman

NOTES AND REFERENCES

1) Blake McKelvey, *Rochester: The Water Power City*.
2) Rochester, *Democrat & Chronicle* 3 March 1974.
3) Kenneth Grant, *Aleister Crowley and the Hidden God*.
4) Isreal Regardie, *The Eye of the Triangle*.
5) For a cryptic reference to 'Son of Sam' in comics, see *Creepy* no. 94, 'Etran to Fulsing'.
6) The Macedon-ian connection may or may not be meaningful, but *Wayne* appears to have twilight language significance: John *Wayne* Gacy; *Wayne* County, home of the Fox sisters, founders of modern spiritualism; *Wayne* Williams, the only suspect in the Atlanta killings thus far, who had one arrest on his record, for impersonating a police officer; recently Wayne figured into a hypnotism angle with regard to the attempted assassination of black activist Veron Jordan; and going from death to sex, a New York City transvestite singer calls himself *'Wayne* County'.
7) *Democrat & Chronicle* 22 Sept 1974.
8) ibid, 30 Nov 1973
9) ibid, 13 April 1976
10) Rochester *Times-Union* 29 Jan 1980.
11) [In recent 'confessions' by Berkowitz - eg see *NY Post* 19 Mar 1981 - from his cell in Attica Jail, he has claimed he was an innocent minor member of a "devil cult", and framed for the murders committed by other cult members. This motion was put forward by Michael Hoffman in his original article in FT30 (Autumn 1979) - Ed.]
12) KNXT-TV, Los Angeles, news broadcast, 28 Jan 1980.
13) Linedecker, *The Man Who Killed Boys*. And in *The Spotlight* 31 Dec 1979.
14) *Times-Union* 5 April 1973.
15) ibid, 22 Oct 1979.
16) Readers are urged to consult the 'Mitre Square' section of Stephen Knight's *Jack the Ripper* (Harrap, 1979; pp175-177), for further information on the role of geomancy in ritual murder.
17) Jim Brandon, *Weird America*. 'Son of Sam' occultists also met in an area hallowed by former black orders - Untermeyer Park, built by a wealthy practicing Satanist. This seems to be a confirmation of the satanist theory I sought to discredit as an exclusive 'solution' in *FT32*. Actually though, it is important to bring some sophistication to this matter of mind control, which is what 'magic' really is after all. Mind control is power and power is what governments and intelligence agencies thrive on. The idea of satanists in goverment as opposed to satanists being hunted down by government is fairly obvious to me.
18) *Times-Union* 16 Nov 1979.

Author's Note: Special thanks to the author of the *Sirius Rising* tapes, to whom I am indebted.

REFLECTIONS OF A TRAVELING AMERICAN FORTEAN

The warmer moths of the year are the times when our thoughts turn to moving, weekend treks, taking vacations, going on holiday, and visiting family and friends in other parts of the country. If your thoughts also have a Fortean bend to them, if you mix your pleasure with furthering your own personal enquiries into the unexplained wonders around you, then you might be interested in some helpful hints toward making your next trip a worthwhile phenomenological investigative adventure.

Before you travel to your destination, there are lots of things you can do at home. A hefty amount of initial background research, before your journey, can save you hours of wasted time in the field. First, I always discovered it was important to find out what the specific locales I was going to and through have to offer. Each researcher has to ask themselves specific questions which apply to their own interests, but in general, I like to know if there are runes, mounds, monster-inhabited lakes, spook lights, Bigfoot country, haunted places, ice caves, panther-frequented valleys, and a whole host of more or less permanent. Fortean wonders in the vicinity of my route or its predetermined end.

Finding these fixed unexplained locations by way of the Fortean literature is becoming easier, if you can get your hands on the right sources. George Eberhart's *A Geo-Bibliography of Anomalies* and Jim Brandon's *Weird America* are two of the best books with individual locale listings. Eberhart's expensive sixty-dollar book may be purchased by a few libraries, and Brandon's quality paperback should be almost as difficult to run across in some bookstores. Both are worth the effort of the search. Brandon's *Weird America* is especially good as it is compact and gives a rather complete rundown on the individual Fortean sites. Since he used his own files as well as the items in the *INFO Journal* and *Fate*, Brandon was able to give a rather nice cross-section of what each state has or has had to offer. *Weird America* is a true Fortean guidebook.

In terms of weirdness and Fortean activity, less helpful is *Amazing America*. This is an exaggerated collection of the biggest, shortest, oldest, etc. (usually manmade) attractions along the way. In fact, it serves as a good negative guidebook for it lets you know what things to avoid, at any cost. *Space-Time Transients* is a book to which you might wish to refer but it is a teaser. *STT* lists some spots from the author's computer printouts, but it leaves a lot out. And be leery, to. The data base is slanted towards Fortean phenomena, as seen through the pages of *Fate*. Because a couple of active writers (myself and Jerry Clark) did many pieces on Illinois mysteries, *STT* has a map demonstrating the especially active nature of Illinois Forteana – which is probably not the case.

Trento's *In Search of Lost America*, Fell's *America B.C.*, and others are good beginning places for individuals looking for ancient anomalous sites. Trento's checklist is not specific enough to be too helpful, but it is a start. The *National Geographic's* 'Guide to Ancient Treasures', however, is excellent for it gives detailed highway, route and by-way travel tips. Also, as I have mentioned before (FT29) ancient sites labeled 'devil', should be examined.

On certain other topics, such as where Bigfoot has been seen, John Green's *The Apes Among Us* gives an easy state-by-state breakdown to follow. Peter Costello's *In Search of Lake Monsters* does a somewhat less than complete job of indicating where to find the watery beasts, but the novice will find it of assistance. Articles with seed catalogue-type presentations can be treasure troves of information on specific locations of particular phenomena. Mark A. Hall's spook-light listing in the *INFO Journal* (No 9) still ranks as my favourite, as it is very detailed as to what to expect to see and where.

Falls of strange items from ice to frogs, for example, appear to be only short affairs, but it is always good to understand a locale in terms of its total Fortean history. Falls and strange appearances are natural candidates for lists, and *Fortean Times* and *INFO Journal* articles on these topics usually have carried tables pinpointing the sites of the occurrences. (For England see Rickard puma listing in *INFO Journal* is a classic.)

Willis' excellent rundown on ice falls, and mine on the appearance of crocs and 'gators are two illustrations of seed catalogues worth having. Another is David Fideler's *Anomaly Research Bulletin's* enjoyable list of kangaroo sightings. Tom Adam's *Stigmata* has had many articles and maps on the mystery of the cattle mutations, for those interested in that pursuit.

Overall, these books and

articles should give you a fairly good idea about where to target some of your efforts on your trip. After going through the literature, you may wish to write some researchers who have been known to do extensive fieldwork in the locale of your interest. The best way to locate such individuals is by taking a deeper dip into the vast underground Fortean pool of organizations, newsletters, and journals. Contact could be made with *Fortean Times*, *Fate*, *INFO*, *VESTIGA SITU*, *ARB*, *NEARA*, and others.

Personally, I enjoy finding out what is the most recent activity in an area I am heading for. Fellow researchers can often give me a lead, but another way I discover if anything unusual is hopping, is by contacting the local area's newspapers before I take my journey. On the road, I also often stop at the regional weeklies to inquiry about any folklore or if I know about some local, well-known wonder (e.g. The Devil's Tramping Ground, Lake Champlain Monster, etc.) then I ask about that specifically. This is lots of fun, and I frequently feel like I am on a Fortean fishing trip. Sometimes I am casting out a line for a Bigfoot account, and I come up with a close encounter with a UFO. It is amazing, and keeps me on my toes.

Getting to, and going through an area. I try to pick up local books published by local people on the regional folklore. Also, sometimes I come across some intriguing maps which have captured local legends in little pictures with quaint names, like the Cape Anywhere Sea Serpent, The Buried Treasure of Some-Place Canyon, or the Headless Horseman of This Valley or That. These local legends are repeatedly new to me, because they are part of the local people's traditions which have not appeared in a national tabloid or on an incredible television program. Undiscovered wonders still do exist. Finding such a Fortean gem can make a trip very worth the time and toil.

Another resource for finding out what unexplained happenings and places abound in any give province is simply talking to the local folks. Gas station attendants are a gold-mine of information if you take the time to get out of your automobile, and chat with them. The people at country stores, craft shops, and yard sales know a good deal about the countryside, and are often willing to share with you some unique incident or story if you are friendly and unjudgemental.

The worst possible source of Fortean knowledge, I have found, is located at the so-called 'Information Bureaux'. These sandtraps of the American vacationer give out not much more than some insights into the nearest or newest tourist attraction. If you go to them with much more than a specific question about a specific location, do not expect much satisfaction. They have been able to tell me where, for example, a well-known haunted house was, but frequently an information bureau has not been able to direct me to an interesting creek close at hand; I had to find out that from a service station operator. Another warning in your travels should be given about 'Mystery Spots'. In 80–90% of the cases, these tourist traps are optical illusions. Unfortunately some completely worthwhile and topnotch Fortean sites, have been labeled a 'mystery something or other'. The most famous example of this is the 4000 B.C. megalithic structures at North Salem, New Hampshire, entitled collectively 'Mystery Hill', a spot well worth a detour. A word to the wise will save you some time, either way.

Well, with all these hints and warnings in mind, it is time to take your trip. Get your tape recorder, camera, paper, pen and money and take a Fortean adventure this summer or next. With careful planning, a little research, and some friendly questions along the way, your journey anywhere in America can be rewarded with some interesting Fortean discoveries. Enjoy yourself. And help enlighten others, after your return.

•

Loren Coleman

March 1979 — While visiting a friend in Atlanta, Georgia (deep in the heart of Dixie), I made a Fortean side-trip to Fort Mountain. As Brandon notes in Weird America, *the giant wall (above) runs 885 feet along the mountainside. At frequent intervals are 29 pits.*
Photo: Loren Coleman

ALL MY EYE AND MISTER MARTIN

'Everything is contained in everything and vice versa' (favourite Dada proverb)

If Nessie happens to be an organic, flesh and blood plesiosaur, then she is no more interesting than a coelacanth; and if Bigfoot is, simply, a type of North American anthropoid ape, he is really no more interesting than a gorilla. No *less* interesting, certainly, but, equally certainly, no more. That's just my opinion. Zoologically speaking, there is nothing 'impossible' about large, long-necked, aquatic creatures or big hairy pongoids. They may be elusive, they may even be improbable, but, from a zoological point of view, they are not impossible. A puma, in the Highlands of Scotland, is a puma... Panthera concolor... a little out of place, perhaps, but, as Ted Noble could tell you, just as physically solid as, for example, a South American coypu living in East Anglia. A black dog, whether it happens to be living in East Anglia, Yorkshire, Devon or Timbuktu, is likely to be nothing more than a black dog. But Owlman ...a winged thing with an owl's face, a man's body and feet like a crab's claws... a mixture of 'zoologically impossible' contradictions is, to me, far more interesting than those other critters just mentioned, unless, of course, our water-dragons, Bigfeet, mystery cats and black dogs behave in a manner which is 'zoologically impossible' too. Forteans know that these creatures often break the physical rules and have been seen to act in ways which could be labelled 'supernatural'. Sincere witnesses of phenomenal animals are regularly said to be 'hallucinating', 'dreaming' or 'imagining' the things which they know they have seen. By which I mean that orthodox science dismisses such phenomena as 'unreal'. The pox on the orthodox! I'm certain that Fortean phenomena – everything from fish-falls to flying saucers – is real, or rather, *Surreal.*

I have successfully invoked some weird beasties through what I will call 'Surrealistic Shamanism'. The high priest of Surrealism, Andre Breton, had written: 'I believe in the future resolution of these two states which are so contradictory in appearance: dream and reality ...a condition of Surreality.' [1] Rene Passeron stresses the fact that, 'The Surrealists are realists first and foremost; they are the most sure of realists, as their title indicates' ... and ... 'The hallucinatory faculty of the Surealists is in fact a game played with reality, the perception of which remains intact.' [2] In the opinion of Michael Edwardes: 'Breton picked up and carried forward the magical tradition. Surrealism rested and revivified the magical view of the world through which the liberated imagination reveals the infinite correspondences of man with Nature, in a universe in which neither man nor god stands at the centre.' It is becoming increasingly obvious to me that, over half a century ago, the shamanic Surrealists had a firm grasp of the principles behind the 'new synthesis' proposed in some recent examples of unorthodox scientific speculation, such as Lyall Watson's 'biology of the unconscious'. [4]

Phenomenal 'monsters' are essentially Surreal. That impossibly contradictory Owlman is an almost classical Surrealist image... 'Surrealism is contradiction become corporeal and incarnate.' [5] The man/bird appears repeatedly in the paintings of Max Ernst, bird-shaman supreme. [6] In fact every kind of monster can be found in Ernst's work, but the man/bird is an obsessive theme. Gaston Diehl tells us that the painter 'became identified for several years with his own creature, the fabulous 'Loplop', half-winged and half-human, who domineers with a sarcastic air over the destiny of anybody and everybody.' [7] This is pure shamanism. 'The wizard's soul is transformed into a bird, the wings and body of the spirit-bird and the shaman's soul are one body.' [8] Unlike the distinguished anthropologist, Weston La Barre, I don't believe that shamanic magic is a 'maladaptive retreat from reality'. However, I'm bound to agree when he says: 'We must not forget the element of entertainment in Surrealism, and in my monster-raising rituals. Midnight, Hallowe'en, 1980, I drunkenly danced and dreamed around a bonfire with a group of sky-clad witches (again!), invoking Fortean beasties in the names of Cernunnos, Ernst and Loplop!

> *'We have only to compare the paraphernalia of the shaman with that traditionally ascribed to the witch to realize that they are one and the same person.' [10]*

Near Mawnan, on the first day of November, three witches capered, widdershins, in a field by the river, and three hawks circled, watching, in the sky above. Later, the witches invoked Morgawr by swimming in the sea off Pendennis Point. These magical activities are 'irrational' but successful. I thumb my nose at the scientific and mystical establishments; play oneiric games on chill November nights and mornings, with naked women; chant absurd incantations whilst beating a dog-skinned drum; stick owl-feathers in my tall conjuring hat; and trace secret spiralling signs in the froth of almost too many pints of Guinness. All this seems to encourage monsters to rise up and electronic gadgets to break down.

Sightings of UFOs, over Cornwall, were reported during the first few days of November. A spokesman for RAF Plymouth suggested 'ball lightning' as an explanation. He was probably right.

Kate Shiels, for her Samhain birthday, received a gift, from twin sister, Meg. It was a book – *Lame Deer. Sioux Medicine Man* – to add to Kate's ever-growing library on shamanism of the Amerinidan kind. My father – a keen afficionado of the 'Old West' (meaning the novels of Jack Schaefer and the films of John Ford) – is constantly entertained by Kate's conversational habit of dropping such names as Black Elk, Sitting Bull and Kicking Bear. On Thursday, Nov 6th, she had been rapping away to him about medicine-men in general and bird-shamanism in particular. Then in the afternoon, she took a stroll on Gyllyngvase Beach, where she encountered a good friend who had just arrived in Falmouth. At tea-time, Kate told her grandfather the name of our chum... 'Attacking Eagle'... a revelation greeted with guffaws of disbelief from the old man! It was true enough. 'Attacking Eagle' is the English translation of the Aztec name of a Mexican painter with strong Surrealist leanings (Cuauh Kamffer). I took this as an interesting omen... if Kate could invoke that eagle-man, maybe Owlman would be next on her list.

'The pit was only as wide as myself, and I was a skinny boy, but that huge bird was flying around me as if he had the whole sky to himself. I could hear his cries, sometimes near and sometimes far, far away. I felt feathers or a wing touching my back and head. This feeling was so overwhelming that it was just too much for me. I trembled and my bones turned to ice.' [11]

On Friday, Nov 7th, Tim Dinsdale came to Falmouth. We had a lunchtime pint in the 'King's Head', and Tim met my wife, Chris, and daughters, Kate and Lucy. I also introduced him to Mike Jams, designer and builder of the 'Fast Worker' boats, two of which we planned to take out, on Sunday, Nov 9th, in a seaborne attempt to sniff out Morgawr. We chatted about all those things you would expect to chat about... everything from scientists to skunk-apes, sea-serpents to Surrealistic shamanism. If anyone deserved to capture Nessie, on film or 'in person', it's Tim Dinsdale, my favourite monster-hunter.

'From a practical viewpoint it is as well to recognise the different types of monster-hunter, and make allowance for them within a certain category.' [12]

Sunday morning, Nov 9th, the weather was bloody awful for seafarers. Inshore winds of Force-8 and biting cold. The white water in Falmouth Bay looked menacing. Mike James, his colleague, Barry Richards, Spike Hopley, Chris, Kate, Lucy and I gathered on Customs House Quay where we were soon joined by a BBC television crew, from *Nationwide*, led by Roy Lipscombe. I climbed aboard the smaller of the two 'Fast Worker' boats, along with Spike (who had spotted Morgawr before, in 1977) and Barry, our skipper. The others were on the large 'Offshore Worker' with Mike at the helm. After a short interview, filmed by a rather nervous-looking cameraman, we moved out of the comparatively cosy harbour and into the mouth of the Fal. The wind hit us hard and the boats bounced, at twenty knots, through the rough sea, rattling our teeth and bones, drenching us with icy salt water every time we smacked through a wave. I wanted to head for the Helford, Spike and Barry were game, but the conditions made filming difficult. Eventually we decided to head up through the Carrick Roads towards Pill Creek and calmer waters. Barry opened up the throttle and we skimmed along at thirty knots. Just past St. Mawes, the three of us in the small boat felt 'something'. I asked Barry to slow down and guide the craft round and round, widdershins, in a gigantic spiral, while I bellowed my incantations. Spike was the first to notice it ...a black hump breaking the surface, ahead of us. I quickly put a wet camera to my eye and snapped two shots. The hump was visible for no more than a couple of seconds but all three of us saw it. 'Offshore Worker', meanwhile, was a long way ahead, pointing in the wrong direction, so the BBC missed what could have been a television 'first'. We spent all morning making magical spirals in the river, and I felt another 'something' directly over a deep 'prawn hole' at Pill Creek, but Morgawr stayed below this time. Mike made the interesting discovery that his sophisticated electronic 'fish-finder' had completely packed up. I was blamed for this happening, and the television sound man was reminded of an occasion, back in 1976, when, during a BBC interview, I psi-zapped an expensive Nagra recorder. Or so they say.

Maggie James, Mike's wife, spent that Sunday morning looking for evidence of the Owlman near Mawnan Church. She didn't see anything but, later, said the atmosphere was 'weird'. When she got home, Maggie planned to do some laundry but her washing

Doc on the Nov 1980 Morgawr hunt off Falmouth. FPL

machine began to behave in a peculiar way, it made odd noises and the door jammed. I was blamed. Who else?

When Mike James arrived home on Sunday evening, he switched on the TV then popped into the kitchen for a moment. There was a loud bang. Mike returned to the sitting room and saw a cloud of black smoke hovering over his new-but-now-useless colour set. I was blamed.

Mike had planned to make a video recording of our TV spot, which was to be broadcast on the Monday night, Nov 10th (a shortened version appeared later in the week on *Nationwide)*, but now his telly was banjaxed. So... Dick Styles, landlord of the King's Head, offered to make a recording for Mike on his own VHS machine. Monday arrived, Lucy and I picked up our very first pairs of specs from the optician, and my darling daughter recalled the time when, as a tiny infant, she had most painfully sliced one of my eyes with a sharp baby fingernail. When we arrived home in the evening, we saw a shadowy figure in the dark lane which leads to the Shiels hovel. Being psychic, I said: 'Hello Jeoff, are you looking for number three?' It was Jeoff Watson, the wandering monster-spotter, and this was our first meeting. He had arrived just in time to see the television version of our Sunday seafaring. Back at the 'King's Head', Dick was amused to note that a strange white line sliced, tele-visually, across my eyes when I talked to the BBC about seeing a sea-serpent. It reminded him of that famous scene in the Dali/Bunuel movie, *Une Chien Andalou*, where a cloud slices the moon and a razor slices the girl's eye (Dick, like so many of us, is an ex-art student!). Synchronistic Surrealism! I was blamed for the strange white line... but a couple of days later, Dick was told that the fault had been caused by candle grease which had, some-how, dropped onto the recording head. It transpired that the wax came from a candle inside a Hallowe'en pumkin lantern, sitting on a shelf above the video machine. During a party, the shelf had, perhaps, been nudged, the candle tipped over and hot wax dripped *through one of the grinning pumkin's eye-holes!* I wasn't sure who or what to blame for that.

Eye-slicing images cropped up in my dreams for several nights. In Amsterdam, my son, Ewan, who is partially blind in the right eye, smashed one of the lenses of his glasses... the right one, which really didn't matter, but it made me think about 'psychic backlash'.

On Thursday, Nov 13th, I had a lunchtime pint in the 'Globe', a Falmouth waterfront pub, where I met a man who said he recognises me from the television broadcast. He was in his late fifties or early sixties and he gave his name as 'Martin'. He told me that he had seen Morgawr himself, the previous afternoon (the 12th), around four o'clock, off Rose-mullion, and that his daughter *and* granddaughter had seen a 'gigantic bird' fly over the Helford River and into the trees above Grebe Beach. He said the sea monster was 'gigantic' too, with a head and neck 'like a python' and a body 'like a whale'. It was dark grey in colour and it moved very fast towards the mouth of the Helford. He watched it for 'two or three minutes' and visibility was good. He couldn't give any real estimate of its size...just 'gigantic'. Mysterious Mr 'Martin' then finished his drink and left the pub.

Kate came into the 'Globe' about half an hour after 'Martin' had taken his leave, and I told her his story. She smiled and said that she, too, had seen Morgawr that very morning (the 13th). About 7 am, from a cave in the jagged South wall of Pendennis Point, Kate did whatever shamanic things she does, then swam, naked, in the sea. It was dark at first – she didn't really want an audience — but, after coming ashore and dressing, she saw Morgawr in the dawn light. I asked Kate to write and sign a statement about her sighting. This is an extract: 'I suddenly noticed a large dark hump rise out of the sea, about three hundred metres offshore. Then a smaller second hump appeared, connected to the first, followed by a long neck. I would say the animal was at least twenty-five feet in length. It hardly moved, just dipping its head up and down, like a swan, for a few seconds, then it sank down under the sea and that was that.' Kate wasn't carrying a camera, she reckons Morgawr would not have appeared to her if she had been.

After lunch, I decided to investigate that area of Pendennis Point myself, with a loaded camera. By mid-afternoon I was clambering around the jagged rocks near Kate's cave. No sign of the monster, just a fleet of Russian factory ships. After a while I decided to climb up onto the road but, near the top, I found my way barred by a thick tangle of thorn bushes. The path looked a little clearer to my right, over towards the Coastguard Station, so I carefully and rather nervously began to edge across the rock above the cave mouth. I was half-way over when the heel of my right boot snapped off! A sudden surge of adrenalin made me grab at the roots of an overhanging bush and haul myself upwards right into a mass of scratching, tearing thorns. When I finally reached the road, my coat was ripped, my camera-case damaged, my hands, arms, legs and face bleeding from hundreds of tiny wounds. 'Backlash', I explained to Chris when I got home. 'Too much Guinness.' said she, wisely.

'Morgawr' is an anagram of 'Ragworm'.

That night the animals in and around our village of Ponsanooth behaved very strangely. Foxes screamed, dogs howled, owls screeched, horses whinnied and cats caterwauled. I didn't sleep too well and when I slept at all I dreamed of having my eyes scratched out by wild beasts.

'The mind of the dreaming man is fully satisfied with whatever happens to it.' [1]

After a satisfying night, I opened my two bleary but functioning eyes to a wet and windy morning. Friday, Nov 14th, the last day of our experiment. I stayed indoors and wrote some letters until late afternoon. The rain still rained, and I picked up a book on Surrealism, intending to read the section concerned with Bunuel and to exorcise my nagging worries about eye-ripping. It fell open a couple of pages before Bunuel's (and Breton's) bit, at Brauner, Victor (Piatra-Naemtz, Rumania 1903 – Paris 1966). I was quite familiar with the name of Victor Brauner and knew his work, but had forgotten something about him which now became disturbingly significant. Let me quote Rene Passeron:

'When we discover that in 1931, shortly before returning to Rumania after his exhibition in Paris in 1934, Brauner painted a Self-Portrait with Enuncleated Eye, *it is difficult not to take the theme of the glass eye and the empty or closed eye — a constant recurring topic at the time — as a premonition of the accident which deprived him of his left eye in 1938.' [2]*

Brauner's 'accident' is described by Marcel Jean: 'During a quarrel to which he was merely a witness, one of the parties to the dispute hurled a glass in a sudden moment of anger; the glass struck him in the face and fatally injured his left eye.' [13] In 1933, Brauner had painted a picture showing a male figure with his eye pierced by a shaft carrying the letter D... the initial of the name of the person responsible for the accident. ('Composition' 1933, reproduced in Jean's book. Dr Pierre Mabille was convinced that Brauner's premonition derived from obsession... a desire to attain inner vision, 'a world that can be seen only with closed eyes.' He also tells us that the painter's father was 'a student of magical experiments'. [14]

Obsessions!

'I saw myself with the head of a kite bird, knife in hand, in the pose of Rodin's 'Thinker', so I thought, but it was actually the liberated pose of Rimbaud's 'Seer'. [15]

On that last night, I dressed myself up in the full rig of Doc Shiels, medicine man: Tall beaver hat with funny feathers, fancy waistcoat with watch-chain and dangling silver skull, charlatan's cloak and wizard's wand. The rain had stopped. I went down to the woods and built a bonfire. When it was burning merrily my witches arrived, the good Paddy whiskey they had thoughfully provided was passed from hand to hand, from mouth to mouth. The 'experiment' ended at midnight... but strange things have happened since then. I'll tell you about them some time.

•

Doc Shiels

REFERENCES

1 Andre Breton. *Les Manifestes du Surrealisme* (Paris 1925).
2 Rene Passeron. *Encyclopedie du Surrealisme* (Editions Aimery Somogy, Paris 1975).
3 Michael Edwardes. *The Dark Side of History* (Hart-Davis McGibbon, London 1978).
4 Lyall Watson. *Lifetide* (Hodder & Stoughton, London 1979).
5 Alfred Schmeller. *Surrealism* (Methuen, London 1956).
6 See the photographs of Max Ernst in feathered fancy dress or at the Paris bird market, in: Patrick Waldberg, *Surrealism* (Thames & Hudson, London 1965).
7 Gaston Diehl. *Max Ernst* (Bonifi Press, Naefels, Switzerland 1975).
8 Joan Halifax. *Shamanic Voices* (E P Dutton, NY 1979; Pelican, London 1980).
9 Weston La Barre. *The Ghost Dance* (Allen & Unwin, London 1972).
10 Paul Huson. *The Devil's Picture Book* (Abacus, London 1972).
11 John Fire/Lame Deer & Richard Erdoes. *Lame Deer: Sioux Medicine Man* (Davis Poynter, London 1973).
12 Tim Dinsdale. *The Story of the Loch Ness Monster* (Allan Wingate, London 1973).
13 Marcel Jean. *The History of Surrealist Painting* (Weidenfeld & Nicholson, London 1960).
14 Pierre Mabille. 'L'Oeil du Peintre', *Minotaure* Nos 12-13 (Albert Skira, Geneva 1939).
15 Max Ernst. *Cahiers d'Art* (Paris 1937).

THE STORY SO FAR: A strange brooch found on the beach has involved our hero with a secret sect, the **Ancient Order of Buffoons**, who manipulate history and control world events. He has been abducted in a Spaceship, and rendered **violently unconscious** three times. NOW READ ON.....

WHEN I AWOKE, I WAS SECURELY BOUND! THESE BUFFOONS SEEMED DETERMINED TO EDUCATE ME....
OOOOOH
AH! GOOD! YOU'RE WITH US AGAIN....
YOU DERIDE OUR ORDER- WELL, I INTEND TO SHOW YOU THAT WE ARE INFINITELY MORE ANCIENT THAN ANY OTHER SECRET SECT.... INDEED, WE TRACE OUR HISTORY BACK TO....
... THE BEGINNING OF THE UNIVERSE ITSELF!!
HMPH! THE IMPUDENCE! TURN ON THE PROJECTOR, LACKEY!
YUS, YOUR FOOLISHNESS, AT ONCE!
IN THE BEGINNING, THE PRIME PARTICLES OF MATTER WERE ALL FALLING TOGETHER IN THE VOID... ALL AT A CONSTANT SPEED!
BUT THERE WAS ONE PARTICLE AMONGST THEM- THE JOKER IN THE PACK, AS YOU MIGHT SAY...
...WHICH GAVE A LITTLE NUDGE!
THE NUDGE ESCALATED... ...MATTER CAME TOGETHER....
POW
FIT
CLOK
BAK
ZIK
SPAN
POON
BAP
PING
POK
CLUNK
PLOT
BIP
TIC
BOP
BIT
DOK
PAK
...AND BINGO! BEFORE VERY LONG, STARS, PLANETS AND ALL THE REST WERE FORMED!
AND WE COMMEMORATE THIS IN OUR SECRET SIGN, THE BUFFONIC NUDGE!
...ABSOLUTE BLOODY RUBBISH...
WHAT??
READ YER LUCRETIUS, MATE - IT'S ALL THERE!
LUCRET
...BUT ALREADY YOU KNOW TOO MUCH....
1 TON
WILL OUR HERO FIND OUT WHY THE BUFFOONS ARE TELLING HIM ALL THIS? WILL THEY STOP BELTING HIM ON THE HEAD? WILL THE NEXT EPISODE FIT INTO IT'S TWO PAGES BETTER THAN THIS? =Find out Next Issue!

Tales from Malaysia.

We welcome to our pages another of our Special Correspondents, **Ahmad Jamaludin,** from Kuantan, in Pahang, Malaysia, whose UFO bulletins from that country have appeared in FSR. Ahmad's interests include Fortean phenomena, and we hope to hear more from him from time to time. This article has been compiled from two items he sent us: the first summarizing events of note from 1979, and the second on events in the first quarter of 1981. Ahmad points out that UFO sightings are quite rare in Malaysia, and earth tremors rarer still, so that to have so many in such proximity to each other in 1979 was quite remarkable.

FORTEANA IN 1979 (relate to map).

• **1:— Butterworth.**
On Jan 2, a RAAF serviceman coming out of a supermarket sighted a round silvery object in the sky at 6.15pm. The object was described as glowing in bright orange colour and had several portholes lining the edge. The witness took 12 shots with his camera but when the film was developed only two shots showing the object came out. The UFO hovered for about 20 minutes before it disappeared.
The National Echo, 4 Jan 1979.

• **2:— Jitra.**
Four farmers going to their rice field at 6.45 in the morning of Jan 5 sighted a small glittering ball floating in the sky. They claimed that the object appeared suddenly before them and they stopped to watch it. No sound was coming from the object but it was moving. The sighting lasted for about 20 minutes.
The New Straits Times, 6 Jan 1979.

• **3:— Penang Island.**
On 7th Feb, at 10.30am, two construction workers were resting under a tree when suddenly both of them caught a glimpse of a round shiny object flying towards the mainland.
Berita Harian, 9 Feb 1979.

• **4:— Penang Island.**
An earth tremor was felt in Penang Island at 11.10pm on March 16. The tremor which occurred twice within a few seconds went unaware by most people.
The New Straits Times, 18 March 1979.

• **5:— Penang Island.**
In March a 3-inch nail appearing from nowhere smashed through a window pane of an institute, whizzed past three members of the teaching staff, hit an iron railing inside the institute office and ricochetted into the arm of a laboratory assistant. The nail made a hole an inch long in the glass pane. The incident occurred at 11.45am.
The New Straits Times (date uncertain)

• **6:— Kampung Pertama.**
Starting from April 20, a display of aerial lights took place near the village for 5 consecutive nights. The strange brightly lit object was elliptical in shape and sparkled like a star. It landed in the rice field which was several miles deep inside the village perimeter. As the UFO landed at about 7pm, it began to get smaller and then the light split into three smaller UFOs. About 20 villagers gathered to watch the spectacle.
The New Straits Times, 25 April 1979.

• **7:— Kuala Lumpur.**
On 27 April, a slight earth tremor was felt by a few people, at 11am sending people on the top floor of at least one building scrambling out. However the tremor went unnoticed in other high-rise buildings in the city.
The New Straits Times, 29 April 1979.

• **8:— Semenyeh.**
In early May a farmer left a buffalo near a disused tin-mining pool and while he was resting under a tree he heard a splash. He ran to the pool but the animal had disappeared. He saw only a whirlpool in the pond. Another farmer had also lost his buffalo there and reported to police that he saw a 'large snake' in the water. Residents there also reported that the 'monster' was spotted at least three times on May 19.
The New Straits Times, 21 May 1979.

• **9:— Bukit Mertajam.**
On 19 May, at 3pm, six schoolchildren encountered a landed UFO and four 3-inch-tall entities near it. One of the students, it is reported, tried to catch one creature but was shot in the hand. The creature then fired another shot at a brick breaking it into two. After the shooting, the creatures scurried back into the tiny object. Another pupil grabbed the UFO with both hands but had to let go when he felt what seemed like an electric current passing through his hands. The object then took off leaving in its wake a shower of falling leaves. A 21-year-old youth playing nearby came to the scene after hearing the commotion just in time to see the shooting and the object taking off.
The Daily Star, 29 May 1979.

• **10:— Kampung Nagalilit.**
On 26 May, between 8–9am, three students were playing in the clearing of a rubber plantation when suddenly they heard a droning sound and turning saw a tiny object coming in slowly for a landing. The UFO appeared to land

and the student rushed to touch it. As they were about to touch the object, which was luminous, an intense beam of light shot out from its outer rim into their eyes, temporarily blinding them; They immediately cried for help which drew the attention of two adults nearby, who rushed to the scene and managed to see the UFO moving slowly into the jungle. The cattle in a nearby shed were very restless and were trying to break away from the posts to which they were tied.

The Daily Star, 30 May 1979, and *The New Thrill*, 1979.

• **11:– Tepoh.**
Several students going to school in the morning saw three mysterious footprints near a bridge. According to the police there were three footprints of various sizes. One measured 3 ft long, the other 2 ft, and the third a little smaller. Hundreds of people have crowded to the bridge to see the prints which were believed to have been made by mysterious entities.

Berita Harian, 9 July 1979.

• **12:– Lumut.**
Since 11 August students of a Vocational Institute have reported that they have been disturbed by three 10-ft-tall hairy creatures. These strange happenings occurred between 10pm and 5am. Several of the students reported that they have seen the entities with their own eyes. These entities have red eyes and they usually disappeared mysteriously into thin air. The Insitute was later temporarily closed and all the students instructed to go home.

Utusan Malaysia, 18 Aug 1979.

• **13:– Pekan.**
Several cases of an encounter with a man with a dog's head were reported in this town. A local resident reported that he had chased a man carrying something in his hands behind his house. The man suddenly vanished when he put the thing that he was carrying on his head. Residents of this small town lived in fear of this mysterious dog-headed phantom for some time until all the excitement died down.

Berita Harian, 6 Oct 1979.

• **14:– Melaka.**
During the month of October, a similar case of a were-dog was reported from this town. But this time a dog was caught and taken to the Veterinary Office to determine what it could be. The animal was tied and locked in a room pending investigation, but the next morning it was found missing. The rope with which it had been tied was not undone, and the lock of the door had not been disturbed. Following the mysterious disappearance of this animal, fear once again gripped the local community. Whatever it was, it was never seen again.

Berita Harian, 22 Oct 1979.

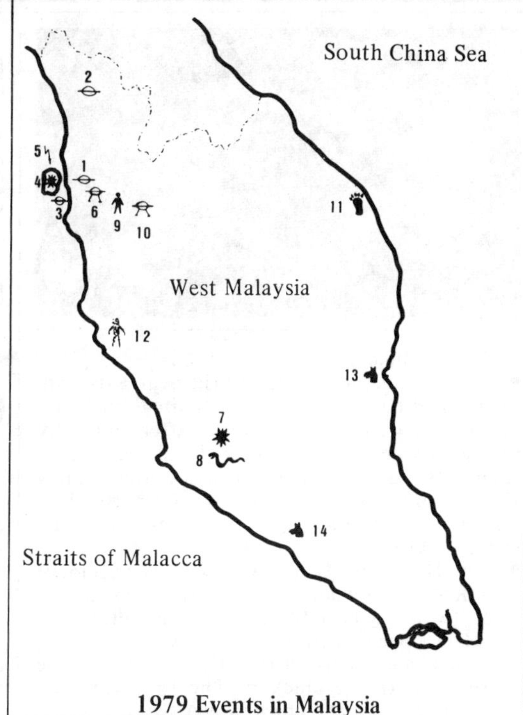

1979 Events in Malaysia

FORTEANA IN 1981 (SO FAR) IN MALAYSIA

• On 13 Feb 1981, at about 9.30am, 20 students out of 100 taking part in a cross-country run suddenly went into hysteria. The incident began when one of the girls started screaming claiming she saw a dark figure in front of her; then she fainted. This was followed by a few more of the students falling to the ground. Things became worse when many more began to faint and they all had to be taken to the hospital.

Utusan Malaysia 15 Feb 1981.

• Sometime in March a rubber tapper was mysteriously killed when the tree he was cutting pushed him several feet into the swamp. His friend nearby reported that he saw the tree falling at an odd angle on the victim. The police and the fire brigade tried for two days to pull the tree out but the cable of the crane snapped. Only after several medicine men chanted prayers could the huge tree-trunk, which had buried itself and the victim, be moved.

New Straits Times March 1981.

• Some time in March a baby buffalo with eight legs was born at Kampung Pondok Bharu (see photo). The baby buffalo was already dead when the owner found it. It was described as a 'Siamese twin' in nature with two bodies joined and had two tails but only one head. The day-old baby buffalo had the size of a two-year-old calf.

Utusan Malaysia 11 March 1981.

• For two nights in mid-April, near Kuantan, many girl students attending an animal husbandry course went into hysteria after allegedly seeing a disembodied black hand waving at them. Its waving seemed to mysteriously draw the students towards it. In an effort to resist the mysterious pull they went into hysteria. (From a witness).

• On 10 April, there was some excitement near Kota Baru when a chicken that was slaughtered twice, by two different people, refused to die. The villagers believed that it was something abnormal and many visited the owner's home to see the strange chicken. The following day after the neck of the chicken was stitched back, the chicken appeared stronger and was able to walk. *(Berita Harian* 19 April 1981). The sad news came a week later when the chicken finally gave up – not that it's ready to go to the dinner table – but it died. This was due to the swelling at the site of the slaughter which did not receive any treatment.

Mingguan Malaysia 26 April 1981.

• As if there is no justice or to see some justice, hundreds of caterpillars swarmed the local courthouse in Bentong in April. The spokesman for the court said that this was the second such invasion; the first was in 1979.

Mingguan Malaysia 26 Apr 1981.

• A 30-year-old man was attacked by a tiger in the jungles of Bukit Ibam while searching for firewood on 21st April. He was attacked from behind and was badly wounded. He nearly died during the struggle with the tiger but his three dogs put up a fight and the tiger ran away. He quickly climbed a tree fearing the tiger might return but in his shock fell down. Although bleeding and in pain, he walked about 8 miles to his village. From there he was taken to the hospital 60 miles away.

Berita Minggu 26 April 1981.

. . . AND IN INDONESIA

• Two gamblers were set on by armed thugs soon after leaving the Jarkarta casino and robbed of more than 100 million rupiahs. The two were thinking of buying a house and while driving looking for one, were jumped by seven knite-weilding bandits who made off with their winnings. The men have two weeks to try to recoup their losses. The casino will be closed from April 1, 1981 under an Indonesian Government ban on gambling.

The Straits Times March 1981.

• A 41-year-old medicine-seller was imprisoned for five-and-a-half months for marrying a girl less than 15 years old. When he was released his youngest wife and 14 others were happy to receive him at the prison gate. All of his 15 wives live in harmony with him in one house. Now here is one man who may be selling some wonderful medicine!

Berita Harian 17 April 1981.

Curiosa.

The owner of this house – a vicar in Murten, Switzerland – returned home after a brief absence to find one of his chimneys twisted a full 180 degrees. A builder who secured it could find no apparent cause for this mystery movement. The vicar checked with the local weather office and was told there were no recent reports of twisters. Besides, adds the confounded cleric, 'The other two chimneys are normal. It's amazing.' [Photo: The Province *(Vancouver, BC) 19 Sept 1980. Credit: David MacAdams.]*

Notes from the
Trashkashic
Records
Bob Tarte + Dave Fideler

TELEVISION FATHERS, FATHER TELEVISION

'If you wish to make an apple pie from scratch, you must first invent the universe. Carl Sagan 'The Lives of Stars' *Cosmos.*

Reporting on a symposium on television that took place in New York City recently, J. Hoberman of the *Village Voice* distilled the thesis of one of the speakers into the statement, 'The real viewer of television is not you but other people – and this is true for everybody.' [1]

Hoberman's remark was aimed at the 'mirage of public opinion' which exists only to the degree that people believe it does', the fact that the typical viewer whose tastes TV supposedly reflects has reality only as a statistic in surveys, or within the demographically twisted minds of advertisers. But his statement is also true in the sense that television reflects the collective psychological layer of its host culture. Opposed to individual expression of insight and creativity which a stereotypically perceived TV-public might find disquieting, television is staunchly committed to upholding established social values.

Harlan Ellison has dubbed the medium 'the glass teat' – and what Jerzy Kosinski caught so successfully in his novel *Being There* is the passiveness of mind that television nurtures. You either watch with full acceptance of its cartoonish conventions or you probably don't watch at all. And so we sit and suck. The extent to which the medium has replaced direct experience in the lives of millions of viewers is a truism that can hardly be overstated. In its function as 'crown control' device [2], TV from a Jungian standpoint serves a patriarchal prupose too; as Erich Neumann writes, 'Creation is always an individual achievement, for every creative work or deed is something new that was not there before .... contrasted with the conventionality of the father, of the collective, of conscience.' [3]

Television's conscience is finely tuned to the spiritual domain of the hawking of goods. The consumer society's superego commands judgement-making on a quantitative rather than a qualitative basis. Though one dog food may claim superiority over its competition, the manufacturer is not concerned with striving towards a Greek Ideal in pet consumables. Large conglomerates may even continue to grind out their rivals' products after they've taken over their firms, hoping to seduce the viewer from one side or the other – if not both. Exclusivity isn't the goal, it's getting the viewer to buy *more* of everything.

With form hoisted over content, it is only initially surprising to find TV's capitalistic eye focused so 'tightly' on sex in puritanical America. When the viewer is invited to leer at Suzanne Sommers' topography in 'Three's Company', packaging is what he is being encouraged to appreciate. He is not to suppose, however, that the lovable Krissy actually makes use of her gonads (which she apparently doesn't). This would direct the libidinous charge of the program inwards towards a personal TV object instead of out at the audience in the collective experience of voyeurism. By the not-so-subtle strategy of innuendo, the show's producers insure that sexual connections occur in the mind of the viewer and not obviously on-screen. In this manner the medium is absolved of sin against social mores, and the viewer may keep much of his enjoyment unconscious, thereby exonerating himself as well.

'Whattya mean we're exploiting Cheryl Ladd for her ass?' a wide-eyed network executive thus can ask with a shadow of conviction. 'That kid's on TV cos she's got a load of talent.'

Whatever depiction of sex does emerge on the tube is all within the boundaries of stereotype – that is, at the collective level of belief. As viewers become bored with TV-reality, it enlarges slightly to accommodate more startling images. Yet these are surprising solely in the context of the medium; 'I didn't think they could show *that* on TV!' is the classic viewer response to something new. Transplanted to a medium with a more individualised audience, however – books, magazines, movies and particularly authentic life experience – the most controversial television rendering grows limp.

But precisely because TV reflects collective values it has, paradoxically an immediacy in our lives that more individualized forms of expression may lack. Watching a few hours of television is a good way of taking 'reality checks', of getting an instant overview of what's happening in society. It's one thing to read Neumann's elegant, coolheaded prose as he describes 'the collapse of the archetypal canon, which has produced such an extraordinary activation of the collective unconscious' [4]; it's another to flick a button and actually see something of this process at work in the presence of increasingly sharply defined patriarchal figures on the tube opposed to the emergence of long-repressed deep layers of our mass psyche.

In the late 50s, the *Ozzie and Harriet* years, TV dads were men who had a basic trust in the equilibrium of the family, giving members a gentle nudge back onto the 'right track' now and then when they violated household standards. On *I Love Lucy*, appropriate to the day, marriage was regarded as a battlefield between masculine and feminine. Lucy and Ricky endlessly hatched secret plots against one another, each striving to be the controlling force in their relationship. At their most intimate, husband and wife relaxed into occasional periods of truce, never a real union.

With the giddy leakage of irrationality that came in the 60s, with its brief hope of counterculture, the video father figure assumed a larger yet often more detached role. In *The Brady Bunch* – as well as in *Family Affair* and *My Three Sons*, where dad as single parent muddled through home rule – the father was an architect by profession. Archetypically the architect represents the erector of culture and on a grander scale maker of the universe. Just ask any Mason. Today as pressures in cultural unconscious mount, the TV patriarch is being blown up into a size blatantly larger than life.

A prime example is Roarke, fulfiller of dreams on *Fantasy Island*. A master of manipulating artifice, like an overinflated Fred MacMurray supreme architect Roarke constructs duplicates of imagined or remembered environments for his clients, in which they act out important situations in their lives that have been denied them in the external world – dad as the ultimate problem-solver. But wait, something's not quite right here. Though Roarke is the one who sets the stage, he quickly becomes irrelevant to the process. His clients' success or failure in their fantasies depends on the acuity with which they resolve unconscious tensions by themselves.

Once a fantasy has begun, it takes on the life of its own which characterizes any complex, and Roarke is powerless to intervene – as he is fond of warning his visitors. Occasionally he does interfere, however, either as a figure from the 'world above' who mouths a few words of advice before vanishing, or more typically to pull his clients entirely out of dreams that threaten to devour their workaday identities. 'Every fantasy must have some basis in reality,' he hissed this season to *Vega$*' co-star Phyllis Davis after rescuing her from the overwhelming desire to be a sex goddess [5] – 'a very dangerous fantasy,' he called it, since such irrational urges are alien to the meticulous Roarke.

Though he may play a part in deflating the unconscious forces that have a firm grip on his clients, Roarke's goal is to stimulate self-knowledge merely to the degree that will permit his visitors to safely return to the social norm. Few depart the island radically changed. Most leave their troubled dreams behind with Roarke, disappearing at the end of each program into the blissful obscurity of the collective, for which Roarke serves as guardian. He's a pop-psychologist in disguise, an anally retentive shaman who alludes to 'dark powers beyond the control of man' when confronted with psychic realities which transcend the personal. He is a symbol *par excellence* of the overinflated ego. Tattoo, the dark, foreign dwarf ever at his side, is his devalued unconscious, a victim of the withering glare of Roarke's white-suited rationalism.

It's remarkable enough to find a fictional TV-character as boldly rendered in his function as Roarke. Even more remarkable is the existence of a champion of the cultural canon who is defined by his real-life identity. On the PBS weekly series *Cosmos*, [now running on BBC, Fridays–Ed] scientist Carl Sagan secularizes the already profane role of TV preachers like Jerry Falwell with his unabashedly materialistic views on the make-up of man and his universe.

As *Time* magazine recently quoted him:

'I am a collection of water, calcium and organic molecules called Carl Sagan. You are a collection of almost identical molecules with a different collective label [sic!]. But is that all? Is there nothing in here but molecules? Some people find this idea somehow demeaning to human dignity. For myself, I find it elevating that our universe permits the evolution of molecular machines as intricate and subtle as we.' [6]

Sagan's reductionist perspective is a lens which muddies history. He sees scientific discovery as proof of man's evolution, believing that progress of technological ideas goes hand in hand with betterment of culture. As a member of the Committee for Scientific Investigations of Claims of the Paranormal, a body predisposed against the phenomena it investigates [7], Sagan is a tireless voice against what he perceives as the growing irrationality of our time. To his way of thinking, there is no distinction between the irrational and the transpersonal. Religion and philosophy are no complement to science, but its rivals.

In a recent episode of *Cosmos*, [8] Sagan accused Pythagoras and Plato of 'extinguishing the light of science and experiment that had been kindled by

Democtritus and other Ionians.' Villifying the Ancient Greek philosophers again on a later show, he stated, 'If the Ionians had won, we might now be going to the stars.' [9]

The notion that an alien culture like the Greeks but for the interference of a philosophical movement would have developed Western-style technology centuries ago is absurd. Furthermore it fails to demonstrate much historical insight. If, as Sagan claims, empiricism is the hallmark of the scientific mind as opposed to mere speculation, then what does that make of a theoretical thinker like Einstein? Pythagorean geometry, based on an abstraction of forms first observed in nature, is scientific discovery through analogy – in much the same manner by which Sagan's cherished Ionian Democritus developed his early concept of atomism by studying seeds and grains of sand.

Lack of space prohibits a discussion of the arbitrariness of the boundaries Sagan draws between the 'materialism' of the Ionians vs. Pythagorean mysticism, or the argument that Pythagorean ideas of the foundation of matter are far closer to modern atomic theory than Democritus' concept. On the level of plain historical accuracy Sagan's reductionism becomes apparent. As history of science writer W.K.C. Guthrie states, 'To some small extent those in the Ionian succession made use of observation, but only spasmodically until the time of Aristotle, and of controlled experiment they had no idea.' [10]

Sagan ascribes a social role to science equivalent to that of religion in Medieval Europe: *'We have a society which is built on science and technology and which uses science in every one of the interstices of national life, and in which the public, the executive, the legislative and the judiciary have very little understanding of what science is all about. That is a clear disaster signal. It has to be suicidal. [11]*

It is as if he is prophesying an apocalypse brought on by lack of public deference to the technological spirit, which he has cast as the only solution to our present cultural upheaval. This is ironic, that the notion of 'reaching for the stars' – which has long stood as a metaphor for total human striving – should be reduced to a dull, literal-minded interpretation, based on the pipe-dream that with the abandonment of planet earth will come the shedding of the undeniable heritage of our collective unconscious. The opposite is more likely to occur. The over-inflation of the rational mind will undoubtedly help release rather than impede what Neumann has referred to as the 'shadow side' of science. [12]

No outward tinkerings with the world and no social ameliorations can give the quietus to the daemon, to the gods and devils of the human soul, or prevent them from tearing down again and again what consciousness has built. Unless they are assigned their place in consciousness and culture they will never leave mankind in peace. [13]

The daemons, it's clear, have begun actively asserting their presence, whether in the powerful fragmented form in millions of individuals of a sense of alienation from any wholeness, or as fullblown compensatory Fortean events. Television is playing its part in their explosive re-emergence but attempting to keep the lid tightened down on unconscious forces that are visible and obvious everywhere – until the day comes when our culture like Kafka's Grego Samsa will awaken in disbelief to a long-neglected side of its personality as it asserts itself in a totally negative manner.

To paraphrase a statement by the Church of SubGenius, a group which has built a satirical religion from the detritus of the collective, not only will the end of the world be much worse and take longer than we thought, but we'll be forced to watch it on TV. [14]

•

Bob Tarte

NOTES

1) J Hoberman, 'Tv or not Tv; What was the Question?', *Village Voice* 5 Nov 1980.
2) Larry Hagman in an interview, *Playboy* Nov 1980: "Think of what people would be doing if they weren't watching television. If they weren't sitting in a little room watching a little box, they'd be out in the streets kicking ass... TV is the opiate of the people."
3) Erich Neumann, *The Origins and History of Consciousness* (Princeton, NJ, Princeton Univ.Press 1973) p379.
4) ibid, p393.
5) This is ironic, considering that Davis plays just that on *Vegas* - a sex symbol. Guest-starring on *Fantasy Island* frequently involves an element of masochism. The media-made personae of such luminaries as Sonny Bono, Barbi Benton and Annette Funicello, among others, have been ridiculed on the show.
6) 'The Showman of Science', *Time* 20 Oct 1980.
7) of D.Scott Rogo, 'Carl Sagan vs the Paranormal', *Fate* April 1980.
8) 'Backbone of Night', *Cosmos.*
9) 'Travels in Space and Time', *Cosmos.*
10) WKC Guthrie, *The Greed Philosophers: From Thales to Aristotle* (NY, Harper & Row 1960) p57.
11) *Time,* ibid.
12) Neumann, ibid, p387.
13) ibid, p393.
14) 'What the HELL do you think you are doing?', pamphlet. Box 140306, Dallas, TX 75214, USA.

Cont from p1

not opening a *new* subscription. We cannot check every name against our records, and so a few have got by the vigilance of Paul Sieveking. The result is a duplication on the overlapping issues of both subs, and this is both expensive to run and to change now that our address labels are generated by computer. If you can bear it, better wait until we send you the renewal form, which we do automatically as a reminder to all subscribers with the penultimate issue on their sub.

Back in the 4th century, when General Yin Hao was cashiered, he did nothing but sit all day tracing in the air with his finger the words 'Oh dear, oh dear! What a strange business!' We know just how he felt, having been confronted with a selection of really odd stories from China in the early part of this year. So here, traced on the printed page, is some very strange business indeed!

• **DOOMSDAY BOOK**: In January we learned that a tome entitled *The Book of Heavenly Prophesy* was circulating underground in Tibet. It had apparently first appeared 20 years previously, but was now gaining such currency that Lhasa Radio felt constrained to denounce it. The book encourages people to eat as much as they can and buy as many clothes as possible, because doomsday is at hand; famine, drought and flood are said to be coming, and the Earth will be destroyed shortly thereafter. All nonsense, says the government controlled radio. But in March, we learned that China was appealing for international aid (700 million dollars worth) because of *famine:* Hebei province suffering from *drought* (23 million people affected) and Hubei province from *flooding* (20 million affected). *Melbourne Herald + Niagara Falls Review*, 21 Jan; *D Telegraph* 1 March; *S Times* 22 March 81.

Then at the end of March about 4000 people in 100 junks sailed to Hong Kong, begging to be allowed to stay until April 10th, because astrologers and/or Taoist priests had predicted that an earthquake would hit the southern province of Guangdong during that period; the prediction being made during the festival of the local god Hang Sing. British and Chinese experts agreed their fears were groundless, landing permission was refused, the junks were escorted back to sea. Come April 9th and whammo! A 10-second earthquake measuring 3-4 points on the Mercalli scale, hits Guangdong, epicentre 85 miles north-east of Hong Kong. *Now* who's got red faces? Sri Lanka *Sun* 1 April; *D Telegraph* 10 April 81.

• **DISTRESSED ROCK**: As if that wasn't bad enough, even the rocks are yelling for help. People are said to have heard cries for help emanating from a rock which juts out of the Dongting Lake, in Hunan province. Speculation is that the rock might be magnetic and have recorded the cries of drowning sailors, and when temperature and sunlight conditions are just right, it 'plays them back'. *D Telegraph* (quoting *Shansi Daily)* 24 February 81.

• **DEVIL'S TRIANGLE**: It must be catching; after the Bermuda farce and the Japanese Devil's Sea, we now learn of a 'Devil's Triangle' in the South China Sea, between Hong Kong, Taiwan and the Philippines. Three vessels, of unknown size but presumed communist registration are said to have disappeared without trace in the area between May 79 and February 80. The area is swept by typhoons, has treacherous currents, reefs and deep water (13,000 feet) anyway, but records tell of hundreds of ships being lost. Court records of 600 years ago speak of ships disappearing on calm, windless days, and of huge waterspouts suddenly appearing, in the grip of which no progress could be made no matter how hard the oars were pulled, until the ships disintegrated. The *Peking Daily* blames whirlpools caused by the interaction of sea-currents and river-flows. *D Telegraph* 5 March; *D Express* 16 March; Sri Lanka *Sun* 28 March 81.

• **ANGRY GOD**: More trouble, this time in a saw-mill at a Canton shipyard. After three successive but unspecified accidents which left a number of men injured, workers and officials decided they had angered the local Tu Di, a guardian spirit of the soil. So, amid exploding firecrackers, they sacrificed a black dog and, according to tradition, held a banquet for the cadres (why should the gods have all the fun, after all?). Naturally, they got told off, in no uncertain terms. Malaysian *Echo* (quoting Canton *Southern Daily)* 20 Feb 81.

• **OLDEST MUMMY**: No longer subject to such vicissitudes is a young woman 'with a very beautiful body' found at the site of the ancient city of Loulan, near Lop Nor, in the western province of Xinjiang. She's dead, of course, having lived 6,470 years ago, and is being claimed as the world's oldest mummy. The corpse is said to be remarkably well-preserved with shoulder-length blonde hair and eyelashes still intact, large eyes, muscles that are still flexible and a face described as 'coldly shimmering but beautiful'. She was wearing a felt hat decorated with two wild goose quills, a woolen dress and leather boots, and the body had been wrapped in more felt and leather before the tomb was covered with wood. The mummification was apparently natural, the area being extremely arid, and the tomb filled with sand by the wind. *D Express + New Straits Times* (Malaysia) + *News-Sun* (Illinois) 18 Feb; *D Telegraph* 19 Feb; *Niagara Falls Review + Sault Star* (Canada) 20 Feb; *China Reconstructs* May 81.

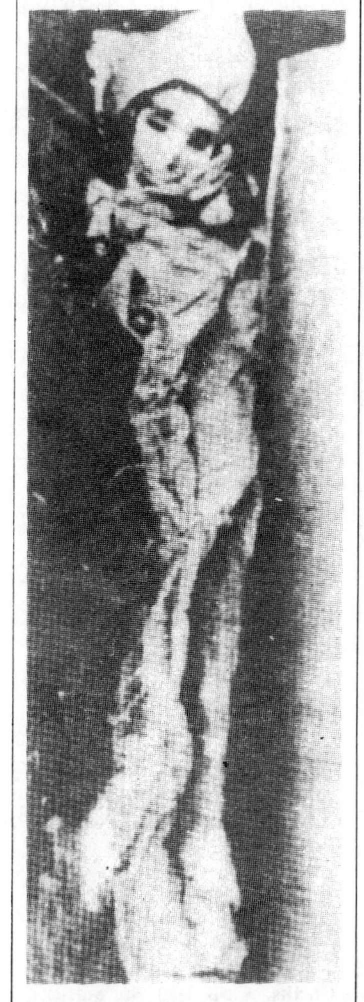

The lady of Loulan. [Photo: Xinhua News Agency.]

• **THE 'TOOTH' ABOUT ANTS**: We learn of a wondrous tonic from 87-year-old Yan Zhongshan: ants. It seems that since 1964 he's been collecting ants, washing them in pure water, drying and grilling them, then grinding them up into powder and cooking them up in an egg omelette, from which he makes pills. One pill a day throughout the winter has given Yan exceptionally sharp eyes and ears; and, having lost his teeth when he was 72, he's now grown a new set, strong enough to crack nuts with! *The* (Penang) *Star* (quoting *Shanghai Wenhuibao)* 13 Feb 81.

• **TREPANED MICE**: Another 'living fossil', apparently surviving from before the Ice Age 11,000 years ago, has been found on 8,200 feet high northern slopes of the Hengduan Mountains between Sichuan and Yunnan provinces. Four specimens have been found of a tiny mouse, weighing less than an ounce, called the 'hole-skulled climbing mouse'. They have two small holes at the front of their skulls. *Houston Chronicle* (Tex) 16 Feb 81.

• **SNAP DRAGONS**: Scientists are said to have found two unnamed girls in Yunnan province who can make tree branches break and flowers bloom by 'mental telepathy'. *D Telegraph* 19 Feb 81.

• **HEY, YOU UP THERE!** In southern Yunnan, in the Gaoligon mountain region, residents simply yell for rain whenever they need it. At the foot of the mountains are a group of pools called 'The Mysterious Lakes' and whenever anyone stands by them and speaks in a loud voice, rain immediately follows. The louder the yell. the heavier the rain; the longer the yell, the longer the rain lasts. 'Experts' theorize that the air round the pools is so wet that the slightest vibration, like a high-pitched voice, can precipitate showers. *Middlesex News* (USA) + *The Post* (Ohio) 24 Feb; *Sault Star* 27 Feb 81. (All quoting Shanghai *Liberation Daily).*

• **HOT AND NAKED**: No, this isn't the porno section. An unidentified boy of 15 in Shiling Commune, Jiangling County, near Nanjing in Jiangsu, is known as 'fire body'. Since falling ill in 1971 he has refused to wear any clothing, even playing naked in the snow during winter. He has not caught colds or other illnesses in the last ten years, and is growing up normally otherwise. He appears to be different from 15-year-old Chen Li, address unknown, congenitally unable to perspire, lacking sweat glands and hair. In summer he has to bathe in rivers a dozen times a day to keep cool and cover himself from head to toe with wet towels before he can fall asleep. Wu Xiaoli, an 18-month-old girl from Miangyang in Sichuan always feels hot and goes naked because she's apparently allergic to clothes. She's nicknamed 'fire baby'; but what they'll call her if she grows up the same way is anybody's guess!

• **TAIL PIECES**: A few tantalising fragments. A report of a child with a tail, said to be five years in advance of other children of his age, but no other details. And that a Peking newspaper had gone to great lengths to prove that a mermaid doesn't exist. And neither does a 'fish with legs', a picture of which (said to be a photo-montage) had been circulating in Peking. *New Thrill* (Malaysia) 21 Feb 81.

Okay, Yin Hao, make room for me! Now, how does it go?

'Oh dear, oh dear! What a strange business!'

Credits: Peter Christie, Loren Coleman, Mark A.Hall, Valerie Martin, Dwight Whalen, Ion Will, Steve Wrathall • **SM.**

From the department that brought you chlorophyll...

THE CRYING PECAN

A 75-foot-tall pecan tree in Needham, Alabama has been whining like a puppy. 'We thought it was a dog sleep-dreaming' said Mrs Linnie Jenkins who owns the tree and first heard the sound on 12 April 1981. A local newspaper ran a report, and soon thousands of tourists started pouring in, many with tape recorders, and cars jammed the narrow roads for miles.

The noise sounds like a crying puppy or the bark of a baby seal. The Jenkinses have done their best to locate it. They've sawed into the tree's base to see if there were hollow roots. They've searched the yard for holes and tunnels that small animals could be trapped in. But it's still a mystery. A forester speculated that the sound could be gas from 'heart rot' seeping through tiny slits in the wood. We are reminded of the moaning rubber plant (FT30p14).

THE WALKING MANGO TREE

Dr Ashok Marathe of Deccan College, Poona, India, claims to have found a walking mango 1,300 years old. The tree grows to a huge size, then lowers one of its branches to the ground some distance away, which then takes root. The parent tree withers and dies. Soniya Ukhadia, a 95-year-old villager, told the scientist that the tree had changed its location at least three times in the last 50 years. We don't know which village the tree is in, nor how Dr Marathe arrived at the extreme age of the tree if it is constantly recycling itself.

Is it a wood or an iron? A curious pine on Spyglass Hill Golf Course, Pebble Beach, California. [Photo: UPI, Lincoln Star *(Neb) 12 March 1980.]*

Meanwhile, in Tewksbury, Gloucestershire, eight lime trees have died, but the willow stakes to which they were tied have taken root and sprouted leaves in their place.

THE MIRACULOUS CHRISTMAS TREE

A 10-foot-high Douglas fir, used as a Christmas tree in 1978, was still fresh and fragrant in February 1980 after more than a year. The fir is supposed to have a life-span no longer than seven weeks after cutting. In October 1979, a private detective sprayed the tree with a substance that will only show up under ultra-violet light, in order to demonstrate that nobody was secretly replacing the tree. They weren't.

Psychic Grace Coveney, who owns the tree, said, 'I knew it was a special tree the first moment I saw it. I could feel the vibrations.' Since the tree arrived, the family have heard strange noises in the house – footsteps, the slamming of drawers, a loud pounding. And the tree ornaments seem to vibrate by themselves. Whether the tree lives on to this day is unknown to us.

THE SMOKING TREE

Finally, an old but interesting note we recently discovered. At East Cowes, Isle of Wight, an old tree was causing concern by smoking like a chimney. Three times in 48 hours firemen were called after smoke billowed out of the old trunk. Spontaneous Tree Combustion? Praps. The *S.Express* 28 April 1974, said there was no apparent cause.

Sources: Kansas City Star 1 May 1980; Sunday Express 7 Oct 1979; Surrey & Hants News 1 July 1980; D.Telegraph 4 Dec 1979; National Enquirer 12 Feb 1980.

Credits: Chris Hall, Steve Hicks, Chris J. Holtzhauzen, Sam, Paul Thomas • **PRAdeGS.**

'There's no fuel like an old fuel' say the inventors of these wonder answers to the oil crisis.

In March 1979, Nick Messemaker, a Director of Solar Reactor Corp. in Miami, announced that his company had discovered a new energy-producing process which would make any amount of energy at virtually no cost and with no environmental problems – in short, a perpetual motion machine.

Hydrogen and chlorine are pumped into a container where, in the presence of oxygen, they are exposed to an energy source – like an artificial light, the sun or low-level radiation from nuclear waste. The result is an ionized hydrochloric gas containing great amounts of energy which can then be recovered for use through a turbine or other means.

According to Messemaker, tests had shown that there is far more energy than should be there. For instance, 47 kilocalories of hydrogen, chlorine and light produced hydrochloric gas containing 241.68 kilocalories of energy. The tests had used artificial light because sunlight is too powerful and the people involved were scared about what might happen. In other processes of combining the two chemicals, the resulting energy is only about half of what goes in.

After the energy has been withdrawn from the gas, it is treated, reconverted to its original components and the process can start again to make a closed system.

'We can't explain it' said Messemaker, before speculating about unidentified light particles and nuclear reactions. The H.P. White Laboratory of Street, Massachusetts and another unnamed laboratory had verified the claims. The process was invented by Robert L. Scragg from West Virginia, who taught himself science and had no academic qualifications.

Two years ago Solar Reactor Corp. was looking for five million dollars backing to create an operational prototype. We have seen no more on this wonderful invention.

•

Back in *Fortean Times* No.11 (then called *The News)*, we wrote of the mysterious Thomas Munson from Blaenau Ffestiniog in North Wales who claimed to have invented a motor fuel costing only 4p a gallon which the *New Scientist* analysed as '95.3% distilled water, benzene, methanol, Iodine crystal, ignitable oil, borax and Fairy washing-up liquid.' The remaining 4.7% included Munson's magic powder 'Tracanath'. Munson vanished on the eve of the big demonstration. Over three years later he was still missing.

In June 1979 another Welshman appeared with a method of running cars which also involved water. Mr Iowerth Thomas' bolt-on device used tapwater to make the engine run more effeciently by burning up the 25% of petrol that is normally wasted. 'It is based on the electrolysis of water and we have found a means of speeding up the process.' he said.

The resultant oxygen eliminated the petrol vapour wastage, while the hydrogen expanded in the cylinders faster than the petrol vapour, cutting the inflow of petrol vapour and reducing the amount of fuel needed. Mr Thomas, 58, has been trying to get a car engine to run on water since 1936. His new device was developed in conjunction with Mr Bert Hoare, boss of a construction engineering company in Brownhills, near Walsall, Staffordshire. They claimed that it not only cut bills by 40% but improved performance and gave a cleaner exhaust.

They had been trying to interest the Energy Department for three years. 'They say it's impossible, which is why we decided to hold the demonstration.' said Mr Thomas. The demonstration on 15th June 1979 was on a 13 bhp Briggs & Stratton stationary engine, which ran for 112 seconds, compared with only 77 seconds on straight petrol, according to the motoring correspondent of the *Daily Telegraph*. Apparently, an Arab consortium was very interested.

The usual objection to any system involving electrolysis is that the energy needed is greater than the energy produced. As the *New Scientist* pointed out, the idea could only be proved to work when the device was put into a car. The equipment would have to be a lot smaller than at the June demonstration, when it took up the space of a room. Mr Thomas was hoping the necessary adaptations would be ready within a month. Why should it work? 'To tell the truth, it's beyond me.' He said. As far as we can make out, this Welshman, like his predecessor, vanished into the woodwork…

or out of the papers anyway. These inventors seem to carry on the tradition of the alchemists of old who flash a powder that turns lead to gold, and vanish after an apparently successful demonstration.

•

Those who see a compensatory facet in mythcraft would expect this breed of trickster-inventor to swarm as the oil taps get disrupted, blocked off or run out. At the beginning of 1980 a Texan called Arnold Burke announced that he had invented a device which would run for ever and generate electricity to power three households if fuelled by three gallons of water each month. The *Daily Mail* tells us that investors from seven states spent half a million pounds for distribution rights before an engineer discovered the machine was secretly plugged to an outlet in the inventor's laboratory. Asked why he did it, Burke said God told him to.

A month later, on 22 February, Dr Hiromu Fushimi, an oil specialist at Tokyo's Waseda University, announced that he was able to produce a blend of 70% petrol and 30% water. 'I'm trying to increase the ratio of water to 40%', he said, adding that he understood US scientists had succeeded in watering petrol by 20%.

He said a go-cart powered by his mixture ran at 12 mph without a cough from its 200 cc engine: financial problems had prevented him from testing his formula on a full-sized car engine. The secret of his method was a chemical medium which he called 'a non-ionic surface agent with a hydrophile-lipophile balance at 4.3' (I trust it hasn't lost any of its poetry in translation). This medium would keep the mixture emulsified for as long as an hour. He had developed a small pump to be installed in a car which would mix the petrol and water just before it was pumped into the engine chamber.

A few weeks after Vancouver readers had been treated to the Japanese announcement, the Sri Lankans were told of the thrilling discoveries of Montedison, the Italian chemicals group. Spokesman Guido Negro said that company researchers in Turin and Lausanne had found a cheap method of producing hydrogen by electrolysis in sufficient quantities for industrial use. It's cheap because it uses sunlight, he added darkly.

•

If water doesn't do the trick, what about magnetism? George Goiri, who runs a farm supply store in Ontario, Oregon, claims that a couple of cow magnets on your petrol intake improves fuel consumption considerably He found this out in March 1980 and as a result the mileage on his truck has improved by eight to nine miles per gallon. He speculates that the magnets, normally used to keep barbed wire accidentally swallowed from piercing cows' stomachs, realign the hydrocarbons which enables them to burn more fumes. Others have different theories.

By last July there was such a nation-wide rush on cow magnets that precious few were left for the poor livestock.

Sources: Washington Post 31 March 1979; D.Telegraph 30 Jan 1975; Sunday Express 31 Dec 1978; D.Mail 15 June, D.Telegraph 16 June, New Scientist 21 June 1979; D.Mail 13 Feb, Vancouver Sun 22 Feb 1980; Sri Lanka Sun 20 Apr 1981; (Portland, OR Sunday Oregonian 20 July 1980.

Credits: Al & Phyllis, Don Boates, Philip Hope Evans, Chris Hall, Sam, Ion Will • **PRAdeGS.**

More things in heaven and earth . . .

YESTERDAY'S NEWS TODAY!

Who discovered Neptune? John Galle in 1846? Nope. Galileo, in 1612. At least, he observed it and recorded it in his notebooks, and also that it had moved relative to the stars; but somehow it seems he never realised what he'd found. One up to Galileo... but I wonder what *he'd* have called Neptune? *Nature*, 25 Sept 80.

But who discovered Jupiter had moons? Galileo? Sorry... a Chinese gent called Gan De, in 364 BC. With the naked eye, too. (And, according to an experiment carried out by the Beijing observatory, it *is* possible to see Jupiter's 3rd moon unaided, under the right conditions.) Only fragments of Gan De's books survive (one on Jupiter, one on astrology), but the appropriate quote is: 'Jupiter is very large and bright. It seems there is a small reddish star attached to it, thus forming a league.' And the 3rd and largest moon is, in fact, red... *Ta Kung Pao* (Hong Kong) 26 March; *Beijing Review* 13 April 1981.

IN A SPIN

The earth span faster in 1980... but only by one second in the year. The only problem that causes is for the folks who have to keep universal (atomic) time and solar time in line; this year they *didn't* have to stop the atomic clock to add in an extra second (no work; that's a problem?) *Guardian* 29 Dec 80; *D Express* 2 Jan 81.

But then later we hear that the earth and moon are *slowing down*, and moving apart, at 1½ inches per year. Maybe there's something wrong with the clockwork? *D Mirror* 19 March 81.

HEY, PLUTO! (ARF, ARF!)
Well, half 'n' half, anyway. It seems that Pluto is actually a double planet. French astonomers have photographed Pluto's moon Charon, and their calculations show that Pluto is 4000 km in diameter, Charon 2000 km. Charon cicles Pluto in just over 6 days, at a distance of 19,000 km; and as it's too big in proportion to Pluto to qualify as a moon, they're now calling the system a double planet... *St Louis Post Dispatch* 20 April; *New Scientist* 2 Oct 80.

SOLAR SPASMS
First noticed in 1976 and confirmed by observations in the Antarctic, the sun is pulsating with a period of 2 hours, 40 minutes. According to theorists' 'standard models', the period ought to be about one hour. But if the sun's central temperature (according to the standard model) was reduced by 10%, that would explain it; and also explain why earth receives only a third of the solar neutrinos that the standard model says it should. Throw out the standard model? Or throw out the observations; because three months later we're told that the period of oscillations varies by 30 minutes a year. Hell, throw the lot out! *New Scientist* 20 Aug; *D Telegraph* 24 Nov 80.

And another idea to toss away. The sun rotates more slowly than other stars of the same age and temperature. The notion is that maybe our sun is slowed down by its family of planets; the implication is that maybe those other sun-like stars don't have planets after all. So maybe we *are* alone, Stephen Spielberg notwithstanding. *New Scientist* 19 June 80.

STELLAR STORIES
6,000 light years away in the constellation Cygnus a gigantic bubble's been found, 1,200 light years in diameter. Detectable only by its X-ray emissions, it contains enough hydrogen gas at a temperature of two million degrees centigrade, to form 10,000 stars like our sun; its energy is 10 times as much as all that emitted by our sun during the last 5,000 million years, and it's still expanding at 10 miles a second. Only supposed explanation is that maybe there's a chain reaction of exploding stars, one going off every 50,000 or 100,000 years. But it's not far away from a huge *cool* gas-cloud known as the Great Rift of Cygnus. Who's forever blowing bubbles? *The Times* 18 Jan; *D Telegraph* 19 Jan; *Laboratory News* 1 Feb 80.

The biggest star in the universe? Maybe. It has the romantic name of R136A, and it's 3,500 times the size of our sun (surely they could have given it a better name; Colosso? Ultramega? The Blob?). It's 150,000 light years away in the Tarantula Nebula, an appendage of the Lesser Magellanic Cloud, but there's only one catch; it probably burned itself out over 100,000 years ago! *Straits Times* (Singapore) 16 Jan; *D Telegraph* 19 Jan 81.

Hubble's constant is in more trouble (see FT31 p33). Basically, according to Hubble, the farther away a galaxy or star is, the more its light-waves will be distended, so the more red it will appear (the red shift). So Quasars, which are very red, have always been assumed to be at the very edge of the universe. But now two Americans, Halton Arp and Cyril Hazard, have discovered three quasars lying in a straight line and apparently close to one another in space, which show wildly differing red shifts. Worse yet, they found another line of three showing the same property. Worse still, using the red shift to calculate distance, it seems that some objects, such as a 'lump' which detached itself from the quasar 3C273, are moving faster than light. Somebody's got it wrong, it seems; but is Relativity relegated? Or Hubble's bubble burst? The old idea about the stars being lamps hung on a crystal dome is starting to sound pretty good to me at the moment! *D Telegraph* 12 Feb; *Guardian* 16 April 81.

Credits: Jim Chambers, Peter Christie, Chris Hall, Mark A. Hall, Valerie Martin, Nigel Pennick, PR.Thomas, Andy Townsend **•SM.**

More problematical peltings, this time frogs and stones. Next time, in this section we hope to have further notes on flying food and cascading cash.

FROGS
• According to the *Bedfordshire Times* 27 July 1979, Mrs Vida McWilliam, of Marten Road, Bedford, found her garden hopping with little frogs after a recent rain. They were all about three-quarters of an inch long, and coloured yellow and black. We enquired at the paper and obtained a photograph, and the address of Mrs McWilliam.

It was November 1980 before we got around to writing, but Mrs McWilliam replied promptly. 'I'm sorry I can't remember the date exactly, but it happened in June 1979. One Sunday we had a really wet day, rain lashing down and windy. It was

One of the tiny frogs that appeared in the Bedford garden of Mrs McWilliam in June 1979. The coin is just over an inch in diameter. [Photo: Bedford County Press.]

very damp and humid the next day. On my patio I have a caged-in area (for my cat) and in it, on the tiles, I noticed what looked like half-grown tadpoles. To my surprise there were tiny frogs everywhere. I told my family it must have rained frogs that Sunday. Later in the week we went down the garden to cut the lawns. It was amazing; the grass was covered with little green and black frogs – and on the bushes hung spawn. We collected up the frogs and put them safely in the garden with the help of my delighted small grandchildren. All the summer they were carefully watched and made a home under the shed. I'm afraid last year [1980] we only had three left, grown to ordinary size.'

We note the discrepancy in the paper's account of their colour, and the fascinating detail of spawn on the bushes. In reviewing the extant records of frogfalls as research for a section in the sequel to *Phenomena*, I have searched high and low for records of tadpoles falling. The very few cases I did find were not as satisfying as I had hoped, being mainly native traditions from Tahiti and New Mexico, with one case of hatching spawn from Haiti. Fort once noted that in all his data he could find no fall of tadpoles. But Mrs McWilliam didn't see tadpoles; there was spawn and very young froglets in the process of absorbing their still visible pollywog tales. This is quite a valuable incident, and more's the pity there is a lack of specific information.

• As we started work on this issue clippings came in on a fall of tiny frogs on the village of Narplion (or Nauplion) in southern Greece – thousands of the little green items rained from the sky early one morning 'recently'. Our source–*Sunday Express* 31 May 1981 – cited scientists at the Meteorological Institute, in Athens, as believing the frogs, weighing a few ounces each, had been sucked up from African marshes by a whirlwind and transported over the sea to Greece. It is remarkable, they thought, that they escaped injury and have taken to their new home, keeping the locals awake, nights, with incessant croaking. Surely a whirlwind that could lift so many frogs of one species and age, and nothing else, and keep them up in the air and together for so long and so far would be more remarkable? And why Africa as a point of origin? Is this a way of confirming the sudden appearance, in Greece, of African frogs? Was the wind direction right for the flight? We have written seeking more info from the Greek meteorologists and will return to this case if we get a reply.

STONES

• Don't mock witchdoctors or you could find yourself being stoned by a poltergeist. That's the conclusion of tennis player Okkie Kellerman, 17, of Cape Town. About the first week in July 1980, he and a friend, Andre Wulfse, 17, travelled to Maritzburg for the Natal Open Tennis Championships when their train pulled into a siding near the city. On the platform they saw a strange-looking man in a white safari suit carrying what seemed to be a doctor's bag. Okkie says: 'I was suffering from a cold and decided to ask him how I could shake it off before the championships. It was all a bit of a joke really. I started by asking him if he was a doctor. He replied that he was, but not the type I meant. He said he was a witchdoctor. Andre and I laughed. Our impression was that witchdoctors wore tribal dress, not Western clothes. He told us not to laugh at him. He said he did have a remedy that would fix my cold – that I should use Vicks. We laughed again. By that stage the train was pulling out and the witchdoctor seemed upset at our attitude. He started wagging his finger at us. We left him standing on the platform with his finger in the air.'

The sequel began the next day after a practice session. 'A small stone suddenly landed on my shoe,' continues Okkie. 'I thought I had kicked it up, but a few metres down the road a bigger stone came out of nowhere and landed next to me. I ducked behind a wall thinking someone was using me for target practice or something. I looked but couldn't see anyone – but I could hear more stones landing in the bushes all round me.' After a while the barrage ceased long enough for him to run to his lodgings. However, the affair was far from over. Every time Okkie and Andre tried to leave the house 'suddenly the stones would be all around us.'

Matters came to a climax on the night of 11 July. Up until then the youths had been safe inside the house, but that night Okkie was woken by a stone dropping off his bed onto the floor. 'Andre was sleeping in the same room but his bed was untouched. Meanwhile I was being pelted with stones. I woke Andre and together we collected the stones and put them on the dressing-table. Then I got back into bed and put the pillow over my head just in case – but more stones kept on coming. I was scared out of my wits.' After three hours of bombardment the lads could take no more and went to spend the night in their landlord's room. The house-owner, Peter Dove, confirmed the events. 'The rocks started flying virtually from the time Okkie and Andre arrived at the house and stopped only when they left.'

Sunday Times (South Africa) 20 July 1980.

• No sign of a poltergeist in the next story. During the night of 21/22 June 1980 a fierce rain rattled against the windows of Mrs Margaret Davies' home, at Hampshire Place, Peterlee, Co Durham. When it had eased off Mrs Davies was surprised to discover her paths and lawns strewn with stone chippings (see photo). Her neighbours too found they had been peppered with gravel in the night. We have no further information.

As far as we can recall, the only other records of non-poltergeist-associated stone-falls in Britain involve a series of occurrences at Birmingham and Wolverhampton in the 1850s and 1860s, a study of which will be presented in a future FT. Once again we have a rare datum, and once again we bewail the lack of detailed information.

Hartlepool Mail 25 June 1980.

• Finally another poltergeist incident – by which we mean that the behaviour of the stones is more *paranormal* than normal. Once again we are frustrated by the dismal standards of today's 'wire' or syndicated journalism – there is no date but we guess the incident occurred not long before the report-date.

Hundreds of stones rained out of the sky on a garage in Aversa, southern Italy, scaring the manager, Nicola Grassia and his 12-year-old son Enzo. During the barrage Grassia spotted a passing police car and stopped it. The officers stepped out into a hail of stones. 'One stone hit a window in the police car shattering it. Another struck the bodywork and badly damaged it,' said Grassia. 'The police were so scared that they fired warning bursts into the air with their machine guns. The chilling thing was that we couldn't see where the stones were coming from.' Searches for culprits failed to find even likely hideouts; the nearest building was at least 25 yards away.

Other factors emerge. It seems Grassia's mother was gunned down by his father at the garage in 1974. Local ghost-hunters have suggested the dead woman's spirit could be using the young boy as a medium for her psychical revenge. Praps.

News of the World 8 Feb 1981.

Credits: Janet + Colin Bord, Chris Holtzhausen, Vida McWilliam, Paul Screeton, PR Thomas • **RJMR.**

The pebbles that fell at Peterlee, in June 1980. [Photo: Hartlepool Mail *25 June 1980.]*

Developments and discoveries in the sciences seem to be coming thick and fast these days, and it's time we gave more space to them. We begin, this issue, with a few biological notes on bacteria . . .

SINGLE-MINDED

Two scientists at the University of Montreal have recently formalized their theory that all the different varieties of bacteria on this earth are not separate individuals but form a single super-organism, intelligent but unconscious. Dr Sorin Sonea, microbiologist, and Dr Marice Panisset, veterinarian, formulated their idea over nine years, collecting many of their papers into a new textbook, *Introduction a la Nouvelle Bacteriologie* (Les Presses de L'Universite de Montreal/Masson, Sept 1980). Based on recent findings in bacteriology, the researchers say that all bacteria share a common three-billion-year-old heritage, each having the ability to transfer its genetic information to another. Conventional bacteriologists see such tranfers as accidental, but recent studies of how pathogenic bacteria become resistant to antibiotics, and how this resistance spreads to other bacteria, cause the researchers to believe that 'isolated bacteria cells sometimes act as if they were linked to a common brain, a brain evidently unconscious and dispersed.' This 'brain' – the 'planetary bacteria organism' (PBO) they call it – appears to coordinate resistance to antibiotics. *Niagara Falls Review* 18 Feb 1981.

MAGNETS AND SQUARES

In April 1979 the National Science Foundation in Washington announced the discovery that bacteria could synthesise an iron-oxide called magnetite (lodestone) from their seawater environment, and use it to orient themselves in the earth's field. The previous year, magnetite had been found in the heads of pigeons and the abdomens of bees. About 25 tiny particles of magnetite were found strung out in the long axis of bacteria from Massachusetts coastal mud, by Dr Richard Frankel of MIT. The bacteria which are tiny and virtually weightless in water, use the orientation to keep them pointed downwards into the mud they adore. Dr Frankel now hopes to find the opposite magnetic orientation in bacteria from the southern hemisphere. *AP: Schenectady Gazette* (NY) 9 April; *Observer* 15 April 1979.

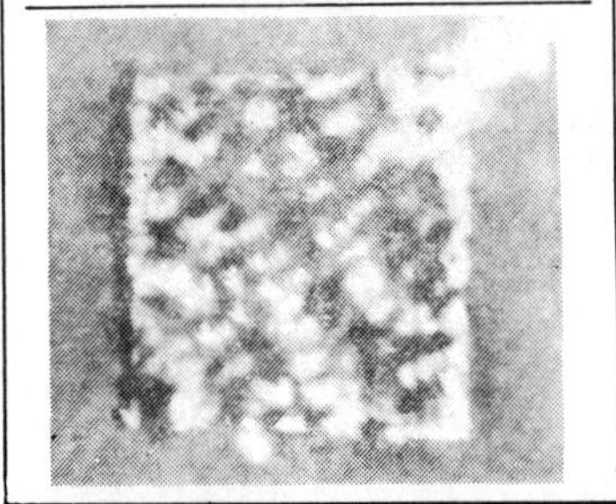

Then comes the startling discovery of a *square* bacterium. It was found by Dr Anthony Walsby, of the marine science labs at Menai Bridge, North Wales, in brine he brough back from a desert pool in the Sinai Peninsula (see photo). The living squares surely one of the strangest of life-forms, reproduces rather like a sheet of postage stamps, forming as many as 16 a 'sheet' before the individual 'stamps' split off on their own. *Daily Mirror* 11 Jan 1980.

Credits: *Dwight Whalen, Joe Zarzynski* • **RJMR.**

Large cats continue to be sporadically sighted in the British undergrowth, where there is no evidence of escape or other origin. Quirky statements from witnesses and 'experts' add further paradoxes to this fun-filled feline fenomenon.

WELSH PUMA RETURNS

Just about the only Fortean phenomena missing from Arthur Machen's memorable and prophetic story, *The Great Return*, is a puma roaming mid-Wales. We chronicled the farce, last issue, of the mystery animal that escaped a siege at a farm near Llangurig, and subsequent sightings of a puma-like animal in the Cwmbelan environs. Well, after laying low since December last year the beast has popped out of the woodwork once more.

About the second week in June sheep and lambs were savaged near Aberystwyth, and seven ewes and five lambs killed between 11-14 June near Ysbytty Ystwyth, only 12 miles from Llangurig. At the scenes of these attacks farmers and RSPCA officers have discovered large paw marks and have told the *Star* that 'experts' have 'thought they could have been made by a panther.' Experts, these days, have a great fondness for the vague and qualified statement! But... if panthers are melanistic leopards their pawmarks should be generally indistinguishable from leopards'. Ah... but one farmer saw the animal and it was black.

Inspector Trevor Caldwell, of the Dyfed-Powys RSPCA said police had 'conclusive' evidence that the animal was a panther. In the next paragraph he is 'almost certain' it is a panther. 'We have had three definite sightings in the last week from very level-headed people. It was described as a long jet-black cat, standing about 2ft 6 in at its head. The countryside here is ideal for a big cat, with old mine shafts and quarries.' He said he and Inspector Blyth of the local police found many tracks during a day's hunt, on 10th June, and set wire traps for it, baited with a leg of meat. 'But we will only catch it if it is hungry, and that is doubtful as there is plenty of food available.' Without a doubt we are almost certain there will be more sightings later this summer. Stay tuned.

Shropshire Star 15 June, *Daily Star* 15 June, *County Times & Express* (Welshpool) 16 June 1981.

AND NOW . . . THE DARTMOOR PANTHER . . .

Back in February, unnoticed by the national Press, a large, black, cat-like creature was padding around the Devon community of Tedburn St Mary. Ben Huggins, 8, and his pal Peter Tremeer, 7, caught sight of the 'Terror of Tedburn' as they walked in woods at Spicery Farm, owned by Ben's dad Michael Huggins. It was prowling through the woods and chased off two dogs. This was on the weekend 21/22 Feb; the next day [I wish papers would give specific dates!] large prints were found in the area. Ben consulted his collection of animal books when he got home and identified it straight away – it was like a puma but black. Huggins *pere* referred to rumours of such an animal in the area in the past. 'A farmer's wife was out riding some years ago when she saw what seemed to be a puma.' He believes it lives on Dartmoor. The cat of the Baskervilles?

A man who regularly drives through the area at night said he had twice seen the animal about two weeks prior to Ben's close shave. Nick Hallett, of Tavistock, had been in his lorry, on the A30 near Cheriton Bishop junction, about 3.30am, when it loped across the road in his headlights, and down a bank into the darkness. 'I knew it wasn't a fox or a dog or a badger because I see those all the time.' The next night it did the same trick, just 50 yards in front of the lorry. The RSPCA were pushing the old 'abandoned pet' theory. Nothing heard of it since.

Western Morning News 26+27 Feb 1981.

AND THE LUTON LION!

Nick Hallett described the animal running through his lorry lights, at Tedburn St Mary as having 'a cantering motion, not unlike a horse'. The loping thing that Adrian Grier saw on a road near Luton, the police suggested to him, might be a cow – or a dog or a deer... but he's certain it was a lion. He was driving towards Toddington on the road from Tebworth at 1.30am on 9 June, when his headlights picked out a large animal on the side of the road ahead. At first he thought it was a Great Dane, but as he got closer he saw clearly it was a lioness. He slowed down, but at about 10 yds the beast broke into a trot and was soon lost in a field. 'It must have been about 6ft long, more than 3½ ft tall, powerfully built and the colour of a Great Dane,' says Adrian. 'It had bloody great feet and was loping along. It didn't look like a cow.' He drove straight to Luton police station, where, after initial skepticism, they took him seriously enough to organise an immediate search, and another later in daylight. Zoos, etc. were queried but none of their lionesses were missing.

Shortly after this incident a creature frightened the life out of another Luton man, walking alone, at 11pm on 11 June, along Waululds Bank Drive, on the Marsh Farm estate. The encounter, which left the man 'white as a sheet', was reported to the paper after the story of Adrian's sighting by the man's wife, requesting anonymity. She said he came in from his walk shaken. 'He said he had just seen the largest dog he had ever seen. It was similar to a Great Dane but the coat was different. It was a bit like an Irish Woolfhound that had had its coat cut. He assumed it was a dog because he couldn't think what else it could be. It followed him and he said he dare not run in case it went for him. He was really scared.' Shades of the old Black Dog stories! Seeing Adrian's account in the paper made them think it might be the same animal.

Another woman, also anonymous, was in turn prompted to report *her* experience after reading of the man shadowed as he walked alone. This lady too was passing through the Marsh Farm area, but in a car driving along Henge Way. Again no date, and not much information. Just: 'The animal was quite huge, streamlined and very fast.' It ran across in front of her car and into the woods. To judge from the road names this is an area with an interesting antiquarian topography too. We have heard nothing more since. But readers are asked to scan their local papers for phantom pussycat appearances – late summer is a favourite time.

Luton Herald (Bedfordshire) 11+18+25 June 1981.

Credits: *Janet + Colin Bord, Peter Christie, Paul Devereux, Peter Smith, P R Thomas, Andy Townsend* • **RJMR.**

ANCIENT MARINER AGAIN?

I thought I might pass on this slight 'Albatross' occurrence as told to me by one Nick Cox of the British Antartic Survey. It seems that a supply ship, the *Brassfield*, was held up for several days whilst making its way to the base in the Falkland Islands:

'The *Brassfield* nearly got here on the 27th (March). She was in view eight miles away when she struck some rocks and was held hard for five hours before she got off with some tears and holes in her hull. A naval ship *HMS Endurance* arrived this afternoon to escort the lame ship home. The crew of the *Brassfield* blame it on an albatross which flew into the ship's radio aerial and was killed on the way here. The bird was put in a fridge to be studied sometime by an ornithologist. Some of the crew wanted to throw it overboard.'

Una Woodruff
Warminster, Wilts

KANGAROO CORRECTIONS

I really cannot let Mr David Rees' letter which was headed 'Giant Kangaroo in Lancs?' (FT32) pass without comment.

While I agree I would be surprised to see a kangaroo grazing freely in the wilds of Lancashire, the proportions and colour of the animal described are not uncharacteristic of a male Red kangaroo. (For the record, the female is known, appropriately, as a Blue Flyer.) It is not unusual for them to grow to a height of 8ft and taller.

I would, however, point out that the posture described, of apparently investigating the foliage with a view to feeding, is an extended one, in which the actual height can extend easily 12" to 18" from the normal upright position.

But, what I wonder most about is Mr Rees' comment that he 'walked into the undergrowth'. In no way can I accept that any of the various gaits of a kangaroo could be described utilising any part of the verb 'walk'. And, when Mr Rees states 'the area was flattened', I wonder if the ground surface were such to show up the pawprints one would expect.

And, turning back the pages of FT32, to 'Swarms and Migrations' and 'The Great Plagues of Australia', I remain on the subject of kangaroos. While it is true that kangaroos have been 'forced out into farmland by droughts', I think the rest of that paragraph (p.38) deserves some qualification.

As provenance to the following remarks, it should be remembered that the current plague of 'roos has developed in the recent years of the US prohibition of imports of kangaroo products. That's the basic reason for what you call 'a baby kanga boom'.

Because of the drought, we are seeing more kangaroos in areas they haven't previously travelled simply out of their need to range beyond their normal territories in search of food and water. Sure, the Reds are coming in from the Centre, but the Greys (of various types) are, also, changing their grazing areas, and for similar reasons: food and water. And their habits are changing. Where, once, they travelled in mobs of extended families, there are now independent mobs of youngsters travelling. They can be seen at the outskirts of towns, in the middle of the day. Normally 'roos travel at around sunrise and sunset.

For each female seen, you can count three more kangaroos. The eldest almost completely independent of his/her mother, another still to some extent dependent on the pouch, and a foetus. But, the youngsters travelling on their own are symptomatic of disruption. It is unusual for them to leave the extended family mob before reaching maturity.

And, while I may appear to be knocking what have seemed strange phenomena, let me add a comment on the locusts: I think the reason they attack 'not only crops but cars and houses' is well included. They will attack anything GREEN!!! Even clothing. The colour is the catalyst. So, if Australia is to take to heart any lesson out of this it is: Don't buy a green car or paint your house green, or even use or wear anything green.

If anyone sees a green kangaroo . . . don't worry! The locusts will get it.

Dr Alyson Lander
Tullamore, New South Wales

I feel I must comment on the letter headed 'Giant Kangaroo' in FT32. It may well be that what your correspondent saw was a wallaby, at least two colonies of which flourish in Britain. [One in Kent, and the other in the Derbyshire peak-district. See Christopher Lever, *The Naturalized Animals of the British Isles* (Paladin 1979)–Ed.] Although wallabies are normally smaller than your correspondent estimates, this would seem to be a more likely explanation than a mystery kangaroo. The colony in the Derbyshire area has given rise to many such stories over the years.

J T Kirkwood
Camberwell, London

WINGED CATS

I wrote about them in my News-Letter (no 548, 1975) and can say what happened to the Oxford animal in 1933 [see FT32p21]. It became a victim of the ANSA syndrome ('Ain't no sich animal!'). The *Daily Mirror* of the time quoted the curator of Oxford Zoo as saying: 'I am somewhat sceptical whether the cat can really fly—I have never seen anything like this – it will be kept at the zoo for a short time and then destroyed if it is not claimed – it is not good policy to keep freaks at this zoo, and I do not think our visitors would like to see it.'

So Dame Nature does her best to fulfil every cat's ambition to get up amongst the birds and to confirm Darwin's theory about the survival of the fittest, whilst zoo-keepers put their faith in Fort (survival of those who survive).

Nevertheless, Nature continues to produce winged cats. Manchester *Evening News*, 23 Sept 1975: a reader asks about a photo of one printed 'some years ago', because he works for a firm in whose yard the animal appeared and he finds it hard to believe. The photo is reprinted with the comment: 'The cat was said to have strayed into a builders' yard (Banister Walton and Co., of Trafford Park) as a kitten. The foreman noticed an unusual growth of fur on the kitten's back which developed into 'wings' after 12 months. They measured about 11 inches from the shoulder-bone to top. The tail was also unusual, being broad and flat.'

Sid Birchby
Editor, *News-Letter*

HORROR-SCOPE

A friend of mine in this magical part of Albion, the astrologer Roger Elliot, recently (March 23rd) suffered one of those disasters that seem shaped by a malign logic. His delightful home, the Old Manor House, Cossington, burned down when his all-electronic-astrological-technology machines spontaneously decided to 'self-destruct'. All of Roger's records and researches have been destroyed, for he worked out of his home (which incidentally is/was situated on a recently dowsed 'black stream' ley). I went to see Roger as soon as I heard of his misfortune and asked him if his work had given him any hint of a portending disaster. He told me that he knew something horrendous was going to happen around that date (infamous in its own right as all Forteans know). One of the reasons given was 'Saturn was making a nasty aspect to my Mars'. Adding fuel to the fire (sorry Roger) was the fact that the day before the blaze he had been doing some astrological work on the two big hotel fires in the USA. A final irony, when poking through the charred remnants of his library, he informed me that the first book he pulled out of the steaming rubble was Harrison's *Fire From Heaven!* Over to you Mr. Fort.

Tony Roberts
'Gondolin', Somerset

[Editor's note: Tony included a postscript to this letter vigorously contesting statements about himself and his book, The Dark Gods, *in Michael Hoffman's letter (FT 34p3f). It is with regret that we have to terminate the correspondence on this subject because of lack of space and the need to move onto other matters. We also offer our apologies to Tony Roberts for inadvertently omitting a line from the beginning of the last paragraph of his letter (FT34 p2) rendering it gibberish. The correct reading should be: 'Most orthodox history is lying bunk but the archetypal metaphysical cadences that sing behind the dry dirge of atonal academic shits are the pure base notes of the pristine Hymn of Creation.']*

HUH?

V2 no brain in me. 50,000 microdots.

June 1970 *The Oregon Journal* show my brain actions my next five years.

Particularly December 15 1980 psychically by ESP forsee F ring Saturn to solve outer twisted ring riddle via Voyager I.

Chuck Eastwood
Astoria, Oregon

WIT AND WISDOM

One of the characteristics of *Fortean Times* which all your readers must appreciate is the capacity of you and your contributors to sustain a sense of humour in the face of the dismaying recalcitrance of things. The Fideler-Tarte article (FT33) is just such an instance – a delicious spoof on the kind of anything-goes theorising we are too often subjected to nowadays by people who should know better. With what splendid mock-solemnity your authors push the old familiar acts onto the stage – Juggling Jung and his Magic Mandalas, the Intrepid Prometheus and his Fabulous Fire, Pretty Pandora and her Bottomless Box, the Amazing Ezekiel with his Egregious Vision! Their witty comment on the Scully cover—'a good deal of feminine cleavage accompanies the return of the matriarchal consciousness' – has just the right blend of apparent perceptiveness with ultimate meaninglessness which typifies serious articles in this genre. And how cleverly your authors satirise the 'why-pick-on-me?' ego-centredness of contemporary writers who fancy that no previous age – no matter how culture-shocked or millenarianistically inclined – can boast such psychic fragmentation as has been inflicted on *them!* In short, a splendid comic travesty, and at the same time a timely reminder of how far some theorists let themselves be carried in their flight from reality.

Hilary Evans
London.

The Authors Reply:

Thanks for your comments, Hilary. Both of us enjoyed the splendid parody of the typical *London Daily Mail* letter, composed with furrowed brow and a rhythmic sense of indignation, a true use of language as pure sound! We also appreciated your article, 'Abducted by an Archetype', which led into ours in the same issue of FT. In contrast to the dense alliteration of the above, that piece came across in a genuinely breezy – if not airy – manner, ideas explored at a pleasantly laconic pace, much like the ripening of a single fruit over an entire growing season. Well done!

Mr. Fideler-Tarte

A BUSY LIFE

Since August 1969 I have been affecting the weather by mental concentration. In August 1976 my concentration seemed to send rain to England and to quiet La Souffriere. Since March 1979 my efforts have cleared skies over 40 times. I was clearing the skies at 11.39 am EDT on May 18 and quietening Mt St Helens which erupted at 8.39am PDT (the same instant).

In January 1980 I found another explanation for Darwin's observations on the Galapagos Islands and now reject evolution. In May 1980 I started locating Atlantis in the Atlantic and in June decided that Bermuda is where it was.

Since May 1977 I have influenced the outcome of many games and matches.

Do any of your readers practice this concentration effort?

Steve Ogden
Ashland, Kentucky

A TELEPORTED TANK?

A patient [Mr Collier is a dental surgeon — Ed.] told me that when he was in the SAS someone pinched a tank; as he said, not an easy thing to do owing to its noisiness etc. It was found, I think, in the Greenwich area, on a roundabout with a low wall and undisturbed grass which had to be wrecked during the removal of the tank. To quote my patient: 'It was as if someone had picked it up and put it down on the island.'

Later the SIB arrived to investigate, and my patient was intrigued enough to try and find out more about the incident — but was firmly told to forget all about what he had seen. Unfortunately, when I started to question him, he clammed up, muttering about the Official Secrets Act, and has not been back since.

Mike Collier
Newhaven, Sussex.

[It's difficult to corroborate stories like these. It sounds like one of those Travellers' Tales/ Barroom Tales/Tumour in the Whale stories, or whatever you want to call them—Ed.]

MARBLE MADONNA

I was wondering if you would be interested in a phenomenon which I came across about four or five years back.

I was at that time taking a course at an art college on illustration architecture and was studying grains of marble. I came across a brochure of the 'Verine' company who manufacture imitation marble effect from actual known marble types for household decor.

One particular marble was a blue grain called 'Vatican Blue' which caught my eye for within the grain was a child's face asleep on his back. Looking closer the most amazing picture presented itself, for above the child's face was the mother with head cloaked looking down upon the child, these were in proportion to each other (see photos).

There were also what appeared to be other figures within the picture, however they were not so clear as the Madonna and Child.

The relation of the name of the title and what is within the picture to my mind is very portentous.

I incidentally approached the 'Verine' company by letter and they replied that they had not seen or noticed the figures before. I also asked if there was a chance to purchase the actual blue marble used for the making of the printers' plate but unfortunately the reply was that the original marble blocks were destroyed after the plates were successfully made.

So all I have is the brochure reproduction in blue and some copies taken off that.

Roger Lowless
Wareham, Dorset

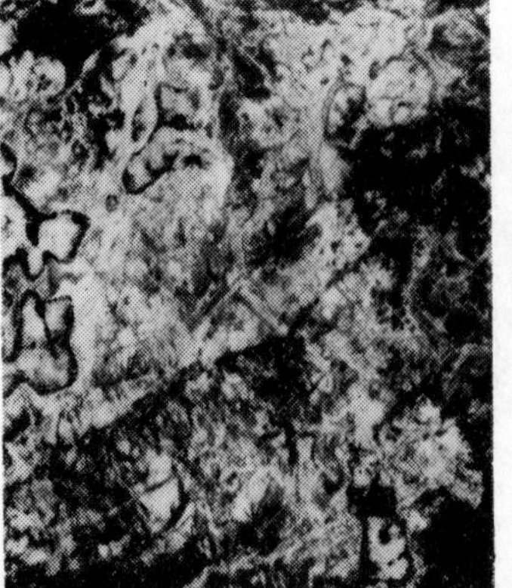

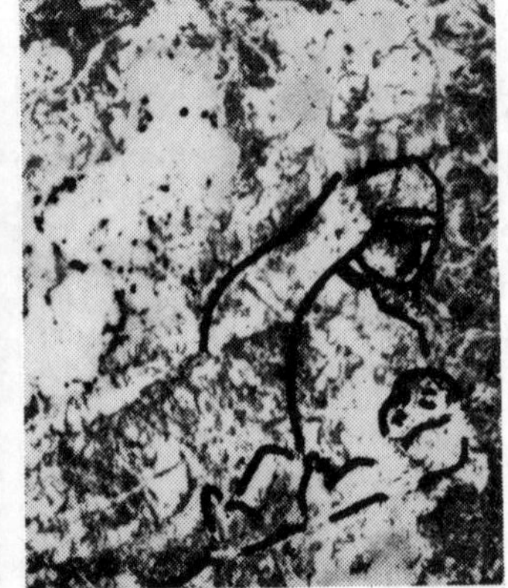

(Left) The slab of Vatican Blue marble. (Right) Madonna and Child revealed.

MEETINGS, etc

• **Fortfest**, the annual Fortean conference organized by the International Fortean Organization, will this year be held over 17-18 October. The venue, as before, will be the University of Maryland, College Park, Washington DC. Speakers booked so far are **Ron Westrum, Joe Zarzynski, Leroy Ellenberger, Larry Arnold, Loren Coleman & Jerome Clark**, with an opening address by **John Keel**. For booking and further information contact INFO: 7317 Baltimore Ave, College Park, MD 20740, USA – or phone US (301) 779 1873.

• **Doc Shiels**, and talented family are enduring a splendidly disorganized withdrawal from Morgawr-haunted Cornwall to take up a nomadic existence in the wilds of Ireland busking and performing his unique (in every sense of the word) plays. You will be able to follow his adventures in his column in FT — but those who are luckier might catch a special travelling show, by Doc and daughter **Lucy**, under the same title, *Words from the Wizard*.

BOOK SERVICE

• We must mention a new enterprise deserving your attention. **Bob Girard** has built up a fine new and used mail-order book business, over the last year, specializing in UFO literature. His 1981 catalogue ($2.50, or $3.50 airmailed outside US) contains over 1100 UFO books and booklets (about half in stock), and 200+ on related subjects including much Forteana. Write to: **Arcturus Book Service**, 263 N Ballston Ave, Scotia, NY 12302, USA. Phone: US (581) 372 2373.

GRANTS, etc

• In their first year of operation, the **Fund for UFO Research** raised over eight thousand dollars in tax-exempted contributions for channelling into UFO research. In May, FUFOR announced a one-thousand-dollar grant to the publishers of *UFO Phenomena International Annual Review* (don't worry, we hadn't heard of it either!), apparently an Italian-based international journal devoted to scientific ufology and described as 'the world's first scientific refereed journal on the UFO phenomenon'. For details of FUFOR, write: Box 277, Mount Rainier, MD 20822, USA. For details of UPIAR, write: c/o Editecs Publishing House, Box 190, 40100 Bologna, Italy.

• Until Forteans can establish some method of funding research projects, perhaps on the lines that FUFOR (above) have done for ufology, the opportunities for external funding are extremely limited. A slim chance, however, is offered by the existence of **The Center for Field Research**, a private, non-profit outfit which has raised over two million dollars for scientific fieldwork. Subjects subsidised to date include: anthropology, archeology, ethology, folklore, marine sciences, meteorology, sociology and zoology. If convinced of the sound base to your research they *might* be able to help you. They say they are not limited to these subjects and also invite interdisciplinary proposals. For further information, write to **Elizabeth E. Caney**, Director of Research, The Center for Field Research, 10 Juniper Rd, Box 127-N, Belmont, MA 02178; or call US (617) 489 3032.

ORGANIZATIONS

• There is much ferment behind the scenes at the moment – suddenly it's new organization time. **The Association for the Scientific Study of Anomalous Phenomena** (ASSAP) has been formed by a group dissatisfied with the rather narrow approach to psychic research of the **Society for Psychical Research**. The ASSAP want to enlarge the scope for interdisciplinary research by acknowledging from the start the great variety, interdependence of phenomena.

Then came news that **Dr Marcello Truzzi**, editor of the impressive *Zetetic Scholar*, has founded a **Center for Scientific Anomalies Research** (CSAR), at Eastern Michigan University. An international society for cryptozoology is currently being formulated around **Dr Bernard Heuvelmans'** unique **Centre de Cryptozoologie**, and its journal, *Cryptozoology*, to be edited by **J. Richard Greenwell**, will be launched soon.

At the same time, your editor has begun a dialogue with other Forteans about the possibility of organizing ourselves around better channels for information exchange. All is in flux at present so I haven't given many details here. But by next issue much will have been resolved.

A GEO-BIBLIOGRAPHY OF ANOMALIES

Compiled by George M Eberhart. *Greenwood Press, Westport, Connecticut, USA + 3 Henrietta St, London WC2E 8LT, 1980; $59.95/£37.25 hb, 1114pp, gloss, map, indexes.*

Behind the clumsy title lies a truly stupendous book – a bibliographic listing of anomaly literature, arranged geographically, crammed in tiny print into about a score more pages than the 1125 of Fort's *Complete Books*.

Having heard infrequent and tantalizing reports of the progress of the *Geo-Bib* over the last few years, its arrival was keenly anticipated. Many books do not live up to their advance publicity, some even disappoint by coming up to expectation and no more. I'm happy to say that the *Geo-Bib* far exceeded my expectations and is a dream reference book for a Fortean researcher. It arrived while I was working on books of my own and immediately proved useful, and in use all those references I've followed up have proved accurate. This is an accomplishment to be sincerely appreciated. And when you realize that here are the references to source books and articles on over 22,100 separate events, grouped under 10,500 geographic place-names Eberhart has certainly earned every ounce of respect you can muster for this mind-boggling feat of research, collation and indexing. Praise too for the publisher for putting out what is obviously not a commercial book, but one aimed at libraries and researchers.

As a librarian Eberhart long ago published articles in *Pursuit* and *INFO Journal* on how to organize your own Fortean library, based on his plan of the arrangement and relationship between Fortean subjects, ufology, para-physics etc, and scientific, historical and geographical anomalies. If you stick to his system it'll work well enough, but to me it seems eccentric. The *Geo-Bib* also incorporates this 'outline of anomalies', but is supplemented with a general listing of types of anomalistic events and processes in the form of a glossary, so that those unfamiliar with such Fortean topics as 'Entombed animals', 'SHC', 'Airship message', 'Falls', 'Phantom animals', or 'Teleportation', can determine their context. The entries are concise, and give in order: place name, type of event, date, principal witness, and then the reference by author, publication, date and page numbers. There is no additional information, so the onus is on the user to be persistent in tracking the material down. There are indexes to ships, witness names, and ethnic groups.

The entries have been drawn from extensive collections of books and back-files of 28 magazines dealing wholly or in part with the range of subjects (from 'Accoustic anomaly' to 'Witch trial'). While not covering whole runs of many of these journals, Eberhart has in fact provided us with the most extensive index yet to such key publications as APRO Bulletin, Doubt, Fate, FSR, INFO Journal, Pursuit, and many dealing with UFOs or American antiquities. The reader's problem is that most of the small specialist journals are not taken by libraries (the excellent New York Public Library has a better record than most in this respect). The range of the *Geo-Bib* covers only North America, so researchers interested in other areas are left in the dark or to their usual devices. The only other hurdle is the price, grim even in these inflated times. But if you are serious in your research please don't let it deter you – you won't get anything like this valuable research tool anywhere else at *any* price. If you have a library, ask them to get it for their reference shelves.

To those of you who can, I say, buy it. Feel its thickness, heft its weight. See how impressively it stands next to those other fat Fortean folios of Fort and Corliss. Above all use it – it will serve you well indeed.

RJMR

INCREDIBLE LIFE: A Handbook of Biological Mysteries

Compiled by William R Corliss. *Sourcebook Project, Glen Arm, MD 21057, USA, 1981; $22.50 hb, 1018pp, illos, index.*

Another fat Fortean reference book in Corliss' series of Handbooks – this time on biological mysteries. Listing some of the headings will give an idea of its scope: Human health and the stars, Hairy men, Hair turning white rapidly, Horned and Tailed men, Humans with gills and other 'Recapitulation Theory' data,

Sleepers and mammals, Chemical transfer of intelligence, Inheritance of acquired characteristics, SHC, Electric and magnetic humans, Rat kings, Animal use of tools, Fascination, Collective action, Population explosions, Lake monsters, Mermaids, Unrecognized species, Curious birds, Bird navigation, Curious bird behaviour, Moa sightings, Two-headed reptiles, Parthenogenesis, Dinosaur evolution, Convergence and mimicry, Do snakes swallow their young?, Animals embedded in rocks, Toads swallowing embers, Sea serpents, Giant snakes, Curious fish, Electric insects, Insect adaptations, Social and magnetic senses of insects, Curiosities of Insect behaviour, Compound animals, Mass deaths, Flatworm memories, Use of tools by worms etc, Globsters, Twisted trees, Luminous plants, Plant adaptations, Compass plants, Synchronous flowering, Unusual cell forms and behaviour, Extraterrestrial life and evolution, Artificial creation of life, Excess DNA, The complexity of genes, Genetic code not fool-proof, Selfish DNA, Life-like chemicals, Biochemical clocks and evolution, Discontinuity of life, Superorganisms, Doubts about Darwinism, Evolution theory, and much more.

...For those new to the Sourcebook concept, Corliss scours the back-files of old and new scientific and other journals for definitive descriptions of anomalous events, processes, animals and things, what he often calls 'the unclassified residuum'. As a reference work on obscure topics, citing hard-to-find sources, the Handbook series, and its companion loose-leaf Sourcebook series, are incomparable as well as invaluable, and *Incredible Life* is a most welcome addition. It almost goes without saying that we readily endorse Corliss' books. If you can't afford them, urge your library to order them, for everyone's sake. *RJMR*

EXCALIBUR BRIEFING
By Thomas E. Bearden.
Strawberry Hill Press, San Francisco, CA 94127, USA, 1980; $8.95 pb, pp266, bib, illos.

Tom Bearden is one of those investigators of the paranormal who have disappeared into a cloud of their own jargon never to be communicated with again. His book is an entertaining example of the scientific explanations and apocalyptic visions of doom that are such a feature of the 20th century. The line now includes such notables as Bertrand Russell, Freud, Lenin, Spengler, Hitler, H.G. Wells, Oppenheimer, Fred Hoyle, Velikovsky, Von Daniken, CND, Friends of the Earth, NATO and the Warsaw Pact.

Bearden's contributions to this line are made quite clear in the last three paragraphs of his introduction: 'This is my rèal goal. Even if the USSR launches Fer-de-Lance, annihilates NATO and China, and obliterates all Western retaliation with a stunning blow, and even if the collective unconsious then psychokinetically lashes back with the violent destruction of the Eurasian continent, linkage is still the goal and the final resolution. Should the apocalypse come to pass, there will still be time, in the midst of the horrendous collapse of civilization, to gain the final solution.'

I seem to have heard all this before.

The book is divided into three sections, a review of paranormal phenomena, a theory of the paranormal and the military and apocalyptic conclusions drawn from the theory. The section on paranormal phenomena is poorly organised, and some events are provided with a partial explanation based upon jargon which is not introduced fully until the second section. One such case study begins with the sentence; 'The magnetic field has more fundamental components which integrate in the virtual state to form it when two successive orthorotational thresholds (quantum thresholds) are breached.' Impressive but utterly meaningless to a simple theoretical physicist such as myself.

The author includes many well known paranormal phenomena which are better described in other works. Those events which Bearden describes from his own experiences are poor indeed. Sometimes he provides insufficient information to duplicate the experiment, and he often supplies irrelevant information in superfluous jargonese. At other times the results of an experiment can easily be explained in conventional terms by any competent physicist or electrical engineer. Two examples of this simplism stand out.

'Hyperfield Generation of Photon Patterns About a Bar Magnet Collector', refers to the pretty patterns that are made when a bar magnet is taped to the screen of a colour television tube. These patterns are a result of the three cathode ray beams of the tube interacting with the magnetic field. The resulting pattern is assymmetric becauss the beams sweep the field in only one direction. Bearden seems to think that he has found some paranormal lights.

'A Deliberate Experiment With Kindling', appears to be nothing more than opening the shutter of a camera in a dimly lit room. The experimenters strained their psychic influences to project a picture on the film. Two photographs are reproduced. One in which 'the camera lens is not quite fully open' shows some stray light. A second in which 'the lens is fully opened' shows more of the same light plus some dim images of the people in the room. This second picture was taken after two hours of 'psychic exercises'.

To my mind the most interesting item in this section is Moray's 'Radiant Energy Device' which it is claimed picks up the zero point energy of the vacuum. As the concept of a vacuum field is a mathematical fiction devised for ease of calculation in quantum field theory this is unlikely. But Moray's story is a fascinating example of how paranoia induces paranoid reactions, confirming the original suspicisions. Moray would not reveal to anyone the secret of his invention. Having therefore failed to get a patent for the device, he finds himself pestered by 'Soviet agents' for its details, and betrayed by a confidant. These events climax with Moray being shot in his laboratory. There appears to be a great deal on record about Moray's demonstrations of his device but Bearden fails to document it.

The collection of UFO pictures presented in the book are most interesting examples, but the comments and inferences drawn from them are facile. Once again there is a lack of documentation of the sources and circumstances. The Soviet UFO reports are even more interesting but again poorly documented. Once well-reported original Fortean event which is included is the Falkville Spaceman.

The second section, a theory of the paranormal, contains the sort of misconceptions of relativity and quantum mechanics that are normally made by people who have culled their knowledge from popularizations of modern physics. Although the reference list cited indicates that this is not strictly true.

There is an interesting discussion of a definition of 'reality' as what is *perceived* by a mind. This is then classified into the private 'reality' of personally perceived emotions, decisions etc. and the public 'reality' of the 'physical' world perceived by *all* minds. Between these two lies the paranormal 'reality' of events which are perceived only by some minds.

This conception is very much in the mainstream of American logical positivism. It rests heavily on the assumption that all science is about *perception* of events, whether objective or subjective, and never involves the *conception* of ideas or theories which affect our perceptions dramatically. The problem of events which are only perceived by some people can easily be explained, if only some people have the required concepts to enable them to perceive those events. The ideas in a person's head can be changed by communication with others, so their perceptions can be changed without interfering with the 'physical' world.

The positivist approach as always leads to the proliferation of parallel 'realities' and the multiplication of jargon terms needed to cope with them all. This situation becomes clear in Bearden's adoption of the 'Many World's Interpretation' of quantum mechanics. Bearden resolves the quantum problem of wave particle duality by splitting the two into separate *perceptual* worlds. By contrast the Copenhagen interpretation of quantum mechanics regards wave and particle as complementary *concepts*.

Consistent with the author's logical positivism, the remainder of the theoretical discussion disappears into a cloud of obscurantist terminology from which he never emerges. A lack of concepts has produced a lack of communication.

...

The basic theme, so far as it holds together, is that any given 'object' can be 'seen' simultaneously in alternative 'orthogonal hyperspace' or alternative worlds. But it is seen in a quite different form in each of these alternative worlds. Bearden assumes that there is continual interaction between these alternative worlds, a point which is inconsistent with Everret's formulation of them.

Bearden uses this assumed interaction as a way to solve the problem of paranormal phenomena. Fortean events occur when objects in a parallel world are projected onto our own. We are back with Plato and the shadow cast on the wall of the cave, but the ideals of Heaven have been reduced to an equally mundane 'parallel world'.

The apocalyptic third section remains as technically obscure as the previous sections, and it lacks the compensation of the visionary emotional grip of Revelations. Bearden argues unconvincingly that the Soviet Union is armed to the teeth with 'psychotronic' weapons capable of destroying the West's entire armoury, and causing earthquakes and cattle mutilations into the bargain. A number of Fortean events are explained in these terms but on the whole it is very patchy.

In summary, as a compilation of Fortean events it is poor, as a theory of the paranormal it is obscurantist, and as an apocalyptic vision it fails to grip the emotions.

Derek C. Banks

ARE WE BEING WATCHED?
By Janet & Colin Bord.
Angus & Robertson, London, 1981; £3.95 hb, 96pp, illos.

Although this is essentially a book for children, it is built around an interesting concept – sightings reported by, or involving, children – making it intriguing for the ufologist too. Seen from this fresh angle even some of the old familiar stories brighten a little – but lest the jaded yawn, the Bords have made efforts to find new and contemporary material (from FSR and other journals).

The book is written intelligently for children around the age of ten, and discusses with examples all categories of UFO experience, from sightings to the high-strangeness abductions. It is stern about hoaxing, practical on UFO-spotting, and calm on what to do if you actually see something. In its straighforward accounts of experiences – omitting boring and lengthy descriptions and details of original reportage – the stories take on a distinct mythological tone which should tingle the spines of young readers. Adults may find the curious colour cover illustration, of two children cringing in the presence of a rosy nipple-topped, breast-shaped metallic UFO both humerous and perversely symbolic. The choice of a well-known hoax photo, and cover words 'True UFO sightings' were presumably made by the publisher and not the Bords. Recommended for presents and school libraries.

RJMR

FENRIS-WOLF, and INSTITUTE OF GEOMANTIC RESEARCH publications.

The arrival of more publications from the tireless Nigel Pennick conjured up a mixture of feelings, of awe at his boundless energy, and appreciation and sympathy for having such a muse/daemon, and appreciation of his wit and intellect. Amongst the latest offerings from Britain's only anarcho-antiquarian pamphleteer: *Ancient Mysteries* (Spring 1981) 65p. *European Troytowns* by Nigel Pennick, 45p. *Welsh Temple of the Zodiac* by Lewis Edwards, *The Cambridge 7-church Ley* by Nigel Pennick & Michael Behrend, *Pre-Christian Geomancy* by Josef Heinsch, *Wandlebury Mysteries* by Nigel Pennick, all 25p each (p+p inc.) *Tunnels Under London* by Nigel Pennick, 85p, now followed by a *Tunnels Under London* newsletter. *Leys of the German Empire* by Kurt Gerlach, 85p. For full list of publications, write to IGR, 142 Pheasant Rise, Bar Hill, Cambridge CB3 8SD, England.

PAPERBACKS OF INTEREST:

Broca's Brain (Coronet, £1.50) essays by Carl Sagan, ranging from his philosophy of science, anthropology and evolution, SF, Velikovsky, robotics, intelligence and awareness, 'Sense and Nonsense at the Edge of Science', and of course astronomy. Intelligent, argumentative, opinionated and fairly safe.

The Quest for Gaia (Paladin, £2.50) the late Kit Pedlar's earnest book about the 'Behemoth of technology' versus the superorganism of Planet Earth's biosphere. High price for such a thin book.

By Lust Possessed (Signet, $1.95) edited by Eric Lombard. Despite the lurid title, a fascinating collection of articles, from various times and publications, about the sexual component of demonic and other types of possession.

Extraterrestrial Encounter (New English Library, £1.35) by Chris Boyce. An SF/astronomy/nuts-and-bolts view of the subject and its problems. Highly skeptical of UFO close encounters.

The Dark Side of History (Corgi, £1.50) by Michael Edwardes. A book not so much about magic, but the persistant and pervasive *belief* in magic. Covers the political use of magic, alchemy, mysticism, natural and scientific magic, subversive magic and the occult underground, surrealism, Nazi occultism. Interesting insights into contemporary unrest.

My Search for the Ghost of Flight 401 (Corgi, £1.00) by Elizabeth Fuller. In the course of writing his own *Flight 401* book, John Fuller met Elizabeth, a stewardess, who helped vitally with his research, and whom he married. This is her own account of her ghost hunt.

Tarotmania (Sphere, £1.40) by Jan Woudhuysen. A history and guide to the Tarot.

The Paranormal (Fontana, £1.50) by Stan Gooch. A parapsychologist's view of Man, The Universe and Everything. A rambling opinionated tour through all aspects of contemporary psychic research. Very interesting.

UFOs: Interplanetary Visitors (Bantam, $2.50) by Raymond Fowler. How the author of that dramatic, subjective experience of Betty Andreasson *(The Andreasson Affair)* can remain so entrenched in the nuts-and-bolts view escapes me, but this title says it all. Despite his narrow interpretation, this is a valuable book, with much astonishing material of high strangeness.

War on the Mind (Pelican, £2.95) by Peter Watson. A fascinating study of the 'Military uses and abuses of psychology'. Delicate though the human mind may be it can accommodate fearful stresses. At once frightening and informative. An eye-opening reference work on aberrations of consciousness and behaviour.

RJMR

Space seems to have been used up quickly in this issue, with many more books to review. We will return to the full number of review pages next issue.

Classified Exchanges.

As a reader service FT welcomes mutual exchanges with any relevant publication, and copies issues received since our last issue earn a listing here. No mag — no mention: All we ask in return is a similar entry in your own journal.

FORTEAN

• **Bigfoot Co-op** – a bi-monthly newsletter of manimal sightings, footprints, etc. Write to Bigfoot Co-op: 14602 Montevideo Drive, Whittier, CA 90605. USA.

• **Bigfoot Times** – an exchange newsletter of the Southwestern Bigfoot Research Team, including general Bigfooteana & news. Contact Danny Perez: 10926 Milano Ave. Norwalk, CA 90650. USA.

• **Common Ground** – exciting, controversial new journal of 'Studies at the Fringe of Human Experience'! Impressive first issue on UFOs, SPR, CE4s, 3rd secret of Fatima, Hallucinations, 'Lobsang Rampa', EVP, Tulpas. Annual sub: £4.00/$15.00. CG: 14 Northfold Rd, Knighton, Leicester.

• **Creature Chronicles** – quarterly Ohio-based coverage of manimals and mystery animal sightings. Annual sub: $6.00. USA and abroad. Hominid Research Group, Box 12049A, Cincinnati, OH45212, USA.

• **INFO Journal** – after a long gap, No 38 arrived, the best for ages. Scheduled to be bimonthly, but subject to delays. Journal of the International Fortean Organization. Annual sub: $10.00. Single copies: $1.75/90p. INFO: 7317 Baltimore Ave, College Park, MD 20740. USA.

• **Full Moon** - Hawaiian journal covering Forteana, folklore, UFO's etc. Juicy Fortean chunks of food for thought. USA $7 /yr; foreign subs please inquire for rates. Jacob A. Davidson: 1981-B St Louis Drive, Honolulu, Hawaii 96816, USA.

• **Journal of Meteorology** – monthly review of weather data and records, with many articles on Fortean-related meteorology. Annual sub: £13.50; overseas £15.50; airmail £21. Inquiries to J. Meteorology: Cockhill House, Trowbridge, Wilts BA14 9BG.

• **Kronos** – serious and scholarly quarterly devoted to discussion of the material and problems arising out of the work of Velikovsky. Annual sub: $15.00 (N. America), $22.00 (overseas airmail). Kronos: Box 343, Wynnewood, PA 19096, USA.

• **Lantern** – quarterly Fortean and folklore journal of East Anglian mysteries. Consistently of interest. Annual sub: UK & Europe £1.20; USA $5.00. Write to BSIG: 3 Dunwich Way, Oulton Broad, Lowestoft, Suffolk, NR32 4RZ.

• **M-Possibilities** – a Fortean newsletter for American mensa. Write to Michael Halm: 620 9th Ave. N, Apt 12, Fargo, ND 58102, USA.

• **New Atlantean Journal** – a quarterly newsprint journal covering parapsychology, UFOs, ancient enigmas, forteana. Annual sub: USA $12.00. airmail $15. NAJ: 5963 32nd Ave N, St Petersburg, FL 33710, USA.

• **Nessletter** – monthly newsletter of the Ness Information Service. Sightings and gossip from the Scottish and other monster-haunted lakes. Annual sub: £2.00; USA $8.00. NIS: Huntshieldford, St John's Chapel, Bishop Auckland, Co. Durham, DL12 1RQ.

• **Nuove Realta** – Fortean journal in Italian. Inquiries to Lorenzo Massai: Via Strozzi No 56, Prato 50047, Italy.

• **Pursuit** – quarterly journal of SITU. Annual sub: USA $10.00; overseas $14.00, airmail $25. SITU: Box 265, Little Silver NJ 07739, USA.

• **Specula** – quarterly journal of the American Association of Meta-science. Much of Fortean interest. Inquiries to AAMS: Box 1182, Huntsville, AL 35807. USA.

• **Stigmata** - occasional report of Project Stigma, investigating the continuing mystery of (mainly) US livestock mutilations. Single issue: $1.50; annual sub $5. Project Stigma:, Box 1094, Paris, TX 75460, USA.

• **Der Ukende** – Danish glossy quarterly on mysteries of all sorts. Write to Der Ukende: Nordvestvej 8, DK 4470, Svebolle, Denmark.

• **Vestigia Newsletter** – quarterly report of Fortean investigating group in New Jersey. Write for details: Vestigia, RD2. Brookwood Rd, Stanhope, NJ 07874. USA.

• **Zetetic Scholar** – really excellent bi-annual review of criticism and bibliography covering the whole range of Fortean interest. Thick, relevant, scholarly. Annual sub: N. America $12 overseas $18 (USA cheques and currency only). Zetetic Scholar: Dept. of Sociology, Eastern Michigan Univ., Ypsilanti, MI48197, USA.

UFOs

• **AFU Newsletter** – in Swedish and English. Write to Archives for UFO Research: PO Box 11027, S-600 11 Norrkoping 11, Sweden.

• **APRO Bulletin** – monthly journal of the Aerial Phenomena Research Association. News, investigations, articles. Annual sub: USA $12.00; overseas $15.00. APRO: 3910 E. Kleindale Rd, Tuscon, AZ 85712. USA.

• **BUFORA Journal** – quarterly of the British UFO Research Association. Write to BUFORA Membership Secretary: 30 Vermont Rd, Upper Norwood, London SE19 3SR.

• **Earthlink** – quarterly. Annual sub: £2.75, overseas £4.00. Single copy £1. Earthlink: 16 Raydons Rd, Dagenham, Essex RM9 5JR.

• **Hypotheses Extraterrestres** – quarterly journal of GEOS, in French. Write to Les Extraterrestres: Saint Denis les Rebais France.

• **Il Senzatitolo** – review journal in Italian. Write for details: IS, c/o Alberto Lazzaro, PO Box 240, 42100 Reggio Emilia, Italy.

• **Inforespace** – bi-monthly journal of SOBEPS in French. Inquiries to SOBEPS: Ave Paul Janson 74. 1070 Bruxelles Belgium.

• **Insolito** – a 94-page UFO journal in Portuguese. Write to: CEAFI, R. Sa da Bandeira 331. 3º, Salas 31/32. Porto, Portugal.

• **Investigation** – official organ of the UFO Investigators Network. Single copy 50p Available from the editor, Martin Keatman: 31 Stuart Close North Walton, Stone, Staffs. ST15 OJU.

• **Magonia** – pioneering quarterly exploring the sociological, psychological and mythological dimensions of UFO study. Highly recommended. Annual sub: £1.75; overseas $5.00. John Rimmer (editor): 64 Aleric Ave, New Malden, Surrey, KT3 4JW.

• **MAPIT Skywatch** – informal journal of UFO discussion. Much of interest. Inquiries to David Rees: 92 Hillcrest Rd, Offerton, Stockport, Cheshire, SK2 5SE.

• **MUFON UFO Journal** – monthly journal of the Mutual UFO Network. Annual sub: N. America $15; overseas $16. MUFON: 103 Oldtowne Rd, Sequin, TX 78155, USA.

• **Nordic UFO Newsletter** – a new publication from Norway, in English. Write for details to the editor: Mentz Kaarbø, Storhaugen 28, 5000 Bergen, Norway.

• **Northern UFO News** – monthly summary of UK cases reported to NUFON. Annual sub: UK £3.60. Write to the editor: Jenny Randles,

8 Whitethroat Walk, Birchwood, Warrington, Cheshire, WA3 6PQ.

• **Odiseja** – UFO journal in Slovenian. They hope to put out an English language quarterly. Write to the editor: Milos Krmelj, Milcinskega 6, 61000 Ljubljana, Slovenija, Yugoslavia.

• **Pre-1947 UFO Bulletin** – an occasional newsletter on the subject from Nigel Watson: Westfield Cottage, Crowle Bank Rd, Althorpe, South Humberside DN17 3HZ.

• **Tijdschrift voor Ufologie** – journal of NOVOBO in Dutch. Inquiries to NOVOBO: Lijnbaan 4, 9982 HJ Uithuizermeeden, Holland.

• **UFO Newsclipping Service** – a monthly collection of facsimilie clippings on UFOs, manimals and Forteana from papers worldwide. Well worth it if you can afford it. For more details see the ad on this page.

• **UFO Ohio** – regional newsletter with rare book and magazine list. Annual sub: $9. UFO Ohio: Box 5012, Rome, OH 44085, USA.

• **Ufologia** – supplement to Italina journal *Clypeus.* Write to Clypeus: Casella postale 82, 10100 Torino, Italy.

PSI

• **EVP Newsletter** – bi-monthly notes, interviews, data etc. on the 'electronic voice phenomenon'. Inquiries to Alan Cleaver: 6 Izane Rd, Bexleyheath, Kent DA6 8NX, England.

• **Metascience Quarterly** – a superb review. Annual sub: USA $14.00. Metascience Quarterly: Box 32, Kingston RI 02881, USA.

EARTH MYSTERIES

• **Ancient Skills and Wisdom Review** – a review newsletter by Paul Screeton, who also puts out the Terrestrial Zodiacs Newsletter. Annual ASWR sub: £2.00/$8.00 ($12.00 air). Paul Screeton, 5 Egton Drive, Seaton Carew, Hartlepool, Cleveland, TS25 2AT.

• **Archaeoastronomy** – quarterly. Annual sub: US $10; overseas $13.00. Write to the Center for Archaeoastronomy: Space Sciences Building, Univ. of Maryland, College Park, MD 20742, USA.

• **Caerdroia Project Newsletter** – the Caerdroia Project is a non-profit-making body, dedicated to researching and preserving turf mazes. Newsletter No. 6, the best so far, is now out. Inquiries to the Caerdroia Project: 53 Thundersley Grove, Thundersley, Benfleet, Essex.

• **Cambridgeshire Ancient Mysteries** – quarterly concentrating on new research into local earth mysteries. Annual sub: UK £2.00. This succeeds the magazine **Ancient Mysteries,** which ended with No. 19. Write to the Institute of Geomantic Research: 142 Pheasant Rise, Bar Hill, Cambridge CB3 8SD.

• **Catastrophism & Ancient History** – bi-annual. Annual sub: $6.00; overseas $8.00; single copies $4. C&AH: 3431 Club Drive, Los Angeles, CA 90064, USA.

• **IG News** – a bi-monthly folklore, occult and earth mysteries magazine. Annual sub: £2.50; overseas $5. IG News: BM Bulletin, London WC1N 3XX.

• **The Ley Hunter** – an essential journal of earth mysteries. Annual sub: UK £3.80; Europe £5, overseas airmail £7.50/$16.00. TLH: Box 13, Welshpool, Powys, Wales.

• **NEARA Journal** – quarterly of the New England Antiquities Association. Annual sub: USA $5; overseas $8. NEARA: 4 Smith St, Milford, NH 03055, USA.

• **Pyramid Guide** – bi-monthly newsletter of pyramidology in all its aspects. Annual sub: USA $9; overseas airmail $13. Write to Life Understanding Foundation: PO Box 30305, 741 Rosarita Lane, Santa Barbara, CA 93105, USA.

• **Quicksilver Messenger** – about earth mysteries in SE England. 60p per issue. Write to Chris Ashton: 26a Wilbury Ave, Hove, Sussex.

OTHERS

• **Gnome News** – newsletter of the Gnome Club of Great Britain. Annual sub: UK £2.50; overseas £3.50. Gnome Club: West Purford, Devon EX22 7XE.

• **Kingdom Voice** – prophesy and related phenomena. Inquiries to Kingdom Revival Crusade: Riverside Cottage, Bridgend, Harpford, Sidmouth, Devon EX10 ONG.

• **Undercurrents** – montly on radical alternatives. Annual sub: UK £4.20; overseas £5.20. Undercurrents: 27 Clerkenwell Close, London EC1R OAT.

Help!

Any reader or researcher requiring help in research, questions answered, or contacts on Fortean topics, may do so free in this column. Just send the details, on a separate sheet, keeping it brief.

• **Children brought up by wild animals** – any examples (with references if possible) on this theme welcome. The 'usual' 64 examples are researched but there has been little in the last ten years or so, and practically nothing from South America. Information to HKD Adamson, 13 Heath St, London NW3.

• Anyone in Lincolnshire interested in forming **a Fortean Group**, please contact Michael Ferrier, 17 Eastfield Rd, Louth, Lincs LN11 7AJ.

• I would be very pleased to hear from anyone who has had personal experience of **clairvoyance, telepathy, premonition, ESP, communications with the dead**, etc, in addition to straightforward hauntings, ghost and poltergeist activity. Please include an SAE with your letter; the cost of acknowledging a thousand stories would be phenomenal! Write: Joy Peach, 31 North View, Winchester, Hants.

• I am researching cases suggestive of a connection between **UFOs and the paranormal,** and would appreciate any lesser-known references or information on UFO cases involving ghostlights, healings, poltergeists, apparitions or mental communications. Write: Mark Moravec, 26 Minnamurra Place, Pymble, NSW 2073, Australia.

• David Fideler and Dennis Keller are looking for **unusual** material on bizarre cults for a possible **board game,** 'KRAZY KULTS: The Monopoly of the New Age.' Also Fideler and Tarte are soliciting clippings and **visuals** for a graphic gallery of **cultural artifacts** as a future Trashkashic installment. Visit your local restaurant today as all contributions will be credited. Send to: Dave Fideler, PO Box 1181, Grand Rapids, MI 49501 USA.

• Adrian Colston is interested in contacting **Forteans** in the Bath/Bristol area. Please write to him at: 14 Down Lane, Bathampton, Bath, Avon.

Errata.

FT27 –

p42 – 'I must argue with the piece about 'Roge' predicting the NYC blackout. That one turned out to be a complete fake. In August '77, 'Roge' made a mess of his prediction trick in Salem, Oregon; then confessed to using a trained stooge in the Seattle caper. Two weeks earlier, a guy called Carl Truchel had blown the gaff on 'Roge' and his methods to the *Seattle Post Intelligencer*. You can never entirely trust predictions which are revealed *after* the event.' Doc Shiels.

FT28

p 50f – Richard Heiden informs us that the mystery kangaroo activity did not happen 'in a suburban area west of Waukesha' as we described. The scene of the unauthorized leaping things was, Heiden writes: 'with but one or two exceptions *east* of Waukesha and west of Milwaukee.'

FT31

p2 – in the leader, the first author's name should be Yuan Zhenxin, (ie without the second z).

p27 – Loren Coleman's column – see below.

FT32

p24f – the undated *Glasgow Herald* clipping was 9 Feb 1980.

p22 – Loren Coleman's column should have carried a 'Copyright Loren Coleman' line, being extracted from his work in progress *Mystery Cats of the World*.

Truss Fund.

...in which we gratefully acknowledge the heartening support of the following whose donations will be applied where they will do most good.

Ron Bishop, James Chambers, Richard Cotton, Michael Ferrier, Steve Hicks, Paul Hindley, J T Kirkwood, Martin Kottmeyer, Al Lopez, Mrs Tojo Melville, Stephen Mooser, S N Morgan, Steve Ogden, Mike Rowe, Mark Ryder, Ion Will •

Next Issue.

We want to see if we can catch up on our lagging schedule by bringing out the next issue as quickly as we can. We've attempted predictions before about what will appear in coming issues but the universe being what it is we are poor prophets. Next issue *may* contain an outline from **Roger Wescott** about the emerging science of Anomalistics; the start of a series by **Peter Christie** extracting Fortean events from that esteemed periodical *The Gentleman's Magazine* begun in 1731; descriptions by **Paul Screeton** of some Toad-in-the-hole cases from the north of England; and a study by **Peter Jordan** using psychics to probe the mystery of cattle mutilations in New Mexico. We should be covering poltergeists, possession, mass-illnesses, falls and a lot more in our data sections.

Published by Fortean Times. Editor: ROBERT JM RICKARD. Editorial Assistants: STEVE MOORE, PAUL SIEVEKING. Contributing Editor: DAVID FIDELER. Art Director: RICHARD ADAMS. Comix Editor and section heading artwork: HUNT EMERSON. Photosetting by WORDSMITH GRAPHICS, 19a West End, Street, Somerset. Reprosetting mostly by PAULA GRAHAM, c/o BCM IT, London WC1N 3XX; and MAGIC INK, 22 Dane Road, Margate, Kent CT9 2AA. Printed by BIJA PRESS, Beeches Green, Stroud, Glos.

FORTEAN TIMES is a quarterly journal of news, notes and reviews and references on current and historical strange phenomena, related subjects and philosophies. A friend to all groups and magazines continuing the work of Charles Fort in investigating, studying and discussing all aspects of strange phenomena. RIGHTS: all articles and artwork in FT is the copyright of the authors unless otherwise stated. Uncredited material is by the editors. The views of the contributors are not necessarily those of Ft, and vice versa. SUBMISSION is invited of articles, artwork, cartoons, and news clippings on related subjects. The publishers can assume no responsibility for unsolicited material, but all reasonable care will be taken while in FT's possession. If the material is to be returned, please enclose S.A.E. CORRESPONDENCE: letters-of-comment and personal experience are welcome. If replies are required please enclose S.A.E. The editor regrets it is not always possible to reply promptly. ADVERTISING and DISTRIBUTION AND SALES ENQUIRIES: contact the editor at the above address, or ring 01 552 5466. SUBSCRIPTION INFORMATION: see index (above)

Don't forget — our new address is: **BM-Fortean Times, London WC1N 3XX, England.**

BACKISSUES £1 (US $2.50)* EACH

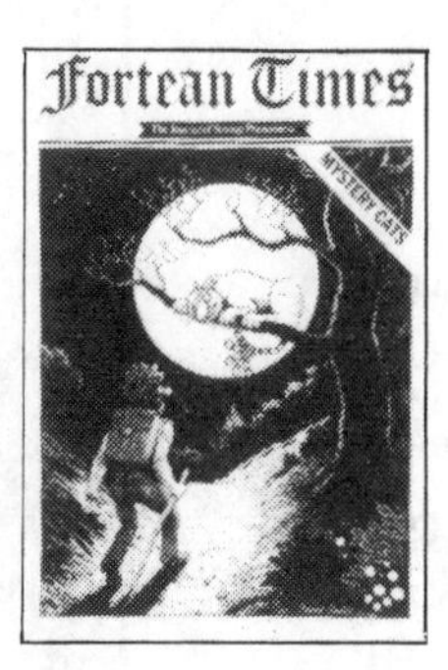

• **FT 31** – The Chinese Wildman by **Yuan Zhenxin & Huang Wanpo**; first part of **Dave Fideler's** Gateways to Mystery; **Michael Goss** on The Touch of Death; plus UFO muggers, mystery cats, ball lightning, synchronous names, little people, fake doctors, etc. etc.

• **FT 32** – **Dwight Whalen** on the Mississauga Blob; **Paul Cropper** on Australian mystery big cats; **Fideler's** Gateways part two; Old Ives' Tales by **Paul Sieveking**; **Michael Hoffman** on American conspiracies and twilight language; plus more cats, old fairy tales come true, Indian Forteana, child sacrifice and much more.

• **FT 33** – **Guy Playfair** on the Enfield Polt; **Hilary Evans** on the mythology and psychology of UFO abductions: a theme continued by **Dave Fideler & Bob Tarte** in Gateways part three; plus the Nottingham 'mass hysteria', simulacra, coffin stories, Jeoff Watson's Nessie pix, the regular columns by **Steve Moore, Nigel Watson** and **Loren Coleman** . . . and other things.

• **FT 34** – Congo dinosaur hunt by **Prof Roy Mackall; Joseph Zarzynski** on the names of lake monsters; **Mike Goss** on phantom hitch-hikers; **Dave Fideler** interviews **Dr Jean Bolen** on synchronicity; **Janet & Colin Bord** on the Welsh 'puma'; plus other UK cat sightings, beached whales, animal saboteurs, nature follows art, ice falls, inept crimes, and the usual columns and comix.

GOOD NEWS!

Founded in 1973 and first called *The News*, FT's humble beginnings have become legendary – well, out of print anyway! We now have high quality xerox facsimilies of the **first sixteen** issues of *Fortean Times*. Available at £1.00 (US $2.50) each, UK and world surface mail included. *£1.50 (US $3.00) each airmail.

"If you are going to read only one Fortean periodical, **Fortean Times** is the one you want."
Fate (USA) May 1979.

Subscribe or Die!

SUBSCRIBE, OR WE DIE! Yes it's a tired old cliche, but true. A sub ensures you get an unthumbed copy delivered to your door wherever you are. A sub also makes a thoughful gift for friends, impoverished scholars, libraries, even enemies, that lasts a whole year (or four issues, whichever takes longest to fulfill). Rate includes postage and banking commission where applicable – **1 year or four issues: £4. Surface: $10.00. Airmail: $17.50.**

GIFT SAMPLE. Have a sample issue, plus our literature sent to a friend or potential subscriber at these reduced rates – **UK: £1.00. Airmail: $4.00.**

PAYMENT – cheques, postal orders, made payable to **Fortean Times.** Dollar cheques acceptable. Overseas subscribers wishing to remit in Sterling may find it easier to ask their bank for a banker's draft drawn on a London bank. If in doubt your bank should be happy to explain. Send your order with payment to us at the address below. NB: surface mail to the USA can take 6-8 weeks. If you think your order has gone astray or is in error, please let us know.

BM-FORTEAN TIMES, LONDON WC1N 3XX, U.K.

Fortean Times

ISSUE No. 36 | The Journal of Strange Phenomena. | PRICE: £1.00 $2.50

MADE IN ENGLAND

16 VIEW FROM THIS SIDE

Photos of the Gods.

An unparalleled collection of over 300 photographs claimed to be evidence of UFOs, sea-serpents, ghost-lights, Bigfoot, parhelia, possession, stigmata, bleeding images, thoughtography, Kirlian photography, levitation, spoon-benders, firewalking, etc. Many in full colour. Plus essay on paranormal photography. Excellent visual reference book. By Bob Rickard (editor of FT) and Richard Kelly. UK £6.00; foreign surface $13.00; foreign airmail $19.00.

SIMULACRA

One of the most remarkable Fortean books around. An erudite survey of the varieties of spontaneous images in Nature. Inspires art, psychology, mysticism. Illustrated with 196 photos and graphics collected by the author over many years. Soft cover only, 128 pages. For reasons hard to understand copies of this essential book have been hard to find here, and are virtually unobtainable in USA, thus robbing *Simulacra* of the success it deserved. Order from FT today. UK £3.60; foreign surface $7.50; foreign airmail $13.50.

THE COMPLETE BOOKS OF CHARLES FORT

Still the greatest compendium of strange phenomena ever written with wit and wisdom. This is a 1974 reprint of the original 1941 edition printed for the old Fortean Society. Contains: *Book of the Damned, New Lands, Lo!*, and *Wild Talents* – with a barely functional index, and introduction by Damon Knight. Hardcover, 1125 pages. Every Fortean should have his own copy. US punters are advised it would be cheaper to get the book from Dover Publications there – it's so heavy the postage is otherwise prohibitive. UK £11.00; foreign surface $24.00.

Recommended introduction to the philosophy of Charles Fort, demonstrating the historical and thematic continuity of 57 kinds of strange phenomena, from stigmata, levitation and fairies to showers of frogs, wild children, ball lightning and spontaneous human combustion. Profusely illustrated. By John Michell (author of *View over Atlantis)* and RJM Rickard (editor of FT) UK £3.50; foreign surface $8.00; foreign airmail $14.00.

At last available. *Fortean Times Occasional Paper No 1:* WILDMAN. A compendium of information on the Chinese equivalent to the Yeti and Bigfoot. Three articles newly (and expensively) translated from the Chinese for the first time, with explanatory material and critical apparatus. Includes new photographs, 12 illustrations and monster-pictures from old Chinese books. 24 pages. FT format. £1.00 (US $2.50) each UK and world surface mail; or US$4.50 airmail.

MAN BITES MAN – The Scrapbook of an Edwardian Eccentric. Edited by Paul Sieveking and published by Jay Landesman Ltd. Large format. Hard-cover. 160 pages. Profusely illustrated with 584 facsimile items from the press-clipping albums of George Ives, from 1890 to 1950. The weird, the dubious, the heroic, the horrific, and the hilarious.
Offered to *Fortean Times* readers at the special price of £6.00 (US $15.00) including p+p UK and world surface mail; or £10.50 (US $26.00) overseas airmail.

Make cheques, money orders etc, payable to **Fortean Times.** Prices include post and packing. Allow up to 10 weeks for surface mail. Send orders to **BM-Fortean Times, London WC1N 3XX, UK.**

Fortean Times

BM-Fortean Times
London WC1N 3XX.

The Journal of Strange Phenomena.

Winter 1982
ISSN 0308.5899

Reprosetting Mostly by Cecelia Boggis: 11 Ashburnham Rd, Bedford. Some by Paula Graham: BCM IT, London WC1N 3XX
Photosetting Wordsmiths: 19 West End, Street, Somerset.

Contents.

ARTICLES
4 **Anomalistics** *Roger Wescott.*
12 **The Runamo Runes** *A Bibliography*
28 **ASSAP & CSAR.**
32 **Photos of the Gods** *Bob Rickard.*
42 **Extracts from the Gentleman's Magazine** *Peter Christie.*

NOTES
13 **Strange Behaviour** *Hermits and Wildmen.*
16 **Strange Tales...***Umm...*
17 **Embeddings** *Toads in the Hole.*
19 **Miracles** *Bleeding Statues and others.*
22 **Forteana Corrigenda** *The Buddha's UFO.*
23 **Medical Curiosities** *DIY Surgery.*
26 **Falls** *Coins, Sand, Ice.*

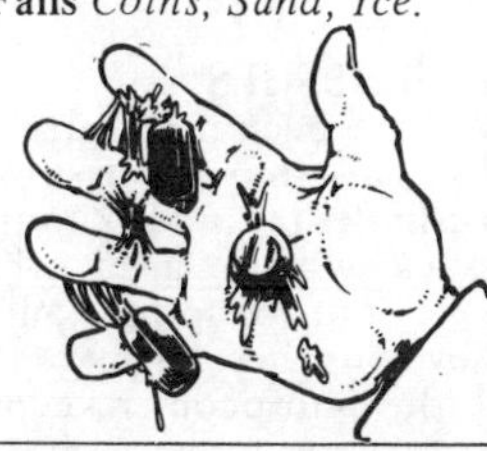

COLUMNS
29 **Soapbox** *Readers' Opinions.*
42 **On The Trail** *Loren Coleman.*
44 **Enigma Variations** *Nigel Watson.*
46 **Tales From The Yellow Emporium** *Steve Moore.*

COMIX
11 **Facts You Might Forget** *Pokkettz.*
30 **Phenomenomix** *Hunt Emerson.*

USUAL STUFF
2 Editorial.
3 Letters.
51 Reviews.
56 Classified Exchange.
62 Subscription info.

LATE AGAIN

Firstly, I have to apologize once again for the lateness of this issue. This is mainly my fault, having taken on much work. Unfortunate domestic problems have been time-consuming, for reasons I won't bore you with, and unexpected production problems added to the delay. None of this is likely to improve dramatically in the near future, and one consequence is that we cannot justify calling ourselves a quarterly any longer. We have every intention of *trying* to get out four issues a year, but it is difficult to guarantee this target. From now on we will be a 'sporadical', to borrow John Nicholson's useful word. We'll peg the subs at £4 for four issues, and subs will last until you've had four issues, however long that takes. Rest assured we won't be as sparse as our illustrious predecessor, *Doubt*, which often had issues spaced years apart!

THIS ISSUE

A slight reorganization of our leading pages gives us room on the Contents Page for a list of our Special Correspondents and those who regularly send us significant quantities of clippings. The editorial team consider these valiant clipsters as much a part of the team as ourselves, and hope they find some satisfaction in this small acknowledgement of their valued efforts. Clippings are FT's lifeblood, so clip something strange today – and keep them coming. Future issues will give more space to our clipping summaries.

This issue sees the appearance of a new column – 'Soapbox' – which is open to any of our readers who wants to sound off on any FT related topic, outside the 'Letters' page. Ideally these should be short pieces, about one page of typing, of a more speculative, critical, or philosophical tone. Our first candidate, Jasper McKee, steps up on page *29*.

We have been aware of the lack of more discursive articles in FT lately – but we can't print what isn't submitted. However, this lack is remedied by Professor Roger Wescott's provocative proposals for turning Forteanism into something more scientifically acceptable – see his article on 'Anomalistics' on page *4* .

BACK ISSUES

We have been pleasantly astonished at the response to the facsimile reprints of our early issues which have otherwise gone out of print, and Paul Sieveking has been kept busy at the photocopier keeping up with your orders. So, you'll be pleased to know that we can now supply copies of all back issues up to FT20 – see ad on the outside back cover.

It has been harder for us to satisfy the demand of out of print issues between 21 and 30. This series saw a dramatic increase in the number of pages; the full A4 size of FT29, which was a nuisance to those who wanted a neat row of FTs on the shelf; and of course, the beautiful full colour covers of FT29 and FT30, by Hunt Emerson and Una Woodruff respectively. All these factors make copying difficult. One solution is to reprint Nos 21-30 in a single, bound volume, to the present format, including the colour covers and possibly an index. Naturally this would mean tying up a lot of capital and we'd have to be sure we could sell a trial printrun of say, 1000. Individually, these back issues would cost you about £10 – there is no doubt we could get the volume price down below that. Please write to encourage us if you think the idea is interesting. If such a volume could pay for itself, we could consider reprinting numbers 1-20 in one volume too. It would be most helpful to know what you think.

BM?

Some of you have asked about the logic of our new address. 'BM' is the abbreviation of British Monomark, perhaps the largest private London mailing address service. The GPO recognizes 'BM', making possible a simpler address. In fact one letter reached us marked only 'Fortean Times, London'!

CIRCULATION

We have not been able to keep you up to date on how well – quite poorly, really – we are doing on the circulation front. So here are the figures for FT33, FT34 and FT35 (in that order) on our survival meter. New subs 113, 203, 89. Lapsed subs 202, 106, 95. Free 100, 92, 88. Total paid subs 907, 1004, 1007.

Remember, our breakeven figure is about 1200 paid subs, so you can see how short we fall. We keep out of the red by the sale of back issues (see below), and books, and through

Cont on p60

THE FAUNA OF DREAMS

The Summer 1980 issue was fascinating as usual. The material on mystery animals in particular brought to mind some ideas I had a few years back concerning a relationship between Fortean events and dreams.

At the time, I was keeping a dream diary and had noticed that I dreamed repeatedly of certain animals but not of others, I often dreamed of large carnivors–dogs, wolves, and unknown doglike creatures, tigers, alligators. I might dream occasionally of monstrous pigs or of a kangaroo in an English garden. But I almost never dreamed of domestic animals like horses and cows, although I live on a farm. I dreamed of large, aggressive birds–wild geese, hostile chickens–but not of small songbirds. I dreamed of prehistoric men and apemen.

I wondered at first what private symbolic significance these creatures might have for me. Then I happened to read Jerome Clark and Loren Coleman's *The Unidentified*, and it began to seem that my dream fauna was more Fortean than Freudian. All the general categories, and some of the specific incidents, were in correspondence with Clark and Coleman's data. I started to pick out further Fortean elements in my dreams: Alien beings with huge, unearthly eyes. Recurrent childhood nightmares of being attacked by featureless monsters that were partly dogs, partly black panthers. Dreams of meteors and other things seen in or falling from the sky. Dreams of levitation, telekinesis, and teleportation.

Except for the special case of UFO-contacts, I have never seen any discussion in print of dreams with Fortean content. If you would print my address, I would be interested in corresponding with anyone who has thoughts or information on this subject.

Cory Panshin
R.R.2, Box 261
Perkasie PA 18944

THE JANOS CASE

Nigel Watson's review of The Janos People [FT34, pp46-48] caught my eye. Whilst he makes some perceptive points, with which I concur, I was a little perturbed by his remarks that Frank Johnson's approach to the Janos case casts a sad reflection on the state of British Ufology, and the validity of UFOIN. I beg the right to reply to such a slap-dash dismissal of affairs.

Whilst it is very true to say that there are many Ufologists (and researchers in all areas of Forteana) who seem to have little idea what the word 'investigation' means, and who seem to think that it somehow equates with proving one particular theory or another, I think Nigel is rather climbing on his hobby-horse to claim that this is typical. Does he seriously believe that nobody else but himself appreciates the need for caution in dealing with CE4s? Or does he think that nobody else sees the glaring psycho-social components of the CE4 cases? Surely not! MAGONIA thrives on such things, and the number of perceptive ufologists is growing, not shrinking. In addition he seems to be unaware of the universal hostility generated against Frank Johnson's book. At a UFOIN/NUFON conference in Birmingham (October 1980), where he lectured, the tone of the audience left no doubt about what they thought of these "investigations". Nigel was present, so was not ignorant of this reaction, mirrored in every review of the book I have read so far.

The case was reported, via Ken Phillips, to me in August 1978. I asked Frank Johnson to follow it up because he was the closest UFOIN member to the scene. He also had produced some excellent reports on medium definition cases, which are still housed in the files for all to see. He had an extensive professional background and was "untainted", in the sense that he had not handled a close encounter before and seemed free from prejudice. I should also point out that, at this time, the case consisted of a multiple witness disc-type encouter and a family who subsequently had apparently got lost. There was no hint of an abduction or even a contact, although the possibility did occur to both Frank and myself. The decision to "send in" Frank was mine. The fact that it is now seen as a mistake proves to be an error of judgement on *my* part, no more.

In November of that year Frank reported on his first discoveries and the fact that the case was now an abduction. This took place at the home of Janet and Colin Bord, who

Cont on p58

Anomalistics: A New Field Of Interdisciplinary Study.

While individual pieces of Fortean research and writing sometimes display the rigour orthodox scientists reserve for themselves, Fortean researches collectively suffer from a lack of direction. No one wishes to impose an 'organization' on our valuable variety of subjects and thinkers, and yet the value of paradigms in organizing data, as demonstrated in the theory of science, is widely acknowledged. The Big Breakthrough in Fortean studies has yet to be made, but many of us feel it will come out work which treats the variety of our subjects and experiences as an inter-related whole—what Fort called an Inclusive Science. This article by **Roger W.Wescott**, professor of anthropology and linguistics, Drew University, USA, is an attempt to bring order out of chaos by searching for an expression of that relationship which would not only be acceptable to science as a discipline, but also provide a useful structure for visualising the 'big picture'. This article orginally appeared in *Kronos* and is reprinted with permission.

Anomalistics may be defined as the serious and systematic study of all phenomena that fail to fit the picture of reality provided for us by common sense or by the established sciences. Although the term itself is my coinage,[1] the area of investigation which it designates is at least sixty years old.

The precursory genius of anomalistics as I define it was the British geneticist John B. Haldane, who was fond of commenting on "the inexhaustible queerness of things" and is widely quoted as having observed that "the universe is not only stranger than we imagine but stranger than we can imagine". The first investigator, however, who made anomalies the primary focus of his activities was the American journalist Charles Hoy Fort. Fort, whom we may fairly regard as the founder of anomalistics, made the first massive compilation of oddities from the world press. Another American journalist, Robert L. Ripley, whose syndicated column "Believe It Or Not" appeared in nearly all United States newspapers, was the first popularizer (or, as his detractors may prefer to phrase it, the first vulgarizer) of anomalistics.

The first organizer of anomalistic field-work was the Scottish-American biologist Ivan Sanderson, who founded The Society for the Investigation of the Unexplained in Columbia, New Jersey. Among living anomalists, the one who probably comes closest to embodying their collective investigatory enterprise is the American engineer William R. Corliss, who publishes the Sourcebook Project, a compilation of anomalistica drawn from scientific periodicals, in Glen Arm, Maryland. The leading patron of anomalistic research, finally, is the American inventor Arthur M. Young, President of the Foundation for the Study of Consciousness, in Philadelphia.

Unfortunately, no consistent typology of anomalies has yet been developed or even proposed in an explicitly reasoned manner. If we follow the lead of the experimental sciences, we can set up a five-part typology basedon a widely accepted (though apparently anonymous) sequential scheme for the goals of science. These frequently cited goals are, in order of progression:

1. description
2. classification
3. explanation
4. prediction
5. control

In these terms, a descriptive anomaly would be a mystical experience, which is characterized by most mystics as ineffable – that is, incapable of being verbalized and therefore, by definition, indescribable. A classificatory anomaly would be the invertebrate taxon onychophora, of which the best known genus is Peripatus. Anatomically, the onychophora are intermediate between the arthropod phylum, including insects, and the annelid phylum, including earth-worms. Some taxonomists therefore classify onychophora as arthropods, others as annelids, and still others as a separate and independent phylum. An explanatory anomaly would be the "sky-quakes" which occurred during the winter of 1978-1979 over the Atlantic Ocean shelf between South Carolina and Connecticut. Although the prevalent explanation of these explosive sounds is that they are sonic booms from Concorde airliners, this explanation fails to account for several peculiarities of the sounds, most obvious of which is the fact that they have been reported by newspapers in the area since 1805. A predictive anomaly would be the adoption, during the middle of the first millennium B.C., of Aramaic as the common language of the ancient Near East between Egypt and India, which it remained till the Islamic conquest of the 7th century A.D. The wide-spread use of any language normally results from military conquest, population explosion, or literary prestige. As far as is known, however, the Arameans were themselves a relatively minor group of pastoral nomads. At the time of the overthrow of the Assyrian and Babylonian empires, a well-informed linguistic prognosticator would probably have predicted that their imperial language, Akkadian, would be superceded by Persian or perhaps by Greek but hardly by any of the West Semitic vernaculars. An anomaly of control, finally, is provided by local weather, concerning which we now have a wealth of information but which we can scarcely even forcast, must less manipulate with any assurance of even minimal success.

The trouble with this typology, of course, is that, having been set up for the natural sciences, it is poorly adapted to religious, humanistic, and social studies. An alternative typology is one that is drawn from within the study of anomalies rather than from outside it. Such a typology, of my own devising, is the following categorization:

1. paradoxes
2 displacements
3. improbabilities
4. deviations
5. unexpected occurrences
6. unexplained phenomena

An example of paradoxical entity is light, which seems not only to consist simultaneously of corpuscles and of waves (an apparent contradiction which some neologists have sought to resolve by referring to photons as "Wavicles") but also to undulate in interstellar space, without a sustaining medium comparable to the fluids or solids through which sound waves move.

An example of displaced entity is provided by the occasional discovery, in quarries and other excavations, of live amphibians or reptiles in small rock cavities without visible outlets.[2] In many such cases, the displacement is not only spatial but temporal as well, since the rock is believed by geologists to have been formed thousands if not millions of years ago.

An example of an improbability is the extraordinary similarity – amounting, with most symbols, to identity – between the Harappan script of the pre-Aryan Indus Valley and the rongo-rongo script of Easter Island. Though both scripts remain undeciphered, it is hard to believe that they are not varities of a single writing system. Yet (in a manner reminiscent of the imprisoned animals just cited) the two scripts are separated by temporal as well as spatial gaps, belonging not only to opposite hemispheres but, by consensual dating, to different and non-adjacent millennia.[3]

An example of a deviation is the behaviour of water, which is the only common substance known that expands rather than contracting when it solidifies. This chemical contrariety has crucial biological consequences. For, if water, like most other substances, were to contract as it solidified, bodies of surface water would freeze from the bottom up and, during protracted cold spells, be converted totally into ice. Under such circumstances, it is doubtful that any multi-cellular organisms, much less higher animals, could survive.

An example of an unexpected occurrence is the development, between World Wars I and II, of that reactionary type of political totalitarianism known as Fascism in Italy, Falangism in Spain, and National Socialism in Germany. Prior to the 1920's virtually all political theorists had foreseen a struggle between liberal capitalism and Marxist communism. But none, apparently, had anticipated this anomalous tertium quid that very nearly conquered the world in the early 1940's.

An example, finally, of an unexplained phenomenon is orogeny, or mountain-building. Although various explanations of our planet's rocky upthrusts have been put forward over the years, the only one currently in wide-spread geological favour is the view that mountain ranges are products of collisions between the drifting tectonic plates on which both continents and sea-floor segments ride. Yet there are major ranges, such as the Rockies of western North America, that seem to be too far from accepted plate boundaries to be accommodated by this explanation.

The difficulty with the preceding categorization, apart from its relative subjectivity, is that its categories lack discreteness. Every displacement, for example, is to some degree paradoxical, improbable,deviant, unexpected and, if not unexplained, at least resistant to explanation.

A third possible typology of anomalies classifies them in terms of the types of questions raised about them by sceptics. For events, the question most often raised is whether they actually occur. Happenings that fall into this category are: ball lightning, human canibalism, and faith-healing. For objects, the question most often raised is whether they exist. Entities that fall into this category are: quarks (hypothesized nuclear particle components), sasquatches (living apemen), totemism (a preliterate ideology involving human descent from non-human ancestors), the mind (as something distinct from the body), and God. And for categories themselves, the question most often raised is whether they are – that is, whether they inhere in nature (in accordance with the so-called "God's Truth" view of categorization) or are merely analytical conveniences for scholars (in accordance with the so-called "hocus-pocus" view of it.) Classes that fall into this category are: numbers, biological taxa (such as genera and species), culture (in its technical enthnological sense), and phonemes (distinctive units of sound in language).

The chief problem with this typology is that it excludes too many interesting anomalies about which these particular questions are rarely raised, though other, equally probing questions may be raised about them. Such anomalies are: retrograde rotation, such as that of the planet Venus; the self-beachings of whales; the seeming senselessness of myths; and the resistance of humour to analytical explanation.

What, if any, typology of anomalies is then left to us? The one used, at least implicitly, by such practicing anoamlists as Sanderson and Corliss is the familiar spectrum of disciplines known to us from university catalogues. Beginning (very scantily) with such "soft" subjects as theology, it proceeds through the humanities to the sciences, which it treats in order of increasing "hardness' – social sciences first, life sciences second, and physical sciences last. At first blush, it might seem that the number of anomalies per subject would vary directly with its softness, since softer disciplines are less tightly organized. In fact, however, quite the reverse is true, for reasons which a moment's reflection makes clear: the softer a subject-matter is, the more difficult it is to distinguish normal from anomalous phenomena within it.

Consequently, it is in the physical sciences that anomalies are most conspicuous, so that a listing of anomalies by disciplinary area ought probably to begin with the physical and end with the "spiritual". In these terms, a good example of a physical anomaly is provided by quasi-stellar objects, or quasars, which are star-sized bodies that appear to radiate as much energy as entire galaxies do. What this implies, in turn, is that quasars are powered by an energy source which exceeds that of thermonuclear energy by about ten orders of magnitude.

A good example of biological anomaly is provided by extinction, the death not just of individual organisms but of entire taxa, ranging in scope from species to phyla. Extinction is anomalous in both a general and a specific sense. In its general sense, extinction is not explained by the prevalent Darwinian theory of environmental unfitness, since the only evidence for that unfitness is the extinction itself. In a specific sense, moreover (as applied to particular taxa), extinction is not merely unexplained but paradoxical, since some groups – of which the best known are the saurischia, or large dinosaurs – seem not merely to have survived but to have flourished immediately before their geologically sudden disappearance.[4]

A good example of social science anomaly is the archaic megalithic complex, of which the best known specimin is probably the great stone circle at Stonehenge, Wiltshire, England. In an apparent effort to contain (since they cannot eliminate) the strangeness of this complex, in which both the methods and the motives of construction remain obscure, archaeologists have written about it as though it were confined to pre-Roman Europe. In fact, however, it is found on every continent but Australia and may date from any or all of the last seven millennia. Associated with it, furthermore, are some artifacts which are so puzzling that most archaeologists do not even try to explain them away; they simply do not mention them at all. In this category as the hundreds of granite and limestone spheres, ranging in diameter from a few inches to eight feet, found in rain forests and even on mountain tops in Costa Rica and Guatamala, none of which seem to have been quarried in the immediate vicinity of their present locations.[5]

Outside the sciences, anomalies are, as we have noted, less clear-cut. But one can cite as anomalous the long-standing philosophical dichotomy of mind and matter, as one can also cite the perennial difficulty of defining religion. Depending both on circumstance and on the definer, religion can consist essentially of a creed, a code, a cluster of rituals, or a response to occult phenomena.

In addition to the anomalistic imbalance between the arts and the sciences, a drawback to the categorization of anomalies by discipline or disciplinary areas is that, during the past generation, a number of new disciplines have appeared which are difficult to locate with any precision on the traditional disciplinary spectrum. Of these, the most conspicuous, though not the most difficult, is parapsychology, the study of such phenomena as telepathy (mind-to-mind communication) and psychokinesis ("mind-over-matter" activity). Though it overlaps to some degree the domains of physics and religion, parapsychology, as its name suggs, has its centre of intellectual gravity in the disciplinary vicinity of psychology among the social sciences. Noetics, the study of consciousness, while clearly related to both psychology and parapsychology, leans in the direction of ontology, epistemology, and other philosophical subdisciplines and ought perhaps, therefore, to be classified as one of the humanities rather than as one of the social sciences. Thanatology, the study of death and attitudes towards death, likewise has psychological affinities. But it also exhibits biological and religious overlaps which make it hard to classify on the spectrum.

Two new disciplines whose ramifications are so broad that they defy placement are futuristics, the study of the future, and "ufology", the study of unidentified flying objects. Because futuristics bears on every subject matter with the possible exception of those laws of God and nature that are regarded as timeless, it can be localized only with regard to its practitioners, most of whom come or came from the social sciences. Ufology (the semi-acronymous term for a field of investigation which I would prefer to call bradyology, meaning "the study of slow-moving objects") is, if anything, an even more polymathic enterprise than futuristics. It involves astronomy, physics, chemistry, oceanography, and meteorology within the physical sciences; zoology, physiology within the social sciences; history and philosophy within the humanities; and ethics and theology within religious studies.

All things considered, the disciplinary typology of anomalies seems to be, despite its occasional drawbacks, the least troublesome one. It is, consequently, the one which we shall use throughout the remainder of this paper.

Closely related to the question of typology is that of terminology. Although in theory it is of no scholarly concern what any datum is called so long as it is consensually defined, in practice names do affect scientists as well as humanists and sometimes even determine their reactions to the topics named. Recently, for example, an article on sky-quakes appeared in *Science* magazine. And one of the reasons why it passed the strict editorial scrutiny characteristic of that journal is, I think, that the anomalous detonations described in it were referred to in the title as brontides – a word of Greek derivation meaning "thunder-like sounds".[6] Another anomaly whose colloquial name may disincline potential investigators to study it is "spook-lights", the small, moving lights, similiar to – but clearly not identical with – ball lightning which have been most recently observed along a one-mile stretch of railway track in Washington Township, N.J.[7] The Hellenic synonym that I have proposed for spook-lights is photophasms, meaning "light phantoms". (Thus far, however, I have not observed any scholarly rush toward either the term or the topic!)

To a large extent, what is or is not considered anomalous depends on the intellectual fashions of the time and place in question. Two decades ago in the United States, any geological evidence suggestive of continental drift seemed anomalous; today, any evidence calling drift into question seems equally anomalous. Much the same is true of the view that life naturally evolves in the universe wherever Earth-like environments occur. The way one answers the question whether continental drift occurs and whether extraterrestrial life exists depends primarily on the paradigm, in Thomas Kuhn's sense,[8] within which one is conducting his scientific deliberations. For this reason, anomalistics is inextricably bound up with what I call paradigmatics,[9] the comparataive study of scholarly presuppositions.

A question that is repeatedly raised with regard to anomalistics is that of its utility, presumably on the assumption that a field of investigation which has no evident use ought not to be admitted to the roster of scholarly disciplines. In response to that question, the anomalist may at first be inclined to reply with a question, as Benjamin Franklin reportedly did when, having been asked of what use electricity is, he answered: "Of what use is a baby?" Apart from its flippant tone, this answer has the merit, at least implicitly, of suggesting the serendipital quality of anomalistics. For, while the anomalist may initially have been drawn to anomalous subjects by nothing more exalted than a penchant for the wild, the weird, and the wonderful, he soon finds that this penchant has unanticipated but valuable results.

Of these valuable results, the one most often mentioned by anomalists is the reformulation of scientific theories as a consequence of discrepancies between them and anomalous data which seem to contradict them. An example of such reformulation is the shift from Renaissance creationism to Victorian evolutionism as a result of the increasing difficulty of fitting fossil organisms into a Biblical framework.

However, since paradigm shifts often seem to have little more to do with ultimate truth than do changes in sartorial fashion with ultimate beauty, I prefer to justify my own anomalistic involvements primarily in terms of the efficacy of anomalistics in linking conventionally disparate disciplines. We have already noted the fact that some anomalies such as fire-walking, require their investigators to involve themselves (however reluctantly) in virtually every disciplinary area of research from theology to physics. It is an exceptional anomaly that permits its investigator to work exclusively in a single discipline. When, in fact, one tries to isolate a narrowly focused anomaly - such as imaginary numbers (like $\sqrt{-1}$) in mathematics – he quickly finds that, by implication at least, the search leads both to philosophical questions, such as the objectivity of numerality, and to psychological questions such as the nature of imagination.

In this connection, what seems to me to be particularly commendable about anomalistics is the fact that it strongly counteracts the besetting sin of contemporary academia – fragmentation. We live in an age in which psychologists, for example, find it difficult to talk not only with non-psychologists but even with one another: psychoanalysts and experimentalists, for example, share almost nothing with one another in terms either of interests or of methods. And anomalists can, I think, make a major contribution to the reintegration of the literally disintegraged scholarship which they encounter in nearly every area of their investigations.

Yet another value of anomalistics, as I see it, is that it restores a proper balance, now missing in most of the conventional disciplines, between search and research. Outside libraries, the term search is rarely even used in contemporary academia. Yet logically, as the late Ivan Sanderson repeatedly observed, not only does search precede research, but search – the (often intuitive) quest for information or insight – can occur in the absence of research, while research is dependent on prior search. Nonetheless, most academicians confine themselves to research, which consists, strictly speaking, of the testing of hypotheses and the verification of investigatory results produced by search. In terms of the Paleolithic life-ways which apparently shaped contemporary human behaviour, we might say that searchers are the hunters who track and capture elusive quarry, while researchers are the camp-bound individuals who dissect and distribute what the hunters bring in. This is not to say that research is unimportant: all scholarship needs to be checked and, ideally, rechecked. My point is, rather, that many scholars who have the intellectual courage and ingenuity to be searchers unnecessarily confine themselves to the role of researchers because they are not fully aware of the primary option that is open to them. Anomalistics, by performing the Zen-like task of shattering the customary presuppositions of conventional scholarship, can help open-minded investigators to take the kind of fresh look at their data which produces new intellectual syntheses.

Because of their inherently disturbing nature, anaomalous data tend strongly to polarize responses to them. A majority of respondents to anomalies may be characterized either as debunkers or as cultists. Debunkers handle unwelcome data by denying their existence. Instead of attempting the difficult task of explaining anomalies, they retreat to the easier procedure of explaining them away – that is, characterizing them as apparent rather than real. Cultists, on the other hand, though equally reluctant to try explaining anomalies, express that reluctance inversely, by revering each anomaly for its own sake and erecting a mystical ethos around it. In no area of anomalistic investigation is this polarization more salient than in that of the study of unidentifed flying objects. Debunkers usually regard such phenomena as being, at best, involuntary misperceptions and, at worst, deliberate hoaxes; while cultists are inclined to respond to UFO experiences or reports by forming religious associations around a doctrine of salvation or instruction by celestial visitors.

At this point a word of caution is in order. Because both the term "debunker" and the term "cultist" are highly emotive, it would be easy – though ill advised – to assume that all debunking is unjustified and every cult a fraud. Most advertising, for example, merits at least partial debunking. And cults are, both etymologically and ethnologically, well-springs of culture, which includes the benefits as well as the burdens of the various ways of life that we have inherited from our ancestors.

Nonetheless, I believe that, in most cases, neither reductionism nor mystification is the best response to anomalous phenomena. What anomalists need, I think, is the ability to tolerate uncertainty indefinitely, if necessary, rather than yielding to the temptation to convert that uncertainty into the certainty of either dogmatic dismissal or equally dogmatic sacralization. Such toleration, of course, is difficult to sustain. If anomalists were to choose a figure from classical mythology to symbolize their enterprise (as futurists have chosen Proteus, the legendary prophet who eluded his questioners by continually changing his shape), that figure would probably have to be Tantalus, the royal demi-god who was punished for offenses against the gods by being kept internally close to the food and drink which he craved but never being allowed to partake of them. All anomalists are, to some degree, tantalized by the anomlies that they study. But none, probably, are more frustrated than those who, in exasperation, decide that they must, somehow, "clear this matter up, once and for all". For, if they are intellectually honest, they usually find that more intensive investigation only increases their puzzlement. At this point, they may be forgiven for toying with the paranoid notion that they are victims of that nearly universal figure in the world's folklore, The Trickster, half god and half animal, who teases and taunts, though he rarely harms, all those who seek to capture or control him.

Of the various scholars who have dared to pit themselves repeatedly against The Trickster, there is none, I think, who has done so more successfully than the Russian-American psychoanalysist Immanuel Velikovsky. Velikovsky has consistently viewed anomalies not as obstacles to understanding but as opportunities for the creation of a new polymathic paradigm, in terms of which the history of our species, our planet, and our solar system must be extensively revised. Among the anomalies that stimulated his grand reformulation are: the sporadicity of ice ages; the missing links between related organic taxa; the relatively sudden extinctions of apparently flourishing animal groups; the relatively sudden collapse of pre-Homeric civilizations in Europe and Asia; the mysteriously vitrified forts of megalithic age; and the virtual universality, in the world's mythologies, of tales of universal destruction by fire and flood. From these and other anomalies, Velikovsky inferred planetary displacements leading to terrestrial cataclysms in both historic and prehistoric times.[10] Though not mentioned by him, there are other anomalies that seem to me to strengthen his hypothesis. Among these are incomplete but widespread pieces of evidence to the effect that some pre-Achaemenid technologies and sciences were more advanced than those of later millennia[11] and that the pre-Viking Americas were visited in significant numbers by at least three different Old World peoples.[12] In each case, protohistoric catastrophes might have destroyed the delicate organizations involved and traumatically converted the memory of them into vague and dream-like oral traditions.

What seems to me to put Velikovsky into a category distinct from such "true believers" as Erich von Daniken and his followers is the fact that Velikovsky's record as a scientific prognosticator far exceeds not only theirs but also that of more conventional scientists whose view of both solar and terrestrial history is rigidly uniformitarian. Among the predictions made by Velikovsky in the 1940's which have been confirmed by subsequent discovery are these: that Jupiter produces radio emissions; that Venus is incandescently hot; and that Earth has a magnetosphere.[13] Although no major representative of the international scientific establishment will explicitly admit that Velikovsky's predictions can be ascribed to anything more than incredibly good luck, some have already admitted it implicitly by adopting his views (without, of course, any public acknowledgement of the fact that they have done so). A conspicuous example of this tactic is provided by Stephen Jay Gould, the widely read science columnist of *Natural History* Magazine. Having gradually abandoned a uniformitarian model of Earth history in favour of a catastrophist model, he has effectively covered his tracks by referring to catastrophic evolution as "punctuational change".[14]

The ostracism of Velikovsky, like that of his anomalistic orientated psychoanalytic precursor Wilhelm Reich,[15] inevitably raises the question of the nature of science. Is it primarily empirical, as it seemed to be with Thomas Edison, or theoretical, as it clearly was with Albert Einstein? Is it basically "common sense," as Bertrand Russell once maintained or "uncommon sense," as I myself have characterized it?[16] Is it invariably sober and austere, as the images both of "the ivory tower" and "men in white" suggest, or is it capable of accommodating what if often stigmatized as a "gee whiz" approach? The only unprejudicial answer to this question must surely be that it is all of these and more, and that the more diversity it can generate and sustain, the more richly productive it will be.

Such a Utopian view of science, however, probably hinders more than it helps us to understand why scientific ostracisms occur. To this end we are doubtless better advised to inquire not so much about the nature of science in the abstract as about the nature of scientific communities as social concretions. When we do, we find that they exhibit as elaborate a complex of rules, roles, and rituals as do most other human social subgroupings. And their prime rule, not surprisingly, is adherence to the basic consensus of the moment, innovative deviation being permitted only in matters of detail. Though intellectual in form, this consensus is emotional in substance: departures from it threaten the scientific community not merely with uncertainty about the nature of reality but, more seriously, with apprehension about the stability of the social order. Challengers to the consensus quickly mobilize retaliatory defences, generated by what Reich called "emotional plague" – that is, rigid conformism and compulsively punitive responses to serious non-conformity.[17]

Many scientists, in justifiable reaction against what they perceive as psychoanalytical reductionism, will object that the emotions of both the orthodox and the heterodox are equally irrelevant and that what must ultimately decide the fate of any theory is its consonance with the facts. To view facts as a court of last appeal, however, seems to be to constitute a fundamental misunderstanding of what "facts" are. Unlike objects and events, facts are not data of experience. Neither the writing of a book nor the book itself, for example, are facts. But that the book exists and that the writing occurred are facts. In other words, facts are not ultimate constituents of reality, but, at most, postulates about those constituents. They are what semanticists call low-level abstractions and so differ more in degree than in kind from theories, which are, in the same parlance, high-order abstractions.[18] Theories may indeed be gaseous, but facts, far from being "hard" as many scientists wishfully conceive them, are at best soft and malleable. To say, then, that one man's fact is another man's fancy is more than a facile quip. It is a realistic recognition of what few scholars readily concede: that no postulate is self-evident

Returning to the subject of scientific ostracism, we may take it for granted, I believe, that no scholar who focuses his attention on scientific anomalies can expect much more than marginal status in his profession. For anomalies subvert the scientific consensus. Yet it would be a mistake, I think, to assume that the more anomalistic an investigator is in his interests, the better scholar he is. Blind conformity can be and often is matched by equally blind non-conformity. And the intellectual rebel who invests more energy in his rebellion than in his intellectuality soon ceases to contribute significantly to knowledge. Moreover, once an anomalist ceases to make an honest effort to explain anomalies – or, worse yet, begins to magnify or even invent anomalies – there is a real danger that he will convert anomalistics into what might well be called "anomalitis": a morbid preoccupation with oddities and abnormalities. The inclination to multiply anomalies unnecessarily might also result from having developed a vested occupational or financial interest in them. (Freak-shows aside, however, such interest still seems to be sufficiently rare as to present only minimal hazard.)

To be sure, before Western science developed the relative rigour which has characterized it for the past three centuries, the scholarly ethos was almost as receptive to marvels, monsters, and mysteries as was the popular ethos. It may be, in fact, that the best way to characterize a magician (in the classical sense, not referring to an illusionist) is as a deliberate creator of genuine anomalies. Such anomalies range from modern medical hypnosis through self-levitation to the miracles described in various scriptures of antiquity. Rather than referring to such practices as unscientific or even anti-scientific, perhaps we should follow William Irwin Thompson in regarding them as examples of "Pythagorean science" as opposed to the "Archimedean science" to which we are accustomed.[19] In any case, as Arthur Clarke reminds us, "Every uncomprehended technology is, in principle, magic".[20]

An anomaly of intellectual history is the fact that alchemy and astrology, two disciplines which are regarded by most modern intellectuals as sterile pseudo-sciences, absorbed much of the intellectual energy of many of the best minds of the Old World ecumene for at least two millennia. While this fact alone need hardly stampede us into an orgy of disciplinary revivalism, it can and should challenge our understanding both of what these studies were and of what they did. In any case, it seems virtually certain that they did more than prepare the way for contemporary chemistry and astronomy.

In conclusion, anomalistics as I have here outlined it seems to be a worthy, if sometimes hazardous, enterprise, with a largely untapped potential for intellectual profit. If, while exploring it, we can preserve a requisitely delicate balance between sceptical imagination and imaginative scepticism, we should find anomalistics a productive as well as an enjoyable endeavour.

Roger W. Wescott

REFERENCES

1. **Roger W. Wescott,** "Anomalistics: The Outline of an Emerging Field of Investigation," Research Division, New Jersey Department of Education, Trenton, N.J., 1974 (reprinted in *Cultures Beyond the Earth,* **Arthur Harkins,** ed., Vintage Books Division, Random House, N.Y., 1975).
2. **Sabina W. Sanderson,** "Entombed Toads," *Pursuit:* (The Journal of the Society for the Investigation of the Unexplained), July, 1973, and Gary Mangiacopra "The Entombed Turtle," *Pursuit,* April, 1976.
3. **James Bailey,** *The God-Kings and the Titans,* St. Martin's Press, N.Y., 1973; p. 199.
4. **Adrian J. Desmond,** *The Hot-Blooded Dinosaurs,* Dial Press, N.Y., 1976.
5. **Eleanor Lathrop,** "The Mystery of the Prehistoric Stone Balls, "*Natural History* Magazine, 1955 (reprinted in *Strange Artifacts,* **William Corliss,** ed., The Sourcebook Project, Glen Arm, Md., 1974).
6. **Thomas Gold,** "Brontides: Natural Explosive Noises," *Science* Magazine, 27 April, 1979.
7. **C. Louis Wiedemann,** "Results of the New Jersey 'Spook Light' Study," *Vestigia Newsletter,* Spring 1977.
8. **Thomas Kuhn,** *The Structure of Scientific Revolutions,* University of Chicago Press, 1963.
9. This term is adapted from **Magoroh Maruyama's** term "paradigmatology." (M. Marayuma, "Paradigmatology and its Application to Cross-Disciplinary Communication," *World Anthropology,* Mouton, 1973.
10. **Immanuel Velikovsky,** *Worlds in Collision,* Doubleday, N.Y., 1950; *Earth in Upheaval,* Doubleday, N.Y., 1955; and *Ages in Chaos,* Doubleday, Garden City, N.Y., 1952.
11. **Andrew Tomas,** *We Are Not the First,* Putnam's, N.Y., 1971.
12. **Cyrus H. Gordon,** *Before Columbus,* Crown Press, N.Y., 1971; **Ivan Van Sertima,** *They Came Before Columbus,* Random House, N.Y., 1976; and **Alexander Von Wuthenau,** *Unexpected Faces in Ancient America,* Crown Press, N.Y., 1975.
13. **Alfred De Grazia,** ed., *The Velikovsky Affair,* University Books, New Hyde Park, N.Y., 1966; **Lewis M. Greenberg,** ed., *Velikovsky Reconsidered,* Doubleday, Garden City, N.Y., 1976; and **C.J. Ransom,** *The Age of Velikovsky,* Kronos Press, Glassboro, N.J., 1976.
14. **Stephen J. Gould** and **Niles Eldredge,** "Punctuated Equilibria: The Tempo and Mode of Evolution Reconsidered," *Paleobiology,* Vol. 3, 1977.
15. **Ola Raknes,** *Wilhelm Reich and Orgonomy,* St. Martin's Press, N.Y., 1970.
16. **Roger W. Wescott,** *The Divine Animal,* Funk and Wagnalls, N.Y., 1969; chapter 9, "Art, Science, and Religion as Windows on Reality".
17. **Wilhelm Reich,** *Selected Writings: An Introduction to Orgonomy,* Noonday Press Division, Farrar, Straus, and Cudahy, N.Y., 1961.
18. **Samuel I. Hayakawa,** *Language in Thought and Action,* Harcourt, N.Y., 1949.
19. **William Irwin Thompson,** *At the Edge of History,* Colophon Books Division, Harper, N.Y., 1972.
20. **Arthur C. Clarke,** *Profiles of the Future,* Harper, N.Y., 1963.

PROFESSOR CLASPROOT'S
FACTS YOU MIGHT FORGET
GOOD EVENING, OR TO BE MORE PRECISE — AVAST ME 'EARTIES
I AM ABOARD THE S.S. NEFERTITI AT THE INVITATION OF MY FRIEND AND COLLEAGUE DR. R. STÜRMKOCH-HARPER, PROFESSOR OF CASSANDRAIC STUDIES AT DANZIG CONSERVATORY. WHERE ARE WE HEADING, MR. MATE? ANY IDEA?
ROCKALL, SIR.
OH MOST EDIFYING... NOW... MYSTERIES OF THE OCEANS HAVE ALWAYS EXERCISED A CERTAIN FASCINATION; ESPECIALLY THE LANDLOCKED VARIETY. TAKE FOR INSTANCE THE BIRMINGHAM TRIANGLE! MY RESEARCHES BEGAN WITH THE DISAPPEARANCE OF A YOUNG CITIZENS' BAND RADIO ENTHUSIAST (MR. KEVIN TROUGH, OR "BIG BINKY" TO HIS CB CHUMS) IN MID-SENTENCE...
OKAY-POKAY GITCHER EARS ON BIG BUDDIES, THIS IS BIG BINKY WACKING A JUBBLY GOON-SQUAT WIDE OPEN 10-8 Y'KNOW? YADIG?
SUDDENLY HE STARTED SPEAKING GIBBERISH
GOOD GRIEF! I SAY, YOU WON'T BELIEVE THIS, BUT THIS ISN'T ON MY AA GUIDE...
WHA...?
Y'WHA?
HUH?
I DON'T COPY BIG BINKY
PUBLIC OPINION WAS UNANIMOUS...
SO WE LOSE A C.B.'ER, ALREADY... HONESTLY — WHO GIVES A TOSS?
BUT THERE ARE OTHER EFFECTS, MY RESEARCHES FIND — HAVE YOU NOTICED...
...SERVICE STATION TOILET ROLLS DISAPPEAR — UNLESS YOU ONLY GO FOR A WIDDLE?
...A MOTORWAY DRIVE LEAVES YOUR CAR MYSTERIOUSLY STREWN WITH HALF-MELTED BOILED SWEETS?
...TIME EXPANDS, ALLOWING YOU TO READ A NEWSPAPER COVER-TO-COVER, SMOKE YOUR LAST CIGARETTE, SNOOZE, DRINK A CAN OF LAGER — AND YET ALWAYS BE 28 MILES FROM WATFORD GAP?
RAPIST GERBIL LATEST
THESE ARE BUT A FEW OF THE MYSTERIES SURROUNDING THE M1, M5, M6 AXIS. I AM ALWAYS PLEASED TO HEAR OF OTHERS. BUT PERHAPS THE MOST ASTOUNDING AND GROTESQUE ENIGMA OF ALL, TO WHICH NO EXPLANATION HAS EVEN BEEN SUGGESTED, IS THIS: WHAT STRANGE POWER BEYOND THE BOUNDS OF REASON DRAWS ANYONE TOWARDS BIRMINGHAM IN TH FIRST PLACE?
GOOD LORD, THE WAVES ARE BREAKING OVER THE... THE...
BULWARKS, SIR
HOW DARE YOU!

The Runamo Runes.

Inexplicably, the bibliography to our article on the Runamo Runes [FT35 pp14-18] vanished into the postal equivalent of the Bermuda Triangle and had to be omitted from last issue. As an addendum we give it here.

BIBLIOGRAPHY

Inexplicably, the bibliography to our article on the Runamo Runes [FT35pp14-18] vanished into the postal equivalent of the Bermuda Triangle and had to be omitted from that issue. As an addendum we give it here.

AA Afzelius, *Svenska Folkets Sagohafder,* vol 1 (Stockholm, 1839).

JJ Berzelius, and **Sven Nilsson,** papers in *Vitterhets-Historiska och Antiqvitets Akademiens Handlingar,* Vols 14-16 (Stockholm, 1838-1841).

Erik Dahlberg, *Suecia Antiqua et Hodierna* (Stockholm, 1661-1678).

Encyclopedias: Danish, *Salmonsens Konversationliksikon,* vols 16 & 20, entries 'Magnusson' and 'Runamo' (Copenhagen, 1924, 1926); Swedish, *Nordisk Familjebok,* vols 17 & 23, entries 'Magnusson' and 'Runamo' (Stockholm, 1912, 1916).

Folke Wiren (ed), *Brakne-Hoby* (Karlshamn, 1962).

Saxo Grammaticus, *Gesta Danorum* (Paris 1514). The standard edition may be *Saxonis Gesta Danorum,* edited by J.Olrik and H.Raeder (1931). There are several editions in Danish.

Olaus Magnus, *Historia de Gentibus Septentrionalibus,* book 5, chapters 3-9 (Rome, 1555). As far as we know there is no modern English edition, but one exists in Swedish, *Historia om de Nordiska Folken* (Stockholm, 1976).

Finnur Magnusson, *Runamo og Runerne* (Copenhagen, 1841). The original Magnusson committee report was published in *Vidensk. Selskabs Hist. og Filos. Afh.,* but is included in his magnum opus *Runamo og Runerne.*

John Michell & RJM Rickard, *Phenomena* (London, 1977).

John Michell, *Simulacra* (London, 1979).

John Michell, *Megalithomania* (to be published by Thames and Hudson, London, in 1982).

August Strindberg, *Svenska Folket,* vol 2 (Stockholm, 1882, 1974).

JJA Worsaae, *Runamo og Braavalleslaget* (Copenhagen 1844).

•

Sven Rosen - Bob Rickard

A copperplate engraving by C F Christensen (in Magnusson's book Runamo og Runerne*) who joined the official expedition to Runamo in 1833. It shows Magnusson himself (left) kneeling to study the marks, and the geologist J G Forschhammer (right), as they follow the natural meander across the clearing.*

They turned their back on the world and became voluntary hermits and wildmen. Here are a few of the tales of today's real outsiders.

HERMITS AND WILDMEN

The Wildman or Wodewose was a durable character in Mediaeval folklore. As the unified mythical coherence of the Mediaeval world dissolved, he gradually transmogrified from an archetype of chaos, insanity and heresy to one of enlightenment and harmony with nature, a symbol of all that man should try to achieve. But his significance was never clear-cut: he could be at once savage and sublime, an image of both desire and punishment. Today, as Raoul Vaneigem puts it, "the wave of materiality has washed out to sea the remains of the myth it has wrecked", but flotsam and jetsam keep floating back. The fascination with the wildman continues and is rekindled with reports of feral children and unknown hairy hominids. The first two cases below exemplify the ambivolent nature of the Wildman. The first is animal-like, the second more akin to Rousseau's Noble Savage.

In February 1980 a man was found in the mountains of Venda in South Africa, and was identified as Daniel Machavi, 36. By the time he was caught, he had already eaten his way through 30 square metres of grass and was seen scampering up and down a tree like a monkey.

"He has difficulty in walking upright and feels more at home on all fours", said Mr Joel Makhuva, secretary-general of Masia. "He understands Venda but has great difficulty in talking. His speech is almost incomprehensible. Luckily he had a reference book on him, which enabled us to identify him. No-one knows anything about him. All he could say was that he wanted grass and water. He rejected cooked food and was uneasy when taken indoors."

The "animal man", whose hands were hardened through years of crawling, made off into the bush before the police could be called. A search revealed no trace of him. (*South African S. Times* 17 Feb 1980.

In 1956, a well-educated Australian of 27 called Michael Fomenko, sickened by the world of humans, retreated into the steamy snake-and-crocodile infested jungles of north-eastern Australia. He hunted wild boar with a knife, and birds wth a bow and arrow which he had made himself. Now—because he has slowed with age and a leg that was ripped open by an attacking pig—he shoots game with a rifle which he bought with his bi-weekly disability cheque of a hundred dollars. He occasionally appears at Smith's Store in the settlement of Ayton on the edge of the jungle, where he spends his allowance on food and sweets for the neighbouring aborigines. (*National Enquirer*, 6 Oct 1981.)

RUNNING FROM THE WARS

D.B. Benson lived wild in the Kiamichi mountains of Oklahoma for 34 years. As an 18-year old he was drafted into the Army Air Corps in September 1942 and was stationed in Texas. He was bullied mercilessly as an illiterate hick, and within a year he went AWOL. Back home in Heavener, Oklahoma, a friend told him the military police were after him and that he faced execution. Believing this to be true, he fled to the mountains with a bundle of clothing, a pistol, some ammo and a knife.

When the ammo ran out, he killed rabbits, squirrels and birds with stones. His throwing arm was deadly. When his Army clothes had become rags he found a coffee can key and sharpened it on a rock to make a needle. An old sock provided thread to mend his clothes. These finally fell away, and he fashioned a loin-cloth out of an old piece of demin he found.

"I completely lost touch with humanity," he said. "I talked to the animals—even sang to the squirrels. Living in the outdoors I rarely got sick. When I did I'd take to a cave for a few days until the illness cleared up. Fresh streams were my bathtub, and fine sand became my soap. Soon I learned how to catch fish bare-handed for food."

After some years, Benson found a dog. He named it "Dog". "We became inseperable. He slept at my feet and hunted for both of us." More years passed and Dog died of old age. Benson felt even more lonely. Middle age was creeping up on him. He could not move around as easily as before, and even a minor injury could keep him down for days.

Finally, in 1977, at the age of 53, he walked up to his parents' home and knocked on the door. His mother and father, aged 90 and 83 respectively, were no doubt suitably astonished. Eighteen months later he obtained an "other-than-honourable" discharge from the Army, and became a free man... or had he lost his freedom? (*National Enquirer*, 14 July 81; *D. Mail*, 1 Aug 79.)

Hiding in the mountains certainly seems preferable to hiding between four walls, like the Ukrainian Dmitri Kozlovsky, who spent 36 years on rotting mattresses in two fetid tomb-like structures in fear of his past. At the beginning of the war he fought in the Soviet

Army but was taken prisoner by the Germans, under whom he worked as a bricklayer. He eventually escaped, but did not join the pro-Soviet Ukrainian restistance, fearing retribution because he had been given extra rations for good work performance. His family hid him in 1944.

The Soviet newspaper *Socialist Industry* said "his eyes grew accustomed to the dark and his hearing became as sharp as a beast." In December 1980, when he was found by police after all his relatives and close friends had died, he had forgotten how to speak and was filthy, unshaven and evil-smelling. He had lost all sense of time. "He stood and trembled as if from fever and cried in a pitiful child's voice and tears poured from his colourless eyes eaten up by the darkness" the newspaper said. It added that he had not been punished and was about to start work at a boiler plant, at the age of 62. (*AP* 12 June 1981)

Also on the run from Stalin —or so they thought—were Stefan Pietroszys and his wife Genovefa, Lithuanians who after the war emigrated to Australia. In 1951 three men dragged Stefan into a car and, believing the KGB were on their heels, the couple went into hiding. For 28 years they lived in virtual secrecy in a cave and crude bush hut only 200 yards from the houses at Killarney Heights, North Sydney. If anyone approached, they melted into the surrounding bush. They wore clothes made from patches of material and would scrounge the bush around their cave for berries and edible roots, occasionally trapping small rodents. For the last ten years they had some contact with the outside world in the person of Major Ivan Unicomb of the Salvation Army, and they occasionally accepted food parcels. Finally, in February 1979, Genovefa Pietroszys died aged 68, and her 81-year-old husband was taken to a hostel. But he said he wanted to go back to the cave to die where his wife had died. (*Reuters* 12 Feb, *Morning Bulletin* (Queensland) 13 Feb 1979.)

Robert Petee of Michigan also spent 28 years in hiding. Posted to Berlin in 1949, he went AWOL in May 1951, after being blamed for something he claims he had not done. He was hidden by his German girlfriend in her mother's two-bedroomed flat in the Freidenau district of West Berlin. The mother became frail with age, and in 1961 Petee's fiancee found a two-roomed flat in the Schoeneberg area. He was smuggled out from one address to the other by night. The new flat had two rooms, but one had a balcony and he feared being spotted. So he spent the remaining 18 years in the other room. In the Autumn of 1978 Petee's fiancee died of cancer and he considered suicide, but found he was unable to jump in front of a train. Finally he turned himself in, aged 52, and in the Spring of 1979 he was in Washington being treated for a hernia.(*D. Telegraph,* 8 May, *Midnight Globe* 5 June 1979.)

Michael Fomenko, a real-life Tarzan [Photo: Nat.Enquirer *6 Oct 1981]*

Men in many countries hid for considerable periods after the Second World War. Many readers will be familiar with the stories of the various Japanese who held out in the Pacific refusing to admit defeat or unaware that the war was finished. One such was Shoichi Yokoi, now 65, who spent 28 years in a cave on Guam. He was finally discovered by shrimp fishermen in 1972. His cave, a four-hour jeep ride through the jungle, is now a tourist attraction and many of his home-made domestic items are on show in the Guam museum in Agana. (*UPI* 25 Feb 1979).

Janez Rus, 62, of Zalna, near Ljubljana in Yugoslavia, was hidden in a loft by his brother for 32 years. He was suspected of collaborating with the Nazis, and was posted missing, believed dead. His bother died in 1977, and he was discovered. The irony was that a Communist court had cleared him of all suspicion in 1947!

Protasio Martin, 77, hid in the basement of his home near Cercedilla, 30 miles from Madrid, when Franco won the Civil War in 1939. He had been an anti-Fascist mayor, and he feared the firing squad. His wife and four children kept him supplied with food and newspapers for 38 years. He even waited two years after Franco's death before emerging in 1977.

Perhaps the most ingenious fugitive was Hsueh Ching Tao who in 1940 had belonged to a Chinese guerilla band under a bandit who surrendered to the Japanese and become a traitor. After three years in which he rose to company commander, Hsueh took some troops and went over to the Communists. But later he fled because he was afraid.

For 24 years he masqueraded as a deaf-mute, sleeping concealed in mosquito netting with a scarf tied around his mouth to keep him from talking in his sleep. Finally he saw an item in a newspaper concerning China's 1st January 1980 criminal law and its time limit for the prosecution of certain crimes. He studied the text of the law carefully, decided it was safe for him to talk, and astonished his fellow-workers in a Jiangxi province crematorium by doing so, according to the *Yangcheng Evening News* (*Sunday People,* 15 Jan 78; *D. Mirror,* 19 July 1977; *New Standard*, 4 Mar 81.)

MODERN CAVE-MEN

Living in caves or tunnels, for reasons other than guilt or fear of the past, is frequently met with. This may be from agroaphobia or some atavistic yearning for a prehistoric life-style.

Keith Payne told us recently of this example of cave-dwelling: In 1706 an illiterate Cornish farm labourer visited the "Cheesecoving", an ancient site on Bodmin Moor near Rilla Mill. The site is made up primarily of wind-eroded stone stacks on some of which are carved a series of related grooves which seem like star patterns. The labourer never came down. Abandoning his wife and seven children, he became a hermit in a small cave made of a huge slab of stone over a fissure. He never spoke again, and after 24 years he died in his cave. On the slab he carved the symbol illustrated here.

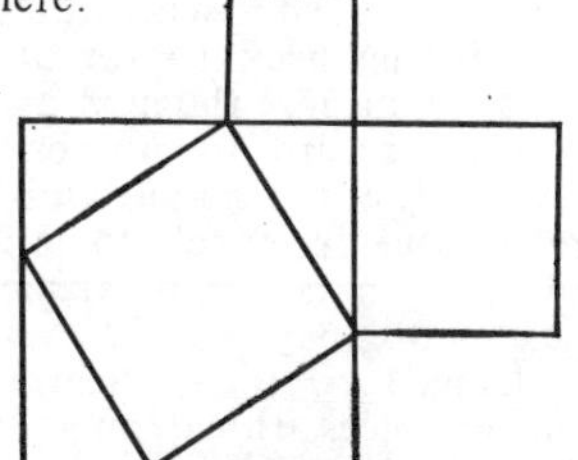

On 11 November 1977, police finally caught up with James Horton, Jr., 42, when they trailed him to a 4-by-6 foot man-made cave in Santa Ana Canyon, California. For over a year this "phantom of the freeway" had been hurling rocks with great strength and accuracy at passing cars. At least 70 cars had shattered windscreens, dented hoods and bodies. A deputy sherriff who gave chase was stabbed. The phantom eluded search parties by building camouflaged bridges across streams and setting false "camp-fires". He told his captors he lived in the hole because he "didn't want to be bothered by people." (*UPI* 14 Nov 77.)

Also in 1977, residents of the far-west Texan community of Post were trying to find out who was living in a nearby cliff dwelling. Garza County Sherriff Jim Pippin had been trying, unsuccessfully, to catch the hermit for three months. The cave was a natural hole in a limestone cliff which had been augmented by mud-and-stone walls on two sides. The sheriff had looked in and discovered canned goods, a home-made wardrobe, a sleeping bag and a CB radio, which he confiscated. (*San Antonio Evening News,* 8 June 77.)

Bricklayer Charlie Port, 44 lived for 18 months in 1977-8 in a disused sewer in the grounds of a mental hospital where he had been sent as a schizophrenic. His letters were addressed to The Tunnel, Knowle Hospital, Fareham, Hants, including his NHS medical card sent by his doctor. He lived on scraps stolen from the wards and pig swill which he made into stew. He was finally arrested in October 1978 after complaints about missing food.

The authorities allowed him to use the day centre where he received one meal a day five days a week. At night and during weekends he lived in the sewer. They refused to accomodate him, saying he was perfectly sane. The rat-infested sewer was 6 foot across, 7 foot high and 30 feet deep, and was next to the hospital's rubbish dump. For five months another patient, Carol Williamson lived with him in the sewer, and left to have his baby

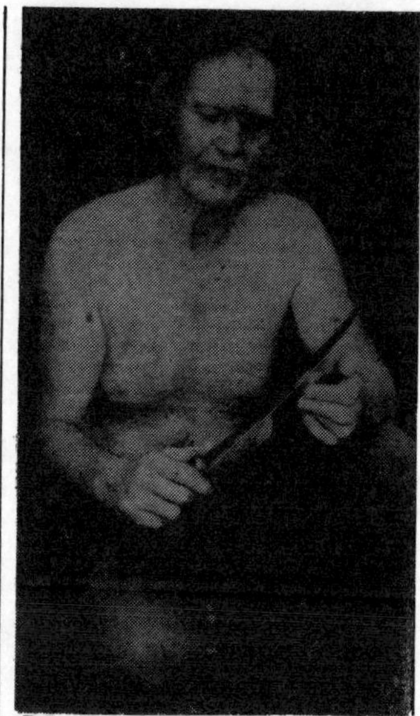

DB Benson, in the woods he called home for 34 years [Photo: Nat.Enquirer *14 July 1981]*

in another hospital. She read him Donne's poems by candlelight as water dripped from the walls. Their one luxury was a spring mattress abandoned by the hospital.

A senior psychiatrist at the hospital, Dr Geoffrey Snape, admitted that nearly all of the staff knew of the tunnel lovers. "We thought it would be an infringement of their personal freedom if we encroached on their adopted way of life", he said.

Meanwhile, another 44-year-old man was living in another mental hospital tunnel. In January 1979 he had been living for two years in the communications tunnels below Langbro Hospital in Sweden. He stole his food from transport trolleys. Dr Gunnar Knave at the hospital rashly called this "a unique case". An Ombudsman intervened, and the man was put in an open ward. He sealed his windows to keep out the daylight, and sometimes he disappeared at night to roam the tunnels again.

The following July, Mr Roy Rohan, 66, a former insurance agent who was swindled out of thousands of pounds in the 1960's, died in the tunnel in Museum Gardens, York, which had been his home for nearly five years...with the blessing of the authorities. He slept on a park bench in the tunnel, and was visited regularly by many friends. Said one: "He was a gentleman and everybody loved him."

A month later, a four-star subterranean home was found in Flanders. Gravediggers at Ledeberg cemetary, near Ghent, opened a three-roomed family crypt in preparation for a burial and found a bed on a coffin, a gas cooker, sewing machine, electric razor, radio, dishwasher, coffee machine, books, records, rifle and rotting food. Electricity was provided by a stolen car batery placed outsdie the grave.

Police said Jules Roberts, 47, a well-known local tramp who had been in jail since 1977, admitted to having lived there, although it was not stated for how long. (*Guardian* & *D. Mail* 15 June; *Sunday People*, 17 June; *D. Telegraph* 29 Mar & 23 July; *Herald Trib* & *D. Telegraph*, 10 Aug 1979.)

For more than 30 years, Paul Wuketsewitz, 79, has lived in his underground home in Petersfield, Manitoba. Only a stove-pipe chimney poking from a barren field identifies his home, which he has shored up with posts, scap lumber and straw. Once or twice a month he peddles his aging bicycle into Clandeboye, 15 kilometres away, to cash his pension cheque and buy groceries. Dim light filters in from a window in the roof, illuminating a vast wood supply which he obtains in exchange for potatoes grown on his garden plots. He emigrated from Vienna 52 years ago, and worked as a labourer in Ontario and Winnipeg, before buying the 16-hectare lot where he now lives.

For 7 years, Andy Fields, 37, known as the Hippie Monster, lived in a coastal cave at Bolinas in California. He survived by poking through trash cans and exchanging his abstract paintings for meals. "He was eccentric, in a grating way," said a neighbour. "He would walk around screeching and whooping like a seagull."

He told a friend that he would be leaving soon on his surfboard to hail passing ships in an attempt to find a dentist to fix his teeth. Sculptor Joyce Clements said she was looking out her window on 13th September 1981 when she saw the Hippie Monster paddling out to sea. "He kept going further and further," she said. "I couldn't believe it. He got about two miles out and I couldn't see him any more." His surfboard was found four miles out to sea, but he had disappeared. (*Niagara Falls Review*, 4 Nov 80 & 18 Sep 81.)

Next issue, I'll continue these withdrawals from society with cases of the Oblomov Syndrome and grisly episodes in family life.

Credits: Tom Adams, Larry Arnold, Janet & Colin Bord, Peter Hope Evans, Mark Hall, Chris Holtzhausen, Valerie Martin, Paul Screeton, Jeff Seward, Anthony Smith, Dwight Whalen, Jake Williams. Ion Will • **PRAdeGS.**

Some tall stories from the other side of this world.

I LEFT MY HEART IN . . . CHIKMAGALUR

Maralyn Rabinovich, 41, single, a San Francisco painter and hypnotherapist, went to India in early 1978, and ended up in Mysore with two friends, Pesho Mehta, 23, and Firdaus Daubush, 25. They went to Chikmagalur intending to visit a 'cursed' cave lying 26 miles northeast. They got their first warning at the hotel in Chikmagalur: 'If you enter the cave with evil reasons, your heart will vanish', and this warning was apparently given them ten times by various people. They didn't pay any attention.

They took a car to the cave, and the driver told them that cars frequently broke down within a mile or two of the place. Theirs did too, and the three of them walked to the cave. Inside they found an old man who appeared to be the cave's keeper, who reeled off a list of Mehta's ancestors before ordering him to sit on a glittering throne. When he got up, he discovered that five hours had passed, though it seemed like he'd just sat down. Before they left the old man warned them again that if they'd come with impure motives, their hearts would vanish.

After leaving, Maralyn claimed to have gained psychic powers in the cave, and was excited at the prospect of using them to make money. But she also told Mehta they must find another car, because they were in danger. So they found another car, and when they were driving back to the airport at Mangalore the next day for their return to Bombay, they saw the first car gutted by fire; and the driver told them it had just burst into flame. Back in Bombay, Maralyn was a changed woman, hearing strange voices threatening to kill her and complaining about dark spirits. On March 26th (but 1978 or 1979 isn't clear), 14 days after visiting the cave, she was found dead in a hotel room locked from the inside. The bed hadn't been slept in.

Comes the post mortem:

Maralyn's body had apparently had a temperature of 100 degrees Farenheit when found, and in her stomach was a "strange luminous green liquid" which it was impossible to analyze. And, of course, she had no heart. There were no visible marks on any part of her anatomy, but the heart was gone, the vena cava, pulmonary artery and vein, and aorta were cut off, and there was no trace of blood in that area.

Okay, that's the story, as told in the *National Enquirer* 21 August 79, but it strikes me even a whale wouldn't swallow a tale like that! Even if we pass by the, uh, 'heart' of the story, the cave isn't identified. What were Maralyn and Daubush doing in the five hours Mehta was on the throne?

Would a hired cabbie wait five hours for his clients? They passed the burned-out car on the way to Mangalore; but Mangalore is south-west of Chikmagalur, and the cave's north-east. And presumably the cabbie was just standing round next to it when they passed, so he could tell them all about it. And who measured the temperature of Maralyn's corpse? If you'd just (presumably) broken into a hotel room and found a corpse, would you take its temperature?

No, tell me another one . . .

DRIVING THEM KWAKU

An oldie but goodie, from the *Daily Mirror* 16 Feburary 1968.

A brave man, was 23-year old Samuel K Nuhu. He actually volunteered to let Kwaku Mark cut his throat. But Kwaku 'the Incredible' was a magician, and obviously one of some repute . . . otherwise Sam's relatives wouldn't have been in the watching crowd in the village of Mando, in Central Ghana, when Kwaku did the dastardly deed. Anyway, Sam got his throat cut, bled to death and was promptly shoved into a coffin and buried. The cops were watching too, though, and if Kwaku didn't make good his promise to resurrect Sam in three days, he was going to have to magic his way out of a jail cell.

Well, the third day arrived, the crowds gathered, and so did a whole detachment of police. Enter Kwaku. A few tricks to warm the crowd up, and then Kwaku ordered the coffin exhumed. The lid was removed, and inside . . .

The coffin was full of tins of Ovaltine, baked beans and baby food!

Uproar!

And then . . . out of the crowd walked Samuel K Nuhu, alive and well, dressed in white, carrying a stick, two parakeets and a bible.

Sam explained that he'd been living under a tree for three days with some animals, and he hadn't been aware of anything since he'd volunteered to help Kwaku.

A happy end to another performance by Kwaku the Incredible. But the crowd . . . would you believe it?

They *booed*!

Credit: *P.R. Thomas.* • **SM**

As a prelude to a forthcoming article on toads-in-the-holes by Paul Screeton, we have gathered a few loose notes on captive croakers here; others may be found in *Phenomena,* and in *Living Wonders* by John Michell & Bob Rickard (to be published later this year).

TOADS IN THE WOODPILE

The commonest form of captive croaker is one imprisoned in stone, but they are also found in isolated cavities deep in the trunks of trees. Examples will be found in *Phenomena* by Michell and Rickard, and in their forthcoming *Living Wonders*, but here are a few that came our way recently.

Our first item is one unearthed by Dwight Whalen during his voyage through the backfile of *The Evening Journal* (St Catherines, Ontario), dated 21 Dec 1865. It reads: "Recently Mr Angus McDonald, of the township of [name looks like 'Mar', the microfilm copy is indistinct], cut down a white ash tree, and on splitting it, a live frog was found embedded in the wood. The tree was about 15 inches in diameter, and perfectly sound; the cavity in which the frog had been enclosed appeared as if carved out for its reception. The question of how the frog got there would be an interesting one for naturalists." Amen.

A similar story was clipped by George Ives from the *D.Star* 30 May 1905 [see FT32p30]: that at Pulham St Mary, Norfolk, a toad quickly died after its liberation from an oak tree by a gang of fellers. This note recently appeared as item 85 in the series 'Notes and Queries' in *Lantern* (Autumn 1981). Curiously Fort did not include much in the way of embedded amphibians, and this is not one of his gleanings, even though 1905 was one of his favourite years.

We also received a letter from Jorg Ehring, in Germany who was responding to *Phenomena*, saying that he had seen a toad released from a wooden prison. "In May 1975, a group of German girl and boy scouts (including myself) made a camp in the ruin of a castle called Sporkenborg, near Bad Ems/Lahn. I and a few other boys went down the hill to look for wood. I pulled out the stump of a felled tree, and cut the base because it was so heavy. I got a terrible shock. Inside was sitting a big toad, bigger than I've ever seen before. The cavity in the wood fitted the form of the toad and was devoid of any crack or connecting hole, until I split the stump. The toad was injured on one leg in the action, but jumped off quickly enough. Our dog caught her and brought her back, but she escaped a second time and could not be found. The toad was like other toads, but bigger and nearly all black."

CONCRETE FROGS

The following account appeared in *Animals* (April 1972 p178), and is a letter from Eric Mackley, a gas-fitter, of Barnstaple, Devon, to Sir Julian Huxley.

"It became desirable to widen the Barnstaple-Ilfracombe road some years ago, taking in part of the long gardens in front of a row of bungalows which had gas meters housed just inside the front gates; these of course had to be moved back to the new front wall line. The meter-houses were brick-walled but rather massively concrete-floored, and the concrete had to be broken up to allow me to get at the pipes for extension. My mate was at work with a sledge hammer when he dropped it suddenly and said, 'That looks like a frog's leg.' We both bent down and there was the frog. Being fond of animals the sledge was set aside and I cut the rest of the block carefully. We released 23 perfectly formed but minute frogs which all hopped away to the flower garden . . ."

Farmer Heino Seppi and the fish that went against the grain [Photo: Vassa *17 Jan 1979]*

We have records going back many centuries and attempts to explain the phenomenon of entombed amphibians fall into similar repetitative categories. The editor of *Animals* offered the perennial favourite: that the tiny creatures, or fertilized spawn fell through minute cracks to hatch and grow. Careful observers – and there have been a few – often discount the idea because of 1) the depth of the cavity in stone or tree, or 2) the readily apparent lack of communicating holes, or 3) the curious detail, often reported, of the cavity and frog or toad being a tight fit, with the former taking the form of the unfortunate within. The editors of *Animals* abandoned their theory when Mr Tackley told them the concrete had been compacted and was without cracks. Mr Tackley's own theory is, "that whoever originally mixed the concrete took up frog spawn with the water from the stagnant stream opposite; the spawn found its way into the middle of the concrete base; and when the tadpoles hatched they cannibalised until the hole was completely filled with small but perfectly formed frogs." The merits of this theory we leave for the criticism of others, but we would have thought that the concrete would have set around the relatively small mass of the spawn-cluster (if that's the way it happened) long before the critters hatched, not giving them much room. Secondly they would have to survive the added hazards of the toxicity of liquid concrete and the heat generated by the setting process on top of the rough and tumble of mixing, pouring and compacting. Another interesting point, says Mackley, is the speed with which the littler sleepers roused from their torpid state and hopped away "after over a quarter of a century".

This case is almost unique in our knowledge. Hardly comparable is the case of a green terrapin, at Fort Worth, Texas, asleep on the ground when wet concrete was poured over it, probably in 1974. According to the Fort Worth *Star-Telegram* 21 August 1975, it had not been completely enclosed by concrete and had lain in its prison for about a year. It died the day after its release.

THE FROG AND PEA PUZZLE

On 9 Dec 1980 a farmer, using a mechanical harvester on pea-fields near Colac, south of Melbourne in New South Wales, stopped to examine his pickings. He was astonished to find tiny frogs in a few of the pods. In fact four were found half out of the 2-inch long pods, each with a pea in its mouth. The farmer said the frogs were dead when he found them. "It looks as though they were born inside the pods, tried to eat their way out, then choked on the peas," he speculated. What? All four of them? Unless Australian frogs have learned how to open pods on the vines and pop in for a pea? If this is a new behaviour pattern, or even if it isn't, neither the farmer nor ourselves have heard the like before.

FISH IN TREE

This has to be one of the strangest datums we have come across. In *Phenomena* is illustrated the image of a duck in a tree (p91), but here we have an apparently genuine record of a fish discovered inside a tree.

In October 1969 farmer Heino Seppi was occupied transporting lumber from the woods of Yrjo Kanto, near Sikasalo, in the Palloneva region of western Finland. The trees had been felled the previous winter and were cut into lengths of a few metres. When Mr Seppi split an aspen log, he found its middle rotten, forming a hollow in which a dried fish over 40cms was found. It resembled a perch, and if so it is a large size for a perch (NB: Mr Ehring's comment about the larger than normal size of his released toad.) There was no clue as to how the fish got there and all who saw the evidence (see photo) were baffled.

Our Finnish correspondent, Tuuri Heporauta, who clipped this story from *Vaasa* 17 Nov 1969, has made heroic attempts to locate the farmer, but had no luck to date – pity!

Credits: *Jorg Ehring, Tuuri Heporauta, Lantern, Gary Mangiacopra, Andy Thompson, Dwight Whalen, Ion Will* • *RJMR.*

We are not ones to swallow tales of miracles without some resistance in the skeptical department, and yet... We accept that there are more things in heaven and earth, Horatio, than you can shake a stick at...

BLOOD AND TEARS

Following the scandal [see FT33p35] of the 'Weeping Madonna' of Lomello, near Pavia, in which suspicion was cast upon the claimed miraculous cures of pilgrims after a man was accused of squirting coloured water at the statue, Italy's latest sensation, a Madonna statue that weeps blood, is holding up well. This effigy is owned by Gaetano Bella, aged 73, and is set in the rock wall of her home in Niscima, Sicily. Mrs Bella and friends were moving the statue from its niche, on 30 August 1980, after prayers, when a trickle of red liquid from its left eye was noticed. News of the prodigy spread quickly and the flow of 'blood' was matched by a flow of pilgrims. It seems that this was not the first time this had happened to Signora Bella's statue. It first bled – or wept blood – back in 1973. At that time it was investigated by Mgr Alfredo Garsia, the Bishop of Caltanisetta, who was not convinced. He ruled that the phenomenon was not supernatural, and banned pilgrimages and veneration – but they came anyway. Over the intervening seven years, crowds must have dwindled, and cynics will find something to nod about in the fact that Mrs Bella's statue started up again only a few days after the 'Weeping Madonna' of Lomello caught the public eye. Naturally the news of the resumption reached the ears of Mgr Garsia, still Bishop of this central region of Sicily. Once more he was unconvinced. "As far as I am concerned," he said, "the conclusions I arrived at seven years ago are still valid." But being a practical man, he ordered the local priest to keep an eye on things, and that a sealed glass case be put around the statue. "I want to find out if the event is attributable to natural or supernatural causes," he explained. The story so far comes from the *Western Mail*, and the *Portsmouth News*, both of 20 August 1980. Both sources say the blood came from the cheek, not the eye, as claimed in *D. Telegraph* 3 Sept 1980.

The usual long silence that we have come to expect after astonishing news ensued. Then we were even more astonished to find a further report. Garsia's skepticism had taken a knock (if you'll forgive the unintended religious pun). Here we learn that the statue, representing the icon known as 'Our Lady of Lourdes', continued to bleed, though sporadically, in its sealed glass case. Eventually the Bishop had to come off his mountain and see for himself – According to the *Saturday Weekly*(M'sia) 7 Feb81 "Monsignor Garcia ran from the grotto, hands flailing in the air, shouting, 'I've seen it! I've seen it!' " A convertion which will improve the pulling power of Mrs Bella's Madonna manyfold.

SANTA LUCRE

Back in FT33, p34 we told of the impounding, by the Public Prosecutor of Piacenza, in Italy's Lombardy, of the enormous assets held by the family of 'Mama Rosa', otherwise known as Rosa Quattrini. The fortune developed after Mama Rosa had a vision of the BVM, high in a pear tree, in the garden of her home at San Damiano on 16 October 1964. Mama was given a message by the Virgin Mary, and afterwards the pear tree bloomed. It is recorded that that October was a mild one; even so it is unusual for trees to bloom so late, but not unknown.

Millions came to pray at Mama's miraculous tree, and despite a proclamation by the Bishop of Piacenza forbidding priests and public to worship there, or to believe in the vision, millions still do. Mama's family were quick to cash in on the pilgrim trade. In 1974 she bought a 109-acre farm and house. Later the family accumulated land and property, pilgrim hotels and millions of pounds in donations. When Mama Rosa died, aged 71, in September 1981, she left her estate, estimated by some to be worth over £2.5 million to the Pope. All the Pope has to do to collect is to revoke the decision of the Bishop of Piacenza and ratify the vision as genuine. Ironically the chief complaint, upon which the Public Prosecutor acted to freeze Mama's assets, came from the Church, who alleged massive fraud. It'll take quite a while to sort this all out – if ever. *Guardian, Shropshire Star* 8 Oct; *D.Mail, The Sun* 9 Oct; *S.Express* 18 Oct 1981.

Outside of the religious context, we have a number of records of trees blooming etc out of season. I can't find them right now, but the most recent one is to hand – *Daily Star* 31 Oct 1981: that an apple tree belonging to Bill Bessey, of Badsley Moor Lane, Rotherham, burst, suddenly and unaccountably, into flower. October again .... If this was Italy and not Yorkshire Mr Bessey might be quids in by now.

HEAVENLY RIDE

Here's one for those who cannot accept that the stuff of folklore is continually created, even today. A coachload of 54 Spanish pilgrims, returning from the shrine at the site of the famous BVM vision at Fatima, Portugal, were somewhat startled to discover that their driver was not driving – he had his head bowed, eyes closed and hands together in prayer. Yet the bus continued at speeds of up to 50mph, turning corners, changing gears, winking lights, in a smooth ride for 20 miles before it pulled into the roadside and the driver, Juan Garcia, 50, woke up. The passengers, including a priest of 40yrs standing, Fr Cesar Trapiello, drew up an affidavit, now being studied by the Bishop of Leon, who has not rejected it outright. According to the priest, at first there was panic, but it soon became clear the bus "was not running out of control, but that somebody, some power, had taken over." Before he woke, the passengers all swear they heard a sombre voice come from the driver's mouth, saying: "I am your brother, Archangel Michael. God had the grace to drive the bus himself as a test of faith for our brother, the driver." Garcia himself remembers nothing, except an overwhelming compulsion to pray, and seems to be genuinely unaware of what happened between closing his eyes and waking up later. There is no date given in either report. *D.Telegraph* 19 Oct; *S.Express* 25 Oct 1981.

GUT REACTION

After John Paul II was shot earlier this year, we learned of an interesting debate occupying the attention of theologians as they waited for the Pope to recover. One of the assassin's bullets damaged the Pope's intestine, and about 25 inches of his inner-tube had to be removed. Now usually internal organs removed from dead Popes during embalming are deposited in large terracotta jars in a vault, closed to the public, in the church known as Sacra Praecordia, near the Trevi Fountain in Rome. As far as we know the question has never before arisen about organs removed from Popes still living. The mood is that the Pope's pipes should be potted for posterity, as a ready-made relic for the undoubted Process of Canonization which will be urged following John-Paul's eventual death. *Toronto Star* 17 May 1981.

AND NOW FOR SOMETHING COMPLETELY DIFFERENT

Bleeding statues and weeping icons you know about – but are you ready for an iron statue of an Indian goddess that menstrates? This bizarre phenomenon came to our attention in an article on the Mahadeva Temple, at Chengannur, in Kerala, in the magazine, *Probe*

India (August 1981).

The origin of the story is lost in antiquity. It is said that Parvati visited the area with Shiva, shortly after their marriage, to see the sage Agastya, when suddenly Parvati began to menstruate. According to tradition she separated from her husband for three days, meditating on a rock, until she was "clean again". A shrine grew up on the site in the reign of King Vanchipuza Tamburan, after blood flowed from the stone when a girl sharpened her sickle upon it. The rock was consecrated according to a tradition which recognizes phallic simulacra as *swayambhu linga* (ie spontaneously formed images of Shiva's penis.) The temple was alleged first built by a legendary genius of that province, Perunthachan, who is also said to have miraculously found and excavated at the site a metal idol of the goddess Bhagawati. According to the chief priest of the temple, the original building burnt down long ago, but a manuscript by Perunthachan had been found which foretold the fire and the location of a secretly buried replica of the first devine image. The temple today contains the *lingam* stone on the eastern side of its inner courtyard, and the replica idol on the western side facing it.

The writer of the article says that at irregular intervals, on holy days when the temple is closed for reconsecration, the white linen loincloth on the idol is removed for washing. Sometimes – as has happened 7 times in the three-year tenure of the present chief priest – the cloth is found stained, and passed to the eldest ladies of the priest's and the ruling family's households for approval. If the ladies announce the goddess has menstruated, she is removed from the temple for three days, then reinstated in fresh clothes at a public festival called *Tripooth Aarat*. Various authorities – a professor and local doctors – are mentioned as believing the statue really menstruates. One dissenting voice comes from "a prominent member of the Rationalists' Association" who explains that the liquid oozing from the statue is formed by a chemical "disintegration of granite." As our source comments, this critic is "temporarily upset when faced by the fact that the idol is made of metal." Much of interest here for students of comparative folklore.

The eastern entrance of the Bhagawati Temple at Chengannur [Photo: Probe India *Aug 1981]*

BVM FLAPS

Exiled Cubans returning to Miami from visiting relations in Havana have brought back stories of an apparition of the Virgin Mary standing on the waters of Havana's bay. The vision is said to be of a smiling olive-skinned woman, dressed in white with long dark hair and with her arms outstretched. One rumour is that a harbour guard lost his nerve and fired at the apparition twice before being carted off blind and crazy. (Compare this with the story of the guard at Windsor Castle who fired at 'something', in FT18, p24f.) The apparition, believed variously to be of Cuba's patron saint, Our Lady of Charity, or the **Virgen de Regla** worshipped in Havana suburbs, has been seen at least three times in the bay, near the fortress Castillo de la Punta. Several Miami newsmen picked up the story from the returning Cubans and included it in the Spanish-language broadcasts of a number of Miami radio stations – the result: a rise in church attendances among the immigrants. Mgr Augustin Roman, Auxiliary Bishop of South Miami, was obliged to make the following statement, to head off the superstitious: "Regarding the apparitions in Cuba, I cannot say anything because I don't know anything about them. All I know is that people are going out on the streets in search of the supernatural without regard for the consequences." Many of the exiles are excited, taking the news as a sign that the prohibition on Catholicism in Cuba is weakening or coming to an end. *The Miami Herald* 14 Nov 1981.

We also have several reports of sightings, by six girls, of a "golden-haired Madonna" in fields near the Yugoslavian town of Citluk, and which has become a bone of contention between the local Catholics and Communist Party. We won't say any more right now, because we are expecting a full report from our Yugoslavian correspondent, Milos Krmelj, hopefully in the next issue. *Guardian* 13 Oct 1981; *AP* 26 Oct 1981.

Credits: *Janet & Colin Bord, Peter Christie, Loren Coleman, Chris Hall, P.R. Thomas, Royce Vassi, Dwight Whalen, Ion Will, Steve Wrathall.*
• RJMR.

Yes, it's righting wrongs time again. Next time under this heading we have some lowdown on the Indian Rope Trick.

THE BUDDHA'S CHARIOT?

For a number of years we have been intrigued by a reproduction of a UFO-like object in association with a Buddha-like figure. The original is a wall painting in the Tivana temple complex at Polonnaruwa, Sri Lanka–but the more familiar version (see A) has been redrawn for its appearance in the Danish periodical *Forteana* No 9 (summer 1979) and before that in *UFO-Information* No 4 (1978).

The commentaries to these reproductions make it clear the viewer is asked to consider the picture in the light of the 'Ancient Astronaut' hypothesis. It is true that above the Buddha hovers the familiar shape of a classic Flying Saucer, and the Buddha, walking down what looks like a ramp, seems to be followed by an amorphous form. A blob-like alien? The scene evokes a much-loved set piece from the genre of SF fiction and films: the humanoid and alien walking together down the ramp of a recently-landed UFO, just before announcing their offer of salvation or destruction.

Too good to be true, we thought, when we first saw it, and filed it away for future investigation. And so it came to pass that FT's intrepid roving reporter was idly kicking heels in Sri Lanka when inspiration jolted him from tropical torpidity. "I know," he said, warming to the adventure, "I'll check out the UFO temple.". Details were wired to Ion, who in his Far Eastern persona of 'The Sahib', set off down jungle tracks to the now-ruined city of Polonnaruwa.

Polonnaruwa had its heyday in the 12th century AD, and although the great artistic traditions of previous centuries were on the decline, the period generated a number of buildings, temples and cave complexes finely decorated in different styles with frescos and statues. The fresco in question is sited behind a ruined statue of a standing Buddha (the Tivana Buddha) and is in an advanced state of disintegration due to exposure to the elements. The fresco now consists of faint browns with large portions missing as The Sahib's photo shows (see B)–the scaffolding is part of general maintainance work–and it needs a simplified drawing to help identify the remaining fragments of the depicted scene. Unfortunately in making their drawing (see A) the proponents of the 'Buddha's UFO' simplified the elements to conform to their view. In fact the original fresco is clearly identi-

The drawn version of the mural Forteana *(Summer 1979)*

The Sahib's photo of the mural disintegrating [FPL]

For comparison, this is a Thai treatment of the same icon [Postcard from Ion Will's collection]

fiable as a particular image from the canons of Buddhist iconography, known as 'Buddha's descent from the Tusita Heaven'. The 'UFO. is seen to be a parasol, and the 'Blob', an attendant walking behind carrying its long handle. What appears to be the outline of a 'dome' over the Blob's (head?) looks more like a wooden pallet or carrying frame worn by the attendant like a backpack. End of mystery–except the interpretation of the 'ramp'. We append a Thai illustration of the same scene for comparison–a postcard from Ion's collection–which shows the Buddha, a stylized umbrella, and the darndest celestial escalator you ever saw!

Additional source: **Ancient Paintings & Sculpture of Sri Lanka** by Nandadeva Wijesekera (No 1 in series 'The Culture of Sri Lanka; Dept of Cultural Affairs, Colombo, 1976, 3rd printing.) • **RJMR.**

Down among the do-it-yourself books in your local library you won't find one on surgery. The heroes (!) of the following stories couldn't find one either, so they did-it-themselves anyway. (Skip this section if you're reading FT while eating.)

PIECE PROTESTS

Perhaps the mildest datum in this bunch is a note, in London *Eve. Standard* 31 Oct 1978. that a craze was sweeping through South Korea in which people were slashing their fingers to write denunciations of Communist North Korea on walls.

Titbits 15 Sept 1979 – that a prisoner in Marseilles, France, was refused parole and protested with a hunger strike. To prevent force-feeding, he sewed up his lips with smuggled-in cotton and needle. But wait, what's this ear? Just part of a plea from another French prisoner, Maurice Locquin, from a jail in Strasbourg. He snipped off his left ear and taped it to the foot (!) of a letter to a judge asking for a re-trial. He claims he is innocent of the charges for which he is serving 12 years. In 1979 he sent the end joint of his little finger to another judge. Cambridge *Eve. News* (AP) 30 May, *Sun* 31 May 1980.

Artist Henry Benvenuti stormed magnificently out of the office of the Soho Weekly News, New York, leaving behind, on the reception counter, his briefcase, a rat trap with a dollar bill in it, and two fingers. Henry had come to see Gerald Marzonati, the paper's art writer. "He said he wanted to rap about the art world," says Gerald. "I told him, 'Look man, I'm on a deadline, finishing a column. Leave your number and I'll call you back." Henry, who had been calling from the reception desk phone, was annoyed at being fobbed off, and left his 'message' on the desk. He calmly took a small axe out of his briefcase and lopped off two fingers. Receptionist, Donna Frost, said: "Nobody screamed. He didn't make a sound. There wasn't much blood, just a few drops. He walked out of here so calmly I thought it was a piece of theatre – until I saw the fingers. You can still see where the blade cut into the counter!" No thank you! Police found Henry in a taxi and took him to Bellevue Hospital, but the fingers could not be reconnected. *St Catherines Standard (AP)* 27 Nov, *Herald Tribune* 1 Dec 1979.

After losing money in yet another card game an Indian farmer, Gopala Reddy, vowed on his father's grave, in the Andhra Pradesh village of Yedduladoddi, never to gamble again – and to make sure, he cut off his right hand with a carving knife. *D. Telegraph* 26 April 1980.

SEW WHAT?

Earlier this year a hardy miner from Darfield in Yorkshire sliced open a finger while ineptly wielding a kitchen knife. Jimmy Poole knew what to do. He sat down with his wife's sewing kit, and selecting a darning needle and some green cotton stitched the wound up so neatly it healed up "beautifully". Doctors were reportedly shaking their heads in disapproval – not so much over Jimmy's colour sense, but over people taking matters into their own hands (as it were). *D. Star* 29 Jan 1981.

I'll give the next item verbatim, because I still don't quite understand what it means by 'do-it-yourself'. *D. Mirror* 30 Oct 1980 – that "A hand that flew out of a New York skyscraper window has been sewn back on to its do-it-yourself owner." Could it have any relationship to the following . . .

NO ARM DONE, Etc.

When James Bradley, 25, strolled into St Charles Hospital, Ladbroke Grove, London, and asked the nice people behind the counter to cut off his arm, he was turned away. Later he returned, but with a tourniquet tied around the remains of his arm, which was missing from above the elbow. "I had a message from God," he explained. He says he was ordered to lose his arm, and after the Hospital's refusal to help he wandered onto the tube line in North Kensington, put his right arm on the track and waited for a train. The deed done, he applied a tourniquet and walked the half mile back to the Hospital. *D. Express* 8 July 1974.

In Aukland, New Zealand, a man learned that his bid for a £3500 State injury compensation, failed when the authorities discovered the man had not been attacked as he claimed. Keith Entwistle, a ship's cook thought he was made for life when he blew his legs off with a bomb after applying tourniquets to them – instead he has made himself a cripple for life. London *Eve. Standard* 30 July 1979.

More recently we heard of another victim who imagined he heard God yell "Cut!" Michael Downing, 40, jobless and living alone in New Cross, London, took a hacksaw and sawed off his left leg below the knee. Neighbours called an ambulance and Michael and leg were taken first to a hospital in Greenwich, then to East Grinstead, where doctors said the amputation was so neat they would have no trouble sewing it back on again. Michael, who should have been unconscious, appeared not to be in shock and chatted to doctors and ambulance men throughout his travel – but he refused to have the leg back, saying "it would be against God's orders." One doctor said: "Mr Downing's condition is outside our normal experience." Michael suffered little loss of blood, no pain and no traumatic shock. After the main report came a second item saying that Michael had been in hospital before, after cutting off several fingers "for practice". An ambulanceman said: "He seems to have an obsession about cutting parts off his body." Michael was being referred to psychiatric treatment after his recovery. *The Sun* 19 & 20 Nov 1981.

HEAD TALES

At an inquest on the death of William Hall, 57, a company director from Belfast, the coroner's court was told that Hall's bizarre death was a suicide and nothing to do with the sectarian violence of Northern Ireland. Hall was found in the garage of his brother-in-law's home at Shrewsbury, where he had bored 8 holes through his skull and brain with a power drill. He had not died quickly – an operation failed to save him and he died the next day of severe cerebral haemorrhage. *Guardian* 25 May 1971.

The doctor giving evidence at Hall's inquest, Dr Michael Symons, said he knew of cases where self-inflicted injuries have included hammering nails and chisels into the brain, but he found it "beyond the bounds of credibility" that anyone could drill eight holes into their head accidentally. Dr Symons asked other pathologists, including Home Office pathologists, but no one knew of a similar case. I'm sure one is mentioned in A. Alvarez' book on suicide, but the reference escapes me. Some bizarre examples of objects penetrating the brain are given in that most Fortean of medical books, *Anomalies and Curiosities of Medicine* (1896) by Gould & Pyle, including a man who hammered three 3-inch nails into his head, and another who bored five holes (with a brace?) in his skull and inserted pieces of wire, nails and needles.

Slightly different is a rather extreme case of face-saving. It concerns a 29-yr-old Brazilian, Alves Pereira, who while riding his moped, collided with a lorry in his village outside Rio. When the bandages came off, he wished he had been killed. His face was so horribly disfigured his fiancee broke off their engagement and he was driven from his barber's job. Soon the whole village turned its back on him – they crossed themselves when they glimpsed him; children threw stones and bullies threw more hurtful taunts – so he became a recluse in the hills, living on church charity, where he lived for 16 years. One day, the priest, his only friend, got him what he had asked for – a book on plastic surgery, and he studied it, reading and planning his own operation. Then he was ready. His equipment consisted of a razor blade, an ordinary needle and cotton, a cracked mirror, alcohol, a vial of local anaesthetic called Novocol, and a syringe. Alves gradually transformed his own face in 15 operations over 10 months, allowing several weeks between for healing. He cut strips off his chest and rebuilt his mouth and nose, and repaired scars, using builders' plaster to seal the new work. When news of this astonishing accomplishment by a simple but determined man reached Rio, one of the country's top plastic surgeons, Prof Ivor Pitanguy, immediately invited Alves to his clinic. The Prof was greatly impressed by "the way this man has been able to master the rudimentary skills of plastic surgery." He added: "His work was not totally successful. But his surgical precision was remarkable. It is amazing that he did not mutilate himself." Then the Prof offered his own services free to complete the job. *S. Express* 29 May 1977. A completely misinformed version of this story appeared in *Weekend* 5 Oct 1977.

WRINKLED RETAINER SACKED

Outdoing their usual sensational selves the *National Enquirer* for 25 Aug 1981 told a first-person story of a French doctor who is literally a self-made woman. At the age of 52, Dr Daniel Kretzschmar was fed up being a divorced father of two. He had always felt himself to be more feminine than masculine, and had been taking a course of hormone treatments. Sex-change operations are illegal in France so Daniel went to Belgium – but an accidental death during a similar operation while he was at the clinic made Daniel decide to look elsewhere. He became convinced that he could castrate himself. "I chose a Sunday, a day I was least likely to be disturbed at home. I began at 9 a.m. I took it one step at a time. It was just like cutting my fingernails, or taking off a wart. I had no pain thanks to a local anaesthetic. My anatomy book was my instruction manual. I just kept cutting. I was totally absorbed in the technical aspects of the surgery. I did the operation in two stages, the left and the right sides." In between, Daniel broke off for lunch and rest, fixing himself steak and veg. "During the operation, I got up to answer the phone three times. I knew I always had the phone nearby and if anything started to go wrong I could ask someone to help me. In fact, in the middle of the second half of the operation I phoned my secretary. I had three patients to see that Sunday. After the surgery I just had time to clean my room. I put all the waste in the trash can, then I saw my patients. Afterward, I went out for a meal in a restaurant." Later, Danielle, as s/he now prefers to be called, acquired female genitals through surgery in Amsterdam. Although his professional and family life have been rebuilt, there are still some patients and members of his family who cannot accept what he has done.

Dr Daniel/Danielle said: "The operation took 6½ hours. I have only two hands and normally you need six to do all the cutting and sewing. I had to do it all myself." Well, he should count himself lucky he did not find himself in the position of Kallie Fortuin, a 19-yr-old South African, who was forced to castrate himself at gunpoint. Fortuin had raped an old lady, and was caught riding her bike the next day by the lady's son and friend. At gunpoint they took him to a remote river bank, gave him a knife used to castrate pigs, and told him it was either snip it or snuff it. Without the aid of books, training or anaesthetics, the youth set to work, and after, the men took him to a police station. When he was brought to trial for the rape, Fortuin told the court he had seen how pigs were castrated, so he "knew what to do"; and a doctor confirmed that he had made a very neat job of it too. In view of this unusual retribution Fortuin escaped both hanging and a life sentence – he got 10 years – and the lady's relatives were simply warned not to take the law into their own hands again. *D. Telegraph* 3 Sept 1981.

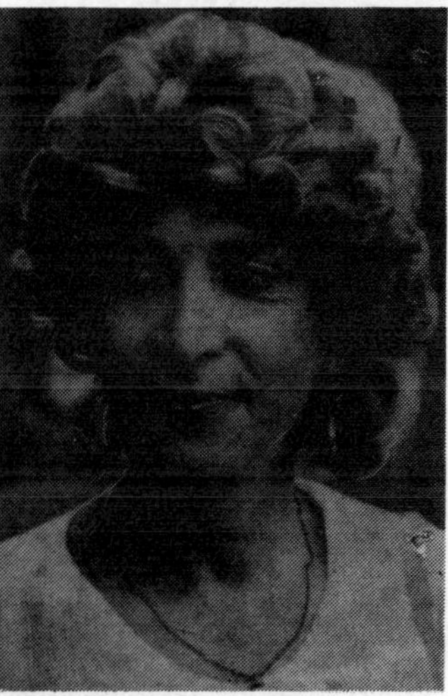

Dr Kretschmar as Daniel and Danielle [Photos: Nat.Enquirer 25 *Aug 1981]*

As we go to press, the *News of the World* 27 Dec 81 [that shows how late we are] carries a story of a doctor who vasectomied himself. Dr Surendra Nath Jain, of the West Park Nursing Home in Wolverhampton, who has performed more than 400 vasectomies, said he did it to demonstrate to patients that the operation is simple, and quick, in an effort to calm their fears. He normally allows 20 minutes for the operation, but performed it on himself in 30 minutes in the Home's theatre, with an anaesthetist standing by. The BMA, when told, were "surprised", adding that Dr Surendra had done nothing unethical. A spokeswoman said: "As far as we know this is the first time its been done." What does she know?

ALL THEIR OWN WORK

With the full permission of a hospital in Colorado, Dr George Balderston removed his own appendix. In the hospital's surgical theatre he sat down, anaesthetized himself, opened up his abdomen, snipped and closed the wound with clamps and stitches unaided within an hour. London *Eve. News* 21 March 1978.

Now the remarkable story of an unidentified 22-yr-old student who castrated himself in one 8-hour operation, and 4 months later performed another 8-hour operation to "denervate his adrenal glands". It is written up in the *AMA Journal* (May 1979) by Dr Ned Kalin of the University of Wisconsin Clinical Services Center in Madison. The student was taking a course of female hormones because he feared, and wanted to suppress his sexual impulses – he strongly denies wishing to change sex, like Dr Danielle (above). With careful preparation he castrated himself, after failing to convince doctors to do it, and then travelled to hospital to have a professional opinion of his efforts. There was a temporary decrease in his sexual impulses, and then real or imagined, they returned. After further reading he planned the second operation to sever the nerves to the adrenal gland above the kidneys in the belief that this would help. He accumulated the necessary instruments, doused his dormitory room with disinfectant, draped sheets over himself, put on surgical gloves, swallowed barbiturates for anaesthetic, and began. He kept a can of vaporized adrenaline to hand in case of shock. Dr Kalin writes: "Lying supine and looking into strategically placed mirrors . . . The incision was made with a scalpel . . . exposure obtained by retractors and the dissection carried out with surgical instruments." After poking around inside himself for eight hours, the student gave up because of the pain when he attempted to move his liver aside to reach the glands above the kidneys. He packed the wound with bandages, cleaned the room and then called the police for emergency transport because of a 'rupture'. At hospital he handed to the dumbfounded duty doctor a set of handwritten instructions on how to treat the deep wound. Doctors found there had been minimal blood loss because blood vessels had been neatly tied with ligatures. They reconnected the plumbing, closed the wound, and the patient recovered quickly in a ward. Dr Kalin said the student had been diagnosed as a paranoid schizophrenic and was undergoing counselling. Even so, said the doctor, doctors had failed the youth, driving him to formulate his own plan to self-help. "He has mastered the concepts and techniques of medicine in an attempt to cure himself. When, in reality, we have little to offer him that would result in effective treatment." The subject of benign forms of schizophrenia, involving self-cures that are drastic to the point of appearing quite insane to the 'normal' concensus, is one psychiatrists admit they know very little about. During his recovery, says Dr Kalin, the student was doing further reading towards solving his problem. This involves the field of spinally administered anaesthetics, and a second assault on his adrenal nerves. We have heard nothing further. London *Eve. Standard* 14 May, *Herald Tribune* & *Indianapolis Star* & *D. Telegraph (UIP + Reuters)* 15 May 1979.

Finally, an even more horrible story of recklessness, from Ithaca, NY – a suitable placename for a tale that reads like part of a Greek tragedy. On 16 August this year, police patrolmen noticed a yound woman wearing a babycarrier inhabited by an obviously newborn and naked baby. As the woman begged for money for cigarettes, the patrolmen were even more alarmed to notice the seat and thighs of the woman's slacks were stained with blood. An ambulance was called and mother and baby, both apparently feeling "remarkably well", were taken to Tompkins Community Hospital, where the story was pieced together. The mother was seven months pregnant and not in labour when she decided she was fed up with her bulge. So she sat down, opened herself up with a penknife, and delivered the baby by caesarian section. She finished up by chewing through the umbilical cord (animals do this naturally), and sewing the wound up with ordinary cotton and thread. Last we heard the mother was "critical" but expected to pull through and face psychiatric care. London *Standard* & *Niagara Falls Review, NY, (AP)* 19 Aug, *D. Star* & *Guardian* 20 Aug 1981.

Yuk! I get queasy if I have to put a sticking plaster on!

Credits: *Peter Christie, Danny Eads, Peter Hope-Evans, Valerie Martin, Nigel Pennick, Dennis Prater, Peter Rogerson, Andy Townsend, Dwight Whalen, Ion Will* ● **RJMR**

The deluge of matter from our skies continues. Next issue: more tales of falling frogs, and—a first for Wales—crabs.

COINS

A genuine case of 'Pennies from Heaven' mystified the parishioners of St Elisabeth's Church, Reddish, between Manchester and Stockport, earlier this year. On the morning of 28 May a young girl claimed to have seen a 50p coin fall "from nowhere" in front of her as she walked through the churchyard. During the day many pounds worth of copper and silver coins were found by children at the same location. The affair came to the attention of the Rector, Rev Graham Marshall, when the owner of a corner shop came to see him wondering if the sudden increase in children buying sweets meant they were raiding his Poor Box. Rev Marshall tracked down the phenomenon to his churchyard and collected numerous plummeting pence to a value of over £2. Investigation quickly eliminated the obvious theories – the nearby church wall (see photo) was too high to conceal a practical joker, and there were no signs of magpie nests, and a number of coins dropping together ruled out the idea of a bird overhead.

We managed to speak to Rev Marshall who confirmed all the details. Children would hear the tinkle of coins on the path and turn to discover them. Only in one case (above) did a girl claim to see one falling. Most curious of all, he told us, was a detail the kids could not have dreamed up – a few coins were found embedded in the ground by their edges. He tried an experiment, hurling a fistful of coins at the ground, but they made no impression. Either the coins fell from a great height (which does not square with the gentle tinkle signalling the arrival of most of them), or we are seeing, in the open, the phenomenon of poltergeist projectiles. Anyone with a modest reading in the latter subject will be familiar with stories of impossible trajectories, sudden acceleration or decelleration, instantaneous loss of momentum, slow falls, and eeerie marksmanship. Whether or not this applies to the Reddish Ready we do not know. Coins fell from an undiscoverable source – and there is some feeling that they might have fallen also the day before, and possibly the day after, the 28th.

Stockport Express 4 June 1981.

SAND AND POLLEN

Sometime in the first week of November, Mr Christopher Newberry, of Sonning, Berks, stepped outside his front door early in the morning and stared in disbelief. His white house had turned pale yellow, as had several neighbouring houses, the road and gardens and a number of parked cars. It was as though someone had been to work with "a giant paint sprayer". Fearing some dire chemical pollution Mr Newberry phoned his Council who sent over an environmental officer. Scraping off a sample of sticky primrose-coloured powder, he identified it as pollen, and sent for Dr Michael Keith-Lucas, of the Reading University botany dept, who in turn identified the goop as cedar pollen. With astonishing powers of observation and deduction he solved the case. "I walked around and there was one cedar of Lebanon which dominates the whole village. I imagine it came from that one," he said with the appearance of certainty. And that's that, except for the question which nags at us: why hadn't such an obvious phenomenon been noticed or recognised in previous years? *S. Express* 8 Nov 1981.

Usually when yellowish dust descends it is hard for educated minds to see clearly. They feel around in the gloom for comfortingly familiar explanations, and if there are none, well then, imagine one. Early September a substance, said to be sand, fell on Mansfield, Nottinghamshire. The sand made 'experts' think of the Sahara, and so it came about that a 'freak wind', for whose real existence no evidence is offered, is blamed for magically whisking a dune or two from the Sahara to Mansfield. See back to FT29p37f for what we think about 'Sahara sand' explanations.

The Sun 18 September 1981.

Rev Graham Marshall at the site of the coin-fall, St Elizabeths, Reddish [Photo: Lancs & Cheshire County Newspapers]

ICE AND HAIL

We have often lamented the habit of modern papers of failing to give us an accurate date for the phenomena they report. That applies to some of the above, and to the next story, from *Sunday Express* 6 September 1981.

At the end of August, or early September, Steven Puckering and Amanda Kaye were on holiday in the south of France at Lac de St Cassien, near Cannes; Steven trying his hand at wind surfing, while 100 yds away Amanda sunbathed on the shore of the lake. Suddenly, out of a calm sky, something struck Steven hard on the head. Although badly stunned he realized it had been a hailstone the size of a tennisball. Then down it came – a blizzard of hailstones of frightening sizes. "One minute I was peacefully sailing over a smooth lake in a temperature of 85 degrees, the next I was in the water in partial darkness, wiping blood from my eyes. I have never been so frightened," he said. He had lost his balance trying to dodge the hail. In the water he tried to shelter under the sail, but "the hail was so fast and heavy it pierced the sail, ripping it to shreds." When he made it to the shore, he found Amanda, bruised, sheltering in bushes. They rushed to their car and were shocked again – the windscreen was smashed

Cont on p 41

CSAR & ASSAP.

Since the last issue there have been two developments which will have far-reaching consequences for our various fields of study. For some years now there has been a growing trend, particularly in the USA, to use the term 'anomalistics' where some of us traditionalists use the term 'Fortean', to gather under a handy umberella much of the variety of strange and paranormal phenomena and related topics. The basic argument for coining a new term is that to use a word based on Fort's name implies a subscription to Fort's views and besides, it is said, Fort is relatively unknown. Naturally I disagree with these views. 'Anomalistics' as a word is far more obscure than 'Fortean' as a descriptive term; the latter having been widely used in books and journals since Fort's death in 1932. Any ignorance of the word could be just as easily remedied by the same amount of publicity as that given to the new word. Secondly, Forteanism as such, has only one tenet, and that is to investigate in the free spirit of inquiry with no allegience to opinion or dogma. I for one will gladly, and proudly, be associated with that view. Fort indulged in many weird ideas, but he did not take them seriously, and his writings are peppered with warnings to the reader not to as well. Those fearing that applying 'Fortean' to their field of study will bring it down to the level of crackpottery do Fort a great injustice, for he was very scientific in referencing his sources and in the dialectics of his arguments. Yet there does seem to be one distinction between the two terms. Anomalistics, as defined by users like Professor Roger Wescott, in his long introductory article on page 30 seems to be restricted to mean anomalies relative to the body of orthodox science. I accept this usage. In comparison Fort was interested in anomalies relative to *any particular dogma*, and dogma, as we know, is not restricted to science alone.

With the July1981 issue of *Zetetic Scholar*, comes the announcement of the formation of **The Center for Scientific Anomalies Research** (CSAR), whose purpose is to "bring together scholars and researchers concerned with furthering responsible scienfic inquiry into and evaluation of claims of anomalies and the paranormal." CSAR aims to become a clearinghouse for scientific anomaly research and to create a network of experts, lecturers, consultants and resource consultants, and to run symposia and conferences. CSAR was formed by Professor Marcello Truzzi, who edits the thick, impressive and valuably useful *Zetetic Scholar*, and Dr Ron Westrum, both of Eastern Michigan University. For further information write to **CSAR: Box 1052, Ann Arbor, MI 48103.**

About the same time, coincidentally, the **Association for the Scientific Study of Anomalous Phenomena** (ASSAP) was being formed here in Britain. The initiative for ASSAP has come from a small but impressive group who left the Society for Psychical Research (SPR) because they believe that psychic phenomena should be studied in its relationship to other, overlapping phenomena which are quite outside the SPR's brief. By virtue of their interests outside psychic research, the SPR dissidents corresponded widely in the fields of ufology, earth mystries and Forteana generally, and all the feedback led to the conclusion that the time was right to form some sort of formal association between them. Britain has some of the best researchers and writers in these fields, some of the most startling phenomena, and a wide range of specialist associations or groups catering for local or individual interest. What it has lacked is a cohesive force - one which reflects the feelings of those seriously interested that all these separate fields are in fact contigious and in need of sound interdisciplinary investigation.

So ASSAP was born, accumulating support from activists in all subjects as it went along. It is true that some people and groups have felt threatened by the existence of ASSAP, and are suspicious of its aims. This is based on a misunderstanding of what ASSAP is. It represents a federal body which has no intention of ousting, dispossessing or pre-empting the status of any group or individual. To the contrary, by working as a representative body for the mutual benefit of its members – who may be groups as well as individuals – ASSAP hopes it will evolve into a general supporting structure in which previously isolated or uncoordinated research can be encouraged in every way. This coordination will not be 'imposed from above' as some fear, but arise from the needs of those involved directly in the work. Major ASSAP programmes will involve: the better representation and reporting of anomalous phenomena inthe media; to seek out funding for research; to establish a national library of works on all anomalous topics for reference and study; to encourage the design and development of specialist databases; to establish a common classification and coding system for subjects etc; to set up specialist information channels to promote data exchanges; to devise a training programme for the different types of investigation of anomalous phenomena; to establish a network of trained observers and investigators; to organize public meetings, lectures and exhibitions, as well as conferences and special study groups; to educate the public and generally encourage interest in the study and investigation of anomalous phenomena. These are all long term projects, and, as far as possible, anyone with any views on these topics will have a chance to voice them to the various working parties.

To begin with it has been necessary to ask a few people who are known to be interested in these areas to take responsibility for getting some sort of programme, study group or working party underway–these appointments being temporary until proper democratic elections can be held at ASSAP's first annual general meeting. For example, I have been asked to devise a programme for the formation of a proper national reference library and archive, and related facilities, something British researchers have long felt the need for. Neither I, nor any of those scholars who have agreed to be part of the initial team, are under any illusion about the difficulties this will involve, or the time-scale and care needed to bring about a practical result.

Many Forteans and others do not feel a strong need for becoming active in any form of association. Like others, I do my best work alone–not in isolation, but untrammelled by red-tape and other formalities. Nevertheless there are times I need the sort of facilities it is intended ASSAP should provide, and the only way they can be achievable is if like-minded people work collectively towards these aims. Also, I feel that our range of subjects has suffered somewhat by being unable to present any coherent collective effort. Fort knows I'm not one to court the approval of Science for the hell of it, but I cannot doubt the benefits that would come from the better organization of our interests and resources. We owe it to ourselves and to our subjects to improve standards all round, and improvements, however brilliant, do not gain ground until they are accepted and utilized by others. ASSAP is only just beginning. Its aims are ones Forteans can endorse, on the whole. It will be a democratic body, so none of us can complain if it develops one-sidedly, or unfairly to our favourite subject, or incorporates policies we disapprove of. ASSAP will have no 'official' opinion, so there should be little dogma. I have always felt that Forteans with their non-specific interests would make good curators of such a body. We have the only sane grasp of the inter-disciplinary nature of things. Join ASSAP and make it a body of practical use to us; one that in all but name will be truly Fortean. Membership will be £6 annually, with benefits and a newsletter. For more info or membership form, write to **ASSAP Membership Secretary, Janice Bagnall, 6 Colwyn House, Cosser St, London SE1 7BY**, or phone evenings 01 928 7531.

•

Bob Rickard

Soapbox.

Each issue, under this heading, we give our readers the opportunity to sound off, speculate on any FT related subject.

A SPECULATIVE NATURE NOTE

Of all the giant reptiles that dominated the earth millions of years ago, the only survivor is one that continues to thrive. The plesiosaur, rarely even seen by man and in academic circles believed to be extinct, roams most of the seas of the world. In its adult state, this shy but formidable creature has no natural enemies.

The creature's breeding cycle, similar to a number of other marine animals but with a unique feature of its own, largely accounts for its survival when mammals drove the other large reptiles to extinction. Plesiosaurs return annually to their birthplace, which is located in a subterranean cavern, partially flooded and accessible only from underwater. There in primeval blackness the huge reptiles lay their eggs. The young return to the sea, where, like many young creatures, most of them are devoured by predators. One of the breeding caverns is located in Scotland, and it is believed there are others elsewhere in the world.

The breeding cavern in Scotland has the unique property of connecting through a good-sized underwater outlet to a large fresh water lake, Loch Ness. From time to time over the centuries of human history–mostly around their breeding season–one of the creatures has entered Loch Ness and thrust its head above water, to the astonishment of any chance human observers. These occurrences led to a long debate, between those who tended to credit the numerous witnesses, and those who did not. During the 1970's photographs were produced whose authenticity was difficult to challenge, and which were taken both above and below the surface. The disbelievers, however, not realizing the existence of the cavern, could still fall back on rather powerful arguments: Loch Ness itself is a preposterously small habitat to sustain creatures of this size in a breeding population over the millenia; further, the most sophisticated sonar searches as well as continuous organized shore watches rarely uncover any evidence of them.

The first specimens which become available are unlikely to be either dramatic or huge, but just a little melancholy. It is anticipated that during the next few years investigators will begin to check the bellies of large fish taken off the coast of Scotland, looking for the remains of young plesiosaurs. When they succeed, no doubt Scottish fishermen will scornfully declare that they have been seeing *those* things for years! •

Jasper McKee

THE STORY SO FAR: THE HERO OF THIS "THRILLING" TALE FINDS HIMSELF INVOLVED WITH, A SECRET SECT, THE ANCIENT ORDER OF BUFFOONS, WHO CLAIM TO BE IN CONTROL OF MANS DESTINY. THEY HAVE KIDNAPPED HIM AND FORCIBLY INDOCTRINATED HIM IN THEIR SECRETS, A PROCESS WHICH APPEARS TO INVOLVE MANY BLOWS ON THE HEAD. AND NOW, BEARING FIVE LUMPS ON HIS NAPPER, HE IS DRAWN INEXORABLY INTO THE FINAL STRETCH OF HIS DESCENT INTO TERROR! NOW READ ON....

I WAS AWARE OF SHADOWY FORMS ALL AROUND – AND EYES GLOWING BENEATH JESTER'S CAPS!

THEN, A FIGURE IN A HIDEOUS MASK DETACHED ITSELF FROM THE GLOOM...
PLOP

SOME STRANGE SIXTH SENSE TOLD ME INSTINCTIVELY THAT IT WAS... THE GRANDE BUFFOON!
GRANDE BUFFOON

SLOWLY–REMORSELESSLY HE APPROACHED ME....

HIS WRINKLED SKRINKLED CLAWS BORE SOMETHING ALOFT!!

MY EYES FIXED ON THIS ARTEFACT! WHAT WAS IT? SOME SORT OF CONTAINER .... A CASKET?... A....A....

AN EGGBOX?!

AFTER THAT, EVERYTHING WENT BLACK! WHEN I REGAINED MY SENSES I WAS BACK ON EARTH.... INDEED, I WAS IN A DITCH, SURROUNDED BY MYSTERIOUS..... er... BOTTLES.....

CIDER

I WENT BACK HOME, TO MY OLD LIFE. BUT THOSE EXPERIENCES HAVE NEVER LEFT MY MIND....PARTICULARLY THE SIX WALLOPS ON THE HEAD EXPERIENCES..... AND NOW, IN THE INTERESTS OF PROFIT, I CAN KEEP SILENT NO LONGER, BUT MUST MAKE THE WORLD AWARE OF THIS STRANGE KNOWLEDGE!

HAS HUMAN HISTORY BEEN MANIPULATED BY A SECRET SUPER-SOCIETY? IS OUR DESTINY CONTROLLED BY BUFFOONS? ALL I KNOW IS THAT SINCE THAT TIME I AM UNABLE TO GET THROUGH ANY SIMPLE SENTENCE WITHOUT SLIPPING IN A CHICKEN JOKE!

...so henjoy yourself....
.... my dear, that's eggstra special....
....clucky for you I can take a yolk...
...I rooster be quite normal...
THE END

Photos Of The Gods.

From our interest in simulacra we began accumulating 'spontaneous images of gods'. Some of these as true 'archeropites' (see FT30p2-7) of the Jesus-on-the-tortilla type are still under study—but in the meantime the category of alleged photographs of gods was in need of some attention. These are extraordinary claims and in all cases the photographic evidence falls far short of proof for all but the blindly faithful. Against this we must weigh the possibility of psychokinetically imposing archetypal images on film, and the claims of spiritualists for almost supernatural causation. This is a subject which involves interesting psycho-social phenomena. Operating at the level of a visual rumour, it constantly renews itself with each wave of media exposure, despite the outrage to scientific 'commonsense', contradictory claims, and degenerating reproductions. FT editor **Bob Rickard**, summarizes the FT file on this tantalizing topic.

Image A Saucer News *vol 15 no 3 [FPL]*

Among the rich variety of paranormal phenomena which interests me, I have a special affection for one of the more preposterous – photos of the gods. It is interesting precisely because it is preposterous, and outrages the notions of 'realists' about our existence. In psychic photography one often encounters claims that peculiar patches of light, not always in human shape, have appeared anomalously in a photo, and represent sentient beings, whether the souls of the dead, spirits, or even angels. Another category of this kind of photograph includes images, some faint and some solid, of definite human form, which are said to be of people not present when the photo was taken. Yet another category is the 'thoughograph', in which an agent has wittingly or unwittingly caused an image to appear on unexposed film, or which bears no relation to the scene which should be on the photo through normal optical processes – and this interferance with a photographic image is attributed to some undefined psychic ability like psychokinesis. The subject of this article goes beyond these categories and involves alleged photos of entities who either existed long before the invention of photography and for whom no authentic evidence exists of what they looked like, or of entities who could more properly be called 'mythical'. It would be easier, one would think, to photograph a dream than a god, and yet there are many claims to have done just that. Though such an accomplishment defies everyday rationality, the gods have the old magic on their side, and to the faithful the very impossibility of the image is evidence of a miracle.

Consider some examples of 'miracles' attributed to Sai Baba, considered by many to be India's greatest living saint. In Howard Murphet's account, *Sai Baba: Man of Miracles* (Muller, London, 1971) are a number of examples of Sai Baba producing, out of thin air it is claimed, photographs of himself, and portraits of himself on medallions, and so on. An interesting instance is given on pages 105-109: following a woman devotee's vision of a cobra which turned into the Hindu deity, Lord Subramaniam, the woman visits Sai Baba who then claims he visited her in her dreams. He shows her a staircase identical to that in her dream of Subramaniam. Then, "to help her understanding, Swami now waved his hand and from the air produced a photograph of himself in the *somasutra* (chariot) of Subramaniam with a cobra circling around him." (p109).

A second, more striking and challenging example is more to the point. Murphet and his wife, and a few other devotees, accompanied Sai Baba to his retreat at Circuit House, in Horsley Hills, some 90 miles north of Bangalore. During a discourse at a sandy area, Sai Baba, drew the outline of a human figure in the sand, and then drew out of the sand a shining silver statue of Vishnu, about 4 inches high. Smoothing out the sand he continued the discourse until he began drawing once again. Then, "with a happy chuckle he felt with his fingertips into the top of the mound and scraped a little sand away; less than an inch down was a photograph. He pulled it out, shook the yellow grains away, and held it up for us to see. It was a glossy back-and-white print, about ten inches by eight. He passed it around for some of us to look at closely, and later I examined it at leisure back at our quarters. It was a photograph of the Hindu gods and avatars, standing in two rows to form a forward-pointing arrowhead, with Lord Krishna in the foreground at the tip. Heads of Satya Sai Baba and Shirdi Baba [his previous incarnation] could be seen as small inserts on the body of Krishna. This print, I felt, was not produced in any earthly studio." (p86).

The print was given to a Mr TA Ramanatha Reddy, and we greatly regret that Murphet did not include the photo as an illustration in in his book. Perhaps a Fortean among the Baba's followers could trace it for us?

Compared with this amazing arrival of a photo of the gods the origins of the remaining subjects of this article are shrouded in a more mundane mystery. As the late Maurice Barbanell told me, after about 40 years of searching for the origins of the 'Christ in the snow' image, he could find no authentification of any claim to have taken the photo, and no satisfactory answer as to who took the photo, where and when. He once trace a lady who claimed to have the 'negative' (see under 'Psychic News' below) but this turned out to be only a copy of a copy, and nowhere approached what the original image must have looked like. When we have accumulated a few more copies of the image, or researched the subject further, we might be in a better position to at least establish some sort of genealogy to the host of differing claims about the origins of each of these images. For example, one of the most recent printings, in *Sunday People* 13 Nov 1977 (see 'Sunday People' below) is only part of a more full image reproduced elsewhere. By comparing the way the light and dark patches have 'blocked in' one could place the different images into some sort of time-scale, because through successive copying -- ie. each time the image is rephotographed and printed – more and more details are lost as the middle grays drop away to form consolidated shapes of solid black and solid white. By such a method of comparison, we can easily accept the *Fate* July 1955 as one of the earliest versions known to us, which lends some weight, in turn, to the priority of the 'Mildred Swanson' story (see under 'Mildred Swanson' and 'Psychic News' below).

I have only three pseudo-points to make as a reason for this article. Firstly I wanted to collect together some 'god-photos' and their explanations that were known to me. If any reader knows of others please write to me at FT.

Secondly, to draw attention to visual forms of the 'whale tumour' type of story through some interesting examples. These are stories for which the origin can never be satisfactorily pinned down. Each claimant implicitly believes their copy is an original or that they know the true story of its origin. These accounts are always given on the authority of a 'friend of a friend' (known as a 'foaf' in the jargon) or some even more esoteric chain of relationships, and these are well reflected in the examples summarized here.

Thirdly, there is the ubiquitous, perhaps even archetypal, nature of this 'god-photo' category. Its forms spread far and wide, even, as we'll see, unto China and where they turn up they seem to exert some strange amnesia over their owners so that how their copy came to them recedes into foggy forgetfulness to be replaced by a more personal myth of its origin which often reaches quite sophisticated forms in elaborateness of detail while appealing to more emotional, religious and mythical needs. Each of these explanations is mutually exclusive, and therefore, to ordinary appearances, not all can be true. Obviously the prior claim would be more authentic – in terms of chronicling the photo's history only, not in itself establishing beyond doubt the event really happened – and with this criterion, it is the 1920 'Mildred Swanson' story, again, which holds the field. There is one earlier story, attributed to 1917 (see under 'Psychic News'), but so far we have found no contemporary evidence to support this. This diversity and contest of claims in the case of the 'Christ in the snow' image did not dismay one faithful, Lewis A. Anthony, who wrote to the West Virginia UFO journal *Saucer News* (see below): "There are several opinions one can take of this matter. One that I prefer is that the duplication of the pictures is further proof of the existence of Christ."

Unable to relax in such all-embracing faith myself, I postulate the other extreme: that someone somewhere cut out a painting of Christ and montaged it with a suitable background, re-photographed it, and circulated the first prints. To test this, I'd like anyone who knows of any classical painting or illustration of Christ in the pose of benediction of the 'Christ in the snow' image, and identifies the two together, to let me know. On the other hand, should proof come to support the paranormal origin of the image, I'd be happy to hear of it also, and perhaps even eat my hat. Apart from that, the adventures of this kind of photo would probably most interest sociologists and psychologists who study the phenomenology of rumour.

It has been quite a headache wondering how best to marshall the information, because in many instances details of dates or places are vague or absent. For better or for worse, I have decided to group the claims under the main headings of the sources in which the information came to light; and under these headings to give all the dated claims in order, followed by the undated ones in no particular order.

•

CHRIST IN THE SNOW

Although the earliest accounts of this photograph, which can be authenticated to some degree, the 'Mildred Swanson' accounts, say the photo was taken of flowers against which the figure of Christ spontaneously appeared where none was seen before, it has become better known as depicting Christ against a snow covered scene. This explanation might have been contrived because it better explains the 'contrasty' black and white areas. In fact where several versions of this image are compared one can see that the real cause of this high contrast is successive copying, with its attendant loss of detail. Each time the photo is circulated or reproduced it generates a new batch of impossible claims, and this is an attempt to catalogue some of them.

THE MILDRED SWANSON ORIGIN

The earliest account of this photo, attributing the taking of it to Mildred Swanson, a Seattle, Washington, housewife, that I can find is an article called 'Jesus of the Flowerbank', by Albert Brandt, in *Fate* July 1955, in which Brandt claims Mrs Swanson took the photo on a bright sunny day, 15 July 1920.

Image B Fate *July 1955*

The story goes like this: Mrs Swanson wished to take a photo of her 7yr-old daughter, Karin, and after returning from loading the Brownie with fresh film, put it down while she posed Karin against a flower bank. Of its own accord the shutter clicked. Fearing she had ruined a frame, Mrs Swanson advanced the film to the next one. It clicked again on its own. The rest of the film behaved normally and she obtained the required photos of Karin – except, when the film came back from the druggist in Rochester, NY, the two 'spoiled' frames contained the image [fig B]. Mrs Swanson tried to duplicate the events with a second film, but that developed normally.

• Some years later, one of our readers, Julian North, of Victoria, BC, Canada, included the photo in an installment of his column 'Incredible but true ...' in *The Victorian* for 8 Sept 1976. Compare his image [fig C], with the *Fate* one [fig B] for differences. North's account too differs from the *Fate* version, alleging it was taken on 15 July, all right, but in 1937, not 1920. North's version runs as follows: Mrs Swanson lived in Winnipeg, but wanted a photo of her flower garden to send to her daughter in Seattle. She put the camera down while she adjusted some flowers, and heard it click on its own. She thought her cat might be responsible but it was not in sight. She continued to take pictures normally, and on receiving the prints from Eaton's (presumably a druggist), she was suprised to find the enigmatic image in place of a spoiled print. The manager of the store asked for and was given permission to sell reprints of "the picture that took itself", and

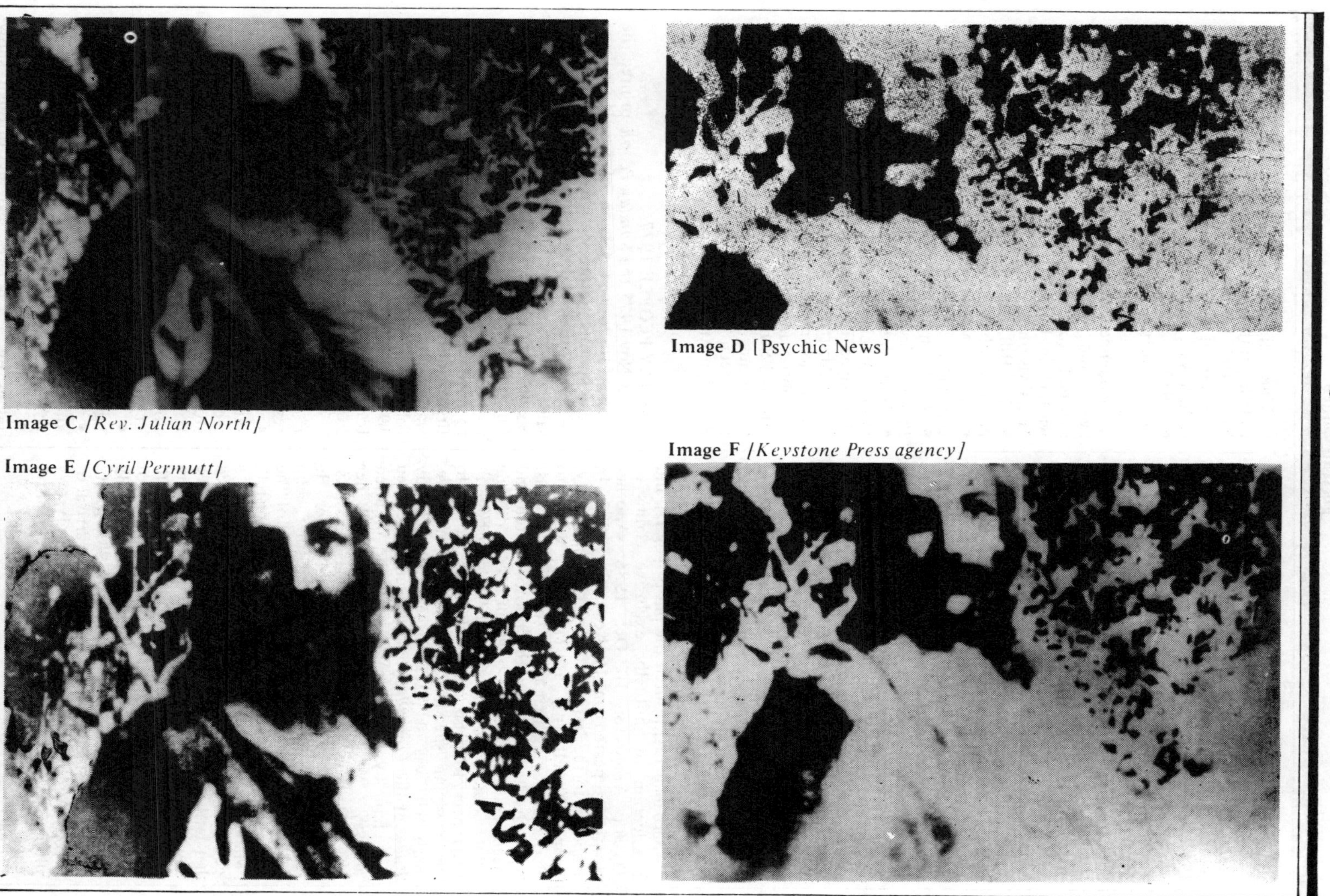

Image C [*Rev. Julian North*]

Image D [Psychic News]

Image E [*Cyril Permutt*]

Image F [*Keystone Press agency*]

hundreds were sold at a nickle each.

In response to my query, North did not seem suprised at another version of the Swanson story, adding: "Most Canadians accept the 1937 version, since it is substantiated in the Winnipeg paper as originating there and then." Unfortunately we do not have this reference on file, so if any reader out there can send a copy we'll use it in a further update of this theme some other time.

THE PSYCHIC NEWS ACCOUNTS

Many times in its long life as Britain's leading spiritualist newspaper, *Psychic News* has printed versions of the famous photo and the various claims of origination. Its late editor, Maurice Barbanell, had made something of a quest to seek out the truth of who took the photo, where and when, and who had the negative, ever since he learned of its existence in the 1930s. Barbanell discovered that a copy was sent to Sir Arthur Conan Doyle in 1926 by a Miss W. Adair Roberts, who had obtained it in Vancouver, BC, where it was causing a sensation. This copy was displayed in the Conan Doyle Museum – part of Sir Arthur's psychic bookshop in Victoria Street, London – for at least ten years, and on the back of the photo was an account which is identical to the first of our two 'Mildred Swanson' versions (see above).

Barbanell first printed the photo [fig D] and a selection of mutually exclusive claims in *Psychic News* for 10 Oct 1936. Another printing appeared on 19 November 1977. In response to the last mentioned printing, a lady, naming herself only as 'Margaret', wrote to Barbanell saying that many times over the last 40 years had she seen the photo printed and been tempted to speak out, but fearing ridicule kept quiet. However seeing Barbanell's references to false claims she was moved to write saying she had the original negative. Barbanell was skeptical because he already knew of the Conan Doyle copy which predated her claim by many years – but he inquired anyway. 'Margaret' said that in 1934 her husband, then a young clerk in Walsall, Staffs, was shown the photo by a colleague. He showed it to her, and she to her father, who was both a spiritualist and a member of the London Photographic Society. It was tested, 'Margaret' claimed, and was pronounced a genuine, untampered-with negative. She closed her letter saying she still had the negative and a few prints. Barbanell's first attempt to obtain the negative (for examination) and a full account of its taking, obviously could not disguise his skepticism, because it brought only and angry and defensive reply from 'Margaret'. A second attempt succeeded with the arrival of a copy print, and hopes for solving the mystery plummeted – it was only another derivative copy. This story is told in *Psychic News* 18 March 1978.

When the *Sunday People* published their fourth printing of the photo, *Psychic News* 19 Nov 1977) countered with yet another selection of false claims, which we summarize as follows:

- 1917 – said to have been "unexpectedly secured in the trenches in France" by a cleric. This is the earliest date we have, though there is no evidence to support it. Many wonderful events and miraculous phenomena have been ascribed to this period of terrible trench warfare in Europe – including the 'Angels of Mons' visions.
- Box Hill, Surrey – taken by two girls on a nature ramble.
- Hayes, Middx – taken by two girls in a cemetary.
- Chobham, Surrey – in 1966 a woman told *Psychic News* she had taken it in the village.
- Himalayas – author and psychic-healer Murdo MacDonald claimed it was taken in the Himalayas. Previously, he claimed he was given it by an Australian patient who obtained it from an unknown woman in California, to whom is attributed an experience like that of our second 'Mildred Swanson' version.
- Various – others credited with the photo have been: a mother in New Zealand, a Salvation Army boy, and a hairdresser in Bristol.

SUNDAY PEOPLE 1977

On 13 Nov 1977 the *Sunday People* printed the image [a cropped version of fig H] as "the most famous picture we have ever printed", to celebrate their 5000th issue. It shows, they said, "Quite simply, a snow scene in the Alps, taken from an aircraft (in which) the face of Christ is etched in the melting snow." There is no information about when the photo was said to have been taken, but the response to their first printing of the photo – on 10 Oct 1958 – was such that they printed it again the following week, and for a third time on 19 Sept 1965. The *People* claimed that 30,000 requests for copies of the picture had been received, and some still arrive almost every week.

A few Sundays later – 11 Dec 1977 – the *People* printed a few letters from readers in response to their image:

- 1919, 1933, 1936 – three different readers said they had an identical photo, taken in a wood near Bristol. Two of them told the same story: that a young girl tripped the shutter of her camera when she slipped and fell. We are not told which of the dates apply to this story, or what the odd story out was.
- Epping Forest, Essex – that a flash of lightning caused the stark contrast.
- Bournemouth, Sheffield, Tunbridge Wells, and Crowborough – said to be of a snow-covered hedge in each place.
- China – the photo is supposed to have been taken by a Chinese, walking through snow-

covered mountains, his soul troubled because of the anti-Christian feeling in China at the time. He heard a voice saying: "Take a photograph." Fortunately he just happened to have his camera with him, and snapped a hillside of melting snow and black earth. On seeing the 'Face' in the developed photo he became a Christian (see 'Goddess in the Sky' below).

THE GLOBE 1980

In their issue for 8 April 1980, the *Globe* summarizes response from readers to a previous printing of a cropped version of image [H]. I do not have the reference to this first printing, but I believe it might have included the stories of the photo's origination in the Alps, England and China.

- 1931-32 – Linda Bragg, of Vallejo, California, claimed the family had the original, taken in this period. "My father's aunt took a picture of her flower garden in Dallas, TX, and what came out was a picture of Christ."
- Oklahoma – Mary Cook, of Silver City, New Mexico received a copy of the photo in Wavrika "41 years ago" (ie. apx 1939). No clue about the date it was taken, but offered this story: a small girl goes into her garden in Oklahoma City. Her mother followed, and finding the girl in prayer, took a photo of the scene. Each time the prints were developed, the scene was obliterated by the image of Christ.
- New Bedford, Massachusetts – Melody Motta, of South Dartmouth, Mass, claimed she had the photo for more than 20 years, and that it was of clouds over New Bedford.
- Bennington, Vermont – Esther Reynolds, of Mesa, Arizona, claimed: "My aunt and I took this picture a long time ago. It is of a bush in front of my grandfather's house in Bennington."
- Ohio – Ruth Brady, of Newark, Ohio, claimed her mother took it with a Kodak camera at "a little place north of New Philadelphia. The picture was of a snowbank, but it wasn't until after my mother developed it that she discovered the portrait."
- Peggy Duchene, of Simi Valley, California, said she found the picture in her grandfather's bible. "I was told it was a photo of a burning bush."

CYRIL PERMUTT'S VERSION

Get your hankies out for this one. The story is undated, but said to concern a young girl, from Victoria, BC, suffering from multiple sclerosis, visiting friends in Portland, Oregon. The girl's photo was taken when she and friends visited Beacon Hill Park. There was a strange man in a Trilby hat, sitting on a bench, chin cupped in his hands, and a hedge of sweet peas in the background. Then, as had been reluctantly promised to the girl beforehand, she was allowed to take off the calipers she had worn for years. But instead of falling down the girl

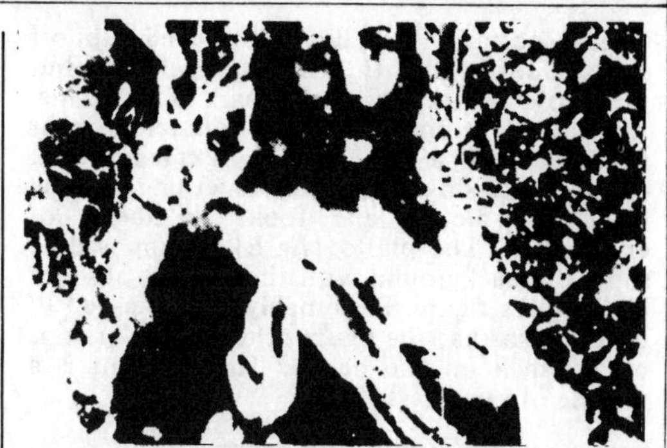

Image G Saucer News *image 4 [FPL]*

Image H *Syndication International, and* The Globe. Saucer News *image 3 is a slightly cropped b otherwise identical version [FPL]*

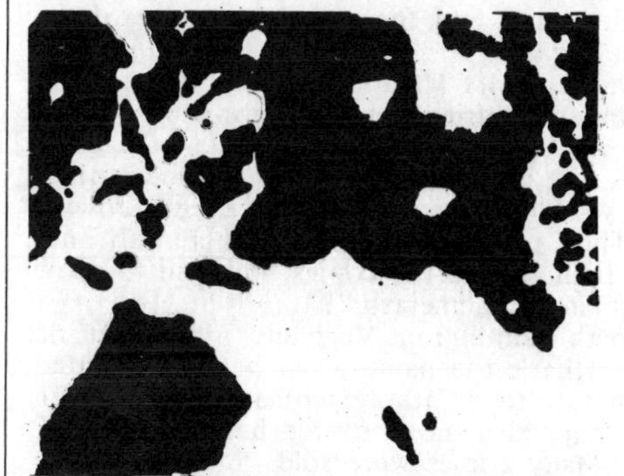

Image I Saucer news *image 2 [FPL]*

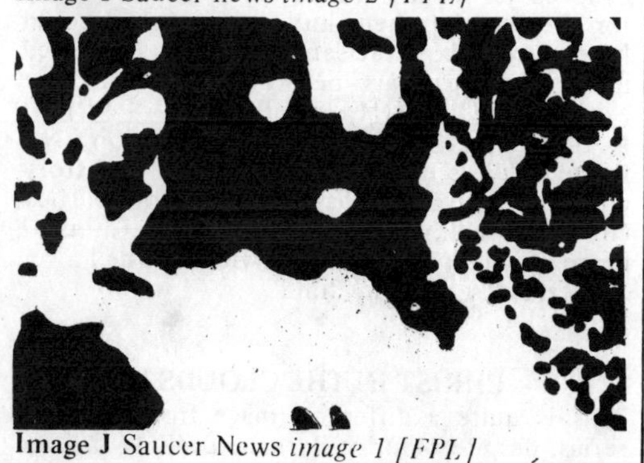

Image J Saucer News *image 1 [FPL]*

walked normally and has not needed support since. Months later the film is developed, but the photo of the girl in the park was missing. An enquiry at the processing counter brought from the back a technician. He explained that during processing he noticed something unusual about the picture and took the liberty of enlarging it. The photo [fig E] is supposed to show the background with the curious absence of the girl's figure. Presumably we are asked to believe also that the figure others call 'Christ' is of the man on the bench. This account is a miracle of vagueness.

THE SAUCER NEWS ACCOUNT

In their issue for Spring 1968, *Saucer News* ran the image [fig J] on their back cover, with the explanation "given to us by a third party" that the photo "was made of a snowy mountain in the Swiss Alps by a vacationeer attempting to photograph a UFO. Yes, that's right. A UFO. A phenomenon is not a phenomenon these days if you can't ascribe it to UFOs or a miracle in the same breath. Anyway this printing brought some responses which the editors included in the issue for Fall/ Winter 1968-69, as follows:

- 1938 – the image [fig I] appeared in a religious tract that explained: in 1938 a Norwegian woman was praying for a sign of God's favour, when a voice told her to take a picture in her garden, with this result.
- 1947 – Mrs Irene Phoenix said the photo was taken in 1947 by a 12yr-old girl in a thunderstorm, and forwarded her copy of the image [fig H].
- 1930s – Mrs Mera Gaskill said the picture was taken by friends near Huntingdon Park in California during a freak blizzard in the early 1930s. "It was taken of an incinerator in their back yard, with trees and shrubs overshadowing it." Their picture [fig G] with more halftones in it than most other copies, was said to show Christ (in the incinerator?).
- North Bennington, Vermont -- Mrs Victoria Cross [that's the name given here] attributed the picture to a Catholic woman in Bennington who snapped a snow-covered bush in her back yard. Many copies were sold "because people believed it was a miracle, and I felt too sorry for them to let them know the truth. I could have shown them the same picture as published in *Fate* some years before with a different explanation." [see 'Mildred Swanson' – ed.]
- China – Edith Chandler, of Union, NJ, wrote: "It is strange how that picture and story crops up in various parts of the world. They circulated many many years ago in China. I heard this from missionaries who returned after 50 years of service in China."

•

CHRIST IN THE CLOUDS I

This is quite a different image from the first series, despite Maurice Barbanell calling the one a variation of the other (PN 19 Nov 1977). The first printing known to us is in *Saucer News* (Fall/Winter 1968-69), and we reproduce this here [fig K]. The story, cited from an undated item in the Ashland, Kentucky *Daily Independent*, runs as follows: a USAF man from Chicago took pictures of a US and a Communist plane during a combat patrol over Korea, and sent the films to Chicago to be developed. He and others were amazed to see the image of Christ, arms outspread, in the sky near the planes. A neighbour of the airman's Chicago family sent a copy to his brother in Ashland, who contacted the *Independent*. Despite such a well-defined route the paper says the names of the people involved are unknown. That has a familiar ring to it. The paper, which comes out on a Sunday, sold out its 14,000 edition; it ran the photo a fortnight later, and that too sold out. Something about this story seemed even more phony than usual. It was not the allegation that the image was formed out of clouds in the sky, since we all have seen examples of faces and other forms in that amazingly plastic medium – see also John Michell's *Simulacra* (1979) – I just couldn't accept a US and a Communist bomber flying so cosily together, in tandem, while in the upper left edge of the photo is the form of the wing of a bomber of identical make, obviously in formation and on the same course.

Sometime after first discovering the above, a different account was told to me by Mr HJ Saddler, of Bristol: "It was taken by a crew-member of a bomber flying over Norway in the year 1954. One of the crew looked out and saw the figure, and with his camera took the picture." That's all he could say – his copy having been borrowed and never returned.

•

CHRIST IN THE CLOUDS II

THE TATTLER TALES

I first came upon this image printed full page on the titlepage of Peter Haining's *Ghosts: The Illustrated History* (Sidgewick & Jackson, London, 1974). It reminded me of that line in an old hymn which goes "Lo! He comes in clouds descending..." I wrote to Haining who said he had obtained the photo from an agency called Fuji Photos, along with an undated clipping from a US magazine, *The Tattler*, written by Tom Valentine. (We are on the track of this clipping and hope it will lead to more positive information.)

The *Tattler* had advertised a prize of $100 for genuine examples of psychic photography, and among the "hundreds" received there were two groups of "Christ-photos'. The first, which is not described fully, nor illustrated in my clipping, simply refers to a portrait of Christ, might refer to the image we have called 'Christ in the snow' (see above). The second image, of a robed figure standing among what look like clouds figured in nearly 20 entries from different people, indicating that it was being copied and widely circulated at the time in the USA. Here are some of the vague stories about it:

- 1972 - during May a photographer in Peoria, Illinois, ended a roll of film by snapping the sky. This result was sent in by Mrs Julian Nelson, of Foley, Minnesota.
- 1968 - Mrs Barbara Poor, of Rhode Island, said her copy of the image was taken by a girl in 1968.
- Pensacola, Florida - Robert W.Stull said it was taken by his son "four years ago" during a tornado alert, as the sky was changing.
- Wilson, Oklahoma - Mrs Hubert Davis, of Lone Grove, Okla, said her friends took the photo at Wilson.

THE FATE ACCOUNTS

In *Fate* August 1977, p59, Ron Anjard, a writer whose name is familiar to readers of a number of small journals, attributed a version of 'Christ in the clouds II' to a Texan. Lou Crowe, photographing a turbulent West Texas sky in the spring of 1975 with a Cannon 35mm camera. This drew the usual responses, two of which were published in the issue of *Fate* for November 1977, p118-9, giving the expected different stories. Anjard replied that he had got his photo from a friend and traced it to this Lou Crowe "who assured me it was taken in a 'tornado-like' sky. Since there are prior claims, we needn't take Crowe's account too seriously.

- The first letter in the Nov 1977 *Fate* is from Oten C.Covington, of Farmville, Virginia, who says that his copy, the third he's seen, came from a worker at the Corning (NY) glassworks who claimed it was taken from a glider in the vicinity. The other two versions known to him came from Virginia, and from Texas (Anjard's version).
- The second letter was more detailed than usual, and came from Grace Terpening, of Imperial, Missouri, whose daughter's friend's friend knew the family involved in taking the photo. A copy of it [fig L] accompanied the letter. Mrs Terpening said it was taken by a 12-yr-old boy, from Thompsonville, Illinois, whose family were camping in the Ozarks in October 1971. They hastily packed up when a dark cloud approached fearing a tornado was coming. They stopped to photograph the cloud, and as they did so lightning flashed. When the boy saw the figure in the sky in his photo he begain shaking and had a nervous breakdown, needing hospitalization in Springfield, Illinois, said Mrs Terpening, who continued: "The film has been carefully examined by experts to prove it is not a hoax. The picture appeared on the front page of the Perryville, Missouri, newspaper on 20 October 1971. I understand

Image K *[Fujifoto agency]*

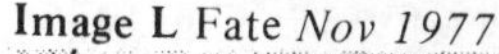

Image L Fate *Nov 1977*

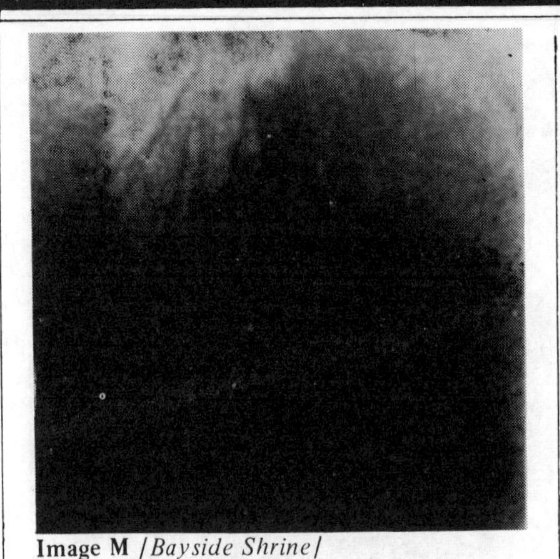

Image M /*Bayside Shrine*/

that as many as 3000 prints have been distributed throughout the world." Although Valentine mentions a claim from 1968 (see 'Tattler' above), it is heartening to have a newspaper date which establised the image's currency at least in October 1971.

A VERSION FROM CANADA

Probably the first appearance of the image in a British newspaper was in the pages of the *Manchester Evening News* for 17 Sept 1976, where it was said to have been snapped by Mrs Janet Wood, of Peel, Isle of Man. I wrote to Mrs Wood and received a reply with the loan of her copy [fig K] . She did not take the photo, she said, but obtained it from a friend in Canada sometime before 1973. She was told it had been taken by a woman in September 1972, flying over California, who was impelled to snap a cloud formation from her plane window; not seeing the figure at the time, only later upon development. Mrs Wood's version contains more half-tones than Haining's or Mrs Terpening's; and all of them have different patterns of 'blocked-in' blacks and whites, indicating possibly that they have all been derived by different routes from a common undiscovered prototype. Note also the suggestion of a treetop in the bottom left corner.

•

CHRIST IN THE CLOUDS III

An image very similar to 'Christ in the clouds II' has been distributed to devotees of Veronica Leuken, the visionary of Bayside, New York (see also FT28pp3-5). I know nothing about this image [imageM] except that it is in colour and came with the caption: "The mystical body of Christ will be without a head..." It does not appear to be identical to 'Christ in the clouds II' because of different folds in the robe of the figure.

•

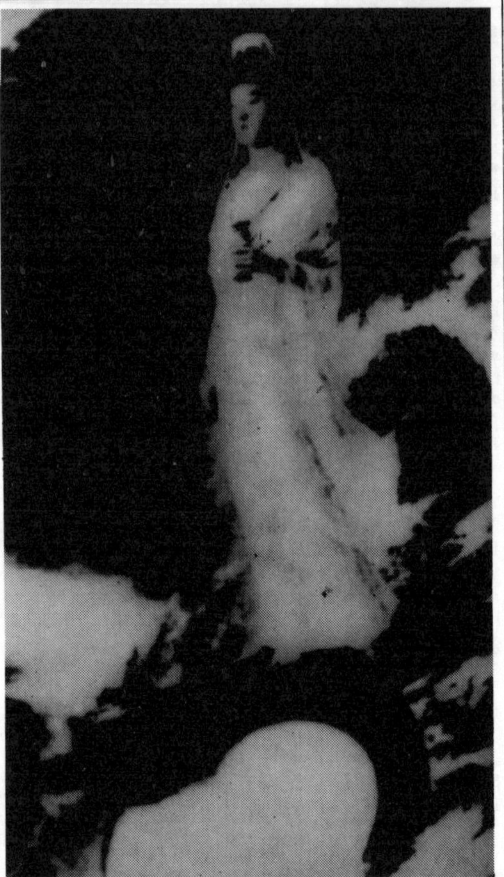

Image N *(One of a mass printing by Great Photo Studio, Singapore, sent to us from Penang, by Dr Yeang. The copy I obtained in Malaysia had even less detail.) [FPL]*

A GODDESS IN THE SKY

As intriguing as they were, I stood little chance in tracking down the references in some of the stories above to Christ photos in China. I simply accepted that should it have happened there, the people being extremely receptive to such claims, then rumours of such photos would abound. In quite a roundabout way, involving the death of a Chinese friend of the family, I found myself looking at two different photos claiming to represent the Buddhist goddess Kwanyin in the clouds.

• Nothing much is known about this first image [fig N] except an unsupported story that it was photographed in 1975 through a plane window. Copies of it are widespread among the Chinese communities of Malaysia. I had seen it in two separate places one in possession of a family, and the other pinned inside a god-cabinet in a temple in Kelang (Klang, Selangor) but our copy was sent to use by our Penang

Image O *[FPL]*

correspondent, Dr Yeang. Despite the loss of the middle tones, one can see the feet of the goddess resting on a curving black shape, which on reflection, takes on the shape of the head and neck of a dragon, also facing to the left. The figure and dragon-head seem to me to be distinctly Japanese in style, and I wonder if the image originated in that country? It looks very much as though someone has photographed a sculptered tableau in a temple or garden somewhere.

• The second image [fig O] came to me from the same Chinese family mentioned above. Although looking more like a painted or drawn image, it is said to be, or represent, a photo. In the inscription which accompanies it there is no date, and no clue as to the identity of the 'Mr Chan' to whom it is addressed. It was translated for us by Susan Lung:

"Mr Chan, from Si-Tsuen –

One day as I was strolling along in the open, I noticed an extraordinary cloud with a funny shape. It seemed to be approaching closer to me. It took on the shape of a respectable lady, but the image was vague. So I took out my camera and took a snap of it. To my surprise it turned out to be an image of our goddess. It hit the headlines at the time – the press and astrologers were all extremely interested. Because of this our humble chemist shop thought it would be nice to make copies from the original so that every household could put one up in their home. The kindness and blessings of our goddess is unlimited.

Signed: A certain chemist, Shin-Tsi."

•

Robert JM Rickard

Credits: The Bayside, New York, shrine of Mary Help of Mothers, the late Maurice Barbanell, Janet and Colin Bord, Loren Coleman, Peter Haining, Ian Lawes, Susan Lung, Rev Julian North, Cyril Permutt, Paul Pinn, Peter Rogerson, HJ Saddler, Paul Screeton, Leslie Shepard, Anthony Smith, Nigel Watson, Janet Wood, Dr CH Yeang.

POSTSCRIPT
A detail from the "Christ in the Snow" being sold as an "optical illusion" poster. Ad in *Nat. Enquirer* 13 May 1980.

Cont from p 27

and a total of £1500 worth of damage done to it by the ice.

Perhaps there is nothing exceptionaly unusual in tales of hail the size of tennisballs, but what about a block of ice of guestimated weight half a hundredweight? This ice bomb fell on the annexe to the farmhouse of Michael Mogridge, of Thornton Farm, Manston, Dorset. And once again the *Sunday Express* (18 October 1981) fails to provide a date – the incident could have been in the preceeding week. Farmer Mogridge had just finished cleaning up after milking his cows and passed through the annexe where it exploded behind him "just like a bomb going off." The huge lump of ice was squatting on the remains of his washing machine. After smashing through a slate roof, it had snapped a six-foot roof beam. The usual 'Fell from a plane' explanation was offered, and, as always, the story ends there. We wrote to Mr Mogridge for details or photos, but to date there has been no reply.

Credits: *J+C Bord, David Rees, Paul Screeton, Anthony Smith*
• **RJMR**

ON THE TRAIL
by Loren Coleman

The look to me is that, throughout what is loosely called Nature, teleportation exists, as a means of distribution of things and materials . . .
Charles Fort in *LO!*

THE SUMMER OF SYNCHRONISTIC SPECIES

Giant out-of-place lizards, all of the same species, have been the plague of Florida during the summer of 1981. Florida is well known for its semi-tropical climate and frequent reports of exotic introduced animals, from walking catfish and piranha, to jaguars and jaguarundis. However, the recent rash of monitor lizard encounters are noteworthy because of the underlying synchronization and the nagging notions of teleportation.

MEANDERING MONITORS

The LaMancha Golf Course in Royal Palm Beach was the site of the first man-lizard meeting. Course Superintendent James Kilgore was crossing the fairway on Saturday June the 20th, when he saw what he at first thought was one of the alligators he often has to chase off of the course.

"It was feeding on something. I never did see what," Kilgore said.

He soon discovered the thing was a six foot, five inch long Nile Monitor lizard. Kilgore pursued the lizard in his pick-up truck, and lassoed its head and body. "I threw the other end of the rope over a tree branch and lifted the lizard off the ground, then I just backed the truck up under him," the Superintendent told reporters.

The folks at Lion Country Safari were given the Nile Monitor by game commission officials, and happily added it to their display of two other Nile Monitors. No-one knew the origin of the golf course monitor, but theories flew. One Lion Country zoologist was quoted as saying: "It must have been imported (from Africa) and then escaped into the canal system."

Perhaps. Anyway, another Nile Monitor popped into official consciousness on Tuesday July 14th. A North Miami man had driven home Monday evening July 13th, and parked his automobile in his driveway. The next morning he opened his hood and found a five foot Nile Monitor lying across his engine. He quickly called game officials. "It's a bit startling to open your hood to change the oil and find a creature like that," noted game commission spokesperson Lt. B.F. Lampton.

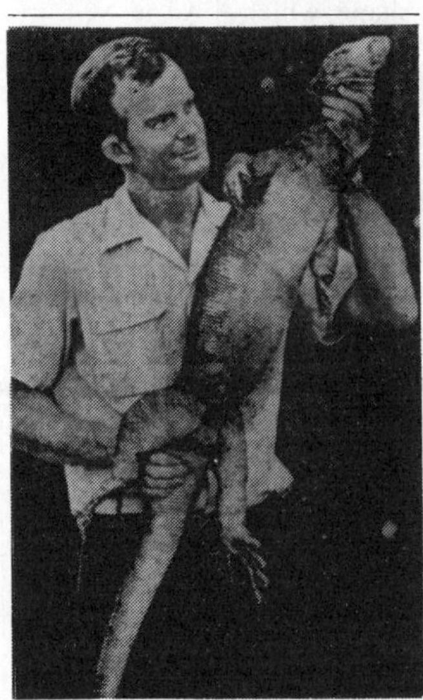
Lindsey Hord and the monitor lizard [Photo: Miami Herald *17 July 1981]*

It must have been a busy week for the Florida Game Commission, because right before the North Miami incident, a drama had begun to unfold in Hypoluxo, north of Boynton Beach, Florida. On Sunday, July 12th, Donald Wilton, a 79-year old retired carpenter and "primitive painter" was sitting in his living room reading. Then, he related later, "around dusk . . . I heard a noise. I opened the door to the garage and the thing scooted by me. It looked like an alligator."

It was no alligator; it was a five foot, thirty pound Nile Monitor.

Wilton called the game officials on Monday, but got brushed aside. They assumed he was talking about a small garden variety lizard, or an iguana. The advice they gave was to merely get a broom and "shoo" it out, or if that did not work, just to leave the garage door open, and it would leave, they said, when it got hungry. It took until Wednesday, and after the North Miami encounter for Wilton to convince them that a biologist and not a broom was needed. On Wednesday night, Alligator Coordinator Lindsey Hord stopped by Wilton's house and was surprised to find a young, five foot long, monitor lizard, and not a foot long gecko. Hord corralled, tied up and taped the lizard's mouth shut. "You always take care of the mouth first," Hord said.

Lt. Lampton of the Florida Game Commission casually noted that two years ago a Nile Monitor had turned up near South Bay, Florida. Behind all the press jokes about the "Dragonslayer" [There seems to be an unintentional allusion to a well-known area of English folklore here. See Paul Screeton's *The Lambton Worm and Other Northumbrian Dragon Legends* (Zodiac House 1978). The title says it all – Ed] Lampton seemed worried: "We have to be concerned since there have been two caught in the past two days." The commission was not even talking about the golf course monitor; we discovered that through contacting newspapers in Florida's east coast. Three Nile Monitors in a little over three weeks. Four in two years.

After the Hypoluxo lizard was taken to commission offices, its adventures continued. It soon escaped from its enclosure (or did it teleport?), and hid behind some filing cabinets. It took three officers several minutes to recapture the Nile Monitor. "I'd rather deal with an alligator any day." Lampton said.

CRAZY CROCODILIANS

For some people in America, alligators were exactly what they were dealing with during the summer of 1981.

Alligators have fascinated me for years, as anyone who has read my articles in *FATE* and *INFO Journal* well knows. Charles Fort was delighted by the croc reports also, and some of his most interesting words on teleportation can be found in his passages on the crocodiles in England. From 1836 through the 1860's, Chipping Norton and Over-Norton in Oxfordshire were visited by young, usually foot long crocs. Along with Fort's work, and my 1973 list of some seventy-odd accounts, the concept of the "crazy crocs" (as Bill Grimstad labelled them) have been firmly planted in the sphere of Fortean study. In the new *People's Almanac #3*, my short piece on alligators-in-the sewers updates the side-branch of erratic croc lore. So it was not surprising that during this crazy summer of 1981, the 'gators would pop up.

Two media exploited stories of escaped alligators kept the press busy. As these 'gators' origins were known perhaps you wonder why they should be of Fortean interest. Mainly for two reasons; first, the closeness in time of the alligators' escapes and captures suggests some synchronization, and second, by virtue of the fact their owners stepped forward bodes well for the teleportation of the large number of supposedly ownerless crocs that keep turning up everywhere.

Briefly then, on June 17th, Albert the Alligator escaped from the Denver Zoo and took up residence in the City Park's Duck Lake. The five foot five inch alligator was recaptured on July 16th. In Indianapolis, Oscar, Charlie Mudd's four foot pet alligator escaped on July 4th (USA's Independence Day). Oscar decided to live in a neighbour's pond in the front yard of Gerald and Joyce Cannon. Oscar was recaptured on July 20th, ending the Indianapolis' most recent croc caper. (Back in September of 1959, the city's Fall Creek was the host for a foot and a half long alligator.)

A short four days after the capture of Oscar, another crocodilian hunting expedition was formed. Officials who probably did not venture close enough to truly identify the animal, began looking for what they said was a four foot long "caiman" in the Kings River, near Laton, south of Fresno, California. Fish and game wardens were especially concerned as this area is a popular swimming spot. This caiman appears to fit more clearly into the Fortean croc catalog than either Oscar or Albert. Or so it would seem at this writing.

California's central valley has a long history of strange animals and crypto-zoological wonders. The Trinity Alps Monster (apparently a giant salamander?) and Folsom Lake's "alligators" intrigue me. In the Tulare Lake Basin, Corcoran, California, a six footer was sighted during the summer of 1930. And in nearby Folsom Lake, a series of sightings of 'gators occurred between September 1957 and June 1958. In recent years, the reported finding of a dead alligator on the shores of Folsom Lake has reached me.

PATTERING OF THE PENGUINS

Folsom Lake's elusive alligators once had to share their watery retreat with another enigmatic beast we Forteans have had to deal with now and then. In April of 1972, a penguin was stolen (by "pranksters", the reports say) from the Sacramento Zoo. After its alleged theft by these alleged pranksters, the penguin was found swimming and feeding in that Fortean hot-spot Folsom Lake. It took six months for officials to end its freedom, and then the animal died three weeks after its return.

Not so strangely, another gateway of Fortean creatures, Loveland, Ohio, had a recent penguin incident. During a later summer's hot spell in September of 1978, two penguins supposedly escaped from a safari exhibit on Kings Island, ten miles from Loveland. One penguin was struck by a car and killed in Foster, but the other black and white creature caused havoc in Loveland for several hours. Darrell Merritt, a service station attendant, said: "I walked in here about 7 o'clock in the morning. Then this guy came to the door and said there was a penguin behind my station. I thought he must have been drunk. I went out and looked. I had to see for myself, you know." What Merritt saw was a penguin. After waddling around the town a bit, the penguin was finally captured by two volunteer firemen.

Loveland, Ohio, is perhaps best known for the frog-mouthed "trolls under the bridge", seen in March 1955, and investigated by Leonard H. Stringfield. Ron Schaffner and Richard Mackay interviewed the police officers involved in the March 1972, Loveland incident in which a four foot tall creature described as a frog, or lizard was seen. Loveland does seem to be one of those focal points we need to watch. Whether for frogs or penguins, who knows?

But back to penguins of late. As 1981's summer came to an end, a strange visitor appeared on the shore of Monmouth Beach, New Jersey – a South American rockhopper penguin. On Saturday, August 29th, the skinny creature was spotted on the beach, and spent the next several days, first in jail, then with the humane society, next at the Bronx Zoo, and finally now at San Diego's Sea World. The origin of the bird remains unknown, and a deep mystery to officials who have been unsuccessful in theorizing an explanation to answer all the questions the rockhopper raised.

And speaking of hoppers, the mystery kangaroos were about as well, in Utah and Oklahoma, but that's another story we will keep for another column.

•

Loren Coleman

U·F·O Commentary by Nigel Watson

HISTORICAL AEROSPATIAL ANOMALIES

At the dawn of this century the skies of our planet were almost as alien to mankind as outer space is to us now. However, once the Wright brothers, at Kitty Hawk on the 17th December 1903, flew the first successful motor-powered heavier-than-air vehicle, the atmosphere quickly became a medium for military and civil exploitation. The progress of aeronautical engineering was spectacular, and the onset of the First World War in August 1914 forced an even quicker pace of production and employment of design innovations and improvements.

Perhaps, the speed of aeronautical progress caused a psychological imbalance in the minds of some people who became worried about the consequences of our invasion into the previously peaceful domain of the birds? I ask because in 1917 someone was led to ask an aviator if he would "Kindly think over all your experiences of flying, and try to recollect if you have had any uncanny experiences in the air. If so, would they lead you to suspect that there is a personality (a real one) invisible but ruling over the power of the air?" Apparently, the gentleman did so, for under the name of 'A Philosophical Aviator' he published them in the *Occult Review,* December 1917, entitled 'Occult Revelations of a Flying Man'.

The first account he dealt with originated from an experienced aviator who had flown before and during The Great War. The pilot "told me confidentially that at a very great height he had seen a curious coloured dragon-like animal apparently floating in the air and approaching him rapidly. The pilot became a little unnerved and at once descended to earth, but for fear of being ridiculed and accused of over-indulgence in alcoholic refreshment he said nothing to anybody till he mentioned the affair to me", wrote the philosophical aviator. Interestingly, aviators today still fear ridicule, but now they do so if they happen to see UFOs outside their cockpits!

On later occasions the pilot was plagued by similar visions, but he could find no explanation for this peculiar phenomenon. The relevant part of his testimony is that which relates to the fact that he was flying at a great height when he saw his 'coloured-dragon' and it is quite possible that he suffered from oxygen starvation which caused him to temporarily hallucinate.

Another interesting aspect of this account is the existence of fictional stories which were published in 1909 and 1913, relating to the same kind of phenomena of the air. In the *Occult Review*, April 1918, a letter from Paris written by Georges Lajuzan-Vigneau was published. He claimed that not long after Bleriot flew over the English Channel on the 25th July 1909, he saw a story in a French newspaper (*Le Journal* or *Le Matin*) which almost paralleled the report given by the philosophical aviator. According to Lajuzan-Vigneau the story "told of three men flying, also at great height, in an aeroplane, and seeing a nearly translucid, vaporous, dragon-like animal, of a blue-green colour, and of considerable size. The animal, floating in the air, caught up to them without apparent effort, and ran a parallel course to theirs. The aviators, who seem to have been of a very un-inquisitive disposition, remembered suddenly a very important appointment somewhere on earth and began to descend. But the dragon, apparently resenting their incivility, or simply yearning for society, made a dive, seized one of them, and carried him away bodily."

Again we can see a correlation between this story and accounts of contemporary aerial abductions contained in the science fiction and UFO literature. But instead of colourful and quaint dragons the modern-world has exchanged heraldic creatures for metallic technological monsters peopled by super beings from another planet or realm beyond our imagination! Unfortunately I have been unable to obtain a copy of the story mentioned by Lajazun-Vigneau.

Aerial serpents were featured in a story by Arthur Conan Doyle who is best remembered for his fictional creation, Sherlock Holmes. The story 'The Horror of the Heights' made its first appearance in the November 1913 edition of *The Strand Magazine*. This noted that with the wreckage of Mr Joyce-Armstrong's monoplane which was strewn over a wide area, a tattered and bloodstained log-book was discovered by an agricultural labourer. Doyle's story includes a full reproduction of this manuscript which reveals why the aviators body was not found amongst the wreckage of the aircraft.

Mr Joyce-Armstrong, an experienced and brilliant pilot, began to ponder the curious sequence of strange accidents which had occurred to aviators as their machines became more powerful and able to ascend to ever greater heights. One instance, was that of an aircraft which crashed but contained no body in it or anywhere in the neighbourhood. Then there was the tragic flight made by Mr Hay Connor who swept down from a great height and on landing muttered the word "Monsters" before he died of fright. Another bizarre accident occurred when Lieutenant Myrtle, RN, attempted to fly to a record height. He plummeted from 30,000 feet and when the wreckage was examined a slimy grease was found on the clothes of the dead pilot. To add to the mystery, the body of the unfortunate Lt Myrtle lacked his head, which was never found.

As he contemplated these events, Mr Joyce-Armstrong became increasingly certain that there were danger zones at around the 30,000 feet level over Pau-Biarritz, France; Homburg-Wiesladen, Germany; and Wiltshire, England. The latter choice of danger zone by Doyle is particularly significant when we recollect that Warminster, Wiltshire, is said to be the centre of British UFO activity by such people as Arthur Shuttlewood and his supporters.

Being an enterprising kind of chap full of chivalry and the good old British stiff upper lip, Mr Joyce-Armstrong resolved to explore the Wiltshire danger zone where he believed unknown terrors resided. Armed with a shot-gun and a bag of oxygen, he took off from his airfield of Devizes, one Thursday morning in September (of what year we are not told, except that it is sometime in the future). At a height of 40,000 feet he encountered a huge diffuse cloud, several acres in size. As he flew through its wispy coils a greasy substance deposited itself upon the bodywork of his monoplane. He even tasted it as it impinged upon his lips. Looking upwards he saw an even more spectacular sight. This was a gigantic pink coloured jelly-fish-like creature the size of St. Paul's dome. The fabric of it displayed channels of green veins, and pulsated with a regular rhythm. From it dangled two pendulous green tentacles. It slowly travelled out of sight, apparently oblivious to his presence. In its wake came a fleet of hundreds of smaller sized creatures of the same species, most of these being about as large as an average balloon.

This quarter of the aerial domain seemed to be teeming with curious life-forms. The beautiful jelly-fish creatures were quickly followed by the more ominous appearance of fast moving, vapour-like serpents, easily 20 to 30 feet in length. One of these grey coloured serpents swept past the pilots face leaving him feeling cold and clammy. Most terrifying of all for the aviator was a new arrival which descended from the heavens at a rapid rate towards him. First he only saw a small purplish patch in the sky above him, but this quickly resolved into something hundreds of feet in size. The thing looked far more substantial than the previous entities of the air he had seen. Two huge eyes lurked on either side of it, and these were bridged by a solid, white, beak-like projection. From its body arose three enormous air-bags which probably served to maintain its position aloft the earth.

It hovered over the aviator for a distance of 20 miles. Its means of propulsion was affected by whipping forward a glutinous streamer and hauling the rest of its body after it. The hideous sight of this leviathan of the air exhibiting a body whch alternated between mauve and purple in colouration, became too sickening even for the British courage of Mr Joyce-Armstrong. But as he tried to escape towards the sanctuary of earth a long tentacle flashed down to grab him. Fortunately the hot monoplane engine, with which it made contact burnt it and forced it to retreat. Another tentacle approached and was mutilated by the aircraft propeller; yet another sought to grab the pilot. The sticky tentacle embraced his waist and attempted to wrench him out of the aircraft. In the dramatic struggle for life and death the pilot's shot-gun blasted one of the air-sacks on the back of the monstrous body of the aerial leviathan. the air-sack exploded and the creature writhed desperately. At this juncture the aviator wisely took the opportunity to return to earth.

Not being a man intimidated by such hideous apparitions, Mr Joyce-Armstrong decided to return to the upper atmosphere in order to capture one of the small jelly-fish creatures, and thus prove to humanity that such creatures exist. In this endeavour he failed, the only record of his last tragic flight is contained on the final page of his logbook. In it, only seconds before his death, he scratched these words: "Forty-three thousand feet. I shall never see earth again. They are beneath me, three of them. God help me; it is a dreadful death to die!"

Such stories feature both the technological marvels of aviation science which were (and are) so awe-inspiring, along with a warning to mankind that we are probably ignorant of many things which exist in our immediate environment. In the case of the allegedly factual encounter with a "coloured dragon-like animal", the acquaintance of the philosophical aviator believed that this was a vision of the devil warning us not to visit his aerial territory. He even believed that Biblical Scripture supported his hypothesis. Whether such stories are fictional or allegedly factual they do indicate that people, at the dawn of the twentieth century, saw the sky as being an alien element where monsters could reside. Much in the same way that superstitious sailors feared the emergence of sea serpents from the hidden depths of the ocean, just as their tales were spread in fictional and factual forms, so writers like Conan Doyle translated the sea serpent legends into the upper atmosphere.

Returning to the philosophical aviator, we discover that he did experience 'occult aerial phenomena' himself. Sometime before The Great War, he was flying a biplane, when he encountered a mist in front of him just as he was preparing to make a landing. He wrote, "I subsequently learned that the mist was illusory. It opened and I plainly saw an aeroplane, similar to the one I was flying, enveloped in flames, the pilot struggling to get away from the temporary furnance." The precognitive vision came true three days later when a friend of his in an aircraft identical to the type in the vision was burnt to death as his flaming aircraft fell earthwards.

It seems that when we seek to conquer new territories with our technological and scientific skills, we have to come to terms with the fears that are conjured up by such incursions into the unknown, where, our imaginations tell us, slimy monsters could very well lurk. With more research it would be interesting to see if any other early aviators were astonished by amazing aeronautical anomalies.

•

Nigel Watson

REFERENCES AND NOTES

1) 'Occult Revelations of a Flying Man' by a Philosophical Aviator, *Occult Review*, December 1917, pages, 350-351. Credit: Granville Oldroyd.
2) Letter to the editor of the Occult Review by Georges Lajuzan-Vigneau, *Occult Review*, April 1918, page 231. Credit: Granville Oldroyd.
3) 'The Horror of the Heights' by Arthur Conan Doyle, *The Strand Magazine*, November 1913.
4) Postal communication from Carl Grove dated 1st September 1980; who noted that the precognitive vision experienced by the philosophical aviator could indicate that "when the rational side of the mind is in a weakened condition, information and experiences, mediated by other forms of cognition, can somehow get through the filters and defences which we normally operate against such phenommena." It seems that when flying alone a person is subject to illusions or delusions that are not normally encountered.
A case in point is the experience related by the late Sir Francis Chichester in his book

Cont on p55

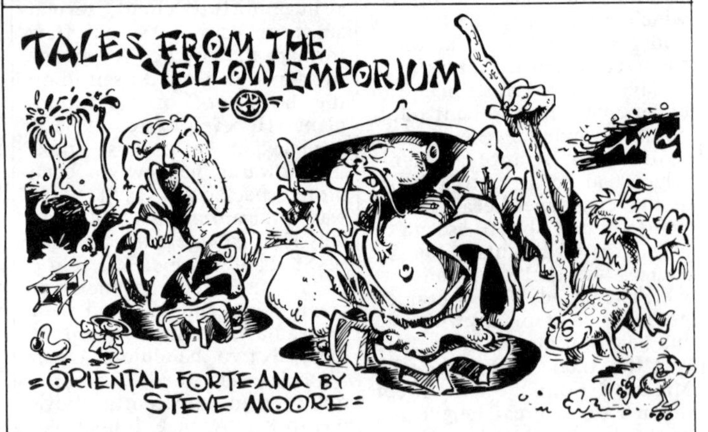
TALES FROM THE
YELLOW EMPORIUM
=ORIENTAL FORTEANA BY
STEVE MOORE=

SORCERY ENCORE

Sorcerers, exorcists and religious maniacs still seem to be running rampant in mainland China, and a steady stream of reports has come in since our last round up (FT 32/32-34). And these are only the cases that have "come to court"...

• Possibly the same case as in FT 32/34 with more details, or maybe a different case: Wang Rongzhen, a witch of Shandong Province, sentenced to ten years in jail for killing a woman she had been treating for hysteria, 31-year old Liu Youju. Wang and her apprentice stamped on the woman's stomach, refusing to stop even when she vomited and passed blood. "The evil has nested in her stomach and if we do not destroy the nest by stamping on her, we cannot get rid of the sickness" Wang explained, stamping on Liu till she fainted. She died the next day. The witch's apprentice was 'detained for education'. *Ceylon Sunday Observer* (quoting *Guangming Daily*) 22 March 1981.

• Sometime in 1979 (?) reports of a 'miracle' in Shanghai were so widespread that the

Wen Wei Pao newspaper published an official denial that the Virgin Mary had appeared in the city. We'd like to know more, but...*Guardian*, 3 July (1980?).

• No location for this but a man claiming to be an immortal stole a peasant family's savings by telling them he could multiply their money by sealing it in a box for 20 days. Nice to see the old alchemist con-man back in business again! *Daily Telegraph* 2 March 1980.

• The Communist party secretary of a farm commune in Southern China arrested for beating to death an exorcist employed by his mother-in-law. The exorcist died after four hours continual beating. *Daily Telegraph* 10 October 1980.

• A member of the provincial congress in the North-eastern Province of Heilungjiang sacked for practising witchcraft...*Straits Times* (Singapore) 29 November 1980.

• Two youths fined for selling horoscopes on the streets of Beijing (Peking). Got them on an 'unauthorised publications' charge. *Straits Times* (quoting *Beijing Daily*) 23 Jan 1981.

• Two peasants beaten to death by witches during exorcism ceremonies in Hailungjiang (again). One witch beat burned and trampled on the chest of a girl for 10 days while attempting to drive out evil spirits. *Daily Telegraph* 25 June 1981.

• A craze for wearing crucifixes grips young people in the northeastern city of Harbin. *Sri Lanka Sun* 7 August 1981.

• Two sorceresses jailed for sabotaging a birth control programme in Guangdong Province, south China. Seems that children can only be born by permission, and the sorceresses were influencing recalcitrant women into praying to the Goddess of Mercy (Guan Yin) for help in concealing their pregnancies. They also put curses on the local officials in charge of the planned parenthood programme. *Observer* 6 September 1981.

• And another official denial, this time from the Beijing *People's Daily*. (Official denials always make our mouths water!) This time the denounced rumour is that ghosts of dancing girls from ancient times have been seen performing on the walls of the Forbidden City in Beijing (the old Imperial Palace). 'Pure rumour' say officials after studying ancient palace records and questioning a man who had worked in the palace for fifty years. Mind you, if I had ghostly dancing girls in my place of work, I don't think I'd say anything about it either! *Herald Tribune* 13 October 1981.

WATER DRAGONS

As we seem to have neglected the subject in these pages, a quick look at a couple of Chinese Lake Monster stories.

• First we had news of a monster in the 800 square km Menbu Lake on the Tibetan Plateau, seen both by farmers and Communist Party officials. Three witnesses reported seeing a strange animal with a body as big as a house, a very long neck, and a comparatively big head. One story tells of a farmer rowing a raft on the lake who was dragged down and presumably eaten. Another that a cow left tied up near the lake disappeared, leaving only traces of having been dragged into the water. *Daily Express* 20 June 1980; *Ta Kung Pao* (Hong Kong) 26 June 1980.

• And three months later, more monsters at the opposite end of China, and this time, even more perplexing. With the Tibetan beasts, the 'experts' could trot out a convenient theory that the Tibetan plateau was under water 300 million years ago, so the monster could be a dinosaur survival; Lake Tian Chi (meaning 'The Lake in Heaven' is actually the flooded crater of the volcanic mountain Baitoushan, which last erupted in 1702...which would make continuous survival rather difficult! The 6400 foot mountain is in Jilin Province, near the North Korean border. The monster is described as having a flat beak like a duck, a head shaped like a cow, and a body bigger than a cow. Later we heard that one Piao Longzhi, a meteorological worker on the mountain fired shots at the beast on 23 August 1980, some of which apparently grazed its head. The beast dived toward the centre of the lake. This time it was described as having a neck longer than a metre, with duck's beak and cow or dog head. A group of five monsters has been reported it seems, and there have been at least five sighting reports, in 1962, 1974 and 1980. *San Francisco Chronicle* 7 October 1980; *News of the World* 12 October 1980; *Mainichi Daily News* (Tokyo) 26 December 1980 (via *UFO Newsclipping Service*).

Credits: *Robin Clauson, Peter Christie, Chris Hall, Y Matsumura, Paul Screeton, Ion Will* • **SM.**

The idea of a magazine, which circulates for the edification of all its readers the clippings and items of interest sent into , it is not new. The principal works for FT today, as it did in the 18th century when *The Gentleman's Magazine* was founded and flourished. **Peter Christie**, who wrote the well-received article on the Grace Pett SHC case in the last issue of FT, has a special affection for the ***Gent's Mag***, here begins a series of chronological extractions for us of the main items of Fortean interest. Such magazines are obviously forerunners of FT and one can only speculate at the Fortean riches which lie buried in the unplundered pages of similiar ancient publications.

Fortean Extracts From *The Gentleman's Magazine*:

Lond Gazette
Londō Jour.
Fog's Journ.
Applebee's ::
Read's ::::
Craftsman ::
D. Spectator
Grubstreet J
W.ly Register
Free = Briton
Hyp = Doctor
Daily Court.
Daily = Post
Dai. Journal
Da. Post-boy
D. Advertiser
Evening Post
St James's Ev.
Whitehall Ev.
Lōdon Ev'ng
lying = Post
Weekly Miscellany.

York 2 News
Dublin 6 :::
Edinburgh 2
Bristol ::::
Norwich 2 ::
Exeter 2 :::
Worcester ::
Northampton
Gloucester ::
Stamford ::
Nottingham
Bury Journ.
Chester ditto
Derby ditto
Ipswich dit.
Reading dit.
Leeds Merc.
Newcastle C.
Canterbury
Manchester :
Boston ::: ¶
Jamaica, &c
Barbados :

Or, Monthly Intelligencer.

The Gentleman's Magazine was a publication first issued in January 1731 that managed to appear monthly for nearly 200 years. In its early period twelve issues made a large bound voume but by the end of the eighteenth century so much material was being printed that it needed two volumes for each year. By the late nineteenth century it had reverted to one volume per year.

In the first volume of the series an 'Introduction' was printed which set out the idea behind the publication which was,

> *to give Monthly a View of all the Pieces of Wit, Humour, or Intelligence daily offered to the Publick in the News-Papers, (which are of late so multiply'd, as to render it impossible unless a Man makes it a Business to consult them all) and in the next Place we*

shall join therewith some other Matters of Use or Amusement that will be communicated to us.

The magazine for the eighteenth century is a real hotch-potch of miscellaneous pieces ranging from turgid theological debate to biting and vicious satire. Also, sprinkled across its closely printed pages are the record of odd events of interest to Forteans. You may recall that Charles Fort did not study pre-1800 records in any depth and it seems a great pity that many intersting records were therefore left unsearched. I have attempted to rectify that to some extent by examining in detail the pages of the *Gentleman's Magazine*. If Bob gives me the space *[It's yours – Ed]* I propose to print a selection of these in chronological order with comments wherever necessary.

1731

• The first odd entry appears in February 1731, where we read:

15 Feb. The Algerine ambassadors went to see Mr Fawkes who, at their request, shew'd them a prospect (picture) of Algier, and rais'd up an apple-tree which bore ripe apples in less than a minute's time which several of the company tasted of. (page 79)

Ultra-fast growth? – not according to a modern magic book which sets out in some detail how sleight of hand was able to present such a spectacle.

• A more Fortean occurrence, however was reported in June of the same year. We hear that:
ported in June of the same year. We hear that,

Benjamin Loder of Lydford, near Wantage, in the county of Berks, has a son, born March 10 1725, who is almost five foot high, and his arms, legs, and other parts proportionable; carries 13 score with ease, takes up to 100 weight with one hand, and half a hundred with one finger. (page 264)

A six-year old strongman was obviously good 'copy' – his abilities would cause raised eyebrows even now.

• The next Fortean entry is from August and is the first of many such reports:

A Tradesman in Southwark has made such Progress in a scheme to accomplish a Perpetual Motion, that he has directed an Engine to be made for that purpose. (page 352)

Another paragraph in December also tells us that,

Mr Andrew Bruce, an half-pay officer, has invented a machine for a perpetual motion, which seems to answer its end to the utmost perfection. (page 542)

One wonders where these machines, if ever constructed, ended up as there are no further references to them in later issues.

• On the 29th of August we hear of:

Newton-meer, a Pond near Elsmere in Shropshire, about a mile in Compass, (where) a surprizing Quantity of Fish rose on the Surface of the Water, which was thought to be poison'd. At first the people eat of the Fish without Damage; but beginning to stink, Labourers and Carts were employ'd several Days to carry them away and bury them. 'Tis hardly conceivable such Multitudes could be contained in so narrow a Compass of Water. (page 353)

Two points of interest are raised and, unfortunately, left unaswered – why did the fish rise to the surface and how come there were so many – a fall of dead fish in a very localised area?

• In December 1731, an Irish woman seemed to have discovered the secret of eternal youth:

In the town of Belfast in Ireland, one Jane Hooks, 112 years of age, had lately all her old stumps drove out by a new set of teeth; which were welcome, because the account affirms her appetite and other faculties are as good as when she was but twenty. (page 542)

• To round off the first year of publication the magazine carried a small but fascinating item:

At Chancy in Champagne was found on a Tree a wild Girl, about eighteen years old, that feeds upon Leaves and Raw Flesh; is as swift as a Hare, and climbs like a Cat. (page 584)

Clearly the writer had a penchant for animal similies – the cat-hare-monkey girl is again one of those interesting items that we hear no more about – perhaps a French reader could follow up this report?

1732

• The year 1732 began quietly from a Fortean point of view, but by March English gentlemen were no doubt horrified to read an item headed 'From Medreyga in Hungary':

That certain dead Bodies called Vampyres, had kill'd several Persons by sucking out all their Blood. The Commander in Chief, and Magistrates of the Place were severally examin'd and unanimously declared, that about 5 Years ago, a certain Heyduke named Arnold Paul, in his Life Time was heard to say he had been tormented by a Vampyre, and that for a Remedy he had eaten some of the Earth of the Vampyre's Graves, and rubbed himself with their Blood. That 20 or 30 Days after the Death of the said Arnold Paul, several Persons complained they were tormented; and that he had taken away the Lives of 4 Persons. To put a stop to such a Calamity, the Inhabitants having consulted their Hadnagi took up his Body, 40 Days after he had been dead, and found it fresh and free from Corruption; that he bled at the Nose, Mouth and Ears, pure and florid Blood; that his Shroud and Winding Sheet were all over Bloody; and that his Finger and Toe nails were fallen off, and new ones grown in their room. By these Circumstances they were persuaded he was a Vampyre, and, according to Custom, drove a Stake thro' his Heart; at which he gave a horrid Groan. They burnt his Body to Ashes, and threw them into his Grave. 'Twas added, that those who have been tormented or killed by the Vampyres become Vampyres when they are dead. Upon which Account they served several other dead Bodies in the same manner.

The many circumstantial details make this a very valuable report. I'm not too well up in vampire lore but I cannot recall reading anywhere about the 'Remedy' poor Arnold Paul tried – getting earth from a vampire's grave would pose no great problem (just locate a vampire!) but how does one go about getting vampire's blood? The stake through the heart of course was still in use in Britain for suicides at this time in order to stop their ghost walking. The last case of 'staking' I believe took place in Portsmouth about 1836 though nowhere have I read of it being applied to 'lay' a British vampire.

1733

• The third year of publication, 1733, saw, in February, an odd case of aerial contamination reported from Brussels:

Feb 3. From Brussels. The Parish Priest of Haaren, imagining that somewhat amiss in the Air was the Occasion of the then Epidemical Colds, stuck a white Loaf upon a high Pole in his Garden, and let it remain 24 Hours; after which he gave a Piece of the Bread to his own Dog, and a piece to his Neighbour's, of which they both burst. (page 105)

Falls of germs? – shades of Fred Hoyle and his theory on diseases from outer space. One wonders what a bursting dog looked like – not a pretty sight.

• In June, we read that:

June 1. The Court of King's-Bench gave Judgement against William Rayner, formerly convicted for publishing a Hieroglphical Paper, call'd Robin's Game, or Seven's the Main, viz. To pay a Fine of 50£ 2 Years Imprisonment, and give Security for his good behaviour for 7 Years. (page 323)

Clearly astrologers were not as tolerated as they are today. One can only presume from the severity of the sentence that Rayner had forecast dire events in store for the government of the day.

• August saw a case of rejuvenation which President Reagan might well envy:

At Guarda in Portugal, one Father Antonio Sequera d'Albuquerque, who had been 86 Years Canon of the Cathedral Church, in May last, when he was 114 Years old, cut an entire new Set of Teeth, small, regular, and white as Ivory: His long, white Beard turn'd black, as did his Eye-brows, and the Hair on his Head. He had retain'd the perfect use of his Senses; his Nerves relax'd by Age, began to contract, and his Muscles seem'd filling out with a Juvenile Robustness; when a Fever seizing him, he died. (page 437)

Perhaps such events might explain mysteries like the Count de St.Germain and the Flying Dutchman – men who repeatedly renewed themselves?

• In that same month, at Chabli in France:

. . .3 Women being a-breast, two of their Heads were struck off by Lightning, and carried 50 Paces, but she in the middled received no Hurt. (page 437)

Clearly divine punishment when it comes is extremely accurate!

1735

• 1734 was 'quiet' in Fortean terms, but in November 1735, we read of a real leprachaun character:

Nov 28. From Ireland. A Man about 18 Inches high, cover'd with strong Hair, was lately taken in a Field near Longford by a Farmer, of whom the little Gengleman demanded why he should be Stopped, for he was travelling for the North in order to pass over for Scotland, but all his Intreaties could not produce him Liberty, the Farmer having been at the Expence of a Box to carry him about, and to make a shew of him. He speaks Irish and mimicks English. (page 680)

One must obviously treat any story emanating from Ireland with caution but it would be nice to believe this tale of the travelling midget and his mimicked English. A month after this report the editor broke into execrable verse to tell us about another midget:

A Dwarf from France arriv'd in Town,
Measuring but Inches twenty one,
At Court a wonder great was shown,
Where he, tho' aged 46
Performed 20 childish Tricks. (page 735)

1736

• The year 1736 opened with yet another small human, though this time the poor creature had other attributes as well as smallness:

Jany 3. One David Ferne was brought to Town, born in the Shire of Ross in Scotland, aged 26, but 30 Inches high and 35 round. All his Features human, but his Hands resembled the Feet of a Seal, and his Feet, those of a Bear. (page 53)

At this period such anomalies were explained by the idea that if a pregnant woman was scared by any event or animal during her pregnancy the event would be reflected in some way in her child (viz. the Elephant Man). One wonders how the eighteenth century medical body explained the seal/bear man.

• A more grotesque production was the calf, born in February 1736.

Feb 4. At Stapleton in Gloucestershire, a monstrous Calf came from a Cow, the Head as large as a Bull's, and bigger than its whole Body; and the Face strangely deform'd, with one Eye on the top of the Nose, and the other under it, near the Mouth; Ears like a Dog's, the Tongue short, and in the Throat; the Heart in the Cavity of a Swelling above the Shoulders; the Navel between the Fore-legs; the Tail short like a Deer but in the Middle of the Back. (page 108)

• I will close this installment by quoting a short paragraph that must, I feel sure, be taken with a pinch of salt:

Sept 1. On the 28th past, a Man passing the Bridge over the Savock, near Preston, Lancashire, saw two large Flights of Birds meet with such Rapidity, that 180 of them fell to the Ground, were taken up by him, and sold in Preston Market the same Day. (page 549)

An unchallengeable excuse for a poacher to sell his illegally taken birds with impunity?

To be continued

•

Peter Christie

VANISHINGS
By Michael Harrison
New English Library, London, 1981; £1.25 pb, 190pp, bib.

The literature about the paranormal is so littered with errors and fraudulent stories that a glance at any shelf of books on the subject will disclose many titles which are little more than fiction. It is to be charitably assumed that the authors of these books are guilty of no more heinous a crime than of copying their material from earlier works without taking the precaution of checking the authenticity of what they write. However, there are a few writers who have deliberately presented as fact information which they know or have good reason to believe to be spurious. Among these odious hacks we must now include Michael Harrison, whose recent book, *Vanishings,* is a monument to Olympian balderdash.

Harrison is a prolific writer on subjects as diverse as cookery and philately to biography and topography and although an earlier venture into the paranormal, *Fire From Heaven*[1], has been the subject of some criticism[2], he has not been widely regarded as a sensationalist writer. It is for this reason that I am at a loss to explain this purile venture into sophism.

Towards the end of *Vanishings*, Harrison says, 'What I want to make clear is that we may fairly accept the fact of a paranormal vanishing only when no more normal reason for disappearance may be adduced.' Accepting this criteria, it seems to me impossible to justify the inclusion in *Vanishings* of cases like that of David Lang[3] or Charles Ashmore, for whom the most assiduous investigations have failed to locate a single scrap of evidence that they ever existed. This *fact* was one of which Harrison was fully aware because he lists my book, *Into Thin Air*[4], in his bibliography and the reasons for believing the Lang case to be spurious are detailed therein.

I am not peeved because Harrison has ignored the results of *my* research. I am concerned because he has elected to ignore it.

Let me say right now that I am not biased against *Vanishings* because Harrison favours conclusions different to mine. I am concerned because he has disregarded what are to my mind hard facts. In the case of David Lang for example, no mention of the Lang family can be found in the highly reliable census records, there is no record of the Lang farm or of a farm which could have been Lang's, no local or State historian has any information whatsoever attesting to the actual existence of David Lang, and no contemporary newspaper with an account of Lang's disappearance has been found. In short, despite every effort to locate corroborative evidence, there is no reason to believe that Lang ever existed.

Faced with such evidence it is difficult to see how Harrison can possibly justify including the Lang story in a book which purports to be factual. But this is just one example of Harrison's dismissiveness. He also makes gross errors and displays bumbling incompetence of considerable magnitude. In fact *Vanishings* is so monumentally bad that it crossed my mind that it was a hoax, but I don't think that even Harrison would sink *that* low and I doubt that in the present economic climate NEL could afford to indulge in such frippary. So proceeding with the notion that Harrison has presented *Vanishings* for serious consideration, let's get down to a few specifics.

It is difficult to know where to start. Like a stage magician with a pack of cards, 'Take a page, any page...'

INACCURATE HARRISON: On page 52, Harrison writes: '...it is sometimes possible to support a rational explanation, as when the rationalists set out to account for the total disappearance of the settlers on Roanoke Island, off the coast of what is now North Carolina. The settlement had been founded by Sir Walter Raleigh, who left then whilst he returned to England for needed supplies and a reinforcement of emigrants. The date of the settlement was 1585. When Raleigh returned to Roanoke, he found no trace of the settlers...The rationalists say that, despairing of ever seeing Raleigh again, the settlers trekked over the mainland until they were either captured by, or voluntarily made common cause with, the Mandan Indians.'

Right from the foreward, Harrison voices contempt for anyone who so much as even dares to suggest that a mystery isn't a mystery and he displays this attitude quite clearly when he writes, '...when rationalists *set out to account for*', the implication being that rationalists –whoever and whatever they might be–have a mind closed to the merest hint of the paranormal and seek prosaic explanations no matter what the cost. Of course such people exist, but there are those amongst us who for a variety of reasons want to clear the paranormal forest of fraudulent stories so that the true mysteries may be better examined. It is nevertheless gratifying to know that Harrison acknowledges that rational explanations do sometimes have some merit, though I think his judgement is misplaced in the case of the Mandan Indians theory.

Harrison gets his facts wrong several times in this short piece: Raleigh never visited the Roanoke settlement, so he could hardly have left it or returned to find the settlers missing. The man who did this was named John White and he was detained in England for three years, during which time the settlers did not receive any message from England, which may explain their subsequent abandoning of the Roanoke settlement. The colony did not arrive in the New World until 1587, not 1585, and they disappeared sometime thereafter. With inadequate supplies and having arrived too late in the year to plant crops for the winter, the settlers are believed to have sought refuge with the friendly Indians on nearby Croatoa[5]. As far as I am aware, the only connection between Europeans and the Mandan culture is the legend of Prince Madoc[6]. It's anybody's guess where Harrison picked up the Roanoke connection.

DISMISSIVE HARRISON: On Page 57 Harrison launches into his account of the troops of the Royal Norfolk Regiment who disappeared at Gallipoli in 1915 and who a veteran of the campaign subsequently claimed to have seen abducted by a cloud. Harrison says that the Norfolks 'were lost in so odd a fashion' that General Sir Ian Hamilton sent Lord Kitchener a special despatch about it. The implications here–and it is no doubt intended to support the abduction story–is that the despatch was sent *because* of the oddity of the disappearance, but this is far from the case. The men who disappeared were part of a brigade engaged in a military operation of considerable importance and which was a failure. It was the failure about which Hamilton sent the despatch, not the disappearance.

Of the veteran's story, Harrison says that it 'was in error in regard to several points, all were unimportant.' He does not give his readers the opportunity to judge the importance of those errors for themselves. Their opinion of their importance might have differed from Harrison's had he done so. The veteran names the wrong battalion, gave the wrong date, located the troops where they were not, and located himself where he probably wasn't at the time...These errors are significant[7].

INCOMPETENT HARRISON: On page 134, Harrison discusses Flight 19–the five bombers which vanished over, or more accurately, in the Bermuda Triangle in 1945 after sending a series of baffling radio messages to Fort Lauderdale. Harrison says, 'Now, it is true what Lieutenant Taylor said when he first reported to the radio operator at Fort Lauderdale...has been touched up a little...but what he did say–and that was almost as frightening–was what was heard and was recorded at Fort Lauderdale...'

This sounds as if Harrison is going to be accurate for once, but, alas, hopes are raised only to be dashed as he launches into the same time-worn tale of how the pilots claimed that they couldn't see land, how everything seemed wrong and strange, and that they didn't know in which direction to fly. This story has now been exposed so many times that it's positively indecent and I would be interested to know how Harrison can justify telling it yet again, particularly since his bibliography lists three sources which describe the real events that December afternoon–sources, of course, which sensationalist Harrison has chosen to ignore.

Now, I come to a part of the book about which I am slightly, eh, cross. Of Flight 19, Harrison writes:

'In several accounts of this highly factual but badly reported happening, there is a great confusion in the timing of successive events. The already quoted Mr Paul Begg[8], says, in his Into Thin Air*: "Not another word was heard from the five bombers. The time was now about 4.30. The Lauderdale tower declared an emergency and within minutes a huge flying boat was heading towards Flight 19s last estimated position. A few minutes later the tower tried to contact the seaplane for a position report. There was no answer. Further attempts to raise the (flight 19) aircraft failed. The flying boat had followed Flight 19 into oblivion."*
The United States Navy report on the affair does not confirm these times. A call... was heard...(from Flight 19) ...at 7.04 pm.'

How does Harrison know what the Navy Report says? He hasn't read it, otherwise he would know that the radio messages he cites are spurious. On the other hand, if he knowingly presented spurious material, what defence can he offer for picking up sombody else's mistake? Whatever the reason, it is academic. I did not make a mistake. Harrison, as usual, did.

In writing *Into Thin Air* I assumed that not everyone would be familiar with the spurious version of the Flight 19 story and I therefore devoted a little over two pages to detailing the account as it is told in the majority of the Bermuda Triangle books. The rest of the chapter on Flight 19 concerns the actual events as revealed by the Navy Report and other reliable documents. Harrison has quoted from my summary of the spurious version of the tale!

Now, it is one thing to present pseudofacts to an unsuspecting public[9], but something else entirely when you unjustifiably shed doubt on the accuracy and reliability of a fellow writer and worker in the field, discrediting him and damaging his reputation in the process.

I hope that Michael Harrison reads this critique. Assuming this to be the case: Mr Harrison, I have made some specific criticisms herein which should be answered for reasons of common decency. I therefore invite you to reply–and to reply in the pages of *Fortean Times*, if you please, where those who have read this critique can also read your defence of *Vanishings.*

REFERENCES

1) *Fire From Heaven,* Pan Books 1977.
2) *Fortean Times* 16 p24; 23 p26
3) *Fortean Times* 18 p6; 29 p55
4) *Into Thin Air,* David & Charles 1979; Sphere 1981
5) D.B. Quinn: *Raleigh and the British Empire,* Collier Books, 1962.
Michael Foss: *Undreamed Shores,* Harrap, 1974.
6) Gwyn A Williams: *Madoc,* Eyre Methuen, 1979
Fortean Times 33 p49. (Review of *Madoc)*
7) *Fortean Times* 27 p35
8) The earlier quote is a reference to my statement in *Into Thin Air* that the strong similarity between the stories of Charles Ashmore, Oliver Larch and Oliver Thomas suggests that they are versions of an original. All are in fact spurious. See *Pursuit* Vol.11, No.3, Summer 1978. 'Fortean Fakes and Folklore' by Robert Schadewald.
9) Books presenting fiction as fact have for some time been a matter of serious concern to many investigators and official bodies, particularly those who have dealings with people claiming contact with ghosts, poltergeists, and other scary things. Books of pseudofact, it seems, are responsible for causing many people considerable fear and upset. In view of this, foisting sophism like *Vanishings* on an unsuspecting public is not something to be lightly dismissed. Authors must take a responsible attitude towards what they write and accept the weighty obligation of ensuring that to the best of their ability what appears under their name as non-fiction is non-fiction.

Paul Begg

ENGLISH MADNESS

By Vieda Skultans.
Routledge & Kegan Paul, Henley, Oxon, 1980; £7.95 hb, pp161, plates, bib, index.

An excellent history of society's changing attitudes to mental illness, illuminating many curiosities of belief and practice along the way, including the special lunacies reserved for masturbators, 'feminine illnesses', and the poor. Some madness, like Melancholy–the 'English madness' – were once thought even to have had social value. Quite apart from helping us understand today's classifications and definitions, Dr Skultan shows just how transient ideas of normality are; and knowing that I for one will be more careful about describing experiential phenomena.

THE ANCIENT SCIENCE OF GEOMANCY

By Nigel Pennick.
Thames & Hudson, London, 1981; £3.95 pb, 180pp, photos, illos, bib, index.

A comprehensive history of the subject, covering every aspect, from city plans, siting and orientation of buildings, holy sites and monuments to ley alignments, symbolic relationships and proportion, turf and other mazes, earth images and terrestrial cosmology. The best introduction to a complex community of subjects to date. Well written and profusely illustrated – stirs up great feeling for our 'lost' heritage as it opens our eyes to the ruins of the ancient landscape about us. *RJMR*

SIGNS OF THE GODS?
By Erich von Daniken.
Souvenir Press, London, 1980; £5.95 hb, pp252, illos, bib, index.

EvD banging the same drum and getting the same old tune, with rather meagre scrapings from the bottom of the 'ancient astronaut' barrel. The high point of the book is that EvD seems to have swallowed the Dale-Sassoon 'manna machine' hoax completely.

RJMR.

RIDDLE OF HANGAR 18
By Timothy Green Beckley.
Global Communications, 303 Fifth Ave, Suite 1306, New York, NY 10016, USA; 1981, S8.95 inc p+p, 68pp, plates.

One of the most intriguing rumours of the last ten years is that of crashed UFOs and recoveries of the alien pilots. The subject was presented to the public in the recent book by Berlitz and Moore, but ufologists have been consistently pursuing and reporting such stories for about 30 years. Where Berlitz and Moore merely summarized, not always accurately, the researches of Stringfield, Beckley and others, you can now read first hand the story of one of the most dramatic of such cases.

The main part of this paperbound typed book develops from what must be a classic 'whale tumour' incident: an unidentified woman phones a Florida radio station, and on the air tells how her unidentified son, while a patient in an unidentified military hospital, wandered into a 'forbidden' area and saw the charred body of a strange looking creature on a mortuary slab. The man was discovered and threatened with dire consequences if he ever revealed what he saw. But he told his mom–and she hung up when pressed for details. Beckley goes on to discuss a number of cases where there is more substantial evidence, some of it impressive, some less so.

The closing portion of the book concerns two photos allegedly showing a charred alien, retrieved from a crashed UFO in July 1948. The material, including an account of the crash and how the photos were taken, was leaked to the Coalition of Concerned Ufologists, who have protected the anonymity of their source while publicizing the case widely. Also included are 2 glossy photo inserts and an analysis of them by GSW of Arizona using computer techniques. GSW conclude, oddly, that the corpse is that of a primate, speculating that in 1948 the US government must have been conducting illegal cross-state firings of test missiles with monkey experiments inside them. This view is contested by Beckley and the CCU, but the result is inconclusive and the reader is asked to make up his own mind.

Altogether a useful and intersting book to have. Whether you believe it all or not, it does document one of ufology's darker mysteries.

RJMR

SERPENT IN THE SKY
By John Anthony West.
Wildwood House, London, 1979; £9.95 hb, pp253, photos, bib, index.

After his sojourn in Egypt (1936–1951) RA Schwaller de Lubicz formulated the idea, through several now rare books, that there was more to ancient Egyptian civilisation that the picture presented by conventional Egyptologists. de Lubicz found that an amazing store of knowledge had been coded into Egyptian art and architecture, involving mystical ideas found in other religions, the use of Pythagoras' Theorem and other mathematical constants and concepts, and above all a sophisticated hermetic symbolism. This upset the orthodox view of Egyptian culture and science, and de Lubicz's work was deliberately ignored. John West undertakes not only a defence of de Lubicz, but to reintroduce his ideas and develop them. The result is a gripping alchemical reinterpretaion of Egyptian science and art.

RSMR.

THE CHEMICAL THEATRE
By Charles Nicholl.
Routledge & Kegan Paul, Henley, Oxon, 1980; £13.50 hb, pp292, illos, notes, index.

ALCHEMY: The Philosopher's Stone
By Allison Coudert.
Wildwood House, London, 1980; £5.95 pb, pp238, illos, bib, index.

Dr Allison Coudert's book is the more readable, being a wide-ranging history of an intellectual adventure which encompassed the lust for gold by kings and rogues; untold numbers of agonising deaths when eager scholars quaffed compounds of antimony, mercury or arsenic; and on more sublime planes poets and artists composed masterpieces of elaborate symbolism. Nicholl's book deals more fully with the latter kind. It is an extremely dense piece of scholarship which sets out to analyse the alchemical structure of Shakespeare's plays – a huge section is devoted to *King Lear* — and poems, and those of many of his contemporaries, particularly Jonson and Donne. But for a layman like myself there was more to be had by Dr Coudert's exploration of Chinese alchemy, the relationship between alchemical symbols and those of religious and psychological experiences, and the alchemical structure of occult ritual (whether of the Catholic Church or of the tribal shaman). Both books are well illustrated from classical alchemical treatises.

RJMR.

BIGFOOT: A Personal Inquiry into a Phenomenon
By Kenneth Wylie
Viking Press, New York, 1980, $14.95 hb, 268pp, photos, appendices, index, bib.

Most of the Bigfoot books so far published have concentrated on sighting reports and have been written by 'true believers'. Wylie is certainly not that, and so the fact that he writes as an outsider gives his book a different flavour from earlier Bigfoot books. Dr Kenneth Wylie is an historian and anthropologist with an interest in Bigfoot lore, and in those who believe in the creature's reality. It is clear that Wylie does not, and although he overwhelms us with evidence showing the impossibility of there being such a creature as Bigfoot, his arguments are often open to question, and also are sometimes marred by factual inaccuracies (especially when he discusses the controversial 1967 Patterson/Gimlin encounter and cine film). His treatment of the Bigfoot scene is fair – there *are* incompetent investigators; there *is* infighting – and no reasonable Fortean would deny that many so-called Bigfoot reports are based on innocent misinterpretation or deliberate hoaxing. Wylie leaves the door open a crack by concluding: 'Then there are those few sightings, impossible to corroborate, that persist and nag at us, to tantalize our sense of mystery.' But the tone of his book is dismissive (he won't even consider the psychic aspects or possibilities!), and he patronises the Bigfoot scene and the participants in the search. Worth reading, though, for its alternative viewpoint, and also for the way it unintentionally points up the overwhelming parallels with ufology: hardcore Bigfooters, like hardcore ufologists, may believe that they are hunting a physical reality, but if so it's tantalisingly elusive, and both phenomena leave physical traces which in the end prove nothing.

Janet Bord

FENRIS WOLF and IGR publications:

Due to overwork and lack of funds and time, the otherwise inexhaustable Nigel Pennick has had to close down his *Ancient Mysteries* journal. But no amount of duplicating paper can staunch his flow of ink, it seems.

IGR: occasional paper 18, *Welsh Temple of the Zodiac* by Lewis Edwards (8pp).

IGR/Cambridgeshire Ancient Mysteries: *Wandlebury Mysteries* by Nigel Pennick (8pp). *The Cambridge 7-Church Ley* by N Pennick and Michael Behrend (6pp). *Prechristian Geomancy* by Joseph Heinsch (4pp). Apply to Institute of Geomantic Research (IGR), 142 Pheasant Rise, Bar Hill, Cambridge CB3 8SD, for details and prices.

IGR/Caerdroia Project:

Cont

Cont from p 46

The Lonely Sea and the Sky (Pan Books, London, orig. pub. 1964, 2nd ed. 1967, pbk). In his successful attempt at the first solo east-west crossing of the Tasman Sea in 1931, he came across an unusual sight on the 10th June, at 2.35pm (local time). Five hours after taking off from Lord Howe Island on his way to Jervis Bay, Australia, he said that "Suddenly, ahead and thirty degrees to the left, there were bright flashes in several places, like the dazzle of a heliograph. I saw a dull grey-white airship coming towards me. It seemed impossible, but I could have sworn that it was an airship, nosing towards me like an oblong pearl." After looking around for any clue as to what it was he looked back to where he had seen the airship and to his amazement he could no longer see it. Instead, he saw several bright flashes of light. Then in front of him to the right another airship appeared out of some clouds. It appeared to come towards him, but when it had got within a mile it had vanished. Not long afterwards it reappeared in approximately the same spot where it disappeared, this time as it advanced it seemed to get smaller, it became transparent and disappeared. Chichester speculated that he had seen clouds which had taken on the appearance of airships, but even he was not convinced that such a phenomena could happen more than once in such a short time, nor does it explain why he saw the brilliant flashes of light in the sky. This is why he could only conclude that "Whatever it was I saw, it seems to have been very much like what people have since claimed to be flying saucers." (page 185).

Chichester admitted that he felt intensely lonely at the time of his sighting and he was probably tired. Today motorway drivers seem to experience weird encounters when they are tired and alone, and on a minor level I've seen grotesque shapes on the roadside late at night which have transmuted into mundane roadsigns or trees on closer observation. At least I've yet to see any coloured dragons, airships, or precognitive visions, but I'm sure it is just a matter of time and a lot more motorway driving!

Ancient and Medieval Labyrinths by E.Trollope (17pp). Apply to Jeff Saward, enthusiastic tredder in the ways of Daedalus, 53 Thundersley Grove, Thundersley, Benfleet, Essex SS7 3EB, for details of the Project (preserving mazes) and price.

Fenris-Wolf: *European Troytowns* by Nigel Pennick (6pp). *The Proof of Ancient Track Alignment* by Alfred Watkins (4pp). Price and details from IGR address above.

Electric Traction Publications: *Tunnels Under London* by Nigel Pennick (3rd edition of this pioneer work on secret and subterranean London, completely revised with additional photos of the parts other tourists never reach. 28pp. £1.20.) *Waterloo and City Railway* by Nigel Pennick (16pp. 75 pence. A eulogy by a Tube buff.) Nigel also publishes a *Tunnels Under London Newsletter*. All inquiries to him at the IGR address above.

Classified Exchanges.

As a reader service FT welcomes mutual exchanges with any relevant publication, and copies issues received since our last issue earn a listing here. No mag — no mention: All we ask in return is a similar entry in your own journal.

FORTEAN

- **Bigfoot Times** an exchange newsletter of the Southwestern Bigfoot Research Team. including general Bigfooteana & news. Contact Danny Perez: 10926 Milano Ave. Norwalk, CA 90650. USA.
- **Common Ground** - studies at the fringe of human experience—now adopted as ASSAP's journal of record. No 3 maintains the interest and vitality of the first issue. Rapidly earned distinction as essential reading for Fortean, ufologists, psi researchers and others. No3 maintains the interest and vitality of the first issue. 4 issues for £4.00/$15. Edited by Kevin McClure: 14 Northfold Rd, Knighton, Leicester.
- **Creature Chronicles** - quarterly Ohio-based coverage of manimals and mystery animals sightings. Annual sub: $6.00/$8.00 abroad. US drafts only, payable to Ron Schaffner: Box 12049A, Cincinnati, OH45212, USA.
- **Griffith Observer** - interesting well-produced monthly journal of the Griffith Observatory, reflecting the interest of editor, Dr Edwin Krupp, in a variety of prehistorical enigmas related to astronomy and cosmology, including so-called archeoastronomy (or astro-archaeology, on this side of the water). $5.00 per year. Griffith Observatory: 2800 East Observatory Rd, Los Angeles. CA 90027, USA.
- **INFO Journal** - back on form. More essential reading for Forteans. $10.00 per yr; $1.75/95p for sample issue. International Fortean Organization: Box 367, Arlington, VA 22210, USA.
- **Journal of Meteorology** monthly review of weather data and records, with many articles on Fortean-related meteorology. Annual sub: £13.50; overseas £15.50; airmail £21. Inquiries to J. Meteorology: Cockhill House, Trowbridge, Wilts BA14 9BG.
- **Kronos** – serious and scholarly quarterly devoted to discussion of the material and problems arising out of the work of Velikovsky. Annual sub: $15.00 (N. America), $22.00 (overseas airmail). Kronos: Box 343. Wynnewood, PA 19096, USA.
- **Lantern** - Quarterly Fortean and folklore journal of East Anglian mysteries. As interesting as ever, and now produced offset-litho in Magonia format (as pioneered by FT) by Magonia Press Services. Annual sub: UK/Europe: £1.50; US/Canada $4.00 airmail. Write to BSIG: 3 Dunwich Way, Oulton Broad, Lowestoft, Suffolk NR32 4RZ.
- **New Atlantean Journal** a quarterly newsprint journal covering parapsychology, UFOs, ancient enigmas, forteana. Annual sub: USA $12.00. airmail $15. NAJ: 5963 32nd Ave N, St Petersburg, FL 33710. USA.
- **Nessletter** monthly newsletter of the Ness Information Service. Sightings and gossip from the Scottish and other monster-haunted lakes. Annual sub: £2.00; USA $8.00. NIS: Huntshieldford, St John's Chapel, Bishop Auckland, Co. Durham, DL12 1RQ.
- **Pursuit** - more essential reading on all Fortean subjects. Recent issues have been very good indeed. Quarterly journal of SITU. Annual sub: USA $10.00, overseas $14.00. SITU: Box 265, Little Silver, NJ 07739, USA.
- **Specula** – quarterly journal of the American Association of Metascience. Much of Fortean interest. Inquiries to AAMS: Box 1182, Huntsville, AL 35807 USA.
- **Stigmata** - occasional report of Project Stigma, investigating the continuing mystery of US cattle mutilations. Single issue $1.50, annual sub $5.00. Project Stigma, Box 1094, Paris, TX 75460, USA.
- **Skeptica** - review journal in Danish for 'off-beat literature'. Write to: Skeptika, PB 8026, DK-9220 Aalborg Ost, Denmark.
- **The Supernaturalist** - a brave venture by Andy Collins (who wrote the entire 64 pages) holding forth on psychic awareness, New Age thinking, a psycho-socio' history of ufology, the Aveley abduction (with new info), ghosts, and history of ley hunting and ley hunters. Published under the aegis of the Parasearch group, Andy hopes to bring out about 4 a year. No sub info - just pay £1.50 for No1, and same again in advance for No2. Illustrated and worth your interest. Andy Collins, 19 St Davids Way, Wickford, Essex, SS11 8EX.
- **Tychonian Society Bulletin** - interesting if convoluted little journal dedicated to the geocentric universe of Tycho Brahe. Free on request, but donations toward costs welcomed. Walter van der Kamp: 14813 Harris Rd, RR1, Pitt Meadows, BC VOM 1PO, Canada.
- **Det Ukendte** - Danish glossy quarterly on all sorts of mysteries. Inquiries to Det Ukendte: Nordvestvej 8, DK-4470 Svebolle, Denmark.
- **Zetetic Scholar** – really excellent bi-annual review of criticism and bibliography covering the whole range of Fortean interest. Thick, relevant, scholarly. Annual sub: N. America $12 overseas $18 (USA cheques and currency only). Zetetic Scholar: Dept. of Sociology, Eastern Michigan Univ., Ypsilanti, MI48197, USA.

UFOs

- **APRO Bulletin** - monthly journal of the respected Aerial Phenomena Research Organization. State of the art thinking by leading investigators plus latest cases. Annual sub: USA $12.00, overseas $15.00. APRO: 3910 E.Kleindle Rd, Tuscon, AZ 85712, USA.

• **BUFORA Bulletin** - a new cheaper printing format and a new title replaces the old glossy *BUFORA Jounral*. For details write to BUFORA: 30 Vermont Rd, Upper Norwood, London SE19 3SR.
• **Hypotheses Extraterrestres** quarterly journal of GEOS, in French. Write to GEOS: Saint-Denis-les-Rebais, 77510 Rebais, France.
• **Inforespace** bi-monthly journal of SOBEPS in French. Inquiries to SOBEPS: Ave Paul Janson 74. 1070 Bruxelles Belgium.
• **Journal of Transient Aerial Phenomena** - bi-annual technical report. £1.80 per copy. Apply to BUFORA address above.
• **Magonia** pioneering quarterly exploring the sociological, psychological and mythological dimensions of UFO study. Highly recommended. Annual sub: £1.75; overseas $5.00. John Rimmer (editor): 64 Aleric Ave, New Malden. Surrey, KT3 4JW.
• **Malaysian UFO Bulletin** - a welcome source of news from the other side of the globe. No sub details known. Write to editor, Ahmad Jamaludin: Makmal Diagnosa, Veterinary Dept, Kuantan, Pahang, Malaysia.
• **MAPIT Skywatch** informal journal of UFO discussion. Much of interest. Inquiries to David Rees: 92 Hillcrest Rd, Offerton, Stockport, Cheshire, SK2 5SE.
• **MUFON UFO Journal** monthly journal of the Mutual UFO Network. Annual sub: N. America $15; overseas $16. MUFON: 103 Oldtowne Rd, Sequin, TX 78155, USA.
• **Northern UFO News** – monthly summary of UK cases reported to NUFON. Annual sub: UK £3.60. Write to the editor: Jenny Randles.
• **Pre-1947 UFO Bulletin** an occasional newsletter on the subject from Nigel Watson: Westfield Cottage. Crowle Bank Rd. Althorpe. South Humberside DN17 3HZ.
• **Probe Report** - glossy quarterly journal of West Country UFO group–serious, knowledgeable, entertaining and much of interest. Annual sub: £2.00 (foreign rates on request.) Probe: 16 Marigold Walk, Ashton, Bristol BS3 2PD.
• **UFO Network** - directory of UFO and related groups and journals. For details write to UFO network: 39 Birkbeck Rd, Mill Hill, London NW7.
• **Project URD** - new English language UFO journal from Sweden. Details from Project URD: Box 454, S-101 Stockholm, Sweden.
• **UFO Research Australia** Newsletter - bi-monthly journal of cases and discussion from Down Under. Annual sub: Aust $10.00; overseas $12.00 (Aust. dollars). UFORAN: Box 229, Prospect, SA 5082, Australia.

PSI

• **EVP Newsletter** bi-monthly notes, interviews, data etc. on the 'electronic voice phenomenon'. Inquiries to Alan Cleaver: 6 Izane Rd, Bexleyheath. Kent DA6 8NX, England.
• **Journal of the Society for Psychical Research.** Annual sub: £13.50/$34.00. For more details write to SPR: 1 Adam and Eve Mews, London W8 6UG.

EARTH MYSTERIES

• **Ancient Skills and Wisdom Review** – a review newsletter by Paul Screeton, who also puts out the Terrestrial Zodiacs Newsletter. Annual ASWR sub: £2.00/$8.00 ($12.00 air). Paul Screeton, 5 Egton Drive, Seaton Carew. Hartlepool, Cleveland, TS25 2AT.
• **Archaeoastronomy** quarterly. Annual sub: US $10; overseas $13.00. Write to the Center for Archaeoastronomy: Space Sciences Building, Univ. of Maryland. College Park, MD 20742, USA.
• **Caerdroia** - lively, interesting and energetic (like its editor Jeff Saward) small journal on mazes. Discussions, preservation projects, etc. No price, but donations welcomed. Caerdroia Project: 53 Thundersley Grove, Thundersley, Essex SS7 3EB.
• **IG News** - now fatter and quarterly. Folklore, occult, EM. Annual sub: UK £2.50; overseas $5.00. IG News: BM-Bulletin, London WC1N 3XX.
• **The Ley Hunter** - another valuable mag beset by financial and production problems, but editor Paul Devereux has pulled off the seemingly impossible. He now has his own mimeography-type system and is largely independent of those horrible price hikes that face FT. The price is greyish printing on what looks like blotting paper, but quite acceptable considering the alternative–extinction. Even the sub price has come down–now £3.75 (UK), £5.00 (Europe) $13.50 (O'seas surf), $18.00 (air), for 3 issues a year. TLH, like FT needs renewals, subs and donations to survive, so help if you can. TLH: Box 13, Welshpool, Powys, Wales.
• **NEARA Journal** quarterly of the New England Antiquities Association. Annual sub: USA $5; overseas $8. NEARA: 4 Smith St, Milford, NH 03055. USA.
• **Quicksilver Messenger** – about earth mysteries in SE England. 60p per issue. Write to Chris Ashton: 26a Wilbury Ave, Hove, Sussex.
• **Stonehenge Viewpoint** - bi-monthly newsprint journal of archeology, astronomy and geology related to earth mysteries. 2yr sub (12 issues): USA $7.50; overseas £5.00. SV: 2821 De La Vina St, Box 30887, Santa Barbara, CA 93105, USA - or via Ley Hunter.

OTHERS

• **Church of the SubGenius** - indescribably - "More laughs and yuks per dollar than any other religious group". Boggle (and laugh) at their unique newspaper *The Stark Fist of Removal.* Send whatever you can donate and get the full rundown from their unspeakable catalogue. SubGenius Foundation: Box 140306, Dallas, TX 75214, USA.
• **Heretic Visions** - delivers what it promises - contemporary anarchic humour, graphics, and writing from a formidable team: John Michell, John Nicholson, Cecilia Boggis, Dedwydd Jones, Hunt Emerson, Heathcote Williams et al. Single copies 60p/$2.00 (payable to Bozo Publications). Obtainable from OHP: 2 Blenheim Crescent, London W11.
• **Mad Scientist D Composer** - stream-of-consciousness anarchic poetry/art (praps). Inquire at: 818 W. 40th St, Balto, MD 21211, USA.
• **The Source** - editor Christine Hayles believes she's in touch with beings from Venus and Orion, and these are her 'translations' from the 'engrams' of 'human/earth consciousness'. Excited? Write to: Oahques Central, Earth Memory Center, Box 1291, Cortez, CO 81321, USA.
• **Outlet** - curious journal of obscure phonography and associated esotera. Single issues 70p; o'seas 80p. Trev Faull: 33 Aintree Crescent, Barkingside, Ilford 1G6 2HD, Essex.
• **Spirals** - native peoples + New Age cosmology. Single issues $1.00. Spirals: Box 29472, San Francisco, CA 94129, USA. *Spirals* also runs a 'Four Corners' Fund to help the Hopi Indian nation state its case at the UN.
• **Triple Echo** - mainly an SF mag, but has Fortean and related interests. Details from Triple Echo: 236 Fletcher Rd, Preston PR1 5HH, Lancs.
• **Undercurrents** montly on radical alternatives. Annual sub: UK £4.20; overseas £5.20. Undercurrents: 27 Clerkenwell Close, London EC1R OAT.

Cont from p 3

were graciously entertaining Frank and me for a meeting on other matters. Janet, Colin and myself were appalled when Frank played some of the interview tapes and advised of how he was handling the case. We were shocked by his naivety and apparent "grilling" of the witnesses. It was immediately obvious to us that we were witnessing the manufacture of an abduction from a strange, but relatively less strange, UFO experience. This was not without interest or merit to UFO studies, of course.

As Janet and Colin will verify, after Frank had left, and in much subsequent correspondence between us, I discussed with them what we should do about the situation. Frank had "abducted" the case, signed a contract to write a book, and refused to even disclose information, let alone widen the scope of the investigation in keeping with UFOIN policy. This was *not* a UFOIN case, since such a complex affair would never be left in the hands of one person only. Frank acknowledged this and over the next couple of months we mutually agreed a couple of important things.

1) He would state, unequivocably, in the book, that he had investigated the case privately and not for any organisation. He *did* do this. Frank has not submitted an investigation report to UFOIN, nor to my knowledge, to any other body.

2) It was decided that as he was not fulfilling obligations to UFOIN that he should no longer continue to investigate for the network. He has not done so since that time.

Consequently, I feel, UFOIN kept its objectives in sight and I fail to see how Frank's handling of this case reflects on the validity of our concept.

Janet and Colin and myself did discuss what might be done after Frank had concluded his dealings with the case, such as a reinvestigation by them. Kevin McClure, another UFOIN member, has also been concerned with this matter (as of course have I). We have kept in mind our primary consideration, the welfare of the witnesses (who were distressed themselves by certain aspects of Frank's cavalier attitude to their experience). However, we concluded that we should leave this decision up to the family themselves, as they had been subjected to considerable pressure. So we made it clear that we were ready to help, if needed. So far they have not requested that help.

I think this episode does in fact teach us a great deal about the UFO phenomenon. Frank, I know, is a serious and dedicated man. He is not a mercenary, or deliberately slip-shod. The fact that this case "took him over" and that he found himself quite incapable of seeing the gross errors he was making (which as a scientist he should have been very aware of under normal circumstances) is a salutary lesson to all investigators of the paranormal. In our book *Alien Contact* (to be published by Neville Spearman in the autumn of 1981) Paul Whetnall and I describe how we tackled these problems in our investigation of a complex CE4. The investigator of high strangeness cases must cultivate a number of special qualities, which at first he has no idea he will require. Some of these are ruthlessness, the incisive ability to disbelieve even your closest friends, and resistance to the temptation of getting personally involved in what feels like the world's greatest mystery. To you it might seem to be this, but to an outsider it will be but a pale, pale shadow. If the investigator of such matters is not ultra-cautious then he will end up being part of the problem, and a subject for investigation himself. Perhaps Frank will eventually see where he took the wrong turn and take time to consult his road map once more! I hope so.

Jenny Randles
Birchwood, Cheshire

CURIOUS HAILSTONES

On the 9th July 1979, I was in Ypsos, about 10 miles north of Kerkira in Corfu, when around 10.30 am there occurred a hailstorm lasting about 15 minutes. The hailstones were about 1" in diameter and shaped like this:

The hailstorm started during the tail end of a thunderstorm and there were many witnesses, including 3 mates of mine, although I don't think they bothered to examine the hailstones. The weather for the rest of the day and the previous day was very hot and sunny!

Paul Pinn
Mottingham, London

PLEISTOCENE PANTHERS

Not long after *FT32* came out – with its emphasis on mystery cat reports – we witnessed the 'beast in the barn' fiasco in Wales, *and* the capture of a puma in Scotland!

What I would chiefly like to comment on, though, is Loren Coleman's theory that American mystery moggies may be survivors of the American lion *(Panthera leo atrox)* of the Pleistocene. To me, this notion seems highly unlikely, for the following reasons:

1. Reports of 'black panthers' and other cats come from various parts of the world; including areas like Australia, where lions and panthers have *never* occurred. The reports from these areas do not differ substantially from the American reports. Also, the latter reports resemble those of 'pumas' and 'lions' spotted in Britain – where lions did occur in prehistoric times: but would anyone seriously argue that they are relict lion populations left in Surrey, for example? If so, what do they eat?

2. Coleman correctly says (page 22, column 2) that only lions (in the Cat family) are social. True. But this negates his own theory. Lions go around in family groups – prides. As far as I know, there

are no reports from America of mystery cats going around in prides. They are usually solitary; occasionally pairs are seen, or a female with young. This is *not* lion behaviour: unless *Panthera leo atrox* differed so markedly from the modern lion.

3. The idea that the 'black panthers' may be melanistic lionesses is an old one. It would be a unique feature in the animal world if *one sex* of any species were to show regular tendencies to melanism (black pigmentation), while the other sex – in this case, the male lion – retained normal colouration. Also, there seems to be no justification whatsoever for the statement that there is a 'tendency towards melanism on the fringes of the lions' range' (page 22, column 3). Some lion populations have black manes and belly hair, but not all these populations are on the edges of the species' distribution. There are *no known* melanistic populations of lions (ie. animals where the actual body is all-over black). Unlike the leopard and jaguar, the lion hardly ever exhibits melanism.

Whatever the answer is to the mystery felines of America –and everywhere else– I doubt that it lies with prehistoric survivors. For my money, these elusive creatures share the same origin as the Owlmen, Skunk-apes, Thunderbirds, and Mothmen which periodically haunt our world. But as to what that origin is . . .

Mike Grayson
London

PASSED-OVER PUMA

Tsk, tsk, Forteans! In FT35, on the "Welsh Puma", you missed out a remarkable synchronistic dimension to the whole affair.

When the first (the very first) Welsh big cat was sighted, it was followed a week later by reports of a *Scottish* puma [see FT34, p18f]. Aha, I thought – the Picts jumping on the bandwagon; the sort of thing some of these new UFOlogists like to claim accounts for goodness knows how many UFO sightings . . . But Lo! What happened! A REAL puma was actually found! And caged! And shown on TV (must be real!)! The matter seems to have gracefully faded away. The whole turn of events was remarkable, the Welsh elusive puma and the Scottish solid puma all occurring within a FORTnight .

But then something really weird happened. The Welsh big cat appeared again as you described [FT35, p44f – we do not know the exact date of appearance, but it was sometime between 11-14 June 1981 – Ed] but you failed to report that the following week a puma was reported AGAIN in Scotland! I have no written source for this, but it was given out on Radio 2 (BBC) news one night when I was travelling up the M6. The newscaster said the sightings were being taken seriously as an actual puma had been captured previously.

I mean, what are the chances against this sort of thing . . . .

Could it be, I wonder to myself, that we are getting glimpses of some insidious Fortean insurrection, and the English will awake one morning to find out-of-place pumas baying on Hadrian's Wall and packs of them crossing Offa's Dyke . . . ?

Paul Devereux
Editor: *The Ley Hunter*

The remains of the New Cross engine sheds – 1863 [Photo: Nigel Pennick]

WIND BLASTS SHED

One of the strangest railway accidents on record took place on Friday, October 30, 1863 (see photo). At about 3.30 pm, the engine shed of the London, Brighton and South Coast Railway at New Cross in South London was struck by a blast of wind. The doors were open at the time, and thewind, unable to escape from the confined space, lifted the roof bodily, and blased open the walls. The roof then fell back upon the debris. The adjacent running line was blocked with debris, and the engine of a passing train was slightly damaged.

The building was 145 feet long by 42 feet wide. It was strongly built of brick work 14 inches thick, strengthened by 23 inch buttresses every 21 feet, yet the sudden blast of wind reduced it to a pile of smashed bricks. The seven locomotives stabled in the shed were covered with rubble. One, number 111, was derailed and severly damaged, being overturned into the ash pit between the rails. The driver and fireman escaped by scrambling into the pit beneath the engine as the roof came in, but a cleaner was crushed to death between the wrecked locomotive and the rubble.

The survivors were dug out of the debris, having been completely trapped. Details of the accident, including an acc-of the scene an hour after the disaster, can be found in *Historic Locomotives and Moving Accidents by Steam and Rail,* written by Alfred Rosling Bennett, 1906. The photograph of the wrecked shed and locomotive appeared in *The Railway Magazine*, Feb. 1945. If any reader has further information on wind accidents to railway premises or vehicles, I would be interested in hearing about them. There was a similiar accident in about 1956 (details please) at Gunnersbury Station in South London, which was totally wrecked by a whirlwind, but I have no further information at present.

Nigel Pennick
Institute of Geomantic Research Cambridge

Help!

Any reader or researcher requiring help in research, questions answered, or contacts on Fortean topics, may do so free in this column. Just send the details, on a separate sheet, keeping it brief.

- I am looking for information on folklore and legends concerning **Black Dogs.** Would appreciate any help in this direction. Kevin Mar tholomew, Maple Cottage, High St, Uckfield, East Sussex. [See Ivan Bunn's article FT17p12f - Ed.]

- I would like each Fortean to conduct a survey among his friends to see when **swarms of frogs** have been seen after rains. Write me your findings. I would also like to hear from anyone who has **affected the weather**, or athletic events, by concentration. I have done it many times. Steve Ogden, 2646 Iroquois Ave, Ashland, KY 41101, USA.

- **Mysterious Airships** - Ufologist is looking for newspaper items, material, etc on 1896-97 US wave, and New Zealand 1909 wave. Could exchange for material on UK 1909-1913 waves. For forthcoming book. Have got all FSR sources. David Clarke, 6 Old Retford Rd, Handsworth, Sheffield S13 9QZ, South Yorks, UK.

Small Ads.

Rates: 10p per word. **Minimum charge** £1.00. Words in *italics* or **bold** 5p extra per word. **Semi-display**: £2.50 per column cm. **Discounts**: two insertions 5%, four insertions 10%. **Payment with order only.** Overseas advertisers remit in US dollars at double UK rates (eg £1=$2). Send to **Advertizing Dept, Fortean Times,**

RESEARCH PROJECT - reincarnation, psychic awareness, UFO/ETs, etc. Discussion groups Birmingham. Booklets 40p each: *Past Lives Access* (methods of facilitating recall); *Psychotherapy in The Light of Esoteric Wisdom.* Details: CONTEXT Research, PO Box 9 Burntwood, Walsall, West Midlands.

NEWSLETTER – An informal postal exchange for studies in paraphysics and the esoteric arts. Founded in 1944 – non-sectarian – non-demanding. For an introductory leaflet send a stamp to NL: 40 Parrs Wood Rd, Didsbury, Manchester M20 OND.

Truss Fund.

...in which we gratefully acknowledge the heartening support of the following whose donations will be applied where they will do most good.

Ron Bishop, Janet + Colin Bord, M Carruthers, Peter Christie, HO Hendricks, Ray Manners, Dave Reissig, Dale Rettig, Bill Sigorski, Martin Straw, Simon Welfare, CAW Worth.

Errata.

FT35

Our apologies to Michael Hoffman, for omitting the title of his column on page 19, 'The Conqueror Worm', an opening fragment of a poem by Poe, and for a typo in the closing line of the Poe poem on page 21 – which should have read: 'And its hero the conqueror Worm.'

FT34

Page 26 - top of col 1 - the correct name of the nuclear generating power station is San Onofre (not San Ofre). Cr: Jim Garlinghouse, who lives near it.

Cont from p 2

kind donations. Our overall gain on the last two issues is a mere 3 new subs, while in the same period 95 people did not renew. This level of dropout is shocking. We prefer to believe it is because of hard times, but if it's because of dissatisfaction then any reader contemplating not renewing is asked to let us know their beef – perhaps we can do something about it. Dropouts make times even harder for us too. On top of everything else the kindly GPO will bring in another penal rise in postage rates this February. More than ever we need your renewals – as well as new readers – to survive.

COMING UP

Next issue we will have a long interview with **Dr Rupert Sheldrake**, formulator of a new scientific paradigm which seems to drive a coach and horses through some hazy areas of orthodox science. A long article by **Peter Jordan**, who asked a handful of psychics to psychometrize photos of cattle mutilations in the hope of new clues to the mystery. Plus clipping summaries of possession murders, 'mass hysteria' illnesses, plants in eyeballs and other odd places, falls of frogs and fish, a 'Corrigendum' on the infamous Indian Rope Trick, strange deaths, fiery and other polts who/which have driven out families from their homes, and more hapless hermits + whatever else we can cram in.

Coming up are: an article on entombed frogs by **Paul Screeton**, articles by **Rex Gilroy** on Australian monsters and MAs, an occasional series on Fort's precursors, and some excellent antiquarian oddities culled from ancient books. You lucky people!

• *Bob Rickard*

Headlines. An occasional feature.

Lobster attacks motorist

Rat horde attacks car

BOULDER, Colo. (UPI) — A city policeman says his patrol car was attacked by thousands of rats in the parking lot of a recycling firm.

Hot dog bites man

Painful surge in biting

WASHINGTON (AP) — More people in New York City are bitten by other human beings than by rats, a new study says.

People were blamed for 892 of the bites reported to the New York City health department in 1977, compared with 229 bites by wild rats.

That put humans in third place among biters after dogs (22,076 reports) and cats (1,152).

Nearly three-fourths of the human bites took place during some aggressive activity — fighting, mugging or resisting arrest. One-fourth of all bites were accidental, occurring during sports, rough-housing and the like.

NIAGARA FALLS REVIEW 2 JAN 80

Policeman bitten by weird dog-man

Police in Roanoke, Virginia, will never forget the bizarre night of the howling dog-man.

Answering a disturbance call, police found a naked man wearing a dog collar, standing on the roof of a shed howling and shouting.

Trying to put cuffs on the man, officer E.L. Mills was bitten on the hand.

Neighbors said the man and a group of dogs had been chasing cars and digging up gardens.

Residents were either laughing or terrified.

"It wasn't just the man who thought he was a dog," said Mills, "the dogs seemed to think he was a dog too. It was uncanny."

WEEKLY WORLD NEWS (USA) 5 FEB 80

France brings downfall of fish

Dog Drops Pistol; Shot Hits Master

Sex attack on pelican

POLICE SAID yesterday that they have charged a young Moroccan man in Syros, Greece, with sexually assaulting a pelican, the mascot of the neighbouring island of Tinos. The pelican died from internal haemorrhage, police said. GUARDIAN 11 AUG 81

Stumped by skunks, city in Utah considers purge

'Kamikaze' mockingbird

Rats eat up Peru's cultural heritage

By Kevin Dunn

LIMA, MAY 13.

Peru's priceless cultural heritage is being eaten by rats.

Slug was eating Ding Dongs

BURNABY, B.C. (CP) — A big black slug has turned up in a box of Hostess Ding Dongs, and health inspectors are trying to figure out how the creature got th...

BATGIRL BITTEN BY VAMPIRE

RABIES serum was flown into a dense Central American

Lustful Elephants Surround Girl

Flying squad

A POLICEMAN at Gillingham, Kent, had to be treated in hospital after a moth got stuck in his ear.

300 EATEN ALIVE BY PIRANHAS

BEES TUNE UP TO EAT HOME

When crabs escaped...

SENKADAGALA: Tourists and the general public were taken by surprise when massive crabs crawled down the main bus stand near the Kandy clock tower.

Orangutan Kisses Nude Woman

JAKARTA (AP) — An orangutan grabbed and kissed a naked woman who was about to take a bath in a river in Borneo, and the woman screamed and fainted, the Antara news agency said Thursday. JAPAN TIMES 14 FEB 81

NIAGARA FALLS REVIEW, WEDNESDAY, MARCH 26, 1980

Dog ate refund cheque

Pet runs down owner

Townspeople Battle Toads

VOLES RAVAGE GRASSLAND

Monkey to plead case

KANGAROOS ON THE RAMPAGE

30,000 fish fall

Man spots 'raccoon with nose of an elephant'

BELTON, Texas (UPI) — Disc jockey J.J. McClain was on his way home early Wednesday when he spotted an animal that looked like a raccoon with the nose of an elephant sitting in the middle of the road.

He was met with skepticism when he called Wes Allen, a member of the KTON radio news staff to report his sighting.

Allen checked with the Bell County Zoo and they reported that sure enough a rare South American coatimundi had escaped from the zoo about a year ago.

WOODPECKERS TAP ELECTRICITY

Wild man. Pen and ink drawing from *Ballade d'une homme sauvage* (France, c.1500). See FT36:13.

F I N I S.